JANE'S WORLD ARMOURED FIGHTING VEHICLES

To my son Robert

JANE'S WORLD ARMOURED FIGHTING VEHICLES

CHRISTOPHER F. FOSS

BOOK CLUB ASSOCIATES • LONDON

This edition published 1979 by Book Club
Associates by arrangement with
Macdonald and Jane's Publishers Limited
Paulton House, 8 Shepherdess Walk
London N1 7LW

Printed in Great Britain by
Purnell & Sons Ltd.,
Paulton (Bristol) and London

CONTENTS

INTRODUCTION

During the past ten years there has been an ever increasing demand for information on current armoured fighting vehicles. It is hoped that *Jane's World Armoured Fighting Vehicles* will meet this requirement.

All types of armoured fighting vehicle are covered in this book, including main battle tanks, light tanks, reconnaissance vehicles including scout cars and armoured cars, armoured personnel carriers and mechanised infantry combat vehicles, internal security vehicles, tank destroyers, self-propelled guns and howitzers, mobile anti-aircraft systems, armoured load carriers, bridgelayers, armoured recovery vehicles and armoured engineer vehicles. In addition to those vehicles in service, some of the known vehicles that are still in development have been included to complete the picture. Such is the pace of development, however, that additional armoured vehicles may well appear before this book is published, whilst some of the older AFVs may well have been phased out of service.

Comparisons have not been drawn between one particular vehicle and another vehicle; to draw such comparisons can be dangerous. Very often one can compare one tank with another on paper and prove that tank A is better than tank B. The tank itself is, however, only a tool; the result of a battle is also determined by the way the crew handle the tank and the tactics used. This has been proved many times in the history of armoured warfare. Tactics and training are in fact being given increasing emphasis in many armies today, especially in tank gunnery and combined arms training.

Over the last few years the Soviets have introduced a new MBT (the T-64/T-70), a new MICV (BMP-1), a new fire support vehicle (the BMD), two self-propelled weapons (SP73 and SP74), and new mobile SAMs (SA-8 and SA-9). They have also introduced new mine warfare equipment and amphibious bridging equipment. All of this has considerably increased the offensive capability of the Warsaw Pact forces.

The West is also developing new equipment, but at the present time most of this exists only in prototype form.

Prototypes of the American XM1 MBT are now being tested but it will not enter troop service until 1980 at the earliest. The XM723 MICV is now well into its test programme and it should enter production in two years' time. The Armoured Reconnaissance Scout Vehicle has been developed over the last five years, but the right vehicle has still to be designed and the Army will have to manage with modified M113A1s until the early 1980s. The M60 tank is being developed further and 1,000 old M48s are being rebuilt under a crash programme in an effort to get some modern tanks into the Reserve units. No new self-propelled artillery is being developed, but improvements are being made to the M110 and M109.

On the European side the Germans are pressing ahead with the new Leopard 2 which is the most advanced tank in Europe, if not the world. No decision has been taken on production, however. Some development work is going on for the British/German FMBT-80 as well as for the British/German/Italian SP-70. The Germans are also carrying out an improvement programme on the Leopard 1 MBT. The Luchs 8×8 reconnaissance vehicle is now in service after a very long period of development.

In France production is continuing of the AMX-30 MBT, and the AMX-10P MICV is now in service in some numbers. Modern artillery and mobile anti-aircraft systems are to be delivered to the French forces in the next few years.

In Britain the Chieftain continues in production for Iran, and the Scorpion series is being produced for export. There is still no sign of a MICV to replace the aging FV432 APCs. The Ferret family was to have been replaced by the Fox and Vixen but the latter has now been cancelled and the Ferret will have to remain in service for some years to come.

8

It would be hoped that the first steps will soon be taken to standardise some of the Army equipment within NATO. At the present time there are just too many different types of weapon in use, be they tanks, guns or missiles. The only way NATO can offset the WPF is by standardisation, training and pushing ahead with advanced technology. The latter includes laser rangefinders, Cannon Launched Guided Projectiles and improved tank ammunition.

In recent years there has been a trend to design vehicles which can be used for a wide variety of roles, eg the Commando, VXB-170 and Panhard M3. Such vehicles can be used as reconnaissance vehicles, APC, Fire Support Vehicles and so on. Whilst this does have certain advantages it has meant in many cases that the vehicle is not really suited to some of the roles which it is called on to perform.

Internal Security vehicles are now being used by more and more countries and their use is likely to increase rather than decrease in these days of urban terrorism.

It should be remembered that during the life of a tank, which is at least twenty years, it is most probable that it will have some modifications carried out to it. This can range from a new armament installation or a new engine to a new radio or fire control system. For example, installation of a new gun may well increase the weight of the tank, which could result in a decrease in its speed and operating range. A new engine may have the opposite effect and increase the speed of the tank and its acceleration. The data in this book relates to a new, well-maintained vehicle, not a thirty-year-old tank which has had little maintenance.

Material for this book has come from many governments, manufacturers, units and individuals all over the world and the author would like to take this opportunity to thank all those who have made this book possible. Additional information and photographs should be sent to the author via the publishers.

Christopher F. Foss

January, 1976

Abbreviations

A/A	Anti-Aircraft	HVAP	High Velocity Armour Piercing
AEV	Armoured Engineer Vehicle	HVSS	Horizontal Volute Suspension System
AFV	Armoured Fighting Vehicle	ICBM	Intercontinental Ballistic Missile
AMX	Atelier des Construction d'Issy-les-Moulineaux	IFF	Identification Friend or Foe
AP	Armour Piercing	inc	including
APC	Armoured Personnel Carrier	IR	Infra-Red
APDS	Armour Piercing Discarding Sabot	IS	Internal Security
APFSDS	Armour Piercing Fin Stabilized Discarding Sabot	JSDF	Japanese Self-Defence Force
APG	Aberdeen Proving Ground	kg	kilogramme
APHE	Armour Piercing High Explosive	kg/cm^2	kilogramme per square centimetre
API	Armour Piercing Incendiary	km	kilometre
ARV	Armoured Recovery Vehicle	km/hr	kilometre per hour
ATGW	Anti-Tank Guided Weapon	Kw	Kilowatt
AVLB	Armoured Vehicle Launched Bridge	LHS	Left-hand side
AVRE	Armoured Vehicle Royal Engineers	LVT	Landing Vehicle Tracked
BAC	British Aircraft Corporation	MBT	Main Battle Tank
BAOR	British Army of the Rhine	m	metre
BARV	Beach Armoured Recovery Vehicle	max	maximum
BHP	Brake Horse Power	mm	millimetre
C & R	Command and Reconnaissance	MG	Machine-Gun
CET	Combat Engineer Tractor	MICV	Mechanised Infantry Combat Vehicle
CEV	Combat Engineer Vehicle	min	minimum
DS	Discarding Sabot	m/s	metres per second
F	Forward	m/v	muzzle velocity
FN	Fabrique Nationale (Herstal, Belgium)	MVEE	Military Vehicles Engineering Establishment
FCS	Fire Control System	NATO	North Atlantic Treaty Organisation
FGR	Federal German Republic	NBC	Nuclear, Biological, Chemical
FVRDE	Fighting Vehicles Research and Development Establishment (now Military Vehicles Engineering Establishment)	o/a	overall
		PTO	Power take-off
		R	Reverse
		RE	Royal Engineer
GB	Great Britain	RHS	Right-hand side
GIAT	Groupement Industriel des Armements Terrestres	ROF	Royal Ordnance Factory or rate of fire
		RMG	Ranging Machine-Gun
GMC	General Motors Corporation	rpm	revolutions per minute
GPMG	General Purpose Machine Gun	SAM	Surface to Air Missile
GPO	Gun Position Officer	SH	Squash Head
HE	High Explosive	SHP	Shaft Horse Power
HEAT	High Explosive Anti-Tank (with T=Tracer)	SPG	Self-Propelled Gun
		SPH	Self-Propelled Howitzer
HEI	High Explosive Incendiary	SPRR	Self-Propelled Recoilless Rifle
HEP	High Explosive Plastic	USMC	United States Marine Corps
HESH	High Explosive Squash Head	V	Volt
HOT	High-subsonic Optically-Guided Tube-launched	w/o	without
		WP	White Phosphorus
HP	Horsepower		

TANKS

After the end of the Second World War there were three basic types of tank. First the light tank (eg the American M41), second the medium tank (eg the American M47) and third the heavy tank (eg the M103). In the last fifteen years, however, the heavy tank has almost disappeared from service apart from the Soviet IS-3 and T-10 tanks, although many would class the Chieftain as a heavy tank.

Light tanks are used mainly in the reconnaissance role: eg the M551 and the PT-76. The medium tank is now known as the MBT or main battle tank, this description including all the current first line tanks including the AMX-30, Leopard, Chieftain, S Tank, Pz.61/68, T-54/T-55, T-62 and so on.

MBTs can range from the AMX-30, weighing only 36,000kg, to the Chieftain, weighing 62,000kg. The AMX-30 was designed to be mobile and to have a good gun and adequate armour, whereas the Chieftain had to have good armour and a good gun, but mobility came last. In future tanks such as the Leopard 2 and XM1, tank designers have been able to design a tank with good armour, a good gun and excellent mobility.

Tanks covered in this section are listed below. The British Scorpion is called a reconnaissance vehicle by the British Army and is therefore in the reconnaissance section.

Country	Designation	Type	Country	Designation	Type
China	T-59	MBT		T-10	Medium/Heavy Tank
	T-60	Light Tank		T-54/T-55	MBT
	T-62	Light Tank		PT-76	Light Tank
	T-63	Tank		IS-3	Heavy Tank
France	AMX-30	MBT		T-34/85	Medium Tank
	AMX-13	Light Tank	United States	XM1	MBT
Germany (FGR)	Waffenträger	Light Tank		New Light Tank	Light Tank
Germany/GB	Kampfpanzer 3/FMBT-80	MBT		M551	Light Tank
	Leopard 2	MBT		M60	MBT
	Leopard 1	MBT		M48	MBT
Great Britain	Vickers Mk.1/3	MBT		M41	Light Tank
	Chieftain	MBT		M47	MBT
	Centurion	MBT		M24	Light Tank
	Comet	Medium Tank		Sherman	Medium Tank
Israel	Sabra	MBT		M3/M5	Light Tank (and M8 SPH)
Japan	Type 74	MBT	Sweden	Ikv-91	Light Tank/Tank Destroyer
	Type 61	MBT		Strv.103 (S Tank)	MBT
Soviet Union	T-64/T-70	MBT	Switzerland	Pz.61	MBT
	BMD	Light Tank (Fire Support Vehicle)		Pz.68	MBT
	T-62	MBT			

CHINA

T-59 MAIN BATTLE TANK
MANUFACTURER – Chinese State Arsenals
STATUS – In service with Albania, China, North Korea, Pakistan, Sudan, Tanzania, Vietnam. In production.

GENERAL

The T-59 is the Chinese copy of the Soviet T-54 MBT. The early models of the T-59 did not have any infra-red driving and fighting equipment and had no stabilization system for the main armament. The T-59 has been used in combat by the Chinese (against Soviet forces), Pakistan (against India) and in Vietnam. It is logical that further development of the T-59 has taken place but no further details of Chinese tank development have become available. It is known, however, that the Chinese have captured at least one Soviet T-62 MBT during border incidents. Physical data are similar to that of the Soviet T-54 MBT.

CHINA

T-60 LIGHT TANK
MANUFACTURER – Chinese State Arsenals
STATUS – In service with China, Pakistan, Sudan, Tanzania, Vietnam. In production.

BASIC DATA (provisional)

CREW:	3 (commander, gunner, driver)	RANGE:	240km
WEIGHT LOADED:	15,000kg	FUEL CAPACITY:	250 litres
LENGTH:	8.2m (gun forward)	FORDING:	Amphibious
	6.91m (hull)	GRADIENT:	60%
WIDTH:	3.1m	VERTICAL OBSTACLE:	1m
HEIGHT:	2.19m (w/o A/A MG)	TRENCH:	2.8m
GROUND CLEARANCE:	.37m	ENGINE:	6-cylinder diesel, 240HP
TRACK:	2.74m		(approx)
TRACK WIDTH:	360mm	ARMAMENT:	1×85mm gun
LENGTH OF TRACK ON			1×7.62mm co-axial MG
GROUND:	4.08m		1×12.7mm A/A MG
GROUND PRESSURE:	.49kg/cm²	ARMOUR	
MAXIMUM ROAD SPEED:	40km/hr	glacis plate:	11mm at 80°
MAXIMUM WATER SPEED:	9km/hr	hull side:	14mm at 0°
		turret:	20mm+

GENERAL

The T-60 is a Chinese development of the Soviet PT-76 Light Amphibious Tank. The hull is of all-welded construction with the driver being seated at the front of the hull on the left side, and provided with a total of three periscopes and a single-piece hatch cover that swings to the left. The turret is in the centre of the hull and is of the same basic design as (but smaller than) that of the T-59 turret, but with a flat roof. The commander is seated on the left of the turret with the gunner on the right side of the turret. Two circular hatches are provided in the turret roof towards the rear. There is a ventilator dome in the turret roof behind the two hatches. The engine and transmission are at the rear of the hull. The suspension is of the torsion-bar type and consists of six road wheels with the drive sprocket at the rear and the idler at the front; there are no track support rollers.

The T-60 is fully amphibious being propelled in the water by two water jets. A trim vane is erected at the front of the hull before the vehicle enters the water.

The vehicle is armed with an 85mm gun which has a fume extractor towards the end of the barrel, and a 7.62mm co-axial machine-gun mounted to the right of the main armament. The 12.7mm anti-aircraft machine-gun is mounted on the gunner's side of the turret. This vehicle has been used in combat in Pakistan and Vietnam. Some reports have indicated that the T-60 may have a four-man crew.

CHINA

T-62 LIGHT TANK
MANUFACTURER – Chinese State Arsenals
STATUS – In service with Albania, People's Republic of Congo, China, North Korea, Sudan. In production.

GENERAL

Little information is available on this vehicle at present. Its turret is believed to be identical to that fitted to the T-60 Light Tank, its chassis has five road wheels, drive sprocket at the rear and the idler at the front. Loaded weight has been estimated at 21,000kg. It is not amphibious.

CHINA

T-63 TANK
MANUFACTURER – Chinese State Arsenals
STATUS – In service with the Chinese Army, Probably in production.

GENERAL

The only information available on the T-63 is that it is armed with an 85mm gun and a 7.62mm co-axial machine-gun. Its chassis has five road wheels with the drive sprocket at the rear and the idler at the front; there are four track support rollers.

FRANCE

AMX-30 – MAIN BATTLE TANK AND VARIANTS
MANUFACTURER – Atelier de Construction Roanne (ARE)
STATUS – In service with Chile (these may not have been delivered), France, Greece, Iraq, Libya, Peru, Saudi Arabia, Spain (some are being assembled in Spain), Venezuela. In production.

BASIC DATA	MBT	ARV	BRIDGE LAYER	ROLAND
CREW:	4	4	3	3
WEIGHT LOADED:	36,000kg	40,000kg	43,000kg	33,000kg
WEIGHT EMPTY:	34,000kg	36,000kg	—	—
LENGTH O/A:	9.48m (inc. gun)	7.18m	11.4m (with bridge)	6.65m
LENGTH HULL:	6.59m	7.18m	6.7m	6.65m
WIDTH:	3.1m	3.14m 3.4m (with blade)	3.95m	3.1m
HEIGHT:	2.85m (O/A) 2.28m (roof)	2.65m	4.29m (with bridge)	3.02m
GROUND CLEARANCE:	.44m	.45m	.4m	.45m
TRACK:	2.53m	2.53m	2.53m	2.53m
TRACK WIDTH:	570mm	570mm	570mm	570mm
GROUND PRESSURE:	.77kg/cm^2	—	—	—
MAXIMUM ROAD SPEED:	65km/hr	60km/hr	60km/hr	65km/hr
RANGE ROAD:	650km	600km	600km	650km
FUEL:	970 litres	970 litres	970 litres	970 litres
FORDING:	2m 4m (with schnorkel)	2m	1m	1.5m
GRADIENT:	60%	60%	60%	60%
VERTICAL OBSTACLE:	.93m	.93m	.93m	.93m
TRENCH:	2.9m	2.9m	2.9m	2.9m
ENGINE:	Hispano-Suiza HS-110, 12-cylinder, water-cooled, multi-fuel engine developing 700HP at 2,400rpm, built in France by Saviem			
ARMAMENT:	1×105mm gun 1×12.7mm co-axial MG 1×7.62mm A/A MG 2×2 smoke dischargers	1×7.62mm MG 2×2 smoke dischargers	none	2 Roland launchers

DEVELOPMENT

France started development on a new MBT in the 1950s. Originally it was intended that France and Germany would both build prototypes, subject them to comparative tests, and then both produce the same tank. In the end the French built the AMX-30 whilst the Germans built the Leopard.

The first prototype AMX-30 was completed in 1960 with pre-production tanks following in 1963. AMX, which is at Satory near Versailles, designed the vehicle, and the 30 stands for the specified design weight.

Prototypes were built with a petrol engine, had different road wheels, no thermal sleeve on the main gun and a simple hatch for the commander. First production tanks were delivered to the French Army in 1966/67, the first unit to be equipped being the 503rd Regiment at Mourmélon.

Initial production was running at ten tanks per month in 1968 but this has now been increased to about twenty tanks per month.

It has been reported that the French are considering updating the AMX-30 in the following areas:
1. Fitting a stabilization system for main armament
2. Fitting a new engine
3. Replacing the 105mm gun with a 120mm smooth-bore gun

DESCRIPTION

The hull of the AMX-30 is constructed of laminated armour plates and welded cast-iron supports. The turret is cast in one piece. The AMX-30 has the thinnest armour of all MBTs at present in service.

The driver is seated at the front of the hull on the left and has a total of three periscopes for observation purposes and a single-piece hatch cover that swings to the left. The other three crew members are in the turret. The commander is seated on the right of the turret with the gunner to his front. The loader, who also acts as the radio operator, is on the left side of the turret.

The commander's cupola is provided with a total of ten periscopes for all-round vision and a single-piece hatch cover that opens to the rear. The commander also has a x10 sight for aiming his 7.62mm machine-gun. The gun is layed and fired from inside the tank, and can be used both in the ground and anti-aircraft roles. The cupola is contra-rotating and this enables the commander to line up the turret with the target whilst still keeping the cupola trained on the target.

The loader has a single-piece hatch cover that opens to the rear, and both the gunner and the loader are provided with observation periscopes. The commander has an M 208 rangefinder which can be used in two ways, either as an aiming telescope or as a rangefinder by means of superimposed images. The gunner has an OB-17-A telescope, with a magnification of ×8.

The suspension of the AMX-30 is of the torsion-bar type and consists of five road wheels with the idler at the front and the drive sprocket at the rear. There are a total of five track support rollers but these support the inner half of the track rather than the whole track. The first and second, fourth and fifth road wheels are mounted on bogies and are provided with hydraulic shock-absorbers. The steel tracks are provided with detachable rubber pads.

The engine is at the rear of the hull. The transmission consists of an automatic clutch, transmission and steering mechanism, brakes and two reducing gears for the drive sprockets. The clutch is of the centrifugal type and is electrically controlled by operating the gear-shift lever. There are a total of five gears of which second to fifth are synchronized. A non-synchronized reverser enables the driver to obtain the same ratios in reverse as forward. To facilitate replacement in the field, the complete engine, steering and transmission are mounted as a complete unit and can in fact be removed from the vehicle in about 45 minutes.

The electrical system is 28v and there are eight 12v 100Amp/hr batteries in two groups of four.

The AMX-30 is fitted with a NBC system and a heater is fitted as standard equipment. An automatic fire-alarm system is provided to warn the driver if there is a fire in the engine compartment.

The AMX-30 can wade to a depth of 2m without preparation. A schnorkel can be fitted in under an hour which enables it to ford to a depth of 4m. Night-driving and night-fighting equipment is provided. The driver has two infra-red headlamps and a dual-purpose periscope which can be used with visible light or infra-red. The gunner can replace his sight with a ×5.4 night-sight, and an infra-red searchlight with a maximum range of 1000m is mounted to the left of the main armament. The commander is provided with an infra-red searchlight with a maximum range of 400m and a telescope with a magnification of ×4.6 is provided for this. Recently an image-intensification periscope has been developed to replace the centre of the driver's periscopes.

The main armament of the AMX-30 is the French 105mm Mk. F1 (CN-105-F1) gun. This is mounted in a turret with a traverse of 360°, elevation limits being +20° and a depression of −8°. The hydraulic control system fitted is the Model CH 27-1S which has been developed by SAMM. The commander has a single control handle and the gunner has a dual control handle; the commander can override the gunner if required.

The 105mm gun is semi-automatic and has a maximum stated rate of fire of eight rounds per minute. The recoil system consists of two diametrically opposed hydraulic brakes and one oleopneumatic recuperator for the counter-recoil of the barrel. The barrel is provided with a thermal sleeve.

A total of five types of ammunition have been developed for the 105mm gun—a non-rotating hollow-charge anti-tank round, an HE round, smoke round, illuminating round and a practice round. This ammunition is not interchangeable with that of other NATO 105mm tanks such as the M60 or Leopard.

Basic data of the ammunition are as follows:

Type	Weight Complete	Weight of Projectile	Muzzle Velocity
Anti-Tank	22.2kg	10.9kg	1,000m/s
HE	21kg	12.1kg	700m/s
Smoke	21.7kg	12.8kg	696m/s
Illuminating	17.8kg	—	290m/s

The anti-tank hollow-charge round has a maximum effective range of 3,000m and will penetrate 360mm of armour at 0° angle of incidence and 150mm of armour at 65° incidence.

The secondary armament consists of a 12.7mm machine-gun or a 20mm cannon mounted to the left of the 105mm gun. This is normally used co-axially with the main armament but can also be elevated independently of the main armament, its maximum elevation of +45° enabling it to be used against low-flying helicopters. A 7.62mm machine-gun is mounted in the commander's cupola. There are also two smoke dischargers mounted either side of the turret.

Fifty rounds of 105mm ammunition are carried, of which 22 are located in the turret for ready use. 600 rounds of 12.7mm and 1,600 rounds of 7.62mm ammunition are also carried.

Above The AMX-30 Main Battle Tank.
Right The AMX-30S MBT for desert operations.

VARIANTS

AMX-30S

This has been developed for operation in the Middle East and is now in production for Saudi Arabia. The main difference between the standard AMX-30 and the AMX-30S is that the latter is provided with a laser rangefinder for the commander, sand-shields have been fitted over the top half of the tracks, the gearbox ratios have been lowered and the engine develops 620HP at 2,400rpm. The AMX-30S has a top speed of 60km/hr.

Basic AMX-30

This is being offered for export. It is essentially an AMX-30 stripped of non-essential items such as the NBC system, night-driving and night-fighting equipment. It also has a simple cupola mounting a 12.7mm machine-gun.

AMX-30 with Rapace

For trials purposes an AMX-30 has been fitted with the Rapace DR-VT-3 radar developed by Électronique Marcel Dassault (EMD). This radar is of the pulsed Doppler type and will detect a tank at a range of 5,000m or a person on foot at a range of 2,000m, range and bearing being displayed on an operating console.

AMX-30 with ACRA Missile System

For trials purposes an AMX-30 was fitted with the ACRA (Anti-Char Rapide Autopropulsé) Missile System, development of which was shelved several years ago. Several thousand test rounds were fired during extensive trials and these proved the basic system. It was shelved primarily for financial reasons. Two types of 142mm ammunition were developed. The guided one had a total of eight fins; the unguided, a total of six.

The guided round was to be used against tanks. The gunner aimed a laser beam at the target and the missile followed the beam for a direct hit. According to GIAT the missile took seven seconds to reach a target at 3,000m range.

155mm GCT Self-Propelled Gun

There is a separate entry for this weapon in the SPG section.

AMX-30D Armoured Recovery Vehicle

This is in service with the French Army and a number of other countries have placed orders for this model. The AMX-30D has a crew of four men—commander, driver who also operates the radio, and two mechanics. It is a AMX-30 chassis with a new superstructure. A hydraulically operated dozer blade is mounted at the front of the hull. This is used both for dozing operations and to stabilize the vehicle when the crane is being used. The main winch has a capacity of 35,000kg and is provided with 90m of cable. The secondary winch has a maximum capacity of 4000kg and is provided with 120m of cable. The crane is mounted on the right side of the hull at the front and can be rotated through 240°. It has a maximum load of between four and fifteen tons depending on the angle of the crane. If required, a spare AMX-30 or similar tank engine can be carried on the rear deck.

The AMX-30D is armed with a cupola-mounted 7.62mm machine-gun and smoke dischargers. It also has night-driving equipment and an NBC system. No provision is made for deep wading.

AMX-30 DI

This has been developed for the French Army by the Pinguely Division of Creusot-Loire. It is similar to the AMX-30D but has a much more powerful hydraulic crane which can lift complete tank turrets.

AMX-30 Bridgelayer

Prototypes of this have been in existence for several years but by late 1975 the vehicle was not in service with the French Army. The mechanism is built by Titan Coder. It is a basic AMX-30 chassis with a folding bridge which is laid in position hydraulically in less than ten minutes. When opened out the bridge is 22m in length and this will span a river or obstacle up to 20m in width. The basic width of the bridge is 3.1m; this can, however, be increased to 3.92m with the aid of widening panels. The bridge will take a maximum load of 50,000kg. The AMX-30 has an NBC system and a crew of three which consists of the commander, driver and bridge operator. Its maximum road speed with the bridge is 50km/hr; without the bridge it can travel at 60km/hr.

AMX-30 Driver-Training Tank

This is simply an AMX-30 MBT with its turret removed and replaced by an observation cupola.

Pluton Weapons System

The Pluton tactical nuclear weapons system became operational with the 3rd Artillery Regiment in 1974. Each Regiment has six Pluton launchers and a total of six Regiments are to be formed over the next few

Top left Close-up of the commander's cupola of an AMX-30 MBT.
Top right The RAPACE radar system mounted on the AMX-30 MBT.
Above AMX-30 MBTs shown fitted with both types of schnorkel for deep fording.
Right The Hispano-Suiza HS-110 12 cylinder engine which is used in the AMX-30.

1

2

3

6▼   4

5   ▼7

1 AMX-30 Armoured Recovery Vehicle from the rear.
2 AMX-30 Armoured Recovery Vehicle from the front.
3 AMX-30 Bridgelayer from the rear in travelling position.
4 AMX-30 with Pluton tactical nuclear missile system ready for launching.
6 Model of the AMX-30 with the Javelot Anti-Aircraft System installed.
5 AMX-30S 401A Anti-Aircraft Tank with twin 30mm cannon.
7 The AMX-30 chassis with the Roland 2 Anti-Aircraft Missile System installed.

years. The missile has a range of between 10km and over 100km and two types of warhead have been developed by the French. One of these is for use when Allied troops are in the area whilst the other is for use against concentrations of enemy troops.

The missile itself is 7.6m in length and weighs 2400kg. It is propelled by a single-propellent rocket motor. The missile is carried in a launcher-box mounted on the rear of a modified AMX-30 chassis. When it arrives at the launch site the front of the launch box is removed and the missile elevated to the firing position. The vehicle has a crew of four and an NBC system is provided. The control centre for the launcher is mounted on a standard Berliet 6×6 truck.

AMX-30 with Javelot Anti-Aircraft System

The Javelot anti-aircraft system is being developed by Thomson-CSF under contract to the American and French Governments. Models have been shown of the system mounted on an AMX-30 chassis although it can be mounted on almost any vehicle, tracked or wheeled.

The Javelot system consists of a set of 64 tubes mounted on a launcher which has a traverse of 360° and a high angle of elevation. The tubes are 40mm in calibre and fire a projectile weighing 1.03kg, of which the warhead amounts to .4kg. The projectile has a velocity of 600m/s when it is launched but this increases to 1,100m/s. Flight time to 2,000m is under 2.6 seconds.

The acquisition function is performed by a radar providing target designation for a fire-control system. This would either be a radar or optical system. In the case of an optical system a TV tracking system or a laser ranging system would also be required.

The basic idea is that salvoes of 40mm projectiles would be fired at low-flying aircraft and a hit from one of these projectiles would be sufficient to damage or destroy it.

By early 1975 the definition study had been completed as had work on the reloading system.

AMX-30 Anti-Aircraft Tank with Twin 30mm Cannon (AMX-30S 401A)

This is basically an AMX-30 tank chassis fitted with the same turret as that mounted on the AMX-13 DCA anti-aircraft vehicle. It has a crew of three which consists of the commander, driver and gunner. Total ammunition supply is 1,200 rounds, of which 600 are for ready use and 600 are in the chassis. For details of the turret and operation refer to the entry for the AMX-13 DCA.

It has been reported that the Saudi Arabian Army has placed an order for this vehicle.

AMX-30 Shahine Anti-Aircraft Missile System

This is under development for the Saudi Arabian Army and should enter service in 1980/81. This system is essentially the Crotale missile system modified and mounted on an AMX-30 chassis rather than on 4×4 wheeled vehicles.

The system comprises two AMX-30 chassis. One of these has a total of six missiles, ie three each side, with additional missiles being carried inside the hull. It also mounts the launch radar which can guide two missiles simultaneously. The other vehicle has a Doppler pulse search and surveillance radar.

A typical firing battery would consist of three launcher tanks and one acquisition tank.

AMX-30 with Roland Anti-Aircraft Missile System

The Roland SAM is a joint German/French development. The Germans mount the Roland on the Marder chassis whilst the French have chosen the AMX-30 chassis. Two systems have been developed, Roland 1 being a clear-weather system developed by the French, and Roland 2 an all-weather system developed by the Germans. France has ordered both the Roland 1 and Roland 2.

The vehicle carries two missiles in the ready-to-launch position with a further eight missiles inside the hull, and two revolver-type magazines each hold four missiles in the launch containers.

The missile itself is 2.4m in length, .16m in diameter, .5m in diameter with fins unfolded, and launch weight is 63kg. The missile and launch container weighs a total of 80kg and is 2.6m in length. The Roland has a maximum speed of Mach 1.6 and a maximum range of 6km. An HE warhead is fitted.

The main components of the Roland 1 are the missile, an omni-directional search radar on the turret rear, complete with IFF system, an optical sight with infra-red detection equipment, a command computer and a command transmitter.

The crew consists of the driver, commander and missile-operator.

The commander is provided with a radar display and passes target-range and bearing to the missile operator. The operator finds the target in elevation and holds the graticule of the optical sight on to the target. The infra-red equipment locks the missile on the line of sight and on receipt of the firing command the missile is launched.

On the Roland 2 the tracking radar is mounted in front of the turret in place of the periscope sight.

The basic chassis has a built-up superstructure. Because of the large amount of electrical equipment, which includes an air-condition system, a 45KW Micro-turbo turbine is provided. It was intended that the French Army would have twenty batteries of Roland missiles but in late 1975 it was announced that only ten would be purchased.

FRANCE

AMX-13 LIGHT TANK
MANUFACTURER – Creusot-Loire, Chalon sur Saône
STATUS – In service with Algeria, Argentina (including bridgelayers, Argentina has been assembling AMX-13s since 1969), Cambodia (few, if any, remain operational), Chile, Dominican Republic, Ecuador, Egypt (very few), France, El Salvador, India, Indonesia, Ivory Coast, Kenya, Lebanon, Morocco, Netherlands (105mm models and ARVs), Nepal (from Israel), Peru, Salvador, Saudi Arabia, Singapore (from Israel), Switzerland (called Pz51s), Tunisia, Venezuela, Vietnam. They are no longer used by Austria (all sold back to France) or Israel (transferred to other countries). Production as required.

BASIC DATA

CREW:	3 (commander, gunner and driver)	TRENCH:	1.6m
WEIGHT LOADED:	15,000kg	ENGINE:	SOFAM Model 8 GXb, 8-cylinder, water-cooled
WEIGHT EMPTY:	13,000kg		petrol engine developing
LENGTH:	6.36m (gun forward)		250HP at 3,200rpm, 8.25
	4.88m (hull)		litres
WIDTH:	2.5m	ARMAMENT:	1 × 90mm gun
HEIGHT:	2.3m (including cupola)		1 × 7.62mm or 7.5mm
GROUND CLEARANCE:	.37m		co-axial machine-gun
TRACK:	2.159m		2 × 2 smoke dischargers
TRACK WIDTH:	350mm	ARMOUR	
LENGTH OF TRACK ON GROUND:	2.997m	hull front:	40mm
		hull sides:	20mm
GROUND PRESSURE:	.76kg/cm²	hull rear:	15mm
MAXIMUM ROAD SPEED:	60km/hr	hull roof:	10mm
RANGE:	350/400km	turret front:	40mm
FUEL CAPACITY:	480 litres	turret sides:	20mm
FORDING:	.6m	hull roof:	10mm
GRADIENT:	60%		
VERTICAL OBSTACLE:	.65m (forwards)		
	.45m (rearwards)		

Note: The above data relate to the current model with the 90mm gun. Height and overall length depend on the model and there are some minor differences between production runs.

DEVELOPMENT

After the end of the Second World War the French Army started development work on three main armoured vehicles—an MBT (which became the AMX-50 but did not enter service), a light tank (which became the AMX-13) and a heavy armoured car (which became the EBR). Design work started in 1946 with the first prototype being completed in 1948/49. The tank was designed by Atelier de Construction d'Issy-les-Moulineaux and it entered production in 1952 with first production tanks being completed in 1953. Initially production was at a French Government tank plant but later Creusot-Loire took over production as the Government tank plant at Roanne was busy with the AMX-30 MBT programme. To date, over 4,000 AMX-13 have been built and in addition thousands of other members of the basic vehicle, including 105mm and 155mm self-propelled guns, anti-aircraft vehicles and armoured personnel carriers. All these vehicles have their own separate entries.

DESCRIPTION

The hull of the AMX-13 is of all-welded construction. The driver is seated at the front of the vehicle on the left side and is provided with a total of three periscopes for driving whilst closed down, and a one-piece hatch cover. The engine, which is built by Saviem, is to his right, and the turret is at the rear of the hull.

   The AMX-13 has torsion-bar suspension, a total of five road wheels, the idler at the rear and the drive sprocket at the front, and three track support rollers (some tanks have been seen with just two). The first and fifth road wheel stations are provided with a hydraulic shock-absorber. The gearbox is manual and has 5F and 1R gears; an automatic gearbox has also been developed. The differential is of the Cleveland type. The electrical system consists of 4×12v batteries (100Amp/hr) and a 4.5Kw generator.

   The AMX-13 can be provided with both infra-red driving and fighting equipment; it has no amphibious capability and does not have a NBC system.

VARIANTS

Model 51 with 75mm Gun

The first model to enter service was the Model 1951. This is still in service in many parts of the world and is armed with a 75mm gun which can fire both HE and HEAT ammunition. Basic data of ammunition are: HE round weighs 12.5kg and has an m/v of 750m/s; HEAT round weighs 14.1kg and has an m/v of 1,000m/s—the French claim that this will penetrate 170mm of armour at 2,000m. During the 1966 Six Day War the Israelis found that this weapon would not penetrate the front of a T 54/T 55 tank although it would pierce the side armour. The turret used is the FL-10 which is similar to the FL-12 described below (ie the 105mm). A total of 37 rounds of 75mm and 3,600 rounds of machine-gun ammunition are carried.

90mm Gun

This is the current production model and it entered service in the early 60s. The FL-10 turret has hydraulic traverse and elevation, and can traverse through 360° in 12 seconds. Elevation limits are elevation $+12\frac{1}{2}°$ and depression $-5\frac{1}{2}°$, elevation speed is 5° a second.

The commander's cupola is on the left and this has a total of eight periscopes and a single-piece hatch cover. The loader is on the right of the turret and has two periscopes and a single-piece hatch cover. The commander is provided with an L 961 periscopic sight with a magnification of ×1.5 and ×6 whilst the gunner has a sight with a magnification of ×7.5.

The 90mm gun fires fin-stabilized shaped charge projectiles and the barrel is provided with an insulating jacket. This allows air to flow between the surface of the barrel and the inner surface of the jacket. A 7.62mm co-axial machine-gun is mounted to the right of the barrel and a 7.62mm machine-gun can be mounted on the roof if required.

The 90mm gun is fed from two six-round revolver magazines and these are loaded via two hatches in the turret roof, towards the rear. This allows the gun to fire one round in five seconds. After each round is fired the empty cartridge case is automatically ejected out through a single hatch in the turret rear. A total of 34 rounds (21 in the turret and 13 in the hull) of 90mm ammunition are carried as well as 3,600 rounds of machine-gun ammunition.

The 90mm gun can fire either HEAT-T, HE or smoke rounds in addition to training rounds. Basic data of ammunition are as follows:
HEAT complete round weighs 8.9kg and has an m/v of 950m/s
HE complete round weighs 10.4kg and has an m/v of 750m/s
Smoke complete round weighs 10.6kg and has an m/v of 744m/s

105mm Gun

This is used by a number of armies including the Netherlands. The 105mm gun is mounted in a FL-12 turret (this is a modified FL-10 turret) and it fires a fin-stabilised HEAT projectile with an m/v of 800m/s and a maximum effective range of 2,700m. It will penetrate 360mm of armour with the complete round weighing 17.7kg. It will also fire HE (weight 18.4kg and m/v 700m/s) and Smoke (weight 19.1kg and m/v 695m/s) rounds.

This turret is also fitted to the Panzerjägers of the Austrian Army.

FL-11 turret with 75mm gun

Very few of these were built for use in Algeria and it is believed that these were left behind for the use of the Algerian Army when France withdrew from North Africa.

AMX-13 Model 51 with SS-11 Missiles

This is in current service with the French Army. It is a basic AMX-13 with two SS-11 anti-tank missiles mounted either side of the main armament. These have a minimum range of 350m and a maximum range of 3,000m. A later model is fitted with the TGA infra-red/optical guidance system.

AMX-13 with HOT Missile System

This is a standard AMX-13 with three HOT missiles mounted either side of the turret. It is expected that this may enter service with the French Army, although the AMX-13 will itself be replaced by the AMX-10C tracked vehicle with a 105mm gun, and the French are also developing a special HOT installation on an AMX-10P chassis.

AMX-13 Training Tank

This is simply an AMX-13 with the turret removed and used for driver training. The French Army is known to have used some AMX-13 tanks with American M24 Chaffe turrets fitted in place of the standard turrets.

AMX-13 Bridgelayer (Char Poseur de Pont AMX-13)

This consists of an AMX-13 tank chassis with the turret removed and a folding class-25 bridge installed. The bridge is made by CODER and is made of two halves connected together by a hinge, with widening panels and guides provided. Basic data of the bridge itself are as follows:

Weight: 4,630kg   Length: 14.01m (unfolded) 7.15m (folded)   Width: 3.05m   Height: 1.12m (unfolded) 1.8m (folded)

The bridge is laid hydraulically over the rear of the vehicle and two spades are provided to stabilize the vehicle when the bridge is being laid. It has a crew of three—commander, bridge operator and driver.
    Basic data of the bridgelayer are as follows:

Weight: 19.700kg (with bridge) 15,000kg (without bridge) Length: 7.75m (O/A) 4.88m (chassis) Width: 3.05m   Height: 4.3m (with bridge) 2.72m (without bridge)   Maximum road speed: 4km/hr (with bridge)   Gradient: 40% (with bridge)

If required, two of these bridges can be laid side by side to take class-50 vehicles.

AMX-13 Armoured Recovery Vehicle (Char de Dépannage Model 55)

This is designed to tow vehicles of the AMX-13 class as well as lifting such components as transmissions, engines and turrets. An A frame is mounted at the front of the hull and when not required this lays down flat on the hull. A winch with a capacity of 16,000kg, and 50m of 25mm cable is provided. It has two speeds. The secondary winch has 120m of 6mm cable. There are a total of four spades at the rear of the hull. When the jib is being used the front suspension can be locked in position and the jib can lift a maximum load of 5000kg. The following safety equipment is provided: a warning light comes on when a load of 14,000kg is being pulled, and when a 17,000kg load is being pulled an automatic switch switches off the magneto. It has a crew of three—commander, driver and winch operator—and is armed with a 7.62mm machine-gun and smoke dischargers.
    Basic data of the vehicle are as follows:

Weight: 15,000kg   Length: 5.515m   Width: 2.6m   Height: 2.682m (jib stowed) 4.65m (jib in use)   Ground clearance: .26m

AMX-13 Model 51 with 75mm gun of the Swiss Army.

AMX-13 of the French Army with a 90mm gun.

AMX-13 Model 51 with four SS-11 ATGWs.

The SOFAM Model 8 GXb 8-cylinder petrol engine as used in all members of the AMX-13 Light Tank family.

AMX-13 Bridgelayer unfolding its bridge during training.

AMX-13 Armoured Recovery Vehicle of the Dutch Army.

GERMANY (FEDERAL GERMAN REPUBLIC)

WAFFENTRÄGER – AIR-PORTABLE TANK
STATUS – Project

GENERAL

In 1974 it was stated that the German Army had a requirement for an air-portable light tank, to be called the Waffenträger 11 LL. It is believed that design work is being carried out by Rheinstahl of Kassel and Porsche of Stuttgart. No data has been released at this time. The tank would probably be carried by the Transall aircraft which has a maximum payload of approx. 15,800kg.

GERMANY (FEDERAL GERMAN REPUBLIC) AND GREAT BRITAIN

KAMPFPANZER 3—FMBT-80
STATUS—Development

GENERAL

Some years ago Germany and Great Britain decided to develop a new MBT. The German Army require a tank to replace the Leopard 1 from the early 1980s and the British require a tank to replace the Chieftain from the early 1980s. There is, however, a possibility that Germany will refit the Leopard 1 and produce larger numbers of the Leopard 2. The British may well decide to carry out a refit programme on the Chieftain and install a new engine, new turret and a new gun.

Germany

The following German companies are known to have been involved in the Kampfpanzer 3 programme: Ing. Hopp of Munich, Krauss-Maffei of Munich, MaK Maschinenbau of Kiel and Rheinstahl of Kassel. Krupp GST of Essen is reported to have built a turretless MBT armed with one or two 105mm rifled guns in a low turret with limited traverse. Until 1972 this company was owned by MaK but in 1974 was taken over by Krupp and it has been reported that it is now no longer involved in armoured vehicle design.

The Kampfpanzer 3 would probably be armed with the new German 120mm smooth-bore tank gun as fitted to the Leopard 2, and have an engine built by MTU.

Great Britain

Both Vickers (Elswick) and the Royal Ordnance Factory at Leeds are involved, as is the Military Vehicles Engineering Establishment (MVEE) where tank design work is carried out, as well as some prototype construction. The British model would be armed with either the German 120mm smooth-bore gun, the British-developed 110mm rifled gun which fires a fin-stabilized APDS round, or the standard 105mm L7A3 rifled gun firing a new American round of ammunition. All three of these weapons were evaluated in England early in 1975 but by late 1975 the results had not been announced. The British tank would probably have a Rolls-Royce engine, laser rangefinder by Barr and Stroud, and an FCS by Marconi Space and Defence Systems Limited.

GERMANY (FEDERAL GERMAN REPUBLIC)

LEOPARD 2 – MAIN BATTLE TANK
MANUFACTURER – Krauss-Maffei AG, Munich
STATUS – Trials in Germany and the United States

BASIC DATA

CREW:	4 (commander, gunner, loader and driver)	LENGTH OF TRACK ON GROUND:	4.72m
WEIGHT:	50,500kg	GROUND PRESSURE:	.83kg/cm²
LENGTH:	9.74m (gun forward)	MAXIMUM ROAD SPEED:	68km/hr
	7.73m (hull)	MAXIMUM CROSS-	
WIDTH:	3.54m (with track skirts)	COUNTRY SPEED:	55km/hr
	3.42m (without track skirts)	POWER-TO-WEIGHT RATIO:	29.75HP/ton
HEIGHT:	2.49m (turret roof)	FORDING:	1m
GROUND CLEARANCE:	.54m (front)		2.35m (with preparation)
	.49m (rear)		
TRACK WIDTH:	635mm	GRADIENT:	60%
TRACK:	2.785m	SIDE SLOPE:	30%

VERTICAL OBSTACLE:	1.15m		chargers, developing
TRENCH:	3m	ARMAMENT:	1,500 HP at 2,600rpm
ENGINE:	MTU MB 873 Ka-500, 4-stroke, multi-fuel, water-cooled, with two exhaust gas turbo-		1 × 120mm gun (or 105mm gun) 1 × 7.62mm co-axial MG 1 × grenade launcher 2 × 4 smoke dischargers

DEVELOPMENT

Development of the Leopard 2 (or Kampfpanzer 2 as it is also called) started in the late 1960s on a low priority. When, however, the American/German agreement for the MBT-70 was cancelled in January 1970, work on the project was given a higher priority. The prototypes were built by Krauss-Maffei, with Wegmann of Kassel building the turrets and AEG-Telefunken working on the electrical side, most of the design work being carried out by Porsche. A total of seventeen prototypes have been built, of which one has been purchased by the United States for comparative trials with the new American XM1 MBT. As of late 1975 it had not been announced when the Leopard 2 would enter production. Krauss-Maffei have stated, however, that if a production order was awarded by late 1975 it would be in production by 1978/79. The German Army has a requirement to replace the 1054 M48 tanks still in service.

DESCRIPTION

The hull and turret of the Leopard 2 is of all-welded construction, and it is known that the hull front and turret is of spaced armour, ie two layers of armour with a space between them.

The driver is seated at the front of the hull on the left side and is provided with a single-piece hatch cover and a total of three periscopes for observation purposes.

The three other crew members are seated in the turret with the commander and gunner on the right and the loader on the left. The commander is provided with a total of eight periscopes for observation purposes as well as a PERI-R-12 panoramic stabilized periscope. This is used for fire control and allows the commander to locate a target and then swing the gun onto it. The gunner has a TZF 1A monocular auxiliary periscope with a magnification of ×8 (as fitted to the Leopard 1) and an EMES-12 combined laser rangefinder and stereoscopic rangefinder with a magnification of ×8 and ×16, both built by Zeiss. The gunner also has an observation periscope. An infra-red/white light searchlight is stowed in the bustle when travelling and can be quickly elevated into position. A passive light-intensification light is also mounted in the turret bustle, which can be traversed through 360° by the tank commander. Three target detection systems are being studied: an AEG Telefunken system, Zeiss/Eltro system and a thermal imaging system.

The turret has an electro-hydraulic system and the commander can override the gunner if required. The gun is fully stabilized and can be layed and fired whilst on the move; the system is essentially the American Cadillac Gage system with some modifications.

The Leopard 2 is armed with a 120mm smooth-bore gun developed by Rheinmetall, which has a drop-type breech block, a fume extractor and a thermal sleeve. Two types of ammunition have been developed for this: a fin-stabilized APDS round and a Multi Purpose round. A hydraulic-assisted loading mechanism positions the fresh round vertically on the loading chute. Both types of ammunition use a semi-combustible cartridge case with a steel baseplate. Some prototypes had a 105mm gun fitted for trials purposes.

A 7.62mm MG-3 machine-gun is mounted co-axially with the main armament and this is operated by the loader; a fume extractor system is provided for this. A grenade launcher is fitted for dealing with infantry. Four smoke dischargers are fitted either side of the turret. The FCS includes the AEG-Telefunken FLER-H computer. The engine and transmission are at the rear of the hull. The engine was in fact originally built for the MBT-70. The complete engine, 20Kw generator, gearbox and steering unit, air filters, engine cooling system, exhaust and brake system is built as a complete unit and can be removed in less than fifteen minutes. The gearbox is an HSWL-354/3 with 4F and 4R gears. The gearbox is of the hydro-mechanical planetary type with combined hydrodynamic/mechanical brakes, converter with bypass and steepless hydrostatic/hydrodynamic regenerative steering.

The suspension is of the torsion bar type; maximum suspension upward movement is 320mm and downward movement is 210mm. There are a total of seven aluminium road wheels, with the idler at the front and the drive sprocket at the rear, and four track support rollers. Friction dampers are provided on the first, second, third, sixth and seventh road wheel stations. The tracks are provided with removable rubber pads and snow grips can be fitted if required.

The electrical system consists of a 20Kw generator on the engine, a 9Kw generator on the auxiliary electrical power system driven by a multi-fuel engine. A total of six 300Amp/hr batteries are fitted, these being provided with a pre-heating system.

Other equipment installed includes an NBC system, two heaters, side skirts, hull escape hatch and night driving equipment.

VARIANTS
A project exists for a Leopard 2 chassis fitted with the Gepard 2×35mm anti-aircraft gun turret.

Austere Leopard
The Leopard 2 being delivered to the United States is an 'Austere' model. Early in 1975 it was stated that the Germans would deliver a Leopard 2 with the following modifications by 1st September, 1976:

Redesign of the turret and hull	Redesigned heating system
Redesigned suspension system	Redesigned engine cooling system
New fire-control system	Increased fuel capacity
New turret drive system	Modified exhaust and final drives
New electrical power supply	New brake system

Top left and right The Leopard 2 armed with a 105 mm smooth-bore gun.
Above The Leopard 2 armed with a 120mm smooth-bore gun.
Left The MTU MB 873 Ka-500 engine which develops 1,500HP at 2,600rpm. This was developed for the German model of the MBT-70 and is now installed in the Leopard 2 MBT.

GERMANY (FEDERAL GERMAN REPUBLIC)

LEOPARD TANK FAMILY–MAIN BATTLE TANK
MANUFACTURER–Krauss-Maffei AG, Munich
Oto-Melara SpA, La Spezia (Italy)
STATUS–In service with Australia, Belgium, Denmark, Germany, Italy, Netherlands, Norway. In production. Future orders could come from Canada, Switzerland and Turkey.

BASIC DATA	Leopard 1	Leopard A4	AEV	ARV	Bridgelayer
CREW:	4	4	4	4	2
WEIGHT LOADED:	40,000kg	42,400kg	40,800kg	39,800kg	45,000kg
WEIGHT EMPTY:	38,700kg	40,400kg	40,200kg	39,200kg	36,400kg (w/o bridge)
LENGTH O/A:	9.543m	9.543m	7.57m (inc. spade)	7.57m (inc. spade)	11.65m (with bridge)
LENGTH/HULL:	7.09m	7.09m	—	—	11.3m (w/o bridge)
WIDTH:	3.25m	3.37m	3.25m	3.25m	4m (with bridge)
HEIGHT O/A:	2.64m	2.64m	2.69m (inc. A/A)	2.69m (inc. A/A)	3.5m (with bridge)
HEIGHT:	2.62m (turret roof)	2.62m (turret roof)	—	—	—
GROUND CLEARANCE:	.44m	.44m	.44m	.44m	.44m
TRACK:	2.7m	2.7m	2.7m	2.7m	2.7m
TRACK WIDTH:	550mm	550mm	550mm	550mm	550mm
LENGTH OF TRACK ON GROUND:	4.236m	4.236m	4.236m	4.236m	4.236m
GROUND PRESSURE:	.86kg/cm²	.88kg/cm²	.86kg/cm²	.85kg/cm²	.95kg/cm²
MAXIMUM ROAD SPEED:	65km/hr	65km/hr	65km/hr	65km/hr	65km/hr
RANGE ROAD:	600km	600km	850km	850km	550km
RANGE CROSS COUNTRY:	450km	450km	500km	500km	400km
FUEL:	955 litres	955 litres	1,410 litres	1,410 litres	955 litres
FORDING:	2.25m	2.25m	2.1m	2.1m	1.2m
FORDING WITH SCHNORKEL:	4m	4m	4m	4m	—
GRADIENT:	60%	60%	60%	60%	60%
VERTICAL OBSTACLE:	1.15m	1.15m	1.15m	1.15m	1.15m
TRENCH:	3m	3m	3m	3m	3m
ENGINE:	All are powered by an MTU MB 838 Ca.M500, 10-cylinder multi-fuel engine which develops 830HP at 2,200rpm.				
ARMAMENT:	1 × 105mm 1 × 7.62mm co-axial 1 × 7.62mm A/A	1 × 105mm 1 × 7.62mm co-axial 1 × 7.62mm A/A	1 × 7.62mm (bow) 1 × 7.62mm (A/A) —	1 × 7.62mm (bow) 1 × 7.62mm (bow) —	— — —
SMOKE DISCHARGERS:	2 × 4	2 × 4	12	12	8
AMMUNITION MAIN:	60	60	—	—	—
MG:	5,500	5,500	4,250	4,250	—
ARMOUR:	According to the manufacturer all data are still classified so the data below should be taken as provisional.				

The data below relate to the Leopard 1 MBT. The Leopard A4 has a spaced armour turret which differs from the Leopard 1 but their hulls are identical.

Nose: 70mm at 55°
Glacis: 70mm at 60°
Glacis top: 25mm at 83°
Sides upper: 35mm at 50°
Sides lower: 25mm at 90°
Hull rear: 25mm at 88°
Hull roof: 10mm
Hull floor: 15mm
Turret front: 52mm
Turret sides: 60mm
Turret rear: 60mm
Turret mantlet: 60mm

The AEV/ARV has the following armour:
Nose: 40mm at 60°
Front: 40mm at 45°
Sides upper: 35mm at 65°
Sides lower: 25mm at 90°
Hull rear: 25mm at 90°
Superstructure sides: 35mm
Superstructure front and rear: 25mm
Roof and decking: 10mm
Hull floor: 15mm

DEVELOPMENT

When the German Army was reformed in 1955 it was initially equipped with the American M47 medium tank and later with the M48 (these still remain in service). In 1955 a project was initiated to design and place in production a new German tank in the 30-ton class. The French were also working on a similar class of tank, and Italy had a requirement for a medium tank as well. The idea was that France and Germany would each build prototypes, test them together, and the best would be produced by both countries. This did not happen and France built the AMX30 and Germany the Leopard.

Initially two Groups were formed to design and build prototypes of a new tank: Group 'A' and Group 'B'. Group A comprised Porsche, Atlas-MaK, Luther & Jordan and Jung whilst Group B consisted of Warneke, Rheinstahl-Hanomag, Henschel. The turret for both tanks was designed by Rheinmetall and Wegmenn.

The first Group A prototype was completed in June 1960, with the second following in August 1960. The first Group B prototype was completed in May 1960. Group B, however, only built four prototypes and it was decided to concentrate on the Group A tank. Over several years this group built a total of 26 prototypes, followed by 50 pre-production vehicles. In 1963 it was decided to place the tank in production and the prime contractor is Krauss-Maffei at Munich. The first production tank, which was then officially called the Leopard, was completed on 9th September 1965. Since then a whole series of vehicles has been developed from the Leopard. Late in 1975 Krauss-Maffei released the following production figures for the Leopard, the first figure being the total number ordered and the second figure the number supplied to late 1975:

	Leopard MBT	Leopard ARV	Leopard AEV	Leopard B/Layer	Gepard	Training	Total
AUSTRALIA:	42	6	nil	5	nil	nil	53
BELGIUM:	334(334)	36(36)	6(6)	nil	55	12(12)	443(388)
DENMARK:	120	nil	nil	nil	nil	nil	120
GERMANY:	2,437(2,437)	444(444)	36(36)	105(105)	420	nil	3,442(2,967)
ITALY:	800(280)	69(69)	12(12)	nil	nil	nil	881(361)
NETHERLANDS:	468(468)	41(41)	14(14)	14	95	12(12)	644(523)
NORWAY:	78(78)	6(6)	nil	5	nil	nil	89(84)
TOTALS:	4,279(3,597)	602(596)	68(68)	129(105)	570	24(24)	5,672(4,323)

DESCRIPTION

The hull of the Leopard is of all-welded construction whilst the turret is cast in one piece.

The driver is seated at the front of the hull on the right side and is provided with a one-piece hatch cover that opens to the right and a total of three periscopes, one of which can be replaced by an infra-red periscope for night driving.

The other three crew members are in the turret with the gunner and commander on the right and the loader on the left. The commander has a single-piece hatch cover and eight periscopes. A zoom panoramic periscope with a magnification of ×6 to × 20 is mounted in front of the commander's hatch, allowing him to locate a target, aim and fire the gun if required.

The gunner has a rangefinder which can either be used in the coincidence or stereoscopic roles. This is a Model TEM 2A and has a magnification of × 16, with a practical range of 4,000m maximum. He also has a TZF 1A sight with a magnification of ×8. The gunner is also provided with a single periscope for observation purposes whilst the loader has two periscopes for observation purposes. Both the commander and loader are provided with a single-piece hatch cover. The commander can replace his sight with an infra-red sight for night operations, this being a Model B 171 II. An XSW-30-U I/Red searchlight is mounted co-axially with the main armament.

The engine and transmission are in the rear of the vehicle. One of the features of the Leopard is that the engine can be removed and replaced in approx. 30 minutes. The transmission is manufactured by Zahnradfabrik Friedrichshafen AG and is a Model ZF 4 HP 250. This is a four-speed planetary-gear steer/shift transmission with torque converter lock-up clutch which is shifted electro-hydraulically. The Leopard is steered by a two-radius cross-drive steering transmission with infinitely variable radii for flat bends, and fixed, speed-dependent radii for sharp bends. The driver can select the following gears: forward road, forward cross country, neutral and reverse.

The suspension is of the torsion-bar type and consists of seven road wheels with the idler at the front and the drive sprocket at the rear. There are four track support rollers. The first, second, third, sixth and seventh road wheel stations are provided with hydraulic shock absorbers. The tracks are of the double-pin type with rubber pads.

The main armament consists of the famous British 105mm L7A3 rifled tank gun which is purchased from England. This has an elevation of +20° and a depression of −9°; traverse is 360° which takes 11 seconds. An electro-hydraulic control system is installed with manual controls for use in an emergency. As built, the Leopard did not have a stabilization system installed.

A 7.62mm MG3 machine-gun is mounted co-axially with the main armament and there is a similar weapon for the use of the commander. Four smoke dischargers are fitted either side of the turret.

A total of 60 rounds of 105mm ammunition are carried, three in the turret and 57 in the hull, a normal load would consist of 31 APDS, 26 HESH and three smoke rounds. According to the manufacturers, the 105mm gun has an 85% probability of hitting another tank at a range of 1,000m, which increases to 98% with the second round. At a range of 2,000m it has a 40% chance with the first round and a 75% chance with the second round. A well-trained crew can achieve better results at longer ranges, however.

The Leopard is provided with an NBC system, and a fire-warning system is also a standard fitting. A hull escape hatch is provided, as is a heater. A dozer blade can be mounted at the front of the hull if required.

The electrical system consists of six 12V batteries with a capacity of 400Amp/hr; these are provided with heaters. An engine-driven 3-phase generator is provided and delivers 28V at 250Amps.

A schnorkel can be fitted over the commander's hatch for deep-fording operations. Air for the engine is drawn in down this tube whilst exhaust leaves the vehicle as normal. The turret ring is sealed by an inflatable rubber ring.

Leopard 1

This is being refitted with the following and will then be known as the Leopard A1:
The main armament will be fitted with a stabilization system.
A thermal sleeve will be fitted to the 105mm gun.
New tracks will be installed as will rubber skirts.
Modified turret hatches.
Modified deep-wading equipment.

Leopard A2

The last 232 Leopard 1s were built with the above modifications but also have:
A turret of stronger cast steel.
More efficient exhaust filtration.
NBC system has been improved.
Passive-image intensification equipment for the commander and driver.

Leopard A3

This has: New turret of spaced armour which incorporates a wedge-shape welded mantlet, turret stowage incorporated into turret contour to accommodate searchlight and other equipment, the loader's periscope is adjustable in elevation and azimuth. It also incorporates most of the modifications of the Leopard A1 and A2. 110 Leopard A3s have been built for the German Army.

According to Krauss-Maffei there are a total of 2,700 companies involved in the production of parts for the Leopard, of which 450 are first-level sub-contractors. For example Rheinmetall deliver the complete Leopard turret with gun to the factory ready to fit on the tank chassis.

The Belgian Army's Leopards are being fitted with a new fire-control system designed by SABCA of Brussels, and a similar system is fitted to the Jagdpanzer Kanones which are now being delivered to the Belgian Army. This includes a DC tachometer, laser rangefinder, pendulum, crosswind sensor and automatic grain temperature sensor.

Gepard Anti-Aircraft Gun System

There is a separate entry for this in the self-propelled anti-aircraft section of this book.

Leopard 155mm GCT Self-Propelled Gun

This is essentially a Leopard tank chassis with the turret of the French AMX-30 155mm GCT self-propelled gun fitted in place of the standard Leopard turret. The first and only prototype was completed in 1973, this being a joint development by Krauss-Maffei and the French GIAT. It is reported that Belgium is showing some interest in this version. For details of the turret the reader is referred to the French GCT entry in the self-propelled artillery section. The chassis is identical to the MBT apart from the following:
1. The NBC system is installed in the turret rather than the hull 2. The right fuel tank has been removed 3. An auxiliary generator has been installed 4. Hull ammunition racks removed.
Basic data are as follows:

Crew: 4 Weight Loaded: 45,500kg Length: 10.6m (gun forwards) Width: 3.25m Height: 3.12m (O/A) 3.02m (turret roof)

Combat Engineer Vehicle (New)
At the present time both MaK and Eisenwerke are reported to be building a new recovery vehicle based on Leopard components. It is believed that this is being designed specifically for preparing river crossing points and exits, as well as for recovering disabled and damaged vehicles from the water.

Leopard Driver Training Tank
This is a Leopard MBT with its turret removed and replaced by a cabin provided with windows. The cabin has three seats, one for the instructor and two for the trainee drivers who can observe the driver under training. If required, the instructor can take over control of the vehicle as he is provided with controls for the accelerator, steering, gear changing and brakes.

Armoured Recovery Vehicle
Development of this was commenced by Porsche when the Leopard MBT was being designed. The first prototype was completed in 1964 and the first production model on the 9th September 1966. All production has been undertaken by MaK of Kiel. The majority of components of the Armoured Recovery Vehicle are identical to those of the MBT. The vehicle has been designed to carry out the following roles:
1. Recovering damaged vehicles   2. Towing disabled vehicles   3. Changing vehicle components and lifting complete vehicles up to 20,000kg   4. Carrying a spare Leopard MBT engine, a complete engine change can be carried out in 30 minutes   5. Carrying out dozer operations   6. Refuelling and defuelling other vehicles
The superstructure is of all-welded construction, and there are two doors in the left side of the hull. The driver is seated at the front of the vehicle and is provided with three periscopes, one of which can be replaced by an infra-red periscope for driving at night, and a single-piece hatch cover. The commander is behind the driver and is provided with a single-piece hatch cover and a total of eight periscopes, one of which can be replaced with an infra-red periscope. There is a further single-piece hatch cover to the rear of the commander's station, which also has three periscopes. There is a swivelling periscope in the roof of the superstructure.
A dozer blade is mounted at the front of the hull; this is used for both dozing operations and to stabilize the vehicle when the crane or winch is being used. The crane is mounted on the right side of the hull and can be traversed through 270°. The hoisting winch is on the right side of the hull.
The main winch is in the centre of the operating compartment and is provided with 90m of 33mm diameter rope. This winch has a capacity of 35,000kg in the lowest cable position and 70,000kg with a guide pulley. All recovery equipment is hydraulically operated. Other equipment installed includes a chain-saw, tools, electric wrench and an electric welding system. Infra-red driving lights are provided.
Armament consists of a 7.62mm machine-gun at the commander's position, and a 7.62mm machine-gun in the bow with an elevation of +15° and a depression of −15°, traverse being 15° left and right. Smoke dischargers are provided.

Armoured Engineer Vehicle
The prototype of this was completed in 1967 with the first production vehicle being completed the following year, all production being undertaken by MaK of Kiel. The chassis and superstructure, and most other components are identical to the armoured recovery vehicle. The main differences are: 1. A heat exchanger has been installed   2. Explosives are carried for demolition work   3. An earth borer is carried in place of a spare powerplant. This can bore a 700mm diameter hole to a depth of 2m   4. The dozer blade can be fitted with scarifiers to rip up the surface of roads, etc. Extension wings can also be fitted to the dozer blade if required, giving the dozer blade a width of 3.75m

Bridgelayer
Prototypes of two different designs of bridgelayers were completed in 1969, these being known as type A and type B. Type B was selected for production and became known as the Biber. MaK of Kiel completed the first production bridgelayer in 1973.
When arriving at the crossing the Biber lowers its spade at the front of the hull. The bridge itself is in two halves which rest on top of each other. The bottom half of the bridge is slid forward until its end is lined up with the end of the other half. The two sections are then locked in position. The bridge is lowered into position by the cantilever arm which is then withdrawn and traffic can cross the bridge. The bridge can be picked up from either end by the Biber. The bridge is constructed of aluminium alloy and can take vehicles up to a maximum weight of 60,000kg. Opened out it is 22m long and can be used to span gaps of up to 20m.

Top Leopard 1 of the 4th production batch for the German Army.
Centre Leopard 1 of the Dutch Army with stowage boxes on side of hull.
Right Leopard 1 of the Belgian Army with FN machine-guns.

1

2

3

4

▲5

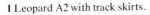

1 Leopard A2 with track skirts.
2 Leopard A3 Main Battle Tank with spaced armour turret.
3 Belgian FN machine-gun as mounted in Leopard tanks of the Belgian Army.
4 Close-up of a Leopard turret with Simfire equipment installed.
5 The Leopard Training Tank.
6 The Leopard Recovery Vehicle in use.
7 The Leopard Engineer Vehicle with auger in position.
8 Biber Bridgelayer with bridge ready to be laid in position.
9 The 155mm Leopard Self-Propelled Gun.
10 The Biber Bridgelayer. Note the spade in position at the front of the vehicle.

6

7

8   9   ▼10

GREAT BRITAIN

VICKERS MAIN BATTLE TANK
MANUFACTURERS – Vickers Limited, Elswick, Newcastle-Upon-Tyne
Avadi Company, Madras, India
STATUS – In service with India and Kuwait. In production in India.

BASIC DATA	Mk.1	Mk.3			
CREW:	4	4	SIDE SLOPE:	30%	30%
WEIGHT LOADED:	38,600kg	38,600kg	VERTICAL OBSTACLE:	.914m	.914m
WEIGHT EMPTY:	36,000kg	36,000kg	TRENCH:	2.438m	2.438m
LENGTH:	9.728m (gun forward) 7.92m (hull)	9.788m (gun forward 7.561m (hull)	ENGINE:	Leyland L60 Mk.4B 6-cylinder water-cooled multi-fuel engine developing 650BHP at 2,670rpm.	General Motors 12V 71T turbocharged diesel developing 800BHP at 2,500rpm
WIDTH:	3.168m	3.168m			
HEIGHT:	2.64m (commander's cupola) 2.438m (turret roof)	2.711m (commander's cupola) 2.489m (turret roof)	ARMAMENT:	1 × 105mm 1 × .50 (12.7mm) RMG 1 × .30 (7.62mm) co-axial MG	1 × 105mm 1 × .50 (12.7mm) RMG 1 × .30 (7.62mm) co-axial MG
GROUND CLEARANCE:	.406m	.406m			
TRACK:	2.533m	2.533m			
TRACK WIDTH:	520mm	520mm			
LENGTH OF TRACK ON GROUND:	4.28m	4.28m			
POWER-TO-WEIGHT RATIO:	16.83BHP/ton	20.7BHP/ton	ARMOUR:		
			hull nose:	80mm	80mm
GROUND PRESSURE:	.87kg/cm²	.87kg/cm²	hull glacis:	60mm	60mm
MAXIMUM ROAD SPEED:	56km/hr	53km/hr	hull sides:	30mm	30mm
RANGE:	480km (road)	600km (road)	hull rear:	20mm	20mm
FUEL:	1,000 litres	1,000 litres	turret front:	80mm	80mm
FORDING:	1.143m	1.143m	turret sides:	40/60mm	40/60mm
GRADIENT:	60%	60%	turret roof:	25mm	25mm

Note: Above data are basic. With such items as NBC pack, flotation screen and so on added, some of the above figures would change.

DEVELOPMENT

In the 1950s Vickers designed a light tank armed with a 20-pounder gun and Vigilant ATGWs. This was not produced and Vickers went on to develop a new tank armed with the 105mm gun as fitted to late Centurions (many of which were built by Vickers). In 1960/61 the Indian Government sent teams to both Germany and Britain to look at designs which could be built in India. In August 1961 Vickers signed an agreement under which they would help set up a factory in India to build a new MBT. The first two prototypes were built in 1963; one was sent to India and the other retained in Britain for trials. This MBT used a suspension system developed for the FV300 series of vehicles (which was cancelled after several prototypes had been built), the engine and transmission of the Chieftain (Vickers are the design parents of the Chieftain), and the 105mm gun.

The first production Vickers MBT was delivered to India in 1965. Meanwhile the factory in India was being built and the first Indian-built tank was completed in January 1969. The Indian name for the tank is the Vijayanta. It has been estimated that over 500 Vijayanta tanks have now been built in India, although some components are still being built in Britain. In 1968 Kuwait ordered 50 Vickers MBTs and these were delivered in 1970/72.

DESCRIPTION

The turret and hull of the Vickers MBT is of all-welded rolled steel construction. The driver is seated at the front of the hull on the right side. He is provided with a single-piece hatch cover that opens to the right and a single wide-angle periscope for observation. To his left is ammunition stowage. The turret is in the centre of the hull with the commander and gunner on the right and the loader on the left.

The commander has a single-piece hatch cover, six periscopes and a sight with a magnification of ×10. The gunner is provided with a single sighting telescope with a ballistic graticule. The loader has a two-piece hatch cover and is provided with a single observation periscope.

The 105mm L7 series gun has an elevation of +20° and a depression of −7°, traverse is a full 360° which takes 13 seconds. Elevation and traverse is powered with hand controls for use in an emergency.

The gun is aimed by the well-tried RMG method, the .50 (12.7mm) ranging machine-gun being mounted to the left of the main armament. This fires three-second bursts of tracer ammunition. A co-axial .30 (7.62mm) machine-gun is mounted to the left of the main armament and a similar weapon can be mounted on the commander's cupola if required. A six-barrelled smoke-discharger is mounted either side of the turret.

Total ammunition supply consists of 44 rounds of 105mm, 600 rounds of .50 and 3,000 round of .30 (7.62mm) ammunition. The 105mm ammunition is stowed as follows: five rounds under main armament, eight on turntable floor, three on LH of turret and 25 rounds to left of driver.

The 105mm gun fires an APDS round with an effective range of 1,800m and a HESH round with an effective range of 5,500m. During trials a Vickers MBT engaged 10 targets at ranges of 600-1,000m in 55 seconds.

The Vickers MBT is fitted with the gun-control and stabilization system type EC517 which has been developed by GEC-Marconi. This has three modes of operation: non-stabilized, stabilized and emergency operation. The system enables the gun to be laid and fired whilst moving across country.

The engine, transmission, steering system and brakes are at the rear of the hull. The L.60 engine has proved a reliable engine when installed in the Vickers MBT. The complete powerpack which consists of the engine, transmission, radiators, fans, coolant, oil filter, can be removed from the vehicle as a complete unit. The TN 12 transmission incorporates an epicyclic gearbox with 6F and 2R gears. The engine is cooled by twin radiators mounted horizontally on each side of the engine compartment, and twin cooling fans are mounted at the rear of the engine compartment.

The suspension consists of six independent torsion bars with a trailing arm, the first, second and sixth road wheel stations having a secondary torsion bar. The idler is at the front and the drive sprocket is at the rear, and there are three track support rollers. The first, second and sixth road wheel stations are provided with hydraulic shock absorbers. The tracks are of cast manganese steel with removable rubber pads.

A 24V generator is mounted on the engine and there is also a Coventry Climax H30 auxiliary engine which drives a second generator. There are a total of four 6V 115Amp/hr batteries, two mounted behind the driver and two in the turret rear.

The Vickers MBT is provided with a fire warning and internal fire-fighting system, and a crew heater. If required the tank can be fitted with a collapsible reinforced nylon fabric flotation screen. This is stowed in a trough around the top of the hull when not required. It takes fifteen to thirty minutes to erect but only two to four minutes to take down. When in the water it is propelled by its tracks at a speed of 6.4km/hr.

Other optional equipment includes an NCB system and infra-red driving and fighting equipment.

VARIANTS
Vickers MBT Mk.2
This was a project only and would have had two integral launchers in each side of the turret rear for two BAC Swingfire ATGW. A Vickers MBT Mk.1 was fitted with four mock-ups of the Swingfire missiles.

Vickers MBT Mk.3
This is now under development and has a new turret. This has a cast front welded to a fabricated armour-plate body. A new cupola gives the commander improved vision. New final drives have been fitted which give the tank increased performance. The 105mm gun on the Mk.3 can be depressed to −10° and total ammunition capacity has been raied to 50 rounds.

Optional equipment for the Mk.3 includes a laser rangefinder by Barr and Stroud and passive night-fighting and driving equipment. An armoured recovery vehicle and a bridgelayer are also being offered by Vickers.

Above Vickers Mk.1 MBT with 105mm gun depressed. This vehicle has the Leyland L60 engine.

Above and below Vickers Mk.I MBT with new commander's cupola, General Motors power pack and thermal sleeve for main armament.

GREAT BRITAIN

CHIEFTAIN – MAIN BATTLE TANK
MANUFACTURERS – Royal Ordnance Factory, Leeds
Vickers Limited, Elswick
STATUS – In service with Great Britain and Iran. In production.

BASIC DATA	Mk.3	Mk.5		Mk.3	Mk.5
CREW:	4 (commander, gunner, loader, driver)	4 (commander, gunner, loader, driver)	FORDING without preparation:	1.066m	1.066m
			FORDING with schnorkel:	4.57m	4.57m
			GRADIENT:	60%	60%
			VERTICAL OBSTACLE:	.914m	.914m
WEIGHT LOADED:	54,100kg	55,000kg	TRENCH:	3.149m	3.149m
WEIGHT EMPTY:	51,460kg	53,500kg	ENGINE:	Both are powered by a Leyland L60, 2-stroke, compression ignition, 12-cylinder vertically opposed multi-fuel engine.	
LENGTH gun forwards:	10.79m	10.795m			
LENGTH hull:	7.52m	7.518m			
WIDTH including searchlight:	3.657m	3.657m			
WIDTH OVER skirts:	3.504m	3.504m	ENGINE MK. NO & BHP:	No 4 Mk.6A 730 at 2,100rpm	No 4 Mk.8A 750 at 2,100rpm
HEIGHT:	2.895m	2.895m			
GROUND CLEARANCE:	.508m	.508m			
TRACK WIDTH:	610mm	610mm	ARMAMENT:	1 × 120mm 1 × 7.62mm co-axial MG 1 × 12.7mm RMG 1 × 7.62mm (commander's cupola)	1 × 120mm 1 × 7.62mm co-axial MG 1 × 12.7mm RMG 1 × 7.62mm (commander's cupola)
LENGTH OF TRACK ON GROUND:	4.8m	4.8m			
GROUND PRESSURE:	.84kg/cm²	.9kg/cm²			
MAXIMUM ROAD SPEED:	48km/hr	48km/hr			
RANGE road:	400/500km	400/500km			
RANGE cross-country:	200/300km	200/300km			
FUEL:	950 litres	950 litres			

DEVELOPMENT

The development of a new MBT to replace the Centurion and Conqueror tanks started in the early 1950s and numerous projects were started and then cancelled. In 1956 Leyland Motors (who built a number of Centurions) built two prototypes of a vehicle called the FV 4202. In appearance this was similar to the Centurion but had five road wheels instead of six, the gun turret did not have a mantlet and the driver was in the reclining position (the latter two features were subsequently adopted for the Chieftain). The characteristics for a Centurion replacement was finally issued in 1958 with a full-scale mock-up being completed early in 1959. The first prototype Chieftain (FV 4201) was completed in September 1959. Chieftain was first seen by the public in 1961 and a further six prototypes were built between July 1961 and April 1962. The Chieftain was accepted for service in May 1963 and two production lines were established, one at the Royal Ordnance Factory at Leeds and the other at Vickers Elswick works. Vickers are the design parents for the Chieftain. The first regiment to be fully equipped with the Chieftain was the 11th Hussars in BAOR, which received their full complement of Chieftains in 1967. The Chieftain is employed by the Royal Armoured Corps in BAOR and in UK. A total of between 700 and 800 Chieftains were built for the British Army, the last one being completed several years ago. A major modernisation programme is now under way on early Chieftains. All Chieftain production today is for the Iranian Army whose original order, placed in 1971, was for about 700 tanks. Since then a further order has been placed and some reports have stated that this is for up to 1,100 Chieftains. The Libyans did place an order for Chieftain but this was subsequently cancelled. There is a possibility that Kuwait may buy 100 Chieftains and a number of other countries may well place orders.

It has been reported that the second batch of Iranian Chieftains will have a Rolls Royce engine rather than the Leyland L60 which has proved somewhat unreliable.

DESCRIPTION

The following description relates to the Mk. 5 which is, in major respects, similar to the Mk. 3.

The nose section is cast with the hull sides, rear and floor being welded into place, and the turret is also cast.

The driver is seated at the front of the hull in the centre, and when driving closed down is in the reclining position. He is provided with a single-piece hatch cover that opens to the right, and a AFV No. 36 Mk. 1 periscope, which can be replaced with an infra-red periscope for driving at night.

The other three crew members are in the turret with the commander and gunner on the right and the loader on the left.

The commander is provided with a cupola which can be traversed through a full 360° by hand, and a single-piece hatch cover. He has a total of 9 AFV No.40 Mk. 2 periscopes and an AFV No. 37 Mk. 4 sighting periscope. An infra-red searchlight (or white light) is mounted on the right side of his cupola.

The gunner is provided with a sight periscope AFV No.59 with a magnification of ×1 and ×8, or a Barr and Stroud laser rangefinder. The latter is designated Tank Laser Sight Unit No. 1 Mk. 1 or 2, and has a magnification of ×10 and is accurate at ranges from 500 to 10,000m. It is accurate to +10m for 90% of the time and a maximum of ten readings a minute can be taken. The gunner also has a monocular sight periscope No. 26 Mk. 1 with a magnification of ×7.

The loader has a folding rotatable periscope AFV No. 30. Mk. 1. Both the commander and gunner can replace their day sights with an infra-red sight with a magnification of ×3.

A dual-purpose infra-red/white light searchlight is mounted on the left side of the turret; effective range in infra-red role is 1,000m and in white light role about 1,500m.

The main armament of the Chieftain Mk. 5 is a 120mm rifled gun designated the L11A5 and made at the Royal Ordnance Factory at Nottingham. This is mounted in a turret without a mantlet; when the barrel needs replacing it is removed through the rear of the turret. The turret can be traversed through 360° between 16 and 28 seconds, elevation being +20° and depression −10°.

The gun has a vertical sliding breech-block and the barrel is provided with a fume extractor and a thermal sleeve. It has a maximum rate of fire of eight to ten rounds for the first minute and six rounds per minute thereafter.

The ammunition is of the separate loading type, ie projectile and charge. The projectiles are stowed alongside the driver, under the gun and in the turret, whilst the charges are stored in pressurised (water) bins below the turret ring.

The following types of ammunition have been developed for the 120mm gun:
APDS with an m/v of 1,370m/s, projectile weighing 10.36kg, and effective range 2,000/3,000m.
HESH with an m/v of 670m/s, projectile weighing 17.08kg, and effective range 8,000m
Smoke, Canister, DS and SH Practice
The Chieftain is fitted with the Marconi FV/Gun Control Equipment No. 7 Mk. 4 which has been developed from the successful FCS fitted in the earlier Centurion. This has four modes of operation: stabilised power control, power control, emergency battery control and emergency hand control. The gun can be laid and fired whilst the tank is moving across country.

A co-axial L8A1 7.62mm machine-gun is mounted to the left of the main armament. The commander's cupola has a 7.62mm L37A1 machine-gun which can be fired from within his cupola. The .50 (12.7mm) ranging machine-gun is mounted over the main armament, firing bursts of three rounds. Early Chieftains' RMG had a range of 1,800m but late Chieftains and modified Chieftains have an RMG with a range of 2,500m. The 6-barrelled smoke dischargers are fitted either side of the turret. The rear of the turret contains the NBC pack and communications equipment.

The total ammunition capacity of the Chieftain is as follows:
120mm ammunition—53 rounds (Mk. 3) or 64 rounds (Mk. 5)   7.62mm ammunition—6,000 rounds in belts of 200 rounds   .50 (12.7mm) ammunition—600 rounds (Mk. 3) or 300 rounds (Mk. 5)

The engine and TN 12 transmission is at the rear of the hull. The TN 12 epicyclic gearbox incorporates a Merritt Brown differential steering system and electro-hydraulic gear selector. The transmission has 6F and 2R gears plus emergency mechanical selection for second gear forward and low reverse.

The suspension is of the well-tried Horstmann type and consists of three bogies each side, each of which has two road wheels and a set of three horizontal springs. The idler is at the front and the drive sprocket is at the rear, there are three track support rollers, and the first road wheel station is provided with a single hydraulic shock absorber. The top half of the track is covered by an armoured skirt which can be removed for maintenance purposes. The tracks are of cast steel with dry pins and rubber pads.

There are a total of six batteries, 4×200Amp/hr in the driver's compartment for the engine and electrical system, and 2×100Amp/hr in the turret for the radio installation.

A Coventry Climax H30 No.4 liquid-cooled three-cylinder (six pistons) engine is installed for charging purposes.

The Chieftain is provided with an NBC system. A fire-warning system and internal fire-extinguishing system is also provided. An infra-red detector is fitted on the turret roof. This has three silicon photo voltaic cells which will detect an infra-red source and locate it an area of approx. 62°. A schnorkel can be fitted for deep fording operations. Other equipment includes a water tank and a heater.

A dozer attachment can be fitted to the front of the hull. This consists of an electro-hydraulic power pack which is fitted in place of the RH front stowage bins. The blade itself is of aluminium construction with a steel cutting edge. The blade is operated by the driver who is provided with a joystick control unit.

Chieftain Marks

Mk.1 First production vehicle with 585BHP engine. Only 40 built for training purposes and issued in
1965/66

Mk.1/2 Mk.1 brought up to Mk.2 standard and used for training

Mk.1/3 Mk.1 with new power pack and used for training

Mk.1/4 Mk.1/2 with new power pack and modified RMG, used for training.

Mk.2 First model to enter operational service in November 1966, 650BHP engine

Mk.3 This entered service in 1969 with the following modifications: improved auxiliary generator, 650BHP
engine, dry-air cleaner element, modified No.15 Mk.2 cupola with L37 7.62mm MG and oil-filled
top rollers, axle arms and track tensioner

Mk.3/G This was a prototype only with turret air-breathing for engine aspiration

Mk.3/2 Modified Mk.3/G

Mk.3/S Production model of Mk.3/G with turret air-breathing and commander's firing switch

Mk.3/3 Mk.3 with extended range RMG, fitted to accept laser rangefinder, modified 720BHP engine, new
low loss air cleaner system, turret aspiration and modified NBC pack

Mk.3/3(P) Export Mk.3/3 for the Iranian Army (from 1971)

Mk.4 Only two built with additional fuel and less RMG ammunition

Mk.5 Developed from Mk.3 with new engine, modified gearbox, modified exhaust and NBC system,
cupola-mounted MG can be elevated to 90°

Mk.5/5(P) Mk.5 for Iranian Army

Mk.6 Mk.2 with new powerpack and modified ranging machine-gun

Mk.7 Mk.3, Mk.3/G, Mk.3/2, Mk.3/S with improved engine and modified RMG

Mk.8 Mk.3/3 with above modifications

Improved Fire-Control System (IFCS)

This is now in its final stages of development by Marconi Space and Defence Systems Limited. The IFCS
is a computer-based digital system that has been designed to exploit the full potential of the Chieftain's
armament. The Marconi 12-12P computer will calculate the ballistic trajectory and aim-off for movement
of the target.

FV 4204 Armoured Recovery Vehicle

Development of an ARV to replace the Centurion ARV commenced in 1966 with the first prototype being
completed in 1971. The second prototype was completed in 1973 with production vehicles following in
1974. The ARV is used by the Royal Electrical and Mechanical Engineers (R.E.M.E.).

The ARV is based on a Mk.5 hull and has been redesigned forward of the engine compartment. It has
two winches which are separated from the crew compartment. These winches are of the double capstan
type and have a capacity of 30,000kg and 3,000kg, the latter winch being provided with a infinite variable
speed control. The 30,000kg winch has 122m of cable whilst the 3,000kg winch has 259m of cable. The
driver controls the winching operations. Power is taken from the main engine via a PTO to an input
gearbox and thence to the capstan winch via an epicyclic selector gearbox; four hydraulic pumps drive the
capstan auxiliary winch and earth anchor rams. The smaller winch is hydraulically driven and controlled.

A hydraulically-operated dozer blade is provided at the front of the hull, and when this is being used the
vehicle can exert a pull of 90,000kg. The Chieftain ARV is armed with a cupola-mounted 7.62mm machine-
gun which can be aimed and fired from within the cupola. Six smoke dischargers are mounted on each side
of the hull. Basic data are:

Crew: 4 Weight loaded: 52,000kg Weight empty: 50,250kg Length: 8.256m Width: 3.518m Height:
2.746m Speed: 41.5km/hr Range: 322km (road), 161km (cross-country) Fuel: 955 litres Engine: Leyland L60
No.4 Mk.7A, 720BHP at 2,250rpm

FV 4205 Bridgelayer

This has been developed to replace the current Centurion bridgelayers (the AVLB and the ARK). The
prototype was built at the Royal Ordnance Factory, Leeds, who have also undertaken production. The
first production tanks were delivered in 1974. Lockheed Precision Products and the Hydraulic Controls
Department of Tubes (Birmingham) were also involved in the development of the Chieftain AVLB. The
vehicle can lay a No.8 Class 60 Bridge in three to five minutes and can recover the same bridge in eight to
ten minutes. A hydraulic pump is driven from the main engine and operates a total of five cylinders which
unfold the bridge in three stages. The bridge itself weighs only 12,200kg and is 24.4m in length when
opened out and 4.16m wide, the road width being 4m. This can span a crossing up to 22.8m in width. The
bridge is built of nickel-alloy with the decking and curbs of aluminium.

A No.9 bridge has also been developed for the Chieftain AVLB. This is 13.4m in length and 4.16m wide,
it weighs 9,144kg and can span a crossing up to 12.2m wide.
Basic data of the Chieftain AVLB are:

Crew: 3 (commander, radio-operator and driver) Weight: 53,300kg (with bridge) Length: 13.741m (with bridge)   Width: 4.165m (with bridge)   Height: 3.885m (with bridge)

AVRE FV 4203
This was a project to replace the FV 4003 Centurion AVRE. With the development of the CET, however, and other RE equipment, the Chieftain AVRE will not be developed, though no official announcement on this has been made.

1

▼2

1 Chieftain Mk.2 (1969 photograph).
2 One of the prototype Chieftains from the rear.
3 Rear view of Chieftain Mk.2.
4 Chieftain with gun in travelling lock.
5 Chieftain of the Queen's Royal Irish Hussars fitted with the Simfire tank gunnery training system.
6 Chieftain Mk.5 with dozer blade installed.

3

4

5▲   **▼6**

1▲

▼2

3▲

▼4

5

6

▼7

1 The Chieftain Armoured Recovery Vehicle.
2 The Chieftain AVLB in travelling position with the
31st Armoured Engineer Squadron (BAOR).
3 Chieftain Bridgelayer laying its bridge in position.
4 The Barr and Stroud laser rangefinder sight as fitted
to late production Chieftains.
5 Hycatrol flexible fuel tank designed and built by FPT
Industries Limited being installed in a Chieftain. This
photograph also shows the track skirts and the turret
front in some detail.
6 Commander's and gunner's infra-red sights built by
MEL Equipment Company.
7 Cupola of the Chieftain ARV designed by the United
Scientific Group.

GREAT BRITAIN

CENTURION–MAIN BATTLE TANK
MANUFACTURERS–Leyland Motors (Leyland)
Royal Ordnance Factory Leeds
Vickers Limited, Elswick
STATUS–In service with Australia (to be replaced by Leopards), Canada, Denmark, India, Iraq, Israel, Jordan, Lebanon, Netherlands, Kuwait, South Africa, Sweden, Switzerland. They are no longer used by Egypt, Great Britain (ARVs, Bridgelayers and other special variants are still used) or Libya. Production of the Centurion is complete although refit programmes are being carried out in Great Britain and Israel.

BASIC DATA	Mk.5	Mk.13		Mk.5	Mk.13
CREW:	4	4	GRADIENT:	60%	60%
WEIGHT LOADED:	50,728kg	51,820kg	VERTICAL OBSTACLE:	.914m	.914m
LENGTH O/A	9.829m	9.854m	TRENCH:	3.352m	3.352m
LENGTH HULL:	7.556m	7.823m	ENGINE:	Rolls-Royce Meteor Mk.IVB 12-cylinde	
WIDTH:	3.39m	3.39m		liquid-cooled petrol engine developing 650BH	
HEIGHT W/O A/A MG:	2.94m	3.009m		at 2,550rpm	
GROUND CLEARANCE:	.457m	.51m	ARMAMENT		
TRACK:	2.641m	2.641m			
TRACK WIDTH:	610mm	610mm	main:	1×83.4mm	1×105mm
LENGTH OF TRACK ON			co-axial:	1×.30(7.62mm)	1×.30(7.62mm)
GROUND:	4.572m	4.572m	A/A:	1×.30(7.62mm)	1×.30(7.62mm)
GROUND PRESSURE:	.9kg/cm^2	.95kg/cm^2	RANGING MG:	nil	1×.50(12.7mm)
MAXIMUM ROAD SPEED:	34.6km/hr	34.6km/hr	SMOKE DISCHARGERS:	2×6	2×6
RANGE ROAD:	102km	190km	AMMUNITION		
FUEL CAPACITY:	458 litres	1037 litres	main:	64	64
FORDING:	1.45m	1.45m	.30(7.62mm):	4,250	4,750
FORDING WITH KIT:	2.74m	2.74m	.50(12.7mm):	nil	600

Note on armour: No data on the armour of the Centurion have been released but the data below, relating to up-armoured Centurions, are believed to be accurate: glacis: 118mm   nose: 76mm   hull sides: 51mm   hull rear upper: 38mm   hull rear lower: 20mm   floor: 17mm   turret front: 152mm

DEVELOPMENT

In 1944 AEC Ltd started development work on a new cruiser tank called the A41, the first mock-up of this being completed in 1944. A total of six prototypes were completed before the end of the War and were sent to Germany but arrived too late to see action. The A41 became the Mk.1 Centurion whilst the A41A became the Centurion Mk.2, armed with a 17-pounder gun. The Centurion first saw action in Korea and since then has served with distinction in many parts of the world, especially with the Israeli Army. In its final form it was armed with the famous 105mm tank gun, and since then this has been adopted by many countries and is now used in the Leopard, M60, Type 64 MBT, Swiss. Pz.61 and Pz.68 tanks, and the Vickers MBT. Total production of the Centurion is believed to have amounted to at least 4,000 tanks, of which about 2,500 were exported.

DESCRIPTION (Mk.13)

The hull of the Centurion is of all-welded construction, its turret cast with the roof welded into place. There is an ammunition resupply hatch in the left side of the turret.

The driver is seated at the front of the hull on the right side and is provided with two hatch covers that open to the left and right, each provided with a periscope. The three other crew members are in the turret, with the gunner and commander on the right and the loader on the left.

The commander is provided with a contra-rotating cupola which has a single-piece hatch cover, a periscopic sight with a ballistic pattern (this is coupled to the gunner's sight) and seven periscopes.

The gunner has a periscopic sight with ballistic pattern graticules linked to a range drum for ranges of between 3,000 and 8,000m.

The loader has two hatch covers which open fore and aft and a periscope which can be traversed.

The engine and Merritt-Brown transmission is at the rear of the hull, the latter has 5F and 2R gears and a differential, incorporated in the gearbox.

The suspension is of the Horstmann type and consists of three units. Each of these carries two pairs of road wheels, these being sprung by one set of concentric coil springs. The drive sprocket is at the rear and the idler at the front, and there are six track return rollers. Shock absorbers are provided for the first and last road wheel units. The tracks are of cast manganese steel and the top half of these are covered by track skirts which can be quickly removed if required.

The electrical system is 24V, and four 6V 115Amp/hr batteries are carried. Charging is accomplished either by DC generator or by an overriding DC generator driven by a 4-cylinder petrol engine developing 13½BHP. The engine compartment is provided with a fire-extinguishing system and a fire-warning system is also fitted. Infra-red driving lights are provided. A heater is fitted as standard. The Centurion does not have an NBC system. A dozer blade can be mounted on the front of the hull. A schnorkel was developed but this was not placed in production.

The 105mm L7A2 gun is mounted in a turret with a traverse of 360°, which takes 26 seconds, elevation is +20° and depression −10°. Elevation and traverse is electric with manual controls for use in an emergency. The gun is fully stabilised and the gunner can select any of the following: manual elevation and traverse, non-stabilised power traverse, stabilised powered elevation and traverse and emergency. If required the commander can override the gunner.

The 105mm rifled tank gun is provided with a fume extractor on the barrel. This gun has an effective range of 1,800m when using an APDS round, or 3,000/4,000m when using HESH. A well-trained crew can fire at least six to eight rounds per minute. The weapon is aimed using a .50(12.7mm) ranging machine-gun. This is mounted co-axially with the main armament, has a maximum range of 1,800m and fires in three-round bursts using tracer ammunition. An infra-red searchlight is mounted to the left of the main armament. The commander's searchlight can be fitted with an infra-red filter if required.

A .30(7.62mm) machine-gun is mounted co-axially with the main armament and there is a similar weapon on the commander's cupola. Smoke dischargers are mounted either side of the turret.

Data of the 105mm ammunition are:

Type	Weight of projectile	Weight of complete round
HESH	11.25kg	21.21kg
APDS (L28)	5.84kg	18.46kg
APDS (L52)	6.48kg	19.14kg
Base Ejection Smoke	19.79kg	26.35kg

SH Practice and DS/T Practice rounds are also available.

83.4mm ammunition for Centurion with 20-pounder guns included APDS with an m/v of 1,432m/s, HE with a muzzle velocity of 601m/s, Cannister with an m/v of 914m/s and smoke with a muzzle velocity of 215m/s.

VARIANTS

There have been the following Marks of Centurion MBT:

Mk.1 with 17-pounder gun – none in service

Mk.2 with 17-pounder gun – none in service

Mk.3 with 20-pounder gun, 7.92mm Besa co-axial machine-gun, not in service, most brought up to Mk.5 standard

Mk.4 was to have been armed with a howitzer but did not enter production

Mk.5 with 20-pounder gun but .30 (7.62mm) machine-gun. When built it could tow a special trailer with additional fuel, still used by some countries. Design parents were Vickers

Mk.5/1 is a Mk.5 with additional armour and designated FV 4011

Mk.5/2 is a Mk.5 with 105mm gun

Mk.6 is a Mk.5 with 105mm gun and additional fuel tank at rear of hull

Mk.6/1 is a Mk.6 with infra-red equipment and stowage basket at turret rear

Mk.6/2 is a Mk.6 with .50 (12.7mm) ranging machine-gun for the 105mm gun

Mk.7 has a 20-pounder gun with 61 rounds, barrel has a fume extractor. Designated FV 4007. Design parents were Leyland

Mk.7/1 is a Mk.7 with additional armour, designated FV 4012

Mk.7/2 is a Mk.7 with 105mm gun

Mk.8 was developed from Mk.7 but with contra-rotating cupola for commander, new gun mantlet and 63 rounds of ammunition

Mk.8/1 is Mk.8 with additional armour

Mk.8/2 is a Mk.8 with 105mm gun

Mk.9 is a Mk.7 with 105mm gun and additional armour, designated FV 4015

Mk.9/1 is a Mk.9 with infra-red equipment and stowage basket on turret rear

Mk.9/2 is a Mk.9 with ranging machine-gun

Mk.10 is a Mk.8 with 105mm gun and additional armour, designated FV 4017. Total ammunition capacity 70 rounds

Mk.10/1 is Mk.10 with infra-red equipment and stowage basket on turret rear

Mk.10/2 is Mk.10 with ranging machine-gun

Mk.11 is Mk.6 with ranging machine-gun, infra-red equipment and stowage basket on turret rear

Mk.12 is Mk.9 with infra-red equipment, ranging machine-gun and stowage basket on turret rear

Mk.13 is Mk.10 with ranging machine-gun and infra-red equipment.

Vickers Modified Centurion

This was first shown in 1973 and two have been converted for the Swiss Army. It is a standard Centurion with the following modifications: modified final drives, new V800 powerpack, TN-12 six-speed semi-automatic gearbox, new 105mm gun, modernised gun-control equipment, ranging machine-gun or Barr and Stroud laser rangefinder, new commander's cupola, ventilation system and night-vision equipment.

The engine, which is a General Motors 12V-71T turbo-charged diesel, is mounted complete with cooling and hydraulic system, filters and generators and can be removed quickly as a complete unit. This centurion has a maximum road speed of 40km/hr and a much-increased operating range over the current Centurion.

Israeli Centurion

The Israelis have rebuilt many of their Centurions with the following modifications: 750HP Continental diesel, 105mm gun, new gearbox with 2 forward and 1 reverse gears, new steering system and oil-cooled brakes. It also has a new electrical system and a more comprehensive fire-fighting system. The Israeli Army have stated that this model has a total weight of 53,000kg and a maximum speed of 45km/hr. Some Israeli Centurions are called the Ben Gurion and are believed to have a French 105mm gun, but few remain in service as most Israeli tanks now have 105mm British guns.

Centurion Mk.5 Bridgelayer (FV 4002)

This is used for launching a Class 80 single-span bridge across gaps up to 13.716m in width. The bridge is carried in the horizontal position and is swung through 180° and laid in position; it is pivoted at the front part of the hull. It takes two minutes to lay the bridge and four minutes to recover it. The bridge is ready for immediate use by A(AFVs) vehicles, by the aid of a hand-laid centre deck between the trackways (these are carried on the sides of the tank), the bridge will accept class B vehicles (ie trucks and jeeps). Basic data are as follows:

Weight loaded: 50,485kg Weight empty: 48,760kg Length with bridge: 16.306m Width with bridge: 4.267m Height with bridge: 3.885m

This is being replaced in the British Army by the new Chieftain bridgelayer. The Dutch have some Centurion bridgelayers with the American type Scissors bridge installed.

Centurion Mk.5 AVRE (FV 4003)

The Centurion AVRE is only used by the British Army. It is armed with a 165mm demolition charge projector which is used to destroy fortifications. A hydraulically-operated dozer blade is fitted at the front of the hull and a fascine or rolled-up length of trackway can be carried at the front of the vehicle. At the rear of the hull is a rotatable towing hook, capable of electrically jettisoning a trailer. This trailer is used to carry stores or the Giant Viper Mine Clearance System. Basic data are:

Weight: 51,810kg Weight empty: 49,627kg Length: 8.686m (with dozer blade) Width: 3.962m (including dozer blade) Height: 3.009m

Centurion Mk.2 ARV (FV 4006)

The first Centurion ARV to enter service was the Mk.1 but it was limited to towing operations. The Mk.2 ARV is a Mk.3 (or later) hull with a superstructure of 30mm armour built to the rear of the driver's position. A winch with a capacity of 31,000kg is provided, this being powered by a 160HP B80 petrol engine. The capacity of the winch can be increased to 90,000kg. A spade is mounted at the rear of the hull and a jib crane with a capacity of 10,000kg can be quickly erected if required. The commander's cupola can be traversed through 360°. Armament consists of a .30 (7.62mm) machine-gun with 2,000 rounds of ammunition, and 2×5 smoke dischargers.

There was to have been a FV4013 ARV on a Mk.7 hull, but this did not enter production. The Centurion ARV Mk.2 is to be replaced in the British Army by the Chieftain ARV.

Basic data are:

Crew: 4 Weight loaded: 50,295kg Weight empty: 47,247kg Length: 8.966m Width: 3.39m Height: 2.895m Rope: 137m of 88.9mm diameter

Centurion Mk.5 ARK (FV4016)

This is used for spanning gaps that cannot be accomplished by the FV4002 bridgelayer. It is to be replaced by the Chieftain bridgelayer. The FV4016 is only used by the British Army. The ARK enters the ditch or obstacle itself and the ramps are then hydraulically opened fore and aft, total span being 22.86m. The vehicle is operated by the Royal Engineers.

Basis data are:

Weight: 51,710kg   Length: 10,363m (travelling)   Width: 3.962m   Height: 3.885m

Centurion BARV (FV4018)

This is a Centurion MBT with the turret removed and replaced by an armoured superstructure enabling it to operate in water up to 2.895m in depth. It has been designed to push landing craft off beaches as well as recovering disabled vehicles. The BARV is used by British Amphibious Forces and is also operational in BAOR.

Basic data are:

Crew: 4   Weight loaded: 40,643kg   Weight empty: 37,848kg   Length: 8.076m   Width: 3.402m   Height: 3.453m

Centurion target tank

This is a specially armoured Centurion tank and is used for training anti-tank crews with the 120mm recoilless rifle and the Carl Gustav weapons.

Other variants

There have been many trials versions of the Centurion including, to name but a few, flame-thrower tanks, self-propelled 25-pounder and 5.5-inch guns, special tank destroyers.

Centurion Pz.57 (Mk.7) of the Swiss Army with 105mm gun, making it the Mk.7/2.

1

2

3▲ ▼4

5

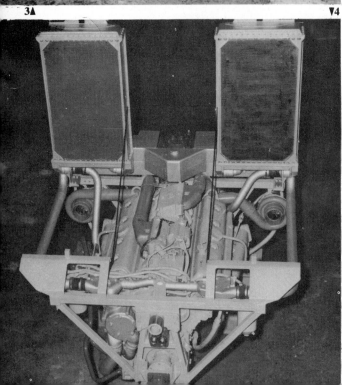

6▲ ▼7

8

9

10

▼11

1 Centurion Pz.55 (Mk.5) of the Swiss Army.
2 Centurion of the Israeli Army with 105mm gun.
3 Canadian Centurion tanks with infra-red searchlights.
4 The powerpack with General Motors GM 12V-71T diesel engine which is being installed in modified Centurions by Vickers.
5 Centurion Mk.2 ARV towing a Chieftain of the Queen's Royal Irish Hussars in Germany.
6 Centurion Mk.5 AVRE.
7 Centurion Mk.5 AVRE towing trailer with Giant Viper mine clearance equipment.
8 Centurion Mk.5 Bridgelayer laying its bridge in position.
9 Centurion Mk.5 ARK Bridgelayer entering a ditch before it unfolds.
10 Centurion Mk.5 Bridgelayers.
11 Centurion of the Netherland's Army with dozer blade.

GREAT BRITAIN

COMET — CRUISER TANK
MANUFACTURER — Leyland Motor Company
STATUS — In service with Burma, Eire, Finland, South Africa. Production complete.

BASIC DATA

CREW:	5 (commander, gunner, loader, bow-gunner and driver)	ARMAMENT:	1×77mm gun with an elevation of +20° and a depression of −12°
WEIGHT LOADED:	33,225kg		1×7.92mm Besa
LENGTH:	7.658m (gun forward)		machine-gun mounted
	6.552m (hull only)		co-axially with main
WIDTH:	3.073m		armament.
HEIGHT:	2.673m		1×7.92mm Besa
GROUND CLEARANCE:	.4m		machine-gun in bow
TRACK WIDTH:	457mm		2×6-barrelled smoke
LENGTH OF TRACK ON			dischargers
GROUND:	3.936m		61 rounds of 77mm
GROUND PRESSURE:	.97kg/cm^2		and 5,175 rounds of
POWER-TO-WEIGHT RATIO:	18.05HP/ton		7.92mm ammunition
MAXIMUM ROAD SPEED:	51.5km/hr		carried
RANGE:	240km (road)	ARMOUR	
	130km (cross-country)	glacis:	32mm
FUEL CAPACITY:	527 litres	hull front:	76mm
FORDING:	1.04m	nose:	64mm
GRADIENT:	60%		
VERTICAL OBSTACLE:	.914m	hull side, outer:	29mm
TRENCH:	2.438m	hull side, inner:	14mm
ENGINE:	Rolls-Royce Meteor	deck:	14mm
	Mk.3, 12-cylinder	hull rear:	25mm
	water-cooled petrol	mantlet:	102mm
	engine developing	turret sides:	64mm
	600HP at 2,500rpm	turret rear:	57mm
		turret roof:	20/25mm

DEVELOPMENT

Design work on the Comet (A34) Cruiser Tank started in 1943, the design and development of the vehicle being undertaken by Leyland Motors. The Comet was a development of the earlier Cromwell but it had a new turret with a new 77mm gun (a development of the 17-pounder anti-tank gun), new hull and a modified suspension system. The first prototype was completed in February 1944, with first production tanks following in September 1944. It entered service early in 1945 and continued in service with the British Army until the late 1950s. About 1,200 Comets were built by Leyland.

DESCRIPTION

The hull of the Comet is of all-welded construction. The driver is seated in the front of the hull on the right side with the bow machine-gun to his left. The driver is provided with a hatch for viewing purposes in the front of the hull plate, and in the roof of his compartment are two periscopes. The bow machine-gunner is provided with a single periscope in the roof of the compartment. Both the driver and bow machine-gunner are provided with a hatch cover that opens sideways in the roof of their compartment.

The turret is in the centre of the hull and is provided with a turret basket.

The commander's cupola is on the left and this can be traversed through 360°. The cupola has twin roof hatches, and a total of eight periscopes are arranged around the hatch to give full view through 360°. The loader's hatch has twin doors and is on the right side of the turret. Periscopes are provided in the roof of the turret for the loader and gunner. The turret is of all-welded construction with a cast front, traverse is through a full 360° by a Lucas electrical system at a speed of 15° a second, and manual controls are provided for use in an emergency. The engine and transmission are at the rear of the hull. A Merritt-Brown Z.5 gearbox is fitted and this has 5F and 1R gears.

The suspension is of the Christie type and consists of five road wheels, drive sprocket at the rear and idler at the front. There are four track return rollers. The first, second, fourth and fifth road wheels are provided with hydraulic shock absorbers.

VARIANTS
There are no variants of the Comet in service. The designation 'Cruiser Tank' was given when the tank entered service; under today's designations it would be called a medium tank.

Comet tank of the Irish Army.

ISRAEL

SABRA — MAIN BATTLE TANK

GENERAL
For the past six years there have been numerous reports that Israel has developed a new MBT armed with the British 105mm gun and an American engine and transmission. To date, however, there has been no confirmation of this tank at all.

   At the present time Israel has sufficient tanks to meet her immediate requirements. Not only is Israel receiving M60A1 tanks from the United States but for many years has been engaged on an extensive rebuilding programme for her Sherman, M48, T54/T55 and Centurion tanks. It could well be that Israel has developed a new MBT to the prototype stage, though this would not be placed in production unless the United States were unable to keep Israel supplied.

JAPAN

TYPE 74 — MAIN BATTLE TANK
MANUFACTURER —Mitsubishi Heavy Industries, Sagamihara, Near Tokyo
STATUS — In service with the Japanese Self-Defence Force. In production.

BASIC DATA

CREW:	4 (commander, gunner, loader, driver)	MAXIMUM ROAD SPEED:	53km/hr (some sources state 69km/hr)
WEIGHT:	38,000kg (loaded)	RANGE:	500km (road)
LENGTH:	9.088m (gun forward)	FUEL:	700 litres
	6.85m (hull)	FORDING:	1m (w/o kit)
WIDTH:	3.18m		3m (with schnorkel)
HEIGHT:	2.675m	GRADIENT:	60%
	(with A/A MG)	SIDE SLOPES:	40%
	2.48m (top of turret; both with ground clearance of .65m)	VERTICAL OBSTACLE:	1m
		TRENCH:	2.7m
		ENGINE:	Mitsubishi 10ZF
	2.03m (top of turret with ground clearance of .2m)		Type 21 WT 10-cylinder air-cooled diesel developing 750HP at 2,200rpm.
GROUND CLEARANCE:	.2m (minimum)		
	.65m (maximum)	ARMAMENT:	1×105mm gun
TRACK WIDTH:	610mm		1×7.62mm co-axial MG
TRACK:	2.7m		
LENGTH OF TRACK ON GROUND:	.4m		1×.50 (12.7mm) A/A MG
GROUND PRESSURE:	.85kg/cm^2		2×3 smoke dischargers
POWER-TO-WEIGHT RATIO:	19.7HP/ton		

DEVELOPMENT

Development of a new MBT to replace the Type 61 MBT started in 1964, design work being carried out by both Mitsubishi and the Japanese Self-Defence Force. Construction of two prototypes started late in 1968 at the Maruko works of Mitsubishi Heavy Industries and were completed in September 1969.

They were known as the STB-1 and featured a semi-automatic loader for the 105mm L7A1 gun, a remote-controlled .50 (12.7mm) anti-aircraft machine-gun towards the turret rear, and a crew of four. Next came the STB-3 in 1971. This had the automatic loader removed as it was found this increased the cost of the tank, and the anti-aircraft machine-gun was on a simple pintle mount forward of the commander's and loader's position. The final model was the STB-6 which appeared in 1973. By this time the STB had been approved for production and the JSDF placed an order for 280 vehicles. Production commenced in 1972 at the new Sagamihara Works of Mitsubishi Heavy Industries.

DESCRIPTION

The hull is of welded construction and the turret is cast. The driver is seated at the front of the vehicle on the left side and is provided with a single-piece hatch cover that opens to the left. His observation equipment consists of three periscopes for day use and an infra-red periscope can be fitted in the driver's hatch for night use.

The commander and gunner are on the right side of the turret with the loader on the left. The commander has a single-piece hatch cover that opens to the rear, five periscopes and a sight. The gunner is provided with a periscopic sight and a telescope sight. The loader's hatch opens to the rear and he is provided with an observation periscope.

The engine and transmission are at the rear of the hull, the latter having 6F and 1R gears, and incorporating a regenerative steering system of the triple differential type.

The suspension is of the hydro-pneumatic type and can be adjusted to suit the tactical situation and the type of terrain being crossed.

There are six road wheels with the drive sprocket at the rear and the idler at the front, but no track support rollers. The tracks are of the double pin type with rubber bushes and rubber pads.

The vehicle is armed with the 105mm L7A3 tank gun built under licence in Japan by the Japan Steel Works, and a Japanese 7.62mm machine-gun is mounted co-axially with the main armament. A .50 (12.7mm) anti-aircraft machine-gun is mounted on the left side of the commander's cupola. Three smoke dischargers are mounted either side of the turret. A total of 50 rounds of 105mm ammunition are carried, of which nine are for ready use.

The turret can be traversed through 360° by an electric/hydraulic system operated by the commander or gunner. Elevation of the main armament is +15° and depression −5°.

The fire-control system includes a laser rangefinder designed and built by Nippon Electric Company Ltd, and a ballistic computer built by Mitsubishi Electric Corporation. A stabiliser is provided which allows the armament to be laid and fired whilst the tank is moving.

An infra-red/white light searchlight is mounted to the left of the main armament and infra-red driving lights are provided. The Type 74 MBT is provided with an NBC system and a schnorkel can be fitted for deep-fording operations. Some models have been fitted with a dozer blade at the front of the hull.

VARIANTS

The only known variant is a 155mm self-propelled gun, although other variants such as bridgelayers and recovery vehicles may be under development.

The 155mm self-propelled gun weights 24,000kg and is armed with a 155mm howitzer in a turret at the rear of the hull. This has a traverse of 360°, elevation limits being from +65° to −5°, and it is believed that the barrel is the same as that fitted to the M109A1 SPG. The engine and transmission have been moved from the rear to the front of the hull and it is powered by a 420HP diesel which gives it a top speed of 50km/hr. A .50 (12.7mm) anti-aircraft machine-gun is mounted on the turret roof.

Left STB-1 MBT from the rear.
Right Close-up of the turret of the STB-1 showing commander's cupola, anti-aircraft machine-gun and smoke dischargers.

JAPAN

TYPE 61 MAIN BATTLE TANK
MANUFACTURER – Mitsubishi Heavy Industries, Maruko, Tokyo
STATUS – In service only with the Japanese Self-Defence Force. Production complete.

BASIC DATA

CREW:	4 (commander, gunner, loader, driver)	GROUND CLEARANCE:	.4m
		TRACK WIDTH:	500mm
WEIGHT:	35,000kg (loaded)	GROUND PRESSURE:	.95kg/cm^2
LENGTH:	8.19m (gun forward)	POWER-TO-WEIGHT	
	6.3m (hull)	RATIO:	17HP/ton
WIDTH:	2.95m	MAXIMUM ROAD SPEED:	45km/hr
HEIGHT:	3.16m (including A/A MG)	RANGE:	200km
		FORDING:	.99m
	2.49 (turret roof)	GRADIENT:	60%

VERTICAL OBSTACLE:	.685m	ARMAMENT:	1×90mm gun
TRENCH:	2.489m		1×.30 (7.62mm)
ENGINE:	Mitsubishi Type 12 HM		M1919A4 co-axial MG
	21 21WT, V-12, 4-cycle,		1×.50 (12.7mm) A/A MG
	direct-injection, turbo-	ARMOUR	
	charged, air-cooled	turret front:	64mm
	diesel developing 600HP	hull glacis:	46mm
	at 2,100rpm.	hull sides:	25mm
		hull rear:	15mm

DEVELOPMENT

Design of a new Main Battle Tank for the Japanese Self-Defence Force commenced in 1954 under the direction of the Technical Research and Development Headquarters of the JSDF. In many respects the Type 61 is a scaled-down American M47 medium tank; the Japanese had several of these for trials purposes in the early 1950s.

The first prototypes were completed from March 1957 and were known as the ST-A1 (two built) and ST-A2 (two built). The ST-A1 had seven road wheels, with the drive sprocket at the front and the idler at the rear, and four track support rollers. An automatic transmission, torque converter and hydraulic steering system was provided. Armament was similar to production tanks.

These were followed by the ST-A3 (two built) and ST-A4) (ten built). These were tested and found to be satisfactory and in April 1961 the tank was standardised as the Type 61 main battle tank and placed in production, the first production tanks being completed in 1962. The 100th tank was completed in 1966 and total production amounted to 400/500 tanks. The Type 61 MBT will be supplemented by the Type 74 MBT which is now in production.

DESCRIPTION

Although the Type 61 Tank has been in service for some thirteen years, full technical information on this is still not available, and the comments and data are provisional. The hull is of all-welded construction whilst the turret is cast. The driver is seated at the front of the vehicle on the right side and is provided with three periscopes and a single-piece hatch cover.

The commander, gunner and loader are seated in the turret. The commander is seated on the right side of the turret and is provided with a cupola which can be traversed through a full 360°. This is provided with a single-piece hatch cover that opens to the rear. The commander's observation equipment includes seven vision blocks, ×12 coincidence rangefinder, and a periscope with a magnification of ×7 and a traverse of 360°.

The gunner is on the right side of the turret and is provided with a ×6 sighting periscope as well as observation equipment. The loader is on the left side of the turret and is provided with an observation periscope and a single-piece hatch cover that opens to the rear.

The engine and transmission are at the rear of the hull. Two axial-flow cooling-fans are mounted over the engine. The transmission has 5F and 1R gears and is operated by a pneumatic servo-mechanism. An auxiliary transmission provides an additional two low ranges.

The suspension is of the torsion bar type and consists of six road wheels with the drive sprocket at the front and the idler at the rear. There are three track support rollers. Shock absorbers are provided on the first, second, fifth and sixth road wheel stations.

The main armament consists of a Type 61 90mm gun built by the Japan Steel Works. This is provided with a fume extractor and a 'T' type muzzle brake. A .30 (7.62mm) M1919A4 machine-gun is mounted co-axially with the main armament. The turret is provided with powered traverse with manual controls for use in an emergency. A .50 (12.7mm) M2 machine-gun is mounted on the commander's hatch and some models have a shield to protect the commander when he is firing the weapon.

The Type 61 has no NBC system and no provision is made for deep-fording. When the tank entered service it did not have any night-fighting capability but recently a number of Type 61s have been fitted with infra-red driving lamps, and an infra-red search light has been mounted on the left side of the main armament.

VARIANTS

Armoured Vehicle Launched Bridge Type 67

This is the basic tank with its turret removed and replaced with an American M48-type AVLB which opens out over the forward part of the vehicle.

Armoured Engineer Vehicle Type 67

This has been designed to carry out engineering work on the battlefield.

Armoured Recovery Vehicle Type 70
This is provided with a dozer blade on the front of the hull, designed to stabilise the vehicle when the crane is being used as well as for dozing operations. The turret has been removed and replaced by a superstructure, and in the rear of this is a winch. An 'A' frame is provided and a full range of equipment is carried, including cutting gear.

	AVLB 67	AEV 67	ARV 70
CREW:	3	4	4
WEIGHT:	35,000kg	35,000kg	35,000kg
LENGTH:	7.27m	7.46m	8.4m
WIDTH:	3.5m	3.2m	2.95m
HEIGHT:	3.5m	2.23m	3.1m
ARMAMENT:	1×7.62mm MG	1×12.7mm MG	1×12.7mm MG
		1×7.62mm MG	1×7.62mm MG
			1×81mm mortar

Type 61 Main Battle Tank showing infra-red driving lights.

Top The Type 61 Main Battle Tank.
Above The Type 67 Armoured Vehicle Launched Bridge.
Left The Type 70 Armoured Recovery Vehicle.
Right T-64 (T-72) MBT on left with a T-70 MBT on the right.

SOVIET UNION

T-64 or T-72—MAIN BATTLE TANK
MANUFACTURER—Soviet State Arsenals. Some of the Warsaw Pact Countries may well undertake production of this tank, including Czechoslovakia.
STATUS—In service with the Soviet Army.

BASIC DATA

CREW:	3 (commander, gunner, driver)	FORDING:	1.4m 5.486m (with schnorkel)
WEIGHT LOADED:	40,000kg	GRADIENT:	60%
LENGTH:	10.1m (gun forward) 7.4m (hull only)	VERTICAL OBSTACLE: TRENCH:	.8m 2.8m
WIDTH:	3.3m	ENGINE:	1,000HP water-cooled
HEIGHT:	2.46m (w/o A/A MG)		diesel
MAXIMUM ROAD SPEED:	60km/hr	ARMAMENT:	1×122mm gun
RANGE:	500km		1×7.62mm co-axial MG
			1×12.7mm A/A MG

The above data are provisional

GENERAL

In the 1960s the Soviets built an experimental tank called the T-70 (or M-1970), armed with the same 115mm gun as the T-62 MBT. This was followed by the T-64 (or T-72) which entered production several years ago and is now in service in some numbers.

The T-64 is armed with a long 122mm smooth-bore gun which fires an Armour Piercing Fin-Stabilized Discarding Sabot (APFSDS) round with a higher muzzle velocity than the 1,680m/s of the similar T-62 round. This is believed to have an effective range of between 1,500m and 2,000m. A co-axial 7.62mm machine-gun is mounted and a 12.7mm machine-gun can be mounted on the commander's cupola for anti-aircraft defence.

The 122mm round is believed to have a combustible cartridge.

The driver is seated at the front of the hull in the centre, the gunner is on the left of the turret and the commander is on the right. All are provided with a single-piece hatch cover.

The fire-control system includes a range-only laser rangefinder as well as a ballistic computer.

The suspension consists of six road wheels with the drive sprocket at the rear and the idler at the front, and three track return rollers. The first two and last two road wheels are provided with hydraulic shock absorbers. The range of the T-64 can be extended by fitting additional fuel tanks at the rear of the hull.

An infra-red searchlight is provided for the commander and there is also an infra-red searchlight for the main armament. An NBC system is provided and a schnorkel can be fitted for deep-fording.

It is possible that the Sagger ATGW is sometimes mounted on the T-64, which could well indicate that the 122mm smooth-bore is not effective at long range.

SOVIET UNION

BMD (Boyevaya Mashina Desantnaya)—LIGHT TANK/FIRE SUPPORT VEHICLE
MANUFACTURER—Soviet State Arsenals
STATUS—In service with the Soviet Army.

BASIC DATA

CREW:	3+3/6	VERTICAL OBSTACLE:	.6m
WEIGHT LOADED:	9,000kg	TRENCH:	2m
LENGTH:	5.3m	ARMAMENT:	1×73mm gun
WIDTH:	2.65m		1×7.62mm MG co-axial
HEIGHT:	1.85m		with main armament
MAXIMUM ROAD SPEED:	50/55km/hr		1×7.62mm MG in each
WATER SPEED:	6km/hr		side of hull
FORDING:	Amphibious		1 launcher for Sagger
GRADIENT:	60%		ATGW

The above data are provisional

DEVELOPMENT

The BMD, which was first known simply as the M1970 light tank, was first seen in public at a parade held in Moscow in November 1973. It is believed, however, that it entered service in 1971. It was first issued to the Soviet Airborne Divisions, as although they have self-propelled anti-tank guns (ASU-85s and ASU-57s), they have no light tanks as part of their divisional equipment. PT-76s have been air-dropped on a number of occasions.

DESCRIPTION

The hull of the BMD is of all-welded construction with the driver seated at the front of the hull in the centre, provided with a one-piece hatch cover and a total of three periscopes for observation purposes. There are additional periscopes to the left and right of the driver's position for crew observation purposes. There is a single 7.62mm machine-gun mounted in each side of the hull, firing forwards.

The turret of the BMD is mounted behind the driver's position and is identical to that fitted to the BMP-1 MICV. The turret has a single-piece hatch cover that opens forwards. The commander is provided with a total of four periscopes arranged around the forward part of the turret on the left side. A white light searchlight is mounted on the right side of the turret, although some vehicles have been observed fitted with an infra-red searchlight.

The 73mm smooth-bore gun has an elevation of +20° and a depression of −5°, and a 7.62mm PKT machine-gun is mounted co-axially with the main armament. A launcher rail for a Sagger wire-guided ATGW is mounted over the gun barrel. During parades the BMD has been shown with a total of six infantrymen seated behind the turret in two rows of three men facing forwards. Each row is provided with a single-piece hatch cover that opens forwards. There is no provision for the infantry to fight from within the vehicle and their only means of exit is via the roof hatches or via the turret.

The engine and transmission are at the rear of the hull but no details of these have become available.

The suspension is believed to be of the torsion-bar type and consists of five road wheels with the drive sprocket at the rear and the idler at the front. There are a total of four track support rollers.

The BMD is fully amphibious. It is propelled in the water by water jets in the rear of the hull, and a trim vane is erected at the front of the hull before the vehicle enters the water. Infra-red driving lights are provided. It is not known if an NBC system is fitted.

VARIANTS

There are no variants known at the present time.

The BMD Light Tank/Fire Support Vehicle with Sagger ATGW over main armament.

SOVIET UNION

T-62—MAIN BATTLE TANK

MANUFACTURER—Soviet State Arsenals. Although the earlier T-54/T-55 MBTs were also manufactured in both Poland and Czechoslovakia, it is not known at the present time if the T-62 is being manufactured in these countries as well.

STATUS—In service with Bulgaria, Czechoslovakia, East Germany, Egypt, Hungary, India (unconfirmed report), Iraq, Israel, Libya, Poland, Romania, Soviet Union, Syria.

BASIC DATA

CREW:	4 (commander, gunner, loader, driver)	ENGINE:	Model V-2-62, V-12, water-cooled diesel developing 700HP at 2,200rpm
WEIGHT LOADED:	36,500kg		
LENGTH:	9.77m (gun forward)		
	9m (gun rear)	ARMAMENT:	1×115mm U-5TS gun with an elevation of +17° and a depression of −4°; axis of bore 1.75m
	6.715m (hull)		
WIDTH:	3.35m		
HEIGHT:	2.4m (w/o A/A MG)		
GROUND CLEARANCE:	.425m		1×7.62mm PKT MG co-axial with main armament
TRACK:	2.64m		1×12.7mm DShK A/A MG (from 1970) tank is known as T-62A
TRACK WIDTH:	580mm		
LENGTH OF TRACK ON GROUND:	4.15m		
GROUND PRESSURE:	.72kg/cm^2		40 rounds of 115mm and 3,500 rounds of 7.62mm ammunition are carried
POWER-TO-WEIGHT RATIO:	19.17HP/ton		
MAXIMUM ROAD SPEED:	50km/hr		
RANGE:	500km	ARMOUR	
FUEL CAPACITY:	912 litres	glacis:	100mm at 60°
FUEL CONSUMPTION:	190 litres per 100km	upper hull side:	70mm at 0°
FORDING:	1.4m	mantlet:	170mm
	5.486m (with schnorkel)	turret sides and rear:	80mm
GRADIENT:	60%	hull rear:	60mm
VERTICAL OBSTACLE:	.8m	roof:	30mm
TRENCH:	2.8m	floor:	20mm

DEVELOPMENT

The T-62 is a further development of the earlier T-54/T-55 series. The tank entered production in 1961/62 and was first seen in public during the parade held in Moscow on 9th May 1965. Since then it has been built in very large numbers and has seen combat with the Egyptian and Syrian forces during the Middle East War of October 1973. In general it was found to be an improvement over the earlier T-54/T-55 series. In appearance the T-62 differs from the earlier tanks as follows: its hull is longer and wider, the turret is a different shape, the commander's and loader's hatches are different, the road wheels are more equally spaced on the T-62 (on the T-54 there is a distinct gap between the first and second road wheels), and the gun is longer and is also fitted with a bore evacuator.

DESCRIPTION

The hull of the T-62 is of all-welded construction with the turret a one-piece casting. The driver is seated on the left side of the hull and is provided with a one-piece hatch cover that swings to the left. He is provided with two periscopes for driving closed down. There is a splash-board on the front of the glacis plate so that water does not rush up the hull front when fording. The other three crew members are in the turret, the commander and gunner to the left and the loader to the right. The commander's cupola can be traversed through 360° and is provided with three periscopes, one in the front and one on either side. His hatch opens forwards and on the forward part of the hatch is an infra-red searchlight. The loader's hatch cover is slightly forward of the commander's cupola and also opens forwards. There is a further small hatch in the turret rear and this is used for ejecting the empty cartridge cases. To the left of this hatch is a turret ventilation dome.

The engine and transmission is at the rear of the hull with the latter having 5F and 1R gears.

The suspension is of the torsion-bar type with five road wheels, drive sprocket at the rear and idler at the front, the first and fifth road wheels are provided with hydraulic shock absorbers.

Like most Soviet tanks, the T-62 can lay its own smoke screen and on the T-62 this is achieved by injecting vaporized diesel fuel into the exhaust system.

The T-62 is fitted with an NBC system and a schnorkel can be fitted for deep-fording operations. Infra-red driving lights are provided and additional fuel can be carried in drums attached to the hull rear, these being jettisoned as required.

The 115mm gun of the T-62 is of the smooth-bore type and fires fin-stabilized fixed rounds, its official rate of fire being seven rounds per minute, though three to four rounds per minute would be a more realistic figure. The barrel has no muzzle-brake but is fitted with a bore evacuator and its breech-block is of the horizontal sliding type. Both powered and manual traverse and elevation are available and the commander can override the gunner's controls. The following types of ammunition are available for the T-62:

HE projectile weighing 17.6kg, indirect sight scale provided

APDS fin-stabilized projectile weighing 6.8kg with a muzzle velocity of between 1,500 and 1,680m/s. This will penetrate 300mm of armour at a range of 1,000m. This round is also known as APFSDS (Armour Piercing Fin-Stabilized Discarding Sabot). This is said to have an effective range of around 1,600m, but there is some dispersion at this range.

HEAT projectile weighs 11.8kg and has a muzzle-velocity of 1,000m/s. This will penetrate 450mm of armour at 1,000m. An infra-red searchlight is mounted to the right of the main armament and this moves with the gun in elevation.

The sighting arrangements are believed to be similar to that of the T-55. The gun is fully stabilized. It has been reported that the Soviets intend to introduce a laser rangefinder at a future date.

A co-axial PKT 7.62mm machine-gun is mounted to the right of the main armament, and there is no bow machine-gun. Since 1970 some T-62s have been fitted with a 12.7mm DShK anti-aircraft machine-gun on the loader's cupola. Also there are some recent T-62s with slightly different loader's cupolas. These tanks, and those with an anti-aircraft machine-gun, are known as T-62As.

VARIANTS

There are no known variants of the T-62. It is logical however that in time armoured recovery and bridgelaying variants will be developed, as the earlier T-55 and T-55 vehicles wear out.

Above Close-up photograph of the rear of a Syrian T-62. Of interest are the hatch in the turret rear, part of the schnorkel on the turret rear and the un-ditching beam at the rear of the hull.

Above T-62 of the Syrian Army captured by Israeli Forces.
Left T-62 MBTs of the Russian Army in convoy.
Below T-62s of the Egyptian Army on parade in Cairo.

SOVIET UNION

T-10 SERIES MEDIUM/HEAVY TANK
MANUFACTURER – Soviet State Arsenals
STATUS – In service with Bulgaria, Czechoslovakia, East Germany, Egypt, Hungary, Vietnam, Poland, Romania, Soviet Union and Syria. Production of the T-10/T-10M has now been completed.

BASIC DATA	T-10	T-10M			
CREW:	4	4	FUEL CONSUMPTION:	360 litres per 100km	360 litres per 100km
WEIGHT LOADED:	50,000kg	52,000kg			
LENGTH:	9.875m (gun forward)	10.6m (gun forward)	FORDING:	1.2m	1.2m
			GRADIENT:	32°	32°
	8.55m (gun rear)	9.28m (gun rear)	VERTICAL OBSTACLE:	.9m	.9m
	7.04m (hull only)	7.04m (hull only)	TRENCH:	3m	3m
			ENGINE:	Model V-2-IS (V2K), V-12 water-cooled diesel engine developing 700HP at 2,000 rpm	
WIDTH:	3.566m	3.566m			
HEIGHT:	2.25m (w/o A/A MG)	2.43m (w/o A/A MG)			
			ARMAMENT:	1×122mm gun	1×122mm gun
GROUND CLEARANCE:	.43m	.43m		1×12.7mm co-axial	1×14.5mm co-axial
TRACK:	2.6m	2.6m		1×12.7mm A/A	1×14.5mm A/A
TRACK WIDTH:	720mm	720mm			
LENGTH OF TRACK ON GROUND:	4.6m	4.6m	ARMOUR		
GROUND PRESSURE:	.76kg/cm^2	.78kg/cm^2	glacis:	120mm at 60°	120mm at 60°
MAXIMUM ROAD SPEED:	42km/hr	42km/hr	upper hull side:	80mm at 45°	80mm at 45°
RANGE:	250km	250km	mantlet:	250mm	250mm
FUEL CAPACITY:	900 litres	900 litres	hull rear:	60mm	60mm
			hull floor:	20mm	20mm
			hull roof:	20/35mm	20/35mm

DEVELOPMENT

The T-10 was first seen on 7th November 1957 and is a logical development of the IS-3 and IS-4 tanks. The T-10 has a more powerful armament, improved armour layout and the same engine as the IS-4.

As far as can be ascertained the T-10 is still in service with most members of the Warsaw Pact Forces and is believed to be in separate battalions, being attached to divisions as and when required. It would probably be used in support of the older T-54 and T-55 MBTs. The T-10 is very well armoured and has a powerful, if rather slow-firing 122mm gun. According to the Israelis it is a very difficult tank to destroy.

The T-10 can be recognised from the earlier IS-3 as it has seven road wheels, idler at the front, drive sprocket at the rear and a total of three track return rollers. It also has stowage boxes along the side of the hull above the tracks. The IS-3 has only six road wheels.

DESCRIPTION

The hull of the T-10 is of cast steel with the turret of rolled steel. The driver is at the very front of the hull and is provided with a one-piece hatch cover that swings to the right. This has a single periscope which can be replaced by an infra-red viewer for night operations.

The gunner, loader and commander are in the turret. The commander's hatch is on the left and hinges forward whilst the loader's hatch cover is on the right and swings to the rear.

The engine and transmission are at the rear of the hull and the gearbox has 5F and 1R gears. The suspension consists of a torsion bar for each road wheel. If required additional fuel tanks can be fitted.

Armament – T-10

The T-10 is armed with a 122mm gun in a turret with a total traverse of 360°, elevation is +17° and depression − 3°, axis of bore is 1.83m. The barrel is provided with a double-baffle muzzle-brake and a fume extractor.

Its co-axial machine-gun is the 12.7mm DShK and it has a similar anti-aircraft machine-gun mounted on the loader's hatch.

A total of 30 rounds of 122mm ammunition is carried, and the ammunition is of the separate loading type which explains its rather low rate of fire of three rounds per minute. A total of 1,000 rounds of 12.7mm machine-gun ammunition are carried. The 122mm gun has a maximum range in the indirect fire role of 16,600m but its effective range in the anti-tank role is 1,200m.

The following types of ammunition are available:

HE round, projectile weighs 27.3kg and has an m/v of 885m/s.

APHE round, projectile weighs 25kg and has an m/v of 885m/s and will penetrate 185mm of armour at 1,000m.

HEAT round with a projectile weight of 14kg, m/v of 900m/s, will penetrate a maximum of 460mm of armour. This is a special non-rotating fin-stabilised round which is only used with the T-10M tank.

T-10M Tank

The T-10M is essentially an improved T-10, the differences being as follows:

1 The 12.7mm DShK machine-guns have been replaced by 14.5mm machine-guns, the co-axial being a KPVT and the anti-aircraft being the KPV
2 The 122mm gun has a multi-baffle muzzle-brake in place of the earlier double-baffle muzzle-brake
3 The main armament is stabilised in both planes
4 The tank can be fitted with a schnorkel for deep-fording operations
5 Some T-10Ms have been fitted with a large sheet metal stowage box on the rear of the turret
6 An infra-red searchlight has been mounted to the right of the main armament and there is also an infra-red searchlight in front of the commander's hatch. Like the T-10, the T-10M has infra-red driving lights
7 Some sources have stated that the T-10M has thicker armour and can carry a total of 50 rounds of ammunition, rather than the 30 rounds carried by the standard T-10, but unless there has been some drastic redesign work inside the hull, this seems rather doubtful. In addition it has been mentioned that the T-10M has an improved 122mm gun and improved ammunition. However it is known that the T-10M fires a more recent HEAT round as mentioned above
8 An NBC system has been fitted

VARIANTS

There are no known variants of the T-10. It is logical, however, that as the older IS chassis for special purposes (ie ARV and carrying various types of tactical and strategic missile systems) wear out, they may well use T-10 chassis in their place.

Above T-10 Heavy Tank.
Left T-10M Heavy Tank. This particular tank does not have the stowage box on the turret rear.

SOVIET UNION

PT-76–LIGHT AMPHIBIOUS TANK
MANUFACTURER–Volgograd Tank Plant
STATUS–In service with Afghanistan, Bulgaria, China (it is also built in China with an 85mm gun as the Model 60 Light Tank), Congo, Cuba, Czechoslovakia, East Germany, Egypt, Finland, Hungary, India, Indonesia, Iraq, Israel, Laos, North Korea, Vietnam, Pakistan, Poland, Soviet Union, Syria, Yugoslavia. Production of the PT-76 is now complete.

BASIC DATA

CREW:	3 (commander, gunner and driver)	VERTICAL OBSTACLE:	1.1m
		TRENCH:	2.8m
WEIGHT LOADED:	14,000kg	ENGINE:	Model V-6, 6-cylinder
LENGTH:	7.625m (gun forward)		in-line water-cooled
	6.91m (hull)		diesel engine developing
WIDTH:	3.14m		240HP at 1,800rpm
HEIGHT:	2.255m (late model)	ARMAMENT:	1×76.2mm D-56T or
	2.195m (early models)		D-56TM gun with an
GROUND CLEARANCE:	37m		elevation of +30° and a
TRACK:	2.74m		depression of −4°, turret
TRACK WIDTH:	360mm		traverse is 360°, axis of
LENGTH OF TRACK ON			bore 1.82m
GROUND:	4.08m		1×7.62mm SGMT MG
GROUND PRESSURE:	.479kg/cm^2		co-axial with main armament
POWER-TO-WEIGHT RATIO:	17.1HP/ton		40 rounds of 76mm and
MAXIMUM ROAD SPEED:	44km/hr		1,000/2,000 rounds of
MAXIMUM WATER SPEED:	10km/hr		7.62mm ammunition are
RANGE:	260km		carried
FUEL CAPACITY:	250 litres	ARMOUR	
FUEL CONSUMPTION:	96 litres per 100km	glacis:	11mm at 80°
FORDING:	Amphibious	upper hull side:	14mm at 0°
GRADIENT:	70%	mantlet:	11mm at 33°

DEVELOPMENT

The PT-76 was developed from the Pinguin cross-country vehicle and has now been in service for some twenty years. Its replacement may well be the new BMD vehicle which was first seen in November 1973. Since the introduction of the PT-76, however, wheeled vehicles of the BRDM type have been used in increasing numbers for the reconnaissance role. The primary role of the PT-76 is that of reconnaissance and the vehicle is found in the Reconnaissance Company of the Soviet Tank Regiments and in the Reconnaissance Battalion of the Tank Divisions and the Motor Rifle Divisions.

The PT-76 is the basic vehicle for many Soviet tracked vehicles, including the BTR-50 and OT-62 APCs, ASU-85 SP A/T gun, ZSU-23-4 SP A/A gun, PVA Amphibious Logging Vehicle, FROG-2, 3, 4 and 5 missile vehicles, GSP Heavy Amphibious Ferry, SAM-6 Missile Vehicle, BMP-1 (BMP-76PB) MICV, M-1970 Tracked Vehicle, GT-T Tracked Transporter and the new 122mm Self-Propelled Gun.

DESCRIPTION

The hull of the PT-76 is of all-welded construction with the driver at the front of the hull, the turret in the centre and the engine and transmission at the rear. The engine is one half of that used in the T-54 MBT and is fitted with a pre-heater to enable it to start easily in cold weather. The gear box has 4F and 1R gears. The suspension is of the torsion-bar type and has a total of six road wheels with the idler at the front and the drive sprocket at the rear. Shock absorbers are fitted at the first and sixth wheel stations.

The PT-76 is fully amphibious, being propelled in the water by two water jets at the rear of the hull. Before entering the water a trim vane is erected at the front of the hull (this is laid flat on the glacis plate when not required) and the two electric bilge pumps are switched on. There is also one hand-operated bilge pump. Some PT-76s have a schnorkel fitted to the rear of the turret. It is believed that this is fitted in case the rear decking becomes awash and the engine cannot draw in air via the normal louvres. Additional fuel tanks are often fitted on the rear decking. These can be of the drum type or similar to those fitted as standard equipment on the sides of T-54s.

The driver is provided with a circular hatch cover that swings to his right and he has a total of three periscopes, the centre one of which can be raised when afloat so that he can see above the trim vane.

The commander and gunner are seated in the turret which is provided with a turret basket. The commander is on the left of the gun and also acts as the loader; the gunner is to the right of the gun.

The turret is provided with a one-piece hatch cover that hinges forward. The commander has three periscopes arranged round the front part of the hatch cover and the gunner has a periscope mounted in the roof of the turret in front of the hatch, in addition to his gun sight.

The 76.2mm D-56T gun is a development of the gun first used in the T-34/76 and KV-1 tanks during the Second World War. This gun has an overall length of 3.455m and weighs 1150kg. Its maximum rate of fire is fifteen rounds per minute but in action six to eight rounds per minute would be a more realistic figure. It has a semi-automatic vertical sliding wedge breech-block, hydraulic buffer and a hydro-pneumatic recuperator; elevation is manual but there does seem to be some confusion as to whether the turret is traversed by hand or power. The sight fitted is the TSh-66. The gun fires fixed rounds as listed below:
HE projectile weighing 6.2kg with an m/v of 680m/s
APHE projectile weighing 6.5kg with an m/v of 655m/s, which will penetrate 61mm of armour at 1000m
HVAP projectile weighing 3.1kg with an m/v of 965m/s, which will penetrate 58mm of armour at 1000m
HEAT projectile weighing 4kg with an m/v of 325m/s, which will penetrate 325mm of armour at 1200m
The maximum range of the 76mm gun is 12,100m, with maximum elevation.

A co-axial machine-gun is mounted to the right of the main armament.

The PT-76 is not fitted with an NBC system. A ventilation fan is fitted in the turret rear. One of the driving lights may be infra-red and the commander has a standard white light searchlight. If required, navigation lights can be erected when swimming. The PT-76 can also lay its own smoke screen, this being achieved by injecting diesel fuel into the exhaust.

The PT-76 has seen combat in both the Middle and Far East and has been easily destroyed on many occasions. Its most useful feature is its amphibious capability which has enabled it to turn up in the most unexpected places.

VARIANTS

Model 1
This has the D-56T gun which has a multi-slotted muzzle-brake and no bore evacuator. This model is rare.

Model 2
This is the most common model and has the D-56T gun with a double-baffle muzzle-brake and a bore evacuator.

Model 3
This is a Model 2 with no bore evacuator.

Model 4
This is also called the PT-76B and has the D-56TM gun which is fully stabilised.

PT-76 Model 1 with turret hatch open.

A column of PT-76s from the rear, showing hydro-jet outlets in the hull rear.

Above PT-76 Model 2 with schnorkel on turret rear.
Below PT-76 Model 2s afloat with trim board erected.

SOVIET UNION

T-54 and T-55 MAIN BATTLE TANK
MANUFACTURER – Chinese Communist (where it is known as the T-59), Czechoslovakia, Polish or Soviet Union State Arsenals. No longer in production in Warsaw Pact countries but still being built in Communist China.
STATUS – In service with Albania, Algeria, Afghanistan, Bangladesh, Bulgaria, Communist China, Cuba, Cyprus, Czechoslovakia, East Germany, Egypt, Finland, Hungary, India, Iraq, Israel, Libya, Mongolia, Morocco, North Korea, Vietnam, North Yemen, Pakistan (both Chinese and Soviet models), Peru, PLA, Poland, Romania, Somalia, South Yemen, Soviet Union, Sudan, Syria, Uganda, Yugoslavia.

BASIC DATA	T-54	T-55			
CREW:	4	4	FORDING:	1.4m	1.4m
WEIGHT LOADED:	36,000kg	36,000kg		5.486m (with	5.486m (with
LENGTH:	9m (gun	9m (gun		schnorkel)	schnorkel)
	forward)	forward)	GRADIENT:	60%	60%
	8.485m (gun	8.485m (gun	VERTICAL OBSTACLE:	.8m	.8m
	rear)	rear)	TRENCH:	2.7m	2.7m
	6.45m (hull)	6.45m (hull)	ENGINE:	Model V-54	Model V-55,
WIDTH:	3.27m	3.27m		V-12 water-	V-12 water-
HEIGHT:	2.4m (w/o	2.4m (w/o		cooled diesel	cooled diesel
	A/A MG)	A/A MG)		developing	developing
GROUND CLEARANCE:	.425m	.425m		520HP at	580HP at
TRACK:	2.64m	2.64m		2,000rpm	2,000rpm
TRACK WIDTH:	580mm	580mm	ARMAMENT	T	
LENGTH OF TRACK ON			main:	1×100mm	1×100mm
GROUND:	3.84m	3.84m	co-axial:	1×7.62mm	1×7.62mm
GROUND PRESSURE:	.81kg/cm²	.81kg/cm²	bow:	1×7.62mm	1×7.62mm
POWER-TO-WEIGHT			A/A MG:	1×12.7mm	—
RATIO:	14.44HP/ton	16.11HP/ton	ARMOUR		
MAXIMUM ROAD SPEED:	48km/hr	50km/hr	glacis plate:	100mm at 60°	100mm at 60°
MAXIMUM RANGE:	400km	500km	upper hull sides:	70mm at 0°	70mm at 0°
FUEL CAPACITY:	812 litres	960 litres	hull rear:	60mm	60mm
FUEL CONSUMPTION:	190 litres per	190 litres per	hull floor:	20mm	20mm
	100 km	100 km	hull roof:	30mm	30mm
			mantlet:	170mm	170mm

DEVELOPMENT

The T-54 is a development of the earlier T-44 medium tank which in turn was a development of the famous T-34 tank of World War II. The first prototype of the T-54 was completed in 1947 with first production models being built in 1949/50. Since then it has been produced in at least four countries and is still being built in Communist China. It is estimated that the Warsaw Pact Forces have built over 40,000 T-54/T-55s. The T-62 MBT is a further development of the T-54/T-55 series. Components of the T-54/T-55 are used in the ZSU-57-2 Self-Propelled Anti-Aircraft Gun, ATS-59 Tracked Artillery Tractor and the PTS Amphibious Vehicles.

DESCRIPTION

The hull of the T-54 is of all-welded steel construction whilst the turret is a one-piece casting with the top containing the two hatches/cupolas welded on. The driver is seated at the front left of the vehicle and is provided with a one-piece hatch cover that swings to the left and two periscopes for driving whilst closed down. To his right are some of the ammunition, batteries and a small fuel tank. There is an escape hatch in the floor of the hull. Early models did not feature a turret basket. The turret is in the centre of the vehicle with the commander on the left and the gunner in front and below the commander. The loader is to the right of the turret.

Both the commander and loader are provided with one-piece hatches. If these are fixed hatches they normally swing forward, if they are cupolas it depends on the position of the cupola. The commander has a total of four periscopes and a TPK-1 target-designation sight. The sight and two of the periscopes are in the forward part of his cupola whilst the other two periscopes are arranged one in each side of the hatch cover. The commander uses his TPK-1 sight as follows: he first rotates his cupola and lines the sight up with the target; he can then line up the turret with the target and the gunner lays the gun accurately on to the target and fires the main gun. The commander can override the gunner if required. The gunner has his own sight and periscope in the roof of the turret. The loader also has a periscope in the roof of the hull.

The engine is mounted transversely at the rear of the hull, and is provided with an electric starter for normal use; in cold weather a compressed-air system is available. The transmission is also at the rear of the hull and this has 5F and 1R gears.

The suspension is of the torsion-bar type and consists of five road wheels with a distinct gap between the first and second road wheels. The idler is at the front and the drive sprocket is at the rear. The first and fifth wheels are fitted with hydraulic shock absorbers. The tracks are of manganese steel and do not have rubber blocks.

The tank can be fitted with a schnorkel for deep-fording operations. This is fitted to the loader's hatch and takes about fifteen to thirty minutes to prepare for operation. There are two types of schnorkel. The training model is very wide but the operational one is very thin and splits into parts so that it can be carried on the rear of the hull when not required. A navigational system is provided so that the driver can navigate the vehicle whilst it is under the water. Early models did not have an NBC system as fitted to late production models. If required the tank can lay its own smoke screen.

Most models are now fitted with the following infra-red equipment—a single infra-red driving light with a range of 40-60m, an infra-red searchlight to the right of the main armament, with a range of 800-1000m, and an infra-red searchlight on the front of the commander's hatch with a range of about 400m. If required additional fuel can be carried in drums on the rear of the hull. On the right running-board are a total of four flat steel tanks. The first, second and fourth are fuel tanks and each holds 93 litres of fuel, and the third is an oil tank. The tanks often carry an unditching beam on the rear of the hull.

As there are many variants of the T-54 and T-55 the different models are listed below, together with a separate note on their armament. It should be noted that some of these have been modified at least twice in their lifetime and it is often difficult to distinguish between models.

T-54 (Early Model)

This was the first model to enter service and is easily recognisable by the bulbous shape of the turret rear, twin cupolas and the lack of any infra-red equipment. This is no longer in front-line service with any of the Warsaw Pact Forces but some were used by the Palestine Liberation Army in their battle with the Jordanian Army a few years ago. This model could not be fitted with a schnorkel.

T-54

This was the second model and had two cupolas and a standard-type turret. The right cupola, like that of the T-54, is fitted with a 12.7mm DShK anti-aircraft machine-gun. This model is built in Communist China. When fitted with infra-red equipment this became known as the T-54(M). The infra-red searchlight on the main armament has a horizontal bracket.

T-54A

This model appeared in 1955/56. The T-54A has the D-10TG gun which is stabilised in the vertical plane only, and the barrel also has a bore evacuator which appeared on all subsequent T-54s. Other modifications include power elevation for the main armament, electric oil pump, bilge pump, modified air filters and an automatic fire-extinguishing system. Infra-red equipment is fitted as standard equipment, although when the T-54A was introduced this was not fitted.

T-54B

This appeared in 1957/8 and was the first model to be built with infra-red fighting equipment. The searchlight to the right of the main armament has a vertical bracket and the 100mm gun D-10T2S is stabilised in both planes.

T-54(X) or T-54C

This is similar to the T-54B but the right-hand cupola has been removed and replaced by a simple hatch that opens forwards. There is no anti-aircraft machine-gun. All T-54s up to and including this model have a turret dome ventilator in front of the loader's hatch.

T-55

This was first seen in public during the parade held in Moscow on 7th November 1961. The T-55 does not have a turret dome ventilator as fitted to the earlier T-54 nor does it have a cupola for the loader. When first introduced it was not fitted with an anti-aircraft machine-gun, although more recently some tanks have had these fitted.

Other improvements over the T-54 include a more powerful engine and modified transmission; the turret is provided with a basket, the armament is stabilised in both planes, and it has an increased ammunition capacity.

T-55A

This was seen for the first time on 1st May 1963. This model lacks the bow machine-gun and the hatches for both the loader and commander are slightly raised. The commander's hatch is smooth at the base rather than bolted on as normal. The older SGMT 7.62mm co-axial machine-gun has been replaced by the more recent PKT machine-gun.

The T-54/T-55 tanks are very compact for their size and have a very good armour arrangement. The main drawbacks of the tank are that it lacks a good fire-control system, the turret is very cramped, the main armament has a very limited depression when compared to Western tanks, the ammunition capacity is limited and the external fuel tanks are a fire risk. Its deep fording capabilities are excellent and its night fighting capability is useful.

ARMAMENT
The basic T-54 is armed with the 100mm rifled gun D-10T, a development of a naval gun and also fitted to the SU-100 assault gun in a slightly modified form. When first introduced the D-10T was not fitted with a bore evacuator, although later this was introduced.

The gun has a horizontal sliding wedge breech-block and the recoil system consists of a hydraulic buffer and a hydro-pneumatic recuperator. Basic data of the gun are: length overall 5.608m, weight 1948kg, and maximum stated rate of fire seven rounds per minute, although three to four rounds would be a more realistic figure. Maximum range at maximum elevation is 14,600m and like most Soviet tanks it is fitted with clinometer for indirect use. The gunner's sight is the TSh 2-22. The D-10T is not stabilised.

The gun fires fixed rounds of the following types:
HE projectile weighing 15.7kg with an m/v of 900m/s.
APHE projectile weighing 15.9kg with an m/v of 1000m/s, which will penetrate 185mm of armour at 1000m.
HEAT projectile weighing 12.2kg with an m/v of 900m/s, which will penetrate 380mm of armour at 1000m. It has recently been reported that fin-stabilised rounds have been introduced for the 100mm gun.

The next model after the D-10T was the D-10TG which was stabilised in the vertical plane only. The gunner's sight for this gun is the TSh 2A-22. This was followed by the D-10T2S which was fitted to the T-54B. The gunner's sight for this model is the TSh 2B-22 or TSh 2-32, and the gun is stabilised in both planes.

The turret traverse on early vehicles was manual, as was elevation; on all late vehicles both traverse and elevation were powered with manual controls for use in an emergency. The turret has a traverse of 360° and the gun has an elevation of +17° and a depression of —4°. Axis of bore is 1.75m.

A 7.62mm SGMT is mounted to the right of the main armament and there is a further 7.62mm SGMT fixed in the centre of the glacis plate and operated by the driver pressing a button on the right steering lever. A 12.7mm DShK anti-aircraft machine-gun is fitted on to the loader's hatch.

Ammunition capacity of the T-54 is only 34 rounds of 100mm ammunition and it is said that of these 20 are HE rounds. A total of 3,000 rounds of 7.62mm and 500 rounds of 12.7mm machine-gun ammunition are carried.

The T-55 is armed with the same D-10T2S which is stabilised in both planes and it has the same traverse and elevation as those of earlier vehicles. The co-axial machine-gun is a 7.62mm PKT, but whereas the T-55 has a bow 7.62mm PKT machine-gun, the T-55A does not. Some vehicles have a 12.7mm DShK anti-aircraft machine-gun. Ammunition capacity is 43 rounds of 100mm and 3,500 rounds of 7.62mm machine-gun ammunition.

VARIANTS
Flamethrower Tank
This is an unconfirmed model and no further details are available.

Dozer Tank
The T-54/T-55 can be fitted with either the BTU bulldozer blade for clearing soil and obstacles, the STU blade for clearing snow. The lugs seen under the nose of some tanks are used for mounting a dozer blade.

Mine-clearing Tanks
The Soviets use at least two types of mine-clearing rollers on the T-54/T-55 tank and these are known as the PT-54 and PT-55. The PT-54 was the first model and this takes eight to twelve minutes to fit to the tank. The more recent model, the PT-55, is somewhat lighter in weight and takes five to ten minutes to fit. Basic data of the tank with these fitted are: weight with PT-54 rollers 44,800kg, width with PT-54 rollers 3.9m; weight with PT-55 rollers 42,700kg, width with PT-55 rollers 3.9m. These rollers clear a path 1.3m wide each side of the tank, leaving a gap in the middle of 1.25m.

The Czechs use two types of mine clearing T-54/T-55. The first of these is of the roller type and is similar to that used by the Soviets. The other is of the plough type. Basically, a plough is mounted in front of each track and this clears a path; between the two tracks is another device that clears smaller mines, ie anti-personnel mines.

Recently some tanks have been seen fitted with rocket-assisted mine-clearing equipment on their hull rears. This would appear to perform in a similar manner to the British Giant Viper, ie the rocket is attached to a line filled with explosive and fired across a minefield. The falling line is then exploded, hopefully clearing a pathway through the mines.

Indian T-54/T-55s
Some of these have been refitted with either the Russian 115mm gun or the British 105mm gun.

Israeli T-54/T-55s
The Israeli Army uses many basic T-54/T-55 tanks without modifications, as well as a number that have been rebuilt. These latter vehicles are known as TI-67s and have new engines, 105mm L7 series guns as fitted to Israeli M48s and Centurion tanks, new fire-control systems, new electrical systems, and air-conditioning systems for desert operations. The Russian anti-aircraft machine-gun has been replaced by a .50 (12.7mm) Browning machine-gun.

Czechoslovakian/Polish T-54/T-55 tanks
Some of these have slightly different rear deckings and many have a stowage box fitted to the left side of the turret.

T-54/T-55 Armoured Recovery Vehicles
There are four models of the T-54/T-55 ARV and these are listed below:
T-54-T ARV – This is a T-54 chassis fitted with a loading platform and a jib crane, and a large spade mounted at the rear of the hull. A schnorkel can be fitted to an extension collar behind the driver's position on the left side of the hull.
T-54-A ARV – This is an East German model and is provided with a schnorkel which is kept in the horizontal position when travelling. No winch is installed although a pushbar is provided at the front of the hull and a jib crane with a capacity of 1000kg is also fitted. Other equipment includes welding gear, and a chemical and radiation detection system. Like the Model B (below) this can also be fitted with mine-clearing equipment.
   Like the Model B, the Model A has neither a spade nor a winch.
T-54-B ARV – This is also an East German model and is identical to the Model A except that it also has a generator and brackets on the rear hull for securing a tow cable.
T-54-C ARV – This is an East German modification and is provided with a heavy-duty hydraulic crane, and a spade at the front of the hull for supporting the vehicle when the crane is being used. Like the Models A and B, the Model C is provided with a stowage platform at the rear of the vehicle. The Model C does not have a winch.
   Basic data are as follows:

Crew: 3   Weight: 34,000kg   Length: 8.5m   Width: 3.4m   Height: 2.65m

MTU-54 or MTU-55 Bridgelayer
The bridge is mounted on a launching frame which moves the bridge over the gap and is then withdrawn, leaving the bridge in place. It can be picked up again from either end. Basic data are:

Crew: 2   Weight with bridge: 34,000kg   Length with bridge: 12.3m   Width with bridge: 3.274m   Height with bridge: 2.865m   Maximum speed: 48km/hr   Length of bridge: 12.3m   Width of bridge: 3.27m   Height of bridge: 1m   Capacity of bridge: 60,000kg   Armament: 1×12.7mm MG

M1967 Bridgelayer
This is similar to the above but the bridge is of box type construction rather than of lattice type. When in the travelling position the ends are folded up to reduce the length of the bridge. The bridge is 20m in length when laid in position and will span a gap 19m wide. Total weight has been estimated at 50,000kg.

MT-55 Bridgelayer
This is a Czechoslovakian design and the bridge is 18.2m in length when opened out and will span a gap of 17m. It is 3.2m wide.

Above T-54 of the Egyptian Army with a German AEG Infra-Red Searchlight.
Below T-54 used by the Israeli Army.

טנק טי 54

תוצרת ברה"מ

טנק: ביצוע

צוות: 4 איש
אורך: 6.3 מ
רוחב: 3.2 מ
גובה: 2.4 מ
משקל: 36 טון

1

2

1 T-55, fitted with the operational schnorkel, leaving a river.
2 T-55 of the Egyptian Army.
3 T-54-T Armoured Recovery Vehicle.
4 The latest T-54/55 Scissors type MT-55 bridgelayer in action.
5 T-54 fitted with dozer blade.
6 T-54 fitted with KMT-3 mine-clearing equipment.
7 T-54 fitted with plough-type mine-clearing equipment.

▼5

4

6

7

SOVIET UNION

IS-3 SERIES – HEAVY TANKS
MANUFACTURER – Soviet State Arsenals
STATUS – IS-2 is still in front line service in both China and Cuba, and it is still used for training and other roles in a number of Warsaw Pact countries. IS-3 is still used by Bulgaria, Czechoslovakia, East Germany, Egypt, Hungary, Poland, Romania, Soviet Union and Syria. In the Warsaw Pact countries it is in reserve or used for training. Production of both the IS-2 and IS-3 was completed many years ago.

BASIC DATA	IS-2	IS-3		IS-2	IS-3
CREW:	4	4	FORDING:	1.3m	1.3m
WEIGHT LOADED:	46,300kg	45,800kg	GRADIENT:	60%	60%
LENGTH:	9.83m (gun forward)	9.725m (gun forward)	VERTICAL OBSTACLE:	1m	1m
			TRENCH:	2.5m	2.5m
	8.23m (gun rear)	8.23m (gun rear)	ENGINE:	Both are powered by the same V-2-IS (V2K), V-12, water-cooled diesel developing 520HP at 2,000 rpm	
	6.77m (hull)	6.77m (hull)			
WIDTH:	3.07m	3.07m			
HEIGHT:	2.74m (w/o A/A MG)	2.44m (w/o A/A MG)	ARMAMENT:	1×122mm gun D-25 M-1943 1×7.62mm DTM co-axial MG 1×12.7mm DShK A/A MG	
GROUND CLEARANCE:	.46m	.46m			
TRACK:	2.41m	2.41m			
TRACK WIDTH:	650mm	650mm			
LENGTH OF TRACK ON GROUND:	4.625m	4.625m			
GROUND PRESSURE:	.84kg/cm^2	.83kg/cm^2	ARMOUR		
POWER-TO-WEIGHT RATIO:	11.23HP/ton	11.35HP/ton	glacis:	105mm at 60°	120mm at 55°
			hull side:	130mm at 12°	60mm at 60°
MAXIMUM ROAD SPEED:	37km/hr	37km/hr	mantlet:	100mm	200mm
RANGE:	150km	150km	floor:	20mm	20mm
FUEL CAPACITY:	520 litres	520 litres	roof:	25mm	25mm
FUEL CONSUMPTION:	350 litres per 100km	350 litres per 100km			

DEVELOPMENT
The standard Soviet heavy tank during the early part of the Second World War was the KV-1 (Klementy Voroshilov). Various marks were developed including the KV-1A (with an improved main armament), KV-1B and KV-1C (both of these being up-armoured). Early models had the same gun as the T-34/76 and a similar, although slightly more powerful, engine. The KV-2 had a much larger turret fitted with a 152mm howitzer. However, this was not a success and was soon withdrawn and replaced by the ISU-122 and ISU-152 vehicles. The KV-IS was developed from the KV-1. It has lighter armour, a number of automotive modifications including a new transmission, a smaller hull, and a commander's cupola, but very few of these were built. Next came the KV-85 which was based on the KV-1 chassis and had the same gun as the T-34/85 but also had a new cast turret. This did not see service on any large scale. In 1943 came the KV-2/1, which had the same 85mm gun as the KV-85; and KV-2/2 had a 122mm gun. The first IS-1 (Iosef Stalin) appeared in 1943, having been designed by a team led by Kotin who also designed the KV-1. The first models had a 85mm gun but later models had a 100mm gun. The first IS-1 was built in 1943, but very few were built as it was replaced in production by the IS-2 from early in 1944. The IS-2 had a redesigned hull and over 2,000 had been built by the end of 1944.

The IS-3 was developed late in 1944 with the first production models being completed early in 1945. Most reports state that the IS-3 arrived at the front just too late to see combat. It did however take part in the Victory Parade held in Berlin on 7th September 1945.

The IS-3 was a new design although it did use the same engine, transmission, suspension and armament as the earlier IS-2. Its most significant features were its new hull and turret. The glacis plate consisted of a number of plates welded together to form an inverted 'V', and the driver was provided with a single-piece hatch cover.

After the war the IS-3 was followed by the IS-4. This had thicker armour than the IS-3 and it also had a 12.7mm co-axial machine-gun rather than the standard 7.62mm machine-gun. The barrel was provided with a fume extractor, the suspension was modified, and a more powerful engine was fitted, the latter being used some years later for the T-10 heavy tank. The IS-4 was not produced in large numbers.

After the IS-4 came the IS-5, IS-6, IS-7, IS-8, IS-9 and IS-10, all of which were built as prototypes. By this time, however, Stalin had died and the IS-10 finally entered service in 1957 as the T-10, a direct decendant of the KV-1.

VARIANTS
IS-2
The IS-2 has a cast hull and a cast turret. The commander is provided with a non-rotating cupola on the left of the turret roof, and the loader has a simple hatch on the right. The engine and transmission are at the rear of the hull and the gearbox has 4F and 1R gears. Additional fuel tanks can be fitted to the rear of the hull if required. The suspension is of the torsion-bar type and consists of six road wheels, idler at the front and driving sprocket at the rear. There are three track return rollers.

The 122mm gun is mounted in a turret with a total traverse of 360°, elevation being +20° and depression −3°, axis of bore 2m. Most IS-2s have a 7.62mm DTM machine-gun in the rear of the turret and very early models had a further 7.62mm DTM machine-gun in a sponson on the right side of the hull. Total ammunition capacity is 28 rounds of 122mm (separate loading type), 250 rounds of 12.7mm and 2,330 rounds of 7.62mm ammunition.

IS-3
The IS-3 has the same gun with the same elevation and depression as the IS-2, but the axis of the bore is 1.95m. The D-25 M1943 gun was a development of the M1931/39 (A-19) towed gun. It has a semi-automatic vertical sliding breech-block and a double-baffle muzzle-brake. A modified version of this gun (the D-25S) is used in the ISU-122 assault gun.

The ammunition is of the separate loading type which accounts for its low rate of fire of about three rounds per minute. The HE projectile weighs 25.5kg and has an m/v of 781m/s whilst the APHE projectile weighs 25kg and has an m/v of 781m/s which will penetrate 160mm of armour at a range of 900m. Maximum range at maximum elevation in the indirect fire role is stated to be 14,600m. The tank is provided with a travelling lock at the rear of the hull and additional fuel tanks can be fitted at the rear of the hull to increase operating range. The IS-3 is not fitted with an NBC system nor does it have any infra-red driving or fighting equipment; a schnorkel was developed but this was not adopted for the vehicle.

310mm self-propelled gun M-1957
This was first seen in Moscow in 1957. It consists of a chassis constructed of IS-3 components, is unarmoured and has eight road wheels, four track return rollers, idler at the rear and drive sprocket at the front. The 310mm gun fires a projectile weighing 320kg with an m/v of 610m/s to a maximum range of 22,860m.

Both HE and nuclear rounds are available. The gun has a maximum elevation of +42° and a depression of −2°, traverse is 4°. Basic data are as follows: weight loaded 63,500kg, length including gun 16m, length hull only 8m, width 3.3m; it is powered by a V-12 700HP engine which gives it a maximum road speed of 24km, the range being 130km. It is most unlikely that this weapon is still in service and its use on the battlefield could cause problems, not only because of its weight but also because it would be difficult to conceal.

420mm self-propelled mortar M-1957 and M-1960
The M-1957 was first seen in Moscow in 1957. Its unarmoured chassis is similar to that of the 310mm self-propelled gun M-1957. The 420mm mortar fires a projectile weighing some 770kg to a maximum range of 18,280m. It can fire both HE and nuclear projectiles, m/v being 610m/s. The mortar is breech-loaded and has a total elevation of +42° and a depression of −2°, total traverse is 4°. In 1960 the M-1960 model was observed. This had a longer barrel, relocated and smaller equilibrators, and in addition additional shock absorbers were fitted to the rear suspension. The position of the cab was changed from the RHS to directly behind the barrel.

Basic data of the M-1960 are as follows: weight 54,400kg, length overall 21m, length hull only 8m, width 3.3m. It is powered by a 700HP V-12 diesel which gives it a top road speed of 24km and a range of 130km. It is most unlikely that this weapon is still in service.

IS-2 Armoured Recovery Vehicle
This is simply an IS-2 with its turret removed and therefore limited to the towing role.

FROG-1 Tactical Missile System
This was one of the first Russian tactical missile systems to enter service. It is based on a IS-3 chassis. The missile has a single-stage, solid-fuel rocket, and both HE and nuclear warheads could be fitted. The missile has no guidance system and a maximum range of 24km. It must now be considered to be obsolete.

SCUD A Missile System
The SCUD A (SS-1b) was first seen in 1957. The missile has a range of about 130km and has a liquid

propellent. It can have either an HE or nuclear warhead. The SCUD B (SS-1c) was originally fitted to a similar chassis but more recently has been fitted to the MAZ-543 (8×8) vehicle.

SCAMP ICBM

This chassis is constructed of IS-3 components and has eight road wheels, five return rollers, drive sprocket at the rear and idler at the front. The SCAMP missile system was first seen in 1965. The missile itself is inside the container and is called the SCAPEGOAT (SS-14). This missile is of the solid propellent type and is basically the first and second stages of the SAVAGE missile.

SCROOGE (SS-XZ) ICBM

This has a similar chassis to the SCAMP but the missile is much longer and has a range of about 5600km.

Top The IS-2 Heavy Tank.
Above The IS-3 Heavy Tank.
Left The IS-2-T Tank Recovery Vehicle.

SOVIET UNION

T-34/85 – MEDIUM TANK
MANUFACTURER – Soviet State Arsenals. Some were also built in Czechoslovakia and Poland.
STATUS – In service with Afghanistan, Albania, Algeria, Bangladesh, Bulgaria, China, Cuba, Cyprus, Czechoslovakia, East Germany, Egypt, Guinea, Hungary, Iraq, Libya, Mali, Mongolia, North Korea, Vietnam, North and South Yemen, Poland, Romania, Somalia, Sudan, Syria, Yugoslavia. In the case of Warsaw Pact countries the tank is only used for training or with second line units, and large quantities are probably held in reserve. Production of the T-34/85 has now been completed.

BASIC DATA

CREW:	5 (commander, gunner, loader, driver and hull gunner)	ARMAMENT:	1×85mm M-1944 (ZIS-S53) gun with an elevation of +25° and a depression of −5°, axis of bore is 2.05m (early models have the M-1943 D5-T85 gun) 1×7.62mm DTM MG co-axial with main armament and one 7.62mm DTM MG in bow 56/60 rounds of 85mm and 2,394 rounds of 7.62mm ammunition are carried
WEIGHT LOADED:	32,000kg		
LENGTH:	8.076m (gun forwards) 7.53m (gun rear) 6.19m (hull)		
WIDTH:	2.997m		
HEIGHT:	2.743m		
GROUND CLEARANCE:	.38m		
TRACK:	2.45m		
TRACK WIDTH:	500mm		
LENGTH OF TRACK ON GROUND:	3.85m		
GROUND PRESSURE:	.83kg/cm²		
POWER-TO-WEIGHT RATIO:	15.62HP/ton	ARMOUR:	
MAXIMUM ROAD SPEED:	50/55km/hr	glacis plate:	45/47mm at 60°
RANGE:	300km	hull sides:	45/47mm at 40° and 90°
FUEL CAPACITY:	560 litres (internal tanks only)	hull rear:	47mm at 50°
		hull roof:	18/22mm
		hull belly:	18/22mm
FUEL CONSUMPTION:	190 litres per 100km	mantlet:	90mm
FORDING:	1.32m	turret sides:	75mm
GRADIENT:	60%	turret rear	60mm
VERTICAL OBSTACLE:	.73m	turret roof:	18/20mm
TRENCH:	2.5m		
ENGINE:	Model V-2-34 or V-2-34m, V-12, water-cooled diesel developing 500HP at 1,800rpm		

It should be noted that due to wartime manufacturing standards in the Soviet Arsenals there are some differences in armour thickness.

DEVELOPMENT
The first model of the T-34 to enter production was the T-34/76. This was armed with a 76mm gun and entered production in June 1940. It was followed by the T-34/85 late in 1943. Production of the T-34/85 continued until 1964 and it is estimated that at least 50,000 were built. The T-34 was followed by the T-44 medium tank at the end of the war, which was then developed into the T-54. The T-44 is not covered in this book as the tank is not used operationally in any country. The T-34 chassis was also used in a number of other roles including the SU-85 and SU-100 assault guns.

DESCRIPTION
The hull of the T-34 is of all-welded construction whilst the turret is of cast armour with the roof welded on. The driver is seated at the front of the hull on the left side and is provided with a one-piece hatch cover that opens upwards on the outside of the glacis plate. To his right is the bow-mounted machine-gun. The turret is in the centre of the vehicle. The commander is seated on the left of the turret and is provided with a fixed cupola and a one-piece hatch cover that opens forwards. He is provided with a sight and five vision blocks around his cupola. In post-war T-34/85s the commander's cupola could be traversed. The gunner is in front of the commander and is provided with a TSh-15 sight and a periscope mounted in the turret roof. The loader has a simple one-piece hatch that opens forwards. He is seated to the right of the main armament and is also provided with a periscope. Towards the rear of the turret roof are two dome-shaped ventilators. The engine and transmission are at the rear of the hull, the latter having 5F and 1R gears. The

suspension consists of five road wheels with the idler at the front and the drive sprocket at the rear. The track is of cast manganese steel.

Additional fuel can be carried in drums fitted to the sides of the rear hull, or on the hull rear. Some post-war models were fitted with a schnorkel for deep-fording. The T-34/85 does not have an NBC system and as far as it is known none has been fitted with infra-red driving and fighting equipment.

The T-34/85 is armed with the ZIS-S53 85mm gun, which is a development of the M-1939 anti-aircraft gun and was also used in a variety of other vehicles including the KV-85. The barrel has no muzzle-brake or bore evacuator, and is provided with a vertical sliding-wedge breech-block, its recoil system consisting of a hydraulic buffer and a hydro-pneumatic recuperator. Its maximum rate of fire is three to four rounds per minute and it can fire the following types of fixed ammunition:

HE projectile weighing 9.5kg with an m/v of 792m/s, maximum range at maximum elevation being 13,300m.

APHE projectile weighing 9.3kg with an m/v of 792m/s, which will penetrate 102mm of armour at 1,000m.

HVAP projectile weighing 5kg with an m/v of 1,030m/s, which will penetrate 130mm of armour at 1,000m. The turret has total traverse through 360° by both hand or power traverse. The 7.62mm DTM machine-gun is mounted to the right of the main armament.

VARIANTS
Flame-thrower Tank
These were developed during the Second World War and none is known to be in service today.

Yugoslav T-34/85
After the Second World War Yugoslavia did modify a few T-34/85s by fitting them with a new turret and modifying the front of the glacis plate.

Bulldozers and Mine-Clearing Tanks
The T-34/85 can be fitted with a dozer blade or mine-clearing rollers as are also fitted to the T-54 and T-55 tanks.

Czechoslovakian Bridgelayer MT-34
This is basically a T-34 tank chassis fitted with a pair of box-girder treadways folded in half. This was first seen in 1960 during a parade held in Prague. Since then a similar bridge has been fitted to the T-54/T-55 chassis so the T-34 model will probably soon be passed over in favour of the more recent model. The bridge is hydraulically operated. The tank complete with bridge weighs 32,000kg and other data are as follows: length 10m, width 3.2m, height 3.7m. When launched the bridge is 20m in length and 3.2m wide. It can take a maximum weight of 45,000kg and it will span a ditch or river up to 18m wide.

North Vietnamese Anti-Aircraft Vehicle
This is a T-34 hull with a new turret mounting twin 37mm Chinese anti-aircraft guns.

Syrian 122m Self-propelled Gun
This is a T-34 with turret removed and a 122mm D-30 howitzer fitted.

T-34 Armoured Recovery Vehicles
There are at least six types of ARV based on modified T-34 tank chassis:
T-34-T Model A ARV – This is simply a T-34 with its turret removed and is therefore limited to the towing role.
T-34-T Model B ARV – This is provided with a winch, jib crane with a capacity of 3,000kg, and a platform over the rear of the hull which can carry spare parts up to 3,000kg in weight. Towed load is 15,000kg.
T-34-T Model B ARV (East German) – This is similar to the Soviet model but in addition has a push-bar on the front of the hull.
WPT-34 ARV (Polish) – This has a large superstructure on the front of the hull and is also provided with a large telescopic schnorkel on the top of the superstructure on the right side. A winch is provided and there is a large spade at the hull rear. A 7.62mm machine-gun is provided in the hull of the vehicle, at the front on the right side.
SKP-5 ARV – This is a T-34 with the turret removed and replaced with a crane which has a capacity of 5,000kg. It has no winch, spade, schnorkel or push-bar.

Czechoslovakian ARV
This is provided with a heavy-duty hydraulic crane mounted in place of the turret. It is used for changing tank components such as turrets but is also used by the engineers in bridging operations. No spade is fitted. Basic data are:

Crew: 2 Weight: 26,000kg Length: 8m Width: 3.05m Height: 2.6m

Top T-34/85 Medium Tank.
Above T-34 with auxiliary fuel tanks on the sides and rear of the hull. These are being refuelled from a field refuelling system.
Right The SKP-5 ARV which is based on a T-34 chassis.

SWEDEN

INFANTERIKANONVAGN 91 – LIGHT TANK/TANK DESTROYER
MANUFACTURER – AB Hägglunds and Soner, Örnsköldsvik
STATUS – In service with the Swedish Army. In production.

BASIC DATA

CREW:	4 (commander, gunner, loader and driver)	MAXIMUM ROAD SPEED:	69km/hr
		MAXIMUM WATER SPEED:	7km/hr
WEIGHT LOADED:	15,500kg	RANGE:	550km (road)
LENGTH:	8.835m (gun forward)	FUEL:	405 litres
	6.41m (hull)	FORDING:	Amphibious
WIDTH:	3m	GRADIENT:	60%
HEIGHT:	2.355m (commander's cupola)	VERTICAL OBSTACLE:	.8m
		TRENCH:	2.8m
	2.155mm (loader's hatch)	ENGINE:	Volvo-Penta Model TD 120 A, 4-stroke, turbo-
GROUND CLEARANCE:	.4m		charged, 6-cylinder in-
TRACK WIDTH:	450mm		line diesel developing
LENGTH OF TRACK ON			295HP at 2,200rpm
GROUND:	3.79m	ARMAMENT:	1×90mm gun
GROUND PRESSURE:	.45kg/cm^2		1×7.62mm co-axial MG
POWER-TO-WEIGHT			1×7.62mm A/A MG
RATIO:	21HP/ton		2×6 smoke dischargers

DEVELOPMENT
In the mid-1960s the Swedish Army drew up its requirements for a new tank destroyer to replace the Strv.74 light tank, Ikv-102 and Ikv-103 SPGs and the Pansarvärnskanonvagn m/43. None of these is covered in this book as they are about to be phased out of service. Three Swedish companies together entered some fourteen different designs. Hägglunds won the contract to design this new vehicle in April 1968. The first prototype of the Infanterikanonvagn 91 (or Ikv-91) was completed in December 1969, with a further two prototypes being completed in 1970. In March 1972 a production contract was awarded to Hägglunds and the Ikv-91 entered production in 1974 with deliveries to the Swedish Army commencing in 1975. The Ikv-91 uses many components of the Hägglunds Bgbv.82 (ARV) and the Brobv.941 (armoured bridgelayer).

DESCRIPTION
The hull of the Ikv-91 is of all-welded construction with the glacis being immune from attack by projectiles up to and including 20mm in calibre. The driver is seated at the front of the vehicle on the left side and is provided with a one-piece hatch cover that opens to the left and a total of three periscopes for driving whilst closed down. To his right is ammunition stowage.

The turret is in the centre of the vehicle and the front of this is also immune to attack from projectiles up to and including 20mm in calibre. The commander is seated on the right of the turret and has a single-piece hatch cover that opens to the rear. The loader's hatch is on the left and also opens to the rear.

The commander's cupola is provided with a ×10° binocular periscope as well as M17 periscopes for all-round vision. The cupola can be traversed through 240° and can counter-rotate. The gunner is also on the right side of the turret and is provided with a ×10° monocular periscope sight with a 6° field of view, built by Jungner Instrument AB and incorporating a Bofors laser rangefinder. The commander can also lay the gun and if required override the gunner's decision.

The gun-control equipment has been developed by AGA Aerotronics AB. The basis of the fire-control system is a hydraulic system for turret traverse and gun elevation, fed through a hydraulic accumulator from an intermittently working electro-hydraulic pump in the turret. The electronic gun-control equipment includes a ballistic computer and electric servos to control the gunner's line of sight. The computer determines the ballistic solution for the 90mm HEAT and HE rounds as well as for the 7.62mm co-axial machine-gun. Total time from when the commander sights the target to when the gun is fired is eight seconds, and twelve seconds to the second round.

The 90mm gun (L54), designed by Bofors, is designated type KV 90 S 73 and is of the low-pressure type. It fires both HE and HEAT rounds of the fixed type, basic data of which are given below: HEAT round has an m/v of 825m/s, complete round weighs 10.7kg of which the projectile itself weighs 4.5kg. A piezo-electric fuze is fitted.

HE round has an m/v of 600m/s and the complete round weighs 12.2kg with the projectile weighing 6.7kg. and impact fuze is fitted.

The co-axial 7.62mm machine-gun is mounted to the left of the main armament with the 7.62mm anti-aircraft machine-gun mounted on the loader's cupola. There are six smoke dischargers mounted either side of the turret.

The turret has full traverse through 360°, the gun having an elevation of +15° and a depression of −10° (except over the rear hull where it is 0°). Maximum traverse rate is 25° per second and maximum elevation rate is 20° a second.

Total ammunition capacity is 59 rounds of 90mm, of which 16 rounds are in ready racks at the loader's station, 18 are to the right of the driver and 25 are behind the turret in the chassis. A total of 4,500 rounds of 7.62mm machine-gun ammunition are carried.

The sides of the hull are of double-skinned construction with the space between them being used for the storage of fuel and other components. There is an emergency hatch in the forward part of the fighting compartment.

The engine and transmission are at the rear part of the hull and separated from the fighting compartment by a fire-proof bulkhead.

The engine, gearbox with torque-converter, bevel gear and steering clutch are mounted as a single unit. The engine is mounted across the engine compartment at an angle of approx 45°. Engine exhaust is used not only to drive the turbo-charger but also to induce a flow of cooling air over the steering brakes by passing it through an ejector.

The gearbox is an Allison model HT 740D with 4F and 1R gears and is fully automatic. The Ikv-91 has the same clutch-and-brake steering system as used in the Pbv.302 armoured personnel carrier. The steering clutch is of the double dry-plate type operated by hydraulic servo. The steering brakes at the end of each end of the drive shafts are used also as main brakes.

The suspension consists of six road wheels, each supported by trailing arms sprung by transversally mounted torsion bars. Heavy-duty shock-absorbers are attached to the first and last wheel stations. The idler is at the front and the drive sprocket is at the rear, there are no track return rollers.

The Hägglunds M70 track is a single-pin, rubber-bushed link with the rubber bushings confined to one link at each joint with the pin being fixed at the other.

The electrical system is 24-Volt and there are two groups each of 2×12V batteries with a total capacity of 228Amp/hr. A 140-Amp alternator is provided.

The Ikv-91 is fully amphibious being propelled in the water by its tracks. Before entering the water the four bilge pumps are switched on, the trim vane is erected at the front of the hull and low screens for the air-inlets and air-exhaust are erected on the rear hull decking.

Infra-red driving lights are provided. The engine is fitted with a pre-heater for use in cold weather and the fighting compartment is also provided with a heater.

An NBC system is provided. An electric fan creates a slight over-pressure by sucking air from the air inlet through a dust filtration system and blowing it through an NBC filter into the fighting compartment.

Above One of the prototypes of the Ikv-91 Light Tank/Tank Destroyer.

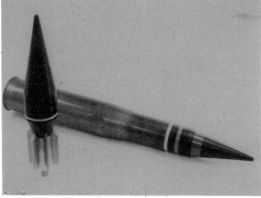

A complete Bofors HEAT round with the projectile on its own in the foreground.

SWEDEN

STRIDSVAGN 103B MAIN BATTLE TANK
MANUFACTURER – AB Bofors, Bofors
STATUS – In service with the Swedish Army. Production complete.

BASIC DATA

CREW:	3 (commander, driver/ gunner, radio operator)	MAXIMUM WATER SPEED:	6km/hr
		RANGE:	390km
WEIGHT LOADED:	39,000kg	FUEL:	960 litres
WEIGHT EMPTY:	37,000kg	FORDING:	1.5m
LENGTH:	9.8m (including gun) 8.4m (without armament)		Amphibious with screen erected
		GRADIENT:	60%
WIDTH:	3.6m	VERTICAL OBSTACLE:	.9m
HEIGHT:	2.5m (with commander's MG)	TRENCH:	2.3m
	2.14m (commander's cupola)	ENGINES:	Rolls-Royce K60 multi-fuel engine developing 240BHP at 3,650rpm and a Boeing 553 gas-turbine developing 490SHP at 38,000rpm
	1.7m (axis of bore)		
GROUND CLEARANCE:	.5m (centre of hull) .4m (sides of hull)		
TRACK:	2.6m	ARMAMENT:	1×105mm gun
TRACK WIDTH:	670mm		2×7.62mm MGs on hull
LENGTH OF TRACK ON GROUND:	2.85m		1×7.62mm MG on commander's cupola
GROUND PRESSURE:	.9kg/cm²		2×4 smoke dischargers
MAXIMUM ROAD SPEED:	50km/hr		

DEVELOPMENT

Development of the Stridsvagn 103 (or Strv.103) can be traced to mid-1956 and an idea from Sven Berge of Swedish Army Ordnance. Various components were tested on a number of vehicles including an M4 Sherman, Ikv-103 and a KRV medium tank chassis. In mid-1958 Bofors was awarded a design contract, this being followed in 1959 by a contract to build two prototype vehicles. The first of these was completed in 1961 and in fact before the prototypes were completed the Swedish Army placed a pre-production order for ten tanks. The first production order was awarded to Bofors in 1965 with production commencing 1966. Production was completed in 1971 after some 300 had been built. Other companies involved in the programme included Volvo (for the engine pack) and Landsverk (for the running gear).

   The first prototype had no flotation screen, no return rollers, no gun barrel support and a total of five machine guns, one on the commander's cupola and two in boxes on each side of the hull. They were powered by a Rolls-Royce 8-cylinder petrol engine and a Boeing 502/10MA gas turbine. Pre-production vehicles had a 12.7mm ranging machine-gun on the right side of the hull in place of two 7.62mm machine-guns, a gun-barrel support and track return rollers. First production vehicles were designated Strv.103As as these did not have a flotation screen. Subsequently all Strv.103As were brought up to Strv.103B standard and provided with flotation screens and dozer blades. The S-tank uses many components of the VK-155 155mm self-propelled gun and the now defunct twin 40mm self-propelled anti-aircraft gun designated the VEAK 40. Several years ago the British Army borrowed a number of S-Tanks for extensive trials in West Germany, the basic idea being to test the concept of a turretless tank in line with BAOR strategy.

DESCRIPTION

The S-Tank is unique in that it has no turret and a crew of three. The driver is also the gunner, the commander can also lay and fire the gun, and the third member of the crew is the radio-operator who can also drive the tank backwards if required. The hull is of all-welded construction and an escape hatch is provided in the bottom of the hull. The driver/gunner is seated on the left side with the commander to the right, and the radio-operator is behind the driver, facing the rear.

The gun is laid by varying the height of the suspension and slewing the tracks, maximum elevation being +12° and depression being —10°. Both the commander and driver have tiller boxes to control the tank, lay the gun, select the ammunition and fire the gun.

The 105mm gun (62 calibres) is designated the L74 and is a longer model of the British L7A1 tank gun. It has a bore evacuator and twin vertical sliding breech-blocks with centre cranks. The gun is fed hydraulically from a 50-round magazine at the rear of the hull. This has ten racks each holding five rounds. Maximum rate of fire is ten to fifteen rounds per minute and the magazine can be reloaded through two hatches in five to ten minutes. Ammunition types are APDS and HESH with a maximum range of 2,000m, as well as smoke and HE (maximum range 5,000m). In an emergency the radio-operator can hand crank ammunition to the gun, the empty cartridge cases being ejected outside the hull automatically. There are two 7.62mm Ksp 58 machine-guns in a box on the left side of the hull. These are lined up with the main armament and fire alternately. A further 7.62mm machine-gun is mounted on the left side of the commander's cupola. This can be aimed and fired at ground targets from within the vehicle and can also be used against aircraft. The machine-guns have a cyclic rate of fire of 700/900 rounds per minute per gun and a total of 2,750 rounds of machine-gun ammunition are carried. Some S-Tanks have been fitted with Lyran flare tubes for illuminating targets at night.

The two engines are in the forward part of the vehicle and are geared together to a common output, the gas turbine being used when additional power is required, eg when in action. Two fire-extinguishers are mounted in the engine compartment. When the engines are removed the glacis plate has to be taken off. The transmission is a Volvo torque converter coupled to a 2F and 2R speed gearbox. The steering is a regenerative double-differential system with a hydrostatic steering drive and is controlled by handle bars on the tiller columns.

The hydro-pneumatic suspension consists of four road wheels with the idler at the rear and the drive sprocket at the front, and two track return rollers. The suspension locks when the main gun is fired, thus providing a very stable firing platform. The road wheels are identical to the Centurion which is used in some numbers by the Swedish Army.

The gunner/driver and commander have a Jungner OPS-1 combined periscope and binocular sight, the latter with magnifications of ×6, ×10, and ×18. In addition, the commander's sight is stabilised in azimuth and elevation. The commander has four periscopes for general observation whilst the driver has one and the radio-operator two. All these periscopes are provided with armoured covers. A laser rangefinder is under development.

The tank commander is also provided with an accelerator and a brake pedal and can take over control of the tank if required. The radio-operator has simple controls and can drive the tank if required.

The electrical system is 24V and 2×12V 114Amp/hr batteries are provided. The K60 engine drives the generator.

A flotation screen is carried around the top of the hull. This takes about fifteen to twenty minutes to erect and the tank can then propel itself across lakes at a speed of 6km/hr. A dozer blade is mounted under the nose of the tank and this can be positioned in a few minutes and is used by the tank to clear obstacles, river bank exits, etc, as well as for preparing firing positions. The blade is static when in use as the tank uses its suspension. The S-Tank is not fitted with an NBC system and the crew have to use their gas masks. Infra-red driving lights are provided.

VARIANTS

There are no variants of the S-Tank.

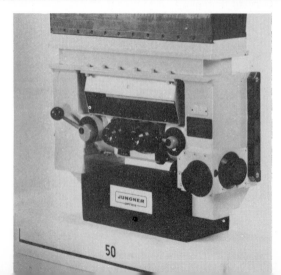

Top Stridsvagn 103B from the side. Note the dozer blade flush with the underside of the hull front.
Above Stridsvagn 103B showing the capabilities of its hydro-pneumatic suspension system. This particular tank is in British Army markings.
Left The Jungner OPS-1 combined periscope and binocular sight as fitted to the S-Tank.

SWITZERLAND

PANZER 61 and PANZER 68 SERIES – MAIN BATTLE TANKS
MANUFACTURER – Federal Construction Works, Thun
STATUS – In service with the Swiss Army. Production complete.

BASIC DATA	Pz.61	Pz.68		Pz.61	Pz.68
CREW:	4	4	MAXIMUM ROAD SPEED:	50km/hr	55km/hr
WEIGHT LOADED:	38,000kg	39,700kg	RANGE:	300km (road)	300km (road)
WEIGHT EMPTY:	37,000kg	38,700kg		160km (cross-	160km (cross-
LENGTH:	9.43m (gun	9.49m (gun		country)	country)
	forward)	forward)	FUEL:	760 litres	760 litres
	8.28m (gun	8.49m (gun	FORDING:	1.1m	1.1m
	rear)	rear)	GRADIENT:	70%	70%
	6.78m (hull)	6.9m (hull)	VERTICAL OBSTACLE:	.75m	.75m
WIDTH:	3.06m	3.14m	TRENCH:	2.6m	2.6m
HEIGHT:	2.85m (with	2.75m (with	ENGINE:	MTU MB 837	8 MTU MB 837
	A/A MG)	A/A MG)		8-cylinder,	8-cylinder,
	2.72m (cupola)	2.74m (cupola)		developing	developing
	1.93m (axis of	1.96m (axis of		630HP at	704HP at
	bore)	bore)		2,200rpm	2,200rpm
GROUND CLEARANCE:	.42m	.45m	ARMAMENT:	1×105mm	1×105mm
TRACK:	2.5m	2.59m		1×20mm (co-	1×7.5mm (co-
TRACK WIDTH:	500mm	520mm		axial)	axial)
LENGTH OF TRACK ON				1×7.5mm (A/A)	1×7.5mm (A/A)
GROUND:	4.13m	4.22m		2×3 (smoke	2×3 (smoke
GROUND PRESSURE:	.85kg/cm^2	.86kg/cm^2		dischargers)	dischargers)
POWER-TO-WEIGHT			ARMOUR:	20mm/60mm	20mm/60mm
RATIO:	17HP/ton	18.9HP/ton			

DEVELOPMENT/VARIANTS/DESCRIPTION

The development of the Pz.58 commenced in the early 1950s with the first of two protoypes being completed in 1958. The first prototype was armed with a Swiss 90mm cannon. The second prototype followed in 1959, this being armed with a British 20-pounder (83.4mm) gun as fitted to the Centurion tanks used by the Swiss Army. These were followed by ten pre-production vehicles in 1960/61. These were armed with the British 105mm gun and were called the Pz.61.

Pz.61

In March 1961 a production order for a total of 150 Pz.61s was placed. Production commenced in 1964 and was completed in 1966.

The hull and turret of the Pz.61 is cast, and is entirely produced in Switzerland. The driver is seated at the front and is provided with a total of three periscopes and a one-piece hatch cover hinged at the rear. The loader is seated on the left of the turret and has a cupola with a split hatch cover and a total of eight periscopes. The gunner is on the right side of the turret and the commander is provided with a total of six periscopes and a single-piece hatch cover that opens to the rear. The engine (which is a diesel made in Germany) and transmission are at the rear of the hull and are separated from the fighting compartment by a bulkhead. An auxiliary engine is provided, and the electrical system is 24-Volt.

The suspension consists of six road wheels with the idler at the front and the drive sprocket at the rear, and there are three track return rollers. Each road wheel is sprung by Belleville washers and the tracks are cast manganese. The driver steers the vehicle with a conventional steering wheel. The semi-automatic transmission has 6F and 2R gears and consists of a double-differential steering system with a hydrostatic steering device.

The 105mm gun is called the Pz.Kan.61 and is a modified version of the British L7A1 built in Switzerland. A 20mm co-axial 5TGK (Masch.Kan.Pz.61) is mounted to the left of the main armament and has a cyclic rate of fire of 800rpm. A 7.5mm machine-gun is mounted on the loader's hatch for anti-aircraft use. A total of 52 rounds of 105mm ammunition are carried, of which eight are in the turret and 22 each side of the driver's position. 240 rounds of 20mm and 3,000 rounds of 7.5mm ammunition are carried. In addition there are 2×3 L.Pz.51 (80.5mm) smoke dischargers either side of the turret. The main types of 105mm ammunition are APDS and HESH although the Swiss also use an HE round.

The commander has a ×8 rangefinder and the gunner a ×6 telescope.

The turret has full traverse through 360° and the 105mm gun has an elevation of +21° and a depression of

−10°. The CH 25 gun-control system was developed for the Pz.61 by the French company of SAMM. The turret takes 9.5 seconds to traverse 360°, elevation speed is 20° per second.

The Pz.61 has infra-red driving lights and a full NBC system.

Pz.68

The Pz.68 is a further development of the earlier Pz.61. A total of 170 production vehicles were completed between 1971 and 1973. The major modifications include the replacement of the 20mm cannon by another 7.5mm machine-gun, and the fitting of a more powerful engine and a modified gearbox. The tank is slightly wider than earlier Pz.61 and its tracks, which are also wider, and are fitted with rubber pads. The suspension has been slightly modified and a stabiliser is provided for the main armament, allowing the tank to shoot whilst on the move. A hatch has been fitted to the left side of the turret so that tank ammunition can be loaded quicker. Total ammunition capacity is: 52 rounds of 105mm and 5,200 rounds of 7.5mm. Like the Pz.61 it is fitted with infra-red driving lights and an NBC system. A laser rangefinder is under development and trials have been carried out with a Pz.68 fitted for deep wading.

Entpannungspanzer 65 (Armoured Recovery Vehicle)

The prototype of the Entpannungspanzer 65 (or Entp.Pz.65) was built on a Pz.61 chassis but production vehicles used the Pz.68 chassis. A hydraulically-operated dozer blade is mounted at the front of the hull, and this is used for dozer operations and for stabilising the vehicle when the 'A' frame is being used. The 'A' frame is pivoted at the front of the hull and has a maximum lifting weight of 15,000kg. The main winch is hydraulically operated and has a maximum capacity of 25,000kg and is provided with 120m of rope. The secondary winch has a capacity of 500kg and is provided with 240m of rope. A full range of tools is carried. The Entp.Pz.65 is armed with a 7.5mm machine-gun and a total of eight smoke dischargers. Performance data are similar to those of the Pz.68:

Crew: 5 Weight: 39,000kg Length: 7.6m Width over blade: 3.15m Width: 3.06m Height: 3.25m Fording: 1.2m

Brückenpanzer 68 (Bridgelayer)

The prototype of this vehicle, which is also known as the Brü.Pz.68, were based on a Pz.61 chassis, but production vehicles used a Pz.68 chassis. Early models had a steel bridge but production models had an aluminium bridge. The bridge can take a maximum load of 60,000kg although for normal operations it is limited to 50,000kg. It takes approx. two minutes to lay in position and five minutes to retract. The bridge itself weighs 6,600kg and is 18.23m in length and 3.79m in width. With the bridge the complete vehicle weighs 44,600kg and the bridge is 20.1m long, 3.9m wide and 3.3m high.

Schweres Panzerzielfahrzeug (Pz.Zielfz.68)

This is an armoured target tank and weighs 36,000kg. Its tracks are protected by side armour and it has a new eight-sided turret with a dummy gun-barrel. The crew consists of two men.

Anti-Aircraft Vehicle

It has been reported that an anti-aircraft vehicle is under development. This could be armed with missiles, eg Roland or Crotale, or with twin 35mm cannon. It should be remembered that the German Gepard A/A tank has Swiss 35mm cannon and these could easily be fitted to the Pz.68 chassis.

Panzer-Kanone 68

The prototype of the Panzer-Kanone 68 was built several years ago. It consists of a Pz.68 chassis fitted with a new turret with a traverse of 360°, and is armed with a 155mm gun with a range of 30,000m. This is a development of a fortress gun already used by the Swiss Army. In addition a 7.5mm machine-gun and six smoke dischargers are provided.

As the Swiss Army purchased 140 American M109Us (these being known as the Panzwehaubitze 66 Pz.Hb.66) suitably modified to meet Swiss Army requirements, it is doubtful if the Panzer-Kanone 68 will enter production in the near future. Basic data of the weapon are given below, and performance is similar to that of the Pz.68 MBT.

Length with gun forward: 9.423m   Length of hull: 6.552m   Width: 3m   Height: 2.628m

1 The Panzer 61 Main Battle Tank with 20mm co-axial cannon.
2 The Panzer 68 Main Battle Tank with 7.5mm co-axial machine-gun.
3 The Brückenpanzer 68 Bridgelayer in travelling order.
4 The Schweres Panzerzielfahrzeug (Pz.Zielfz.68) Armoured Target Tank.
5 The Panzer-Kanone 68 with 155mm gun at high elevation.
6 The Entpannungspanzer 65 Armoured Recovery Vehicle with blade lowered and 'A' frame erected.

1

2

▼5

3

4

6

UNITED STATES

XM1–MAIN BATTLE TANK
MANUFACTURERS–Chrysler Corporation of Warren, Michigan.
Detroit Diesel Division of General Motors Corporation of Indianapolis, Indiana
STATUS–Trials. Not yet in production.

GENERAL

On 1 August 1963 the United States and German Governments signed an agreement to develop a new MBT which became the MBT-70. This was, however, cancelled in January 1970. The United States then went on to develop a more austere model of the MBT-70 called the XM803, but this too was cancelled. The Germans developed the Leopard 2 MBT.

In February 1972 the United States Army formed a group to formulate the concept for a new tank for the Army. The final programme was approved in January 1973. On 28th June 1973 contracts were awarded to Chrysler and Detroit Diesel to design and construct prototypes and test rigs. The prototypes were completed in 1975 and handed over to the Army for trials early in 1976. This first stage is known as the Prototype Validation Phase (PVP).

After the two prototypes have been tested one of the companies will be selected to undertake full-scale engineering, development and production. The Army has a total requirement for 3,312 XM1s. Production should start in 1979 at a rate of ten tanks per month with full production of 30 tanks per month being reached late in 1980. The XM1 will replace some but not all of the M60s in the active Army Fleet.

Cost of the XM1 is estimated at $507,000 per tank (in Constant Fiscal Year 1972 dollars) but this includes government-furnished equipment. The Research, Development, Test and Evaluation cost of the XM1 Programme in FY 72 dollars is estimated to be $391.9 million. In December 1974 the United States Army announced that it was considering the Leopard 2 as a possible contender for this programme and a contract has been awarded to FMC for a number of modifications to the Leopard 2, one of which was shipped to America for trials late in 1976.

At this time few details of the XM1 have been released. It will, however, have a number of improvements over the current M60 series, including improved armour (ie spaced armour), a lower profile, an improved fire-control system, higher cross-country speed, greater acceleration and easier maintenance. Prototypes will be armed with the same 105mm gun as fitted to the M60 and this may well be fitted to production tanks. A Bushmaster co-axial cannon will be installed (see ARSV entry), a .50 (12.7mm) machine-gun will be mounted on the commander's cupola, and a 7.62mm machine-gun will be mounted on the loader's hatch. The United States has recently developed two new rounds for the 105mm gun. The XM735 being a APFSDS round with a tungsten alloy core whilst the XM774 has a projectile of depleted uranium.

The Army has released the following comparisons between the M60A1 and the XM1:

	M60A1	XM1
Combat weight:	48,081kg	56,000/58,000kg
Acceleration 0-32km/hr:	14.1 secs	6/9 secs
Cross-country speed:	29/35km/hr	40/48km/hr
Maximum road speed:	48km/hr	56/64km/hr
Speed on a 10% slope:	19km/hr	32/40km/hr
Speed on a 60% slope:	3.54km/hr	4.8/8km/hr
Horsepower:	900	1,500

The fire-control system will include a thermal night-sight, day-sight, solid state computer, laser rangefinder developed by Hughes, and a stabilization system. The Detroit Diesel XM1 will be powered by a Teledyne Continental variable-compression ratio engine which will develop 1,500HP. The Chrysler tank will have an Avco-Lycoming AGT 1500 gas turbine. This features a stationary heat exchanger, twin-spool compressors, free-power turbine with built-in reduction gear, and variable turbine nozzle geometry.

In October 1974 it was announced that the XM1 will be named the Abrams.

Above United States Army drawing of the possible configuration of the XM1.

UNITED STATES

NEW LIGHT TANK
STATUS – Project.

NOTES
In the Department of Defense Appropriations for 1976, Lt Gen. H. H. Cooksey, Deputy Chief-of-Staff for Research and Development and Acquisition, mentioned that it would be possible to develop a new light tank weighing 16-17 tons. This would be armed with a new very high-velocity gun firing a kinetic energy round with a calibre of between 60 and 75mm. Other sources have stated that a 73mm round and gun is well under development. This new light tank will be airportable by aircraft and helicopter and would enter service in the 1985-90 time frame. Both the Army and Marine Corps appear to have a requirement for this new light tank. No further details are available at the present time.

UNITED STATES

M551 – LIGHT TANK/RECONNAISSANCE VEHICLE
MANUFACTURER – Allison Division of General Motors Corporation, Cleveland Tank-Automotive Plant
STATUS – In service only with the United States Army, Production complete.

BASIC DATA

CREW:	4 (commander, gunner, loader, driver)	FUEL:	598 litres
		FORDING:	Amphibious
WEIGHT LOADED:	15,830kg	GRADIENT:	60%
WEIGHT EMPTY:	13,589kg	SIDE SLOPE:	40%
LENGTH:	6.299m	VERTICAL OBSTACLE:	.838m
WIDTH:	2.819m	TRENCH:	2.54m
HEIGHT:	2.946m (with A/A MG) 2.272m (turret roof)	ENGINE:	Detroit Diesel Model 6V53T, 6-cylinder, water-cooled, developing 300BHP at 2,800rpm with turbo-charger
GROUND CLEARANCE:	.48m		
TRACK:	2.348m		
TRACK WIDTH:	444mm	ARMAMENT:	1×152mm gun/missile launcher
LENGTH OF TRACK ON GROUND:	3.66m		1×7.62mm co-axial MG
GROUND PRESSURE:	.49kg/cm²		1×.50 (12.7mm) A/A MG
MAXIMUM ROAD SPEED:	70km/hr		8 smoke dischargers
MAXIMUM WATER SPEED:	5.8km/hr		
RANGE:	600km		

DEVELOPMENT

Development of the XM551 started in January 1959, when technical feasibility and preliminary concept studies commenced. A number of companies submitted proposals for the vehicle and in May 1960 General Motors were awarded a contract for the development of a vehicle called the Armoured Reconnaissance Airborne Assault Vehicle. This was to replace the M41 light tank and the M56 self-propelled anti-tank guns at that time in service. The final mock-up was approved in December 1961 and a test rig was running by this time. It had been decided that the vehicle would be armed with the XM81E7 gun/missile launcher which was also being developed. In July 1962 an XM551 turret was fitted to an M41 light tank chassis for an extensive series of trials, during which a total of 590 missiles were fired. A total of twelve prototypes were built, the first of which was completed in 1962. These prototypes had a box-type hull and buoyant road wheels and were fully amphibious without the need for a flotation screen. In November 1965 the XM551 was type classified as Limited Production type and the first production order was placed. It then became known as the M551 or Sheridan. In May 1966 it was type classified as Standard A. The first production model was completed in June 1966 and the vehicle continued in production for four years and a total of approx. 1,700 were built. In 1968/69 64 Sheridans were deployed in Vietnam where numerous problems were found. Since then, however, the vehicle has shown itself to be a rugged and reliable vehicle. It is deployed in the reconnaissance platoon of armoured cavalry squadrons in armoured, infantry and airborne divisions and in the reconnaissance platoons of armoured cavalry regiments. It is in service in the United States, Germany and Korea.

DESCRIPTION

The hull of the Sheridan is of aluminium construction with the driver seated at the front of the vehicle. His hatch cover has a total of three M47 periscopes, the centre one of which can be replaced by an M48 infra-red periscope for night-driving. His hatch cover is unusual in that when driving in the head-out position it is swung inside the vehicle, behind the driver.

The turret is of welded steel with the loader on the left and the commander and gunner on the right. The commander's cupola has a total of ten vision blocks and his hatch cover is of the split type. The loader has a single-piece hatch cover and an M37 periscope which can be rotated through 360°. The gunner has an M119 telescope linked to the main armament, with a magnification of ×8 and a 8° field of view. For night use he has an infra-red periscope with a 6° field of view and a magnification of ×1 or ×8. The commander has a portable night-vision sight.

The engine and the aluminium and magnesium cross-drive transmission (a model TG-250; whilst under development it was the XTG-250-1A) are at the rear of the vehicle with the aluminium cross-flow radiator in the forward part of the engine compartment. The transmission has 4F and 2R gears (high and low) with a torque converter and semi-automatic gear-shift. The suspension is of the torsion-bar type and consists of five road wheels with the idler at the front and the drive sprocket at the rear. There are no track return rollers. The first and fifth road wheel stations are provided with hydraulic shock absorbers.

The Sheridan is fitted with a flotation screen which takes about five minutes to erect and is propelled in the water by its tracks. The Sheridan has infra-red driving lights and most models now have an infra-red searchlight over the main armament. The crew are provided with uncontaminated air via their face masks which are connected to a central system. The fighting compartment is provided with a heater and a ventilator. The engine compartment is fitted with a fire extinguisher which is operated by the driver. The electrical system is 24V DC and two batteries are normally carried; in a cold climate an additional two batteries are fitted. A 300Amp generator is provided.

The turret has full powered traverse through 360°, traverse being 48° a second. The gun/launcher has an elevation of +19° and a depression of —8°. Manual controls are provided for use in an emergency.

The main armament of the Sheridan is the M81 (XM81E12) gun/launcher which can fire the Shillelagh missile or conventional type ammunition with a combustible cartridge.

The Shillelagh missile is designated MGM-51A and was developed by Missile Command and the Philco-Ford Corporation. Production commenced in November 1964. The Shillelagh missile is 1.155m in length, weighs 26.76kg and has a maximum velocity of 689m/s. It has a solid propellent and this burns for 1.18 seconds. Most reports put its range at 3,000m. Its shaped charge warhead is effective against all armour. The missile is fired by the gunner who simply has to keep the cross-hairs of the sight on the target and the missile will impact where required. Basically the missile tracker measures the deviation of the missile's flight-path from the line of sight, and the signals are converted into commands that are transmitted by the infra-red transmitter (which is above the main armament) to the receiver in the missile. Normal rate of fire is two missiles per minute. The following types of conventional ammunition are available: M409 HEAT-T-MP which weighs 22kg, has a length of .68m, an m/v of 683m/s and a maximum range of 9000m; M410 WP, M411 Target Practice; and a Canister round which has an effective range of 400m. When firing conventional ammunition four rounds per minute can be fired. A 7.62mm M73 machine-gun is mounted to the right of the main armament and there is a .50 (12.7mm) Browning M2 machine-gun on the commander's cupola for anti-aircraft use. The latter has a maximum elevation of +70° and a depression of —15° and most are now fitted with shields. The mix of missiles/conventional ammunition depends on mission requirements. A typical load would be eight missiles and twenty conventional rounds. A total of 1,000 rounds of .50 and 3,000 rounds of 7.62mm ammunition are carried, most of which are outside the turret. There are four smoke dischargers either side of the turret, towards the front.

In 1971 Hughes were awarded a contract for $8.3 million to design a laser rangefinder which will fit the front of the commander's cupola.

VARIANTS
The Sheridan was to have been the basic member of a whole family of vehicles but none of these entered production and in most cases only reached the drawing-board stage:

Mauler anti-aircraft missile carrier with a total of nine missiles in ready-to-launch position.
Flamethrower.
Mortar carrier with 107mm mortar.
155mm self-propelled gun.
Bridgelayer, this has now reached the prototype stage, its bridge is 18.28m in length when opened out and can take a load of 30,000kg.
Engineer vehicle.

Fitted with 105mm gun, developed to prototype stage.
Fitted with 76mm gun M76, developed to prototype stage.
Mechanized Infantry Combat Vehicle.
Armoured Crane.
Anti-Aircraft gun vehicle.
Cargo carrier, similar to the M548.

Above One of the prototypes of the M551 firing a Shillelagh missile.

Above M551 with flotation screen raised just leaving a river in Germany.
Below The M551, fitted with a lightweight aluminium bridge, undergoing trials in the United States.

UNITED STATES

M60 SERIES—MAIN BATTLE TANK
MANUFACTURER—Chrysler Corporation, at Detroit Tank Plant, Michigan.
STATUS—In service with Austria, Ethiopia, Iran, Israel, Italy, Jordan, Saudi-Arabia, Somalia, South Korea, Spain (AVLB only), Turkey, United States (Army and Marine Corps). Production of the M60 and M60A2 is complete. Production of the M60A1, M60A3, M728 and M60 AVLB continues.

BASIC DATA	M60	M60A1	M60A2	M728
CREW:	4	4	4	4
WEIGHT LOADED:	46,266kg	48,987kg	51,982kg	52,163kg
WEIGHT EMPTY:	42,184kg	43,999kg	41,459kg	48,500kg
LENGTH OVERALL:	9.309m	9.309m	7.283m	9.3m (with boom)
LENGTH HULL:	6.946m	6.946m	6.946m	7.88m (inc. blade)
WIDTH:	3.631m	3.631m	3.631m	3.7m (inc. blade)
HEIGHT:	3.213m	3.257m	3.108m	3.2m
GROUND CLEARANCE:	.463m	.463m	.463m	.463m
TRACK:	2.921m	2.921m	2.921m	2.921m
TRACK WIDTH:	711mm	711mm	711mm	711mm
LENGTH OF TRACK ON GROUND:	4.235m	4.235m	4.235m	4.235m
GROUND PRESSURE:	.78kg/cm^2	.79kg/cm^2	.86kg/cm^2	.87kg/cm^2
MAXIMUM ROAD SPEED:	48.28km/hr	48.28km/hr	48.28km/hr	48.28km/hr
MAXIMUM RANGE:	500km	500km	500km	500km
FUEL LITRES:	1,457	1,420	1,457	1,420
FORDING:	1.219m	1.219m	1.219m	1.219m
FORDING WITH KIT:	2.438m	2.438m	2.438m	2.438m
FORDING WITH SCHNORKEL:	4.114m	4.114m	3.114m	4.114m
GRADIENT:	60%	60%	60%	60%
VERTICAL OBSTACLE:	.914m	.914m	.914m	.914m
TRENCH:	2.59m	2.59m	2.59m	2.59m
ENGINE:	All are powered by a Continental 12-cylinder diesel developing 750BHP at 2,400rpm			
ENGINE MODEL:	AVDS-1790-2	AVDS-1790-2A	AVDS-1790-2A	AVDS-1790-2A
ARMAMENT:				
main:	1×105mm	1×105mm	1×152mm	1×165mm
co-axial:	1×7.62mm	1×7.62mm	1×7.62mm	1×7.62mm
A/A:	1×.50 (12.7mm)	1×.50 (12.7mm)	1×.50 (12.7mm)	1×.50 (12.7mm)
AMMUNITION				
main:	60	63	46	30
(7.62mm):	5,950	5,950	5,560	2,000
.50 (12.7mm):	900	900	1,080	600
ARMOUR:	No armour data have been released. The M60, M60A1, M60A2 (hull) and M728 armour is similar to the M48 series. The M60A2 turret's armour is believed to have been improved over the M60.			

DEVELOPMENT

In 1956 a meeting was held in the United States on the future development of the current M48 series of MBT. The first step was the installation of an AVDS-1790-P engine in an M48. This was followed in 1958 by three prototypes which were known as the M48A2E1. Late in 1958 it was decided that the new tank would have the British 105mm L7A1 gun (built in the United States) as its main armament. The initial production order was placed in April 1959 and it entered production shortly afterwards, entering troop service as the M60 in 1960. This was followed by M60A1, the development designation of this being the M60E1. The M60A1 replaced the M60 in production from October 1962, and since then has been in continuous production at the Detroit Tank Arsenal which is managed by Chrysler. Average production has been 360 tanks per year. Early in 1975 an Army spokesman stated that 3,010 M60/M60A1 had been built for the United States Army, 115 for the United States Marine Corps and 913 for export. Several years ago a major programme was launched to increase M60A1 production and this is now being achieved. Initially 30 tanks per month were being built, by April 1975 this had been increased to 48 tanks per month, by February 1976 it should reach 72 a month and by February 1977 it should reach a peak of 103 tanks a month. Further development has resulted in the M60A2 and M60A3. Even when the XM1 enters service, 70% of the US Army tank fleet will comprise M60 series tanks.

DESCRIPTION (M60A1)

The hull is cast with additional sections welded into position, and the turret cast as one complete piece. A turret stowage basket is provided at the turret rear.

The driver is seated at the front of the hull and is provided with a single-piece hatch cover and a total of three M27 periscopes, of which the centre one can be replaced by an M24 infra-red periscope for night operations.

The other three crew members are in the turret with the commander and gunner on the right and the loader on the left. The commander's cupola can be traversed through a full 360° and this is provided with a single-piece hatch cover, an M28C sight and eight vision blocks. The gunner is provided with an M31 periscope with a magnification of ×8 and an M105C telescope with a magnification of ×8. The loader has a single-piece hatch cover that opens to the rear and is also provided with an M37 periscope. Both the commander and gunner can change their day sight for an infra-red night sight. The coincidence rangefinder has a magnification of ×10 and a range of between 500 and 4,400m.

The engine and Allison cross-drive transmission is at the rear of the hull, the later is a model CD-850-6 with 2F and 1R ranges. The suspension is of the torsion-bar type and consists of six road wheels with the idler at the front, drive sprocket at the rear and three track return rollers. Hydraulic shock absorbers are fitted on the first, second and sixth road wheel stations.

The main armament of the M60/M60A1 consists of the 105mm M68 gun, this being the British 105mm L7 series gun built in the United States. The turret is provided with an electro-hydraulic control system with manual controls for use in an emergency. The turret can be traversed through 360° in fifteen seconds, elevation being +20° and depression −10°.

The barrel is provided with a bore evacuator and the gun has an effective range of 2,000m. Average rate of fire is stated to be six to eight rounds per minute. The M60A1 carries 63 rounds of ammunition: 26 in the driver's position (ie left and right of driver), 13 ready rounds, 21 in turret bustle and 3 under gun. The following types of ammunition are available for the M60 series:

Ammunition Type	Designation	Muzzle Velocity	Weight of Complete Round
APERS-T	XM494E3	823m/s	24.95kg
APDS-T	M392A2	1458m/s	18.6kg
HEAT-T	M456 series	1173m/s	21.78kg
HEP-T	M393 series	classified	classified
Smoke WP-T	M416	731.5m/s	20.68kg
TP-T	M393A1(E1)	1173m/s	21.78

There are also additional training rounds. The latest rounds are the M726 APDS-T. The following have been mentioned as being under development: XM735 (APFSDS), and the XM774 which is said to have a depleted uranium projectile.

The M85.50 (12.7mm) machine-gun in the commander's cupola has an elevation of +60° and a depression of −15°. The co-axial machine-gun is a 7.62mm M73.

The electrical system is 24V and a total of six 12V 100Amp/hr batteries are mounted under the floor. Charging is carried out by a 300Amp, 24Volt engine-driven DC generator.

A central air filtration system is provided and this pipes fresh air to each crew member by a tube. Other equipment includes an infra-red/white light searchlight mounted over the main armament (maximum range 2,000m), heater in the crew compartment, hull escape hatch, fire-fighting system in the engine compartment and infra-red driving lights. A Radiac NBC detection meter can be fitted if required. A schnorkel can be fitted to the commander's hatch for deep-fording operations and a dozer blade can be fitted at the front of the hull if required.

M60A2

This is essentially an M60 chassis with a new turret mounting the Shillelagh weapons system. Development started in 1964 with the prototypes being known as the M60A1E1 and M60A1E2, the first prototype being completed in September 1965. Production commenced in September 1966, although trials had not been completed as the system was unsuitable on a number of counts. Over the following six years the problems were sorted out and the first battalion was formed in 1974 with a total of 59 M60A2s. A total of six battalions will be deployed for operations in Europe, the first one being operational in late 1975. The role of the M60A2 is long-range anti-tank operations, as its Shillelagh weapons system has an effective range of over 3,000m. Total production of the M60A2 amounted to 526 tanks.

The new turret has a total of three hatches, one each side just above the turret ring and the other in the commander's cupola on the top of the turret. The turret can be traversed through a full 360° in 9.1 seconds, elevation limits being +20° and depression —10°. The turret is fully stabilised in both elevation and traverse. The gunner has a telescope with a magnification of ×8 (this being the primary missile sight), a periscope with a magnification of ×8 and a night sight with a magnification of ×10. The commander has a periscope with a magnification of ×8 and a night periscope with a magnification of ×10. The commander's cupola has a single-piece hatch cover and a total of ten vision blocks. It is armed with a .50 (12.7mm) M85 anti-aircraft machine-gun. The commander's turret is also fully stabilised and the commander can line up the main armament if required. A laser rangefinder is provided, as is a ballistic computer. An AN/VSS2 infra-red/white light searchlight is mounted on the left side of the turret, with a range of 1,500m. The loader is on the left side of the turret and he is provided with a periscope. The co-axial machine-gun is a 7.62mm M73 and four smoke dischargers are mounted either side of the turret.

The 152mm M162 gun/missile launcher can fire the Shillelagh missile or a range of ammunition with a combustible cartridge case.

The Shillelagh missile has a HEAT warhead and is a single-stage, solid-propellent missile. It is guided to its target by a two-way infra-red command link which eliminates the need for the gunner to estimate the lead, windage and range to the target.

The ammunition is stowed as follows:

	Missile	Conventional Ammunition	Total
Turret	7	15	22
Hull	6	18	24
Total	13	33	46

The following types of conventional ammunition have been developed:

Type	Designation	Muzzle Velocity	Weight of Complete Round
Canister	XM625	683m/s	21.77kg
HE-T	XM657E2	683m/s	22.68kg
HEAT	XM409E5	683m/s	22.59kg
TP-T	XM411E3	683m/s	22.13kg

M60A3

This shows a major series of improvements over the M60A1 tank, some of which will be installed in production tanks and some fitted to tanks in service. When a tank has all these modifications it will become the M60A3.

The improvements are as follows:
Main armament fully stabilised in elevation and traverse.
Top Loading Air Cleaner installed.
AN/VSS3A searchlight to replace existing AN/VSS1 searchlight.
T97 track to be replaced by new T142 track with removable pads.
Tube over bar-suspension system on first, second and sixth road wheel stations.
Laser rangefinder with a range of 5,000m, being developed by Hughes.
Solid-state M21 computer installed.
AVDS-1790-2A RISE (Reliability Improved Selected Equipment) engine installed.
650Amp oil-cooled alternator fitted.
Passive night-vision equipment fitted.
Thermal sleeve for main armament fitted.
Of the above the first four are already in production and service. Other improvements being developed are a new engine and transmission (the existing engine has developed up to 900HP for trials purposes), new final drives and a thermal night system.

Chrysler K Tank

This was a Chrysler Project and was essentially an M60A1 with a long-barrelled Shillelagh system installed.

M60 AVLB (Armoured Vehicle Launched Bridge)

This consists of an M60 chassis without the turret and fitted with a hydraulic cylinder assembly and a scissors bridge, as fitted to the M48 AVLB which is still used by the United States Army. The bridge is constructed of aluminium alloy, and basic data are:
Crew: 2 Weight Complete: 55,746kg Weight of chassis: 41,685kg Weight of Bridge: 14,061kg Length Bridge folded: 9.6m Length bridge emplaced: 19.202m Length of chassis: 8.648m Length travelling: 11.048m Width of bridge: 4.002m Width of chassis: 3.657m Height of chassis: 3.162m Height with bridge: 4.038m Maximum span: 18.288m Emplacement time: 3 minutes Retrieval time: 10-60 minutes

M60 Lightweight AVLB

This is being developed by the US Army Mobility Equipment Research and Development Center at Fort Belvoir, and an 18.288m bridge has already been built and tested. The 27.432m AVLB is a hydraulically-operated double-folding bridge with orthotropic place-deck and space-frame truss-structure in high-strength weldable aluminium alloy. The bridge consists of four tapered ramp panels and two centre panels which are pin-connected through a non-eccentric (double-centred) hinge to form two treadways. Horizontal and vertical bracing join the treadways to complete the bridge. A new folding and unfolding system using two hydraulic cylinders eliminates the conventional quadrant and cable system used on the present AVLB. The bridge is 28.956 long and will span a 27.432m gap. It weighs only 8618kg, less than the existing AVLB.

M728 Combat Engineer Vehicle (CEV)

The M728's development designation was the T118E1. It is based on a modified M60A1 tank chassis and was standardised in 1963, entering production in 1965 and service in 1968. It is employed by Engineer Battalions and can be used for a variety of roles including destroying fortifications, filling in trenches, removing obstacles and preparing defensive positions. It is provided with an 'A' frame which is mounted at the front of the hull, and a hydraulically-operated dozer blade. A two-speed winch with a capacity of 11,340kg is mounted on the rear of the turret.

The main armament consists of a 165mm demolition gun, M135. This fires an M123A1 HEP round and turret rotation speed is 1.6° a second. Other armament consists of a co-axial 7.62mm machine-gun and a .50 (12.7mm) machine-gun in the commander's cupola. An infra-red searchlight can be fitted if required.

1

1 The M60 has the same turret as the M48 but with a 105mm gun.
2 This is the equipment carried inside an M60A1, including ammunition, radios, machine-guns and personal kit.
3 M60A1 showing turret details.
4 One of the prototype M60A1E2s loading up with a Shillelagh missile. This was standardized as the M60A2.
5 M60A1 of the Austrian Army.

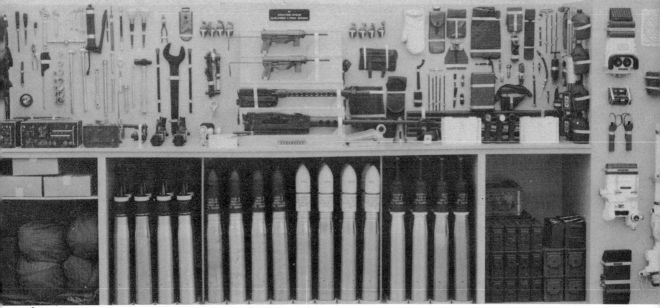

ON VEHICLE EQUIPMENT
FOR
TANK. COMBAT. FULL TRACKED
105 M.M GUN. M 60A1

2

3▲

▼4

5

Above Side view of an M60A2 Main Battle Tank.
Below The M60A1E3 which will be standardized as the M60A3.
Left The standard M60 AVLB crossing a Medium Girder Bridge.

Top Right The M728 Combat Engineer Tank on exercises in Germany. Note the 'A' frame stowed on the rear deck in the travelling position.
Bottom Right The new lightweight AVLB being tested at Fort Belvoir, Virginia.

UNITED STATES

M48 SERIES – MAIN BATTLE TANK
MANUFACTURERS – Fisher Body Division of General Motors Corporation
Ford Motor Company
Chrysler Corporation
STATUS – In service with Germany, Greece, Israel, Jordan, Morocco, Norway, Pakistan, South Korea, Spain, Taiwan, Thailand, Turkey, United States, Vietnam. Production complete but conversion programme under way (see text).

BASIC DATA	M48	M48A1	M48A2	M48A3	M48A5	M67A2
CREW:	4	4	4	4	4	3
WEIGHT LOADED:	44,906kg	47,173kg	47,173kg	47,173kg	47,180kg	48,990kg
WEIGHT EMPTY:	42,240kg	43,999kg	43,999kg	44,452kg	44,460kg	46,800kg
LENGTH OVERALL:	8.444m	8.729m	8.686m	7.442m	9.302m	8.157m
LENGTH HULL:	6.705m	6.87m	6.87m	6.882m	6.87m	6.87m
WIDTH:	3.631m	3.631m	3.631m	3.631m	3.631m	3.631m
HEIGHT OVERALL:	3.241m	3.13m	3.089m	3.124m	3.086m	3.089m
GROUND CLEARANCE:	.393m	.387m	.385m	.406m	.406m	.387m
TRACK:	2.921m	2.921m	2.921m	2.921m	2.921m	2.921m
TRACK WIDTH:	711mm	711mm	711mm	711mm	711mm	711mm
LENGTH OF TRACK ON GROUND:	4m	4m	4m	4m	4m	4m
GROUND PRESSURE:	.78kg/cm²	.83kg/cm²	.83kg/cm²	.83kg/cm²	.83kg/cm²	.86kg/cm²
MAXIMUM ROAD SPEED:	41.8km/hr	41.8km/hr	48.2km/hr	48.2km/hr	48.2km/hr	48.2km/hr
MAXIMUM RANGE:	113km	113/217km	258/402km	463km	482km	258/402km
FUEL LITRES:	757	757	1,268	1,420	1,420	1,420
FORDING:	1.219m	1.219m	1.219m	1.219m	1.219m	1.219m
FORDING WITH KIT:	2.438m	2.438m	2.438m	2.438m		2.438m
GRADIENT:	60%	60%	60%	60%	60%	60%
VERTICAL OBSTACLE:	.915m	.915m	.915m	.915m	.915m	.915m
TRENCH:	2.59m	2.59m	2.59m	2.59m	2.59m	2.59m
ENGINE:	All are powered by a Continental 12-cylinder air-cooled engine					
ENGINE MODEL:	AV-1790 5B/7/7B/7C	AV-1790 7C	AV-1790-8	AVDS-1790 -2A	AVDS-1790 -2D	AVI-1790-8
HP/RPM:	810/2,800	810/2,800	825/2,800	750/2,400	750/2,400	810/2,100
ARMAMENT						
main:	1×90mm	1×90mm	1×90mm	1×90mm	1×105mm	Flame gun
co-axial:	.30 (7.62mm)	.30 (7.62mm)	.30 (7.62mm)	.30 (7.62mm)	.30 (7.62mm)	.30 (7.62mm)
A/A:	.50 (12.7mm)	.50 (12.7mm)	.50 (12.7mm)	.50 (12.7mm)	.50 (12.7mm)	.50 (12.7mm)
ARMOUR (all tanks)						
hull front:	101/120mm					
hull sides front:	76mm					
hull sides rear:	51mm					
hull top:	57mm					
hull floor:	12.7mm-63mm					
hull rear:	44mm					
turret front:	110mm					
turret sides:	76mm					
turret rear:	50mm					
turret top:	25mm					

DEVELOPMENT

In October 1950 Detroit Tank Arsenal commenced design work on a new medium tank armed with a 90mm gun. On 8th December 1950 a letter of intent was given to the Chrysler Corporation and design work commenced on 22nd December 1950. A total of six pilot models were built, the first of these being completed in December 1951. This was called the T48 and was essentially a T42 with a new turret and other modifications. First contracts went to Chrysler but latter contracts were awarded to Ford (who built 900 at Livonia) and Fisher Body Division of General Motors Corporation. Production ran from April 1952 to May 1956. The M48 has seen combat in the Middle East (with Israeli Forces), in the Far East (with American and Vietnamese Forces) and in the Indo/Pakistan conflict of 1971.

Further development of the M48 has resulted in the M60 series of tanks. Many components of the M48 were common to the M88 Armoured Recovery Vehicle (refer to separate entry), M53 SPG (separate entry) and M55 SPG (no longer in service).

DESCRIPTION (M48A3)

The hull of the M48 is of cast construction with additional sections welded in. The turret is also of cast construction.

The driver is seated at the front of the hull and is provided with a single-piece hatch cover and a total of three periscopes for observation purposes. One of these periscopes can be removed and replaced by an infra-red periscope for night operations. The other three crew members are in the turret with the commander and gunner on the right and the loader on the left. The commander is provided with an M1 cupola (this being fitted to the M48A1, M48A2, M48A2C and the Flamethrower tanks). This can be traversed through 360° by hand and is provided with an M28 sight, vision blocks and a single-piece hatch cover. The machine-gun can be elevated from −10° to +60°. The gunner has a periscope with a magnification of ×8 and a telescope with a magnification of ×8. The commander also has a periscope which is linked to the gunner's sight. The loader has a single-piece hatch cover that opens to the rear. The engine and cross-drive transmission is at the rear of the hull. The suspension is of the torsion-bar type and consists of six road wheels with the idler at the front and the drive sprocket at the rear. There are a total of five return rollers and a tension-adjusting idler is situated between the sixth road wheel and the drive sprocket. Hydraulic shock absorbers are provided for the first, second and sixth road wheel stations.

The electrical system is 24V and a total of four 14V 100Amp/hr batteries are provided.

Other equipment includes an NBC system, infra-red driving lights, and an infra-red/white searchlight mounted over the main armament with a maximum range of 2,000m. A heater is provided and a hull escape hatch is fitted.

The 90mm gun fires the same ammunition as the M47 tanks and the M56 self-propelled anti-tank gun. The 90mm M41 is mounted in a turret with full powered traverse and elevation, elevation being +20° and depression −9°, one complete turret rotation taking 15 seconds. The turret system is electro/hydraulic with manual controls for use in an emergency, and the commander can override the gunner if required. A rangefinder of the coincidence type is mounted in the turret, and this has a magnification of ×10 and can be used from 480 to 4,400m, and is coupled to a ballistic computer.

The following types of ammunition have been developed, though not all of these are now used:

Ammunition type	Designation	Muzzle Velocity	Complete Weight of Round
APERS	XM580E1	914m/s	18.71kg
Canister	M336	875m/s	18.86kg
HE	M71	823m/s	18.82kg
HE-T	M71A1	731m/s	17.91kg
HEAT-T	M431	1219m/s	14.97kg
HEP-T	T142	823m/s	Classified
APC-T	M82	884m/s	19.39kg
AP-T	M77	823m/s	19.06kg
AP-T	M318	853m/s	19.94kg
Smoke WP	M313	853m/s	19.94kg
HEAT	M348A1	853m/s	15.78kg

The M48/48A1 carries a total of 60 rounds of ammunition: 19 to the left of the driver, 11 to right of driver, 6 under gun, 16 in turret and 8 in the ready rack.

Total ammunition capacity of the series is:

	.30/7.62mm	.50(12.7mm)	90mm	105mm
M48 and M48C	5,900	180	60	nil
M48A1	5,900	500	60	nil
M48A2	5,590	1,365	64	nil
M48A3	6,000	630	62	nil
M67 and M67A1	3,500	600	nil	nil
M48A5	6,950	900	nil	57

All series have a Browning M2 .50 (12.7mm) anti-aircraft machine-gun. All series have a .30 M1919A4E1 co-axial machine-gun although the M48A3, M67s and M48A5 now have a 7.62mm M73 machine-gun The following types of optical equipment are fitted:

	M48	M48A1	M48A2	M48A3	M48A5
Rangefinder	M13	M13	M13A1	M17B1C	M17B1C
Ballistic computer	M13	M13A1	M13A1C	M13A1C	M13B1C
Telescope	M97C	M97C	M97C	M105	M105

All series have a General Motors Corporation (Allison Division) cross-drive transmission with 2F and 1R ranges. The following models are fitted:

M48	CD-850-4/4A/4B
M48A1	CD-850-4B
M48A2	CD-850-5
M48A3	CD-850-6
M67A1	CD-850-5

VARIANTS

M48

This was the first model to enter service and its distinguishing features are as follows: the commander's cupola has a .50 machine-gun in an open mount rather than a turret; a small driver's hatch; five return rollers and no tensioning idler; no dust shields on the fenders, and it can have either a 'T' type or cylindrical blast deflector on the barrel.

M48C

This is similar to the M48 but has a hull of mild steel and is not suitable for combat but training only.

M48A1

This model has the larger driver's hatch and cupola. It has fender dust shields, rear track idler wheel and five support rollers and a 'T' type blast deflector is provided.

M48A2

Development of the M48A2 started in 1954 under the designation T48E2, the first prototype being completed the following year. There were numerous improvements over the earlier tanks and these included a fuel injection system for the engine, larger fuel tanks, improved engine deck to minimize infra-red detection, constant pressure turret control system, improved fire-control system, modified commander's cupola, and long-range fuel tanks could be fitted at the rear of the hull though these are no longer used. A stowage basket has been fitted to the rear of the turret, the main armament has a 'T' blast deflector, and there are three track return rollers. The first production order went to Alco Products Incorporated of Schenectady, New York in 1955. This was followed in 1957 by an order to the Chrysler Delaware Defense Plant (Lenape Ordnance Modification Center) at Newark, Delaware.

M48A2C

This is almost identical to the M48A2 apart from slight differences in the optical and fire-control equipment; most M48A2Cs do not have the track tensioner wheel.

M48A3

This had the development designation of M48A1E2 and features a diesel engine rather than the petrol engine fitted to earlier models, improved fire-control system and revised commander's cupola. The latter modification comprised a circular ring with vision blocks being fitted between the turret top and the commander's cupola. M48A3s can be seen with both three or five track support rollers. They also have 'T' type blast deflectors and fender dust shields.

M48A4

This model did not enter service. At one time it was intended that the turrets removed from M60s after they had been fitted with the new turret mounting the Shillelagh missile system would be fitted on the M48A1 chassis. Six prototypes were completed in 1960 but the project was then cancelled.

M48A5

This project started at Anniston Army Depot in 1975 and should run through to 1978. A total of 1210 M48A1 and M48A3 tanks will be rebuilt to almost M60 standards. It takes three months to convert an M48A3 and four months to convert an M48A1. These will be issued to United States Army Reserve formations rather than to regular units. The modifications to the M48A3 include fitting a 105mm gun, T142 track, modified ammunition racks, gun travel lock, fitting a top-loading air cleaner and numerous other improvements. At a latter stage it is hoped to fit a new cupola, M60D co-axial machine-gun, increase the ammunition stowage and fit two pintle mounts for M60D machine-guns at the loader's station.

M67 Flamethrower Tank
A total of 74 were built for the United States Marine Corps, development designation being T67. This is essentially an M48A1 with the 90mm gun replaced by an M7-6 flame gun which is slightly shorter than the main armament of an M48 and is also thicker. This has an elevation of +45° and a depression of −12°. The M67 is not deployed at the present time.

M67A1 Flamethrower Tank
This is similar to the above but is based on an M48A2 chassis and has an M7A1-6 flame gun. This was developed for the Army but is not at present deployed.

M67A2 Flamethrower Tank
This is based on the M48A3 and was developed for the United States Marines but is not at present deployed.

M48 Armoured Vehicle-Launched Bridge
This is essentially an M48 chassis with the turret removed and a hydraulically operating scissor's bridge fitted. No armament is fitted although early models had two turrets each with a .50 (12.7mm) machine-gun fitted. Basic data are:

Crew: 2   Weight: 55,700kg (with bridge)   Length: 9.6m (with bridge)   Width: 4.012m (with bridge)   Height: 4.038m (with bridge)   Time to emplace bridge: 3 minutes   Time to retract bridge: 10-30 minutes   Length of bridge opened out: 19.202m   Width of obstacle bridge will span: 18.288m

M48 with gas turbine
Avco-Lycoming is using an M48 as a testbed for the gas turbine that is being developed for the XM1 MBT.

German M48s
Have 4 smoke dischargers mounted each side of turret and a AEG infra-red/white searchlight mounted with the main armament.

Israeli M48s
Many have been fitted with a British 105mm gun and have a commander's cupola designed and built in Israel.

Dozer blade attachment
A dozer blade can be fitted to members of the M48 family: Type M8 for the M48, M48C and M48A1, weighing 3980kg.
Type M8A1 for the M48A2, M48A3 and M48A5, weighing 3810kg.
Trials models—there have been various trials models including fender machine-gun kits, fitted with SS 10 ATGW, fitted with Shillelagh installation. Various types of mine-clearing systems have been tested on the M48 tank but none of these has been standardized.

Above A Pakistani M48 knocked out in the 1971 Indo/Pakistan campaign.

1

2

4

▼3

1 A rear view of an M48A2 tank of the German Army.
Note smoke dischargers on turret.
2 M48A3 tank with turret traversed to the rear.
3 The M48A5 which has a 105mm gun and many other
improvements.
4 M48A2 of the German Army crossing a bridge laid
by a Biber (Leopard) Bridgelayer.
5 M67A2 Flamethrower Tank of the United States
Marine Corps in action in Vietnam.
6 M48 Bridgelayer of the German Army shown being
laid in position.

5▲

▼6

UNITED STATES

M41 – LIGHT TANK
MANUFACTURER – Cleveland Tank Plant
STATUS – In service with Argentina, Austria, Belgium, Bolivia, Brazil, Chile, Denmark, Ecuador, Ethiopia, Greece, Japan, Lebanon, Nationalist China, New Zealand, Pakistan, Philippines, Portugal, Saudi-Arabia, Spain, Thailand, Tunisia, Turkey, Vietnam. The M41 is no longer in production.

BASIC DATA

CREW:	4 (commander, gunner, loader, driver)	ENGINE:	Continental or Lycoming. M41/M41A1 have AOS-895-3. M41A2/M41A3 have AOSI-895-5. 6-cylinder, air-cooled, supercharged petrol engine developing 500BHP at 2,800rpm
WEIGHT LOADED:	23,495kg		
WEIGHT EMPTY:	18,457kg		
LENGTH:	8.212m (gun forward) 5.819m (hull)		
WIDTH:	3.198m		
HEIGHT:	3.075m (including A/A M/G) 2.726m (cupola)	ARMAMENT:	1 × 76mm gun M32 1 × .30 (7.62mm) Browning M1919A4E1 co-axial MG 1 × .50 (12.7mm) Browning H2 HB A/A MG
GROUND CLEARANCE:	.45m		
TRACK:	2.602m		
TRACK WIDTH:	533mm		
LENGTH OF TRACK ON GROUND:	3.251m		
GROUND PRESSURE:	.72 kg/cm^2	ARMOUR	
MAXIMUM ROAD SPEED:	72km/hr	hull glacis:	25.4mm at 30°
RANGE:	161km	hull nose:	31.75mm at 45°
FUEL CAPACITY:	530 litres	hull sides:	19mm – 25.7mm
FORDING:	1.016m 2.44m (with kit)	hull rear:	19mm
		hull top:	12mm – 15mm
GRADIENT:	60%	hull floor:	9.25mm – 31.75mm
SIDE SLOPE:	30%	turret front:	25.4mm
VERTICAL OBSTACLE:	.711m	turret roof:	12.7mm
TRENCH:	1.828m	turret mantlet:	38mm

DEVELOPMENT

Shortly after the end of World War II the United States Army started work on a new light tank designated the T37. Three different models were built – T37 Phase 1, T37 Phase 2 and T37 Phase 3. The first of these was completed in 1949. The Phase 2 model became the T41 and later the T41E1.

The first production M41 was completed in mid-1951, production being undertaken at the Cleveland Tank Plant which was run by the Cadillac Car Division of General Motors Corporation. At first the M41 was to have been called the Little Bulldog, but this was changed to Walker Bulldog in 1951 when General W. W. Walker was killed in Korea. The full designation of the M41 is Tank, Combat, Full-Tracked: 76mm Gun, M41. The M41 has been replaced in the United States Army by the M551 Sheridan tank.

DESCRIPTION

The hull of the M41 is of all-welded construction with the driver being seated at the front of the vehicle on the left side. He is provided with a single-piece hatch cover that swings to the right and a total of four M17 periscopes, three to his front and one to his left. A hull escape hatch is provided.

The turret is of cast and welded construction. The commander and gunner are on the right of the gun with the loader on the left. The commander's cupola has a single-piece hatch cover that opens to the rear and a total of five vision blocks are provided as well as an M20A1 periscope which can be traversed through 360°. The loader has a single-piece hatch cover, and an M13 periscope. A stowage box is mounted on the rear of the turret with the domed shaped ventilator being in the turret roof towards the rear. The M41 is provided with a heater.

The engine and transmission are at the rear of the hull and separated from the fighting compartment by a fire-proof bulkhead. A fire extinguisher is mounted in the engine compartment. The transmission is a GMC Allison Division Cross-Drive Model CD-500-3 with 1F and 1R range.

The suspension is of the torsion-bar type and consists of five road wheels, idler at the front and drive sprocket at the rear, and three track return rollers. The first, second and fifth road wheel stations are provided with hydraulic shock absorbers.

The electrical system is 24V, the main generator is 150Amp with the auxiliary generator 300Amp, and a total of four 6TN batteries.

The turret has hydraulic/electric traverse through 360°, one complete turret rotation taking 10 seconds. The gun has an elevation of +19° 45 minutes and a depression of −9° 45 minutes.

The 76mm gun M32(T91E3) is in mount M76(T138E1), and a .30 co-axial machine-gun is mounted to the left of the main armament though at one time it was intended to mount a .50 co-axial machine-gun. The M41A1 tank has the M32A1 gun in mount M76A1. The .50 anti-aircraft machine-gun has an elevation of +65° and a depression of −10°. Traverse is a full 360°.

The 76mm gun has a vertical sliding breech-block and a spring actuated, inertia percussion firing mechanism. The recoil mechanism is of the concentric hydrospring type. The barrel is provided with a bore evacuator• and a T type blast deflector. Total ammunition capacity is 76mm 65 rounds, .50 2,175 rounds and .30 5,000 rounds. The following types of ammunition were developed:

AP-T with an m/v of 975m/s, a range of 4,572m at an elevation of 2° 16 minutes.

HE, complete round weighs 19.05kg and has an m/v of 731m/s.

HVAP-T with an m/v of 1,260m/s, complete round weighs 16.78kg and has a range of 4,572m with an elevation of 1° 8 minutes.

HVAP-DS-T with an m/v of 1,257m/s, a range of 4,572m and an elevation of 2° 28 minutes.

WP with an m/v of 731m/s, complete round weighing 19.05kg.

TP-T, Blank and Canister.

A total of 1,802 M41s were built, the M41A1 following the M41 in production. The development designation of the M41A1 was the T41E2. The M41A1, M41A2 and M41A3 have modified elevating and traversing mechanism whilst the M41A2 and M41A3 also have a fuel injection engine.

Cadillac developed a simplified and improved gun control system to replace the pulsing relay system of the M41. The system consists of a manual and hydraulic power traverse for the gunner with direct mechanically-linked control of the oil gear pump in lieu of electrical control of the M41, dual power traverse by commander and manual, mechanical, rank-and-pinion type elevation for the gunner, and slewing motor elevation control for the commander.

The M41 is not provided with a NBC system. Most models are fitted with infra-red driving equipment and some countries have fitted infra-red fighting equipment; for example Denmark has fitted her M41s with a B30 (AEG) infra-red searchlight and a B8V (Eltro) infra-red sight. The M41 has no amphibious capability although it can be fitted for deep wading.

VARIANTS
There have been many trials variants of the M41 including an M41 with a Sheridan-type turret which was used in early trials of the Shillelagh missile system and the T49 light tank. This was an M41 with a 90mm gun. Components of the M41 are also used in the M42 self-propelled anti-aircraft gun, the M44 155mm SPG and the M52 105mm SPG. A recent model of the M41 is the QM41, used by the United States Navy as a remote-controlled tank for testing new air-to-surface missiles.

Left M41 Light Tank of the Belgian Army.
Right M41 Light Tank of the Brazilian Army.

UNITED STATES

M47 – MEDIUM TANK
MANUFACTURERS – Detroit Arsenal and American Locomotive Company.
STATUS – In service with Austria, Belgium (Reserve), Brazil, Greece, Iran (being phased out), Italy (being phased out), Jordan, Pakistan, Portugal, Saudi-Arabia, South Korea, Spain, Taiwan, Turkey, Yugoslavia. They are no longer used by France or Germany; most of theirs were sent to other NATO countries or expended as targets. The Germans fitted the 90mm guns to the Jagdpanzer Kanone. Production complete.

BASIC DATA

CREW:	5 (commander, gunner, loader, driver and bow machine gunner)	ENGINE:	Continental Model AV-1790-5B, 7 or 7B, V-12, 4-cycle, air-cooled petrol engine developing 810BHP at 2,800rpm
WEIGHT LOADED:	46,170kg		
	42,130kg		
LENGTH:	8.508m		
	6.362m	ARMAMENT:	1 × 90mm gun
WIDTH:	3.51m		1 × .30 (7.62mm) co-axial M/G
HEIGHT:	3.352m (A/A M/G)		
	2.954m (w/o A/A M/G)		1 × .30 (7.62mm) bow M/G
GROUND CLEARANCE:	.469m		
TRACK:	2.794m		1 × .50 (12.7mm) A/A M/G
TRACK WIDTH:	584mm		
LENGTH OF TRACK		ARMOUR	
ON GROUND:	3.911m	hull front upper:	101mm at 60°
GROUND PRESSURE:	.935kg/cm²	hull front lower:	76/89mm at 53°
MAXIMUM ROAD SPEED:	48km/hr (early models 58km/hr)	hull sides forward:	76mm at 0°
		hull sides rear:	50.8mm
RANGE:	130km	hull top:	22mm
FUEL:	875 litres	hull floor front:	25.4mm
FORDING:	1.219m	hull floor rear:	12.7mm
GRADIENT:	60%	gun shield:	115mm
VERTICAL OBSTACLE:	.914m	turret front:	101.6mm at 40°
TRENCH:	2.59m	turret sides:	63.5mm at 30°
		turret rear:	76.2mm at 30°
		turret roof:	12.7mm

DEVELOPMENT

At the end of the 2nd World War the M26 Pershing was the heaviest and most powerful armed tank in American Army service. Further development work on this produced the M46 Medium Tank (M26E2) which was also known as the Patton, and next the M46A1 (M46E1). Development of a new medium tank was also started after the war and this was known as the T42. This was basically a new turret on a modified T40 chassis. The Korean War meant that a new tank was urgently required so a modified M46 chassis was fitted with the T42 tank turret mounting a 90mm T119 gun. Modifications to the chassis included improved glacis armour protection, improved cooling system, improved fan control and a new electrical system. The end result was the M47. The M47 was replaced in production after several years by the M48 which was a direct development of the M47.

DESCRIPTION

The hull of the M47 is of cast sections welded together, with two escape hatches in the hull floor. The driver is seated at the front on the left with the bow machine-gunner to his right. Both are provided with a one-piece hatch cover with an integral M13 periscope.

The turret, which is cast, is mounted in the centre of the hull, with the loader on the left and the commander and gunner on the right. The loader has a single-piece hatch cover and an M13 periscope. The commander's cupola has a total of 5 five-vision blocks, and an M20 periscope is also provided. The gunner has an M20 periscope and an M12 rangefinder.

The engine and transmission are at the rear of the hull, the latter being an Allison Model CD 850-4, 4A or 4B cross-drive with 2F and 1R ranges. The electrical system is 24V and there are 4 × 12V batteries. The generator is driven by a Wisconsin TFT two-cylinder petrol engine which can be run when the main engine is switched off. A fire extinguisher system is provided in the engine compartment.

The suspension is of the torsion-bar type and consists of six road wheels with the idler at the front and the drive sprocket at the rear. There are three return rollers and most models have a tensioning wheel between the sixth road wheel and the drive sprocket, though some countries have removed these. The first, second, fifth and sixth road wheel stations have hydraulic shock absorbers.

The rifled 90mm gun M36 (T119E1) is in mount M78. The breech-block is of the vertical sliding type and the recoil mechanism is of the concentric hydrospring type and the firing mechanism percussion. The barrel is provided with either a cylindrical or a 'T' shaped blast deflector. The turret has full powered traverse through 360° in ten seconds. Elevation is + 19° and depression − 5°, elevation speed is 4° a second. A .30 (7.62mm) M1919A4E1 co-axial machine-gun is mounted to the left of the main armament. At one time it was intended that the co-axial machine-gun would be a .50 (12.7mm) type. There is a .30 (7.62mm) M1919A4E1 machine-gun in the bow of the tank, but some countries have taken this out in favour of increased ammunition stowage – ie a total of 105 rounds. The .50 (12.7mm) Browning M2 HB machine-gun is mounted on the turret roof for anti-aircraft defence. Some countries have provided the M47 with smoke dischargers, German Army tanks were fitted with four each side of the turret. Total ammunition stowage is 90mm 71 rounds, .30 4,125 rounds and .50 440 rounds. The ammunition used in the 90mm gun is the same as that used for the 90mm M54 gun which is fitted to the M56 Self-propelled Anti-Tank Gun and the 90mm M41 gun which is fitted to the M48 Tank. The ammunition is of the fixed type and the following types have been used with the gun:

Type	M/V	Range	Weight	Type	M/V	Range	Weight
APERS-T	914m/s	4,400m	18.71kg	APC-T	792/853m/s	19,568m	19.89kg
AP-T	914m/s	17,355m	—	HE	823m/s	17,716m	19.01kg
HE-T	731m/s	15,330m	17.93kg	HEAT-T	1,219m/s	8,138m	14.96kg
Smoke (WP)	823m/s	17,716m	18.86kg	TP–T	914m/s	21,031m	19.91kg
Canister	874m/s	183m	19.89kg	HVAP-T	1,020m/s	13,835m	16.84kg

In addition HEP-T and TP-T rounds are available. It should be noted that the ranges stated above in most cases are at maximum elevation. Most of the anti-tank rounds, ie HEAT-T and AP-T, have an effective range of around 2,000m. The M47 is normally fitted with infra-red driving lights and a number of countries have fitted an infra-red searchlight over the main armament. No NBC system is fitted although there is a ventilator fan in the rear of the turret in the roof. It is not amphibious although an amphibious kit was developed.

Above M47 Medium Tanks of the Austrian Army.

VARIANTS

The American Army developed few variants of the M47 as it was in production for only a few years and was replaced by the M48. Many other countries have however developed variants of the M47.

Austria

Has fitted an M47 with a new diesel engine for trials purposes and may well refit her fleet of M47s with this new engine.

France

The GIAT/DTAT have for a number of years shown a modified M47 at the Satory Exhibition, the modifications including a new 105mm gun similar to that fitted to the AMX-30. They have also suggested a new engine, but so far this has not been adopted.

Italy

Oto-Melara has for some years been offering a rebuilt M47 with the British 105mm gun, new engine, transmission and electrical system of the M60 MBT which they built some years ago for the Italian Army. Oto-Melara has also rebuilt many M47s for other NATO countries.

Other Variants
Belgium/UK

The British Aircraft Corporation (GW Division) did fit an M47 with Swingfire ATGWs. This never entered service.

Below M47 with General Motors 12V 71T engine fitted by the Astra Company of Piacenza, Italy.

Italy
The Italian company of Astra, Piacenza, have developed to the prototype stage the Tank bridgelayer A20 which can be mounted on the M47, M48 or Centurion chassis. The scissors type bridge has an overall length of 22m, a width of 4m and takes a maximum load of 54,000kg. It is unusual in that the ends of the bridge can swing at an angle of 90° (vertical) to the angle of the bridge and two A20 bridgelayers can be used to cross a wide ditch. Astra have also fitted an M47 with the General Motors 12V 71T engine as well as new transmission, fire-control system, modified final drives, and a new generator.

Korea
Has a number of M47s converted to the armoured recovery role. The 90mm gun has been removed and a winch is fitted in the turret. An 'A' frame is mounted on the front of the hull with the cable being taken out through the old gun-shield position. This vehicle is limited to changing tank components rather than full recovery work.

USA
The M102 Combat Engineer Vehicle on the M47 chassis is no longer in service. The T66 flame thrower tank reached development stage only. There were a number of trials versions but none of these saw service. The older M26 is still used by Greece and Turkey but will probably be phased out in the near future.

Spain
A retrofit programme is being carried out by Chrysler Espana SA. This consists of replacing the petrol engine with a Continental AVDS-1790-2A diesel, and modifying the cooling system, fuel tanks (fuel capacity has been increased by 50%), suspension, transmission and electrical system.

Above M47 of the Republic of Korea Army converted to the ARV role.
Below A20 Bridgelayer preparing to lay a bridge on top of another bridge previously laid by an A20 Bridgelayer. This system can also be fitted to other tanks including the Centurion and M48.

UNITED STATES

M24 – LIGHT TANK
MANUFACTURER – Cadillac Motor Company and Massey Harris
STATUS – In service with Austria, Cambodia, Ethiopia, France (reserve), Greece, Iran, Iraq, Japan, Laos, Nationalist China, Norway, Pakistan, Philippines, Saudi Arabia, Spain, Thailand, Turkey, Uruguay, Vietnam. Production complete.

BASIC DATA

CREW:	5 (commander, gunner, loader, driver, radio-operator/assistant driver)	ENGINES:	2 × Cadillac Model 44T24, V-8, water-cooled petrol engines developing 220HP at 3,400rpm (each engine develops 110HP)
WEIGHT LOADED:	18,370kg		
WEIGHT EMPTY:	16,440kg		
LENGTH:	5.486m (gun forward) 5.028m (hull only)	ARMAMENT:	1 × 75mm gun M6 1 × .50 (12.7mm) M2 A/A M/G
WIDTH:	2.95m		1 × .30 (7.62mm) M1919A4 co-axial M/G with 76mm
HEIGHT:	2.77m (including A/A M/G) 2.463m (commander's cupola)		1 × .30 (7.62mm) M1919A4 M/G in bow
GROUND CLEARANCE:	.457m		
TRACK:	2.438m	ARMOUR	
TRACK WIDTH:	406mm	hull upper front:	25.04mm at 60°
LENGTH OF TRACK		hull lower front:	25.04mm at 45°
ON GROUND:	2.844m	hull upper side front:	25.04mm at 12°
GROUND PRESSURE:	.78kg/cm²	hull lower side rear:	19.05mm at 12°
MAXIMUM ROAD SPEED:	55km/hr	hull rear:	19.05mm
RANGE:	173km	hull top:	12.7mm
FUEL CAPACITY:	416 litres	floor:	19.05mm
FORDING:	1.016m	turret mantlet:	38.1mm
GRADIENT:	60%	turret sides:	25.04mm
VERTICAL OBSTACLE:	.914m	turret roof:	12.7mm
TRENCH:	2.438m		

DEVELOPMENT

Development of a new light tank to replace the M3/M5 light tanks commenced in April 1943 and was designated the T24. The first of two prototypes was completed in October 1943 by the Cadillac Motor Car Division of the General Motors Corporation. The T24 was standardized as the M24 in mid-1944, after production had commenced. Cadillac completed their first production M24 in April 1944 at Detroit. Massey-Harris also built M24s and their first production vehicle was completed in July 1944, at their Plant at Milwaukee. A total of 4070 M24s were completed by June 1945. The M24 was supplied in small numbers to the British who called it the 'Chaffee'.

The M24 chassis served as the basic member of a whole series of vehicles called the 'Light Combat Team'. Other members were the M19 twin 40mm self-propelled anti-aircraft gun, M37 105mm Howitzer Motor Carriage, M41 155mm Howitzer Motor Carriage (and supply vehicle T22E1), and the T6E1 recovery vehicle. None of the other members of the family remain in service today, although the M41 155mm Howitzer was used until the early 1960s by the French Army. The T24E1 had an air-cooled Wright engine and torque converter transmission, though this was not standardized.

The M24 saw combat during the closing months of both the European and Pacific campaigns and since the War has served with distinction with the American Army in Korea, the French Army in Indo-China, the South Vietnamese Army, as well as Cambodian and Laotian forces. The M24 will continue in service for a good many years yet. It was replaced in the United States Army by the M41 Light Tank.

DESCRIPTION

The hull of the M24 is of all-welded construction and a hull escape hatch is provided. The driver is seated at the front of the vehicle on the left side with the assistant driver/radio operator/bow machine-gunner to his right. Both the front two crew members were provided with a single-hatch cover and a periscope. Dual controls were provided.

The turret is in the centre of the vehicle and can be traversed through the full 360°, traverse power being operated with manual controls for use in an emergency. Elevation and depression of the main armament are manual.

Left M24 of the Japanese Self Defence Force.
Right M24 rebuilt in Norway with a 90mm gun, new engine and transmission.

The commander's cupola is on the right of the turret and provided with a total of 6 vision blocks and a periscope in the cupola roof. The gunner and loader are seated on the left of the turret, and a single-piece hatch cover is provided over their position, which opens to the front. There is a pistol port in the right side of the turret.

The engines and transmission are at the rear of the vehicle. The two engines, which are the same as those fitted to the M5 light tank, are interchangeable. The driver has a manual shift transfer unit, with 2F and 1R speeds, incorporated in the gear train used to couple the engines together. A controlled differential for steering and braking is mounted in the front of the hull and a large access plate on the glacis allows easy access to this. A synchronizer incorporated in the transfer unit permits a speedy shift from the low to the high range or vice versa. This allows the driver a total of eight speeds forwards with an overlap of third and fourth speeds in the low range and with the first and second speeds in the high range. Four speeds can be obtained in reverse, maximum speed in reverse being 29km/hr.

The suspension is of the torsion-bar type and consists of five road wheels, drive sprocket at the front, idler at the rear and three track return rollers. Shock absorbers were provided on the first, second, fourth and fifth road wheel stations. The T72E1 track is of the steel block, single-pin, rubber-bushed with centre guide type.

The 75mm gun, which was a development of an aircraft gun, and the .30 co-axial machine-gun (mounted to the right of the main armament), are in Combination Gun Mount M64. The recoil mechanism of the 75mm gun is of the concentric type. The main armament has an elevation of $+15°$ and a depression of $-10°$, and the following types of ammunition could be fired: armoured piercing capped with an m/v of 625m/s, high explosive and WP smoke. The .50 anti-aircraft machine-gun was mounted on the rear of the turret. Total ammunition stowage was: 75mm 48 rounds, .50 440 rounds and .30 3,750 rounds. Production vehicles were fitted with a two-inch mortar but these were taken out after the war, and a gyrostabilizer provided for the main armament.

The M24 has no amphibious capability, no NBC system and no infra-red equipment. Many countries have however fitted their vehicles with both infra-red driving lights and an infra-red searchlight. The M24 could also tow a maximum load of 9979kg.

VARIANTS
The United States built many trials versions of the M24 both during and after the Second World War, but none of these entered service. The French fitted at least one Chaffee with the turret of an AMX-13 light tank, and also fitted an AMX-13 with a turret of the Chaffee. The latter, it is believed, were used for training purposes.

In the early 1960s the French Groupement Industriel des Armements Terrestres looked at many older vehicles for possible updating with new armament and engines, one of which was the M24, and a modified vehicle was shown at the Satory display in 1973. The GIAT produced the gun whilst the manufacturer or overall contractor was Thune-Eureka A/S of Oslo, Norway. Thune-Eureka completed the first prototype in January 1973 and a total of 54 vehicles were scheduled to be delivered to the Norwegian Army between the 15th January 1975 and the 15th October 1976. The modifications have been very extensive and the whole vehicle has been rebuilt. These modifications are:

Armament—replacing the 75mm gun with the French 90mm low-pressure gun D/925, fitting a new muzzle brake, modifying the breech assembly (breech-ring, breech-block and extractor), the sighting telescope, and adjusting the ammunition racks to accept the 90mm ammunition. The recoil mechanism and the gyrostabilizer are not modified. The gun fires a fin stabilized shaped charge round and the following types of ammunition are available:

HEAT weighing 7kg complete, projectile itself weighs 3.65kg, with an m/v of 750m/s and will penetrate 340mm of armour.

HE round weighing 9kg, with an m/v of 640 m/s and a range of 3,000m. Smoke round weighing 9kg with range and m/v identical to HE round. Practice rounds for HEAT and HE are available.

The bow machine-gun has been deleted and the co-axial .30 machine-gun has been replaced by a .50 machine-gun, the .50 anti-aircraft machine-gun has been retained. Four German type smoke dischargers are mounted either side of the turret. Total ammunition capacity is 41 rounds of 90mm and 500 rounds of machine-gun ammunition. Engine—the two existing engines have been replaced by one supercharged Detroit Diesel Model 6 V-53 T 5063-5299 which develops 250HP at 2,800rpm. There ar two radiators with hydraulically-driven and thermostatically governed fans and four heat exchangers for the cooling of the oil. Two heat exchanges are for the transmission and differential, one for the additional gearbox and one for the oil of the hydraulic system.

The transmission has been replaced by an Allison MT 650, fully automatic with converter driven PTO. There are a total of 5F and 1R gears and automatic shifting for second through fifth gears. The torque converter is a Model TC 370-2.4. With the new engine and transmission the M24 has a top road speed of 57km/hr, a cross-country speed of 26/30km/hr and a road range of 400km.

Other optional equipment includes replacement of the original tracks with German Diehl or Swedish Hägglund type tracks, installation of an air-conditioning system, new shock absorbers, new communications equipment, installation of a laser rangefinder, fitting infra-red head lamps and infra-red periscope for the driver, fitting infra-red searchlight, or image intensification driving and fighting equipment. The crew has been reduced from five to four as the vehicle has no bow machine-gun.

UNITED STATES

SHERMAN SERIES – MEDIUM TANK
M32 AND M74 – ARMOURED RECOVERY VEHICLES
MANUFACTURERS – Baldwin Locomotive Works, Detroit Tank Arsenal, Pressed Steel Car Company, Pullman Standard Car Manufacturing Company, Lima Locomotive Works, Pacific Car and Foundry Company, Fisher Tank Division of General Motors, Federal Machine and Welding Company, Ford Motor Company and the American Locomotive Company
STATUS - The Sherman is in service with Argentina (including Firefly), Brazil, Chile, Colombia, Guatemala, India, Iran, Israel, Japan, Lebanon, Mexico, Pakistan, Paraguay, Peru, Portugal, Philippines, South Korea, Uganda and Yugoslavia (including Firefly)
The M32 is still used by Austria, Brazil, Israel, Japan and Yugoslavia.
The M74 is still used by Belgium, Spain, Turkey and Yugoslavia.

BASIC DATA	M4A3	M4A3E8	M32	M74
CREW:	5	5	4	4
WEIGHT LOADED:	31,070kg	32,284kg	28,123kg	42,525kg
LENGTH O/A:	5.905m	7.518m	5.82m	7.95m
WIDTH:	2.667m	2.667m	2.616m	3.095m
HEIGHT:	2.743m	3.425m	2.467m	3.11m
GROUND CLEARANCE:	.434m	.434m	.434m	.394m
TRACK:	2.108m	2.26m	2.108m	2.26m
TRACK WIDTH:	419mm	584mm	419mm	584mm
LENGTH OF TRACK ON GROUND:	3.733m	3.831m	3.733m	3.831m
GROUND PRESSURE:	.924kg/cm²	.72kg/cm²	.935kg/cm²	.956kg/cm²
MAXIMUM ROAD SPEED:	42km/hr	48km/hr	42km/hr	34km/hr
RANGE:	161km	161km	165km	161km
FUEL:	636 litres	636 litres	651 litres	636 litres
FORDING:	.914m	.914m	1.219m	.914m
GRADIENT:	60%	60%	60%	60%
VERTICAL OBSTACLE:	.609m	.609m	.609m	.609m

TRENCH:	2.26m	2.26m	1.879m	2.28m
ENGINE:	Ford GAA 8-cylinder petrol developing 450HP at 2,600rpm	Ford GAA 8-cylinder petrol developing 450HP at 2,600rpm	Continental R975-C1 9-cylinder petrol developing 350HP at 2,400rpm	Ford GAA 8-cylinder petrol developing 450HP at 2,600rpm
ARMAMENT				
main:	1 × 75mm	1 × 76mm	—	—
co-axial:	1 × .30 (7.62mm)	1 × .30 (7.62mm)	—	—
bow:	1 × .30 (7.62mm)	1 × .30 (7.62mm)	1 × .30 (7.62mm)	1 × .30 (7.62mm)
A/A:	1 × .50 (12.7mm)	1 × .50 (12.7mm)	1 × .50 (12.7mm)	1 × .50 (12.7mm)
AMMUNITION				
main:	97	71	—	—
.50:	300	600	300	1,050
.30:	6,000	6,250	2,000	2,000
ARMOUR:	12mm-75mm	12mm-75mm	12mm-51mm	12mm-51mm

Note: Slight differences will be found between the same models as Shermans were built by many manufacturers.

DEVELOPMENT

The Sherman tank was developed early in the Second World War and replaced the earlier Grant/Lee tank in production. The M3 Sherman was standardized in October 1941 and first saw combat with the British Eighth Army in the Middle East. The Sherman was continuously developed during the war and the 75mm gun was replaced by a 76mm gun, a new turret was designed and finally a new suspension system was also designed. Total Sherman production amounted to just over 48,000 tanks of all types.

The Sherman continued in service with the United States Army after the war and saw combat in Korea. Since then it has seen combat with the Indian Army in the India/Pakistan battles and with the Israeli Army in the 1956, 1966 and 1973 campaigns. Many countries have modified their Shermans and fitted them with new guns and in some cases with new engines.

DESCRIPTION

The Sherman has a crew of five. The driver is seated at the front of the hull on the left with the bow machine-gunner to his right. Both are provided with an individual hatch cover with an integral periscope. The other three crew members are seated in the turret. On early models the only hatch in the roof was the commander's on the right side, this being provided with a two-piece hatch cover. Late production models, ie the M4A3E8, have a new turret. On this the commander has a cupola with a total of six vision blocks whilst there is also a hatch for the gunner. All Shermans have an escape hatch in the floor of the hull.

Armament. A typical Sherman is the M4A3, which is armed with a 75mm gun in mount M34A1. The turret has hydraulic power traverse through a full 360°, elevation is manual from +25° to −10°, a stabilizer is provided although most Shermans today probably have them removed. The 75mm gun fires a variety of ammunition; World War II types included the M48 HE, M72 Armour Piercing and the M61 Armour Piercing Capped, which had a muzzle velocity of 619m/s and would penetrate 80mm of armour at a range of 914m. An M1919A4 machine-gun is mounted to the left of the main armament and there is a similar machine-gun in the bow of the tank. The M2 .50 (12.7mm) Browning machine-gun is operated by the commander.

Later Shermans had a 76mm gun M1A1 or M1A2 in mount M62. This fired the M42A1 HE round, M8 Smoke Round and the M62 Armour Piercing Capped round. The latter had a muzzle velocity of 792m/s and would penetrate 101mm of armour at a range of 914m.

The engine is mounted at the rear of the hull and power is transmitted to the transmission and steering unit at the front of the vehicle by a propeller shaft. The suspension consists of three units each of which has two road wheels and a return roller. The drive sprocket is at the front and the idler at the rear. Late production vehicles had the Horizontal Volute Suspension System (HVSS) including the M4A3E8. This gave a much better ride and was more reliable. Early Shermans had a cast hull but this was changed to a welded hull which greatly speeded up production.

VARIANTS

There are separate entries for the following vehicles which use a Sherman type chassis:

Sexton 25 Pounder Self-Propelled Gun (Canada)

L-33 Gun/Howitzer (Israel)

M7 105mm Self-Propelled Howitzer (United States)

M10 and M36 Self-Propelled Anti-Tank Guns (United States)

M32 Armoured Recovery Vehicle

The M32 was developed during World War II to fulfil an urgent requirement for a vehicle to repair tanks in the field. The M32 is essentially a Sherman tank with its turret removed and replaced by a superstructure. An 'A' frame is mounted at the front of the hull and a winch with a capacity of 27,216kg has been installed behind the driver's position. The following models of the M32 were built:
M32 based on the M4 welded hull. M32B1 based on the M4A1 cast hull. M32B2 based on the M4A2 welded hull. M32B3 based on the M4A3 welded hull. M32B4 based on the M4A4 welded hull.
The 12.7mm (calibre .50) machine-gun is mounted on top of the superstructure. When built these were also provided with an 81mm mortar.

M74 Armoured Recovery Vehicle

This is a post-war design and is based on the M4A3 tank with HVVS system. A dozer blade is mounted at the front of the hull, which can be used for both dozing operations and to stabilize the vehicle when the 'A' frame is being used. A winch is provided inside the hull and the M74 can tow a maximum of 45,359kg. The .50 (12.7mm) anti-aircraft machine-gun is mounted on the superstructure of the vehicle. Total ammunition supply was 1,050 rounds of .50 (12.7mm) and 2,000 rounds of .30 (7.62mm).

Sherman Firefly

This was introduced into British Army service in early 1944. It was essentially a Sherman chassis mounting the 17-pounder anti-tank gun. A bulge was added to the turret rear to take the radio, the turret itself was modified and the bow machine-gun was removed. This proved an excellent tank in Normandy and the 17-pounder round could penetrate both the Panther and Tiger tanks of that time.

Israeli Modifications

In addition to the L-33 155mm Self-Propelled Gun/Howitzer which has its own entry, Israel has the following Sherman Variants:
Mine Clearing– Two types have been mentioned, one being a flail type model and the other a remote-controlled type.
Ambulance– Some Shermans have been converted for the ambulance role.
Artillery Observation Vehicle– This is a Sherman with its turret removed and a hydraulically operated observation platform installed.

155mm Self-Propelled Howitzer

This is a rebuilt Sherman or Priest with a French 155mm M1950 weapon mounted in the rear. Ammunition is stowed under the gun and a ramp folds down at the rear so that the crew can operate the weapon. At least two 7.62mm or 12.7mm anti-aircraft machine-guns are provided.

160mm Self-Propelled Mortar

This has been designed and produced by the Soltam Company. It has vertical hull sides and when deployed in action the front folds down into the horizontal position. The 160mm mortar is breech-loaded and has a maximum range of 9,600m. A wide range of ammunition has been developed including high explosive and two types of smoke bomb. A total of 56 mortar bombs are carried and average rate of fire is 5 rounds per minute. The complete vehicle and ammunition weighs approx. 36,654kg and it has a crew of 4/7 men. A 7.62mm or 12.7mm machine-gun can be mounted on each side of the hull.

Super Sherman

This is a Sherman with a French 75mm gun as fitted to the AMX13 Light Tank. The turret has been modified and two smoke dischargers have been fitted either side of the turret. As the AMX13 has been phased out of service many of these have been modified to other roles.

Isherman

This is a Sherman with a French 105mm gun and a French hydraulic power traverse mechanism. A Pratt and Witney R-1340-AN-1 500HP engine has been installed and numerous other modifications have been carried out to the transmission, steering and exhaust systems. Some Ishermans have the standard 419mm track whilst others have the wider 584mm track. As the Israeli Army now has large numbers of M48, M60, Centurion and captured Russian tanks, it would seem likely that Sherman gun tanks will become increasingly used in the support role, ie converted to artillery or mortar carriers. Israel did have some Shermans that she captured from Egypt with the AMX13 turret but it is doubtful if these are in service. Some reports have mentioned that Israel had fitted some Shermans with the 20-pounder gun of the Centurion, as the latter has been upgunned to 105mm.

Japanese Bridgelayer

Some years ago Japan did fit at least one Sherman tank with a scissors type bridge. It is believed that it was a trials installation as the Japanese then fitted a similar bridge on the standard Type 61 Main Battle Tank and called it the Type 67 Armoured Vehicle Launched Bridge.

Above Sherman with French 105mm gun and SAMM hydraulic control system.
Below Sherman M4A3E8 with 76mm gun.

Above M32B1 Recovery Vehicle of the Austrian Army.
Below M74 Armoured Recovery Vehicle.

Israeli Sherman with 160mm Soltam mortar installed.

UNITED STATES

M3 and M5–LIGHT TANKS
M8–75mm SELF-PROPELLED HOWITZER
MANUFACTURERS–M3: American Car and Foundry Company
M5: Cadillac Motor Car Division of GMC, Massey Harris, American Car and Foundry
M8: Cadillac Motor Car Division of GMC
STATUS
M3s are in service with Bolivia, Brazil, Chile, Dominican Republic, Ecuador, Guatemala, Haiti, Honduras, Indonesia, Mexico, South Korea, Taiwan, Uruguay, Venezuela. M5s are used by Mexico and the M8 is also used by Mexico. Production of the M3, M5 and M8 was completed in 1944.

BASIC DATA	M3A1	M5	M8
CREW:	4	4	4
WEIGHT LOADED:	12,927kg	15,397kg	15,694kg
LENGTH:	4.54m	4.838m	4.438m
WIDTH:	2.235m	2.286m	2.24m
HEIGHT:	2.298m	2.298m	2.298m
GROUND CLEARANCE:	.42m	.35m	.42m
TRACK:	1.854m	1.854m	1.854m
TRACK WIDTH:	295mm	295mm	295mm
LENGTH OF TRACK ON GROUND:	2.971m	2.971m	3.073m
GROUND PRESSURE:	.74kg/cm^2	.88kg/cm^2	.88kg/cm^2
MAXIMUM ROAD SPEED:	56km/hr	58km/hr	58km/hr
ROAD RANGE:	120km	160km	160km
FUEL CAPACITY:	212 litres	310 litres	310 litres
FORDING:	.914m	.914m	.914m
GRADIENT:	60%	60%	60%
VERTICAL OBSTACLE:	.609m	.457m	.457m
TRENCH:	1.828m	1.625m	1.625m
ENGINE:	Continental W670-9A 7-cylinder petrol, developing 250HP at 2,400rpm Or Guiberson T-1020-4 9-cylinder diesel developing 220HP at 2200rpm	Both the M5 and M8 were powered by two V-8 Cadillac Series 42 petrol engines developing 110HP (each) at 3200 rpm	
ARMAMENT			
main:	1 × 37mm gun	1 × 37mm gun	1 × 75mm Howitzer
co-axial:	1 × .30 (7.62mm)MG	1 × .30 (7.62mm)MG	nil
bow:	1 × .30 (7.62mm)MG	1 × .30 (7.63mm)MG	nil
A/A:	1 × .30 (7.62mm)MG	1 × .30 (7.62mm)MG	1 × .50 (12.7mm)MG
main:	108	147	46
.30 (7.62mm):	6,890	6,500	nil
.50 (12.7mm):	nil	nil	400
ARMOUR			
hull front upper:	38.1mm	28.5mm	28.5mm
hull front lower:	15.87-44.5mm	50.8-63.5mm	44.5mm
hull sides and rear:	12.7mm	28.5mm	25.4mm
hull top:	9.5mm	12.7mm	12.7mm
hull bottom:	9.5-12.7mm	9.5-12.7mm	9.5-12.7mm
turret front:	38.1mm	44.4mm	38.1mm
turret sides:	31.7mm	31.7mm	25.4mm
turret top:	12.7mm	12.7mm	9.5mm

DEVELOPMENT/DESCRIPTION/VARIANTS
M3 Series
The M3, or Stuart as it is often called, is a development of the earlier M2 series of light tank whose development can be traced back to the early 1930s. The M3 was standardised for production in July 1940 and entered production in early 1941. It saw extensive service with the British Army in North Africa and with the United States Army (and Marines) in the Far East. The first model was the M3 followed by the M3A1 and finally the M3A3. This was further developed into the M5 Stuart.

Early Stuarts had a hull and turret of riveted construction, later changed to a riveted hull and a welded turret, and finally to an all-welded hull and turret. The driver is seated at the front of the hull on the left with the bow machine-gunner to his right. The other two crew members being in the turret. The engine is at the rear of the hull and the transmission and differential are at the front. The suspension is of the vertical volute type and consists of four road wheels, drive sprocket at the front, idler at the rear and three track return rollers. Some models could be fitted with a deep fording system whilst others could have long range fuel tanks on the hull rear.

The 37mm gun M5 or M6 was mounted in a turret with a traverse of 360°, elevation being +20° and depression −10°, and a variety of ammunition could be fired. World War II types included the M51B1 APC round, M51B2 APC round, M63 HE round and the M2 cannister round.

M5 Series

The M5 was standardised in February 1942 and was developed from the M3A2 light tank. Other improvements included an auxiliary power plant and redesigned hull interior. The armament consisted of a 37mm gun M6 and a co-axial .30 (7.62mm) Browning M1919A5 machine-gun, with a similar machine-gun in the bow and another on the turret. Like some M3s the M5 could be fitted with sand shields.

M8 75mm Howitzer Motor Carriage

This is based on an M5 chassis with a new turret, modified driver's position and bow machine-gun removed. The howitzer is mounted in a turret with a traverse of 360°. The 75mm Howitzer M2 or M3 has an elevation of +40° and a depression of −20°. A .50 (12.7mm) Browning M2 machine-gun is mounted on the turret for anti-aircraft defence. The 75mm gun can fire the following types of World War II ammunition: M48 HE, M61 APC and M72 AP. The M48 round has a maximum range of 8,786m an m/v of 381m/s. The turret of the M8 was also used on the T17E3 Staghound armoured car.

Left M3A3 Light Tank.
Above M8 75mm Self-Propelled Howitzer on display at Aberdeen Proving Ground, Maryland.

RECONNAISSANCE VEHICLES

Both tracked and wheeled reconnaissance vehicles are covered. In many countries light tanks such as the M551 (United States) and AMX-13 (France) are used for the reconnaissance role. Reconnaissance vehicles are normally very small and lightly armoured and rely on their speed to escape detection. Their armament ranges from a 7.62mm machine-gun up to a 90mm gun. They are often fitted with ATGWs and a wide range of sensors. In addition many armoured personnel carriers such as the M113, Commando, VXB-170 and Panhard M-3 are used for the reconnaissance role.

The following vehicles are covered:

COUNTRY	DESIGNATION	TRACKED OR WHEELED	COUNTRY	DESIGNATION	TRACKED OR WHEELED
Belgium	FN 4RM/62F AB	Wheeled	Hungary	FUG-70	Wheeled
Brazil	Cascavel EE-9	Wheeled		FUG	Wheeled
	Cutia-Vete T1 A1	Tracked	Israel	Rby.Mk.1	Wheeled
France	AMX-10RC	Tracked and Wheeled	Italy	Fiat/Oto Melara 6616 M	Wheeled
	VP-90	Tracked	Soviet Union	BRDM-2	Wheeled
	Panhard AML	Wheeled		BRDM-1	Wheeled
	Panhard EBR	Wheeled		BA-64	Wheeled
	Hotchkiss Carriers	Tracked	United States	XM800 ARSV	Tracked and Wheeled
Germany	Radspahpanzer 2	Wheeled			
	Radspahpanzer 3	Wheeled		XR311	Wheeled
Germany (GDR)	Sk-1	Wheeled		Lynx	Tracked
Great Britain	Scorpion	Tracked		M114	Tracked
	Fox	Wheeled		Staghound	Wheeled
	Shorland	Wheeled		M8	Wheeled
	Saladin	Wheeled		M20	Wheeled
	Ferret	Wheeled		M3A1	Wheeled

BELGIUM

FN 4RM/62F AB–LIGHT ARMOURED CAR
MANUFACTURER – Fabrique Nationale, Herstal
STATUS – In service only with the Belgium Gendarmerie. Production complete.

BASIC DATA	MG VERSION	90mm VERSION		MG VERSION	90mm VERSION
CREW:	3	3	FORDING:	1.1m	1.1m
WEIGHT LOADED:	8,660kg	7,880kg	GRADIENT:	60%	60%
LENGTH			ENGINE:	FN Model 652, 6 cylinder, in-line,	
gun forward:	—	5.42m		OHV petrol, 4.75 litres, develop-	
hull:	4.5m	4.5m		ing 130HP at 3,500rpm. Accelera-	
WIDTH:	2.26m	2.26m		tion 0-80km/hr in 65 secs	
HEIGHT OVERALL:	2.37m	2.52m	ARMAMENT:	2 × 7.62mm	1 × 90mm
GROUND CLEARANCE:	.324m	.324m		MG	CATI gun
TRACK:	1.62m	1.62m		1 × 60mm	1 × 7.62mm
WHEELBASE:	2.45m	2.45m		grenade	co-axial MG
TYRES:	9.00 × 20	9.00 × 20		launcher	1 × 7.62mm
TURNING RADIUS:	6m	6m		6 × 6 smoke	A/A MG
MAXIMUM ROAD SPEED:	110km/hr	110km/hr		dischargers	6 × 2 smoke
RANGE AT 80km/hr:	550/600km	550/600km			dischargers
FUEL CAPACITY:	180 litres	180 litres	ARMOUR:	6.5 – 13mm	6.5 – 13mm

DEVELOPMENT

The FN 4RM/62F AB was designed for the Belgian Gendarmerie by FN and is based on the FN 4RM 4 × 4 tactical truck. The first prototype was completed in 1962 and the second in 1965. A total of 62 production vehicles were built commencing in 1971. Although offered for export none was sold. An armoured personnel carrier was projected but not built.

DESCRIPTION

The hull of the armoured car is of all-welded construction. The driver is seated at the front of the vehicle and is provided with a one-piece hatch cover that opens upwards. A total of three periscopes are provided in this hatch and the steering wheel can be removed to assist the driver in leaving the vehicle via this hatch. In the lower half of the driver's hatch is a smaller hatch which, when opened, uncovers a small bullet-

The FN 4RM/62F AB Armoured Car armed with a 90mm gun.

proof window. There is a single door in each side of the hull, the door on the right side being provided with a small pistol port/observation cover.

The turret is in the centre of the hull and has electric traverse with two speeds, fast and slow. The commander/loader is seated on the right and the gunner on the left. There are two different turret models:

Machine-Gun Model
This is armed with twin 7.62mm GPMGs with an elevation of $+55°$ and a depression of $-10°$. A 60mm grenade launcher is mounted to the right of the machine-guns, with an elevation of $+75°$ and a depression of $-10°$. Elevation is manual with two speeds. The machine-guns and mortar can be elevated separately or in parallel. Ammunition stowage is: 60mm – 46 rounds, 7.62mm – 4,830 rounds and 36 smoke grenades for the six smoke dischargers mounted either side of the turret.

The commander's cupola is provided with a total of eight periscopes and his single-piece hatch cover opens towards the rear. The gunner is provided with a single-piece hatch cover that also opens to the rear and three periscopes and a sight.

90mm Gun Model
This has a similar turret to the machine gun model but is armed with a 90mm CATI gun and a co-axial 7.62mm machine-gun to the right of the main armament. The main armament has an elevation of $+27°$ and a depression of $-12°$. The 90mm gun can fire a HEAT round with an m/v of 649m/s, the complete round weighing 3.54kg, with an effective range of 1,000m. In addition an Anti-Personnel (Canister) round is available. This weighs 5.1kg complete, has an m/v of 338m/s and a maximum range of 1,800m. A 7.62mm machine-gun is mounted on the commander's cupola for anti-aircraft defence and there are six smoke dischargers mounted either side of the turret.

Ammunition stowage is: 90mm – 40 rounds, 7.62mm – 3,680 rounds, smoke grenades – 36.

The engine and transmission are mounted at the rear of the hull and an automatic fire extinguisher is installed in the engine compartment. The gearbox has 4F and 1R gears and a two-speed transfer box.

The suspension consists of semi-elliptical springs front and rear with rubber auxiliary load-springing. Shock absorbers are fitted front and rear. The brakes are hydraulically operated with two separate circuits for front and rear wheels, servo-assisted. Four × 12V batteries are fitted.

The vehicle is provided with an NBC system but has no amphibious capability. Steel channels are carried which enable the vehicle to cross ditches. Infra-red driving and fighting equipment is not provided.

VARIANTS
There are no variants of the FN 4RM/62F AB Light Armoured Car.

The FN 4RM/62F AB Armoured Car armed with twin 7.62mm machine-guns and a 60mm grenade launcher.

BRAZIL

CASCAVEL EE-9 – ARMOURED CAR
MANUFACTURER – Engesa SA, São Paulo
STATUS – In service with the Brazilian Army. 20 have been ordered for Qatar (see text). In production.

BASIC DATA

CREW:	3 (commander, gunner, driver)	SIDE SLOPE:	30%
		VERTICAL OBSTACLE:	.6m
WEIGHT LOADED:	10,750kg	TRENCH:	1.5m
WEIGHT EMPTY:	10,000kg	ANGLE OF APPROACH:	60°
LENGTH:	5.998m (gun forward)	ANGLE OF DEPARTURE:	72°
	5.18m (hull)	ENGINE:	Mercedes-Benz (Brazil)
WIDTH:	2.44m		Model OM-352-A, 4-
HEIGHT:	2.33m (turret roof)		cycle, direct injection,
	1.515m (top of hull)		turbo-charged, 6-
GROUND CLEARANCE:	.35m		cylinder, in-line diesel,
TRACK:	1.9m		developing 172HP at
WHEELBASE:	2.093m + 1.415m		2,800rpm
TYRES:	11.00 × 20 (bullet-proof)	ARMAMENT:	1 × 90mm gun
			1 × 7.62mm co-axial
TURNING RADIUS:	7m		MG
MAXIMUM ROAD SPEED:	100km/hr		2 × 2 smoke
RANGE ROAD:	880km		dischargers
FUEL:	260 litres	ARMOUR:	6-12mm (hull-estimate)
FORDING:	1m		
GRADIENT:	60%		

DEVELOPMENT

Development of the Cascavel (a Brazilian Rattlesnake) EE-9 was started by Engesa Engenheiros Especializodos in July 1970 with the first prototype being completed in November 1970. The EE-9 uses many components of the earlier EE-11 Urutu armoured personnel carrier. The first export order was from Qatar for 20 vehicles, and these will be built in Brazil and shipped to France where their H-90 turrets will be fitted. They will then go direct to Qatar. The Brazilian Army calls the EE-9 the CRR, Carro de Reconhecimento sobre Rodas.

DESCRIPTION

The hull of the EE-9 is of all-welded construction. The driver is seated at the front of the vehicle, with the turret in the centre and the engine and transmission at the rear.

A Clark gear box with 5F and 1R gears is fitted and hydraulically operated. There is a one-speed transfer case between the engine and the gear box and a two-speed transfer case between the gear box and the axles. The front axle has a Rockwell differential mounted in an independent front suspension, with coil springs and double-action, air-cooled shock absorbers.

The rear suspension is of the Engesa 'Boomerang' type, consisting of a rigid axle (attached to the vehicle by leaf springs) which holds two lateral walking-beams. Power from the drive shaft to the four rear wheels is via gears inside the walking beams. The rear suspension is also provided with double acting, air-cooled shock absorbers. The main brakes are air over hydraulic on all six wheels. Steering is hydraulic. The electrical system is 12V and a Bosch 14V/35Amp alternator is provided.

Various armament can be provided ranging from 20mm cannon to a 90mm gun. The prototype was armed with a turret-mounted 37mm gun, co-axial 7.62mm machine-gun and a 12.7mm anti-aircraft machine-gun mounted on the turret roof.

For export Engesa are offering the vehicle fitted with the French H-90 turret and a co-axial 7.62mm machine-gun. The 90mm gun is the model D-921 and fires two main types of ammunition:
HEAT with an m/v of 760m/s and an effective range of 1,500m. The complete round weighs 7.077kg whilst the projectile itself weighs 3.65kg.
HE with an m/v of 650m/s and an effective range of 1,500m. The complete round weighs 8.662kg with the projectile itself weighing 5.27kg.

Total ammunition capacity is 20 rounds of 90mm and 2,400 rounds of machine-gun ammunition. Additional data on the turret is given in the entry for the Panhard AML-90 Armoured Car.

The EE-9 is not amphibious and is not provided with an NBC system. Infra-red driving and fighting equipment can be provided. The vehicles for Qatar will most probably be fitted with an air-conditioning system.

VARIANTS

See text above.

Left Cascavel EE-9 Armoured Car with turret-mounted 90mm gun.
Below Rear view of the EE-9 Armoured Car with 90mm gun.

BRAZIL

CUTIA-VETE T1 A1–TRACKED RECONNAISSANCE VEHICLE

BASIC DATA

CREW:	4
WEIGHT:	2,720kg
LENGTH:	3.66m
WIDTH:	1.83m
HEIGHT:	1m
SPEED:	80km/hr
RANGE:	370km
ENGINE:	4-cylinder petrol
ARMAMENT:	1 × 7.62mm M/G

GENERAL

According to the information available at the present time, design work on the Cutia-Vete T1 A1 commenced in 1966, with about 100 so far built for the Brazilian Army. Another report states that it has only reached the prototype stage.

The personnel compartment is at the front of the vehicle with the driver on the left and the machine-gunner on the right. The other two crew members are seated behind the driver and gunner. The engine and transmission are at the rear of the hull. The suspension consists of five road wheels with the idler at the front, drive sprocket at the rear and two support rollers. The tracks are very narrow and the quoted speed of 80km/hr would appear to be rather high. The personnel compartment has no overhead protection at all.

VARIANTS

There are no known variants.

FRANCE

AMX-10RC–ARMOURED RECONNAISSANCE VEHICLE (ARMOURED CAR)
MANUFACTURER–See Text
STATUS–On order for the French Army. Not yet in production. See text.

BASIC DATA

CREW:	4 (commander, gunner, radio-operator, driver)	RANGE (road):	800km
		FORDING:	Amphibious
WEIGHT LOADED:	15,000kg	GRADIENT:	60%
LENGTH:	6.243m (hull)	SIDE SLOPE:	30%
WIDTH:	2.84m	VERTICAL OBSTACLE:	.7m
HEIGHT:	2.565m (O/A)	TRENCH:	1.6m
	2.215m (turret top)	ENGINE:	Hispano-Suiza HS-115,
	1.565m (top of hull)		water-cooled, 8-cylinder
GROUND CLEARANCE:	.3m		supercharged diesel
TRACK:	2.425m		developing 280HP at
WHEELBASE:	1.55m + 1.55m		3,000rpm.
TYRES:	14.00 × 20	ARMAMENT:	1 × 105mm gun
MAXIMUM ROAD SPEED:	85km/hr		1 × 7.62mm co-axial MG
MAXIMUM WATER SPEED:	7.2km/hr		2 × 2 smoke dischargers

DEVELOPMENT

The AMX-10RC is a development of the tracked AMX-10P MICV, with the same engine and transmission as the latter. The first prototype AMX-10RC was shown at the 1973 Satory exhibition and in 1975 it was announced that it would be entering production for the French Army in 1977/78. It is assumed that it is the replacement for the 8 × 8 Panhard EBR heavy armoured car and that it will be built at the Atèlier de Construction Roanne (ARE) where the AMX-10P is at present being built.

DESCRIPTION

The hull of the AMX-10RC is of all-welded construction. The driver is seated at the front of the vehicle on the left and is provided with a one-piece hatch cover that swings to the right. This has a total of three periscopes, the centre one of which can be replaced by a passive periscope for driving at night.

The turret is in the centre of the hull. The loader is on the left and has a one-piece hatch cover. The gunner and commander are on the right of the gun and a single hatch cover is provided for the commander.

The engine and transmission are at the rear of the hull. The suspension can be adjusted to suit the ground conditions and consists of six road wheels. Each road wheel station has an oleo-pneumatic suspension jack which acts as both a pneumatic suspension spring and as a shock absorber. These have been designed and built by Messier Auto Industrie and are controlled by the driver with a four-position lever. The front and rear wheels have disc brakes and the centre two wheels have two hydro-mechanically controlled disc brakes on the transmission. The vehicle is steered in the same way as the tracked AMX-10P, ie skid steering. The AMX-10RC is fully amphibious being propelled in the water by two hydro-jets at the rear of the hull. Before entering the water a trim vane is erected at the front of the hull. An NBC system is provided.

The 105mm MECA gun has an elevation of +20° and a depression of −8° and traverse is a full 360°. The CH 49 electro-hydraulic control system has been developed by SAMM for this vehicle, which also has manual controls for use in an emergency. The gun itself weighs 750kg and has a double baffle muzzle brake. It has a length of 48 calibres without the muzzle brake, and a recoil length of 600mm. It fires a fin-stabilized range of ammunition, details of which are listed below:

TYPE	CARTRIDGE WEIGHT	M/V	PROJECTILE WEIGHT
HEAT-T	13.9kg	1,090m/s	6.2kg
HE	13.5kg	800m/s	7.2kg
DUMMY-T	13.9kg	1,090m/s	6.2kg

The effective range of the 105mm gun is stated to be 1225m. The HEAT-T round will penetrate 350mm of armour at zero angle of incidence or 150mm of armour at 60° angle of incidence. A MECA/APX fin-stabilized shaped charged projectile is also under development. The complete round weighs 16.5kg of which the projectile itself weighs 7.5kg. The complete round is 1.08m in length with the projectile being 735mm in length. This round has an m/v of 1,000m/s and a maximum velocity of 1,500m/s, and effective range is given as 1,650m. A co-axial 7.62mm machine-gun is also provided and there are two smoke dischargers each side of the turret.

Below and following page The AMX-10RC 6 × 6 model. Note in the second photograph that its suspension has been adjusted to give maximum ground clearance.

The gunner has the APX M 401 optical sight and laser rangefinder which has been developed by Sopelem and CILAS (Compagnie Industrielle des Lasers) under contract to the DTAT/APX. It consists of the gunner's telescope with a magnification of ×10 and an optical compensator for automatic inputs of fire-control corrections in the telescope. The laser rangefinder has a range of not less than 10,000m, depending on the visibility, and is accurate to +5m. In addition a techymetric device on both axis, an automatic cant sensor, meteorological sensors and a deviation computer which caculates the firing data from the measured parameters are provided.

The commander has an APX M389 panoramic periscope mounted in the roof of the turret. This is used for all-round observation, acquisition of target located by the gunner, target designation for the gunner and for aiming and firing the co-axial machine-gun. It can also be used to fire the main gun if required. It has a magnification of ×2 and ×8, elevation is +24° and depression −12°. Additional periscopes are provided for the three turret crew members in the front, sides and rear of the turret.

A night TV system developed by Thomson-CSF (Division Équipements Avioniques) is fitted in the AMX-10RC. The camera itself is mounted to the left of the main armament and is aligned to the axis of the gun. The TV screen is inside the turret and the aim axis is represented by an electronic reticle displayed on the TV screen.

VARIANTS
The AMX-10C tracked vehicle was shown for the first time at the 1975 Satory Exhibition and apart from its tracks has an identical hull, turret, engine and so on as the AMX-10RC. It has a loaded weight of 14,500kg.

Top The AMX-10RC showing its amphibious capabilities.
Centre The AMC-10C tracked vehicle which has the same turret and hull as the wheeled AMX-10RC.
Lower The APX M 401 optical sight and laser rangefinder which is used in both the AMX-10RC and the AMX-10C.

FRANCE

VP 90 – TRACKED VEHICLE
MANUFACTURER – LOHR, SA, Hangenbieten
STATUS – Prototypes tested. Available for production.

BASIC DATA

CREW:	1 + 1	GROUND PRESSURE:	.268kg/cm²
WEIGHT LOADED:	2,700kg	TURNING RADIUS:	2.5m
WEIGHT WITHOUT		MAXIMUM ROAD SPEED:	85km/hr
ARMAMENT:	2,200kg	RANGE:	400km
LENGTH:	3.6m	FUEL CONSUMPTION:	15/20 litres per hour
WIDTH:	1.85m	GRADIENT:	70%
HEIGHT:	1.05m (without	SIDE SLOPE:	60%
	armament)	TRENCH:	1m
GROUND CLEARANCE:	.31m	ENGINE:	Liquid-cooled petrol
TRACK:	1.62m		engine developing 90 or
TRACK WIDTH:	230mm		130HP
LENGTH OF TRACK		ARMAMENT:	See text
ON GROUND:	1.84m		

DEVELOPMENT

The LOHR Company is at least the third company to try to market the VP 90 (Voltigeur Patrouilleur). The last company to market the vehicle was Hotchkiss-Brandt, but they closed their vehicle side down some years ago and LOHR build it under licence from them.

DESCRIPTION

The hull of the VP 90 is of all-welded steel construction and apart from the very front of the vehicle it is unarmoured. The crew are at the front of the vehicle and operate it in the prone position, ie lying flat, with the engine and transmission at the rear of the hull. The latter is a four-speed (4F and 1R) semi-automatic gearbox and is coupled to a differential which incorporates self-ventilated disc brakes and which transmits power to the drive sprockets.

The suspension consists of five light alloy road wheels with the drive sprocket at the rear and the idler at the front. There is a single support roller. The flexible suspension system uses rubber rings. The track consists of an endless rubber belt reinforced internally with a synthetic fabric.

Steering and braking are controlled hydraulically with a mechanical safety device. To overcome obstacles the nose can be raised to a maximum of +9° and the tail to a maximum of +4° by an electrical system which is interconnected with the suspension of the vehicle.

As the vehicle has no overhead armour at all it relies on its low overall height for its survival. The manufacturers state that it would be a very useful vehicle for commando and anti-tank units as its small size would make it difficult to detect and it is easily deployed by aircraft and helicopters.

VARIANTS

A wide range of roles has been suggested, including the following:
Anti-Tank vehicle armed with a Milan ATGW launcher and four missiles.
Anti-Tank vehicle armed with a recoilless rifle.
Anti-Tank vehicle armed with six SS-11 ATGWs.
60mm mortar mounted in the front of the hull, plus a machine-gun.
Towing a 120mm mortar.
Fitted with a flamethrower and a 7.62mm machine-gun.
Fitted with 20mm cannon plus a machine-gun.
Cargo vehicle carrying driver and 600kg of cargo.
Armoured carrier carrying driver and three men.
Ambulance with driver, orderly and two patients.
Command vehicle with driver and three men.

Above VP 90 Tracked Vehicle towing a Brandt 120mm mortar.
Below VP 90 Armed with a Brandt breech-loading mortar.

FRANCE

PANHARD AML – ARMOURED CAR
MANUFACTURER – Société de Constructions Mécaniques Panhard and Levassor, Paris
STATUS – In service with Abu Dhabi, Algeria, Angola, Burundi, Cambodia (few, if any, are operational), Chad, Congo, Ecuador, Eire, Ethiopia, France, High Volta, Iraq, Israel (one), Ivory Coast, Kenya, Libya, Malaysia, Mauritania, Morocco, Nigeria, Portugal, Rhodesia (from South Africa), Rwanda, Saudi Arabia, Senegal, South Africa (built under licence), Spain, Tunisia, Venezuela, Zaire. In production.

BASIC DATA

CREW:	3 (commander, gunner and driver)	FORDING:	1.1m Amphibious with kit (see text)
WEIGHT LOADED:	5,500kg		
LENGTH:	5.11m (gun forward)	GRADIENT:	60%
	3.79m (hull)	SIDE SLOPE:	30%
WIDTH:	1.97m	VERTICAL OBSTACLE:	.3m
HEIGHT:	2.07m	TRENCH:	.8m (with 1 channel)
	1.385m (top of hull)		3.1m (with 4 channels)
GROUND CLEARANCE:	.33m	ENGINE:	Panhard Model 4 HD 4-
TRACK:	1.62m		cylinder air-cooled petrol
WHEELBASE:	2.5m		engine developing 90HP
TYRES:	11.00 × 16		at 4,700rpm
TURNING RADIUS:	6m	ARMAMENT:	1 × 90mm gun
SPEED:	100km/hr		1 × 7.62mm co-axial MG
RANGE:	600km (road)		2 × 2 smoke dischargers
FUEL CAPACITY:	156 litres	ARMOUR:	8mm-12mm

Note: Above data relates to the AML-90.

DEVELOPMENT

The AML (Automitrailleuse Légère) was designed and developed by Panhard in the late 1950s to meet a French Army requirement. The first prototype was completed in 1959 with production commencing in 1961. The vehicle has the Panhard Model Number 245. The AML has been built in very large numbers (approx. 3,000) and has been exported to most parts of the world. It is being manufactured in South Africa by Sandock-Austral Limited of Boksburg, and total production in South Africa has amounted to at least 1,000 vehicles. The AML90 is known as the Eland Mk. 5 in South Africa. The Panhard M3 Armoured Personnel Carrier (refer to separate entry) uses 95% of the automotive components of the AML.

DESCRIPTION

The hull of the AML is of all-welded construction. The driver is seated at the front of the vehicle and is provided with a one-piece hatch cover that swings to the right to open and has three integral periscopes. The turret is in the centre of the hull – full details are given below. There is an entry door in each side of the hull. The engine and transmission are at the rear of the hull and there are two access doors in the hull rear allowing access to the engine.

The gearbox has 6F and 1R gears. It is located crosswise and consists of two gearboxes in one, coupled on both sides of the bevel pinion. The low-range box comprises two low gears, a top gear and one reverse gear for use in rough terrain. The high-range box is for normal use and has three low gears and one overdrive. When the low-range box is in normal drive the four ratios of the high-range box command the four upper gears of the range (sixth, fifth, fourth and third). Panhard type ball differentials are located in the gearbox and in each transfer box. These automatically prevent wheel slip.

Drive is transmitted from the gearbox to two lateral transfer boxes via pinions to the rear wheels and via driveshafts that run along the inside of the hull to the front wheels.

The independent suspension consists of coil springs and hydro-pneumatic shock absorbers acting on the trailing arms of the wheel mechanism. The tyres have unpuncturable inner tubes. There are two hydraulic braking systems, one for the front wheels and one for the rear wheels.

The AML has no NBC system but can be fitted with infra-red or image-intensification driving and fighting equipment. The basic vehicle can ford to a depth of 1.1m but Panhard have developed a kit for the AML which allows it to float. This consists of a metal box attached to the hull and filled with expansive polyurethane. According to Panhard this has the following advantages:

1. It forms a hollow charge screen. 2. If hit by an incendiary bullet it will not catch fire. 3. It is unsinkable.

When afloat it is propelled in the water by a propeller at a speed of 6-7km/hr and is steered by its wheels. Total weight of an AML90 with this kit is 5,750kg, length 5.65m, width 2.3m, height 2.07m and it will climb a 58% gradient. The kit is retained after the vehicle leaves the water and is normally kept on the vehicle as part of its normal equipment.

VARIANTS
Most of the turrets described below are built by CNMP-Berthiez at their factory at Le Havre.

AML with H-90 Turret
This is armed with a D 921 90mm gun with a 7.62mm machine-gun mounted to the left of the main armament; if required, a further 7.62mm machine-gun can be mounted on the turret roof. The gun has an elevation of +15° and a depression of −8°, turret has full 360° traverse and one turret rotation takes twenty seconds. Elevation and traverse are manual. The turret is provided with two circular hatches that open to the rear, eight periscopes and an AMX M262 telescope. The 90mm gun fires HE and HEAT projectiles, both of which are fin-stabilized. Basic data of these projectiles are:
HE round has an m/v of 650m/s, the complete round weighs 8.662kg, the projectile itself weighs 5.27kg, and effective range is 1,500m.
HEAT round has an m/v of 760m/s, the complete round weighs 7.077kg with the projectile weighing 3.65kg, and it has an effective range of 1,500/2,000m. The HEAT projectile will penetrate 320mm of armour at an incidence of 0°, or 140mm of armour at an incidence of 60°. Two smoke dischargers are mounted either side of the turret. Total ammunition capacity is twenty rounds of 90mm and 2,400 rounds of 7.62mm. This was also offered with two SS-11 or ENTAC missiles mounted either side of the main armament.

AML with HE 60-7 Turret
This is armed with twin 7.62mm machine-guns (on the left) and a single 60mm mortar on the right. The machine-guns have an elevation of +60° and a depression of −15° whilst the mortar has an elevation of +76° and a depression of −15°. Two types of mortar are available – the Hotchkiss-Brandt Model CM 60A1 or the DTAT Model CS. This can be used in both the direct role (up to 300m) or indirect role (up to 1,700m). 53 rounds of 60mm and 3,800 rounds of 7.62mm ammunition are carried, and there are slight differences in the amounts of ammunition that are carried if additional radios are installed. The turret has a large two-piece hatch cover that opens front and rear. A total of seven periscopes (type L794B) are provided as well as an M112/3 sighting periscope. This was also offered with four ENTAC missiles mounted on the rear of the turret, two of which slide out of rails each side of the turret to be launched.

Above AML with H-90 turret fording a stream.

AML with HE 60-12 Turret

This is the same turret as above but armed with the 12.7mm machine-gun and a 60mm mortar. The machine-gun has an elevation of +60° and a depression of −15°, whilst the mortar has an elevation of +76° and a depression of −15°. Total ammunition capacity is 53 mortar bombs and 1,300 rounds of 12.7mm ammunition.

AML with HE 60-20 Turret

This has the same turret as the above but is armed with a 60mm CS DTAT mortar and a 20mm cannon. The mortar has an elevation of +76° and a depression of −15°, whilst the 20mm cannon has an elevation of +50° and a depression of −8°. If required a 7.62mm machine-gun can be mounted on the turret roof. Ammunition capacity is 39 rounds of 60mm and 300 rounds of 20mm plus 1,000 rounds of 7.62mm. The 20mm cannon fires both AP and HE rounds with an m/v of 1,040m/s and a cyclic rate of fire of 700/750 rounds per minute.

AML 30

This is a new turret armed with a 30mm Hispano-Suiza 831A or 831SL cannon with an elevation of +45° and a depression of −8°. The 30mm cannon has a cyclic rate of fire of 650 rounds per minute and the gunner can select either single shots, bursts or fully automatic. The turret has either manual or hydraulic traverse and elevation. The hydraulic model has been developed in association with the Marrel company, and has a maximum speed in traverse of 80° a second and a maximum speed in elevation of 40° a second. The commander has four L793B periscopes whilst the gunner has three L794D periscopes and an M112/3 sight for aiming the gun. Turret armour is 15mm front, 12mm sides and 8mm on the roof. Total ammunition capacity is 200 rounds of 30mm (of which 155 are for ready use), and 2,200 rounds of 7.62mm. Two smoke dischargers are mounted either side of the turret.

AML with S530 Turret

This anti-aircraft turret has been developed by SAMM (Société d'Applications des Machines Motrices) and has been purchased by Venezuela. It is armed with twin AME 621 20mm cannon, which have full 360° traverse, an elevation of +70° and a depression of −10°. Maximum elevation speed is 40° per second and maximum traverse speed is 80° per second. A total of 600 rounds of 20mm ammunition are carried and the empty cartridge cases are ejected externally. Turret armour is 15mm thick at the front and 7mm at the side and rear. Overall height of this model is 2.315m. Two smoke dischargers are mounted either side of the turret rear.

A wide range of ammunition can be fired including HE-T with an m/v of 900m/s, HE with an m/v of 1,026m/s, HEI with an m/v of 1,026m/s and AP with an m/v of 1,000m/s, the latter able to penetrate 23mm of armour at 1,000m. Cyclic rate of fire is 740 rounds per minute per barrel. The gunner can select either single shots, bursts, or full automatic.

AML with NA2 Turret

This was developed by Nord-Aviation (now Aerospatiale) and could be fitted with either four SS-11 or two SS-12 anti-tank guided missiles. In addition two 7.62mm machine-guns and two ACL 89 anti-tank launchers were provided. As far as is known this has not been adopted by any country.

Left AML with HE 60-7 turret.
Above Loading the Hotchkiss-Brandt Model CM 60A1 60mm mortar on an AML.

The AML 30 with its 30mm cannon at high elevation.

AML with S 530 turret-mounting twin 20mm cannon.

Above Rear view of the Panhard AML Light Armoured Car.
Below AML with 30mm gun and fitted with the flotation kit shown leaving the water.

AML with H-90 turret fitted with the Panhard developed flotation kit.

FRANCE

PANHARD EBR 75 – HEAVY ARMOURED CAR
PANHARD EBR ETT – ARMOURED PERSONNEL CARRIER
MANUFACTURER – Panhard and Levassor, Paris
STATUS – The EBR 75 is in service with France, Mauritania, Morocco, Portugal and Tunisia. The EBR ETT is only in service with Portugal. Production of both the EBR 75 and EBR ETT is complete.

BASIC DATA	EBR FL-10	EBR FL-11	EBR FL-11	EBR ETT
CREW: (commander, gunner and two drivers)	4	4	4	3 + 12
WEIGHT LOADED:	15,200kg	13,500kg	13,500kg	13,000kg
LENGTH TURRET FORWARD:	7.33m	6.15m	6.15m	—
LENGTH HULL:	5.56m	5.56m	5.56m	5.21m
WIDTH:	2.42m	2.42m	2.42m	2.44m
HEIGHT				
8 wheels:	2.5m	2.32m	2.32m	2.19m
4 wheels:	2.58m	2.24m	2.24m	2.32m
GROUND CLEARANCE				
8 wheels:	.42m	.41m	.41m	.41m
4 wheels:	.32m	.33m	.33m	.33m
TRACK:	1.74m	1.74m	1.74m	1.74m
TYRES:	9.75 × 20	9.75 × 20	9.75 × 20	9.75 × 20
TURNING RADIUS:	7.974m using the front wheels only 3.962m using both the front and rear wheels			
GROUND PRESSURE:	.8kg/cm²	.75kg/cm²	.75kg/cm²	.7kg/cm²
MAXIMUM ROAD SPEED:	105km/hr	105km/hr	105km/hr	105km/hr
RANGE (road):	650km	650km	650km	650km
FUEL CAPACITY:	380 litres	380 litres	380 litres	370 litres
FORDING:	1.2m	1.2m	1.2m	1.2m
GRADIENT:	60+%	60+%	60+%	60+%
VERTICAL OBSTACLE:	.4m	.4m	.4m	.4m
TRENCH CROSSING:	2m	2m	2m	2m
ENGINE:	All are powered by a Panhard 12-cylinder air-cooled petrol engine developing 200HP at 3,700rpm			
ARMAMENT:				
main:	1 × 75mm	1 × 75mm	1 × 90mm	1 or 2 7.62mm
co-axial:	1 × 7.5mm or 7.62mm MG			Nil
driver:	1 × 7.5mm or 7.62mm MG front and rear			front only
ARMOUR				
hull front:	40mm	40mm	40mm	40mm
hull rear:	40mm	40mm	40mm	—
hull sides:	16mm	16mm	16mm	15mm
hull roof:	20mm	20mm	20mm	15mm
hull floor:	16mm	16mm	16mm	20mm
turret front:	40mm	40mm	40mm	—
turret rear:	20mm	20mm	20mm	—
turret roof:	10mm	10mm	10mm	—

DEVELOPMENT

In 1937 Panhard started the development of the AMR 201 Armoured Car for the French Army. Construction of the first prototype started in 1938 and this was completed in December 1939. This was armed with a 25mm gun and a 7.5mm machine-gun and it had a crew of three men, commander, gunner and driver. When war broke out this vehicle was taken to North Africa where it was subsequently lost. After the war the French Army drew up requirements for three basic armoured vehicles—a heavy tank (this became the AMX-50 which was developed to prototype stage only), a light tank (which became the famous AMX-13) and a heavy armoured car. The latter requirement was filled by the Panhard Company who designed a new armoured car called the EBR 75, Panhard number being model 212. This new vehicle was similar in concept to the pre-war vehicle. The first prototype was completed in July 1948. After trials a production order was given to Panhard and the first production vehicle was completed in August 1950. Production continued until 1960, by which time some 1,200 vehicles had been built, the majority for the French Army. After production of the EBR 75 (EBR stands for Engin Blindé Reconnaissance) was completed, Panhard started production of the AML 245 and later the M3 series, which are still in production. The EBR is still in front-line service with the French Army though early replacement is intended as many of these vehicles are now twenty years old. Its replacement will be the new AMX-10RC which is armed with a 105mm turret-mounted gun.

DESCRIPTION

The hull of the EBR is of all-welded construction, and there are a number of features of the vehicles which make it unique. First of all it has two drivers, one in the front and one at the rear. For normal operations the front driver has control of the vehicle. If however the tactical situation is such that a high speed exit is required, then the rear driver takes over. The vehicle can travel 105km/hr in either forward or reverse. Both drivers are provided with a two-piece hatch cover and three periscopes for viewing when closed down. In addition each driver has a 7.5mm or 7.62mm fixed machine-gun mounted in the bottom of his compartment. When first built the EBR had 7.5mm machine-guns, as this was the standard French Army calibre, but more recently they have adopted the 7.62mm round, and machine-guns of this calibre are fitted for both the driver and co-axial positions.

The EBR has a total of eight wheels. For normal road operations it travels on the four-tyred wheels which are puncture-proof. When rough country is encountered, the four center wheels, or intermediate wheels as they are also known, are lowered. These powered wheels have steel gousers and increase the cross country capabilities of the vehicle. Steering is power assisted. The front and rear wheels are provided with concentric coil springs and a damper. The intermediate wheels are lowered or raised by a hydro-pneumatic unit.

The turret is in the centre of the vehicle with the commander on the left and the gunner on the right. The commander is provided with a cupola with periscopes for all-round observation. The loader has a single-piece hatch cover and three periscopes are arranged round the front of his hatch.

The turret is of the oscillating type and has two halves. The top half mounts the main armament and this pivots on the bottom half. The Panhard 12 H 6000 engine is mounted under the floor of the vehicle. The engine in fact is only 22cm in height and weighs approx 360kg, consisting of two opposed groups of six cylinders. The carburettor and ignition system can be checked from within the vehicle. Air is drawn into the vehicle through oval holes between the top of the hull and the bottom of the turret. This then passes over the engine and leaves the vehicle by similar oval holes at the rear of the turret. There are two gear boxes mounted in tandem, each of which has four gears, giving a total of sixteen gears in each direction.

EBR Armoured Car shown steering on front and rear wheels.

VARIANTS

EBR 75 with FL-11 turret
This was the first model to enter service and is armed with a 75mm gun with an elevation of +15° and a depression of −10°. A total of 56 rounds of ammunition are carried. Two smoke dischargers are mounted either side of the turret.

EBR 75 with FL-10 turret
This is also known as the EBR 75 Model 51 Type 55-10. It has the same turret as is fitted to the AMX-13 light tank. The 75mm gun has an elevation of +13° and a depression of −6°. The gun is fed by two revolver type magazines in the rear of the turret and each of these hold a total of six rounds of ammunition. Once these two magazines have been expended they must be reloaded from outside the turret. A total of 38 rounds of ammunition are carried and like the earlier model two smoke dischargers are fitted either side of the turret. The turret is power operated (complete rotation in twelve seconds) with manual controls for use in an emergency. While increasing the firepower this turret also increased the overall height of the vehicle as well as its weight.

EBR 75 with FL 11 turret and 90mm gun
Early in the 1960s it was decided to fit the FL-11 turret with a new 90mm gun firing fin-stabilized rounds, ie HE and hollow charge. The modifications to the vehicle included the fitting of a new barrel, modification of the breech mechanism and the modification of the existing ammunition racks. The hollow charge round will penetrate 320mm of armour at 0° or 120mm at 60°. This model is in service with the French Army.

Anti-Aircraft Vehicle
Only one of these was built in 1952. This consisted of a basic chassis with a new turret mounting twin 30mm cannon and no radar fire-control system was provided. An EBR 75 with an FL-11 turret was modified to have a 12.7mm machine-gun mounted in the turret for anti-aircraft defence, but this was not adopted.

EBR ETT Armoured Personnel carrier.
This was also known as the Panhard Model 238 and only 30 were built, the first prototype being constructed in 1957. This was designed as an armoured personnel carrier for use in the colonies and could be fitted with two small turrets, one at the front and the other at the rear, each being armed with a 7.62mm machine-gun, or no armament at all. Hatches were provided in the front, sides and rear of the vehicle so that the crew could fire their weapons from within the vehicle. On this model only one driver was carried and he was seated at the front of the vehicle. The rear driver's station was taken away as twin entry doors were provided at the rear of the hull. Trials were carried out with a model that had the intermediate steel wheels replace by conventional tyres for use in the desert. This model is no longer used by the French Army and some turned up in Portugal during the troubles in 1974.

EBR on the left has FL-10 turret whilst the EBR on the right has FL-11 turret.

EBR ETT Armoured Personnel Carrier with turret-mounted machine-gun.

FRANCE

HOTCHKISS CARRIERS – RECONNAISSANCE, COMMAND and AMBULANCE VEHICLES
MANUFACTURER – Hotchkiss-Brandt, Paris. Some were also assembled in Germany by Klöckner-Humboldt-Deutz
STATUS – In service only with the German Army. Production complete.

BASIC DATA	RECCE. SP.1A	MORTAR SP.1B	COMMAND SP.111	AMBULANCE SP.1V
CREW:	5	4/5	5	3/5
WEIGHT LOADED:	8,200kg	8,200kg	7,500kg	8,000kg
LENGTH:	4.51m	4.66m	4.51m	4.6m
WIDTH:	2.28m	2.28m	2.28m	2.29m
HEIGHT:	1.97m	1.84m	1.688m	1.84m
GROUND CLEARANCE:	.35m	.35m	.35m	.35m
TRACK:	1.918m	1.918m	1.918m	1.918m
TRACK WIDTH:	308mm	308mm	308mm	308mm
LENGTH OF TRACK ON GROUND:	2.3m	2.3m	2.3m	2.3m
GROUND PRESSURE:	.58kg/cm²	.58kg/cm²	.55kg/cm²	.57kg/cm²
MAXIMUM ROAD SPEED:	58km/hr	58km/hr	58km/hr	58km/hr
RANGE (Road):	390km	320km	400km	350km
FUEL CAPACITY:	330 litres	375 litres	345 litres	295 litres
FORDING:	1m	1m	1m	1m
GRADIENT:	60%	60%	60%	60%
VERTICAL OBSTACLE:	.6m	.6m	.6m	.6m
TRENCH:	1.5m	1.5m	1.5m	1.5m
ENGINE:	Hotchkiss 4-stroke, 6-cylinder, in-line, OHV, water-cooled petrol engine developing 164HP at 3,900rpm			

ARMOUR:				
hull nose:	15mm at 62°	hull floor rear:	8mm	
hull glacis:	10mm at 21°/24°	turret front:	15mm at 40°	
hull sides:	8mm at 60°/66°	turret sides:	12.5mm at 68°	
hull rear:	8mm at 66°/75°	turret rear:	12.5mm at 68°	
roof:	8mm	turret roof:	8mm	
hull floor front:	15mm			

Fuel consumption is 85 litres/100km on roads and 35 litres/100km cross country.

DEVELOPMENT

In the early 1950s Hotchkiss developed a series of tracked vehicles under contract to the French Army but the latter did not place any production orders for these vehicles. At that time the German Army was being reformed and was in urgent need of modern vehicles. The Germans tested the French prototypes and placed an order with Hotchkiss for a series of vehicles based on the earlier Hotchkiss carriers, with a number of modifications.

All of these used the same basic engine, transmission, tracks and suspension and many parts of their hulls were identical. Production started in 1958 and was completed in 1962. Total production for the German Army amounted to 2,374. In recent years these vehicles have started to be phased out of service and replaced by more modern vehicles. For example the SPZ.11-2 reconnaissance vehicle is now being replaced by the new 8 × 8 Spähpanzer 2. Hotchkiss developed numerous other variants of the vehicle, but none of these reached production. Hotchkiss also developed the TT A 12 tracked armoured amphibious personnel carrier from this range of vehicles, but these were not placed in production and Hotchkiss then closed down their vehicle side and concentrated on mortars, ammunition and anti-tank weapons.

DESCRIPTION

The hull is of all-welded construction. The engine is mounted at the front of the hull on the right. The driver is seated on the left and is provided with three periscopes for driving whilst closed down and a single-piece hatch cover. The roof hatch layout differs according to the variant, all models having twin doors at the rear of the hull. All models have an escape hatch in the hull floor.

The transmission/steering assembly consists of the clutch, gearbox and differential steering system. The conventional type gearbox has 4F and 1R gears, the second, third, and fourth being synchronized. The steering system consists of a differential operated by normal Cleveland-type pinions, and the shafts from the differential steering system drive the sprockets directly without reduction gearing.

The suspension is of the torsion-bar type and consists of five road wheels with the drive sprocket at the front and the idler at the rear. There are three track return rollers. The first, second, fourth and fifth road wheels are provided with hydraulic shock absorbers. The track consists of 98 steel alloy shoes with detachable rubber blocks.

The electrical system is 24 Volt and four 12V/100Amp batteries are provided. The Hotchkiss vehicles do not have an NBC system and are not amphibious. Two heaters are provided, one in the driver's compartment and one in the rear fighting compartment.

The Hotchkiss SP.1A, or SPz 11-2 as it is called by the German Army.

VARIANTS

Reconnaissance Vehicle SP.1A
This is known in the German Army as the SPZ.11-2 Halbgruppe Kurz; a radio model is known as the SPZ.31-2 Funk Kurz. It is armed with a turret-mounted Hispano-Suiza 20mm cannon. This has an elevation of $+75°$ and a depression of $-20°$, and traverse is a full 360°. The turret has a hatch in the roof and a periscope with a magnification of $×4$ and $×15$. A total of 500 rounds of 20mm ammunition are carried and most vehicles have three smoke dischargers mounted either side of the turret. This model has a total of three hatches in the rear fighting compartment roof. The crew of five consists of the commander, gunner, radio-operator, rifleman and driver.

Mortar Carrier SP.1B
This is known in the German Army as the SPZ.Panzermörser 81mm SPZ.51-2, and it is believed that few of these remain in service. It is armed with an 81mm mortar firing forwards. This has a traverse of 30° left and 30° right, elevation being between $+45°$ and $+90°$. A total of 50 mortar bombs are carried. A 7.62mm machine-gun and 500 rounds of ammunition are also provided. The roof is covered with twin hatches hinged on the sides. This model has a crew of four, commander, driver and two mortar-men. Some models have been fitted with the American AN/TPS-33 radar system, and are known as the Radarpanzer Kurz or SPZ.2.

Command Vehicle SP.111
This model has a crew of five – commander, driver, observer, radio operator and rifleman. The Germans call it the SPZ.22-2 or Artilleriebeobachter. The commander's cupola is on the left and the right hatch has a 7.62mm machine-gun mounted on it. A total of 500 rounds of ammunition are carried for this. A periscope with a 120° field of view is mounted in the forward part of the roof for observation purposes. As it is used in the command/artillery fire-control role a total of three radios are fitted.

Ambulance SP.1V
This is known in the German Army as the SPZ.2-2 or Kr.Kw.Krankenwagen. It is unarmed and can carry two stretcher and one sitting patients in addition to the driver and two medical orderlies. A further two stretchers could be carried on the roof.

Cargo Carrier
The German Army did have a number of cargo models called the SPZ.Kurz.Nachschubpanzer. These had four road wheels each side instead of five and were powered by a four-cylinder petrol engine. As far as is known these have been withdrawn from service.

Hotchkiss carriers on the production line in Paris, France.

GERMANY (FEDERAL GERMAN REPUBLIC)

SPÄHPANZER 3–RECONNAISSANCE VEHICLE
STATUS–Project.

BASIC DATA

CREW:	3 (commander, gunner, driver)	MAXIMUM WATER SPEED:	10km/hr
		RANGE:	600/800km
WEIGHT:	10,600kg	FORDING:	Amphibious
LENGTH:	5.95m	ENGINE:	Diesel
WIDTH:	2.5m	ARMAMENT:	1 × 20mm cannon
HEIGHT:	2.5m		1 × 7.64mm MG
GROUND CLEARANCE:	.405m		2 × 4 smoke dischargers
MAXIMUM ROAD SPEED:	90km/hr		

GENERAL

This is only a project and will use some components of the 8 × 8 Radspähpanzer amphibious reconnaissance vehicle now in service with the German Army. It will have the same turret and armament as the latter and will be fully amphibious, with two propellers.

GERMANY (FEDERAL GERMAN REPUBLIC)

RADSPÄHPANZER 2 LUCHS–RECONNAISSANCE VEHICLE
MANUFACTURER–Rheinstahl Wehrtechnik, Kassel
STATUS–In service with the German Army. In production.

BASIC DATA

CREW:	4 (commander, gunner, driver and rear driver/ radio-operator)	FUEL:	500 litres
		FORDING:	Amphibious
		GRADIENT:	60%
WEIGHT:	19,500kg	VERTICAL OBSTACLE:	.6m
LENGTH:	7.743m	TRENCH:	1.9m
WIDTH:	2.98m	ANGLE OF APPROACH:	59°
HEIGHT:	2.84m	ANGLE OF DEPARTURE:	50°
	2.056m (top of hull)	ENGINE:	Daimler-Benz Type OM 403 VA, 10-cylinder, 4-stroke, with fuel injection and turbo-charger, this develops 390HP when used with diesel fuel or 300HP when used with petrol
GROUND CLEARANCE:	.405m		
TRACK:	2.54m		
WHEELBASE:	1.4m + 2.365m + 1.4m		
TYRES:	14.00 × 20		
TURNING RADIUS:	11.5m (all 8 wheels) 19.4m (4 wheels only)		
MAXIMUM ROAD SPEED:	90km/hr	ARMAMENT:	1 × 20mm cannon
WATER SPEED:	10km/hr		1 × 7.62mm MG
ACCELERATION 0/80km/hr:	65 seconds		2 × 4 smoke dischargers
RANGE:	800km		

DEVELOPMENT

In 1964 the German Ministry of Defence started drawing up plans for a new family of military vehicles which would include an 8 × 8 amphibious reconnaissance vehicle, 4 × 4 and 6 × 6 amphibious load carriers and 4 × 4, 6 × 6 and 8 × 8 trucks, some of which were to be amphibious. A year later, in 1965, a Joint Project Office was formed to develop this range of vehicles, comprising the following companies: Büssing, Klöckner-Humboldt-Deutz, Krupp, MAN and Rheinstahl. Daimler-Benz did not join the JPO but developed a range of vehicles as well. Both teams built prototypes of the 8 × 8 amphibious reconnaissance vehicle and these were completed in 1967/68. In 1971 it was decided that Daimler-Benz would concentrate on the armoured vehicles (ie the 8 × 8 reconnaissance vehicle and the 4 × 4 and 6 × 6 load carriers) whilst the JPO concentrated on the new family of tactical trucks.

In December 1973 the German Ministry of Defence awarded a contract to Rheinstahl for the production of 408 Radspähpanzer 2 reconnaissance vehicles at a total cost of DM300 million. The first production vehicles came off the assembly line in May 1975 and production should continue until 1977. The vehicle will replace the old Hotchkiss 11-2 vehicles at present used in the reconnaissance role. There is a separate entry for the Transportpanzer 1 and 2, which may well enter production after the reconnaissance vehicle contract has been completed.

DESCRIPTION

The hull and turret of the vehicle are of all-welded steel construction, and an entry door is provided in the left side of the hull.

The driver is seated at the front of the hull on the left side and is provided with a single-piece hatch cover that opens to the right and a total of three periscopes.

The turret is behind the driver, the commander being on the left and the gunner on the right. Both the commander and gunner are provided with a single-piece hatch cover and a full range of vision equipment.

The turret is power operated and the 20mm Rh.202 cannon is the same as that used by the Marder MICV and the German Air Force in the anti-aircraft role. A 7.62mm MG3 machine-gun is mounted on a ring mount over the commander's hatch. This can be quickly traversed through 360°, elevation limits being −15° to +55°. An infra-red/white searchlight is mounted on the left side of the turret, and this is elevated with the main armament.

The second driver, who also acts as the radio-operator, is behind the commander and faces the rear of the vehicle. He has a single-piece hatch cover and a total of three periscopes for observation purposes.

The engine and transmission is to the rear of the turret. The complete engine, transmission, air filter and oil filter are mounted as a complete unit and can be removed from the vehicle very quickly. The radiator and fans are at the rear of the hull.

The transmission is a type ZF 4 PW 96 H1, is fully automatic and is provided with a hydro-dynamic torque converter. The vehicle has a top speed of 90km/hr both forwards and backwards.

The suspension consists of rigid Daimler-Benz AM 7 axles with control rods in conjunction with coil springs, telescopic shock absorbers and intermediate suspension arms. Steering is of the recirculating ball type and is power assisted. The driver can select either the front four wheels, rear four wheels or all eight wheels for steering. Dual circuit hydraulic brakes are provided.

The vehicle is fully amphibious with two propellers, one on each side of the hull rear. Steering is achieved by swivelling the propellers. The trim vane is erected hydraulically by the driver before the vehicle enters the water.

The Luchs is provided with an NBC system and an automatic fire-extinguishing system is fitted in the engine compartment. A heater is also provided and this can heat the engine if required.

Wherever possible standard well-tried commercial components such as the engine and axles have been used in the design of the vehicle.

VARIANTS

No variants have been announced.

Cutaway drawing of one of the prototypes of the Luchs, the LG 494.

The Spähpanzer 2 Luchs Reconnaissance Vehicle.

GERMAN DEMOCRATIC REPUBLIC (EAST GERMANY)

SK-1–ARMOURED CAR
MANUFACTURER–Robur Garant (chassis), State Arsenals (body)
CURRENT STATUS–In service in East Germany. No longer in production.

BASIC DATA

CREW:	5	FORDING:	.54m
WEIGHT:	5,400kg	GRADIENT:	40%
LENGTH:	4m	VERTICAL OBSTACLE:	.4m
WIDTH:	2m	ENGINE:	Model 30K, 4-cylinder,
HEIGHT:	2.8m		air-cooled, in-line diesel
GROUND CLEARANCE:	.28m		developing 55HP at
TRACK:	1.5m (front) 1.45m (rear)		2,800rpm.
WHEELBASE:	3.77m	ARMAMENT:	1 × 7.92mm MG-34 MG
TYRES:	7.50 × 20		mounted in a turret
MAXIMUM ROAD SPEED:	80km/hr		with a traverse of 360°.
RANGE:	350km		900 rounds of MG
FUEL CAPACITY:	70 litres		ammunition are carried.
FUEL CONSUMPTION:	16 litres per 100km	ARMOUR:	8mm (maximum)

DEVELOPMENT

After the troubles in East Germany in June 1953 the East Germans designed two vehicles for internal security duties. These were the SK-1 (4 × 4) Armoured Car and the SK-2 (6 × 6) Armoured Water Cannon. As the SK-2 is not strictly an Armoured Fighting Vehicle it is beyond the scope of this book for a detailed description. Basically it consists of a standard German G-5 (6 × 6) truck chassis with an armoured cab. Over this cab is a turret-mounted high-pressure water cannon. The unarmoured water tank is at the rear of the vehicle and contains 4,000 litres of water. The water tank can be refilled from within the vehicle if required. The SK-2 positions itself over a water main manhole, the operator inside the vehicle opens a hatch in the floor of the vehicle and lowers a filler pipe down the manhole. It takes a maximum of eight minutes to refill the tank. Basic data of the SK-2 are as follows: weight 9,100kg loaded, length 7.5m, width 2.5m, height 4.3m, crew 3 men, speed 48km/hr and it has a maximum range of 585km.

The SK-1 Armoured Car is essentially a Robur Garant 30K truck chassis with a shorter wheelbase, fitted with an armoured body. The first production models were completed in 1954 and the vehicle was not built in large numbers. In appearance it is very similar to the Soviet BA-64 armoured car, but the SK-1 has dual rear wheels, is much heavier than the BA-64 and is also somewhat larger. It should be remembered that the East German Army does not use the SK-1; it is used only by Police, Security Units and Workers Militia.

DESCRIPTION

The hull of the SK-1 is of all-welded construction with the engine at the front of the hull. The driver is on the left and he is provided with a windscreen which can, if need be, be covered by a steel hatch. There is a similar windscreen and hatch cover for the co-driver. There are vision slits in the sides of the hull and firing ports in the sides and rear of the hull. The turret has hand traverse and is provided with twin hatch covers and vision slits. There are doors in each side of the hull with an additional door in the rear of the hull. The SK-1's gearbox has 4F and 1R gears and a two-speed transfer case. No NBC or infra-red driving equipment is fitted.

VARIANTS

There are no known variants in service.

SK-1 Armoured Car being used by an East German Militia unit.

GREAT BRITAIN

COMBAT VEHICLE RECONNAISSANCE (TRACKED) SCORPION FAMILY

MANUFACTURER – Alvis (British Leyland) Limited, Coventry, and at Malines Plant in Belgium
STATUS – In service with Abu-Dhabi, Belgium, Great Britain, Iran, Nigeria, Saudi-Arabia. In production.

BASIC DATA	SCORPION FV101	STRIKER FV102	SPARTAN FV103	SAMARITAN FV104	SULTAN FV105	SAMPSON FV106	SCIMITAR FV107
CREW:	3	3	3 + 4	3 + 4	5/6	3	3
WEIGHT LOADED:	7,960kg	8,221kg	8,172kg	7,710kg	7,918kg	8,002kg	7,893kg
LENGTH O/A:	4.388m	4.759m	4.839m	4.991m	4.991m	4.934m	4.743m
LENGTH HULL:	4.388m	4.759m	4.839m	4.991m	4.991m	4.934m	4.743m
WIDTH:	2.184m	2.184m	2.184m	2.184m	2.184m	2.184m	2.184m
HEIGHT O/A:	2.096m	2.21m	2.25m	2.016m	2.016m	2.023m	2.115m
HEIGHT HULL TOP:	—	1.727m	1.718m	—	—	1.718m	—
GROUND CLEARANCE:	.356m	.356m	.356m	.356m	.356m	.356m	.356m

TRACK:	1.7m	1.7m	1.7m	1.7m	1.7m	1.7m	1.7m
TRACK WIDTH:	432mm	432mm	432mm	432mm	432mm	432mm	432mm
LENGTH OF TRACK ON GROUND:	2.49m	2.49m	2.49m	2.49m	2.49m	2.49m	2.49m
POWER-WEIGHT RATIO:	18.61	17.4	17.5	18.6	18.1	17.9	18.61
GROUND PRESSURE kg/cm^2:	.345	.345	.345	.345	.345	.345	.345
MAXIMUM ROAD SPEED:	87km/hr	87km/hr	87km/hr	87km/hr	87km/hr	87km/hr	87km/hr
WATER SPEED:	6.44km/hr	6.44km/hr	6.44km/hr	6.44km/hr	6.44km/hr	6.44km/hr	6.44km/hr
RANGE:	644km	644km	644km	644km	644km	644km	644km
FUEL LITRES:	391	364	364	364	364	364	391
FORDING:	1.067m	1.067m	1.067m	1.067m	1.067m	1.067m	1.067m
GRADIENT:	70%	70%	70%	70%	70%	70%	70%
VERTICAL OBSTACLE:	.508m	.508m	.508m	.508m	.508m	.508m	.508m
TRENCH:	2.057m	2.057m	2.057m	2.057m	2.057m	2.057m	2.057m
ENGINE:	Jaguar OHC 4.2 litres 6-cylinder in line petrol engine developing 195BHP at 4,750rpm						

Note. The Scorpion will accelerate from 0–48km/hr in 16 seconds and fuel consumption is 1.77km/litre.

DEVELOPMENT

In the early 1960s the FVRDE (now MVEE) designed a number of vehicles to meet a British Army requirement for an Armoured Vehicle Reconnaissance (AVR). The end result was that two different vehicles were developed, these being:
Combat Vehicle Reconnaissance (Wheeled) Fox
Combat Vehicle Reconnaissance (Tracked) Scorpion
In 1964 a test vehicle known as the TV15000 was built, powered by a Rolls-Royce B60 petrol engine which developed 130BHP. This was however replaced by a Jaguar XK engine in 1966. The vehicle was followed by two Test Rigs. In 1967, Alvis Limited of Coventry (who were at that time building the FV600 series) were awarded a contract for a total of 17 prototypes, the first of which was completed in January 1969. The prototypes were first shown to the public and press in September 1969. In May 1970 Alvis received a production order for the British Army which amounted to some 2,000 vehicles. The next order was placed by Belgium in October 1970. This was for a total of 701 members of the Scorpion family; some components of the Scorpions for the Belgium Army are built in Belgium. The other large export orders have been from Iran (for 250-350 vehicles) and Saudi-Arabia (250). The Scorpion was entered for the American ARSV contest by Teledyne-Continental.

The first production Scorpion was completed early in 1972. Late in 1975 it was stated that a Scorpion fully equipped with night vision equipment cost approx. £90,000.

The Scorpion is airportable and two can be carried in a Lockheed C-130 Hercules transport aircraft.

DESCRIPTION

The hull and turret of the Scorpion is of all-welded aluminium armour construction. The driver is seated at the front of the hull on the left side and is provided with a single-piece hatch cover and a wide-angle periscope which can be replaced by a passive periscope if required.

The other two crew members are seated in the turret with the commander on the left and the gunner on the right. The commander has seven periscopes and a sight with a magnification of ×1 and ×10, but limited traverse. The gunner has a sight with a magnification of ×10 or ×1 and two periscopes. A Rank passive sight is mounted to the right of the main armament and has two ranges: high magnification (×5.8) and low magnification (×1.6). Both the commander and gunner have a single-piece hatch cover that opens to the rear.

The main armament of the Scorpion is a 76mm gun, which is a lighter model of that used in the Saladin armoured car. The gun has an elevation of +35° and a depression of −10°, traverse being a full 360°. Traverse and elevation are manual although a powered system has been fully developed. A 7.62mm machine-gun is mounted to the left of the main armament and can also be used as a ranging machine-gun. Two three-barrelled smoke dischargers are mounted either side of the turret. The following types of fixed ammunition are available: HESH, HE-T, Canister, Smoke and Practice-T. The HESH round weighs 7.4kg of which the projectile wieghs 5.39kg. The HE-T round weighs 7.33kg of which the projectile weighs 5.36kg. The smoke round weighs 10.2kg.

Total ammunition supply is 40 rounds of 76mm (if the NBC pack is not installed an additional 20 rounds can be carried) and 3,000 rounds of 7.62 ammunition in belts of 200 rounds.

The suspension is of the torsion-bar type and consists of five aluminium road wheels with the drive sprocket at the front and the idler at the rear. There are no track support rollers. Hydraulic shock absorbers are fitted on the first and fifth road wheel stations. The lightweight tracks are fitted with rubber pads.

The fuel tank, which is rubber, is at the rear of the hull. This is built by FPT Industries Limited. The engine is to the right of the driver and is a derated version of the famous car engine, also used in the Fox armoured car. If required a GM diesel could be installed in place of the petrol engine, which would give the Scorpion increased range. The Scorpion has a TN-15X cross-drive transmission which provides seven speeds in each direction. This was developed from the Chieftain tank transmission. A mixed flow fan draws air through the radiator which is situated over the gearbox, then over the engine and out through the louvres.

The electrical system is a nominal 27/28.5V and a total of four 6TN 100Amp/hr batteries, two of which are in the turret for use with the radios and two in the hull for starting, lighting, etc. A generator has an output of 140Amps at 28V.

The Scorpion is provided with a flotation screen which is stowed collapsed around the top of the hull, and can be erected in less than five minutes by the crew. It is propelled in the water by its tracks at a speed of 6.44km/hr, but a propeller kit has been developed and this gives a water speed of 9.65km/hr.

The NBC pack is mounted in the hull rear. Optional equipment includes an NBC detection kit, navigation system and an air-conditioning system for use in hot climates. The latter has been developed by Normalair-Garret Limited of Yeovil and has been fitted to the Scorpions purchased by Abu-Dhabi.

VARIANTS
As of December 1975, the only variant in production apart from the basic Scorpion was the Scimitar. The other members of the family will be placed in production during the next few years.

FV102 Anti-Tank Guided Weapon Vehicle Striker
The driver is in the same position as in the basic Scorpion. The commander is seated behind the driver and has a No.16 cupola with eight periscopes and a sight with a magnification of ×1 and ×10. A 7.62mm machine-gun is mounted on the right side of the cupola and can be laid and fired from within the turret. A total of 3,000 rounds of ammunition are carried for this. The missile controller is to the right of the commander and he has a monocular sight with a magnification of ×1 and ×10, this being of the split-field type. The sight can be traversed 55° left and right. Both the commander and missile controller have a single-piece hatch cover.

On the rear of the hull roof is a launcher box with five BAC Swingfire ATGWs. This launcher box is normally in the horizontal position and is elevated before the missiles are launched. A further five missiles are carried in the hull rear, and these have to be loaded into the launcher from outside the hull. There is a single door in the hull rear. Two Lyran launchers are provided on the front of the hull for target illumination at night. Two four-barrelled smoke dischargers are fitted on the hull front.

FV 101 Scorpion CVR(T) in desert livery.

Top Detailed section drawing of a FV 101 Scorpion CVR(T).
Above FV 101 Scorpion CVR(T) with flotation screen raised.
Left A FV 101 Scorpion having its TN-15X transmission removed during exercise Advent Express held late in 1975.
Right FV 102 Striker launching a BAC Swingfire ATGW.

FV103 Spartan Armoured Personnel carrier
This has a similar hull to the Striker and its crew consists of commander, gunner/radio-operator, driver (same facilities and position as the Scorpion), and four infantry. The gunner has a similar cupola to that fitted to the Striker and also has a night sight. The commander is to the right of the gunner and has three periscopes and a single-piece hatch cover that opens to the right.

The personnel compartment is at the rear and this has hatches in the roof and a single door in the hull rear. There are two periscopes in each side of the hull roof and a single vision block in the rear door.

A total of 2,000 rounds of 7.62mm ammunition are carried and smoke dischargers are also provided. A ZB.298 ground surveillance radar can be fitted on top of the hull if required. A variant of the Spartan with the American TOW anti-tank missile is under development.

The Spartan will not replace the FV432 APC, and will be used as a missile resupply vehicle for the Striker and for other roles such as carrying Royal Engineer Demolition teams.

FV104 Samaritan Armoured Ambulance
This has the same hull as the Sultan command vehicle but with an additional .304m of height. Its crew consists of commander/medical orderly, driver and four stretcher patients or two stretcher and three sitting patients or six sitting patients. The commander has a single-piece hatch cover that opens to the rear and a total of five periscopes. There is a single door in the hull rear. This model is unarmed.

FV105 Sultan Armoured Command Vehicle
This has a higher roof than other members of the family and has a crew of up to six men—commander, radio-operator, driver and two to three staff members. The rear of the vehicle is provided with radios and mapboards and an additional set of batteries. A penthouse can be erected at the rear of the hull to increase the working area. The commander has a single-piece hatch cover that opens to the rear and three periscopes. Armament consists of a pintle-mounted 7.62mm machine-gun and 2,000 rounds of ammunition. Smoke dischargers are also fitted.

FV106 Sampson Armoured Recovery Vehicle
This has the same hull as the Spartan APC. A heavy-duty main winch is mounted in the rear of the hull. This is driven from the main engine and has a variable speed of up to 122m/min. 229m of wire rope are provided. Maximum pull with a 4 : 1 block is 12,000kg. Spades are provided at the hull rear. Both the commander and gunner have single-piece hatch covers and three periscopes.

FV107 Scimitar
This has the same hull and turret as the Scorpion but the latter has been modified to accept the 30mm Rarden cannon. A full description of the Rarden is given in the entry for the CVR(W)Fox.

The 30mm cannon has an elevation of +40° and a depression of −10°, and the turret can be traversed through 360°. A 7.62mm machine-gun is mounted to the left of the main armament and smoke dischargers are also provided. Total ammunition capacity is 165 rounds of 30mm and 3,000 rounds of 7.62mm ammunition.

FV 103 Spartan Armoured Personnel Carrier.

The FV 104 Samaritan Ambulance which is unarmed.

The FV 105 Sultan Command Vehicle. Note the penthouse stowed at the rear of the vehicle.

The FV 106 Sampson Recovery Vehicle with spades in position.

The FV 107 Scimitar armed with the 30mm Rarden Cannon.

GREAT BRITAIN

FOX – ARMOURED CAR (COMBAT VEHICLE RECONNAISSANCE, WHEELED)
MANUFACTURER – Royal Ordnance Factory, Leeds
STATUS – In service with Great Britain, Iran, Nigeria and Saudi Arabia. In production.

BASIC DATA

CREW:	3 (commander, gunner, driver)	MAXIMUM ROAD SPEED:	104km
WEIGHT LOADED:	6.386kg	MAXIMUM WATER SPEED:	5km/hr
	5,733kg	FUEL CAPACITY:	145 litres
LENGTH:	5.359m (gun forward)	FORDING:	1.016m
	2.242m (hull)		Amphibious with screen up
WIDTH:	2.134m	GRADIENT:	50%
HEIGHT:	2.2m	VERTICAL OBSTACLE:	.5m
	1.981m (top of turret)	TRENCH:	1.22m (with channels)
GROUND CLEARANCE:	.3m	ENGINE:	Jaguar 4.2 litre 6-cylinder petrol,
TRACK:	1.753m		developing 195BHP at 5,000rpm
WHEELBASE:	2.464m		(4,235cc).
TYRES:	11.00 × 20		
GROUND PRESSURE:	.46kg/cm²	ARMAMENT:	1 × 30mm Rarden cannon
POWER TO WEIGHT RATIO:	30BHP/TON.		1 × 7.62mm co-axial M/G
TURNING RADIUS:	6.1m		2 × 4 smoke dischargers

DEVELOPMENT

Development of the Fox (FV 721) started in 1965 at FVDRE (now MVEE), and in 1966 a contract was awarded to Daimler's at Radford, Coventry to build prototypes. Construction of the first prototype started in 1966 and was completed in 1967. A total of 15 prototypes were built by Daimler's.

The production contract was, however, awarded to the Royal Ordnance Factory at Leeds, who were building (and still are) the Chieftain MBT. The first production Fox was completed in May 1973. With the awarding of the production contract to the ROF and the running down of the Ferret production line, Daimler closed down their fighting vehicle section which had been building wheeled armoured vehicles for over thirty years. Daimler is now part of the British Leyland Motor Corporation and two divisions of BLMC are supplying parts of the Fox to the Royal Ordnance Factory at Leeds; Jaguar supply the engine and Alvis the turret.

The Fox has been designed to replace some of the Ferret scout cars in service and it is a logical development of the Ferret vehicle.

DESCRIPTION

The hull and turret of the Fox is of all-welded aluminium armour, the armour being produced by Alcan Industries. Fox is the first armoured car in the world to be constructed of aluminium. Some of the late production Ferrets (the Mk. 5) did have some aluminium components.

The driver is seated at the front of the vehicle and is provided with a one-piece hatch cover that lifts and swings to the right to open. The hatch has an integral wide-angle periscope which can be replaced by an infra-red or image-intensification periscope for night operations.

The turret is in the centre of the hull and is provided with a turret basket. The commander, who also acts as loader for the Rarden gun, is seated on the left, and the gunner is seated on the right. Both the commander and gunner are provided with a single-piece hatch cover that opens to the rear.

The commander has one periscope binocular ×1 and ×10 in a rotating mounting in front of his hatch, and in addition there are a total of seven periscopes arranged around his hatch cover to the sides and rear. The gunner has two observation periscopes and a periscope binocular linked to the main armament with a magnification of ×1 and ×10.

The image-intensifier night sight is mounted to the right of the main armament and has been developed by Rank Pullin Controls (a division of Rank Precision Industries) and is called the SPAV (or L2A1 by the Army). It has two ranges – high-range with a magnification of ×5.8 and a 8° field of view, and low-range with the magnification of ×1.6 and a field of view of 28°. It has two objectives mounted one within the other; the outer ×5.8 is used for gunnery and the inner is used for surveillance. When the gun is fired the image-intensifier tube is protected from muzzle flash by a shutter. An illuminated ballistic graticule is automatically injected into the optical system when high magnification is selected. The window is provided with a screen wiper and a washer. The night sight will also detect infra-red devices. If required the vehicle can be delivered without the image-intensifier.

The Fox is armed with the Rarden 30mm cannon which has been developed by the Royal Armament Research and Development Establishment at Fort Halstead and the Royal Small Arms Factory at Enfield

Lock, Middlesex, where it is now in production. The Rarden is mounted in a turret with a traverse of 360° by hand, the internal turret ring diameter being 1.27m. The gun can be elevated from −14° to +41°, and no stabilization system is fitted at the present time. One of the features of the Rarden gun is that the gun mechanism is housed within a compact light alloy casing, with a short inboard length. The overall length of the Rarden is 3.15m of which only 43cm is inboard. It weighs 100kg, which is less than that of the comparable Swiss HS 831.

The Rarden can fire either single, aimed shots or bursts of up to six rounds. Maximum rate of fire is 90-100 rounds per minute, but this would soon use up the ammunition as only 99 rounds are carried. Ammunition is fed to the gun in clips of three rounds and the empty brass cartridge cases are ejected outside the vehicle. Not only does this mean the turret is not cluttered up with shell cases but also there are no powder fumes in the fighting compartment.

The Rarden gun can fire all types of Hispano 831L ammunition and in addition two special rounds have been developed – the APDS-T (Armoured Piercing Discarding Sabot – Tracer) and the more recent APSE-T (Armour Piercing Special Explosive—Tracer). The APDS-T round has an effective range of over 1,000m, can defeat light armoured vehicles and will penetrate the sides of MBTs. The APSE-T penetrates the armour before exploding. The British rounds have the following features: the round is not armed until it is 20m away from the barrel, and if the target is not hit in 7-10 seconds the shell will destruct. Nor will it function if it hits foliage, etc. Basic data on the ammunition are given below:

	British		Hispano		
	APSE-T	APDS-T	HE(UIAT)	AP(RINT)	PRACTICE
WEIGHT OF PROJECTILE gram:	360	290	360	360	360
WEIGHT OF FILLING (HE) gram:	28	—	28	—	—
WEIGHT OF CARTRIDGE CASE gram:	366	350	350	350	350
WEIGHT OF COMPLETE ROUND gram:	886	780	870	872	870
MUZZLE VELOCITY m/s:	1,080	1,200+	1,100	1,080	1,080

The 30mm cannon and the co-axial 7.62mm machine-gun are electrically operated but with manual over-riding control. If required one man can operate the weapon. The co-axial machine-gun is mounted to the right of the main armament and a total of 2,600 rounds of ammunition are carried for this. There are four smoke dischargers mounted either side of the turret and these are fired electrically from within the vehicle.

The Rarden cannon is also fitted to the FV 107 Scimitar and the complete Fox turret is mounted on a modified FV 432 for use with Mechanised Battalions. There has also been a trials mount for the M113.

The engine and transmission are mounted at the rear of the hull. The Jaguar XK militarized engine is the same as that used in the CVR (T) Scorpion and has been developed from the famous sports car engine. It has a modified induction system and a reduced compression ratio. A Ki-gas cold-starting system is fitted.

The cooling system comprises twin radiators horizontally disposed across the top and rear of the engine, and a pair of ducted centrifugal fans are sealed to the radiator. Drive is transmitted to all four wheels through a fluid coupling, and a five-speed pre-selective epicyclic gearbox and a transfer box provide a total of five speeds in each direction. An oil-water heat exchanger serves both the engine and the transfer case.

The Fox has independent suspension on all four wheels. Each wheel has an upper and a lower wishbone, coil spring and a hydraulic telescopic damper. The steering is power-assisted and Lockheed disc brakes are mounted front and rear. These, too, are power-assisted and hydraulically operated. Tyres are of the run flat type.

A 24V electrical system is mounted together with two 6TN batteries giving 100 Amp/hour capacity. A rectified AC generator gives 140 Amps output.

The Fox can ford to a depth of 1.016m. A flotation screen is carried around the top of the hull. This can be erected in 70 seconds and is held in position by stays. The Fox is propelled and steered in the water by its wheels.

If required the Fox can be fitted with the ZB 298 Radar System, a navigational system and an NBC kit. Infra-red or image-intensification driving equipment are also available.

VARIANTS
There are no variants of the Fox. There was a development of the Fox called the Combat Vehicle Reconnaissance (Wheeled) Liaison Vixen (FV 722). This was developed to replace the Ferret in the liaison role. It used many automotive components of the Fox but with a new hull. The Vixen, was however, cancelled in the Defence cuts of December 1974. It is expected that the Ferret will be suitably modified to replace the cancelled vehicle.

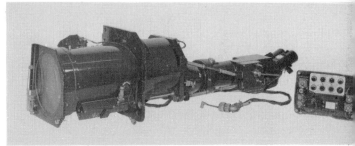

Top One of the prototypes of the CVR(W) Fox.
Above One of the first production CVR(W) Fox.
Above right The Rank Precision L2A1
Image-intensifier Nightsight as fitted to the CVR(W)
Fox.
Right One of the prototypes of the now cancelled
CVR(L) Vixen vehicle.

GREAT BRITAIN

SHORLAND – ARMOURED PATROL VEHICLE
MANUFACTURER – Short Brothers and Harland Limited, Belfast, Northern Ireland
STATUS – In service with 20 countries including Argentina, Brunei, Great Britain (Ulster Defence Regiment), Libya, Persian Gulf States and Thailand. In production.

BASIC DATA

CREW:	3 (commander, gunner and driver)	RANGE:	257km (standard tank) 514km (long-range tank)
WEIGHT LOADED:	3,360kg	FUEL CAPACITY:	64 litres (standard tank)
WEIGHT EMPTY:	2,931kg		128 litres (long-range tank)
LENGTH:	4.597m		
WIDTH:	1.778m	VERTICAL OBSTACLE:	.23m
HEIGHT:	2.286m (including turret)	ENGINE:	Rover 6-cylinder petrol engine developing 91BHP at 1,750rpm
GROUND CLEARANCE:	.21m (minimum)		
TRACK:	1.358m		
WHEELBASE:	2.768m	ARMAMENT:	1 × 7.62mm MG (see text)
TYRES:	9.00 × 16		
TURNING RADIUS:	8.84m	ARMOUR:	8.25-11mm
MAXIMUM ROAD SPEED:	88.5km/hr		

Note: The above data relate to the Shorland Mk.3

DEVELOPMENT

The Shorland was designed to meet the requirements of the Royal Ulster Constabulary and they used them until they were taken over by the British Army. The first prototype was completed in 1965 as was the first production vehicle. These were built at Newtownards and were known as the Mk.1. They were powered by a four-cylinder Rover petrol engine which developed 67BHP at 4,100rpm and their hull armour was 7.25mm thick. These were followed by the Mk.2 which had thicker armour (hull thickness being 8.25mm) and were powered by a four-cylinder petrol engine developing 77BHP at 4,100rpm. These had a range of 322km on a standard fuel tank, or 644km on a long-range tank. Production is now undertaken at the main Belfast plant of Short Brothers and Harland, with the current production model being the Mk.3. By mid-1975 Shorts had sold over 400 Shorlands to twenty countries.

DESCRIPTION

The Shorland armoured patrol vehicle is essentially a Land Rover (Long Wheelbase) chassis fitted with an armoured body. It is available in both LHD and RHD models. The chassis has a number of modifications to suit it to its new role, including a larger radiator, modified and stronger axles and different final drives. The hull is of all-welded construction and provides the crew with complete protection from both 7.62mm rifle and machine-gun fire. The floor is of reinforced fibreglass construction.

The driver and commander are seated at the front of the vehicle and each is provided with a windscreen which can be covered by an armoured hatch with an integral vision block. They are each provided with a side door in the top of which is a hatch that can be opened from the inside.

The turret runs on nylon runners and is traversed by the gunner's feet. It can be locked in position if required. The turret is provided with a seat and the roof of the turret folds forwards whilst the rear folds downwards.

An escape hatch is provided in the rear of the crew compartment and the air extraction system is installed in this hatch. The petrol tank is enclosed within the armour-plated boot, with the filler cap being released from within the vehicle. The spare wheel is also stowed in the boot.

The inside of the hull is lined with thick polyurethane foam faced with plastic sheeting, which provides additional thermal insulation for the crew.

The turret can be fitted with a variety of weapons, the most common being a .30 Browning machine-gun or a 7.62mm FN GPMG. The weapon is aimed by a combined periscope sight, and a searchlight is mounted on the right side of the turret, which moves in elevation with the main armament. A total of 1,500 rounds of machine-gun ammunition are carried. If required a tear gas discharger can be mounted in place of the machine-gun and loaded from within the vehicle. Smoke dischargers can be mounted either side of the turret or on each mudguard.

The engine compartment is armoured on both sides, as is the roof. Armoured louvres are fitted to the front of the radiator and the bonnet can only be opened from inside the vehicle.

The gearbox has 4F and 1R gears and a two-speed transfer case. The electrical system is 24V negative earth. The suspension consists of heavy semi-elliptical springs front and rear with hydraulic shock absorbers, and in addition anti-roll bars are provided front and rear.

VARIANTS

A Shorland was fitted with a Vigilant ATGW either side of the turret but this was not adopted. There was also a project to fit a Shorland with a water cannon but this was dropped. Shorts have recently designed a companion vehicle to the Shorland called the SB.301, and for this there is a separate entry. The Shorland can be fitted with a variety of radio installations and a loud-hailer if required.

Above Shorland Mk.3 Armoured Patrol Car with smoke dischargers mounted on turret.
Left Shorland Armoured Patrol Car as used in Northern Ireland.

GREAT BRITAIN

ALVIS SALADIN – ARMOURED CAR
MANUFACTURER – Alvis Limited (now part of the British Leyland Motor Corporation), Coventry
STATUS – In service with Abu Dhabi, Bahrain, Great Britain (mainly with Territorial units), German Border Police, Ghana, Indonesia, Jordan, Kenya, Kuwait, Libya, Muscat and Oman, Nigeria, Portugal, Qatar, Sudan, Tunisia, Uganda, Yemen. No longer in production.

BASIC DATA

CREW:	3 (commander/loader, gunner and driver)	VERTICAL OBSTACLE:	.46m
		TRENCH:	1.52m
WEIGHT LOADED:	11,590kg	ANGLE OF APPROACH:	60°
WEIGHT EMPTY:	10,500kg	ANGLE OF DEPARTURE:	50°
LENGTH:	5.284m (gun forward) 4.93m (hull)	ENGINE:	Rolls-Royce B80 Mk.6A, 8-cylinder petrol engine developing 160HP at 3,750rpm
WIDTH:	2.54m		
HEIGHT:	2.93m (top of gunner's periscope)	ARMAMENT:	1 × 76mm gun
	2.19m (top of turret roof)		1 × .30 (Browning) (7.62mm) co-axial MG
	1.854m (axis of bore)		1 × .30 (Browning) (7.62mm) A/A MG
GROUND CLEARANCE:	.426m		6 × 2 smoke dischargers
TRACK:	2.038m		
WHEELBASE:	1.524m + 1.524m	ARMOUR	
TYRES:	12.00 × 20	hull glacis:	12mm at 45°
GROUND PRESSURE:	1.12kg/cm^2	nose:	14mm at 42°
TURNING RADIUS:	7.31m	hull sides:	16mm at 20°
MAXIMUM ROAD SPEED:	72km/hr	hull rear:	16mm
RANGE:	400km (road)	hull roof:	10-12mm
FUEL CAPACITY:	241 litres	hull floor:	8-12mm
FORDING:	1.07m	turret front:	32mm at 15°
	2.13m (with kit)	turret sides and rear:	16mm
GRADIENT:	42%	turret roof:	10mm

DEVELOPMENT

Shortly after the end of the Second World War the British Army issued a requirement for a new armoured car. Design work started in 1947 and a contract was awarded to Alvis Limited to build two prototypes of a 6 × 6 armoured car designated the FV 601. The first mock-up was completed in 1948 and it was proposed to arm the vehicle with a two-pounder gun. This model was known as the FV 601(A). The two-pounder was soon dropped and it was decided to arm the FV 601(B) with a new 76mm gun. The first two prototypes were completed by Alvis in 1952/53. These were followed by six pre-production vehicles, built by Crossley Motors of Stockport, which had a different turret to production vehicles. After further modifications the FV 601(C) entered production at Coventry in late 1958 with first production vehicles being completed in 1959. Production continued until 1972. The production vehicle was known as the Saladin Mk.2 or FV 601(C) Armoured Car 76mm (Alvis Saladin Mk.2 6 × 6). In British Army service it was issued to both Regular and Territorial Reserve Armoured Car Regiments, and is still in service with the latter although most Regular Regiments have now replaced the Saladin with the Scorpion CVR(T) which is also built by Alvis and has a similar 76mm gun. The vehicle has seen operational service in many parts of the world including Borneo, Malaya, Aden, Jordan and North Africa.

DESCRIPTION

The hull of the Saladin is of all-welded construction with the driver seated at the front of the vehicle. He is provided with a total of three No.17 periscopes, one in front of him and one on either side. The hatch to his immediate front folds forwards. The turret is in the centre of the hull and there is an escape hatch in each side of the hull just below the turret ring. The engine is at the rear of the hull and is separated from the fighting compartment by a fireproof bulkhead. The three fuel tanks are also in the engine compartment. Air for the engine compartment is drawn in via six louvred engine covers by two fans. It then passes through the radiators and is expelled through grilles at the very rear of the hull. The layout from the rear of the engine compartment is: radiator, engine, fluid flywheel, preselector gearbox, transfer box and differential and thence to the six wheels. The coupling is a Daimler fluid coupling and the gearbox is an epicyclic five-speed. The transfer box has a bevel and helical gear and incorporates a reverse and differential unit. There are six bevel boxes, ie one for each wheel, of the spiral bevel type. The final drives (ie one for each wheel) consist of articulating axle shafts from the bevel box connecting an epicyclic wheel hub reduction gear through two tracta constant velocity joints. The drive shafts are inside the hull.

The suspension is of the fully independent type fitted with torsion bars and sleeves, and double acting hydraulic shock absorbers. The steering is of the re-circulating ball type and is power-assisted. Steering is on the front four wheels. Disc brakes are fitted on all wheels.

The electrical system is 24V negative earth and there are two 12V batteries with a capacity of 60Amp hours. A two-speed automatic generator with a maximum output of 75Amps is provided.

The commander is seated to the right of the gun and the gunner to the left. Both are provided with a single-piece hatch cover that opens to the rear. The commander has four No.17 periscopes arranged around the forward part of the hatch and a single swivelling periscope to the rear of the hatch cover. The gunner has a periscope with a × 6 sight and a × 1 observation window. This periscope is provided with a wiper. A fan extractor is fitted inside the turret. The turret has full traverse through 360°, and traverse is powered with manual controls for use in an emergency. The 76mm L5A1 gun has an elevation of + 20° and a depression of − 10°. It has a vertically sliding breech-block and a hydro-spring recoil mechanism. A .30 M1919A4 (L3A3/L3A4) machine-gun is mounted to the left of the main armament and a similar machine-gun is mounted to the right of the commander's hatch. Total ammunition capacity is 43 rounds of 76mm and 2,750 rounds of machine-gun ammunition.

The following types of 76mm ammunition are carried:
HESH, complete round weighs 7.4kg with the projectile weighing 5.39kg.
HE, complete round weighs 7.33kg with the projectile weighing 5.36kg, and maximum effective range of 5,000m.
Smoke (Base Ejection) complete round weighs 10.2kg with the projectile weighing 8.51kg.
Canister, deadly when used against infantry at a range of around 100m.
Squash Head Practice training round.
The Saladin is not fitted with an NBC system and does not have any infra-red fighting aids. It would be simple to fit the latter.

VARIANTS
FV 601(D)
This is used by the German Border Police (*Bundesgrenzschutz*) and does not have a co-axial machine-gun. It has German type lights and German type smoke dischargers. Its German designation is Geschützter Sonderwagen 111 (SW 111) (Kfz 93). There was a project to fit a Fox turret to the Saladin and this may well be still available to those countries still using the Saladin.

The Australian Army have fitted the Saladin turret to an M113 vehicle and have renamed it the M113A1 Fire Support vehicle. This is in service with the Australian Army. A feasibility study was carried out between Alvis and the Guided Weapons Division of the British Aircraft Corporation to fit Swingfire to Saladin. This reached the mock-up stage. It basically consisted of a standard Saladin with a single Swingfire in the ready-to-fire position either side of the turret, with a further two missiles in reserve at the rear of the turret.

A Saladin was also fitted with a flotation screen but this was not adopted for service.

Left Saladin armoured car of the Queen's Own Hussars on patrol in Hong Kong in 1969.
Right Saladin armoured car of the Royal Armoured Corps Centre, Bovington.

GREAT BRITAIN

DAIMLER FERRET–LIGHT SCOUT CAR/RECONNAISSANCE VEHICLE

MANUFACTURER–Daimler Company, Coventry
STATUS–In service with Abu Dhabi, Bahrein, Brunei, Burma, Cameroon, Canada, Ceylon, France (Foreign Legion, some of which are armed with a 75mm recoilless rifle), Gambia, Ghana, Great Britain, Iran, Indonesia, Iraq, Jamaica, Jordan, Kenya, Kuwait, Libya, Malagasy, Malaysia, Malawi (from South Africa), Muscat and Oman, New Zealand, Nigeria, Qatar, Ras Al Khaimah, Rhodesia, Sierra Leone, Somali, South Africa, South and North Yemen, Sudan, Uganda, Upper Volta, Zaire, Zambia. Production of the Ferret is now complete.

BASIC DATA	Mk.1/1 FV701	Mk.1/2 FV704	Mk.2/3 FV701	Mk.2/6 FV703	Mk.4 FV711	Mk.5 FV712
CREW:	2-3	3	2	2	2-3	2
WEIGHT LOADED:	4,210kg	4,370kg	4,395kg	4,560kg	5,400kg	5,890kg
WEIGHT EMPTY:	3,510kg	3,660kg	3,684kg	3,680kg	4,725kg	4,980kg
LENGTH:	3.835m	3.835m	3.835m	3.835m	3.962m	3.962m
WIDTH:	1.905m	1.905m	1.905m	1.905m	2.133m	2.133m
HEIGHT:	1.448m	1.651m	1.879m	1.879m	2.336m	2.044m
GROUND CLEARANCE:	.33m	.33m	.33m	.33m	.41m	.41m
TRACK:	1.549m	1.549m	1.549m	1.549m	1.75m	1.75m
WHEELBASE:	2.286m	2.286m	2.286m	2.286m	2.286m	2.286m
TYRES:	9.00 × 16	9.00 × 16	9.00 × 16	9.00 × 16	11.00 × 20	11.00 × 20
TURNING RADIUS:	5.795m	5.795m	5.795m	5.795m	5.795m	5.795m
MAXIMUM ROAD SPEED:	93km/hr	93km/hr	93km/hr	93km/hr	80km/hr	80km/hr
RANGE (road):	300km	300km	300km	300km	300km	300km
FUEL CAPACITY (litres):	96	96	96	96	96	96
FORDING (w/o kit):	.914m	.914m	.914m	.914m	.914m	.914m
FORDING (with kit):	1.524m	1.524m	1.524m	1.524m	Amphibious	Amphibious
GRADIENT:	46%	46%	46%	46%	46%	46%
VERTICAL OBSTACLE:	.406m	.406m	.406m	.406m	.406m	.406m
TRENCH (with channels):	1.22m	1.22m	1.22m	1.22m	1.22m	1.22m
ENGINE:	All are powered by a Rolls-Royce B60 Mk.6A, 6-cylinder, in-line, water-cooled petrol engine developing 129BHP at 3,750rpm.					

ARMOUR thickness is given below and applies to all Ferrets except Mk.5 (where it applies to the hull but not to the turret):

hull front:	12mm at 50°	driver's floor:	10mm
hull front:	16mm at 35°	floor, apart from driver's:	6mm
hull side:	12mm at 20° and 15°	turret front:	16mm at 15°
hull sides:	16mm at 15°	turret sides:	16mm at 15°
hull rear:	12mm at 45°	turret rear:	16mm at 15°
hull rear:	6mm at 45°	turret roof:	8mm at 75° and 90°

Fuel consumption is 3.2km/litre whilst travelling on roads and 1.7km/litre whilst travelling across country.

DEVELOPMENT

Shortly after the end of the Second World War the War Office drew up a requirement for a new 4 × 4 scout car. The development contract went to Daimler who, during the war, had built large numbers of armoured and scout cars for the British Army. The first prototype, a Mk.1, was completed in 1949 and delivered to the Army for trials in 1950. It was placed in almost immediate production with the first production vehicles (Mk.2s) coming off the production line in mid-1952. The first Mk.1 came off in October 1952. The Ferret remained in production until 1971 and the last vehicles built were a small quantity of Mk.2/6 with Vigilant ATGW for Abu Dhabi. Total production of the Ferret amounted to 4,409 vehicles. The Ferret was to have been replaced by the Fox and the Vixen CVR(W) vehicles. Daimler developed the Fox CVR(L) from the mid-1960s, but the production contract was awarded to the Royal Ordnance Factory at Leeds and Daimler closed down the AFV side after thirty years of design and production. The Vixen was cancelled in the December 1974 Defence cuts and it was stated that Ferrets would continue in service for at least a further ten years. A number of Ferrets will probably be fitted with a more up-to-date armament installation and a flotation screen and bigger wheels.

DESCRIPTION

The hull of the Ferret is of all-welded construction with the driver at the front, fighting compartment in the centre and the engine at the rear of the hull.

The driver has hatches to his sides and front, which swing up to give added visibility, and each hatch is provided with a No. 17 Mk.3 periscope. The other two crew members are seated in the centre of the hull. Either side of the fighting compartment is a small glass observation block. And in the rear of the compartment are two small hatches which can be opened for observation purposes. A spare wheel is carried on the left side of the hull and there are stowage bins on the right.

The clutch is a Daimler Fluid Coupling and the gearbox a Daimler pre-selective, five-speed unit. The transfer box has forward and reverse gear trains with spiral bevel directional control gears with positive dog engagement and a double helical drop-down gear to a single central bevel type differential. This, in combination with the gearbox, provides 5F and 5R gears.

Power is transmitted from the engine through the fluid coupling to the pre-selective gearbox and thence to the transfer box which in turn transmits power to the four propeller shafts. Each wheel station has a bevel box and the wheel hubs have reduction gears.

Steering is of the recirculating ball type on the front wheels and is not power assisted. The brakes are hydraulic and run-flat tyres are provided. The road wheels are mounted on fully independent coil springs with wishbone linkages. The single coil spring encloses the double acting hydraulic shock-absorber. Access to the engine is via roof hatches. The electrical system is 24V and two × 12V, 60Amp/hr batteries are carried. A two speed generator (automatic), with an output of 25 Amps at 600rpm is fitted.

The Ferret does not have infra-red driving lights nor does it have an NBC system. The basic model is not amphibious although a deep fording kit is available. The latter consists of a bellow type unit over the commander's hatch and an extension unit over the radiator at the rear.

There are minor differences between production models in such things as thickness of armour and type of threads. All Ferrets have three smoke dischargers mounted on the sides of the hull.

VARIANTS

Ferret Mk.1/1 FV701(J)
Full designation is Scout Car Liaison. This is the basic model and is armed with either a 7.62mm Bren LMG or a Browning .30 (7.62mm) MG. The vehicle has an open roof which can be covered by a canvas cover when required.
Total ammunition capacity is 450 rounds. Some Mk.1/1s have a flotation screen.

Ferret Mk.1/2(FV704)
This is identical to the above model but has a small flat turret and is armed with an externally mounted Bren LMG.

Ferret Mk.2/2
This was a local modification carried out in the Far East and was not produced in large numbers. It is essentially a Ferret Mk.2 with an extension collar between the top of the hull and the machine-gun turret.

Ferret Mk.2/3
This is the basic Mk.1 hull with a turret armed with a .30 (7.62mm) Browning machine-gun. The turret is traversed by hand through a full 360°. The machine-gun has an elevation of +45° and a depression of −15°. The weapon is aimed using a No.3 Mk.1 periscope which is mounted in the roof of the turret. Total ammunition capacity is 2,500 rounds. The Ferret Mk.2/4 is a Mk.2/3 with additional armour whilst the Mk.2/5 is a Mk.2/1 brought up to Mk.2/4 standard. The Mk.2/3 can be fitted with the ZB 298 ground surveillance radar.

Ferret Mk.2/6(FV703)
The full designation of this model is Scout Car Reconnaissance/Guided Weapon Mk.2/6. It is essentially a Mk.2/3 with a single British Aircraft Corporation (Guided Weapons Division) Vigilant ATGW mounted in a launcher box on each side of the turret. Both missiles have a common elevating mechanism and are launched from within the vehicle or away from the vehicle with the aid of a combined sight/controller and separation cable. A further two spare missiles are carried in their launcher boxes on the left side of the hull in place of the spare wheel. The Vigilant ATGW has a minimum range of 200m and a maximum range of 1,375m. The missile itself weighs 14kg and is wire guided. A hollow charge warhead is provided. The Mk.2/6 retains its .30 machine-gun.

Ferret Mk.2/7
This is a Mk.2/6 with Vigilant missile installation removed, and is almost identical to the Mk.2/3.

Ferret Mk.3
This is a Mk.1/1 with a collapsible flotation screen, bigger wheels and modified suspension. It is in service only with the British Army.

Ferret Mk.4(FV711)

This is a Mk.2/3 but with stronger suspension units, disc brakes in place of the drum brakes on earlier models, larger wheels and tyres. A flotation screen is carried around the top of the hull, which can be quickly erected and the vehicle can propel itself across rivers and streams by its wheels. The Mk.4 is only in service with the British Army.

Ferret Mk.5(FV712)

This was to have been built in large numbers but in fact less than 50 were built and these were conversions of earlier vehicles. Its full designation is Scout Car Reconnaissance/Guided Weapon Mk.5. It consists of a basic Ferret hull with modified suspension, bigger wheels and tyres, flotation screen and a new turret. The turret is of aluminium armour and can be traversed through a full 360° by hand. A 7.62mm machine-gun is mounted in the front of the turret for local protection. There is a total of four British Aircraft Corporation Swingfire ATGWs in the turret, two each side. These are elevated to fire and can be launched from within the vehicle or away from the vehicle with the aid of a combined sight/controller and a separation cable. A further two missiles are carried under armour, one each side of the hull.

The Swingfire ATGW is wire guided and has a maximum range of 4,000m and a minimum range of less than 150m. Additional information on the Swingfire is given in the entry for the FV438 vehicle in the FV432 APC entry. The Ferret Mk.5 is employed only with the British Army.

1

2

3

4

5

6

▼7

1 Ferret Mk.1/1 from the rear.
2 Ferret Mk.1/1 from the front.
3 Ferret Mk.2/3.
4 Ferret Mk.2/3 showing turret detail.
5 Ferret Mk.2/6 firing Vigilant ATGW.
6 Ferret Mk.4 complete with flotation screen.
7 Ferret Mk.5 with Swingfire ATGW being launched.

HUNGARY

FUG-70–AMPHIBIOUS SCOUT CAR   (FUG Felderítö Úszó Gépkocsi)
MANUFACTURER–Hungarian State Arsenals
CURRENT STATUS–In service with East Germany and Hungary. Probably still in production

BASIC DATA

CREW:	3+6	GRADIENT:	30°
	(commander, gunner,	VERTICAL OBSTACLE:	.4m
	driver and 6 passengers)	TRENCH:	.6m (with channels)
WEIGHT LOADED:	7,000kg	ENGINE:	Raba-MAN D-2156,
LENGTH:	5.79m		6-cylinder, in-line water-
WIDTH:	2.362m		cooled diesel
HEIGHT:	2.525m (including turret)	ARMAMENT:	1 × 14.5mm KPVT MG with
GROUND CLEARANCE:	.305m		500 rounds, 1 × 7.62mm
TRACK:	1.9m		PKT MG with 2,000 rounds.
WHEELBASE:	3.2m		These are mounted in a
TYRE SIZE:	30.00 × 18		turret with a traverse of 360°,
MAXIMUM ROAD SPEED:	100km/hr		elevation of weapons is
WATER SPEED:	10km/hr		from −5° to +30°
RANGE:	500km	ARMOUR:	10mm

DEVELOPMENT

The FUG-70 was first seen during a parade held in Budapest on 4th April 1970. The FUG-70 was a development of the FUG-66 which was first seen in September 1966. The FUG-66 had a very small turret which was armed with a 23mm cannon and a 7.62mm machine-gun. In effect the FUG-66 served as a prototype to the FUG-70, as the FUG-66 was built in small numbers and has not been seen in recent years.

DESCRIPTION

The hull of the FUG-70 is of all-welded construction and has a different superstructure that extends the full width of the hull when compared to the OT-65(FUG). Doors are provided in each side of the hull. The driver is provided with two armour-plated windows. When in action these are covered by two steel hatch covers, each of which is provided with a vision block. There are also two roof hatches over the driver's compartment. The turret, which is in the centre of the vehicle, has no hatch cover. The 7.62mm machine-gun is on the left of the turret with the 14.5mm machine-gun in the centre. The searchlight is to the right of the 14.5mm gun and moves with the armament. Vision blocks are provided in the front, sides and rear of the hull, and in addition there are two firing ports in each side of the hull.

The FUG-70 is fully amphibious, being propelled in the water by two water jets, which, when not in use, are covered by two covers. Before entering the water a trim vane is erected at the front of the vehicle.

Apart from the shape of the superstructure the FUG-70 can be distinguished from the OT-65 as the FUG-70 has a turret and no belly wheels, and unlike the Soviet BRDM, the engine of the FUG-70 is at the rear. The lack of belly wheels does mean that the vehicle does not have the same cross-country capability as the BRDM and OT-65. It does however mean that there is more room inside the vehicle and it is also powered by a more powerful engine which gives it increased road and water speed. The FUG-70 is fitted with a central type pressure regulation system, NBC system and infra-red driving lights.

The actual role of the FUG-70 is unclear as it can carry a total of six men in addition to its crew of three. These additional men could well be used as a further extension of the vehicle's reconnaissance capability.

VARIANTS

There is known to be a turretless model of the FUG-70 but the present status of this model is uncertain. It would, however, be useful in the command role.

The FUG-70 4×4 Reconnaissance Vehicle.
Right FUG M-1963 Amphibious Scout Car.

HUNGARY

FUG – AMPHIBIOUS SCOUT CAR   FUG M-1963 = Felderítö Úszo Gépkocsi (Hungarian Army); the Czechoslovakian Army called their vehicles the OT-65 (Obrneny Transporter)
MANUFACTURER – Hungarian State Arsenals
CURRENT STATUS – In service with Czechoslovakia, Hungary, Poland, Romania. Production is now complete.

BASIC DATA

CREW:	5	GRADIENT:	32°
WEIGHT LOADED:	6,100kg	VERTICAL OBSTACLE:	.4m
LENGTH OVERALL:	5.79m	TRENCH:	1.3m
WIDTH:	2.362m	ENGINE:	Csepel D-414.44, 4-cylinder water-cooled diesel, in-line developing 100HP at 2,300rpm
HEIGHT:	1.91m (without armament) 2.25m (OT-65A with turret)	ARMAMENT:	1×7.62mm SGMB MG pintle mounted with an elevation of $+23\frac{1}{2}°$, a depression of $-6°$ and a total traverse of 90°. 1,250 rounds of ammunition are carried. Czechoslovakian vehicles have an M59 7.62mm MG
GROUND CLEARANCE:	.305m		
TRACK:	1.91m		
WHEELBASE:	3.2m		
TYRE SIZE:	12.00×18		
MAXIMUM ROAD SPEED:	87km/hr		
WATER SPEED:	9km/hr		
RANGE:	500km		
FUEL CAPACITY:	140 litres		
FUEL CONSUMPTION:	24 litres per 100km	ARMOUR:	10mm

DEVELOPMENT and DESCRIPTION

The FUG is the Hungarian equivalent of the Soviet BRDM(BTR-40P) Amphibious Scout Car. The Hungarian vehicle differs from the Soviet vehicle in a number of ways. The FUG has its engine at the rear and has a different hull and superstructure. Like the Soviet vehicle it has two sets of belly wheels, one set each side. These are powered by a PTO, which not only enables it to cross trenches but also gives it increased mobility across rough country. These belly wheels are lowered into position by the driver when they are required. The FUG is fully amphibious being propelled in the water by two water jets at the rear of the hull. These are covered when not in use. A trim vane is mounted at the front of the vehicle and this is erected before the vehicle enters the water. Bilge pumps are provided. The FUG has a central tyre pressure regulation system and is believed to be fitted with an NBC system. Infra-red headlights are fitted as standard equipment and some models have been fitted with an infra-red searchlight.

The hull of the FUG is of all-welded construction. The driver is at the front of the vehicle and is provided with direct vision through two glass plates. In action each of these is covered by a steel hatch provided with an observation block. The only means of entry and exit for the crew is via the twin roof hatches which open one each side of the vehicle. There are two firing ports in each side of the hull and a further two in the rear of the superstructure. There is also a vision slit in each side of the vehicle.

VARIANTS

Ambulance
The Czechoslovakians are known to use some of these vehicles in the ambulance role, although the vehicle has obvious limitations for this role.

Radiological-Chemical Reconnaissance Vehicle
This carries out a similar mission to the Soviet BRDM(BTR-40P-rkh). Mounted either side on the rear of the hull are specials racks which carry flag dispensers. As the vehicle finds a safe way through a contaminated area the flags are fired into the ground so that following vehicles can follow the same route.

Czechoslovakian OT-65A
This is basically a FUG fitted with the same turret as that fitted to the Czechoslovakian OT-62B tracked armoured personnel carrier. This turret is fitted with a 7.62mm machine-gun, and in addition a T-21 82mm recoilless rifle (also known as the Tarasnice) is fitted externally on the right side of the turret. This can be fired from within the vehicle, but must then be reloaded from outside. The crew enter and leave this model via a small twin hatch cover behind the turret.

ISRAEL

RBY. Mk. 1 – ARMOURED RECONNAISSANCE VEHICLE
MANUFACTURER – Ramta Structures and Systems (a division of Israel Aircraft Industries), Beer Sheva
STATUS – In production and service.

BASIC DATA

CREW:	2 + 6 (commander, driver and 6 men)	FUEL CAPACITY:	140 litres
		FORDING:	.4m
WEIGHT EMPTY:	3,600kg	GRADIENT:	60%
LENGTH	5.023m	ANGLE OF APPROACH:	60°
WIDTH:	2.03m	ANGLE OF DEPARTURE:	50°
HEIGHT:	1.66m (without armament)	ENGINE:	Dodge Model 225.2, 6-cylinder water-cooled petrol engine developing 120HP
GROUND CLEARANCE:	.48m (hull) .35m (transfer case)		
TRACK:	1.665m	ARMAMENT:	See text
WHEELBASE:	3.4m	ARMOUR:	8mm (hull sides, front and rear) (MIL-S-12560) 10mm (hull floor) (SAE-1020)
MAXIMUM ROAD SPEED:	100km/hr		
RANGE:	550km (road) 400km (cross country)		

DEVELOPMENT
The RBY. Mk. 1 was announced by Israel Aircraft Industries at the May 1975 Paris Air Display. At that time it was stated that the vehicle was in production and service. It is not known if the Israeli Army uses the vehicle. IAI did however state that the RBY. Mk. 1 was available for export.

The vehicle has been designed primarily as a cheap reconnaissance vehicle, although it can also be used for other roles including anti-aircraft, anti-tank and as an ambulance. It is air-transportable by both aircraft and helicopter, ie the Sikorsky S-65 (CH-53) which is used by the Israel Defence Force. Wherever possible standard commercial components have been used in the construction of the vehicle.

DESCRIPTION
The hull of the RBY. Mk. 1 is of all-welded construction. The driver is seated at the front of the fighting compartment on the left side with the commander to his right. The front of the fighting compartment can be folded flat to give increased visibility, and it has two observation hatches that open upwards on the outside. There is also an observation hatch either side of the commander and driver. The other six crew members are seated three each side of the hull with their backs to each other. They have no hatches as they have direct vision outside. There is no overhead protection at all to the fighting compartment. The Israelis have found in their many campaigns that eyes are far better for observation purposes than viewing systems.

The wheels are placed at the extreme ends of the hull so that in the event of the vehicle striking a mine the main force of the blast will be as far away from the fighting compartment as possible. In addition the bonnet and fenders are constructed of glass fibre so that they will give way in the event of a mine exploding.

The engine and transmission are at the rear of the vehicle. The transmission has 4F and 1R gears and a two-speed transfer case. Front and rear suspension consist of semi-elliptical springs and hydraulic shock absorbers. The steering is power-assisted and brakes are hydraulic. The electrical system is 24V and $2 \times 12V$ batteries are provided together with a 60Amp alternator. A winch with a capacity of 2,722kg can be provided. The spare wheel can be mounted at the front or rear of the hull.

A wide range of armament can be installed, including a 106mm M40 Recoilless Rifle (made by Israel Military Industries), 2×20mm anti-aircraft cannon (made by Ramta Structures and Systems) and up to four 7.62mm or 12.7mm machine-guns mounted around the top of the hull.

VARIANTS
There are no variants at the present time.

Above and below RBY Mk.1 4 × 4 Armoured Reconnaissance Vehicle. Note that there are minor differences between these two vehicles, including the mudguards and the drivers' hatches.

ITALY

FIAT/OTO MELARA TYPE 6616M – ARMOURED CAR
MANUFACTURER – Fiat of Turin and Oto Melara of La Spezia, Italy
STATUS – In production.

BASIC DATA

CREW:	3 (commander, gunner and driver)	ARMAMENT:	1 × 20mm Mk.20 Rh.202 cannon
WEIGHT LOADED:	7,400kg		1 × 7.62mm co-axial MG
WEIGHT EMPTY:	6,900kg		
LENGTH:	5.235m		1 × 40mm XM-174 grenade launcher on roof
WIDTH:	2.5m		
HEIGHT:	1.98m (top of turret) 1.48m (top of hull)		1 × smoke grenade launcher mounted in turret roof
GROUND CLEARANCE:	.51m (hull) .37m (axles)		2 × 3 smoke dischargers mounted either side of turret.
TRACK:	1.977m		
WHEELBASE:	2.7m		
TYRES:	14.50 × 20		
TURNING RADIUS:	6.8m (land) 7.5m (water)	AMMUNITION:	250 rounds of ready-use 20mm plus a further 150 rounds in reserve;
ANGLE OF APPROACH:	45°		300 rounds of 7.62mm ready-use ammunition
ANGLE OF DEPARTURE:	45°		
MAXIMUM ROAD SPEED:	95km/hr		plus 700 rounds in reserve. 12 × 40mm grenades ready-use
WATER SPEED:	4.5km/hr		
RANGE:	750km at 70km/hr 20km (water)		plus 300 in reserve. Total of 39 smoke grenades for roof mounted grenade launcher
FUEL CAPACITY:	120 litres		
FORDING:	Amphibious		
GRADIENT:	60%		
VERTICAL OBSTACLE:	.45m		
ENGINE:	Fiat Model 8062.22, 6-cylinder, direct injection, turbo-charged liquid-cooled diesel developing 147HP at 3,200rpm	ARMOUR	
		hull front and sides:	8mm
		turret front and sides:	8mm
		hull and turret roof:	6mm
		hull floor:	6mm

DEVELOPMENT
The Fiat/Oto Melara 6616M (4 × 4) armoured car is a joint development of the Fiat Company and Oto Melara. The first prototypes were completed in 1972/73 and the first order is for a total of 50 vehicles. Of these 30 will go to the Italian Carabiniere and the other 20 will go to the Italian Army for trials, primarily with reconnaissance units. After these trials the Italian Army may place further orders. The 6616M has the same basic mechanical components as the Type 6614 (4 × 4) Armoured Personnel Carrier for which there is a separate entry.

Production vehicles will differ from the prototype in a number of small points, for example the turret front will be redesigned. Production will be shared between the following companies – Breda will build the turret, Officine Reggiane the hull, Fiat will supply the transmission, engine, suspension and other mechanical components, Oto Melara will assemble the turret and the 20mm Mk.20 Rh.202 cannon, which is standard equipment in the German Army (also fitted to the Marder MICV, Spähpanzer and so on). This cannon will be built in Italy by Whitehead Moto Fides who obtained a licence from Rheinmetall in 1974.

DESCRIPTION
The hull of the Type 6614M armoured car is of all-welded construction which, according to the manufacturers, provides effective protection against small arms fire and splinters from small calibre artillery bursts.

The driver is seated at the front of the vehicle on the right side. He is provided with a total of five direct vision blocks which give him a 200° field of view. He also has a single-piece hatch cover that swings to the right to open, and on production models this may be provided with a periscope. His seat can be adjusted for head-out operation. The commander and gunner are seated in the turret which is provided with a turret basket. The commander is seated to the left of the turret and has a one-piece hatch cover that opens to the rear. In the roof of his hatch is a grenade launcher which is loaded and fired from within the vehicle. There are a total of nine periscopes arranged around the commander's hatch. The gunner is to the right of the armament and is provided with a one-piece hatch cover that opens to the rear. In front of his hatch is a combined sight/observation periscope. Both the commander's and gunner's seats are adjustable for height.

The engine, transmission and radiator are at the rear of the hull and these are separated from the fighting compartment by a fireproof bulkhead. The transmission has 5F and 1R gears and a two-speed transfer case. Independent suspension is fitted front and rear and hydraulic shock absorbers are provided for all wheels. Anti-roll bars are fitted. The steering is power assisted and the tyres are of the run-flat type. Brakes are of the air/hydraulic type. A winch is mounted at the front of the vehicle and this has a capacity of 3,000kg on the first layer. It is powered by a PTO from the transmission.

The 6616M is fully amphibious without preparation and is propelled in the water by its wheels.

A ventilation, heating and filtered NBC system is mounted in the rear of the hull.

The turret has full power traverse through 360° at a speed of 40° per second, this being electrically operated with manual controls for use in an emergency. The guns have a maximum elevation of +35° and a depression of —5°, maximum elevation is 25° per second. Armament is electrically fired with manual controls for use in an emergency.

The 7.62mm machine-gun is mounted above the 20mm cannon and the empty 20mm cartridge cases are automatically ejected outside the vehicle. In addition the ammunition container is sealed to prevent gases escaping into the turret. For a full description of the 20mm Mk.20 Rh.202 cannon refer to the section on the German Marder MICV.

The smoke grenade launcher in the commander's hatch is fired from within the vehicle. The 40mm grenade launcher can fire a variety of grenades including HE, Smoke and Anti-Personnel. This is operated by the commander with his turret hatch open. The smoke dischargers mounted outside the turret are German Wegmann models as fitted on most German AFVs including the Leopard MBT.

If required the 40mm grenade launcher can be replaced by an ATGW system, for example the French/German Milan or the American TOW.

VARIANTS
The Type 6616M could also be fitted with the French H-90 turret with a 90mm gun as fitted to the Panhard (4 × 4) AML-90 Armoured Car. Under development in Italy is a 2 × 20mm anti-aircraft turret. Other standard turrets could be fitted according to individual Army requirements.

Above and previous page The Fiat/Oto Melara Type
6616M 4x4 Armoured Car undergoing trials.

SOVIET UNION

BRDM-2 – RECONNAISSANCE VEHICLE
MANUFACTURER – Soviet State Arsenals
CURRENT STATUS – In service with Angola, Bulgaria, East Germany, Egypt, Israel, Mali, Poland, Romania, Soviet Union, Syria and Yugoslavia. Still in production.

BASIC DATA	BRDM-2	BRDM-2 (SAGGER)			
CREW:	4	2	FORDING:	Amphibious	Amphibious
WEIGHT:	7,000kg	7,000kg	GRADIENT:	60%	60%
LENGTH:	5.75m	5.75m	VERTICAL OBSTACLE:	.4m	.4m
WIDTH:	2.35m	2.35m	TRENCH:	1.25m	1.25m
HEIGHT:	2.31m	2.01m	ENGINE:	GAZ-41.V-8	
GROUND CLEARANCE:	.335m	.335m		water-cooled	
TRACK:	1.84m	1.84m		petrol engine	
WHEELBASE:	3.1m	3.1m		developing	
TYRES:	13.00 × 18	13.00 × 18		140HP	
MAXIMUM ROAD SPEED:	100km/hr	100km/hr	ARMAMENT:	1 × 14.5mm	Launcher with 6
WATER SPEED:	10km/hr	10km/hr		KPVT MG	
RANGE:	750km	750km		1 × 7.62mm	Sagger ATGW
FUEL CAPACITY:	290 litres	290 litres		PKT MG	
FUEL CONSUMPTION:	35/45 litres	35/45 litres	ARMOUR:	10mm	10mm
	per 100km	per 100km		(maximum)	(maximum)

DEVELOPMENT
The BRDM-2 (which is also known as the BTR-40-P2 or BTR-40PB) is the replacement for the earlier BRDM-1 (BTR-40P) vehicle. The main improvements are its more powerful engine which gives it a higher speed, larger radius of action and a turret-mounted fully enclosed weapons system. The above data relate to the current production models. Early models were powered by twin M-21 four-cylinder petrol engines that developed 70HP at 4,000rpm (each engine). The BRDM-2 entered service in the early 1960s and was seen for the first time in public in 1966.

DESCRIPTION
The hull of the BRDM-2 is of all-welded construction with the engine, transmission and fuel tank at the rear of the hull. A winch is mounted internally at the front of the hull.

The suspension consists of semi-elliptical springs with hydraulic double-acting shock-absorbers. Like the BRDM-1, the BRDM-2 has a central tyre pressure regulation system and powered belly wheels that can be lowered for crossing difficult terrain and trenches.

The driver and commander are at the very front of the hull, with the driver on the left and the commander on the right. They are both provided with a windscreen for direct observation, and when in action this is covered by a steel hatch. Periscopes are provided in the roof of the vehicle for both the commander and driver. The only means of entry and exit are via the two hatches in the roof just behind the commander's and driver's position.

The commander is provided with an infra-red searchlight that can be operated from within the vehicle. In each side of the hull are three small vision blocks and a single firing port.

The turret is identical to that fitted to the BTR-60PB Armoured Personnel Carrier. The machine-guns have a maximum elevation of + 30° and a depression of − 5°, axis of bore being 2.13m. The turret has no hatch cover and can be traversed through 360° by hand. The gunner has an integral seat and the weapons are aimed by using a telescope to the left of the 14.5mm machine-gun. An infra-red sight can be fitted if required. A total of 500 rounds of 14.5mm and 2,000 rounds of 7.62mm ammunition are carried.

The BRDM-2 is fully amphibious being propelled in the water by a single water jet at the rear of the hull, covered when not in use. Before entering the water the bilge pumps are switched on and the trim vane is erected at the front of the hull.

Infra-red driving lights are fitted as standard and a complete NBC system is installed.

VARIANTS
BRDM-2U Command Vehicle
This is the basic vehicle with its turret removed and replaced by a simple one-piece hatch that opens forwards. It has additional radios and a total of two radio aerials. A generator is mounted externally on the roof to the rear of the roof hatch.

BRDM-2-rkh Radiological-Chemical Reconnaissance Vehicle
This fulfills a similar role to the BTR-40kh and BTR-40P-rkh as it dispenses marker flags in contaminated areas. A land navigation system is fitted.

The basic BRDM-2 with turret-mounted 14.5mm and 7.62mm machine-guns.

BRDM-2 Sagger ATGW Vehicle

This has no turret and a redesigned hull top. Inside are six launching rails for Sagger ATGWs, these being raised for firing complete with their overhead armour. A further eight missiles are carried in reserve. The driver is on the left as in the basic vehicle, and to his right is the missile controller who is provided with a periscope to control the missiles from within the vehicle. If required the missiles can be controlled away from the vehicle with the aid of a separation cable and the standard control box. In addition the individual missiles can be dismounted from the vehicle and fired from their normal mounts. The Sagger ATGW weighs 11kg and is 815mm in length and has a diameter of 120mm. Its minimum range is 500m and its maximum range 3,000m. It will penetrate 400mm of armour.

This vehicle was extensively used in the Middle East in the October 1973 conflict, and numbers were captured by the Israeli Army. A typical BRDM-2 (Sagger) detachment is reported to have consisted of one basic BRDM-2 and a further three vehicles fitted with the Sagger ATGW system.

BRDM-2 Anti-Aircraft Missile System

This entered service with the Soviet Army in 1972 and some were supplied to the Egyptian and Syrian Armies shortly before the October 1973 War. The first models consisted of a BRDM-2 with the turret removed and replaced by eight launchers for a modified version of the SA-7 Strela (or Grail) missile.

The second version to enter service has a further modification of the missile which is now designated SA-9. This is also mounted on a BRDM-2 but with four launchers. The SA-9 also has an infra-red homing device which is said to be an improvement over the earlier infra-red homer which did not prove very effective in the Middle East. The SA-9 also has a longer range. Some reports have suggested that the SA-9 is a modified version of the Atoll air-to-air missile of the Soviet Air Force.

Above The BRDM-2 Sagger ATGW vehicle with missiles in the ready-to-launch position. This photograph was taken during a parade in Cairo, Egypt.
Left The SAM-9 mounted on a BRDM-2. This particular vehicle has two missiles, most however have four, two each side.

SOVIET UNION

BTR-40P/BRDM-1 SERIES–AMPHIBIOUS RECONNAISSANCE VEHICLE
MANUFACTURER–Soviet State Arsenals
STATUS–In service with Albania, Bulgaria, Congo, Cuba, East Germany, Egypt, Israel, Poland, Soviet Union, Syria, Uganda. Production complete.

BASIC DATA	BRDM-1	BRDM-1 (Sagger)			
CREW:	5	2	FORDING:	Amphibious	Amphibious
WEIGHT LOADED:	5,600kg	5,600kg	GRADIENT:	60%	60%
WEIGHT EMPTY:	5,100kg	5,100kg	VERTICAL OBSTACLE:	.47m	.47m
LENGTH:	5.7m	5.7m	TRENCH:	1.22m	1.22m
WIDTH:	2.225m	2.225m	ENGINE:	Both are powered by a	
HEIGHT:	1.9m (w/o armament)	2m (missiles retracted)		GAZ-40P, 6-cylinder, in-line water-cooled petrol engine developing 90HP at 3,400rpm	
GROUND CLEARANCE:	.315m	.315m			
TRACK:	1.6m	1.6m	ARMAMENT: (BRDM-1)	1 × 7.62mm SGMB MG; with an elevation of $+23\frac{1}{2}°$ and a depression of $-6°$. Total traverse 90°. Or a 12.7mm DShK MG. 1,250 rounds of 7.62mm ammunition are carried	
WHEELBASE:	2.8m	2.8m			
TYRES:	12.00 × 18	12.00 × 18			
MAXIMUM ROAD SPEED:	80km/hr	80km/hr			
MAXIMUM WATER SPEED:	9km/hr	9km/hr			
RANGE:	500km	500km	ARMAMENT: (BRDM-1 sagger)	6 × Sagger ATGW.	
FUEL CAPACITY:	150 litres	150 litres			
FUEL CONSUMPTION:	30 litres 100km	30 litres 100km	ARMOUR:	10mm (maximum)	

DEVELOPMENT
The BRDM-1, or BTR-40P as it used to be called, was first seen early in 1959 and was the replacement for the earlier BTR-40 reconnaissance vehicle. The BRDM-1 has now been replaced in many first line units by the improved BRDM-2, which is itself a logical development of the BRDM-1. The BRDM-2 has a separate entry.

DESCRIPTION
The hull of the BRDM-1 is of all-welded construction with the engine and transmission at the front and the crew compartment at the rear. The transmission has 4F and 1R gears and a two-speed transfer case. The driver is seated on the left side of the vehicle with the commander to his right. Both the commander and driver are provided with a bullet-proof windscreen for direct observation, and when in action this can be covered by a steel hatch cover provided with an integral vision block. Two firing ports and one vision slit are provided in each side of the crew compartment. At the rear of the compartment are twin doors, and each of these has a firing port. The vehicle has an armoured roof with two hatch covers that open to the rear in the forward part of the roof. As far as it is known the BRDM-1 is not provided with an NBC system.

The vehicle is fully amphibious, being propelled in the water by a single water jet at the rear of the hull. Before entering the water a trim vane is erected at the front of the hull and carried under the nose of the vehicle when not required.

Two small powered wheels are mounted in each side of the hull and these are lowered by the driver when required, to increase both the cross-country and trench-crossing capabilities of the vehicle. A central tyre pressure regulating system is fitted. Some models have been provided with infra-red driving lights.

Most BRDM-1s are armed with a single 7.62mm machine-gun on top of the vehicle towards the front. Some models, however, have a 12.7mm machine-gun at the front and a 12.7mm machine-gun at the rear.

VARIANTS

BRDM-1 rkh Radiological-Chemical Reconnaissance Vehicle (BTR-40P-rkh)
This is used for marking lane lines through contaminated areas. Two boxes are mounted on the rear of the hull. When in action these are swung out and dispense marking flags into the ground.

BRDM-U Command Vehicle (BTR-40PU)
This is the basic vehicle adapted internally to the command role. It is distinguishable from the basic BRDM-1 which has one aerial because the BRDM-U has four aerials.

Anti-Tank Vehicles

The BRDM-1 has been adapted to carry all three of the current Soviet anti-tank guided weapons, the Sapper, Swatter and Sagger. The latter are now the most common models. In each case the rear of the vehicle has been redesigned so that the armour extends to the rear of the hull. The missiles are carried inside the hull and are raised to be fired. They are normally fired from within the vehicle. All the missiles are wire guided and have a HEAT warhead.

BRDM-1 Snapper

The three missiles are raised and the overhead armour slides down either side of the hull. This model has off-vehicle control enabling the commander to aim and launch the missiles away from the vehicle. This model has been replaced in most of the Warsaw Pact Forces by the vehicles listed below.

BRDM-1 Swatter

The four missiles are raised on their launcher. The overhead armour slides down either side of the hull and on this model the rear of the missile compartment hinges downwards when the missiles are raised.

BRDM-1 Sagger

This model is the most common and was first seen in 1965. The six Sagger missiles are raised complete with their overhead armour.

MISSILE NAME:	SNAPPER	SWATTER	SAGGER		SNAPPER	SWATTER	SAGGER
MISSILE NUMBER:	AT-1*	AT-2	AT-3	EMPLOYMENT:	UAZ-69(4)	BRDM-1(4)	BRDM-1(6)
MISSILE LENGTH:	1.14m	1.14m	815mm		BRDM-1(3)	Helicopter	BRDM-2(6)
MISSILE DIAMETER:	140mm	132mm	120mm				BMP-1(1)
MISSILE WEIGHT:	24kg	20kg	11kg				BMD(1)
MAXIMUM RANGE:	2,000m	2,500, 3,500**	2,500m				Manpack
							Helicopter
ARMOUR PENETRATION:	300mm	400mm	400mm				

* Russians call it the 3M6 'Shmel' or Bumblebee
** Extended range model

Above BRDM-1s on a reconnaissance mission.
Left BRDM-1 being used as a radio/command vehicle.

BRDM-1 Model A with three Snapper ATGWs.

BRDM-1 Model B with four Swatter missiles in the ready-to-launch position.

Below BRDM-1 with six Sagger ATGWs in the ready-to-launch position. This variant is known as the Model C.

SOVIET UNION

BA-64 – ARMOURED CAR
MANUFACTURER – Soviet State Arsenals
CURRENT STATUS – In second line service with a number of countries including Albania and North Korea. No longer in production.

BASIC DATA

CREW:	2	ENGINE:	GAZ-MM, 4-cylinder in-line water-cooled petrol engine developing 50HP at 2,800rpm
WEIGHT LOADED:	2,400kg		
LENGTH:	3.66m		
WIDTH:	1.74m		
HEIGHT:	1.9m	ARMAMENT:	1 × 7.62mm DTM MG in a turret with a traverse of 360°. Axis of bore is 1.775m. 1,070 rounds of 7.62mm ammunition are carried
GROUND CLEARANCE:	.21m		
TRACK:	1.448m		
WHEELBASE:	2.13m		
TYRES:	7.00 × 16		
MAXIMUM ROAD SPEED:	80km/hr		
RANGE:	600km	ARMOUR	
FUEL CAPACITY:	90 litres	hull front:	15mm
FUEL CONSUMPTION:	15 litres per 100km	hull sides:	6mm
FORDING:	.47m	hull rear:	4mm
GRADIENT:	60%	turret:	6mm (late models 15mm)
VERTICAL OBSTACLE:	.4m		

DEVELOPMENT

The BA-64 (BA=Broni Avtomobil) 4 × 4 armoured car entered service early in 1943 and is based to some extent on the German Sd.Kfz.221 and Sd.Kfz.222 Armoured Cars. Post-war the vehicle continued in front line service until it was replaced by the BTR-40 and BTR-40P reconnaissance vehicles. The BA-64, which is also sometimes known as the Bobby, was also encountered in Korea but is no longer in front line service with any members of the Warsaw Pact Forces. It is normally found in Workers Militia and similar second line units.

DESCRIPTION

The hull of the BA-64 is of all-welded construction with the engine at the very front of the vehicle. Its gearbox has 3F and 1R gears and a two-speed transfer case; some reports, however, state that it has 4F and 1R gears and no transfer case. Its tyres are bullet proof. The suspension consists of semi-elliptical springs front and rear and steering is on the front pair of wheels and is not power assisted. There are firing ports/vision ports in the sides and rear of the vehicle. The driver is provided with a one-piece hatch cover that opens upwards. The turret is of the open-top type. The BA-64 is very similiar in appearance to the East German SK-1 Armoured Car.

VARIANTS

There are no known variants in service. During World War II, however, various weapons were fitted in place of the 7.62mm machine-gun, the most common being a 14.5mm PTRD Anti-Tank Rifle.

Left The BA-64 Armoured Car without armament installed.

UNITED STATES

XM800 ARMOURED RECONNAISSANCE SCOUT VEHICLE
MANUFACTURERS – Wheeled Model – Lockheed Missiles and Space Company, Sunnyvale, California
Tracked Model – FMC Corporation, San Jose, California
STATUS – Trials. Not in production. See text.

BASIC DATA	TRACKED	WHEELED			
CREW:	3	3	MAXIMUM SPEED IN	7.2km/hr	8km/hr
WEIGHT LOADED:	8,618kg	7,697kg	WATER:		
WEIGHT EMPTY:	7,980kg	—	ACCELERATION	10 seconds	8 seconds
LENGTH:	4.673m	4.914m	0–48km/hr:		
WIDTH:	2.438m	2.438m	RANGE:	725km	725km
HEIGHT:	2.399m (O/A)	2.489m (O/A)	FUEL:	397 litres	341 litres
	1.663m (top		FORDING:	Amphibious	Amphibious
	of hull)		GRADIENT:	60%	60%
GROUND CLEARANCE:	.406m	.406m	SIDE SLOPE:	40%	40%
TRACK:	1.955m	1.981m	VERTICAL OBSTACLE:	.762m	.914m
TRACK WIDTH:	482mm	—	TRENCH:	1.828m	—
WHEELBASE:	—	3.682m	ENGINE MODEL:	GM 6V53AT	GM 6V53T
LENGTH OF TRACK ON	2.743m	—	ENGINE TYPE:	Diesel	Diesel
GROUND:			ENGINE HP/RPM:	280/2,800	300/2,100
GROUND PRESSURE:	.32kg/cm^2	.42kg/cm^2	ARMAMENT:	1 × 20mm	1 × 20mm
MAXIMUM ROAD SPEED:	88.5km/hr	104.6km/hr		cannon	cannon
MAXIMUM REVERSE	40.23km/hr	—		1 × 7.62mm	1 × 7.62mm
SPEED:				MG	MG

DEVELOPMENT

In 1965, Australia, Canada, the United Kingdom and the United States tried to formulate a common reconnaissance vehicle. In the end, however, Canada purchased the FMC Lynx whilst England developed the Scorpion series of CVR(T). After this a number of American companies were approached about a new reconnaissance vehicle for the United States Army. On the 15th October 1971 the Army issued a Request for Proposal (RFP) for a replacement for the M114 Command and Reconnaissance Carrier. Six companies put forward proposals, these being Chrysler, CONDEC, FMC Corporation, Ford Corporation, Lockheed Missiles and Space Company and Teledyne Continental (who entered a modified version of the Scorpion). On 23rd May 1972, Lockheed Missiles and Space Company and FMC Corporation were awarded a contract called 'Expanded Contract Definition'. Under this contract each company was to build four prototypes (three for the Army and one to be retained by the Company), test rigs and a hull for ballistic tests. These prototypes were delivered to the Army for trials. After this, one of the two companies should have been awarded an Advanced Production Engineering/Limited Production contract. This did not happen for a number of reasons, which included: the ARSV could not operate for a continuous 24-hour period, it did not have sufficient surveillance equipment, it had no anti-aircraft armament apart from the 7.62mm machine-gun. Early in 1974 it was stated that a total of 39,500,000 dollars had been spent on the programme.

In January 1974 the Armoured Reconnaissance Task Force was established at Fort Knox to carry out a Force Development Test and Evaluation (FDTE). This was undertaken in three phases, the last of which was completed in July 1975. The following vehicles were tested:

Lockheed ARSV/FMC ARSV/FMC AIFV/Modified FMC Lynx (with turbo-charged engine and tube over bar suspension)/FMC XR311(4 × 4)/V150 Commando Armoured Car/British Scimitar/Modified M551 Sheridan/Suzuki 185cc Motor Cycle/Modified M113A1 APC

At the time of writing the best vehicle had yet to be announced, but it did appear that the tracked FMC ARSV was superior to the Lockheed wheeled ARSV.

DESCRIPTION

Tracked FMC Scout

The hull and turret of the vehicle is of all-welded aluminium construction. The driver is seated at the front of the vehicle and is provided with a single-piece hatch cover that opens to the rear and a total of five vision blocks. The driver has two foot pedals, brake and accelerator, transmission range selector and a steering wheel. His instruments include a Light-Emitting Diode (LED) display which provides him with a digital read-out for such things as fuel, speed, rpm and so on. A door is provided in each side of the hull.

The turret is in the centre of the vehicle, with the commander/gunner on the right and the observer on the left. Both crew members are provided with a hatch cover. The commander has five M17 and two M27 periscopes whilst the observer has five M17 and one M27 periscopes.

The vehicle is armed with a 20mm M139 cannon with an elevation of + 65° and a depression of − 20°. Turret traverse is a full 360°. Production vehicles would have the 20mm cannon replaced by the 20/30mm Bushmaster system which is being developed by Philco-Ford. Five hundred rounds of 20mm linked ammunition are carried and the empty cartridge cases are ejected outside the hull. A 7.62mm M60D machine-gun is mounted on a skate mount on the observer's hatch. This can be traversed through a full 360°. 2,000 rounds of 7.62mm ammunition are carried.

The all-electric power control system has been developed by General Electric. The commander pulls a handle right or left which slews the turret right or left, the slew rate is determined by the amount of pull. The elevation and depression of the gun is controlled by pulling the top or bottom of the handle. Elevation and traverse speed is 90°/second maximum. The commander can select manual, powered or stabilized modes of operation.

The day night/sight has been developed by the Delco Electronics Division of General Motors and is mounted on the right side of the turret. It has high and low power day channels and high and low power night channels, both integrated into an articulated periscope configuration.

The engine and transmission are at the rear of the hull and there is an access panel in the hull rear. The transmission is an Allison X200 cross-drive torque converter with lock-up clutch with 4F and 2R gears. Steering is hydrostatic. The air cleaner is mounted on the left side of the engine compartment and the radiator and air outlet grille are on the right side.

The suspension system is of the torsion-bar type and consists of four road wheels with the drive sprocket at the rear and the idler at the front. There are no track support rollers. Shock absorbers are provided on the first and last road wheel stations. The tracks are of forged aluminium and of the double pin type, and are provided with detachable rubber pads.

The electrical system consists of four 6TN batteries with a capacity of 100Amp/hr each. A generator with a capacity of 180Amps is provided.

The ARSV is fully amphibious being propelled in the water by its tracks, and before entering the water a trim vane is erected at the front of the hull.

Equipment carried includes binoculars, weapon sight, laser rangefinder, Radiac meter and NBC detection kit. A fire suppression system is installed in the engine and crew compartments.

Wheeled Lockheed Scout

The Lockheed entry was based on their experience obtained in designing and building the 8 × 8 Twister series of vehicles. This Twister is not included in this book as development has now been completed and no production order was placed.

The Lockheed vehicle's hull is of aluminium construction with a layer of dual hardness steel appliqué armour. The turret is of cast aluminium and also has appliqué steel armour.

The Lockheed ARSV is a two-body 6 × 6 vehicle with roll articulation between the two bodies. The front body contains the front wheels, front suspension, steering, fuel tank and front differential. The rear body contains the crew compartment, turret, engine, transmission and rear wheels assembly.

The driver is seated towards the front of the vehicle and is provided with a total of five vision blocks which are mounted in an integral hatch cover which swings to the inside of the hull when the driver is driving in the head out position. A night vision periscope is provided. Entry doors for the crew are provided in both sides of the hull. The commander and observer are provided with a total of twelve vision blocks and a day/night dual observation/fire control system is provided for the commander who is seated on the left side of the turret. This has a magnification of × 3 and × 9.

The armament installation is similar to the FMC vehicle but it has an electric power control and stabilization system developed by Honeywell. The 7.62mm M60D machine-gun is mounted externally on the right side of the cupola. Total ammunition supply is 500 rounds of 20mm and 2,000 rounds of 7.62mm.

The engine is at the rear of the hull and is coupled to an Allison MT6500 automatic transmission with 5F and 2R gears. The front suspension is of the double 'A' arm type with hydraulic shock absorbers enclosed in a coil spring. The roll joint between the two bodies allows for + 25° roll articulation. The rear suspension is of the walking beam type. Power steering, disc brakes and radial tyres with a run-flat capability are provided. The electrical system is 24V and two type 6TN batteries are provided.

The vehicle is fully amphibious being propelled in the water by a single water jet in the rear hull. A trim vane is erected at the front of the hull before the vehicle enters the water.

Equipment carried includes an AN/TVS-5 Image Intensification Night Sight, Binoculars, AN/GVS-3 laser rangefinder, navigation system, Radiac set, AN/PPS-15 surveillance set, Infra–Red Alarm System, and a Radar Illumination Detector set.

Above The FMC Tracked Armoured Reconnaissance Scout Vehicle.
Below The Lockheed Wheeled Armoured Reconnaissance Scout Vehicle.

UNITED STATES

XR311–HIGH MOBILITY WHEELED VEHICLE
MANUFACTURER–FMC Corporation, San Jose, California
STATUS–Prototypes completed testing by United States Army. In service with Israeli Army. Available for production.

BASIC DATA

CREW:	3	MAXIMUM ROAD SPEED:	129km/hr
WEIGHT LOADED:	2,767kg		84km/hr on a 10° forward slope
WEIGHT EMPTY:	2,087kg		
LENGTH:	4.343m		16km/hr on a 60° forward slope
WIDTH:	1.93m		
HEIGHT:	1.6m (without armament)	ACCELERATION:	0 to 96km/hr in 12 seconds
GROUND CLEARANCE:	.279m (hull centre) .355m (hull sides)	RANGE (road):	480km
		FUEL:	98 litres
TRACK:	1.625m	FORDING:	.75m (without kit)
WHEELBASE:	3.073m	GRADIENT:	60%
TYRES:	12 × 16	SIDE SLOPE:	50%
TURNING RADIUS:	6.51m	VERTICAL OBSTACLE:	.2m
ANGLE OF APPROACH:	75°	ENGINE:	Chrysler V8 petrol engine, OHV, developing 187HP at 4,000rpm
ANGLE OF DEPARTURE:	50°		
		ARMAMENT:	See below

DEVELOPMENT

Development of the XR311 commenced as a private venture in 1969 with the first of two prototypes being completed in 1970. As a result of the trials of these two prototypes the United States Army purchased ten improved or second generation models in 1971. Of these ten vehicles, four had the TOW missile installation for use in the anti-tank role, three had a .50 (12.7mm) machine-gun for use in the reconnaissance role and three had 7.62mm machine-guns and the crew armour kit for use in the escort/security role. These trials were completed in 1972. They were then tested by the 2nd Armoured Division. In 1974 they were also tested in the 2nd Armoured Reconnaissance Scout Vehicle competition along with a number of vehicles including the original FMC and Lockheed designs, the British Scimitar, Commando armoured car, M113A1, Lynx, modified M551 Sheridan and a Suzuki motor cycle. It has been stated that an XR311 with TOW missile installation costs around $50,000. The XR311 has been designed to carry out a wide variety of roles including anti-tank, reconnaissance, convoy escort, command and communications, medical evacuation, military police, mortar carrier, internal security and forward air defence communications vehicle.

DESCRIPTION

The XR311 is built around a tubular-steel frame safety cage which protects the passenger compartment if the vehicle turns over. This cage is covered by heavy-gauge sheet metal. An electrical winch with a capacity of 5,000kg can be mounted at the front of the vehicle if required, and the windshield can be removed.

The passenger compartment is in the centre of the vehicle with the driver on the left and two passenger seats to his right. There is space for .93m³ of cargo behind the passenger seats.

The engine and transmission are at the rear of the hull and there is a load-carrying space above this which can take a maximum load of 386kg. A full length skid pan protects the hull and allows the vehicle to slide over obstacles. The transmission is a Chrysler A-727 fully automatic with a torque converter, there are 3F and 1R gears – the XR311 is in 4 × 4 drive all the time. Limited-slip clutches, in front and rear, and inter-axle differentials automatically distribute more torque to those wheels with the most grip.

The independent suspension is of the double 'A' design with a torsion-bar spring and hydraulic telescopic shock absorber at each station. A stabilizer bar is provided for the rear suspension.

The steering is power-assisted and the tubeless tyres have a high-pressure tube inner tyre which provides a built-in spare for each tube as well as eliminating rim leaks during high speed cornering. The tyres are self-cleaning and disc brakes are fitted on all four wheels.

The electrical system is 24V DC and two batteries with a capacity of 45Amp/hr are provided. The alternator is of the integral rectifier and regulator type.

The XR311 is provided with a heavy duty towing pintle as well as a trailer wiring harness receptacle. It is air-transportable and can be air-dropped.

Below XR311 with .50 (12.7mm) machine-gun on a ring mount.
Right XR311 with 7.62mm machine-gun on a pintle mount.

VARIANTS
The following kits are available for the basic vehicle:
Crew compartment armour kit, consisting of high-hardness steel doors, side body panels, toe panel, firewall, bullet-proof windshield and bullet-proof side windows.
Armoured radiator.
Armoured fuel tank.
Top and door kit (water-proof fabric with plastic windows and hinged doors).
Various communications installations.
High output alternators, 100 or 180Amp.
Litter-carrying kit.
Jump seat for two additional passengers.
Explosion resistant reticulated foam fuel-tank filler.
Radial ply tyres or bullet-proof foam-filled tyres.
Extreme climate kits for winterization or desert temperatures.
Tool kit and portable fire extinguisher.

Anti-tank Vehicle
There are two models:
1. A recoilless 106mm rifle mounted above the crew compartment and a total of six rounds of ammunition.
2. TOW installation with a total of ten TOW missiles.

Reconnaissance
Fitted with a ring-mounted .50 (12.7mm) machine-gun with 360° traverse.

Convoy Escort/Security Vehicle
This can be provided with pintle-mounted 5.56mm or 7.62mm light machine-guns, 40mm grenade launcher XM174 and various other similar weapons. These weapons can also be mounted on the reconnaissance model on the ring mount.

Communications Vehicle
Communications equipment for ground-to-ground and ground-to-air roles can be mounted behind the crew compartment with the radio aerials on the engine compartment cover.

UNITED STATES

LYNX – COMMAND AND RECONNAISSANCE VEHICLE
MANUFACTURER – FMC Corporation, San Jose, California
STATUS – In service with Canada and The Netherlands. Production complete.

BASIC DATA	C & R	LYNX		C & R	LYNX
CREW:	3	3	GROUND PRESSURE:	.46kg/cm^2	.48kg/cm^2
	(commander, driver, radio-		MAXIMUM ROAD SPEED:	70.8km/hr	70.8km/hr
	operator/gunner)		MAXIMUM WATER		
WEIGHT LOADED:	8,477kg	8,775kg	SPEED:	6.6km/hr	5.6km/hr
WEIGHT AIR DROP:	7,409kg	7,725kg	RANGE:	523km	523km
LENGTH:	4.597m	4.597m	FUEL:	330 litres	303 litres
WIDTH:	2.413m	2.413m	FORDING:	Amphibious	Amphibious
WIDTH REDUCED:	2.266m	2.266m	GRADIENT:	60%	60%
HEIGHT WITH	2.108m	2.171m	SIDE SLOPE:	30%	30%
ARMAMENT:			VERTICAL OBSTACLE:	.609m	.609m
HEIGHT TOP OF HULL:	1.651m	1.651m	TRENCH:	1.473m	1.524m
GROUND CLEARANCE:	.406m	.406m	ENGINE:	Detroit Diesel (GMC) Model	
TRACK:	1.885m	1.885m		6V53, 6-cylinder, 2-stroke,	
TRACK WIDTH:	381mm	381mm		water-cooled diesel	
LENGTH OF TRACK ON				developing 215 HP 2,800rpm	
GROUND:	2.39m	2.39m	ARMAMENT:	See text	See text

DEVELOPMENT
The Command and Reconnaissance vehicle was developed by FMC as a private venture with the first prototype being completed in 1963. It is sometimes referred to as the M113½. The vehicle was offered to the United States Army but they chose the M114 (see under separate entry) and the M114 is now to be replaced by a new ARSV for which the Lynx has been entered. The reader is referred to the ARSV entry for full details of this programme. The Lynx uses many components of the M113A1 Armoured Personnel Carrier.

DESCRIPTION
The hull of the Lynx is of all-welded aluminium construction with the engine and transmission at the rear. The transmission is an Allison TX100 with torque converter and there are 3F and 1R gears. The DS200 controlled differential is at the front of the hull. The suspension is of the torsion-bar type and consists of four road wheels with the idler at the rear and the drive sprocket at the front. The tops of the tracks are covered by a rubber cover which can be removed to reduce the overall width of the vehicle. The vehicle is fully amphibious being propelled in the water by its tracks.

Before entering the water a trim vane is erected at the front of the hull and covers are erected around the air inlet and air exhaust louvres on the top of the hull.

The Lynx is provided with infra-red driving lights but does not have an NBC system.

Lynx (Armoured Full Tracked Command and Reconnaissance Carrier) for Canada
The first production vehicle was completed in May 1968. The driver is seated at the front of the vehicle on the left side and is provided with a single-piece hatch cover with an integral periscope. There are a total of five periscopes in front of the driver's hatch. The commander has an M26 cupola with a single-piece hatch cover that opens to the rear. The cupola is in the centre of the vehicle, offset slightly to the right, and a total of eight vision blocks is provided. The .50 (12.7mm) M2 machine-gun can be aimed and fired from within the vehicle and the turret has full 360° traverse (unpowered). There is a further hatch on the left side at the rear, with a single-piece hatch cover and four periscopes arranged around it. A .30 (7.62mm) Browning machine-gun is mounted at this station. There are three smoke dischargers mounted on each side of the glacis plate. Total ammunition capacity is 1,155 rounds of .50 (12.7mm) and 2,000 rounds of .30 (7.62mm). The Canadians purchased a total of 174 Lynxes.

Command and Reconnaissance Vehicle for The Netherlands
The Netherlands purchased 250 vehicles, the first of which was completed in September 1966. The vehicle is similar to the Canadian vehicles except that the radio operator is to the right of the driver.

The driver is at the front on the left and has a single-piece hatch cover with an integral periscope. In addition there are four periscopes in front of the hatch cover. The radio-operator/gunner has a single-piece hatch cover and four periscopes in front of his hatch. A .30 (7.62mm) machine-gun can be mounted in front of his hatch if required.

A .50 (12.7mm) Browning machine-gun is mounted on the M26 cupola. This can be aimed and fired from within the vehicle. The commander has a single-piece hatch cover and there are a total of eight vision blocks arranged around the cupola. This model also has an access door in the right side of the hull, which is not fitted to the Canadian vehicle. Total ammunition capacity is 1,000 rounds of .50 (12.7mm).

Modified Netherlands Vehicle

In May 1974 the Netherlands Army ordered a total of 266 25mm Oerlikon turrets to be fitted to their Command and Reconnaissance Vehicles. The turret is armed with the 25mm cannon which has two rates of fire, low at 150/250 rounds per minute and high at 570 rounds per minute. Two ammunition boxes are provided, one holding 80 rounds (normally APDS-T) and the other 120 rounds (normally HEI-T), allowing the gunner to change from one type of ammunition to the other. The turret has traverse through full 360°, elevation being +55° and depression −15°. Various types of ammunition have been developed including HEIT with an m/v of 1,100m/s, APDS-T with an m/v of 1,460m/s, APHEI-T and HEP-T. The APDS-T round will penetrate 25mm of armour at 1,000m. The weapon has an effective range against armoured vehicles of 1,500m, and can also be used in the anti-aircraft/anti-helicopter roles. The day sight has a × 2 and × 6 magnification whilst the night infra-red sight has a × 4 magnification. There is a total of six vision blocks.

Other variants

FMC also offer the following armament installations:
Model 100-E Cupola with a .30 (7.62mm) or a 7.62mm M73 machine-gun.
Model 74 Cupola with twin 7.62mm M73 or twin .30 (7.62mm) M37 machine-guns.
XM27 Cupola (modified XM26) with a 20mm Hispano-Suiza 820 cannon.
M113 type cupola with a .50 (12.7mm), .30 (7.62mm) or 7.62mm machine-gun pintle-mounted.
FMC Pedestal Mount with a .30 (7.62mm), .50 (12.7mm), 20mm or 25mm cannon, loaded and fired from within the vehicle.
ATGWs mounted in launcher boxes on the roof of the vehicle.
106mm recoilless rifle mounted on the roof of the vehicle.
Rheinmetall fitted a Dutch C & R vehicle with a Rh.202 20mm cannon, but this was for trials purposes only and the contract eventually went to Oerlikon for the 25mm cannon.
A C & R vehicle with a turbo-charged engine and a new tube-over-bar suspension system has been tested in the recent ARSV competition.

Above Command and Reconnaissance Vehicle of the Dutch Army.

Below Rear view of a Dutch Command and Reconnaissance Vehicle showing the access panel in the hull rear and the side hatch.
Left Command and Reconnaissance Vehicle of the Dutch Army with new Oerlikon turret mounting a 25mm cannon.
Bottom Lynx Command and Reconnaissance Carrier of the Canadian Armed Forces.

UNITED STATES

M114 and M114A1–COMMAND AND RECONNAISSANCE CARRIER
MANUFACTURER–Cadillac Division of General Motors Corporation, Cleveland, Ohio
STATUS–In service only with the United States Army. Production complete.

BASIC DATA

CREW:	3 or 4 (commander/ gunner, radio-operator/ gunner and driver)	MAXIMUM WATER SPEED:	5.4km/hr
		RANGE:	440/480km
WEIGHT LOADED:	6,928kg	FUEL:	416 litres
WEIGHT EMPTY:	5,687kg	FORDING:	Amphibious
LENGTH:	4.463m	GRADIENT:	60%
WIDTH:	2.33m	VERTICAL OBSTACLE:	.508m
HEIGHT:	2.155m (including armament)	TRENCH:	1.524m
		ENGINE:	Chevrolet 283 V8, OHV, liquid-cooled petrol engine developing 160HP at 4,600rpm
GROUND CLEARANCE:	.362m		
TRACK:	1.912m		
TRACK WIDTH:	419mm		
LENGTH OF TRACK ON GROUND:	2.311m	ARMAMENT:	1 × .50 (12.7mm) or 1× 20mm cannon 1 × 7.62mm MG
GROUND PRESSURE:	.36kg/cm²		
MAXIMUM ROAD SPEED:	58km/hr		

Note: Above data relates to the M114A1

DEVELOPMENT

Development of the M114 commenced in January 1956, and the first prototype was completed several years later. This was designated the T114 and had a turret-mounted .30 (7.62mm) machine-gun. In December 1961 the T114 was cleared for limited production and was type classified as standard 'A' in May 1963. By this time however the M114 was in production and the first production vehicle was handed over to the Army in 1962. The first production contract was for a total of 1,215 M114s, of which 615 were built to M114 standard whilst the remainder were built to the M114A1 standard with a number of other internal modifications. The second contract was for 1295 M114A1s and the third contract was for 1200 M114A1s.

The M114 was used in Vietnam in the C and R (command and reconnaissance role) but was withdrawn as it was found it had poor cross-country mobility. It is still in use by the United States Army although it was to have been replaced from 1977 by the new ARSV (see separate entry for this), but this has been cancelled. In 1975 a TACOM spokesman stated that the M114/M114A1 would be phased out of service by 1980.

DESCRIPTION

The hull of the M114 is of all-welded aluminium armour. The driver is seated at the front of the hull on the left side and he is provided with a single-piece hatch cover that opens to the left, three M26 periscopes and an M19 (infra-red) periscope which is mounted in the roof of his hatch. The commander's station is in the centre of the hull on the left side and is described below. The third crew member is at the rear of the vehicle on the right side. He is provided with a single-piece hatch cover with an integral M13 periscope which can be traversed through 360°. A seat is provided for a fourth crew member if required. The ventilator is located on the top of the hull on the left side at the rear. At the rear of the hull is a large circular hatch which can be used for entry and exit purposes by the crew.

The suspension is of the torsion-bar type and consists of four road wheels with the drive sprocket at the front and the idler at the rear. There are no track support rollers. One telescopic shock absorber is provided per pair of road wheels. The track is of the rubber band type.

The power train is at the front of the hull on the right side. This consists of the engine, Detroit Model 305MC transmission with 4F and 1R gears, universal joint, Allison GS100-3 geared-steer clutch-brake unit, from which power is transmitted to the drive shafts. The air inlet and exhaust grille are over the engine compartment.

The electrical system is 24V and consists of two 12V batteries and a 100Amp alternator. When operating in cold climates an additional two batteries can be installed. Infra-red driving lights are provided.

The M114 is fully amphibious being propelled in the water by its tracks. Before entering the water a trim vane is erected at the front of the hull and the bilge pump switched on.

VARIANTS
M114
This was the first model to enter service and was armed with a pintle-mounted .50 (12.7mm) Browning M2 machine-gun at the commander's station. This could not be fired from within the vehicle. The commander's cupola had manual traverse, eight vision blocks and split hatch covers. A 7.62mm M60 machine-gun on an M142 mount is mounted at the third crew member's station. This can be mounted in two places.

M114A1
This was the same armament as the above but the .50 machine-gun can be laid and fired from within the hull. The commander has eight vision blocks and a single-piece hatch cover.

The commander's cupola can be traversed through a full 360° by a handwheel with two speeds, 2° or $\frac{1}{2}$° of traverse per revolution. The machine-gun can be elevated from +61° to —16$\frac{1}{2}$° at a rate of 1.41° per handwheel revolution. The .50 Browning machine-gun is recoil operated and fed by a link belt. It can be fired in two ways: electrically by a firing trigger on the elevating mechanism handle, or manually by a solenoid trigger on the back plate of the gun. The gunner can select either single shots, burst or full automatic. Total ammunition supply is 1,000 rounds of .50 (12.7mm) and 3,000 rounds of 7.62mm ammunition.

M114A1 with 20mm cannon
This is armed with a 20mm M139 cannon built in the United States under licence from Hispano-Suiza of Switzerland. It entered service with the United States Army in 1968/69. The commander can select five rates of fire:

single shots, 200 rounds per minute (cyclic), 820/1,000 rounds per minute (cyclic), 5 round burst at 200 rounds per minute (cyclic), 5 round burst at 820/1,000 rounds per minute (cyclic).

Types of ammunition include HEIT (High Explosive Incendiary Tracer), APIT (Armour Piercing Incendiary Tracer), and TPT (Target Practice Tracer). The ammunition feed box holds 75 rounds and there are a further 25 rounds in the feed chute.

EXPERIMENTAL MODELS
There have been a number of experimental models which include:
Fitted with 25mm TRW 6425 gun system. Fitted with turret of AML 90 armoured car with 90mm gun. Fitted with the now cancelled DART ATGW. Fitted with the 20mm Vulcan gun.

Above The M114A1 with 20mm M139 cannon. The rear door is shown in the open position.
Previous page The M114 Command and Reconnaissance Carrier with pintle-mounted .50 machine-gun.

UNITED STATES

T17E1 STAGHOUND–ARMOURED CAR
MANUFACTURER–Chevrolet Division of General Motors Corporation.
STATUS–In service with Cuba, Honduras, Lebanon, Rhodesia, Saudi Arabia and South Africa (reserve).

BASIC DATA

CREW:	5 (commander, gunner, loader, driver and bow-gunner)	ENGINES:	Two GMC Model 270, 6-cylinder, in-line water-cooled petrol engines developing 97HP at 3,000rpm (each)
WEIGHT LOADED:	13,925kg		
LENGTH:	5.486m		
WIDTH:	2.692m	ARMAMENT:	1 × 37mm gun
HEIGHT:	2.362m		1 × .30 (7.62mm) gun
GROUND CLEARANCE:	.381m		co-axial with main
TRACK:	2.26m		armament
WHEELBASE:	3.048m		1 × .30 (7.62mm) A/A MG
TYRES:	14.00 × 20		1 × .30 (7.62mm)
GROUND PRESSURE:	1.26kg/cm²		co-axial MG
TURNING RADIUS:	8.38m	ARMOUR	
MAXIMUM ROAD SPEED:	90km/hr	hull front:	22m
RANGE:	724km	hull sides:	19mm
FUEL CAPACITY:	519 litres	hull rear:	9.5mm
FORDING:	.812m	hull top:	12.7mm
GRADIENT:	57%	hull floor:	6.35mm-12.7mm
VERTICAL OBSTACLE:	.533m	turret front:	45mm
		turret sides and rear:	31.75mm
		turret top:	12.7mm
		shield:	25.4mm

DEVELOPMENT
Development of the T17E1 was started by the Chevrolet Division of General Motors Corporation in 1941 with construction of the first prototype being authorised in October 1941. The T17 was a 6 × 6 armoured car whereas the T17E1 was a 4 × 4 armoured car. In January 1942 a production order for 2,000 T17E1s was placed, followed by a further order for 1,500 in April 1942. Production commenced in October 1943 with production being completed in December 1943 after 2,844 vehicles had been built. The vast majority of these were supplied to the British who called them the Staghound. The T17E2 was an anti-aircraft vehicle. This was a basic T17E1 hull with a new Frazer-Nash turret-mounting twin .50 (12.7mm) machine-gun. Only 789 of these were built. The T17E3 only reached the prototype stage and had the complete turret of the M8 SPG with a 75mm howitzer. The British Army developed two models of the Staghound, the Staghound 11 being armed with a 76.2mm gun for close support work whilst the Staghound 111 had the complete turret and six-pounder gun of the Crusader tank fitted in place of the standard turret.

DESCRIPTION
The hull is of all-welded construction whilst the turret is cast. The driver and bow machine-gunner are seated at the front of the hull, with the other three crew members in the turret. The engine and transmission are at the rear of the hull. The 37mm gun is in mount M24A1 together with the co-axial .30 M1919A4 machine-gun. A similar machine-gun is mounted in a ball mount on the right side of the hull front and another on the turret roof for anti-aircraft use. Wartime vehicles were also provided with a two-inch mortar. The turret had full 360° traverse, maximum elevation was + 40° and depression − 7°. Total ammunition capacity is 103 rounds of 37mm and 5,250 rounds of .30 ammunition. The Staghound has no amphibious capability.

VARIANTS
See development.

The T17E1 Staghound Armoured Car (Second World War Photograph).

UNITED STATES

M8 – LIGHT ARMOURED CAR
M20 – ARMOURED UTILITY CAR
MANUFACTURER – Ford Motor Company
STATUS – M8 and/or M20 vehicles are used by the following countries: Brazil, Cambodia, Cameroon, Colombia, Congo, Dahomey, Ethiopia, Greece, Iran, Laos, Malagasy, Mexico, Morocco, Niger, Norway, Peru, Saudi Arabia, Senegal, South Korea, Taiwan, Thailand, Togo, Tunisia, Turkey, Upper Volta, Venezuela, Vietnam, Yugoslavia.
Production of these vehicles has been completed.

BASIC DATA

	M8	M20		M8	M20
CREW:	4 (commander, gunner, driver and co-driver)	2-6 (commander, driver)	ENGINE:	Hercules JXD, 6-cylinder in-line petrol engine developing 110HP at 3,000rpm	
WEIGHT LOADED:	7,892kg	6,576-7,937kg	ARMAMENT:	1 × 37mm gun M6	1 × .50 (12.7mm) M2
WEIGHT EMPTY:	—	5,805kg		1 × .30	MG
LENGTH:	5.003m	5.003m		(7.62mm)	
WIDTH:	2.54m	2.54m		M1919A4 MG	
HEIGHT:	2.247m (without A/A MG)	2.311m (without A/A MG)		1 × .50 (12.7mm) M2	
GROUND CLEARANCE:	.29m	.29m		MG	
TRACK:	1.93m	1.93m			
WHEELBASE:	2.032m+ 1.219m	2.032m+ 1.219m	ARMOUR:		
			hull front upper:	15.87mm	15.87mm
TYRES:	9.00 × 20	9.00 × 20	hull front lower:	19.05mm	19.05mm
TURNING RADIUS:	8.534m	8.534m	hull sides:	9.52mm	9.52mm
MAXIMUM ROAD SPEED:	90km/hr	90km/hr	hull rear:	9.52mm	9.52mm
RANGE:	560km	560km	hull top:	6.35mm	6.35mm
FUEL CAPACITY:	212 litres	212 litres	hull floor:	3.17-12.7mm	3.17-12.7mm
FORDING:	.609m	.609m	turret front:	19.05mm	—
GRADIENT:	60%	60%	turret sides and rear:	19.05mm	—
VERTICAL OBSTACLE:	.304m	.304m			

DEVELOPMENT

In October 1941 development of the 37mm Gun Motor Carriages T22 and T23 started. Contracts were awarded in November 1941 to the Ford Motor Company for the T22, and to the Fargo Division of the Chrysler Corporation for the T23. A short while later it was decided to build 4 × 4 models and these were designated T22E1 and T23E1. Early in 1942, however, it became apparent that the 37mm Gun Motor Carriages were already outclassed and in March 1942 their designations were changed to light armoured cars.

After trials with prototypes further work on the T22 was undertaken and this resulted in the T22E2. This was standardised as the M8 in June 1942. Work on the other vehicles was stopped.

Production of the M8 commenced at the Ford Plant at St Paul and the first production vehicles were completed early in 1943; production continued until 1945 by which time 8,523 vehicles had been built. The M8 was supplied to the British Army in small numbers and they called it the Greyhound.

The Tank Destroyer Command also wanted an A/A vehicle, a command vehicle and a personnel carrier. These became the T69 Multiple Gun Motor Carriage, T26 Armoured Command Car and the Personnel-/Cargo Carrier T20. The T69 was built but was not placed in production. It was found that the role of the T26 and the T20 could be carried out by just one vehicle and this was the T26 Armoured Utility Car. This was standardised as the M10 in April 1943, only to be changed to the M20 in May 1943 to avoid confusion with the M10 Tank Destroyer.

The M20 was basically an M8 with the turret removed, the superstructure raised and a ring mount M49 (later M66 ring mounts were fitted) fitted on top. The M20 entered production in July 1943 and a total of 3,791 vehicles were built by the time production was completed in 1945. The M20 was used as a reconnaissance vehicle, personnel carrier, load carrier or ambulance.

DESCRIPTION

The hull of the M8 is of all-welded steel construction. The driver and co-driver are seated at the front of the vehicle and each is provided with a hatch which opens forwards, whilst the hatch above their head opens to the left or right. The turret has an open roof and can be traversed through 360° by hand wheel, and seats are provided for the commander and gunner.

The 37mm gun has an elevation of $+20°$ and a depression of $-10°$. A co-axial machine-gun is also provided and both of these are in mount M23A1. The 37mm gun can fire an M51B1 or M51B2 Armour Piercing Capped projectile with an m/v of 884m/s, which will penetrate 46mm of armour at 914m. In addition, the M63 High Explosive and M2 Canister rounds could be fired. A .50 Browning machine-gun is mounted on a pintle at the rear of the turret. Total ammunition capacity is: 37mm 80 rounds, .50 500 rounds and .30 1,500 rounds.

The engine and transmission are at the rear of the vehicle. The latter has 4F and 1R gears and a two-speed transfer case. Hydraulic brakes are provided. The suspension consists of semi-elliptical springs.

The M20 is similiar to the M8 but does not have a turret. The .50 machine-gun can be traversed through a full 360° and a total of 1,000 rounds of ammunition are carried for this.

VARIANTS

The Brazilian Army has a number of M8s fitted with rocket launchers. At the 1973 French Armaments display at Satory, the GIAT exhibited a modified M20. This consisted of a basic M20 with its superstructure removed and the same turret fitted as mounted on the Panhard AML 90 armoured car. The turret is designated H 90 and is built by CNMP-Berthiez. To date no known orders have been placed for this vehicle. It is aimed at those many countries who wish to update their existing armoured vehicles rather than buy expensive new ones. For details of the turret refer to the entry on the AML 90.

Above M8 Light Armoured Car (Second World War Photograph).
Left M20 Armoured Utility Car (Second World War Photograph).
Right A M3A1 Scout Car with roller at front of vehicle.

UNITED STATES

M3A1 – SCOUT CAR
MANUFACTURER – White Motor Company
STATUS – In service with Brazil, Cambodia, Chile, Congo, Greece, Laos, Liberia, Mexico, Nicaragua, Peru, Thailand, Turkey, Yugoslavia. Production complete.

BASIC DATA

CREW:	8	GRADIENT:	60%
WEIGHT LOADED:	5,920/5,624kg	VERTICAL OBSTACLE:	.304m
LENGTH:	5.625m	ENGINE:	Hercules Type JXD 6-
WIDTH:	2.032m		cylinder in-line petrol
HEIGHT:	1.993m		engine developing 87HP
GROUND CLEARANCE:	.4m		at 2,400rpm
TRACK:	1.657m	ARMAMENT:	1 × .50 (12.7mm) M2
WHEELBASE:	3.327m		Browning MG with 750
TYRES:	8.25 × 20 or 9.00 × 20		rounds
ANGLE OF APPROACH:	37°		1 × .30 (7.62mm)
ANGLE OF DEPARTURE:	35°		M1919A4 MG with 8,000
TURNING RADIUS:	4.343m		rounds
MAXIMUM ROAD SPEED:	90km/hr	ARMOUR	
RANGE:	400km	front:	12.7mm
FUEL CAPACITY:	113 litres	hull sides and rear:	6.35mm
FORDING:	.711m		

GENERAL

The M3 4 × 4 Scout Car was standardised in 1939. It is essentially a 4 × 4 truck chassis fitted with an armoured body. The engine is at the front of the hull and the radiator is protected by armoured shutters which are operated by the driver. The driver and commander are behind the engine and each is provided with a side door. The top half hatch of this has a vision port and can also be folded down if required. The windscreen is bullet-proof and can be covered by covers which are provided with vision ports. The personnel compartment is at the rear of the hull. If required a canvas cover can be fitted over both the driver's and personnel compartments. The machine-guns are mounted on a skate rail which runs round the personnel compartment.

The gearbox has 4F and 1R gears and a two-speed transfer case is also fitted. The suspension consists of semi-elliptical leaf springs with shock absorbers. The brakes are hydraulic. A roller is mounted at the front of the vehicle to assist the vehicle in overcoming ditches and other obstacles.

ARMOURED PERSONNEL CARRIERS

Today there are four basic types of armoured personnel carrier:
1. The MICV or Mechanised Infantry Combat Vehicle. This is designed to carry men about the battlefield and be a part of the tank/infantry team. Its crew can aim and fire their small arms from within the hull. Armament normally comprises at least a 20mm cannon and many have an anti-tank capability as they are provided with an ATGW launcher. All MICVs are tracked.
2. The APC or Armoured Personnel Carrier. This covers such vehicles as the M113 which can carry troops but has no capability for the troops to fight from within the vehicle. Some have turret-mounted weapons and others some AT capability. There are both tracked and wheeled APCs, the latter being useful in the IS role.
3. Internal Security Vehicles. These are designed to transport men in IS operations and are always wheeled. Many IS vehicles use standard commercial automotive components to keep costs to a minimum. Among these are the Shorts SB.301, the Sankey 104/105 and the German UR-416. In addition wheeled vehicles such as the Commando and VXB-170 are used for IS operations.
4. Amphibious Assault Vehicles. These are used to transport men and supplies from ships off-shore, across beaches and if required inland as well. The United States Marines are the largest users of these vehicles.

The following personnel carriers are covered:

COUNTRY	DESIGNATION	TRACKED OR WHEELED	TYPE
Austria	Saurer 4K FA	Tracked	APC
Brazil	Urutu EE-11	Wheeled	APC
China	Type 55	Wheeled	APC
	Type 56	Wheeled	APC
	Type K-63	Tracked	APC
Czechoslovakia	OT-64	Wheeled	APC
	OT-62	Tracked	APC
	OT-810	Half-Track	APC
Egypt	Walid	Wheeled	APC
Eire	Timoney	Wheeled	APC
France	VAB	Wheeled	APC
	Panhard M3	Wheeled	APC
	AMX10P	Tracked	MICV
	VXB-170	Wheeled	APC
	AMX-VCI	Tracked	APC/MICV
Germany	Marder	Tracked	MICV
	UR-416	Wheeled	APC
	HWK-11	Tracked	APC
	Spz.12-3	Tracked	APC
Great Britain	AT104/AT105	Wheeled	IS
	SB.301	Wheeled	IS
	FV432	Tracked	APC
	Saracen	Wheeled	APC
	Humber 1T	Wheeled	IS
Italy	O-F 24 Tifone	Tracked	MICV
	Fiat 6614 CM	Wheeled	APC
Japan	Type 73	Tracked	MICV
	Type SU 60	Tracked	APC
Netherlands	YP-408	Wheeled	APC
Romania	TAB-70	Wheeled	APC
Spain	Pegaso 6 × 6	Wheeled	APC

Soviet Union	GT-T/M1970	Tracked	APC
	BMP-1	Tracked	MICV
	BTR-60	Wheeled	APC
	BTR-50	Tracked	APC
	BTR-152	Wheeled	APC
	BTR-40	Wheeled	APC
	AT-P	Tracked	APC
Sweden	Pbv.302	Tracked	APC
Switzerland	MOWAG Piranha	Wheeled	APC
	MOWAG Tornado	Tracked	MICV
	MOWAG Grenadier	Wheeled	APC
	MOWAG Roland	Wheeled	APC
	MOWAG MR 8-01	Wheeled	APC
United States	XM723	Tracked	MICV
	AIFV	Tracked	MICV
	Commando	Wheeled	APC
	M113	Tracked	APC
	M59	Tracked	APC
	M75	Tracked	APC
	Half-Tracks	Half-Track	APC
	Landing Vehicle Assault	Tracked	APC (Assault)
	LVTP-7	Tracked	APC (Assault)
	LVTP-4	Tracked	APC (Assault)
Yugoslavia	M60	Tracked	APC
Other APCs:			
	Refer to entry for		*Name of APC*
France	EBR-75	Wheeled	EBR ETT
Great Britain	Scorpion	Tracked	Spartan

AUSTRIA

SAURER 4K 4FA – ARMOURED PERSONNEL CARRIER
MANUFACTURER – Saurer-Werke (now part of Steyr-Daimler-Puch AG)
STATUS – In service only with the Austrian Army. Production complete.

BASIC DATA

CREW:	2 + 8 (commander/ gunner, driver and 8 infantry)	MAXIMUM ROAD SPEED:	60.4/61.7km/hr
		RANGE:	370km
		FUEL CAPACITY:	184 litres
WEIGHT LADEN:	15,000kg (maximum with 20mm turret)	FORDING:	1m
		GRADIENT:	75%
	12,500kg (standard model with 12.7mm MG)	SIDE SLOPE:	50%
		VERTICAL OBSTACLE:	.8m
WEIGHT EMPTY:	11,100kg	TRENCH:	2.2m
LENGTH:	5.4m	ENGINE:	Saurer type 6FA, 4- stroke, 6-cylinder diesel developing 250HP at 2,400 rpm
WIDTH:	2.5m		
HEIGHT:	2.1m (including MG) 1.95m (axis of bore of MG)		
		ARMAMENT:	1 × .50 (12.7mm) M2 Browning HB MG *or* 1 × 20mm Oerlikon 204 GK cannon
	1.65m (hull top)		
GROUND CLEARANCE:	.42m (centre of hull)		
TRACK:	2.12m		
TRACK WIDTH:	375mm	ARMOUR	
LENGTH OF TRACK		hull nose:	20mm at 45°
ON GROUND:	2.9m	hull glacis:	20mm at 30°
GROUND PRESSURE:	.52kg/cm^2	hull sides:	14mm
POWER-TO-WEIGHT		hull rear:	12mm
RATIO:	22HP/T	hull roof:	8mm

DEVELOPMENT

Saurer started development of a tracked armoured personnel carrier in 1956 and the first models were the 3K3H (1958) and the 4K3H (1959). Both of these were powered by a 200HP Saurer diesel and were quite different from latter vehicles. They had five road wheels, idler at the rear, drive sprocket at the front and no track return rollers. The shape of their hulls was also different. Next came the 4K2P which was powered by a 250HP Saurer diesel. The first production models were the 4K4Fs in 1961. These were powered by a 200HP Saurer diesel. Later models were the 4K3KA and 4K4FA. A wide range of vehicles has been developed and these are described below. Production has now been completed and approx. 450 vehicles were built for the Austrian Army.

DESCRIPTION

The hull of the Saurer APC is of all-welded construction. The driver is seated at the front of the hull on the left side and is provided with three periscopes for driving when closed down and twin hatch covers that open left and right. The commander/gunner is seated behind the driver's position and he also has twin hatch covers. A single periscope is provided for observation purposes. The transmission has 5F and 1R gears, and the engine is to the right of the driver. The personnel compartment is at the rear of the vehicle and infantry are provided with two bench seats, one down each side of the vehicle. There are two long hatches in the roof of the compartment and twin doors at the rear of the troop compartment. Each of these doors has an observation port.

First models were armed with a .50 machine-gun and had provision for mounting a total of four 7.62mm MG 42 machine-guns round the top of the personnel compartment. Later models have a 20mm cannon; these are described below.

The suspension is of the torsion-bar type and consists of five road wheels with the drive sprocket at the front, idler at the rear and two track support rollers.

VARIANTS

The first production models were armed with a .50 machine-gun in an open mounting. These were later fitted with an armoured shield with the hatch covers giving vertical protection when the commander was firing the weapon.

The last production model was the 4K 4FA-G. This is armed with an Oerlikon GAD AOA turret which has a 20mm Type 204 GK belt-fed cannon. This can be used against both ground and air targets. Maximum elevation is + 70° and depression − 12°, traverse is a full 360°. Both elevation and traverse are manual: the turret traverses 5.46° for one rotation of the handle, and 8.1° in elevation for one rotation of the handle. The gun-turret, gun and 100 rounds of ready-use ammunition weigh approx. 1,030kg. The empty cartridge cases and links are automatically ejected outside the turret. Armour on the turret varies between 15 and 25mm.

The following specialized versions are in service:

4K 4FA-San (Sanitatspanzer San) Ambulance. Crew consists of driver and medical orderly, can carry 4 sitting patients and 2 stretcher patients

4K 3FA-FU (Command Vehicle)

4K 3FA-FU/A (Artillery Command Vehicle)

4K 3FA-FU/FIA (Anti-Aircraft Command Vehicle)

4K 3FA-F2S (Radio Vehicle)

GrW1 81mm mortar carrier

GrW2 120mm mortar carrier (not adopted for service)

Rocket-launcher vehicle with twin multiple launchers for Oerlikon 80mm rockets.

There was also a 120mm rocket-launcher, but it appears that these did not enter service. In addition there have been various trials versions and many projects such as anti-aircraft and anti-tank vehicles.

The Saurer APC is not fitted with an NBC system although provision was made in the design for such an installation. It has no amphibious capability and no infra-red driving or fighting equipment, though this could be provided.

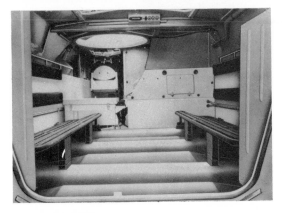

Top Saurer Armoured Personnel Carrier with .50 (12.7mm) M2 machine-gun.
Above Saurer 4K 4FA-G armed with a turret-mounted Oerlikon Type 204 GK Cannon.
Left Interior photograph of a Saurer Armoured Personnel Carrier.

BRAZIL

URUTU EE-11 – ARMOURED PERSONNEL CARRIER
MANUFACTURER – Engesa SA, São Paulo
STATUS – In service with the Brazilian Army and Marines. In production.

BASIC DATA

CREW:	2 + 13 (commander/ gunner, driver and 13 infantry)	RANGE ROAD:	600/700km
		RANGE WATER:	60km
		FUEL CAPACITY:	250 litres
WEIGHT EMPTY:	10,500kg (Marine model)	FORDING:	Amphibious
	9,000kg (Army model)	GRADIENT:	75%
LENGTH:	5.76m	SIDE SLOPE:	30%
WIDTH:	2.44m	VERTICAL OBSTACLE:	.6m
HEIGHT:	2.45m (with Commando type turret)	TRENCH:	1.5m
	2.00m (top of hull)	ENGINE:	Mercedes-Benz (Brazil) Model OM-352-A, 4-
GROUND CLEARANCE:	.5m		cycle, direct injection,
TRACK:	2.1m		turbo-charged, 6-
WHEELBASE:	2.093m + 1.415m		cylinder, in-line diesel
TYRES:	11.00 × 20 (bullet-proof)		developing 165HP at
TURNING RADIUS:	7.7m		2,800rpm
MAXIMUM ROAD SPEED:	95km/hr	ACCELERATION:	0-30km/hr in 18 seconds,
MAXIMUM WATER			0-60km/hr in 48 seconds
SPEED:	10km/hr	ARMAMENT:	See text
		ARMOUR:	6-12mm (estimate)

DEVELOPMENT

The Urutu EE-11 armoured personnel carrier has been designed for the Brazilian Army by Engesa Engenheiros Especializados SA of São Paulo with the assistance of a number of other establishments and companies in Brazil. The Urutu EE-11 is called the CTRS by the Brazilian Army. This stands for Carro De Transporte Sobre Rodas Anfíbô. Design work started in January 1970 with the first prototype being completed six months later in July 1970. The first production vehicles were ordered in early 1972. The EE-11 shares many components with the EE-9 Cascavel armoured car.

DESCRIPTION

The hull of the EE-11 is of all-welded composite steel construction, which gives the crew complete protection from small arms fire.

The driver is seated at the front of the vehicle on the left side and is provided with a total of three periscopes for driving with his hatch closed. When driving in the head out position his seat is raised and the hatch cover retracts inside the hull. The engine is to the right of the driver.

There is a single door in each side of the hull and a large door in the rear of the hull. A circular hatch is provided in the centre of the hull roof, which can accept a wide variety of armament installations including a ring-mounted 12.7mm machine-gun, United States Commando type turret with various combinations of 7.62mm, 12.7mm and 20mm weapons, Swedish Hägglunds turret with a 20mm cannon, right up to a 90mm gun turret. There are a total of six hatches in the roof of the personnel compartment, ie three down each side of the vehicle.

The personnel are provided with bench seats down each side of the hull, and a bench seat across the troop compartment behind the driver's position. There are a total of five firing ports in each side of the hull with a further firing port in the rear hull door.

The gearbox has a total of 5F and 1R gears and a two-speed transfer box. The front differential has hypoid single reduction gears, optionally lockable. The rear differential has double reduction hypoid-helical gears, and these are lockable.

The front suspension is of the independent type with coil springs and double-action air-cooled telescopic shock absorbers. The rear suspension is of the Engesa independent 'Boomerang' type with double-elliptical leaf springs. This is a well tried design which Engesa have been using on their tactical trucks for many years.

Steering is hydraulic, power assisted. Brakes are air over hydraulic. Electrical system is 12V with a 60Amp alternator. A winch with a capacity of 10,000kg can be mounted at the front of the hull if required.

The basic Army version is fully amphibious and can propel itself across lakes and streams with its wheels. The Brazilian Marines however required a vehicle capable of operating in heavy seas.

The Marine version is powered by a Chrysler 318 HP V-8 petrol engine. It is fitted with four schnorkel type tubes, two each side of the hull, which are raised pneumatically by the driver when entering the water. When on land they are stowed horizontally. These tubes provide a constant flow of fresh air into the troop compartment. Air for the operation of the engine is drawn from the troop compartment into the engine compartment since the engine space is at a slightly reduced pressure.

It is propelled in the water by two propellers at the rear of the vehicle, run from a PTO from the transfer case. It is steered in the water by two rudders operated by the steering system. Before entering the water the trim vane at the front of the vehicle is extended pneumatically by the driver and locked in position.

Two power-operated bilge pumps are provided in addition to the hand-operated pump. Optional fittings include infra-red driving lights, fire extinguishers and so on.

The vehicle can also be fitted with other engines including a Perkins diesel, Chevrolet 292 petrol or a Ford 292 petrol engine.

VARIANTS
Variants are described above.

Above Urutu EE-11 Armoured Personnel Carrier with schnorkels in the raised position.
Right Urutu EE-11 Armoured Personnel Carrier with ring-mounted .50 (12.7mm) machine-gun.

CHINA

TYPE 55 ARMOURED PERSONNEL CARRIER
MANUFACTURER – Chinese State Arsenals
STATUS – In service with Chinese Army and probably exported to those countries which have received Chinese aid. No longer in production.

GENERAL

The Type 55 Armoured Personnel Carrier is the Chinese version of the BTR-40 Armoured Personnel Carrier, and physical data is almost identical. The Chinese model probably uses Chinese automotive components such as engine and transmission.

CHINA

TYPE 56 ARMOURED PERSONNEL CARRIER
MANUFACTURER – Chinese State Arsenals
STATUS – In service with the Chinese Army and probably exported to those countries which have received Chinese aid. It is doubtful if the Type 56 is now in production.

GENERAL

The Type 56 Armoured Personnel Carrier is the Chinese version of the BTR-152 (6 × 6) Armoured Personnel Carrier, and has similar physical data to the Soviet model. The Chinese model probably uses some Chinese automotive components. It is probable that the Chinese have developed anti-aircraft and command versions of the Type 56.

CHINA

TYPE K-63 ARMOURED PERSONNEL CARRIER
MANUFACTURER – Chinese State Arsenals
STATUS – In service in China, Albania, Vietnam. In production.

GENERAL

The K-63 has also been known as the M-1967 or the M-1970 Armoured Personnel Carrier. It is a full tracked vehicle with four road wheels with the drive sprocket at the front and the idler at the rear. The driver is seated at the front of the hull on the left side and is provided with a single-piece hatch cover that opens to the left. The commander is on the right side of the hull and his hatch cover opens forwards. A 12.7mm Type 54 heavy machine-gun is mounted on the roof of the vehicle. This is a Chinese copy of the Soviet DShKM machine-gun. The engine is in the forward part of the hull between the driver and commander. There are hatches over the troop compartment in the hull rear and normal means of entry and exit is via doors in the rear of the hull. The K-63 is fully amphibious being propelled in the water by its tracks. Before entering the water a trim vane is erected at the front of the hull.

The K-63 is believed to use some components of the T-60 Light Tank which is a development of the Soviet PT-76 Amphibious Tank.

Left Type K-63 Armoured Personnel Carriers on parade in Albania.

CZECHOSLOVAKIA

OT-64 SERIES – ARMOURED PERSONNEL CARRIER
OT=Obrneny Transporter (Czechoslovakian)
SKOT=Stredni Kolowy Opancerzony Transporter (Polish)
MANUFACTURER – Czechoslovakian State Arsenals
CURRENT STATUS – In service with Czechoslovakia, Egypt, Hungary, India, Libya, Morocco, Poland, Sudan, Syria, Uganda. Still reported to be in production.

BASIC DATA

CREW:	2 + 18 (commander, driver and 18 infantry)	VERTICAL OBSTACLE:	.5m
		TILT:	23°
WEIGHT LOADED:	14,300kg	TRENCH:	2m
LENGTH:	7.44m	ENGINE:	Tatra Model T 928-14, V-8, air-cooled diesel engine developing 180HP at 2,000rpm
WIDTH:	2.5m		
HEIGHT:	2.03m (excluding armament)		
GROUND CLEARANCE:	.46m	ARMAMENT:	1 × 7.62mm SGMB MG with 1,250 rounds of ammunition, or a Czechoslovakian M59 7.62mm MG. This weapon has an elevation of +23½° and a depression of −6°, total traverse is 90°.
TRACK:	1.86m		
WHEELBASE:	1.3m + 2.15m + 1.3m		
TYRE SIZE:	13.00 × 18		
MAXIMUM ROAD SPEED:	94.4km/hr		
WATER SPEED:	9km/hr		
RANGE:	710km (road)		
FUEL CAPACITY:	320 litres		
FUEL CONSUMPTION:	45 litres per 100km		
GRADIENT:	60%	ARMOUR:	10mm (maximum)

Note: The above data relate to the OT-64A.

DEVELOPMENT

The OT-64 was designed jointly by Czechoslovakia and Poland and both of these countries use the vehicle in place of the Soviet BTR-60. Design work commenced in 1959 and by 1964 the vehicle was in large-scale service. It has also been exported to many countries.

DESCRIPTION

The hull of the OT-64 is of welded construction round a tubular frame. The driver and commander are at the front of the vehicle, behind them is the engine compartment and behind this is the personnel compartment. The driver is on the left side and has his own door and hatch cover, and the commander is to the right of the driver and also has a door and a hatch cover. The driver is provided with three vision blocks in his cupola and the commander has a periscope that can be traversed through 360°. In addition, both the driver and commander have vision blocks in their respective side doors. Hatches are provided over the engine compartment. The OT-64A is provided with a total of five hatches in the rear part of the roof. The first two and rear two are hinged at the sides and the centre hatch opens towards the front of the vehicle. Some early models did have a slightly different hatch arrangement. From the OT-64B onwards most of them have, behind the turret, a single hatch that opens forwards and two hatch covers that open either side. Some late production vehicles have four hatch covers on the rear hull top. The infantry enter and leave the vehicle via the two rear doors, each of which is provided with a firing port. In addition there are two or three (depending on the model) firing ports in each side of the hull. The troops are provided with seats down each side of the interior, which fold up when not in use and allow the vehicle to be used for the cargo role.

The OT-64 is fitted with a complete NBC system. It is also fully amphibious, being propelled in the water by two propellers at the rear, these being driven from a PTO. It is steered in the water by rudders. A trim vane is fitted at the front of the vehicle and this is erected before the vehicle enters the water, and at the same time the bilge pumps are switched on.

The OT-64 is an 8 × 8 vehicle, its semi-automatic transmission has 5F and 1R gears × 2 × 2. A central tyre pressure regulation system is fitted and there is a front mounted internal winch.

VARIANTS

OT-64A (or SKOT)

This was the first model to enter service. The Czech vehicles had no armament fitted although the Polish vehicles were fitted with a 7.62mm machine-gun on a pedestal mount.

OT-64B (or SKOT 2)

This was used only by the Polish Army and its armament consists of a 12.7mm or a 7.62mm machine-gun on a pedestal mounted with a curved shield. This was mounted just behind the engine compartment.

OT-64C(1) (or SKOT-2AP or OT-64 Model 3)

This has a similar hull to the earlier vehicles and the most significant improvements are the fitting of a fully enclosed turret and the installation of a new engine. Basic data is similar to the OT-64A except that it has a loaded weight of 14,500kg and the overall height with the turret is 2.68m.

The OT-64C (1) is powered by a Tatra Model T 928-18, V-8, air-cooled multi-fuel engine developing 180HP and performance is identical to the earlier model. This model does however carry only 15 infantrymen instead of the 18 of the earlier model. The turret is identical to that fitted to the Soviet BTR-60PB (8 × 8) and the BTR-40P-2 (4 × 4) vehicle. This mounts a 14.5mm KPVT machine-gun (on the left) and a 7.62mm PKT to the right. The turret, which is provided with a seat for the gunner, has a total traverse of 360° and its armament can be elevated for −4° to +29°. A total of 500 rounds of 14.5mm and 2,000 rounds of 7.62mm ammunition are carried. The API round of the KPVT machine gun will penetrate 32mm of armour at 0° at 500m. Practical rate of fire is 150 rounds per minute.

OT-64C(2) (or SKOT-2AP or OT-64 Model 4)

So far this has only been seen in service with the Polish Army. This model has the same turret as fitted to the OT-62C (TOPAS-2AP) armoured personnel carrier. This is armed with the same weapons as the OT-64(1) but these are capable of being elevated from −4° to +89½°, enabling them to be used in the anti-aircraft role. The maximum effective range of the KPVT in the anti-aircraft role is 1,400m or in the ground role 2,000m. In 1974 some Polish vehicles were fitted with a single Sagger ATGW either side of their turrets.

OT-64 Anti-Tank Vehicle

This is a Model 1 (or OT-64A) fitted with two Soviet Sagger ATGW over the rear of the troop compartment. Additional missiles would be carried inside the vehicle.

OT-64 Command Vehicles

There are at least two command models of the OT-64, known as the R2 and R3.

Above and below OT-64 Model 1s shown leaving the water.

Above OT-64 Model C, or SKOT-2AP which has the same turret as the Soviet BTR-60PB and BRDM-2 vehicles.

CZECHOSLOVAKIA

OT-62 – ARMOURED PERSONNEL CARRIER
MANUFACTURER – Czechoslovakian State Arsenals
CURRENT STATUS – In service with Bulgaria, Czechoslovakia, Egypt, Hungary, India, Israel, Libya, Poland, Romania. Probably still in production.

BASIC DATA	OT-62B	OT-62C		OT-62B	OT-62C
CREW:	2 + 18	3 + 12	RANGE:	450km	550km
WEIGHT LOADED:	15,000kg	16,390kg	FUEL CAPACITY:	417 litres	520 litres
LENGTH:	7.08m	7m			(estimate)
WIDTH:	3.14m	3.225m	FUEL CONSUMPTION:	90 litres per	90 litres per
HEIGHT:	2.23m (with	2.725m (with		100km	100km
	turret)	turret)	FORDING:	Amphibious	Amphibious
GROUND CLEARANCE:	.37m	.425m	GRADIENT:	70%	70%
TRACK:	2.74m	2.74m	VERTICAL OBSTACLE:	1.1m	1.1m
TRACK WIDTH:	360mm	360mm	TRENCH:	2.8m	2.8m
LENGTH OF TRACK ON GROUND:	4.08m	4:08m	ENGINE:	Model PV-6, 6-cylinder in-line, supercharged, water-cooled diesel developing 300HP at 1,200rpm	
GROUND PRESSURE:	.53kg/cm²	—			
MAXIMUM ROAD SPEED:	58.4km/hr	60km/hr	ARMAMENT:	See text	See text
MAXIMUM WATER SPEED:	10.8km/hr	10.8km/hr	ARMOUR:	14mm (maximum)	14mm (maximum)

DEVELOPMENT

The OT-62 is the Czechoslovakian-built model of the Soviet BTR-50PK Armoured Personnel Carrier. In appearance, however, it is almost identical to the BTR-50PU Model 2 Command Vehicle. The OT-62 was introduced into service in Czechoslovakia in 1964 and into the Polish Army in 1966. The Poles call their vehicles the TOPAS, standing for Transporter Obojzivelvý Pásový Stredni.

The Czechoslovakian vehicles are however much more powerful than their Soviet counterparts as their engine is supercharged. In addition they have a fully enclosed troop compartment provided with a complete NBC system.

DESCRIPTION

The hull of the OT-62 is of all-welded construction. There are two hatches over the personnel compartment, opening to the left and right. Most models have a single door in each side of the hull. There are two projecting bays at the front of the hull, each provided with three vision blocks. The left bay is the commander's and he is provided with a single-piece hatch cover that opens forwards. On most models the right bay has no hatch cover, but on some models, including the OT-62C, this bay has a hatch cover. The driver is in the centre of the hull front between the two projecting bays. He is provided with a one-piece hatch cover with an integral viewing block. This hatch cover swings upwards and in addition there are three viewing blocks below this hatch cover.

Like the Soviet BTR-50PK, the OT-62 is fully amphibious being propelled in the water by two water jets. Before entering the water a trim vane is erected at the front of the hull and the bilge pumps are switched on.

Infra-red driving lights are provided and it is probable that infra-red searchlights can be fitted for the use of the commander.

VARIANTS

OT-62A (also known as the Model 1)
This model has no fixed armament. Like all OT-62s this model can carry and fire the 82mm M59A recoilless rifle on the rear decking.

OT-62B (also known as the Model 2)
This model is only used by the Czechoslovakian Army and has a small turret mounted on the right projecting bay. This is the same turret as that fitted to the OT-65A 4 × 4 reconnaissance vehicle. This turret is armed with an M59T 7.62mm machine-gun, with a maximum elevation of +20° and a depression of −10°, total traverse is 360°. Also mounted externally on the turret, on the right side, is an 82mm recoilless gun T-21. Although this can be fired from within the vehicle it can only be reloaded from outside. A total of 1,250 rounds of 7.62mm ammunition and 12 rounds of recoilless ammunition is carried.

OT-62C (also known as the Model 3)

This is a Polish modification and they call it the TOPAS-2AP. Basically it is the basic model fitted with the same turret as that fitted to the OT-64C(2) 8 × 8 Armoured Personnel Carrier. This turret is armed with a 14.5mm KPVT machine-gun and a 7.62mm PKT machine-gun, elevation is +78° and depression is −5°, turret can be traversed through 360° and can be used against both ground and aerial targets. A total of 500 rounds of 14.5mm and 2,000 rounds of 7.62mm ammunition is carried. The OT-62C is also used to carry two 82mm mortar squads, ie a total of eight men, two mortars and ammunition.

WPT-TOPAS

This Polish developed vehicle is based on the OT-62 and is used for the recovery of disabled vehicles, especially during amphibious operations. In appearance it resembles the basic OT-62A. The WPT-TOPAS has a winch with a capacity of 2,500kg, a small hand-operated crane with a capacity of 1,000kg and various tools. Armament consists of a pintle-mounted 7.62mm PK machine-gun plus an RPG-7 anti-tank weapon, small arms and grenades.

Command and Ambulance Vehicles

There are known to be command and ambulance models of the OT-62 in service.

OT-62A of the Polish Marines.

OT-62C (Model 3) of the Polish Army.

Below The OT-62D of the Egyptian Army. This has the same turret as that fitted to the OT-62B and the OT-65A (4 × 4) reconnaissance vehicle.

CZECHOSLOVAKIA

OT-810 – ARMOURED PERSONNEL CARRIER
MANUFACTURER – Various German and Czechoslovakian companies were involved in the production of this vehicle
CURRENT STATUS – In service only with the Czechoslovakian and Romanian Armies. Production complete.

BASIC DATA

CREW:	2 + 10	RANGE:	320km
WEIGHT LOADED:	8,500kg	FUEL CAPACITY:	160 litres
LENGTH:	5.8m	FUEL CONSUMPTION:	50 litres per 100km
WIDTH:	2.1m	FORDING:	.5m
HEIGHT:	1.75m (excluding armament)	GRADIENT:	24°
		VERTICAL OBSTACLE:	.255m
GROUND CLEARANCE:	.3m	TRENCH:	1.98m
TRACK:	1.65m (wheels) 1.6m (tracks)	ENGINE:	Tatra 6-cylinder in-line air-cooled diesel developing 120HP
TRACK WIDTH:	300mm		
GROUND CONTACT:	1.8m	ARMAMENT:	1 × 7.62mm M59 MG
GROUND PRESSURE:	.843kg/cm²	ARMOUR	
TYRES:	7.50 × 20	hull front:	12mm
MAXIMUM ROAD SPEED:	52.5km/hr	hull sides:	7mm

DEVELOPMENT

The OT-810 is the Czechoslovakian designation for the Second World War German Half-Track Vehicle Kfz.251. This vehicle was built in very large numbers during the war and there were at least 23 different models. The chassis were built by a number of companies including Alder, Auto-Union, Hanomag, Borgward and Skoda (Czechoslovakia). The armoured bodies were built by various companies including Ferrum, Schoeller and Bleckmann, Bohemia and Steinmueller.

When the Germans retreated from Czechoslovakia at the end of the Second World War they left behind large numbers of the Kfz.251 which the Czechoslovakians pressed into service.

DESCRIPTION

Initially the Czechs used the basic vehicle without any modifications. In the early 1950s however they carried out an extensive modernization programme to the vehicle, and modifications included the replacement of the German engine by a Czech Tatra engine and the fitting of armoured roof hatches over the personnel compartment at the rear of the hull.

The engine is at the front of the vehicle with the driver's and commander's compartment in the centre and the personnel compartment at the rear. The front two wheels are powered and its gearbox has 4F and 1R gears and a two-speed transfer case. Normal means of entry and exit are via the twin doors at the rear of the vehicle.

The driver is on the left side of the vehicle with the commander on the right. The commander is provided with a single-piece hatch cover that hinges to the rear, and the 7.62mm machine-gun, which has no shield, is used by him. There are two vision blocks in the front of the vehicle and one each side of the commander and driver. Some OT-810s have firing ports in the rear hull.

VARIANTS

The only known variant is the anti-tank vehicle. This is basically an OT-810 with an 82mm M59A recoilless rifle carried in the rear of the vehicle. This can be fired from within the vehicle or dismounted for ground use. When not in action the gun and its crew are protected by front and side armour. This can be quickly folded down when required. The rear of the hull is modified on this model. The M59 has a maximum elevation of +25° and a depression of −13°, traverse is 360° at 0° elevation or 60° at 25° elevation, all these figures relating to when the weapon is dismounted for ground use. It fires an HE round which has an m/v of 565m/s and a projectile weight of 6kg, or a HEAT round with an m/v of 745m/s and a weight of 6kg. The HEAT round will penetrate 250mm of armour at 1,000m.

Overleaf OT-810 fitted with a 82mm M59A recoilless rifle in the rear compartment and more ammunition stowage on the right side.
Inset OT-810 with firing ports in the rear troop compartment.

EGYPT

WALID – ARMOURED PERSONNEL CARRIER
MANUFACTURER – Egyptian Government Factories/Arsenals
STATUS – In service with Algeria, Egypt, Israel, PLO and the Yemen. Production is now believed to have been completed.

GENERAL

To date hardly any information on this has become available. It is however known that it is powered by a German Deutz air-cooled diesel engine and the vehicle may well be based on a standard commercial truck chassis. In appearance it is similar to the Soviet BTR-40 armoured personnel carrier which has been supplied to Egypt.

The hull of the Walid is of all-welded steel armour construction with the engine at the front of the hull, driver and commander behind the engine and the personnel compartment at the rear. Both the commander and driver are provided with a side door, the top half of which has a vision port and can be folded down. Each windscreen can be covered by an armoured hatch if required, and this too is provided with a vision port. The personnel compartment has an open roof and there are three firing ports in each side of the hull. Normal armament consists of a 12.7mm or a 7.62mm machine-gun.

EIRE

TIMONEY ARMOURED PERSONNEL CARRIER
MANUFACTURER – Technology Investments Limited, Dublin
STATUS – Prototypes built and tested. Pre-production vehicles being built.

BASIC DATA	APC	RECCE VEHICLE			
CREW:	12	9	SPEED:	4.8km/hr	4.8km/hr
WEIGHT LOADED:	8,164kg	8,164kg	RANGE:	483km	483km
WEIGHT EMPTY;	6,350kg	6,803kg	FUEL:	273 litres	273 litres
LENGTH:	4.95m	4.64m	FORDING:	Amphibious	Amphibious
WIDTH:	2.406m	2.406m	GRADIENT:	60%	60%
HEIGHT WITH TURRET:	2.475m	2.14m	SIDE SLOPE:	30%	30%
HEIGHT HULL TOP:	2.032m	—	ANGLE OF APPROACH:	35°	—
GROUND CLEARANCE:	.381m	.381m	ANGLE OF DEPARTURE:	45°	45°
TRACK:	1.93m	1.93m	VERTICAL OBSTACLE:	.762m	.762m
WHEELBASE:	2.867m	2.867m	ENGINE:	Both are powered by a	
TYRES:	11.00 × 20 or 12.00 × 20	11.00 × 20 or 12.00 × 20		Chrysler Type 360 CID, 8-cylinder, water-cooled petrol	
TURNING RADIUS:	6.1m	6.1m		engine developing 200BHP at	
MAXIMUM ROAD SPEED:	98km/hr	98km/hr		4,000rpm	
MAXIMUM WATER			ARMAMENT:	See text	See text

Note: Above data for the APC relate to the Mk.3

DEVELOPMENT

Development of the Timoney armoured personnel carrier started in January 1972 with the first prototype being completed in mid 1973. Since then a further two prototypes have been built and a pre-production batch is planned. The Timoney APC has been designed to meet an Irish Department of Defence requirement for a vehicle for use both in Ireland and abroad as part of United Nations Forces.

So far Armoured Personnel Carriers Mk.1, 3 and 4 have been developed. Other projects include the Mk.2 Armoured Reconnaissance Vehicle and a 4 × 4 amphibious load carrier.

DESCRIPTION

The hull of the armoured personnel carrier is of all-welded construction and provides complete protection from small arms fire including 7.62mm armour-piercing rounds.

The driver is seated at the front of the hull and is provided with a large bullet-proof windscreen to his front. This can be opened and used as an emergency exit if required, and there is a smaller bullet-proof window each side of the driver's station. There is a door in each side of the hull and a further door in the rear of the hull. There are two firing ports in the right side of the hull, three in the left and two in the hull rear, one each side of the door. A turret-mounting twin 7.62mm machine-gun is mounted in the roof of the vehicle. This has manual traverse and is provided with a total of five vision blocks. The turret has a two-piece cover, the top part opens forwards and the rear part folds downwards to provide a seat for the commander. Smoke dischargers can be mounted each side of the hull and other armament installations are possible.

The engine, which is identical to that used in the M113 Armoured Personnel Carrier, is behind, and slightly to the right of the driver. This is connected to an Allison AT 540 automatic transmission comprising a hydro-kinetic torque converter driving a multi-stage epicyclic gearbox with 4F and 1R gears. This is connected to a two-speed (road and cross country) transfer gearbox to drive shafts running front and rear to the axles which incorporate 'No-Spin' differentials. From the axles power is carried by universal joints to the wheels, and an epicyclic hub reduction gear is incorporated. Air is drawn in through the forward part of the hull above the driver's station by a cooling fan, and used to cool the engine and water. This air is also used to cool the automatic transmission oil. There is an exhaust pipe on each side of the hull roof, one for each bank of cylinders. The independent suspension consists of wishbone linkages anchored to the hull and supported by helical coil springs with telescopic hydraulic shock-absorbers.

Disc brakes are fitted on all wheels and run-flat tyres are standard. The steering is of the rack-and-pinion type and is power-assisted. The electrical system was developed for the vehicle by the Gabriel Company of Leon, France and is 24V and battery capacity is 128Amp/hrs. The Gabriel Company in fact designed the complete electrical system to the requirements of Technology Investments Limited, including the instrument panel, heater, bilge pumps, gun-firing system, rotary junction and radio control box. The APC is fully amphibious being propelled in the water by its wheels. A kit is being developed which will increase water speed from 4.8km/hr to 11.3km/hr. Electric bilge pumps are provided. It is possible to install an air-condition system.

Other roles envisaged for this vehicle include use as a command or ambulance vehicle. It is also possible to build a 6 × 6 APC which can carry a total of 17 men, using Timoney components.

Timoney Mk.3 Armoured Personnel Carrier with twin machine-guns.

VARIANTS

Armoured Reconnaissance Vehicle

This will have a lower hull than the armoured personnel carrier and will have a crew of three—driver, commander and gunner. It will also be able to carry six infantrymen. On this model the driver is at the front, turret and personnel compartment are in the centre, and the engine at the rear of the hull. There is an entry door in each side of the hull. The turret has full powered traverse through 360° and both the commander and gunner will have individual hatch covers. A variety of armament installations are possible including 20 or 30mm automatic cannon, 75mm or 90mm guns, or a recoilless rifle.

A flotation screen is carried around the top of the hull, which can be quickly erected so that the vehicle can swim across rivers and streams.

Amphibious Load Carrier

This will be fully amphibious and will be able to carry 5,080kg of cargo on both land and water.

Infantry dismount from their Timoney Mk.3 Armoured Personnel Carrier.

FRANCE

SAVIEM/CREUSOT-LOIRE VAB – ARMOURED PERSONNEL CARRIER
MANUFACTURER – Société des Materiels Speciaux Saviem/Creusot-Loire
STATUS – In production for the French Army.

BASIC DATA	4 × 4 MODEL	6 × 6 MODEL			
CREW:	2 + 10	2 + 10	ROAD RANGE:	1,300km	1,100km
WEIGHT LOADED:	13,000kg	14,000kg	FUEL:	300 litres	300 litres
WEIGHT EMPTY:	11,000kg	12,000kg	FORDING:	Amphibious	Amphibious
LENGTH:	5.98m	5.98m	GRADIENT:	60%	60%
WIDTH:	2.49m	2.49m	SIDE SLOPE:	30%	30%
HEIGHT:	2.06m (w/o armament)	2.06m (w/o armament)	VERTICAL OBSTACLE:	.6m	.6m
			TRENCH:	—	1m
GROUND CLEARANCE:	.4m	.4m	ANGLE OF APPROACH:	45°	45°
TRACK:	2.035m	2.035m	ANGLE OF DEPARTURE:	45°	45°
WHEELBASE:	3m	1.5m + 1.5m	ENGINE:	Saviem HM-71 2356,	
TYRES:	14.00 × 20 (run flat)	14.00 × 20 (run flat)		6-cylinder water-cooled diesel developing 230HP	
MAXIMUM ROAD SPEED:	100km/hr	100km/hr		at 2,220rpm	
MAXIMUM WATER SPEED:	7km/hr	7km/hr	ARMAMENT:	See text	See text

---

Note: The above data relates to first prototypes. Production vehicles may differ.

DEVELOPMENT

In 1969 the French Army issued a requirement for a VAB (Véhicule de l'Avant Blindé) or Front Armoured Vehicle. This was required to supplement the AMX-10P MICV which was considered expensive for some roles. The VAB would be used to bring men and supplies to the front, and in addition a wide range of other roles was envisaged.

Both Panhard and Saviem built prototypes of both 4 × 4 and 6 × 6 vehicles, and these were subjected to extensive trials by the French Army.

Saviem built a total of five prototypes, the first of which was completed in 1971 and armed with a ring-mounted .50 (12.7mm) Browning M2 machine-gun.

In 1974 it was announced that the Saviem vehicle had won the contract. The first production order was awarded to Saviem in 1975. The French Army will initially have the 4 × 4 vehicle. The first pre-production vehicles should be completed at the St Chamond factory in late 1976/early 1977. The production vehicles will be built in a new factory. The French Army is said to have a total requirement for 4,000 of these vehicles, and there is little doubt they will be exported, as Saviem and Creusot-Loire (who have built the hulls) have set up a joint company to market the vehicle.

DESCRIPTION

The hull of the VAB is of all-welded construction and provides the crew with protection from small arms fire and shell splinters. The driver and commander are seated at the front of the vehicle. They are both provided with a bullet-proof windscreen which can be covered by a steel hatch, a door in the side of the hull which also has a bullet-proof windscreen which can be covered by a hatch, and finally a roof hatch over their seats.

The engine, transmission and fuel tank are mounted as an integral unit behind the driver's and commander's position, offset to the left, thus enabling the crew to have access to the troop compartment at the rear. The troops sit on bench seats down each side of the hull. Over the troop compartment is a circular hatch to which a variety of armament installations can be fitted, whilst in the rear of the roof are two hatch covers. The troops enter and leave the vehicle via two doors in the rear of the hull, each provided with a vision/firing port. There are a total of three observation windows in each side of the troop compartment and these can be covered by a steel hatch cover when required. Both the 4 × 4 and 6 × 6 models have identical components. Wherever possible standard commercial components have been used in the VAB.

Saviem are offering two gearboxes: manual gearbox with 6F and 1R gears and a transfluid gearbox with 5F and 1R gears and a disconnectable torque converter. Axles—differential reduction gear with double reduction and differential locking. The suspension is of the torsion-bar type with hydraulic shock absorbers. Steering is power assisted: on the 6 × 6 models the front four wheels are steered. The electrical system is 24V.

The VAB is fully amphibious being propelled in the water by twin water jets at the rear of the hull. A trim vane is erected at the front of the hull before the vehicle enters the water. An NBC pack is standard as is a fire-extinguishing system for the engine compartment.

Optional extras include infra-red (or image intensification) night-driving equipment, heater, air-conditioning system and a winch with 60m of cable.

VARIANTS

It has not been disclosed what armament installation will be provided for the French Army VAB, but below is a list of some of the options that manufacturers have suggested:

H-90 turret with 90mm gun and co-axial 7.62mm machine-gun as fitted to Panhard AML-90 armoured car.
Anti-aircraft gun (20mm or 30mm) or missile (Roland) vehicle.
Load carrier carrying 2,000kg of cargo, rear load area being 2.46m long and 2.376m wide.
Recovery vehicle.
Ambulance carrying 4 stretchers plus medical crew.
Command and radio vehicle.
Internal security vehicle.
Fitted with mountings for AGTWs, ie HOT, TOW, MILAN, SS11.
Towing a 120mm Brandt mortar.
An 81mm mortar in the rear of the hull, firing through a modified roof with a 7.62mm machine-gun at the front.
Twin 7.62mm machine-guns in a TL 21 80 turret.
Turret with 20mm M-693 cannon and 7.62mm machine-gun as fitted to AMX-10P MICV.
Hotchkiss-Brandt 60mm breech-loaded mortar at front and 7.62mm machine-gun at rear.
Single 12.7mm machine-gun or 20mm cannon.
Turret with 60mm mortar and twin 7.62mm or 7.5mm machine-guns, as fitted to AML.
CB 20 turret with 20mm cannon.

Above The 4 × 4 model of the VAB with a single 7.62mm machine-gun.

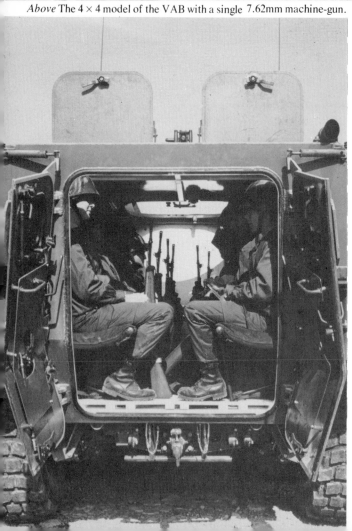

Above and below The 6 × 6 model of the VAB.

Left The 4 × 4 model of the VAB with rear doors open.

FRANCE

PANHARD M3 – ARMOURED PERSONNEL CARRIER
MANUFACTURER – Société de Constructions Mécaniques Panhard and Levassor, Paris
STATUS – In service with Abu-Dhabi, Angola, Congo, Eire, France, Iraq, Kenya, Lebanon, Malaysia, Portugal, Saudi-Arabia and Spain. In production.

BASIC DATA

CREW:	2 + 10 (commander, driver and 10 men)	RANGE:	600km
		FUEL CONSUMPTION:	26 litres per 100km
WEIGHT LOADED:	6,100kg	FUEL CAPACITY:	165 litres
WEIGHT EMPTY:	5,300kg	FORDING:	Amphibious
LENGTH:	4.45m	GRADIENT:	60%
WIDTH:	2.4m	SIDE SLOPE:	30%
HEIGHT:	2.48m (with TL.2.1.80 turret) 2m (without armament)	VERTICAL OBSTACLE:	.3m
		TRENCH:	.8m (with one channel) 3.1m (with 5 channels)
GROUND CLEARANCE:	.35m	ENGINE:	Panhard Model 4 HD, 4-cylinder, horizontally-opposed petrol engine developing 90HP at 4,700rpm
TRACK:	2.05m		
WHEELBASE:	2.7m		
TURNING RADIUS:	6.55m		
ANGLE OF APPROACH:	68°		
ANGLE OF DEPARTURE:	50°	ARMAMENT:	See text. Most models have 2 × 2 smoke dischargers
MAXIMUM ROAD SPEED:	100km/hr		
MAXIMUM WATER SPEED:	4km/hr	ARMOUR:	8mm–12mm

Note: Weight and height depend on armament installation.

DEVELOPMENT
The prototype of the M3 was built by Panhard in 1969. This prototype differed from production vehicles in that it had vertical sides, a flat roof and a single small machine-gun turret. The first production vehicles with the new hull design were completed in 1971 and since then large numbers have been built, most of which have been exported. 95% of the mechanical components of the M3 are identical to those of the Panhard AML Light Armoured Car.

DESCRIPTION
The hull of the M3 is of all-welded construction with the driver seated at the front of the vehicle. A total of twelve men are carried – three each side of the hull facing outwards, three in the rear facing the rear and two in the centre of the vehicle, plus the driver.

The driver is provided with a one-piece hatch cover with three integral periscopes. The hatch lifts and swings to the right to open. There are three hatches in each side of the hull which lift upwards and enable the crew to fire their weapons from within the vehicle. In the rear of the hull are two large doors, each of which is provided with a firing port. In addition there is a single large door each side of the hull.

There are two hatches in the roof, one to the rear of the driver and one at the rear and various armament installations can be provided for these.

The engine and transmission are situated behind the driver. Air is drawn in via louvres just to the rear of the driver on the roof, with the exhaust pipes running along either side of the roof.

The gearbox has 6F and 1R gears and is located crosswise. It consists of two gearboxes in one, coupled on both sides of the bevel pinion. The low range box comprises two low gears, top gear and one reverse for use in rough country. The high range box has three low ranges and one overdrive. When the low range box is in direct drive, the four ratios of the high range box command the four upper gears of the range (ie sixth, fifth, fourth and third). Drive is transmitted from the main gearbox to the two lateral boxes, and these transmit power to the front wheels by pinions and to the rear wheels by driveshafts that run along the inside of the hull.

The clutch is of the centrifugal type with electro-magnetic control. Ball type differentials, located in the gearbox and in each of the rear lateral transfer boxes, prevent the wheels slipping without the driver having to take action.

The suspension consists of coil springs and hydro-pneumatic shock-absorbers acting on suspension arms of the wheel mechanism. The tyres have puncture-proof Hutchinson inner tubes. Brakes are hydraulic, one line for front and one line for the rear.

The M3 is fully amphibious being propelled in the water by its wheels. When afloat it has a freeboard of .73m. Infra-red driving equipment can be fitted if required.

VARIANTS

The M3 can be fitted with a wide variety of armament installations as listed below. In addition there are a number of variants of the vehicle and these are also listed.

TL.2.1.80 turret with twin 7.62mm machine-guns, elevation +55°, depression −13°, traverse 360°.

TL.52.3.S turret with 7.62mm machine-gun and three STRIM rocket launchers.

TL.52.S turret with single 7.62mm machine-gun and one STRIM launcher.

CB.127 ring mount with 12.7mm machine-gun with an elevation of +65° and a depression of −15°.

STB ring-mount, hatch opens forward to form a shield, armed with a 7.62mm machine-gun.

CB.20. M621 with 20mm cannon.

STR for rear hatch, half circle type rail on which is mounted a 7.62mm machine-gun, traverse 180°, elevation +45°, depression −15°.

MAS T 20.13.621 turret with AME 621 20mm cannon, elevation +75°, depression −10°, traverse 360°.

VPM (Véhicule Porte Mortier)

This is currently undergoing final development. It has a new turret with an 81mm breech-loaded mortar. A total of 60 mortar bombs can be carried, which include Smoke, Illuminating, Armour-Piercing and HE. Data of the HE mortar bombs follows:

FA 32 with a weight of 3.2kg and a range of 4,500m.

ML 61 with a weight of 4.25kg and a range of 5,500m.

Super M with a weight of 5.3kg and a range of 6,500m (m/v 335m/s).

The vehicle has a crew of five which consists of vehicle commander, gunner, two loaders and the driver.

VAT (Repair Vehicle)

This has a crew of five – commander, driver and three mechanics. It carries a welding set, generator, tools, bench, vice and lifting tackle. A spare engine can be carried inside the hull if required.

VTS (Ambulance)

This is similar to the standard M3 but has a large one-piece rear door rather than twin doors as on standard M3s. It has a crew of three – driver and two medical orderlies. It can carry four stretcher patients or six seated patients or two stretcher and three sitting patients.

VPC (Command)

The front of the vehicle is the command area with tables and five seats with the radio compartment and two radio operators at the rear. It has four batteries instead of the normal two and a total of six aerial sockets are provided.

M3 (Cargo)

When used in the cargo role the vehicle can carry 1,350kg of cargo.

1

1 Panhard M3 with Creusot-Loire turret Type TL.2.1.80 with twin 7.62mm machine-guns, showing its amphibious capabilities.
2 Panhard M3 with same turret as above. This shows side and rear doors open. Note generator over rear wheel.
3 Panhard M3 armed with two 7.62mm machine-guns showing its cross country capability.
4 Panhard M3 with 7.62mm machine-gun.

M3 VTT 60 B

This is armed with a 60mm Hotchkiss-Brandt CM 60 A1 smooth-bore mortar. This has an elevation of +75° and a depression of −10°, and total traverse is 360°. The mortar can be either breech-loaded or muzzle-loaded. The following types of ammunition can be fired: HE (M 61 bomb has a range of 2,000m and the M35/47 has a range of 1,600m), Canister and Illuminating. A light machine-gun is mounted at the rear of the vehicle.

M3 HOT Anti-Tank Vehicle

This was shown for the first time at the 1975 Satory Exhibition near Paris and will enter production early in 1976. It is a standard M3 hull on the roof of which has been built a small superstructure. On top of this are four launchers (two each side) for the Euromissile HOT ATGW. The HOT has a minimum range of 75m and a maximum range of 4,000m. Ten missiles are carried inside of the hull in addition to the four on the launchers. The vehicle has a crew of three – commander, missile controller and driver. The HOT M3 is 2.7m in height.

M3 VDA Anti-Aircraft Vehicle

This was first shown at the 1975 Satory Exhibition. It is an M3 hull with a new turret designed by the following companies: Oerlikon (armament), Galileo (optical sights), CNMP (turret) and Electronique Marcel Dassault (radar system). It has a crew of three – commander, gunner and driver. The turret, which has been designated the TA 20, is armed with twin 20mm HSS 820 SL guns with a cyclic rate of fire of 800/1,050 rounds per minute. Each gun has 325 rounds of ready-use ammunition. The gunner can select left or right guns or both as well as single shots, bursts or full automatic. There is a single 7.62mm machine-gun on the roof of the turret. The turret has a traverse of 360°, elevation being +85° and depression −5°. Traverse speed is 180° in three seconds and elevation speed is 90° in two seconds.

The radar has a detection range of 8km. When in action the vehicle is supported on four hydraulic jacks. Basic data are similar to the standard M3 except that the VDA has an overall weight of 6,300kg and a height of 2.995m.

2   3   ▼4

Top Panhard M3 with 81mm breech-loaded mortar known as the VPM.
Centre Close-up of a Hotchkiss-Brandt 60mm Mortar on a Panhard M3 APC.
Left The M3 with four HOT ATGWs mounted in a turret on top of the hull.
Above Panhard M3 VDA Anti-Aircraft Vehicle with twin 20mm cannon.

FRANCE

AMX-10P – MECHANIZED INFANTRY COMBAT VEHICLE
MANUFACTURER – Atelier de Construction Roanne (ARE)
STATUS – In service with the French Army and entering service with at least two other Armies, reported to include Greece and Saudi-Arabia. In production.

BASIC DATA

CREW:	2 + 9 (driver, commander and 9 infantrymen)	FORDING:	Amphibious
		GRADIENT:	60%
		SIDE SLOPE:	30%
WEIGHT LOADED:	13,800kg	VERTICAL OBSTACLE:	.7m
WEIGHT EMPTY:	11,300kg	TRENCH:	1.6m
LENGTH:	5.778m	ENGINE:	Hispano-Suiza HS 115-2,
WIDTH:	2.78m		V-8, water-cooled
HEIGHT:	2.54m (o/a)		supercharged diesel
	1.87m (top of hull)		developing 276HP at
GROUND CLEARANCE:	.45m		3,000rpm
GROUND PRESSURE:	.53kg/cm²	ARMAMENT:	1 × 20mm gun
POWER TO WEIGHT RATIO:	20HP/ton		1 × 7.62mm co-axial
MAXIMUM ROAD SPEED:	65km/hr		machine-gun
MAXIMUM WATER SPEED:	7.92km/hr		2 × 2 smoke
RANGE (road):	600km		dischargers

DEVELOPMENT

The requirement for a new tracked vehicle to replace the AMX VC1 was issued in the early 1960s. The first prototypes were completed in 1968 and were shown at the 1969 Satory Exhibition. The prototypes weighed 12,000kg and were powered by a multi-fuel engine. The commander had his own cupola as did the gunner, and the gunner's turret had a single 20mm cannon. The hatches over the rear troop compartment were also different on the prototypes. In 1972 a production order was placed for the AMX-10P and the first pre-production vehicles were delivered to the 7th Mechanized Brigade at Rheims in 1973, the next unit to be re-equipped being the 10th Mechanized Brigade.

DESCRIPTION

The hull of the AMX-10P is of all-welded alloy construction, with the driver seated towards the front of the vehicle on the left side with the engine to his right. The driver is provided with a single-piece hatch cover that opens to the rear and a total of three periscopes for observation purposes. The turret is in the centre of the hull and is described below. The troop compartment is at the rear of the hull and is provided with two hatches in the roof, these being hinged in the centre. There are two periscopes in the left side of the roof, three in the right side and two in the rear, these being for the use of the infantry. Normal means of entry and exit is via the electrically operated ramp in the rear of the hull. This is provided with two doors, each of which has a firing port. Unlike most MICVs there are no firing ports in the hull sides of the AMX-10P. The nine infantrymen are provided with individual seats which can be folded up so that stores and cargo can be carried.

The suspension is of the torsion-bar type and consists of five road wheels with the drive sprocket at the rear and the idler at the front. There are a total of five track support rollers. Double-acting lever-type shock absorbers are provided for the first and fifth wheel stations. There is an access panel in the front of the hull to give access to the transmission and steering units. The transmission consists of a hydraulic torque converter coupled to a preselective gearbox with 4F and 1R gears. The AMX-10P is fully amphibious being propelled in the water by its tracks and two water jets, one each side of the hull rear. If required the vehicle can be delivered without these water jets. Before entering the water a trim vane is erected at the front of the hull.

The AMX-10P is provided with an NBC system similar to that provided for the AMX-30 MBT and is also fitted with a DOM 410 radiation meter. The vehicle can be supplied without the NBC pack if required.

One of the driver's periscopes can be replaced by a combined day/image intensification unit if required.

The Toucan 2 turret has two roof hatches which open to the left and right, and both the vehicle commander and the gunner have individual seats in this turret. The turret has full powered traverse through 360°, traverse speed being 50°/sec and elevation speed 30°/sec. Manual controls are provided for use in an emergency, ie 26°/sec in traverse and 10°/sec in elevation. The commander can override the gunner at any time. There are a total of seven periscopes arranged around the turret. The gunner has a sight with a magnification of ×6 whilst the commander has a sight with a magnification of ×1 and ×6. An image intensification sight can be fitted for night operations.

The turret is armed with a 20mm M693 cannon with dual feed—ie the gunner can select either AP or HE rounds—and a co-axial 7.62mm machine-gun. If required a French 20mm M621 or a German Rh.202 cannon could be fitted in place of the M693. Total ready-use ammunition is 350 rounds of 20mm and 900 rounds of 7.62mm. Total ammunition supply is 800 rounds of 20mm and 2,000 rounds of 7.62mm. The 20mm cannon has a cyclic rate of fire of 740 rounds per minute, and the gunner can select single round, limited burst or a continuous burst as required. The weapon fires the HS 820 range of ammunition which includes HE, HE-1 and AP rounds. These have an m/v of 1,050m/s and a time of flight to 1,000m of 1.25 seconds. In addition the French have developed a special AP round with an m/v of 1,300m/s, and a time of flight to 1,000m of only .85 seconds. This will penetrate 20mm of armour at an angle of 60° at a range of 1,000m. Tracing distance is 1,700m.

Two smoke dischargers are mounted on each side of the hull rear.

VARIANTS

AMX-10P with RATAC

This is now in service with the French Army. It is a basic AMX-10P with the RATAC (Fire Radar for Field Artillery) mounted in place of the gun turret. It has a crew of five which consists of a driver, two radar operators, radio operator and tracing table operator. The radar head is provided with an automatic elevation and slant corrector. A tracing table, servo-controlled by the radar, enables the moving target to be followed on a map.

AMX-10P with HOT

It was intended that the German/French HOT missile would be mounted on the AMX-13 light tank. It was then decided that it would be mounted on the AMX-10P. At first two models were developed of a model called the AMX-10M, one armed with an ACRA long range anti-tank system mounted in the glacis, which had a new hull, and the second model with a 20mm cannon in a small turret and two launchers for HOT missiles either side. Development of both these has stopped as they were too expensive. The first prototypes of the AMX-10P with HOT were shown at the 1975 Satory Exhibition. The new turret has two HOT launchers either side in the ready-to-launch position with a further 15/20 missiles carried inside the hull. The turret has seats for both the vehicle commander and the missile controller, and has powered traverse through a full 360°, elevation being +18° and depression −12°. Traverse speed is 50°/sec powered and 10°/sec manual, and elevation speed is 18°/sec powered and 22°/sec manual.

The HOT missile is aimed using the M509 sight which has a magnification of ×4 for acquisition purposes, ×12 for aiming purposes. A laser rangefinder called the M427 is under development. This will have a range of 8,000m and an accuracy of ±5m. A 7.62mm machine-gun can also be mounted, with 200 rounds of ready-use ammunition. Total ammunition supply is 2,000 rounds and this is aimed using an M309 sight with a magnification of ×3.

When the HOT missiles have been fired they have to be reloaded from outside the hull, unlike vehicles such as the British FV438 which can be reloaded from within the hull. Total crew consists of five men—commander, missile-controller, two loaders and a driver.

AMX-10 TM (Mortar Towing)

This is in its final stages of development and is expected to enter production in the near future. It is a basic AMX-10P with its turret replaced with a more simple single-seat turret with manual controls and a 20mm cannon. Inside the hull are racks for 60 120mm mortar bombs, and the mortar is towed behind the vehicle. The rear ramp is modified and has just one door rather than two as on the standard AMX-10P. It has a crew of six men.

AMX-10 PC (Command)

This is now in service with the French Army and has a crew of six—driver, two radio operators and command staff. On each side of the vehicle is an awning which is folded up when not required. Two vehicles can be backed up together and joined by a canvas cover. Inside the rear compartment are additional radios, maps and so on. A generator is mounted on top of the hull at the rear and this can be removed and set up away from the vehicle when in use for extended periods.

AMX-10P Training Vehicle

This is a basic AMX-10P with its turret removed and replaced by a greenhouse-type cupola. The driver is seated at the front in the normal position with the instructor and a trainee driver in the cupola. The driver at the front of the hull can be monitored by the instructor who can also stop the vehicle if required. A further four trainee drivers can be carried in the hull rear. This model is now in service with the French Army.

AMX-10 ECH Repair Vehicle

At one time this was to have been known as the AMX-10D. The AMX-10 ECH has a crew of five consisting of a chief engineer, three mechanics and the driver. Its physical characteristics are identical to those of the AMX-10P except that it has a T 20-13 turret known as Toucan 1. This has manual traverse and elevation, traverse is a full 360°, elevation being +50° and depression −13°. It is armed with a 20mm cannon and co-axial 7.62mm machine-gun. Total ammunition supply is 576 rounds of 20mm and 2,000 rounds of 7.62mm ammunition. This has been designed to carry out repair work on other members of the AMX-10P family.

Future modifications to the AMX-10P

At least three modifications have been suggested for the AMX-10P: 1. A stabilization system for the 20mm turret.   2. Fitting a Milan ATGW to the turret or hull rear.   3. Trials are under way with an AMX-10P fitted with a Saviem Transfluid transmission installed. This consists of a hydro-kinetic torque converter with automatic clutch disengagement and an aligned gearbox in constant mesh with 5F and 1R gears.

AMX-10P Ambulance

This is the basic vehicle with armament removed. It has a crew of three and carries a range of medical equipment. It can carry between four and nine men, either sitting or on stretchers.

AMX-10RC 6 × 6 Wheeled Reconnaissance Vehicle

There is a separate combined entry for the AMX-10RC (6 × 6) Wheeled Reconnaissance Vehicle and the AMX-10C tracked vehicle with the same turret as fitted to the AMC-10RC.

Wheeled Members of the AMX-10 Series

Apart from the AMX-10RC mentioned above there were to have been the following additional wheeled vehicles using similar components:
AMX-10RP – Prototype was shown in 1971.   AMX-10RM – With HOT ATGW.

It is assumed that these are still under development but no official announcement has been made on them for several years.

AMX-10P MICV of the French Army.

AMX-10P MICV with crew, infantry and equipment carried in the vehicle.

AMX-10P fitted with the RATAC radar system in place of turret.

Infantry dismount from their AMX-10P MICV.

AMX-10P with HOT ATGW installation.

The AMX-10 PC Command Vehicle from the rear.

Left AMX-10 TM towing a 120mm Hotchkiss-Brandt Mortar.

FRANCE

BERLIET VXB-170–ARMOURED PERSONNEL CARRIER
MANUFACTURER–Automobiles Berliet, Bourg
STATUS–In service with the French Gendarmerie and on order for a number of African countries including Senegal. In production.

BASIC DATA

CREW:	1 + 11	MAXIMUM ROAD SPEED:	85km/hr
WEIGHT LOADED:	12,700kg	MAXIMUM WATER	
WEIGHT EMPTY:	9,800kg	SPEED:	4km/hr
LENGTH:	5.99m	RANGE:	750km
WIDTH:	2.5m	FUEL:	220 litres
HEIGHT:	2.05m (w/o armament)	FORDING:	Amphibious
GROUND CLEARANCE:	.45m (transfer box)	GRADIENT:	60%
TRACK:	1.91m	SIDE SLOPE:	30%
WHEELBASE:	3m	ENGINE:	Berliet V-8 diesel
TYRES:	14.00 × 20		developing 170HP at
TURNING RADIUS:	7.8m		3,000rpm, 6.92 litres
ANGLE APPROACH:	45°	ARMAMENT:	See text
ANGLE DEPARTURE:	45°	ARMOUR:	7mm

Note: The weight and height of the vehicle depends on the armament installation.

DEVELOPMENT
In the mid-1960s Berliet, who are the largest manufacturers of military trucks in France, commenced development of a 4 × 4 armoured personnel carrier as a private venture. The first prototype of this vehicle, known as the BL-12, was completed in March 1968 and shown at the Satory Exhibition in 1969. A second prototype was built for the French Army, but they did not place a production order for the vehicle. The French Gendarmerie became interested in the vehicle and a further five improved models were built, the first of these being completed in 1971. These were known as the VXB (Véhicule Blindé à Vocations Multiples), or Multi-Purpose Armoured Vehicle. After further trials the French Gendarmerie ordered a batch of 50 vehicles, with production commencing in 1973. The French Gendarmerie have a total requirement of around 400 vehicles. The VXB was entered for the VAB competition but it was unsuccessful. The basic vehicle has been designed to carry 12-13 fully armed men. Wherever possible, standard automotive components have been used in the vehicle.

DESCRIPTION
The hull of the Berliet VXB is of all-welded construction. The driver is seated at the front of the hull on the left and is provided with a one-piece bullet-proof windscreen which can be covered by a two-piece armoured cover. In addition there is a smaller bullet-proof window either side of the driver's position. The driver is provided with three periscopes in the roof for driving when the armoured cover is in position. The commander is to the right of the driver and is provided with a one-piece hatch cover that opens to the right. This is provided with an integral swivelling periscope.

There are a total of three doors, one in each side of the hull and one in the hull rear to the right of the engine. On the standard model there are a total of seven firing ports. On the Internal Security Model, however, bullet-proof windows are provided (two each side in the hull and one in the rear hull door). These can also be opened to allow the infantry to fire their weapons from within the vehicle.

A total of four roof hatches are provided. One towards the front, where the main armament is normally installed, two in the centre of the roof and a circular hatch to the right of the engine compartment.

The engine is mounted at the rear of the hull on the left side, and access to this is via louvred covers in the roof and a cover in the rear of the hull. The pre-selective gearbox with electric-pneumatic control has 6F and 1R gears. The VXB has permanent 4 × 4 drive with two ratios, road and cross country. The front and rear wheels have planetry reduction gears in each wheel. The rear axle has a pneumatically controlled interwheel differential lock and a differential lock can be provided for the front axle if required. The suspension consists of a concentric helical spring with a hydraulic shock absorber at each wheel station. Steering is power assisted and disc brakes are provided on all wheels. A winch with a capacity of 3,500/4,500kg can be mounted in the front of the hull on the right side.

VARIANTS
The VXB has been designed to undertake a wide variety of roles apart from its basic role as an armoured personnel carrier. These other roles are:

VLC (Véhicule Léger de Combat) or Light Combat Vehicle.
VRL (Véhicule Reconnaissance Légère) Light Reconnaissance Vehicle.
Maintien de L'Ordre or Internal Security Vehicle.

The basic APC (or VTT – Transport de Troupe) is normally armed with light automatic weapons such as 12.7mm or 7.62mm machine-guns. In addition the following optional extras are available: hydraulically operated obstacle-clearing blade on the front of the hull, heater, NBC system, public address system and various radio installations. The standard model is fully amphibious being propelled in the water by its wheels, and it also has bilge pumps. If required, however, the vehicle can be delivered without these pumps and with unsealed doors and hatches.

The full range of armament installations and roles is as follows:
Mortar vehicle with 81mm mortar and 100 mortar bombs.
Turret-mounted 20mm cannon as mounted on the AMX-10P MICV.
Turret-mounted twin 7.62mm machine-guns.
Various 20mm, 12.7mm and 7.62mm weapons in open mounts.
Turret-mounted 90mm gun as used on the Panhard AML-90 armoured car.
Anti-tank missile vehicle with HOT or Milan missile installation.
Command vehicle with eight men.
Fire control or radio vehicle.
Cargo vehicle carrying 2,000kg of cargo.
Ambulance with driver, orderly, four stretcher patients and three sitting patients.
Anti-aircraft vehicle with twin 20mm cannon (ie as fitted to Panhard AML or M3).
Twin 80mm rocket launchers.
Turret-mounted 60mm mortar and twin 7.62mm machine-guns (as on Panhard AML).
Turret-mounted 20mm cannon and 60mm mortar (as on Panhard AML).
Other weapons installations are also available.

Above VXB-170 with 7.62 mm machine-gun.
Left VXB-170 with obstacle-clearing blade at front of hull.

FRANCE

AMX VCI – MECHANIZED INFANTRY COMBAT VEHICLE
MANUFACTURER – Creusot-Loire, Chalon-sur-Saone
STATUS – In service with Abu Dhabi, Argentina (assembled in Argentina), Belgium, Ecuador, France, Indonesia, Italy, Netherlands, Venezuela. Production as required.

BASIC DATA

CREW:	1 + 12 (driver and 12 infantry, one of the latter acts as commander/gunner)	TRENCH:	1.6m
		ENGINE:	SOFAM Model 8 GXb, 8-cylinder, water-cooled petrol engine developing 250HP at 3,200rpm, 8.25 litres
WEIGHT LOADED:	14,000kg		
WEIGHT EMPTY:	11,700kg		
LENGTH:	5.544m	ARMAMENT:	1 × 20mm cannon or
WIDTH:	2.51m		1 × 12.7mm machine-gun
HEIGHT:	2.32m (with turret)		or
	1.92m (w/o turret)		1 × 7.62mm or 7.5mm machine-gun (see text)
GROUND CLEARANCE:	.48m		
TRACK:	2.159m	ARMOUR	
TRACK WIDTH:	350mm	troop compartment front:	30mm
LENGTH OF TRACK		troop compartment side:	20mm
ON GROUND:	2.997m	troop compartment roof:	15mm
GROUND PRESSURE:	.7kg/cm²	hull rear:	15mm
MAXIMUM ROAD SPEED:	65km/hr	hatches:	15mm
RANGE:	350/400km	hull glacis:	15mm
FUEL CAPACITY:	410 litres	floor forward:	20mm
FORDING:	.6m	floor rear:	10mm
GRADIENT:	60%		
VERTICAL OBSTACLE:	.65m (forwards) .45m (reverse)		

Note: As this vehicle has been manufactured on and off for 20 years, and there are many different models, there are some variations in the above figures between particular vehicles.

DEVELOPMENT
The AMX VCI (Véhicule de Combat d'Infanterie) is based on a modified AMX-13 light tank chassis. Design work started in 1954 with the first prototype being completed the following year. The first production vehicles were completed in 1956. Initially the vehicle was produced by French Government tank plants but when the AMX-30 was placed in production, Creusot-Loire took over the manufacture and marketing of all the AMX-13 family, including the VCI. The VCI was without doubt one of the first MICVs, as it has an NBC system and provision for the crew to fight from within the vehicle. First vehicles had an unprotected machine-gun but a turret soon replaced this. The AMX VCI has started to be replaced in the French Army by the new AMX-10P MICV. The AMX VCI has also been called the following at various times:
AMX Model 1956 Armoured Personnel Carrier
TT.CH.Mle.56 (Transport de Troupe Chenillé Model 56)
AMX-VTP (Véhicule Transport de Personnel)

DESCRIPTION
The hull of the VCI is of all-welded construction. The driver is seated at the front of the hull on the left side and is provided with a total of three periscopes for driving when closed down and a one-piece hatch cover that opens to the left. The engine, which is built by Saviem, is to the right of the driver with the exhaust pipe in the right side of the hull.

The gunner's position is behind the driver. Early models were armed with a 7.5mm or 7.62mm machine-gun on a pintle mount, with the gunner having a cupola with a total of eight observation devices—in fact the same cupola as that fitted to the AMX 13 Light Tank. This was sometimes called the Model A APC. The other two models in service are: all-cast turret with a roof hatch and armed with a 7.5mm or 7.62mm machine-gun with an elevation of +45° and a depression of −15°, total traverse being 360°. The Belgian Army has some of these with .30 machine-guns in place of the French weapons. The second model has a .50 (12.7mm) machine-gun on a ring mount. Which can be fired by remote control from within the vehicle. In this case it has an elevation of +5° and a depression of −10°, with the gunner in the head-out position. The gun has an elevation of +68° and a depression of −10°. At the 1975 Satory Exhibition an AMX VCI was shown fitted with the GIAT Toucan cupola-type T 20.13. This is armed with a 20mm cannon with a co-axial 7.62mm machine-gun as an optional extra. There is also a hatch to the right of the gunner's station which is provided with a total of four periscopes.

The personnel compartment is at the rear of the vehicle and entry to this is via two doors in the rear of the hull, each provided with an observation/firing port. The personnel are seated in the centre of the vehicle on benches with their backs to each other. On each side of the personnel compartment are two sets of hatches. Each hatch has two parts, and the lower part, which has two observation/firing ports, folds downwards horizontally whilst the upper part folds back on to the roof.

The suspension is of the torsion-bar type and consists of five road wheels with the drive sprocket at the front and the idler at the rear. There are three (some models have four) track support rollers. Shock absorbers are provided on the first and fifth road wheel stations.

The gearbox has 5F (second, third, fourth and fifth have synchromesh) and 1R gears and steering is through a Cleveland type differential. The electrical system consists of four 12V batteries and a 4.5kw generator.

The vehicle is fitted with an NBC system and many have both infra-red driving lights and an infra-red searchlight fitted to the gunner's cupola. It has no amphibious capability.

VARIANTS
There have been many trials versions of the AMX VCI and current service vehicles and some of the recent trials vehicles are described below. In addition the 105mm and 155mm self-propelled howitzers and the 30mm self-propelled anti-aircraft system have their own entries.

Battery Command Post
This has a crew of seven and is provided with additional radios, plotting board, fire calculating board and a loud speaker. It can also tow the four-wheeled ammunition trailer.

ENTAC Missile Launching Vehicle
This is in service with the Belgian Army and has two retractable launchers, one each side at the rear. Each of these holds two missiles in the ready-to-fire position and may be elevated and retracted manually or electrically. These can be elevated from $-15°$ to $+45°$. A total of 26 ENTAC missiles are carried, and these have a minimum range of 400m and a maximum range of 2,000m. The missiles can be fired from the vehicle or away from the vehicle. It has a crew of five and retains its machine-gun turret.

81mm Mortar Vehicle
This is called the AMX-VCPM (Véhicule Chenillé Porte-Mortier) and is armed with a 81mm mortar firing through the forward part of the roof (ie where the gunner's turret is normally fitted). The mortar has a total traverse of $40°$, elevation limits being $+43°$ to $+80°$. It has a crew of six and a total of 128 mortar bombs can be carried. A baseplate is carried on the front of the hull, enabling the mortar to be fired away from the vehicle if required.

120mm Mortar Vehicle
This is also called the AMX-VCPM. It has a 120mm mortar and a crew of five. A total of 60 mortar bombs are carried. The mortar has a total traverse of $46°$, elevation limits being $+45°$ to $+77°$.

Command Vehicle
This is called the Véhicule de Commandement and has a crew of four to nine men depending on its role. It is provided with additional radios and map boards.

Ambulance
This is called the Véhicule Sanitaire and is unarmed. It can carry three stretcher patients, four sitting patients, two orderlies, driver and commander.

Roland Anti-Aircraft Vehicle
This was the trials vehicle for the French/German Roland 1 (clear-weather) anti-aircraft missile system. Production systems are mounted on the AMX-30 (France) or Marder (Germany).

AMX-VCA
This is used to support the 155mm Self-Propelled Howitzer MK F3. It has a crew of eight—the driver and seven artillery men. It carries 25 155mm projectiles, 25 cartridge bags, 39 nose fuses and can also tow an ammunition trailer. It retains its normal armament. The trailer is the ARE 2T F2, weighing 4,400kg loaded and 2,500kg empty. It can carry 30 155mm projectiles, 26 slow bags, four fast bags and six nose fuses.

AMX VCI with TOW Anti-Tank Missile Installation
DAF of Eindhoven, Holland, under contract to the Royal Netherlands Army, have fitted the American TOW missile system to a VCI for trials purposes.

Cargo Vehicle

When used as a cargo vehicle it can carry a maximum of 3,170kg.

Mine-Laying Vehicle

This was developed six years ago and when moving at a speed of 3km/hr could lay approximately 500 mines an hour at 5m intervals. A total of 600 mines were carried in the vehicle and these were packed in containers. This was not developed further than the prototype stage.

Combat Engineer Vehicle

This is known as the Véhicule de Combat du Génue (or VCG). The prototype was simply an AMX VCI fitted with a dozer blade at the front of the hull. The hydraulic equipment consists of a pressure pump driven by the main engine, a distributor for the control of the dozer blade and winch, two operating rams for the dozer blade, remote control unit for operating the dozer blade and a hydraulic winch with 60m of cable and a capacity of 3,500/4,500kg.

The dozer blade is 2.85m in width. The A frame is pivoted at the front of the hull and when the vehicle is travelling it rests on the superstructure. It has a total crew of eleven men and is armed with a turret- or cupola-mounted machine-gun and smoke dischargers. It can also tow a four-wheeled trailer similar to that used by the AMX-VCA. This can be uncoupled from within the vehicle by remote control. The VCG has similar capability to the VCI. Other data are as follows:

Weight loaded: 17,800kg Length o/a: 6.37m Width o/a: 3m Height with sheer legs in working position: 3.61m Height with sheer legs resting on tripod: 3.46m Height travelling: 2.46m

Top AMX VCI with unprotected 7.5mm machine-gun mounting.
Left AMX VCI with turret-mounted 20mm cannon.
Above AMX VCI of the Belgian Army with ENTAC missile launchers in rear troop compartment.

Top AMX Ambulance of the Netherlands Army.
Above AMX VCI of the Netherlands Army fitted with the American TOW ATGW system by DAF of Eindhoven.
Left The Combat Engineer Vehicle which is known as the Véhicle de Combat du Génue.

GERMANY (FEDERAL GERMAN REPUBLIC)

MARDER – MECHANIZED INFANTRY COMBAT VEHICLE
MANUFACTURER – Rheinstahl Sonderfertigung, Kassel and Atlas Mak of Kiel
STATUS – In service only with the German Army. It is believed Saudi-Arabia has expressed an interest in
buying the Marder.

GERMANY (FEDERAL GERMAN REPUBLIC)

CREW:	10 (commander, driver, 2 gunners and 6 infantrymen)	FORDING:	1.5m 2.5m (with kit)
WEIGHT LOADED:	28,200kg	GRADIENT:	60%
LENGTH:	6.79m	VERTICAL OBSTACLE:	1m
WIDTH:	3.24m	TRENCH:	2.5m
HEIGHT:	2.95m (including searchlight) 2.86m (turret top)	ENGINE:	MTU MB 833 Ea-500, 6-cylinder diesel developing 600HP at 2,200 rpm
GROUND CLEARANCE:	.45m	ARMAMENT:	1 × 20mm Rh 202
TRACK:	2.62m		cannon
TRACK WIDTH:	450mm		1 × 7.62mm MG 3 MG
LENGTH OF TRACK			co-axial with above
ON GROUND:	3.9m		1 × 7.62mm MG 3 MG
GROUND PRESSURE:	.8kg/cm²		on hull rear
MAXIMUM ROAD SPEED:	75km/hr		6 smoke dischargers
RANGE ROAD:	520km		on turret
FUEL:	652 litres		

DEVELOPMENT
In 1959 the German Army drew up a requirement for a new type of armoured personnel carrier. This was not only to transport men but would also allow the infantry to fight from within the vehicle. In addition the vehicle was to have heavier armour and a more complex armament installation. The vehicle was to be a member of a new family of tracked vehicles, the other main members being the Jagdpanzer Kanone and Jagdpanzer Rakete. However, development and production of these latter two vehicles was pushed ahead of the Marder MICV.

In 1960 three companies were awarded contracts to build prototype vehicles: Hanomag built three vehicles called the RU 111, RU 112 and RU 122, Henschel built the 1HK 2/1 and 1HK 2/2, whilst the Swiss MOWAG Company built the HM 1 and HM 2. These were followed by the second series of prototypes which were completed in 1961/63. Hanomag built the RU 241, RU 261, RU 262 and RU 263, whilst Henschel built the RU 264 and MOWAG the 2M 1/1, 2M 1/2 and 2M 1/3. Finally came the third and final series of prototypes: Hanomag built the RU 361, RU 362 and RU 363, Henschel the RU 364, RU 365, RU 366 and RU 368, and MOWAG the 3M 1/1, 3M 1/2 and 3M 1/3.

The Marder, or Schützenpanzer Neu, was then cleared for production and the production contract signed in October 1969. Rheinstahl built 1,926 vehicles whilst Atlas MaK of Kiel built 875 vehicles. The first Marder was officially handed over to the German Army on 7th May 1971. When the Marder first entered production Rheinstahl were building them at the rate of 30 per month. However this was reduced towards the end of the above contracts. In 1974 a further contract for 210 Marders was placed. There are many sub-contractors to the Marder including MOWAG of Switzerland who build the rear seating units, ball machine pistol mounts and the rear machine-gun position, Rheinmetall who build the weapons, and so on.

DESCRIPTION
The hull of the Marder is of all-welded construction. The front of the hull is immune to attack from 20mm rounds whilst the rest provides the crew with protection from small arms fire and artillery splinters.

The driver is seated at the front of the hull on the left side and steers the vehicle with a conventional steering wheel. He is provided with a single-piece hatch cover that opens to the right and a total of three periscopes for driving whilst closed down. The engine and transmission are to the right of the driver. There is a further seat behind the driver and a single-piece hatch cover with an integral periscope is provided. The turret is in the centre of the hull and is described below.

At the rear of the hull is the troop compartment and in each side of the hull are two MOWAG type ball mounts which allow the infantry to fire their weapons from within the vehicle. Three periscopes are provided in the roof on each side of the troop compartment. There are a total of four circular roof hatches over the troop compartment. The six infantrymen are provided with a central seating unit, which can also be used as a bunk unit. At the rear of the hull, in the roof, is a remote-controlled machine-gun, details of which are given below. Normal means of entry and exit for the infantrymen are via the ramp in the hull rear.

The road wheels are supported on swing arms and have torsion-bar springing. There are a total of six road wheels with the drive sprocket at the front and the idler at the rear and three track support rollers. The Marder has Diehl tracks with removable rubber pads.

The Marder is provided with a Renk four-speed HSWL-194 planetry gearbox and a stepless hydrostatic steering unit. It can travel the same speeds backwards as forwards. The main gun turret has been designed and built by Keller and Knappich of Augsburg and weighs 2,300kg complete with ammunition. The turret has full powered traverse through 360°, elevation being from − 17° to + 65°. Maximum traverse speeds are 60° a second and elevation speed is 40° a second. Manual controls are provided for use in an emergency. The Rheinmetall 20mm Rh 202 cannon has a cyclic rate of fire of 800/1,000 rounds per minute and is provided with a three-way belt feed which allows the gunner to select the required type of ammunition for a given target. A variety of ammunition is available including HE and AP rounds. Both the turret members (commander and gunner) are each provided with a Periz 11 periscope which has a magnification of ×2 and ×6, and these can be changed to infra-red for night operations. An infra-red/white light searchlight is mounted to the left of the turret. The commander, who sits on the right of the turret, has a total of eight periscopes for observation purposes whilst the gunner has three, and both are provided with an individual hatch cover. There are six smoke dischargers on the left side of the turret front. Total ready-use ammunition for this turret is 345 rounds of 20mm and 500 rounds of 7.62mm ammunition. Total ammunition supply for the vehicle is 1,250 rounds of 20mm and 5,000 rounds of 7.62mm ammunition.

In the rear of the hull roof is a remote-controlled 7.62mm machine-gun with a traverse of 180°, an elevation of + 60° and a depression of − 15°.

The Marder is provided with an NBC system and infra-red driving equipment. A small schnorkel can be quickly fitted, which enables it to ford to a depth of 2.5m. More recently trials have been carried out with a special amphibious kit consisting of a cigar-shaped flotation bag fixed to each side of the hull and a small bag on the glacis plate. The Basic Marder can also be used as a cargo vehicle or ambulance if required.

1 Marder showing both turrets with armament at high elevation.
2 Marder leaving a Landing Craft of the German Navy.
3 The Roland 2 Anti-Aircraft Missile System installed on a Marder chassis.
4 Marder with the new LWT-3 stabilized turret.

1

2

3

4

VARIANTS

Schützenpanzer, Neu, Mösertrager

A total of 245 of these vehicles were ordered for the German Army in 1969 but the vehicle did not eventually reach the production stage. The reason for this was that the Germans felt that the M113 fitted with the 120mm Tampella mortar could perform the same role at a much reduced cost. Rheinstahl have to date fitted over 500 M113s with the 120mm mortar for the German Army.

Schützenpanzer, Neu, Waffenträger ROLAND

This is a Marder chassis fitted with the German/French Roland surface-to-air missile system. Roland 1 is a clear-weather system, whilst Roland 2 is the all-weather system. The French will mount theirs on an AMX-30 chassis whilst the Germans have chosen the Marder chassis. Basic data of this model are length 6.91m, width 3.21m, height 2.92m (travelling) and a loaded weight of 32,500kg. Two missiles are carried in the ready-to-launch position whilst a further eight missiles are carried inside the hull. The missile itself is 2.4m in length, 160mm in diameter and weighs 63kg at launch. It is fired from a sealed launcher which weighs a total of 73kg with the missile. The missile has a maximum range of about 6,300m and a minimum range of 500m. Radar range is 18km.

Brazil has ordered four Roland systems but it is not known what vehicles the system will be mounted on. Roland will be built in the United States by Boeing and Hughes and will install it on a 4 × 4 GOER chassis or a MICV chassis. In December 1975 it was announced that the German Army had placed an order for 143 Marders with the Roland 2 missile system for delivery from 1978/79 at a unit cost of £1.4 million. Five units will be delivered in 1977, five in 1978 and 133 units between 1979 and 1982. A total of 5,000 missiles have also been ordered.

Marder with Rapier

This was a project only and was first shown at the 1970 Farnborough Air Display.

Beobachtungs Panzer Artillerie

This was developed in 1970 but not placed in production. It is a Marder with its turret removed and replaced by a large cupola complete with artillery fire-control equipment. Its remote-controlled 7.62mm machine-gun in the rear of the hull is retained.

Tieffliegerüberwachungsradar

This was built in 1971 and is simply a Marder chassis with its turret removed and replaced by a radar scanner mounted on a hydraulic arm. It has not been placed in production.

Marder with 105mm gun turret

There is a project to fit a Marder chassis with a new turret at the rear of the hull mounting a 105mm gun.

Marder with LWT-3 turret

This is a standard Marder fitted with a new turret designated the LWT-3. This has been developed by Rheinstahl and mounts the same 20mm cannon as the existing Marder turret. This turret is fully stabilized and allows the weapon to be fired accurately whilst on the move.

Other members of the original family

SPz Krkw armoured ambulance – prototype built, no production.
Rak Werfer Multiple Rocket Launcher – prototype built, no production.
SPz Fü/Fü – no production.
Flak Zwilling – anti-aircraft gun vehicle, prototypes built, role taken over by Gepard anti-aircraft tank.
Spähpanzer – based on Jagdpanzer Kanone chassis, prototypes built, no production, role taken over by Leopard and new 8 × 8 Spähpanzer.

Left Roland missile being launched from a Marder vehicle during trials.

GERMANY (FEDERAL GERMAN REPUBLIC)

UR-416—ARMOURED PERSONNEL CARRIER/INTERNAL SECURITY VEHICLE

MANUFACTURER—Rheinstahl Sonderfertigung, Kassel
STATUS—In production. In service with numerous countries in all parts of the world. Known customers include the Netherlands and Peru.

BASIC DATA

CREW:	2 + 8 (commander, driver and 8 men)	ANGLE DEPARTURE:	51°
		MAXIMUM ROAD SPEED:	80km/hr
WEIGHT LOADED:	6,300kg	RANGE:	700km (road)
WEIGHT EMPTY:	4,800kg	FUEL CAPACITY:	150 litres
LENGTH:	4.99m	FUEL CONSUMPTION:	20 litres per 100km
WIDTH:	2.26m	FORDING:	1m
HEIGHT:	2.18m (top of hull)	GRADIENT:	70%
	2.24m (top of turret ring)	VERTICAL OBSTACLE:	.55m
	2.52m (turret)	ENGINE:	Daimler-Benz Model OM 352, 6-cylinder, 4-stroke,
GROUND CLEARANCE:	.44m		water-cooled, direct
TRACK:	1.616m		injection diesel
WHEELBASE:	2.9m		developing 110HP at
TYRES:	12.5 × 20		2,800rpm
TURNING RADIUS:	6.45m	ARMAMENT:	According to role
ANGLE APPROACH:	47°	ARMOUR:	9mm

DEVELOPMENT

The UR-416 basically consists of a standard Mercedes-Benz Unimog truck chassis fitted with an armoured body. The first prototype was built in 1965 with the first production vehicles being completed in 1969. Since then well over 400 vehicles have been sold all over the world. The primary role of the UR-416 is that of internal security, although Rheinstahl (who also build the Marder MICV) have put forward various other proposals. The Unimog vehicle is well known for its excellent cross-country capabilities and is in widescale civilian and military use all over the world.

DESCRIPTION

The hull of the UR-416 is of all-welded construction and is proof against 7.62mm rounds and shrapnel.

The driver is seated at the front of the vehicle on the left side with the commander to his right. Both the driver and commander are provided with a bullet-proof windscreen, which, when in action, is covered by a steel hatch cover. Each of these hatch covers is provided with a periscope for observation when the hatch is closed.

There is a door in each side of the hull and another in the rear of the hull. All the doors are in two halves, the top half opening outwards, left or right, and the bottom half folding down to provide a step for easy access to the vehicle. In the roof there is a circular hatch that can be provided with a variety of armament installations. Towards the rear of the roof is a rectangular hatch that opens forwards.

There are five firing ports in each side of the hull (including one in each side door), and there are two firing ports in the rear hull door. The spare wheel is normally fitted to the rear door.

The eight men in the rear of the vehicle are each provided with a folding seat. Three men sit each side facing outwards and the other two men are at the rear of the vehicle facing the rear. Each of the men can use one of the firing ports if required.

Two fans draw fresh air into the interior via two ducts. Adjustable air-outlet ports distribute fresh air throughout the crew compartment.

The engine and transmission are at the front of the vehicle, and the latter has 6F and 2R gears. For normal road use it is a 4 × 2 vehicle and when off the road it is a 4 × 4 vehicle. The control lever for all-wheel drive and differential locks may be operated whilst the vehicle is being driven and without operating the clutch.

The brakes are hydraulic with a mechanical handbrake that operates on the rear wheels. Steering is power assisted. The vehicle has two 12V batteries with a capacity of 100Amp/hr and a three-phase alternator is provided. Internal and external lights are provided and various radio installations are available. If required the vehicle can be fitted with special combat tyres on which the vehicle can be driven up to 80km after its tyres have been punctured. Other optional equipment includes a machine-gun rail on the rear hatch and a winch. The engine compartment can be fitted with a semi- or fully-automatic Graviner fire-extinguishing system. A heater can be installed for operating in cold climates.

Special spherical mountings can be fitted in place of the firing ports. These enable the crew to use their SMGs with complete safety from 45° left and right, and from −20° to +25° in elevation.

The hull and the chassis can be quickly separated for repair or maintenance requirements. The lifting equipment consists of three simple jacks though these are not normally carried on the vehicle. One is fitted to each side of the hull and the third jack is fitted at the rear. The two side jacks are operated whilst the chassis pivots on the rear jack. Once the body has been lifted clear the chassis can be driven away. Only four screws and one electric connection have to be loosened before the hull is removed from the chassis.

VARIANTS

The basic model is armed with a 7.62mm machine-gun which is provided with a small shield. The gun can be traversed through 360°, elevation limits being −10° to +75°. An infra-red sight can be fitted if required. A horseshoe-shaped mount is also available, on which the machine-gun can be traversed through 270°. Four smoke dischargers can be fitted either side of the hull if required. The following variants of the basic model are available:

Ambulance
This can carry eight sitting or four lying, or four sitting and two lying patients plus the crew of two. No armament is normally fitted.

Armoured Command Vehicle or Fire-Control Vehicle
This is the basic vehicle fitted with tables and additional communications equipment.

Scout Car
This is fitted with a small turret armed with a 7.62mm machine-gun. The turret has a traverse of 360°, elevation limits of the machine-gun being −10° to +60°. A similar model has twin 7.62mm machine-guns.

Scout Car
Armed with a turret-mounted Rheinmetall Rh 202 20mm gun, the turret has a traverse of 360° and elevation limits of the cannon are −8° to +60°.

Scout Car with 90mm Recoilless Gun
This has a turret-mounted 90mm recoilless gun. The weapon has a traverse of 45° left and 60° right. Elevation limits are +15° and depression −10°. A total of 23 rounds of 90mm ammunition are carried.

Anti-Tank Vehicle COBRA
This carries a total of nine COBRA wire-guided anti-tank missiles, each of which has an effective range of 2,000m. These are launched from two launchers, each of which can be extended through hatches in each side of the hull. This model has a crew of four men and is also armed with a 7.62mm machine-gun.

Anti-Tank Vehicle TOW
This is armed with a TOW missile launcher and a total of 10 TOW missiles. Crew consists of four men. The TOW has a range of 4,000m.

Repair Vehicle
This is provided with tools, benches, vice, welding equipment and so on. A jib crane can be erected at the front of the hull if required.

Police Vehicles
In addition to the basic vehicle a number of models have been developed specifically for the use of Police Forces.

Observation Cupola Model 1
This is provided with a one-piece hatch cover and a total of seven bullet-proof vision blocks. A firing port with a window above it is provided. The firing port has been designed to accept a rifle or sub-machine-gun. The weapon can be used from −5° to +25° in elevation and 15° left and right.

Observation Cupola Model 2
This is similar to the above but has a double row (ie 14) of bullet-proof vision blocks and two firing ports, each with a window. This model has been designed for use against snipers. The lower firing port has the same capabilities as the Model 1 but the second firing port can accept a weapon to be used up to +65°.

Obstacle Clearing Blade
This is simply the basic vehicle fitted with a blade suitable for clearing obstacles. The blade is hydraulically operated by the driver from within the vehicle. The blade can be quickly removed and stowed at the rear of the vehicle.

Above UR-416 with turret mounted 20mm cannon.
Below UR-416 showing its cross-country capabilities.

GERMANY (FEDERAL GERMAN REPUBLIC)

HWK 10 SERIES
MANUFACTURER – Henschel-Werke (Kassel) now Rheinstahl
STATUS – In service only with the Mexican Army. Production complete.

BASIC DATA (of the HWK 11 APC)

CREW:	2 + 10 (commander, driver and 10 infantry)	RANGE:	320km (on roads at a speed of 40km/hr)
WEIGHT:	11,000kg (loaded) 9,000kg (empty)	FUEL CAPACITY:	300 litres
		FORDING:	1.2m
LENGTH:	5.05m	GRADIENT:	60%
WIDTH:	2.53m	VERTICAL OBSTACLE:	.68m
HEIGHT:	1.585m (without armament)	TILT:	30%
		TRENCH:	2m
GROUND CLEARANCE:	.435m	ENGINE:	Chrysler (361 B) 75M, V-8, OHV petrol engine developing 211HP at 4,000rpm
TRACK:	2.2m		
TRACK WIDTH:	330mm		
LENGTH OF TRACK ON GROUND:	2.87m	ARMAMENT:	1 × 7.62mm or 1 × 12.7mm M/G
GROUND PRESSURE:	.55kg/cm²		
POWER TO WEIGHT RATIO:	19.5HP/ton	ARMOUR hull front, sides and rear:	14.5m
MAXIMUM ROAD SPEED:	65km/hr	floor and roof:	8mm

DEVELOPMENT
The HWK (Henschel-Werke Kassel) 10 series were developed in the late 1950s by Henschel-Werke of Kassel, Germany, who have since become a part of Rheinstahl. The basic idea was to develop a series of light tracked vehicles that would fulfil a wide variety of roles, all using the same basic components. They were aimed primarily at the export market. The first prototypes were built in 1963 with production vehicles following in 1964. A total of 40 HWK 11 APCs were built and only 2 HWK 13 reconnaissance vehicles were built.

Below An HWK 11 Armoured Personnel Carrier on trials in Germany before delivery to Mexico.
Right An HWK 13 Reconnaissance Vehicle with a turret-mounted 20mm cannon and a co-axial 7.62mm machine-gun.

DESCRIPTION

The hull is of all-welded construction with the transmission at the front of the hull with the engine on the right and the driver and commander on the left. The driver is provided with a single-piece hatch cover that opens to the right, and a total of three periscopes are mounted in front of this hatch cover and give a coverage of 180°. The commander's hatch is behind the driver's and this opens to the rear. He is provided with a single periscope in front of his hatch that can be traversed through 360°. There are two hatches over the troop compartment at the rear of the vehicle. These are hinged in the centre of the vehicle and can be opened up vertically for loading purposes or opened half way to give overhead protection to the infantry when they are firing their weapons. The infantry are provided with benches down each side of the hull. At the rear of the hull are two rear doors.

The HWK 11 is provided with a total of five road wheels, the first, second and fifth provided with hydraulic shock absorbers. The drive sprocket is at the front and the idler is at the rear and there are two track return rollers. The suspension is of the torsion-bar type and the tracks have rubber pads.

The engine is the same as that fitted to the standard M-113 armoured personnel carrier, as is the transmission. The transmission is an Allison TX-200-2A with a hydraulic torque converter, and a total of 6F and 1R gears are provided with the following ratios:

1st 5.296:1   2nd 3.810:1   3rd 2.690:1   4th 1.936:1   5th 1.390:1   6th 1.000:1   Reverse 6.042:1

The vehicles delivered to Mexico have no infra-red equipment and no NBC systems, although these were available as optional extras. The vehicle has no amphibious capability.

VARIANTS

HWK 10 – This was an anti-tank rocket vehicle and had a total of eight ATGWs on launchers and a further two missiles in reserve. (A TOW model has also been built.)

HWK 11 – Armoured Personnel Carrier – described above. Machine-gun mounted for use of the commander.

HWK 12 – This was an anti-tank vehicle and was fitted with a turret at the rear of the hull armed with a 90mm gun.

HWK 13 – Reconnaissance vehicle fitted with a two-man turret armed with a 20mm cannon and a 7.62mm co-axial machine-gun. Different hull to APC, with engine, transmission and drive sprocket at the rear.

HWK 14 – Similar hull to the above, fitted with an 81mm or 120mm mortar firing forwards.

HWK 15 – Basically an APC hull used either for command, radio or fire-control roles.

HWK 16 – Basically an APC hull used for the ambulance role. Could carry four stretcher patients or ten sitting patients, plus crew of two.

GERMANY (FEDERAL GERMAN REPUBLIC)

SCHÜTZENPANZER SPZ 12-3 – ARMOURED PERSONNEL CARRIER
MANUFACTURER – Henschel and Hanomag (Germany) and Leyland (Great Britain)
STATUS – In Service only with the German Army. Production complete.

BASIC DATA	SPZ 12-3	JPZ 3-3		SPZ 12-3	JPZ 3-3
CREW:	8	3	GRADIENT:	60%	60%
WEIGHT LOADED:	14,600kg	13,600kg	VERTICAL OBSTACLE:	.6m	.6m
WEIGHT EMPTY:	11,700kg	—	TRENCH:	1.6m	1.6m
LENGTH:	6.31m (inc. gun)	—	ENGINE:	Rolls-Royce B.81 Mk.80F, 8-cylinder petrol engine developing 235HP at 3,800rpm	
	5.56m (hull)	5.56m (hull)			
WIDTH:	2.54m	2.55m			
HEIGHT:	1.85m (inc. turret)	2.6m (including missile)	ARMAMENT:	1 × 20mm cannon	1 SS 11 ATGW launcher
	1.63m (W/O turret)	1.71m (excluding missile)		1 × 7.62mm MG	
GROUND CLEARANCE:	.4m	.33m		2 × 4 smoke dischargers	2 × 4 smoke dischargers
TRACK:	1.92m	1.92m			
TRACK WIDTH:	305mm	305mm	ARMOUR		
LENGTH OF TRACK ON			hull front:	30mm	30mm
GROUND	2.3m	2.3m	hull sides:	15mm	15mm
GROUND PRESSURE:	.75kg/cm²	—	hull roof:	8mm	8mm
MAXIMUM ROAD SPEED:	58km/hr	58km/hr	hull floor:	8-20mm	8-20mm
RANGE (road):	270km	270km	turret front:	30mm	—
FUEL:	340 litres	340 litres	turret sides:	20mm	—
FORDING:	.7m	.7m	turret roof:	10mm	—

DEVELOPMENT

The SPZ 12-3 has a very short and unusual development. In 1955 the Swiss company of Hispano-Suiza built a light self-propelled anti-aircraft gun on a tracked chassis. At that time the German Army was being reformed, much of the original equipment coming from the United States including M7 SPGs and M47 tanks. At the same time Germany wanted to start building armoured vehicles again. In 1956 Hispano-Suiza were awarded a contract to build prototypes of a tracked APC which became known as the HS-30. A year later production contracts were awarded to Leyland in England and Hanomag and Henschel in Germany for quantity production of the vehicle. Production began in 1958 and was completed in 1962. As soon as the vehicle entered service numerous problems showed up, primarily because of the rushed development period. After these had been solved the vehicle gave good service. The SPZ 12-3 was replaced in many units by the Marder from 1970, although according to the German Army as of October 1973 they had 758 SPZ 12-3s in active use as well as 270 120mm mortar carriers with additional vehicles in reserve.

DESCRIPTION

The hull of the SPZ 12-3 is of all-welded construction. The driver is seated at the front of the vehicle on the left and is provided with a single-piece hatch cover that opens to the left and three periscopes for observation purposes. On some models the driver's hatch opens to the rear. Behind the driver's hatch is a further hatch cover that opens to the rear.

The gun turret is to the right of the hull at the front and is provided with a single-piece hatch cover that opens forwards. There are two rectangular hatch covers over the troop compartment and these are hinged on the sides of the vehicle. The infantry normally leave the vehicle by jumping over the sides. In the rear of the hull, on the left side, is a small two-piece door. The engine is at the rear of the vehicle on the right side. The transmission has 8F and 1R gears. The suspension consists of five road wheels with the idler at the front and the drive sprocket at the rear and there are three track return rollers. The electrical system is 24V.

The 20mm Hispano HS 820 (built in Germany by Rheinmetall) has an elevation of +75° and a depression of −10°. The turret has full traverse through 360°. A 7.62mm MG-3 machine-gun is often mounted forward of the hatch behind the commander's hatch. Four smoke dischargers are fitted at the front of the vehicle on each side. A total of 2,000 rounds of 20mm ammunition are carried.

The HS-30 has no NBC system and no amphibious capability. Some models have been fitted with infra-red driving lights.

VARIANTS
Hispano-Suiza built a number of other vehicles on the HS-30 chassis including a multiple rocket launcher and an anti-tank vehicle with a turret-mounted 90mm gun.

Jagdpanzer JPZ 1-3
This was developed to prototype stage and was an HS-30 chassis with a 90mm gun mounted in the front of the vehicle.

Panzermörser SPZ 52-3
On this model the 20mm turret has been removed and a 120mm mortar mounted in the troop compartment, firing forwards. It has a crew of four and is armed with a 7.62mm MG-3 machine-gun and eight smoke dischargers.

Panzermörser SPZ 51-1
This was developed to prototype stage only and was armed with a 81mm mortar. The Germans felt that this mortar was too light and therefore adopted a 120mm mortar.

Jagdpanzer Rakete JPZ 3-3
This is a basic SPZ 12-3 hull with the turret removed. It is provided with two launchers for the French SS-11 ATGW missile, but only one launcher is visible at once as the other is being reloaded. This model has a crew of three. The SS-11 ATGW is wire-guided and has a maximum range of 3,000m.

SPZ 21-3 Funkpanzer
This is a command and radio vehicle.

SPZ 81-3 Feuerleitpanzer
This is an artillery fire-control or command vehicle.

SPZ 12-3 with TOW ATGW system
This was tested in 1971. It is a basic APC with the turret removed and an American TOW missile system fitted. The system is known as the PARS.3.
The basic APC is also in service fitted with the American M40A1 106mm Recoilless Rifle, with various radar systems, and some have been fitted with the French/German Milan ATGW for trials purposes. The vehicle is also used to carry or tow assault boats. In the latter case two poles are tied to the rear of the vehicle and the boat lashed to the poles.

Above The Spz.12-3 Armoured Personnel Carrier from the rear.

The Jpz.3-3 launching a SS 11 ATGW.

Spz.12-3 with Milan ATGW system in place of turret.

GREAT BRITAIN

AT104 and AT105 – INTERNAL SECURITY VEHICLES
MANUFACTURER – GKN Sankey Limited, Wellington, Shropshire
STATUS – AT104 is in service with Royal Brunei Malaya Regiment and Dutch State Police. In production.
AT105 has completed its trials and is expected to enter production in the near future.

BASIC DATA	AT104	AT105		AT104	AT105
CREW:	2 + 9	2 + 8	RANGE:	640km	643km
WEIGHT LOADED:	8,900kg	9,144kg	FUEL CAPACITY:	160 litres	160 litres
WEIGHT EMPTY:	8,000kg	8,230kg	FORDING:	.7m	1.12m
LENGTH:	5.486m	5.17m	ENGINE:	6-cylinder	Bedford 500
WIDTH:	2.438m	2.489m		Bedford petrol	6-cylinder diesel
HEIGHT (cupola):	2.489m	2.59m		developing	developing
GROUND CLEARANCE				134BHP at	146BHP at
hull:	.457m	.36m		3,300rpm	2,800rpm
axles:	.33m	.34m		or	or
TRACK				6-cylinder	Rolls-Royce
front:	2.076m	2.06m		Bedford diesel	B.81 8-cylinder
rear:	2.057m	2.302m		developing	petrol engine
WHEELBASE:	3.302m	3.07m		98BHP at	developing 164BHP
TYRES:	12.00 × 20	12.00 × 20		2,600rpm	at 3,000rpm
TURNING RADIUS:	7.62m	7.15m	ARMAMENT:	See Text	See Text
MAXIMUM ROAD SPEED:	80km/hr	88.5km/hr	ARMOUR:	6mm-12.5mm	6mm-12.5mm

DEVELOPMENT
In 1970 GKN Sankey, who built the FV432 series of tracked armoured personnel carriers for the British
Army, realised that there was a requirement for a well armoured internal security vehicle. The first model
built was the 4 × 2 AT100 which was completed in 1971, but this was not placed in production. It was
followed by the 4 × 4 AT104 in 1972 and the 4 × 4 AT105 in 1974.

DESCRIPTION/VARIANTS AT104
The hull of the AT104 is of all-welded steel construction. The engine is at the front of the vehicle and is
armoured. The driver is seated behind the engine and is provided with a total of three bullet-proof glass
vision blocks. Both LHD and RHD models are available. The personnel compartment is at the rear of the
vehicle and there is a single door in each side of the hull, one of these being for the driver, and twin doors
in the rear of the hull. A total of seven vision/firing ports are positioned around the hull, and GKN have
developed a ball-type mount so that men can fire their weapons from within the vehicle. The commander's

cupola is in the centre of the roof and is provided with a single-piece hatch cover and a total of four bullet-proof vision blocks. The troops sit on padded seats down each side of the hull. The AT104 is fitted with an Allison AT540 automatic transmission with 4F and 1R gears and there is provision for a power take-off. All vehicles have power-assisted steering. Brakes are hydraulic with servo-assistance. Run-flat tyres are standard. The suspension consists of Bedford semi-elliptical springs and hydraulic shock absorbers as fitted to the Bedford MK truck. The electrical system is 24V with a battery capacity of 100Amp/hr, charged by an engine-driven alternator with a 790watt output.

A wide range of armament installations and optional fittings are available, including a turret-mounted machine-gun, pintle-mounted machine-gun, grenade dischargers, air conditioning, heater, searchlights, auxiliary electrical generator, barricade-remover hydraulically operated, hydraulic winch with a pull of 5,000kg, and other fittings.

Whenever possible all essential components are within the armoured body. This includes the engine, transmission, fuel tanks and brakes.

DESCRIPTION/VARIANTS AT105
The first prototype was completed late in 1974 and this went on a sales tour to South America early in 1975. The main improvement over the earlier AT104 is that the wheelbase of the AT105 is shorter and the engine is now completely within the armoured envelope. The driver's position has been moved right forward so that he has a better view of the road, and on the AT105 the personnel can use both side doors rather than just one as on the AT104.

The commander's cupola is welded on to an oblong sheet of armour which is bolted on to the roof of the vehicle. This serves two roles. First, it can be quickly removed so that other armament installations can be installed, and second, when this is removed the engine can be easily removed through the roof of the hull.

The AT105 has the same transmission as the AT104 but also has a British Twin Disc transfer box with 4 × 2 and 4 × 4 drive. Like the AT104, the AT105 can be fitted with a wide variety of armament installations

Under development is a Fire Support Vehicle based on the AT105. This is essentially the hull bottom of the AT105 with a turret mounting a 76mm gun and a 7.62mm co-axial machine-gun.

The gun has an elevation of +35° and a depression of −10°. Overall length of the vehicle is 5.17m, width 2.49m and height to top of turret is 2.67m.

Above The GKN Sankey AT104 Internal Security Vehicle with searchlights and obstacle-clearing blade.

Left Rear view of the AT105 with rear doors open.

Below Interior view of the AT104 with driver's position on the left.

Bottom The AT105 without armament installed.

GREAT BRITAIN

SHORT SB.301–ARMOURED PERSONNEL CARRIER
MANUFACTURER–Short Brothers and Harland Limited, Belfast, Northern Ireland
STATUS–In service with two unnamed countries. In production.

BASIC DATA

CREW:	2 + 6 (commander, driver and 6 men)	TURNING RADIUS:	8.87m
		MAXIMUM ROAD SPEED:	96km/hr
WEIGHT LOADED:	3,543kg	RANGE:	368km
LENGTH:	4.292m	FUEL CAPACITY:	100 litres
WIDTH:	1.764m	ENGINE:	Rover 6-cylinder petrol
HEIGHT:	2.159m		engine developing
GROUND CLEARANCE:	.21m (minimum)		91BHP at 4,500rpm
TRACK:	1.358m	ARMAMENT:	Nil
WHEELBASE:	2.768m	ARMOUR:	8.25mm
TYRES:	9.00 × 16		

DEVELOPMENT
The Short SB.301 armoured personnel carrier was developed as a companion vehicle to the Shorland armoured patrol vehicle (see separate entry). The first prototype was completed in 1973 with the first production vehicle being completed in 1974. An earlier vehicle designed by Short's was called the Shorland Trooper, but this was not placed in production.

DESCRIPTION
The hull of the SB.301 is of all-welded construction and provides the crew with complete protection from small arms fire including 7.62mm rifle and machine-gun fire. The floor is constructed of glass-reinforced plastic. The driver and commander are seated at the front of the vehicle and are each provided with a conventional windscreen which can be quickly covered by an armoured hatch that has an integral observation block. They are also each provided with a side door in the top of which is an observation hatch which is hinged at the bottom and opens outwards. There are two firing ports in each side of the hull. Entry for the personnel is via twin doors in the rear of the hull, each of which has a firing port.

The six men are seated three each side down the rear passenger compartment, facing each other. Each man is provided with a safety belt, and a grab rail is suspended from the roof.

Over each of the firing ports, tops of the doors and over the windscreen is a gutter so that burning fuel from petrol bombs does not enter the vehicle. There is also a gutter for a similar purpose under the junction of the bonnet and the windscreen.

The inside of the hull is lined with thick polyurethane foam faced with plastic sheeting. This provides additional thermal insulation for the crew. An air extractor is provided.

No armament is mounted although smoke or tear gas dischargers can be mounted if required. A searchlight is mounted in the forward part of the roof and this can be operated by the vehicle commander or driver from within the vehicle. The gearbox has 4F and 1R gears and a two-speed transfer case. The suspension consists of heavy duty semi-elliptical springs with telescopic shock absorbers, and anti-roll bars are fitted front and rear. Run-flat tyres can be fitted if required and various radio installations are available.

 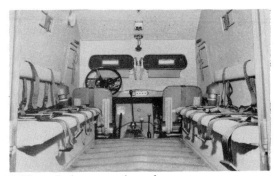

Left The Short SB.301 Armoured Personnel Carrier fitted with CS gas dischargers on the roof.
Right Interior of the Short SB.301 Armoured Personnel Carrier.

GREAT BRITAIN

FV432 SERIES – ARMOURED PERSONNEL CARRIER
MANUFACTURER – GKN Sankey Limited, Wellington, Shropshire
STATUS – In service only with the British Army. Production complete.

BASIC DATA	FV432 APC	FV434 REPAIR	FV438 ATGW
CREW:	2 + 10	4	3
WEIGHT LOADED:	15,280kg	17,750kg	16,200kg
WEIGHT EMPTY:	13,740kg	15,040kg	12,510kg
LENGTH:	5.251m	5.72m	5.105m
WIDTH O/A:	2.8m	2.844m	2.972m
WIDTH OVER TRACKS:	2.527m	2.527m	2.527m
HEIGHT:	2.286m (machine-gun)	2.794m (crane)	2.705m
	1.879m (roof)	1.891m (roof)	—
GROUND CLEARANCE:	.406m	.35/.46m	.406m
TRACK:	2.184m	2.184m	2.184m
TRACK WIDTH:	343mm	343mm	343mm
LENGTH OF TRACK ON GROUND:	2.819m	2.819m	2.819m
GROUND PRESSURE:	.78kg/cm²	—	.84kg/cm²
MAXIMUM ROAD SPEED:	52km/hr	47km/hr	52km/hr
MAXIMUM WATER SPEED:	6.6km/hr	6km/hr	6.6km/hr
RANGE (road):	580km	580km	480km
FUEL CAPACITY:	454 litres	454 litres	454 litres
FORDING:	1.066m	1.066m	1.066m
GRADIENT:	60%	60%	60%
VERTICAL OBSTACLE:	.609m	.609m	.609m
TRENCH:	2.05m	2.05m	2.05m
ENGINE:	Rolls-Royce K60 No.4 Mk.4F, two-stroke, 6-cylinder, twin crankshaft, multi-fuel engine developing 240BHP at 3,750rpm		
ARMOUR:	6mm – 12mm	6mm – 12mm	6mm – 12mm

DEVELOPMENT

The FV432 series of tracked armoured vehicles is a development of the earlier FV420 series. These were developed to prototype stage but were not placed in production. The first prototypes were completed in 1961 and were known as the Trojan. This name was subsequently dropped as it clashed with a car company of that name. In 1962 GKN Sankey were awarded a contract to build the FV432 and the first production models were completed in 1963, production continuing until 1971. A whole series of tracked vehicles has been developed from the basic FV430 chassis. The FV431 was a load carrier but this did not enter production. The FV433 Abbot 105mm self-propelled gun uses many components of the FV432 and there is a separate entry for this.

DESCRIPTION

The hull of the FV432 is of all-welded steel construction. The driver is seated at the front of the vehicle on the right side, with the engine to his left. He is provided with a single-piece hatch cover that opens to the left, in the roof of which is a single AFV No.33 Mk.1 wide-angle periscope. This can be replaced with an image-intensification periscope for driving at night. The commander is seated behind the driver and has a single-piece hatch cover and a total of three AFV No.32 Mk.1 periscopes. A 7.62mm machine-gun is mounted at the commander's station and eight boxes containing 200 rounds are provided. Some FV432s when being used by rear units have a 7.62mm Bren LMG and 50 magazines each holding 28 rounds. Two three-barrelled smoke dischargers are mounted at the front of the hull. The troop compartment is at the rear of the vehicle and five infantry are seated down each side of the hull. The seats can be folded upwards so that cargo and stores can be loaded. Over the troop compartment is a four-piece circular hatch. Normal means of entry and exit for the infantry is the single door in the rear of the hull, which is hinged on the right and has an integral vision block. The FV432 has torsion-bar suspension which consists of five road wheels with the drive sprocket at the front and the idler at the rear. There are two track return rollers. The first and last wheel stations have a hydraulic shock absorber. The steel tracks are rubber padded and rubber bushed.

The steering unit is mounted at the front of the hull and there is an access plate in the front of the glacis plate for this. The steering unit is coupled to the GM Allison TX200-4A (made in UK) transmission by a universally jointed propeller shaft. Power is transmitted from the steering unit to the drive sprockets. The engine can be removed from the vehicle as a complete unit, ie engine and oil tank.

The electrical system is 24V negative earth with two AC generators. These are current-rectified to DC for battery charging and general purposes. A total of six batteries with a capacity of 100Amp/hr are provided.

The FV432 is provided with an NBC system which is mounted in the right-hand side of the hull and provides fresh air via ducts to the troop and driver's compartments. A fire-extinguishing system is installed and this expels BCF (gas) through a network of perforated tubes. Early models had infra-red driving lights. The FV432 is provided with a flotation screen around the top of the hull. This can be erected in a short time and a trim vane is erected at the front of the hull and the vehicle propelled in the water by its tracks.

VARIANTS
The first Marks to enter service were the Mk.1s. These were followed by the Mk.1/1, Mk.2 and Mk.2/2. On the late production models the NBC filters are almost flush with the right side of the hull. The FV432 can be used for the following basic roles:

Mortar
This is armed with the British 81mm mortar firing through the roof. The mortar is mounted on a turntable enabling it to be traversed through 360°.

A total of 160 rounds of ammunition are carried. This model has a crew of six and a laden weight of 16,400kg. There are normally six of these in each Mechanized Infantry Battalion support company.

Command
This is fitted with two map boards, radios, and has a total crew of seven and a laden weight of 15,500kg. A penthouse measuring 3.66m × 2.74m × 1.98m can be quickly erected at the rear of the hull to increase the working space for the command staff.

Ambulance
This is unarmed and has a crew of two plus four stretcher patients or two stretcher patients and five walking wounded.

Cargo
The FV432 can be used in the cargo role and can carry a maximum of 3,670kg.

Recovery
This model has a winch with a maximum line pull with two-part tackle of 16,270kg. An earth anchor is provided and a total of 107m of cable is carried. The winch is powered from a power take-off on the engine transfer case.

Wombat
A 120mm Wombat anti-tank recoilless rifle is mounted over the rear troop compartment. This can be fired from the vehicle or away from the vehicle. It is loaded on to the FV432 by means of small ramps and a hand-operated winch. This model has a crew of four and carries 14 rounds of HESH ammunition. Total weight is 15,870kg. There are six of these in each Mechanized Infantry Battalion support company.

Minelayer
The FV432 is used by the Royal Engineers to tow the Bar Minelaying System. This consists of a plough-type two-wheeled trailer which is towed behind the vehicle. The Bar Mines are laid on to the conveyor inside the hull and are then laid and buried. Maximum laying speed can be as high as 600 Bar Mines per hour.

Carl Gustav
A Swedish Carl Gustav anti-tank launcher can be mounted on a bar across the rear hatch.

Radar
Some FV432s are fitted with the ZB 298 ground surveillance radar which can detect both men and vehicles. The ZB 298 is a non-coherent pulsed doppler radar that operates in the X-band from a 24V DC supply. It has a maximum range of 10,000m.

Navigation
For trials purposes a FV432 has been fitted with the Sperry navigation system.

Face
This is a FV432 fitted with the Field Artillery Computer Equipment developed by Marconi Space and Defence Systems Limited. It is deployed by the Royal Artillery at battery level.

FV432 with Cymbeline
This has been developed as a replacement for the Green Archer Mortar Locating Radar System which is mentioned below. This is an FV432 with the Cymbeline radar, which has been developed by EMI Limited, mounted on top of the hull. It is now in service with the Locating Regiments of the Royal Artillery.

Ranger Anti-Personnel Mine System
This is still undergoing trials. It has been developed by EMI Limited for the Royal Engineers. The complete system is mounted on top of a standard FV432 which can still be used for other roles, for example towing the Bar Mine System. The idea would be to cover the Bar Mine field with Ranger Anti-Personnel Mines. Ranger consists of a bank of 72 tubes each of which holds 20 Ranger mines. These are ejected from the vehicle to a range of about 100m.

FV432 Towing Giant Viper
The Royal Engineers use the FV432 to tow the Giant Viper mine clearance system.

FV432 with Rarden gun
This is basically a standard FV432 fitted with the same turret as that fitted to the Fox armoured car. A full description of the 30mm Rarden cannon is given in the entry for the Fox armoured car. Each Mechanized Infantry Battalion will eventually have 17 of these vehicles.

FV432 with turret-mounted 7.62mm machine-gun
This was undergoing trials in 1974/75 and is a standard FV432 fitted with a turret mounting a 7.62mm machine-gun over the rear troop compartment.

FV432 with twin 7.62mm GPMGs
This entered service in 1975 and is a standard FV432 with twin 7.62mm machine-guns mounted on the commander's cupola for use in the anti-aircraft role.

FV432 Sonic Detection Vehicle
This is used to detect hostile artillery fire and is used by the Royal Artillery.

FV434 Carrier Maintenance Full Tracked
This is used by the Royal Electrical and Mechanical Engineers for changing power plants, gun barrels and so on. The FV434 has a crew of four or five men and is provided with a full range of tools. An HIAB 61 hydraulic two-piece hinged jib with three-position telescopic extension is provided. This is driven from a PTO in the transmission and can be slewed through 190°. The crane can lift 3,050kg at a radius of 2.26m to 1,250kg at a radius of 3.96m. The front and rear hydraulic shock absorbers can be locked to give stability when using the HIAB crane.

FV436 Self-Propelled Mortar-Locating Radar System Green Archer
This has a modified rear hull so that it can accept the EMI Green Archer Mortar-Locating Radar System. The FV436 has a crew of three. The Green Archer is being replaced by the Cymbeline Radar System which is also mounted on the FV432.

FV437 Pathfinder Recovery Vehicle
This was a trials vehicle only and was designed to recover vehicles from river crossings.

FV438 Swingfire ATGW Vehicle
The FV438 is issued on the scale of six per Armoured Regiment and three per Mechanized Infantry Battalion. On the top of the hull are two launcher boxes for the British Aircraft Corporation Swingfire ATGW. The Swingfire is wire-guided and has a maximum range of 4,000m. It can be launched from the vehicle or away from the vehicle with the aid of a separation sight and controller. In the latter case the vehicle can be out of sight, with a maximum separation distance of 100m.

After the missile is launched it is gathered in the operator's field of view by an automatic programme generator built into the ground equipment, and the operator guides the missile on to the target. A total of 14 missiles are carried. In addition the vehicle has the standard 7.62mm GPMG mounted on a cupola.

FV439 Signals Vehicle
This is used by the Royal Corps of Signals and has a comprehensive range of radio installations installed as well as a high radio aerial mounted on the roof of the vehicle.
Note: It is possible for an FV432 to be quickly converted from the APC role to a load carrier or an ambulance. Most other variants, ie the FV434, FV436, FV438, FV439, Cymbeline models, etc., cannot be converted from one role to another. In addition there have been numerous trials versions.

Above FV432 armed with a turret-mounted 30mm Rarden cannon.
Left An FV432 of the 1st Battalion, The Royal Regiment of Wales.

Top An FV432 armed with twin 7.62mm General
Purpose Machine-guns.
Above BAC Swingfire long range ATGW being
launched from an FV438 vehicle.
Left FV432 with 120mm Wombat Recoilless Rifle.

GREAT BRITAIN

ALVIS SARACEN – ARMOURED PERSONNEL CARRIER
MANUFACTURER – Alvis Limited (now part of the British Leyland Motor Corporation), Coventry
STATUS – In service in Abu Dhabi, Brunei, Great Britain, Hong Kong (police), Indonesia, Jordan, Kuwait, Libya, Nigeria, South Africa, Sudan, Thailand, Uganda, Qatar. Production of the Saracen has been completed.

BASIC DATA

CREW:	2 + 10 (commander, driver and 10 men)	TRENCH:	1.52m
		ANGLE OF APPROACH:	53°
WEIGHT LOADED:	10,170kg	ANGLE OF DEPARTURE:	53°
WEIGHT EMPTY:	8,640kg	ENGINE:	Rolls-Royce B80 Mk. 6A
LENGTH:	5.233m (including tow hook)		8-cylinder petrol engine developing 160HP at 3,750rpm
WIDTH:	2.539m		
HEIGHT:	2.463m (including turret)	ARMAMENT:	1 × .30 Browning (7.62mm) machine-gun
	2m (top of hull)		1 × Bren 7.62mm machine-gun
GROUND CLEARANCE:	.432m		2 × 3 smoke dischargers
TRACK:	2.083m		
WHEELBASE:	1.524m + 1.524m	ARMOUR	
TYRES:	12.00 × 20	hull glacis:	12mm at 40°
GROUND PRESSURE:	.98kg/cm²	nose:	10mm at 40°
TURNING RADIUS:	7m	hull sides:	12mm at 20°
MAXIMUM ROAD SPEED:	72km/hr	hull roof:	8mm
RANGE:	400km	hull floor:	12mm
FUEL CAPACITY:	200 litres	turret front:	16mm at 10°
FORDING:	1.07m	turret sides:	10mm at 15°
	1.98m (with kit)	turret rear:	8mm at 13°
GRADIENT:	42%	turret roof:	8mm
VERTICAL OBSTACLE:	.46m		

Note: Above data relate to FV 603(C) Saracen with Reverse Flow Cooling.

DEVELOPMENT
Development of the Saracen Armoured Personnel Carrier started in 1948/49 with production vehicles following in 1952/53. The vehicle was urgently required for use in Malaya and hence its development was pushed forward over the Saladin armoured car, development of which had started earlier. The Saracen uses many components of the Saladin and these are also used in the FV 622 Stalwart High Mobility Load Carrier and the Salamander Fire Engine.

First Saracens were the Mk. 1 followed by the FV 603(B) and the FV 603(C). The latter is the most common and differs in minor details to the earlier vehicles. Production of the Saracen was completed in 1972.

DESCRIPTION
The hull of the Saracen is of all-welded construction with the engine at the front of the hull and the personnel compartment at the rear.

The driver is seated behind the engine and is provided with a total of three No. 17 periscopes, one to his front and one each side. These periscopes are mounted in hatch covers that fold forwards to give him a better view of the terrain when not in combat.

The section commander is seated behind the driver to the left and the radio operator is behind the driver to the right, both facing forwards. The other eight men are seated four each side of the hull, facing each other. The commander is seated in the turret.

Normal means of entry and exit is via the twin doors in the rear of the hull, each of which is provided with a firing port. There are three firing ports in each side of the hull as well as an escape hatch in each side of the hull. A ventilating system is provided for the personnel compartment.

The machine-gun turret is in the forward part of the roof and can be traversed through 360° by hand. The top of the turret folds forwards whilst the rear folds down to provide a seat for the commander when travelling. The machine-gun has an elevation of +45° and a depression of −15° (except over the rear part of the hull), and a No. 3 Mk. 1 sight is provided for both observation and aiming purposes. A total of 3,000 rounds of ammunition are carried.

A Bren light machine-gun is mounted on a ring mount at the rear of the roof, and access to this is via a sliding hatch from the personnel compartment. Some TAVR units have replaced the Bren with a .30 Browning machine-gun.

The Saracen has fully independent double wishbone suspension with torsion bars and sleeves. Two telescopic double-acting hydraulic shock absorbers are fitted to the front and rear wheel stations, whilst the centre wheel stations have a single shock absorber.

Steering of the front and centre wheels is by positive mechanical linkage hydraulically assisted between the steering wheel and road wheels. The Saracen can operate with one front wheel missing each side. Hydraulic brakes are provided on all wheels.

Power is transmitted from the engine by way of a fluid coupling, five-speed pre-selective gearbox, a transfer box embodying forward and reverse ranges, a differential traverse, drive direct to each centre wheel hub through universally jointed shafts. Each wheel hub houses an epicyclic train which provides the final gear reduction to the wheels.

Layout of components from the front of the vehicle is as follows: radiator, engine, fluid flywheel, gearbox, transfer box and then fuel tanks, the latter under the personnel compartment. Air enters at the front of the vehicle and is expelled via the four hatch covers over the engine compartment.

The electrical system is 24V negative earth and consists of $2 \times 12V$ batteries with a capacity of 60Amp/hr, and an automatic two-speed generator with a maximum output of 25 Amps. The Saracen has no NBC system and no infra-red equipment.

VARIANTS

FV 603(C) with Reverse Flow Cooling

This was designed specifically for operations in desert-type climates. On this model air is drawn in through raised louvres at the back of the engine compartment, passed forward over the engine by the fans, the blades of which have been reversed, and expelled through the radiator and front louvres. A cowl has been mounted on the front of the vehicle to prevent air rushing into the radiator and therefore impeding passage of air through the radiator in the opposite direction. The vehicle is easily recognisable by the cowl and the raised engine louvres.

FV 603(C) with Open Roof

A number of these were built for Kuwait. It is a standard Saracen with Reverse Flow Cooling and the roof, complete with machine-gun turret, removed.

Above Saracen APCs with reverse flow cooling system installed.
Right Saracen FV610 Command Vehicle with tent erected on right side.
Far right The standard FV603 Saracen APC.

FV 603(C) with Normalair-Garret Air-Conditioning System

Normalair-Garret have fitted a Saracen with their air-conditioning system. The engine for this is mounted on the right running boards towards the rear. During trials the outside temperature was 120°F whilst inside it was 90°F. The company have also developed a system for the Scorpion and this has been fitted to a number of production vehicles for export.

Saracen Mk. 3

Five years ago Libya ordered a number of Saracens fitted with Reverse Flow Cooling, but these were not delivered for a number of reasons and were stored at Coventry Airport. At about this time the situation in Northern Ireland became worse and the British Army took over the vehicles and sent them to Northern Ireland still in their desert camouflage. Some reports have suggested that these vehicles have a modified suspension system.

FV 603(C) with Swingfire ATGW

This progressed only as far as a mock-up. It was basically a standard Saracen with two Swingfire ATGWs mounted either side of the hull in the ready-to-launch position. A periscope for guidance purposes was mounted in the roof behind the machine-gun turret and additional missiles were carried inside the hull.

FV 604 Command Vehicle

This is the basic FV 603 modified to fulfil the command role. It has a crew of six – three staff officers, two radio operators and a driver. Early vehicles retained the machine-gun turret but most vehicles were not fitted with this as the ring mount for an LMG was moved forwards to the turret position. Stowage baskets are provided each side of the hull as well as other equipment including an auxiliary charging plant and additional batteries. A tent can be erected at the rear if required. Inside the hull mapboards are provided. There was to have been a command vehicle called the FV 602 but this was cancelled as was the FV 605 ambulance.

FV 610 Command Vehicle

The full designation of this is Armoured Carrier 6 × 6 Command GPO/CPO FV 610(A). It has a much higher and wider hull as it would be used in the static role for longer periods than the FV 604. Like the FV 604 the FV 610 is provided with an auxiliary charging plant, extra batteries, additional stowage, and a tent can be erected at the rear. It has a crew of six. The FV 610 is also used by the Royal Artillery to mount the FACE (Field Artillery Computer Equipment). It was also used to mount the Robert Radar System but this was not adopted for service.

FV 611 Ambulance

Reference has been made to the FV 611 Ambulance but it is not in service in large numbers (if at all). It has an FV 610 hull and can carry ten seated patients, or three stretcher and two seated patients, or two stretcher and six seated patients in addition to the driver and medical orderly.

Other variants

There have been numerous trials versions and projects including a Saracen Mine exploder and a Saracen 25 Pounder SPG, though the latter never left the drawing board.

	FV603 (Open Roof)	FV604	FV610
WEIGHT LOADED:	9,647kg	10,170kg	10,700kg
LENGTH:	5.233m	4.81m	4.81m
WIDTH:	2.539m	2.515m	2.515m
HEIGHT:	2m	2.057m	2.362m

GREAT BRITAIN

HUMBER 1-TON TRUCK – ARMOURED PERSONNEL CARRIER
MANUFACTURER – Chassis were built by Humber and armoured bodies by GKN Sankey and Royal Ordnance Factory at Woolwich
STATUS – In service with British Army (in Northern Ireland) and Portugal. No longer in production.

BASIC DATA

CREW:	2 + 6/8 (commander, driver and 6/8 men)	TYRES:	11.00 × 20
		MAXIMUM ROAD SPEED:	64km/hr
WEIGHT LOADED:	5,790kg	RANGE:	402km
WEIGHT EMPTY:	4,770kg	FUEL CAPACITY:	145 litres
LENGTH:	4.926m	ENGINE:	Rolls-Royce B60 Mk.5A,
WIDTH:	2.044m		6-cylinder petrol engine
HEIGHT:	2.12m		developing 120HP at
TRACK:	1.713m		3,750rpm
WHEELBASE:	2.743m	ARMAMENT:	Nil

Note: the above data relate to the FV 1611 without additional armour.

DEVELOPMENT

In the late 1940s and early 1950s a whole series of 1-Ton 4 × 4 tactical vehicles were developed by Humber/Rootes, the basic model being known as the FV 1601. At that time the Saracen APC was being built but not in sufficient numbers. It was therefore decided to modify the chassis and fit it with an armoured body. A total of about 1,700 were eventually built both by GKN Sankey and the Royal Ordnance Factory at Woolwich. These were issued to most arms of the Army for carrying men and supplies. With the introduction of the FV 432 many were sold as scrap in both the UK and overseas, only to be repurchased when the troubles broke out in Northern Ireland.

DESCRIPTION

The hull of the vehicle, which is most commonly known as the Pig, is of welded construction with the engine at the front and the personnel compartment at the rear. The driver and commander are each provided with a windscreen which can be covered by an armoured hatch complete with an observation block. Both the driver and commander are provided with a side door, the top of which can be opened if required. A circular hatch is provided over both the commander's and driver's position.

There are two firing/observation ports in each side of the hull and the crew enter and leave the vehicle via the twin doors in the rear of the hull, each of which has a vision/firing port.

The gearbox has 5F and 1R gears and the suspension is of the torsion-bar type with hydraulic shock absorbers on all wheels. Brakes are hydraulic.

VARIANTS

The first armoured models were the FV 1609 but the most common are the FV 1611 which can be used as an armoured personnel carrier, load carrier or for towing the Green Archer Mortar-Locating System. The FV 1612 is a radio vehicle whilst the FV 1613 is an ambulance, the latter having a crew of two (driver and orderly) and able to carry eight sitting or three stretcher or one stretcher and four sitting patients. The FV 1620 Markara missile-launching vehicle known as the Hornet was replaced by the Ferret Mk.5 some years ago.

In 1972/73 it was found that the IRA in Northern Ireland were using AP rounds which would penetrate the armour of the Pig in certain circumstances. All 500 of the Pigs in Northern Ireland were returned in batches to the UK where they were up-armoured. The additional weight also meant that the rear axle and suspension had to be modified as the vehicle now weighed around 7,000kg. In addition vision blocks were fitted to the firing ports and when the rear doors are open an armour shield drops down so that when troops are behind the vehicle people cannot fire under it from the front and hit them in the legs. Some Pigs have had tear gas launchers fitted to the tops of their hulls.

Above The Humber Pig 4×4 Armoured Personnel Carrier as built.
Below The Humber Pig 4×4 Armoured Personnel Carrier modified for use in Northern Ireland.

ITALY

O-F 24 TIFONE–MECHANIZED INFANTRY COMBAT VEHICLE
MANUFACTURER–Oto Melara, La Spezia
STATUS–Project.

BASIC DATA

CREW:	3 + 6 (commander, gunner, driver and 6 infantry)	MAXIMUM ROAD RANGE:	500km
		FORDING:	1.8m
		GRADIENT:	60%
WEIGHT LOADED:	22,800kg	SIDE SLOPE:	40%
WEIGHT EMPTY:	18,800kg	VERTICAL SLOPE:	.9m
LENGTH:	6.8m	TRENCH:	2.4m
WIDTH:	3.15m	ENGINE:	V-8, two-cycle, turbo-charged diesel developing 530HP
HEIGHT:	2.325m (o/a) 1.855m (top of hull)		
GROUND CLEARANCE:	.44m	ARMAMENT (Mk.1):	1 × 76mm gun
TRACK:	2.7m		1 × 7.62mm machine-gun co-axial with above
TRACK WIDTH:	450mm		2 × 7.62mm machine-guns in individual
LENGTH OF TRACK ON GROUND:	3.9m		mounts at rear of hull
GROUND PRESSURE:	.65kg/cm²		2 × 3 Smoke dischargers either side of turret
POWER TO WEIGHT RATIO:	23.2HP/ton		
MAXIMUM ROAD SPEED:	70km/hr		

DEVELOPMENT
The Tifone was announced by Oto Melara early in 1975 and it is based on the Swiss MOWAG Tornado.

DESCRIPTION
The hull of the Tifone is of all-welded construction. The driver is seated at the front of the hull on the left side. The gun turret is to the right of the driver. As different turrets can be installed these are described under Variants. The engine, cooling system, air cleaner and exhaust system are mounted as a complete unit in the centre of the hull and can be quickly removed for repair or replacement.

The personnel compartment is at the rear of the hull and is provided with two circular roof hatches, one each side, and two remote-controlled MOWAG type machine-gun mounts, again one each side. There is a single MOWAG type ball mount in each side of the hull. The personnel are seated three each side, facing outwards, and there is a hull escape hatch in each side of the personnel compartment. The infantry enter and leave the vehicle via a ramp in the hull rear.

The suspension is of the torsion-bar type and consists of six road wheels, drive sprockets at the front, idler at the rear and three track support rollers. The front two and rear two road wheels are provided with hydraulic shock absorbers. The tracks are fitted with rubber pads.

The Mowag-built Taifun from which Oto Melara have developed the Tifone.

The steer/shift transmission is at the front of the hull and an access panel is provided in the glacis plate. The gearbox has six gears in forward and reverse. The electrical system is 24V and four batteries with a capacity of 200Amp/hr are provided together with an alternator. Infra-red driving equipment can be installed as can an NBC system.

VARIANTS

Tifone Mk.1
This is fitted with a Scorpion type turret with limited traverse. This is armed with a 76mm gun and a co-axial 7.62mm machine-gun. Elevation is +35° and depression −10°. The commander is provided with a sight with ×10 and ×1 magnification, whilst the gunner has a sight with a magnification of ×8 and ×1. Total ammunition supply is 40 rounds of 76mm and 3,000 rounds of 7.62mm. 76mm types of ammunition available are HESH, HE, Smoke, Canister and Illumination.

Tifone Mk.2
This is fitted with the same turret as that mounted on the Fiat/Oto Melara 6616M 4 × 4 Armoured Car. This is armed with a 20mm Rh 202 cannon and a co-axial 7.62mm machine-gun. A smoke grenade launcher is mounted on the commander's hatch and a 40mm grenade launcher can be mounted if required, or a TOW missile launcher. The turret has powered elevation and traverse, elevation being +35°, depression −5°, and traverse a full 360°. Ready-use ammunition consists of 250 rounds of 20mm, 300 rounds of 7.62mm and 12 40mm grenades. Reserve ammunition consists of 150 rounds of 20mm, 700 rounds of 7.62mm and 300 40mm grenades.

Tifone Mk.3
This is armed with twin 20mm Rh 202 cannons in a turret with a traverse of 360°, elevation being +85° and depression −5°. Elevation and traverse are powered, elevation speed being 70°/second and traverse speed being 90°/second. Cyclic rate of fire is 1,000 rounds per gun per minute.

ITALY

FIAT 6614 CM – ARMOURED PERSONNEL CARRIER
MANUFACTURER – Fiat of Turin
STATUS – Trials. Not yet in production.

BASIC DATA

CREW:	2 + 8 (commander, driver and 8 men)	MAXIMUM WATER SPEED:	4.5km/hr
WEIGHT LOADED:	7,000kg	RANGE:	700km (road)
WEIGHT EMPTY:	5,850kg		20km (water)
LENGTH:	5.56m	FUEL:	120 litres
WIDTH:	2.37m	FORDING:	Amphibious
HEIGHT:	1.68m (top of hull)	GRADIENT:	60%
GROUND CLEARANCE:	350mm (hull)	SIDE SLOPE:	30%
TRACK:	1.92m (front and rear)	VERTICAL OBSTACLE:	.45m
WHEELBASE:	2.8m	ENGINE:	Fiat Model 8062,
TYRES:	10.00 × 20		6-cylinder water-cooled
TURNING RADIUS:	6.8m		diesel developing 128HP
	15m (water)		at 3,200rpm
ANGLE OF APPROACH:	45°	ARMAMENT:	See text
ANGLE OF DEPARTURE:	45°	ARMOUR	
MAXIMUM ROAD SPEED:	96km/hr	hull front, sides and rear:	8mm
		hull roof and floor:	6mm

DEVELOPMENT
The Fiat 6614 CM is a development of the Fiat 6614 BM. The latter vehicle was shorter than the current model and had a wheelbase of 2.4m and was powered by a 6-cylinder petrol engine which developed 115HP at 5,000rpm. It could only carry six men plus the driver. The 6614 BM did not enter production.

DESCRIPTION
The hull of the Fiat 6614 CM is of all-welded steel construction. The driver is seated at the front of the vehicle and is provided with a single-piece hatch cover that opens to the right and a total of five vision blocks for driving whilst closed down. There is a door in each side of the hull and these are provided with a

single firing port and a vision block. There are a further three firing ports and three vision blocks in each side of the hull. At the rear of the hull is a large power-operated ramp which is hinged at the bottom and provided with two vision blocks and two firing ports. In the centre of the roof is a cupola with a total of five periscopes and a single-piece hatch cover. There is a smaller circular hatch in the roof towards the rear, and this hatch opens forwards.

The engine is mounted to the right of the driver. The manual gearbox has 5F and 1R gears and a two-speed transfer case.

Independent suspension is fitted on all wheels. This is of the strut and link type with a helical spring and rubber bump stop. Each wheel station has two hydraulic shock absorbers.

Drum brakes are fitted on all wheels and run-flat tyres are standard. The steering is power assisted. The electrical system is 24V and two 12V (90Amp/hr) batteries are provided as is an alternator.

The Fiat 6614 CM is fully amphibious being propelled in the water by its wheels. Optional equipment includes an NBC system and infra-red driving lights. The prototypes were armed with a single .50 (12.7mm machine-gun) although other armament installations are possible, including 20mm cannon and various ATGWs. Many of the components of the Fiat 6614 CM Armoured Personnel Carrier are identical to those of the Fiat 6616 4 × 4 Armoured Car which is now in production.

VARIANTS
Fiat have suggested that the 6614 CM can be adopted for a wide variety of other roles including load carrier and an ambulance. Late in 1975 Fiat announced a new model called the Fiat 6614 M. This has a slightly more powerful engine which develops 147HP at 3,200rpm. Combat weight is 7,200kg, length 5.86m, width 2.5m, height to top of hull 1.78m, wheelbase 2.9m and track (front and rear) is 1.977m. Tyres are 14.5 × 20 and are of the run-flat type.

Above The Fiat 6614 CM 4×4 Armoured Personnel Carrier with ramp lowered.
Left The Fiat 6614 CM 4×4 Armoured Personnel Carrier without armament fitted.
Right SUB-1 MICV on the left and the SUB-2 MICV on the right. Note the different armament installations.

JAPAN

TYPE 73 – MECHANIZED INFANTRY COMBAT VEHICLE
MANUFACTURER – Mitsubishi Heavy Industries Limited, Sagamihara, near Tokyo
STATUS – In service with the Japanese Self-Defence Force. In production.

BASIC DATA

CREW:	2 + 10 (driver, commander and ten infantry)	VERTICAL OBSTACLE:	.65m
		TRENCH:	1.6m
		ENGINE:	Mitsubishi V4, 2-cycle, air-cooled supercharged diesel developing 300HP at 2,200rpm
WEIGHT:	14,000kg (loaded)		
LENGTH:	5.6m		
WIDTH:	2.8m		
HEIGHT:	1.7m	ARMAMENT:	1 × .50 (12.7mm) MG
GROUND CLEARANCE:	.4m		1 × .30 (7.62mm) bow MG
MAXIMUM ROAD SPEED:	60km		2 × 3 smoke dischargers
FORDING:	Amphibious		
GRADIENT:	60%		

Note: The above data are provisional

DEVELOPMENT

Design work on the Type 73 MICV commenced in 1967/68 with the first prototypes being completed in 1970. In 1972 the vehicle was standardized as the Type 73 MICV and this is now in production for the JSDF and will supplement the older Type SU 60 APC.

Two types of prototypes were built, the SUB-1 and the SUB-2, sometimes referred to as the Type 70 MICV. The SUB-1 had a cupola-mounted 12.7mm machine-gun which could be fired from within the vehicle, and three smoke dischargers were mounted either side of the hull rear. The SUB-2 had a turret-mounted 12.7mm machine-gun with three smoke dischargers mounted on each side of the turret and an infra-red searchlight mounted on the left side of the turret. Both had a hull-mounted 7.62mm machine-gun.

DESCRIPTION

The hull of the Type 73 is of all-welded aluminium construction. The driver is seated at the front of the vehicle on the right side and is provided with a single-piece hatch cover that opens to the right and a total of three periscopes for observation purposes. The bow machine-gunner is seated on the left side of the hull and is provided with a single-piece hatch cover that opens to the left. This has an integral observation periscope in the roof of the hatch. The commander's cupola is between and behind the driver's and bow machine-gunner's position, and is provided with observation blocks and a single-piece hatch cover that opens to the rear.

The engine is on the left side of the hull with the armament installation on the right side of the hull. At the present time it has not been revealed what the exact armament installation of the Type 73 will be, ie a cupola or a turret. Hatches are provided over the rear troop compartment and the infantry enter and leave the vehicle via a single ramp in the hull rear. This is provided with a door in the right side in case the ramp fails to open. Two 'T' type firing ports are provided in each side of the hull and there is also a 'T' type firing port in the hull rear.

The suspension is of the torsion-bar type and consists of five road wheels with the drive sprocket at the front and the idler at the rear. There are no track return rollers.

The Type 73 is fully amphibious being propelled in the water by its tracks. Before entering the water a trim vane is erected at the front of the hull.

The vehicle is provided with an NBC system and night-vision equipment is fitted as standard.

VARIANTS

None announced. Variants such as mortar carriers are no doubt under development.

Above Rear view of a SUB-1 MICV showing the rear ramp with door, and smoke dischargers.
Above right The Type SU 60 Armoured Personnel Carrier.
Right The Type SX 60 107mm (4.2-inch) Mortar Carrier.

JAPAN

TYPE SU 60 – ARMOURED PERSONNEL CARRIER
MANUFACTURER – Mitsubishi Heavy Industries, Maruko (Tokyo)
STATUS – In service only with the Japanese Self-Defence Force. Production complete.

BASIC DATA

CREW:	2+8 (commander, driver and 8 infantrymen)	GRADIENT:	60%
		VERTICAL OBSTACLE:	.6m
		TRENCH:	1.82m
WEIGHT:	11,800kg (loaded)	ENGINE:	Mitsubishi Model HA-21
	10,600kg (empty)		WT, V-8, air-cooled,
LENGTH:	4.85m		4-cycle, turbo-charged
WIDTH:	2.4m		diesel developing
HEIGHT:	2.31m (including MG)		220HP at 2,400rpm
	1.70m (hull top)	ARMAMENT:	1 × .50 (12.7mm) M2
GROUND CLEARANCE:	.4m		MG
GROUND PRESSURE:	.57kg/cm^2		1 × .30 (7.62mm)
MAXIMUM ROAD SPEED:	45km/hr		M1919A4 MG
RANGE:	230km		
FORDING:	.76m		

Left The Type SU 60 Armoured Personnel Carrier from the rear.

DEVELOPMENT
Development of the Type 60 Armoured Personnel Carrier commenced in 1956 with the programme being managed by the Technical Research and Development Headquarters of the Japanese Self-Defence Agency.

Prototypes were built by Mitsubishi Heavy Industries and the Komatsu Manufacturing Company. The Komatsu prototype was known as the SU1 and was powered by a 6-cylinder horizontally-opposed diesel engine in the forward part of the hull. The Mitsubishi vehicle was known as the SU2, and was powered by an 8-cylinder diesel engine mounted in the forward part of the hull, just to the right of centre. These prototypes were completed in 1957 and were tested between 1957 and 1958. The SU2 was found to be the best design and a modified SU2 was built with the engine moved to the left side of the hull. This was accepted for service and became the Type SU 60 Armoured Personnel Carrier. The first production vehicle was completed in 1960 and by the time production had been completed in 1970, about 430 had been built. The Type 60 will be replaced by the new Mitsubishi Type 73 MICV which is now in production.

DESCRIPTION
The hull of the Type 60 is of all-welded steel construction. The driver is seated in the forward part of the hull on the right side and provided with a single periscope for driving whilst closed down and a single-piece hatch cover that opens to the right. The bow machine-gunner is on the left side of the hull and has a single periscope and a single-piece hatch cover that swings to the left. The commander is seated between and to the rear of the driver and bow machine-gunner's positions. His cupola has a single-piece hatch cover and five vision blocks. The .50 (12.7mm) machine-gun is mounted on the right side behind the driver, and the weapon is provided with a simple shield. The gunner has a two-piece hatch cover that opens left and right.

The troop compartment is at the rear of the hull and the forward part of the troop compartment roof hatch opens forwards, whilst the rear half opens left and right. The crew enter and leave the vehicle via twin doors in the rear of the hull.

The suspension is of the torsion-bar type and consists of five road wheels with the drive sprocket at the front and the idler at the rear. There are three track support rollers. Shock absorbers are provided for the first, second and fifth road wheel stations. The engine is on the left side of the hull, behind the bow machine-gunner's position, with the louvres in the roof.

The Type 60 APC has no NBC system, no infra-red equipment and is not amphibious.

VARIANTS
Type SV 60 81mm Mortar Carrier
This has a crew of five and an 81mm mortar is mounted in the rear of the hull. A base plate and stand are mounted on the glacis plate which enables the mortar to be dismounted from the vehicle and fired away from the vehicle if required. The SV 60 retains its .50 (12.7mm) and .30 (7.62mm) machine-guns.

Type SX 60 4.2-inch Mortar Carrier
This has a crew of five and a 4.2-inch (107mm) mortar is mounted in the rear of the hull. The rear hull of this vehicle differs slightly to that of the SV 60 mortar carrier. A base plate and stand are mounted on the glacis plate enabling the mortar to be fired away from the vehicle if required. The SX 60 retains its .50 (12.7mm) machine-gun but the bow machine-gun is covered by the base plate.

Type SY 105mm Self-Propelled Howitzer
This was also known as the Type 56 Self-Propelled Howitzer and was developed to prototype stage only. It was armed with a 105mm howitzer and a .50 (12.7mm) anti-aircraft machine-gun.

NETHERLANDS

YP-408 – ARMOURED PERSONNEL CARRIER
MANUFACTURER – DAF (Van Doorne's Automobielfabrieken), Eindhoven, The Netherlands
STATUS – In service only with the Royal Netherlands Army. Production of the YP-408 has now been completed.

BASIC DATA

CREW:	2 + 10 (commander/ gunner, driver and 10 infantry)	FUEL CAPACITY:	200 litres
		FUEL CONSUMPTION:	250km per 100 litres
		FORDING:	1.2m
WEIGHT LOADED:	12,000kg	GRADIENT:	60%
WEIGHT EMPTY:	9,500kg	VERTICAL OBSTACLE:	.7m
LENGTH:	6.23m	TRENCH:	1.2m or 2.9m (diagonally)
WIDTH:	2.4m	ENGINE:	DAF Model DS 575,
HEIGHT:	2.37m (top of MG)		6-cylinder in-line, water-
	1.8 (hull top)		cooled direct injection
GROUND CLEARANCE:	.518m (hull)		diesel (turbo-charged),
TRACK:	2.054m (front)		developing 165HP at
	2.08m (rear)		2,400rpm
TYRES:	11.00 × 20 (run-flat)	ARMAMENT:	1 × .50 (12.7mm) M-2
TURNING RADIUS:	9m		Browning MG in a DAF
ANGLE OF APPROACH:	42°		mount with a traverse
ANGLE OF DEPARTURE:	70°		of 360°, elevation
MAXIMUM ROAD SPEED:	80km/hr		being +70°
	60km/hr (cruising speed)		and depression —8°
RANGE:	500km (road)		2 × 3 smoke dischargers
	400km (cross-country)	ARMOUR:	8-15mm

DEVELOPMENT

Design work on the YP-408 commenced in 1956 with the first mock-up being completed the following year. The first prototype was built in 1958. This had different hatches in the troop compartment from the production model and was powered by a Hercules JXLD petrol engine developing 133HP. After extensive trials DAF were awarded a production contract for the YP-408. The first production vehicles were completed in 1964 with production finally being completed in 1968. In all some 750 YP-408s were built for the Netherlands Army.

DESCRIPTION

The hull of the YP-408 is of all-welded construction. The radiator, engine and transmission are at the front of the hull. The driver is seated behind the engine on the left side with the commander/gunner to his right. The driver is provided with a one-piece hatch cover that opens to the left, and in this hatch cover is a periscope that can be traversed through 360°. There is also a periscope to the driver's front and another in the left side of the hull. The commander is provided with a periscope to his front and another to his right, and he has two hatch covers that open vertically. These give him some protection when he is using his machine-gun.

The troop compartment is at the rear of the vehicle and the ten infantry sit facing each other, ie five down each side of the hull. There are a total of six hatches in the roof, three each side. Normal means of entry and exit for the infantry is via the twin doors in the rear of the hull, and both of these are provided with a single firing port.

The YP-408 uses many components of the DAF YA 328 (6 × 6) military truck. The gearbox has 5F and 1R gears and the auxiliary gearbox has both high and low ranges. The vehicle steers on the front two axles and the steering is power-assisted. The second front axle is not driven, ie the vehicle is an 8 × 6. The foremost front wheels are independently suspended on two trailing arms with traverse torsion bars. The wheels of the second front axle are also independently suspended, but the torsion bars are mounted longitudinally for reasons of space. The rear tandem axle consists of a centre axle with equalising beams and leaf springs. Vertical movement of the equalising beams is restricted by steel cables between the beams and the vehicle hull.

The vehicle is provided with air/hydraulic brakes and the tyres have reinforced side walls. These enable the vehicle to be driven 50km at a reduced speed if they become punctured.

The YP-408 is not amphibious and has not been fitted with an NBC system. Infra-red driving lights can be fitted as can an infra-red searchlight for the machine-gun, and an infra-red periscope for the driver.

VARIANTS

PWI-S(GR)

This is the basic member of the family – PWI-S(GR) stands for Panzer Wagen Infanterie – Standard (Group).

PWI-S(PC) Platoon Commander's Vehicle

This is basically the PWI-S(GR) fitted with additional radios. It has a crew of nine men – platoon commander, gunner, driver, and six infantrymen.

PWCO (Company or Battalion Commander's Vehicle)

This has been modified internally, ie the seats have been retained on the right side of the vehicle but on the left side a folding table and map shelf has been fitted. Additional radios are fitted and externally it can be recognised by its three radio aerials. If required a tent can be erected at the rear of the hull to increase the working area. The PWCO, like the PWI-S(PC), has an additional periscope with a traverse of 360° fitted in the roof at the rear of the vehicle. The PWCO has a crew of six comprising driver, gunner and four staff men including the commander.

PW-GWT (Ambulance)

This model is unarmed and has a crew of three – driver and two medical orderlies. It can carry two stretcher and four sitting patients and additional spare stretchers are carried outside the vehicle.

PW-V (Freight)

This has a crew of two – driver and commander/gunner. The PW-V (Freight) has been designed to carry 1,500kg of cargo in the immediate battlefield area. If required the PW-V (Freight) can be converted into the ambulance role and is the only member of the family that is not fitted with a radio.

PW-MT (Mortar Tractor)

This tows the French 120mm Brandt Mortar as well as carrying the mortar crew, stores and 50 rounds of mortar ammunition. It has a crew of seven men – driver, gunner, mortar group commander and four mortarmen. The rear doors on this model are slightly different from the standard vehicle as they have been shortened at the bottom so that they can still be opened when the mortar is hooked up to the vehicle.

Above The DAF YP-408 PWI-S Armoured Personnel Carrier.

The DAF YP-408 PW-MT vehicle towing a 120mm Brandt Mortar.

ROMANIA

TAB-70 – ARMOURED PERSONNEL CARRIER
MANUFACTURER – Romanian State Factories
STATUS – In service with the Romanian Army. In production.

GENERAL
The TAB-70 is reported to be a late production model of the Soviet BTR-60 8 × 8 Armoured Personnel Carrier, several hundred of which have been built. No further details are available.

SOVIET UNION

GT-T/M-1970 – MULTI-PURPOSE TRACKED VEHICLE
MANUFACTURER – Soviet State Arsenals
STATUS – In service with Soviet Army

BASIC DATA

CREW:	3 + 10 (commander, driver, gunner and ten men)	MAXIMUM WATER SPEED:	5km/hr
		RANGE:	400km
WEIGHT LOADED:	10,000kg	FORDING:	Amphibious
LENGTH:	6.35m	GRADIENT:	60%
WIDTH:	2.8m	VERTICAL OBSTACLE:	1.1m
HEIGHT:	2.25m	TRENCH:	1m
GROUND CLEARANCE:	.35m	ENGINE:	Model IZ-6, 6-cylinder,
TRACK WIDTH:	360mm		in-line, water-cooled
LENGTH OF TRACK ON			diesel developing 200HP
GROUND:	4.08m		at 1,800rpm
MAXIMUM ROAD SPEED:	55km/hr	ARMAMENT:	1 × 7.62mm PKT MG

Note: The above data are provisional.

DEVELOPMENT
This vehicle was first observed in 1970 and is variously known as the M-1970 Multi-Purpose Tracked Vehicle or the GT-T. It is used for a large variety of roles including use as an armoured personnel carrier, command and radio vehicle, fire-control vehicle, cargo carrier and as a prime mover for various types of artillery including anti-tank guns and 122mm howitzers. Some sources state that this vehicle is based on the GT-T tracked load carrier, others that it is based on the PT-76/BTR-50 series of vehicles. It is believed that this is to replace the AT-P armoured tracked artillery tractor.

DESCRIPTION
The hull of the GT-T is of all-welded construction. The driver is seated at the front of the vehicle on the left side and is provided with a single-piece hatch cover to his immediate front which opens upwards. There is a similar hatch to the right of the driver. The driver is provided with a hatch cover over his position and periscopes for driving whilst closed down. To the right of the driver is a turret-mounted 7.62mm PKT machine-gun. The commander's hatch is between and to the rear of the driver's and gunner's positions. The personnel compartment is at the rear of the hull and entry to this is via twin doors in the rear of the hull, each of which is provided with a firing port and a vision block. There are hatches in the roof of the personnel compartment and at least one firing port and vision block in each side of the hull.

The engine and transmission are at the front of the hull. The suspension is of the torsion-bar type and consists of six road wheels with the drive sprocket at the front and the idler at the rear. There are no track support rollers.

The vehicle is fully amphibious being propelled in the water by water jets (some reports have suggested that it is propelled in the water by its tracks only), and before entering the water a trim vane is erected at the front of the hull. Infra-red driving lights are provided and it is believed that an NBC system is provided. The GT-T can carry approx 2,000kg of cargo, and maximum towed load is about 4,000kg.

VARIANTS
It is reported that a model of the GT-T/M-1970 has been fitted with the Pork Trough fire-control radar system.

122mm M-1938 (M-30) Howitzers being supported by GT-T/M-1970 tracked vehicles.

SOVIET UNION

BMP-1 – MECHANIZED INFANTRY COMBAT VEHICLE
MANUFACTURER – Soviet State Arsenals
STATUS – In service with Czechoslovakia, East Germany, Egypt, Iraq, Libya, Poland, Soviet Union and Syria. Still in production.

BASIC DATA

CREW:	3+8 (commander, driver, gunner and 8 infantrymen)	TRENCH:	2.7m
		ENGINE:	Model V-6, 6-cylinder in-line water-cooled diesel developing 280HP at 2,000rpm
WEIGHT LOADED:	12,500kg		
LENGTH:	6.75m		
WIDTH:	3m	ARMAMENT:	1 × 73mm smooth-bore gun with an elevation of +20° and a depression of −5°, axis of bore is 1.4m
HEIGHT:	2m		
GROUND CLEARANCE:	.4m		
TRACK:	2.54m		
TRACK WIDTH:	300mm		1 × 7.62mm PKT MG co-axial with main armament
LENGTH OF TRACK ON GROUND:	3.6m		1 × launcher rail over main armament for Sagger ATGW
GROUND PRESSURE:	.57kg/cm^2		
POWER TO WEIGHT RATIO:	22.4HP/ton		30 rounds of 73mm and 1,000 rounds of 7.62mm ammunition are carried
MAXIMUM ROAD SPEED:	55km/hr		
WATER SPEED:	8km/hr		5 Sagger missiles (1 on launcher and 4 inside vehicle)
RANGE:	300km		
FUEL:	300 litres		
FORDING:	Amphibious		
GRADIENT:	60%		
VERTICAL OBSTACLE:	.9m	ARMOUR:	14mm (maximum)

Russian BMP-1 without Sagger ATGW.

DEVELOPMENT

The BMP-1 was first seen in public during the display held in Moscow on the 7th November 1967. When first seen it was simply called the M-1967 Armoured Personnel Carrier, and later the BMP-76PB. Recently it had been established that its correct designation is the BMP-1, and more recent models are known as the BMP-2. The BMP-1 was the first MICV to enter service and is still considered by many to be ahead of many other vehicles of this type. It uses many components of the PT-76 Light Amphibious Tank family.

DESCRIPTION

The hull of the BMP-1 is of welded magnesium construction. The driver is seated at the front of the vehicle on the left side and is provided with a total of three periscopes and a single-piece hatch cover that swings to the right. The commander is seated behind the driver and he is provided with a one-piece hatch cover that opens forwards. Three periscopes are arranged around the forward part of the hatch and there is also an infra-red searchlight mounted in front of the hatch.

The engine is at the front of the vehicle to the right of the driver and the radiator and exhaust grilles are to the right of the vehicle commander. The turret is in the centre of the hull and is provided with a one-piece hatch cover towards the turret rear. This opens forwards. The gunner is provided with a total of four periscopes arranged around the front and sides of the hatch, and the gun-sight is in the turret roof on the left side. A white light searchlight is mounted on the right of the turret, but this may well be replaced in the future by an infra-red searchlight.

The eight infantrymen are seated back to back in the rear of the vehicle. There are a total of four roof hatches, two each side, and these are hinged in the centre of the roof. The main means of entry is via the twin doors at the rear of the hull, and these doors also contain fuel tanks.

There are four firing ports and four periscopes in each side of the rear compartment. Both rear doors have periscopes whilst the left door also has a firing port. These enable the infantrymen to fire their weapons from within the vehicle and it is reported that special fans are fitted in the compartment to take the fumes out of the vehicle. An SA-7 (Grail) surface-to-air missile is carried inside the vehicle and this can be fired by one of the infantrymen through one of the roof hatches.

The suspension consists of six road wheels with the idler at the rear and the drive sprocket at the front. There are three track support rollers and the first and sixth road wheels are fitted with hydraulic shock absorbers. The 73mm gun is of the low pressure type and can fire HEAT, HE or canister rounds. The HEAT round is fin-stabilized and has a range in excess of 1,000m. This is said to be rocket-assisted and will penetrate over 100mm of armour. Stated rate of fire is 8 rounds per minute, the automatic loader holds 30 rounds of ammunition. The 7.62mm PKT machine-gun is mounted to the right of the main armament. The Sagger ATGW has a range of 3,000m. It is said that the launcher can be reloaded from within the vehicle and there is a small hatch in the forward part of the turret that could be used for this purpose. It does seem, however, that at least one member of the crew must expose himself during the reloading operation.

The BMP-1 is fully amphibious and is propelled in the water by its tracks. Before entering the water a trim vane is erected at the front of the vehicle, and when not required this is carried flat on the glacis plate.

The BMP-1 is fitted with an NBC system and infra-red driving lights.

Since the vehicle was first introduced there have been a number of modifications to the vehicle and these have resulted in the new designation of BMP-2. These modifications include the lengthening of the bow, and the deflector shroud at the rear has been extended; both modifications improving its amphibious characteristics. Because of its very low free-board it is capable of operating in calm waters only, though if a shroud were fitted around the air intake and exhaust, this would improve its amphibious capabilities.

The BMP-1 was used in combat in the Middle East Campaign of October 1973 and numbers were captured by the Israeli Army. Without doubt the BMP-1 is a most useful vehicle, but the infantry at the rear must work in very cramped conditions and there is much debate at the present time of the relative merits of an MICV type vehicle.

VARIANTS

There is reported to be a command model of the BMP-1 and the Polish Army has some which are believed to be fitted with a 23mm cannon in place of the 73mm gun.

The turret of the BMP-1 is also used on the new Soviet light tank/reconnaissance vehicle BMD (or M-1970) which was seen for the first time in public on the 7th November 1973.

In addition there is an artillery fire control model of the BMP. This has a somewhat larger turret, on the rear of which is a radar scanner which is folded down when in the travelling position. This has a crew of five men and there are no large hatches over the rear troop compartment, merely a single hatch at the rear of the roof on the left side.

Top BMP-1 with track guards removed and different type road wheels.
Above Rear view of a BMP-1 of the Egyptian Army. Note the side firing ports are open.
Right Close-up of the turret of the BMP-1 with Sagger ATGW on launcher rail over 73mm gun.

SOVIET UNION

BTR-60 SERIES – ARMOURED PERSONNEL CARRIER
MANUFACTURER – Soviet State Arsenals
CURRENT STATUS – In service with Afghanistan, Algeria, Bulgaria, Cuba, East Germany, Egypt, Hungary, Iran, Iraq, Israel, Libya, Mongolia, North Korea, Poland, Romania, Soviet Union (Army and Marines), Syria, Yugoslavia, Vietnam. Production of the BTR-60 has probably now been completed.

BASIC DATA	BTR-60PK	BTR-60PB		BTR-60PK	BTR-60PB
CREW:	2 + 16	2 + 14	GRADIENT:	30°	30°
WEIGHT LOADED:	9,980kg	10,300kg	VERTICAL OBSTACLE:	.4m	.4m
LENGTH OVERALL:	7.56m	7.56m	TILT:	25°	25°
WIDTH:	2.825m	2.825m	TRENCH:	2m	2m
HEIGHT			ENGINES:	Both are powered by two
without turret:	2.055m	—		GAZ-49B, 6-cylinder in-line
with turret:	—	2.31m		water-cooled petrol engines
GROUND CLEARANCE:	.475m	.475m		developing 90HP each at
TRACK:	2.37m	2.37m		3,400rpm
WHEELBASE:	1.35m+ 1.525m + 1.35m	1.35m × 1.525m + 1.35m	ARMAMENT:	1 × 7.62mm SGMB or PKT MG,	1 × 14.5mm KPVT and 1 × 7.62mm
TYRE SIZE:	13.00 × 18	13.00 × 18		pedestal-	PKT MG,
MAXIMUM ROAD SPEED:	80km/hr	80km/hr		mounted	turret-mounted
WATER SPEED:	10km/hr	10km/hr			
RANGE:	500km	500km	ARMOUR		
FUEL CAPACITY:	290 litres	290 litres	hull:	10mm	10mm
FUEL CONSUMPTION:	58 litres per 100km	58 litres per 100km	turret:	—	14mm

DEVELOPMENT

The BTR-60P (BTR=Bronetransporter, 60 the year it entered production, and P for Plavayushchiy – amphibious) was first seen during the parade held in Moscow on the 7th November 1961. It is the replacement for the older BTR-152 (6 × 6) APC. Today it is used extensively by most members of the Warsaw Pact (except Czechoslovakia and Poland who use the OT-64 8 × 8 APC) as well as by many foreign armies. It is normally deployed in the Motorised Rifle Divisions. The Tank Divisions normally have BMP-1 or BTR-50P tracked APCs. Since the BTR-60P has entered service it has been continuously developed to meet the changing requirements of the battlefield, but has now probably reached the end of its development.

BTR-60Ps with open roof on exercise.

DESCRIPTION

The hull of the BTR-60P is of all-welded steel construction. The driver and commander are at the front of the vehicle with the troop compartment behind them. The engines are at the rear of the hull and these are the same as those fitted to the BRDM (BTR-40P) vehicle. All eight wheels are powered and the front four are used for steering, the steering being power-assisted. The suspension is of the torsion-bar type and the first and second road wheels are each provided with two hydraulic shock absorbers whilst the third and fourth wheels have single hydraulic shock absorbers. All models are provided with central tyre pressure regulation system and most vehicles have a front-mounted winch. The gearbox, which is manual, has 4F and 1R gears and a two-speed transfer case.

The BTR-60P is fully amphibious being propelled in the water by a single hydro-jet at the rear of the hull. Before entering the water the trim vane, which is carried under the nose of the vehicle when not required, is raised into position, and a single bilge pump is provided. The models of the BTR-60P with overhead armour are all fitted with an NBC system.

The driver is seated at the front of the vehicle on the left with the commander to his right. On all models both the commander and driver are provided with direct vision windscreens at the front of the hull and when in combat these are covered with a steel hatch cover provided with a direct vision block. All models have infra-red driving lights and most vehicles have an infra-red searchlight for the commander which can often be controlled from within the vehicle.

It should be noted that there are often minor differences between vehicles in a given production batch, especially in the arrangement of their hatches, firing ports and vision devices.

VARIANTS

BTR-60P

This was the first model to enter service and has an open top to the troop compartment with the seats running across the vehicle. If required the troop compartment can be fitted with steel hoops and a canvas cover to keep out the rain. The normal means of entry and exit for the crew is via the two half-doors in each side of the vehicle. There are three firing ports in each side of the hull. In addition to the vision blocks in the commander's and driver's steel windscreen covers there is also a vision block at the front of the vehicle, between the hull front and hull side, one each side. Various types of machine-guns can be fitted. The most common are a 12.7mm and a 7.62mm, each on a pedestal mount on the top of the hull at the front, and a 7.62mm each side of the hull on an outrigger. None of these weapons is provided with a shield.

BTR-60PK (also known as the BTR-60PA)

This model entered service in 1961 and is provided with armour protection over the complete roof. The commander and driver are each provided with a single-piece hatch cover that opens forwards, and also with a periscope in the roof of the vehicle. Behind the driver's and commander's hatches is a single-piece hatch cover that opens to the rear. In front of this hatch is a single 12.7mm DShK machine-gun or a single 7.62mm SGMB or PKT machine-gun; this has an elevation of $+23\frac{1}{2}°$ and a depression of —6°, total traverse being 90°. Mounted either side of this hatch is a further 7.62mm SGMB or PKT machine-gun. There is a further roof hatch at the rear of the vehicle. The only means of entry and exit in this model is via the roof hatches. The troop compartment is provided with seats that run along the sides of the hull.

BTR-60PB (also known as the BTR-60PKB)

This is the latest model to enter service and is similar to the BTR-60PK except that it has a turret similar to that fitted to the BRDM-2 (4 × 4) scout car and the OT-64C (8 × 8) armoured personnel carrier.

This turret is armed with a 14.5mm KPVT machine-gun and a 7.62mm PKT machine-gun. Elevation is +30° and depression —5°, total traverse, by hand, being 360°. A total of 500 rounds of 14.5mm and 2,000 rounds of 7.62mm ammunition are carried. This model has a small door in each side of the hull just forward of the turret. In addition there are two roof hatches behind the turret. The commander and driver are provided with a number of direct viewing devices around their positions. These are in place of the viewing blocks in the steel hatches that cover their windscreens. Some models have three firing ports in either side of the hull as well as one direct vision block.

BTR-60PU Command Vehicle

This is the basic BTR-60P fitted with a canvas roof, map tables and additional communications equipment.

BTR-60PB Forward Air Control Vehicle

This is similar to the BTR-60PB with its armament removed from the turret and its place taken by a plexiglass window. On the rear deck is a portable generator which is covered up when not in use, and a similar generator is fitted to the BRDM-2 command vehicle.

Top BTR-60Ps showing their amphibious capabilities.
Left BTR-60PKs from the rear. The water jet
propulsion system is covered by the two cam-type
doors in the rear of the hull.
Above BTR-60PBs on exercise.

SOVIET UNION

BTR-50 SERIES – ARMOURED PERSONNEL CARRIER
MANUFACTURERS – Soviet State Arsenals. It is also built in Czechoslovakia as the OT-62. Refer to separate entry for this vehicle
STATUS – In service with Afghanistan, Albania, Algeria, Bulgaria, Communist China, Czechoslovakia (OT-62), East Germany, Egypt, Finland, Hungary, India, Iran, Israel, Libya, Vietnam, Poland, Romania, Somalia, Soviet Union, Sudan, Syria, Yugoslavia. Production of the BTR-50 series has now been completed.

BASIC DATA

CREW:	2 + 20 (commander, driver and 20 infantry)	GRADIENT:	70%
WEIGHT LOADED:	14,200kg	VERTICAL OBSTACLE:	1.1m
LENGTH:	7.08m	TRENCH:	2.8m
WIDTH:	3.14m	ENGINE:	Model V-6, 6-cylinder in-line water-cooled diesel developing 240HP at 1,800rpm
HEIGHT:	1.97m		
GROUND CLEARANCE:	.37m		
TRACK:	2.74m	ARMAMENT:	1 × 7.62mm SGMB pintle-mounted with an elevation of + 23½° and a depression of − 6°, total traverse being 90° 1,250 rounds of 7.62mm ammunition are carried
TRACK WIDTH:	360mm		
LENGTH OF TRACK ON GROUND:	4.08m		
GROUND PRESSURE:	.51kg/cm^2		
POWER TO WEIGHT RATIO:	16.9HP/ton		
MAXIMUM ROAD SPEED:	44km/hr	ARMOUR	
WATER SPEED:	11km/hr	glacis:	11mm at 80°
RANGE:	260km	upper hull side:	14mm at 0°
FUEL CAPACITY:	250 litres	hull roof:	10mm
FUEL CONSUMPTION:	96 litres per 100km	hull rear:	10mm
FORDING:	Amphibious	hull floor – maximum:	10mm

Note: The above data relate to the BTR-50PK

DEVELOPMENT

The BTR-50P was first seen in public during a parade held in Moscow in November 1957. Basically the vehicle consists of a PT-76 Light Amphibious Tank chassis and hull with an armoured superstructure welded to the front part of the hull. Since it was first introduced the BTR-50 has been further developed and is still quite a useful vehicle. The Czechoslovakian model of the BTR-50, the OT-62, is a further improvement over the Russian vehicle.

The BTR-50 is used by the Motor Rifle Regiment of the Tank Division and its replacement is the BMP-1 (BMP-76PB).

DESCRIPTION

All models of the BTR-50 have the same basic chassis and differ only in their superstructures. The different models are described later.

The hull of the BTR-50 is of all-welded steel construction with the personnel compartment at the front and the engine and transmission at the rear. The engine is fitted with a pre-heater for starting in very cold weather and the transmission has 5F and 1R gears.

The suspension consists of six road wheels with the drive sprocket at the rear and the idler at the front. There are no track return rollers. The first and sixth road wheels are provided with hydraulic shock absorbers.

All members of the BTR-50 family are fully amphibious and are powered in the water by two water jets at the rear of the hull–again, similar to the PT-76. Before entering the water a trim vane is erected at the front of the hull, and this is carried on the glacis plate when not required. Two electric and one manual bilge pumps are provided.

On all models the driver is seated in the front of the vehicle, in the centre. He is provided with a one-piece hatch cover that opens upwards on the outside, and a vision block is provided in this hatch. In addition there are three periscopes below the bottom of the hatch, and the centre periscope can be raised above the trim vane when it is erected. In all models the commander is seated in the left-hand projecting bay at the front of the hull. This has a one-piece hatch that opens forwards, and there are three vision blocks in the front of the bay. There is a further vision block in the front of the superstructure to the right of the driver.

Most BTR-50s have at least one infra-red driving light and most also have an infra-red searchlight mounted on the front of the superstructure on the right side. All models can carry additional fuel in tanks or drums on the rear deck. It should be noted that there are many minor differences in BTR-50s, especially in such areas as side doors, vision blocks and firing ports.

VARIANTS

BTR-50P
This was the first model to enter service and the troop compartment has an open roof and benches are provided across the compartment for the infantry.

Loading ramps are provided on the rear deck so that 57mm, 76mm and 85mm anti-tank guns can be carried and fired from the vehicle, even in the water. When the vehicle was first introduced they were not fitted with any armament. Some vehicles have a side door in the troop compartment.

BTR-50PA
This is similar to the BTR-50P but does not have the loading ramps at the rear, and a ring-mount with a 14.5mm KPVT machine-gun is fitted to the roof of the commander's cupola.

BTR-50PK
This version has full overhead armour protection and is believed to be fitted with an NBC system. There is a dome-shaped ventilator on the right side of the superstructure and some models have been provided with two firing vision ports in the sides of the superstructure. There are two hatches in the roof and these are hinged either side. This model is not normally fitted with any armament although some members of the crew use their LMGs when the roof hatches are open.

BTR-50PU (Command Vehicle)
There are two models of the BTR-50PU Command Vehicle. Model 1 has a single projecting bay whilst Model 2 has two projecting bays. These command vehicles have two roof hatches which are oval in shape rather than oblong as in the BTR-50PK. There is also a circular hatch cover in the roof behind the driver's position and this is provided with a periscope. Internally additional radios have been fitted along each side of the hull and there is a long table in the centre of the compartment. Also fitted is a comprehensive navigation system which includes a co-ordinate indicator and a map course plotter. The command models also have additional stowage boxes on the rear deck and some are also fitted with a generator on the rear deck. There are four or five radio aerials fitted. The right projecting bay on the Model 2 is not fitted with a hatch cover.

Top left BTR-50P Armoured Personnel Carrier.
Above BTR-50PK Armoured Personnel Carrier.
Left BTR-50PU Command Vehicle of the Egyptian Army.

SOVIET UNION

BTR-152 SERIES – ARMOURED PERSONNEL CARRIER
MANUFACTURER – Soviet State Arsenals
CURRENT STATUS – In service with Afghanistan, Albania, Algeria, Bulgaria, Cambodia, Ceylon, China (the BTR-152 has been built in China as the Type 56 Armoured Personnel Carrier), Congo, Cuba, Cyprus, East Germany, Egypt, Guinea, Hungary, India, Indonesia, Iran, Iraq, Israel, Mongolia, North Korea, North Yemen, Palestinian Liberation Army, Poland, Romania, Somalia, Soviet Union, Sudan, Syria, Tanzania, Uganda, Yugoslavia. Production of the BTR-152 is now complete.

BASIC DATA	BTR-152V1	BTR-152A (Anti-Aircraft)		BTR-152V1	BTR-152A (Anti-Aircraft)
CREW:	2 + 17	4	TRENCH:	.69m	.69m
WEIGHT LOADED:	8,950kg	9,600kg	ENGINE:	Both are powered by a	
LENGTH:	6.83m	6.83m		ZIL-123 6-cylinder, in-line	
WIDTH:	2.32m	2.32m		water-cooled petrol engine	
HEIGHT:	2.05m			developing 110HP at	
	(excluding	2.8m (with		2,900rpm	
	armament)	armament)	ARMAMENT:	1 × 7.62mm 2 ×14.5mm	
GROUND CLEARANCE:	.295m	.295m		SGMB MG MGs	
TRACK				with elevation	
front:	1.742m	1.742m		of + 23½°, de-	
rear:	1.72m	1.72m		pression of − 6°	
WHEELBASE:	3.3m + 1.13m	3.3m + 1.13m		and a total	
TYRES:	12.00 × 18	12.00 × 18		traverse of 90°.	
MAXIMUM SPEED:	75km/hr	65km/hr		1,250 rounds of	
RANGE:	650km	650km		ammunition are	
FUEL CAPACITY:	300 litres	300 litres		carried	
FUEL CONSUMPTION:	46 litres per 100km	46 litres per 100km	ARMOUR		
			hull front:	13.5mm	13.5mm
FORDING:	.8m	.8m	hull sides:	11.5mm	11.5mm
GRADIENT:	30°	30°	hull rear:	9mm	9mm
VERTICAL OBSTACLE:	.6m	.6m	hull top:	6mm	6mm

DEVELOPMENT

The BTR-152 was the first Soviet-built Armoured Personnel Carrier. The first prototypes were built shortly after the end of the Second World War and the vehicle was first seen in quantity in 1950. The first production models were based on the ZIL-151 (6 × 6) truck chassis but later production models (from and including the BTR-152V) were built on the ZIL-157 (6 × 6) truck chassis. Over the years the BTR-152 has been continuously developed and is still used in some numbers by most members of the Warsaw Pact. The Soviets have replaced most of their front line BTR-152s with the BTR-60P (8 × 8) APC. Not only was the BTR-152 used as an APC but it was also used to carry mortar and anti-tank squads complete with their weapons, cargo carrier, and towing various heavy mortars, artillery pieces and anti-tank guns.

DESCRIPTION

The BTR-152 has a hull of all-welded steel construction with the engine at the front. Behind this is the driver's seat with the personnel compartment at the rear of the hull. There are two types of seating arrangements, the first of which consists of wooden bench seats down each side of the vehicle and the second of three rows of seats across the hull. Both the driver and vehicle commander are provided with a windscreen and when in action this is covered by a steel hatch that is provided with an integral vision block. Both the driver and commander are provided with a side door, the top of which can be folded down. Most vehicles also have a single vision block in this door, although some just have a vision slit. Most vehicles have three firing ports in each side of the hull and two at the rear of the hull. Normal means of entry is via twin doors at the rear of the hull.

The gearbox has 5F and 1R gears with a two-speed transfer box. Fifth gear has an overdrive. Suspension consists of leaf springs with hydraulic shock absorbers.

The normal armament of the BTR-152 is a single 7.62mm SGMB machine-gun mounted on the roof behind the driver and commander's positions but some vehicles are fitted with a 12.7mm or 14.5mm machine-gun in place of the 7.62mm weapon. In addition a 7.62mm machine-gun can be mounted on either side of the hull top.

The BTR-152 is not amphibious and is not fitted with an NBC system.

VARIANTS

BTR-152

This was the first model to enter service and has an open top, no winch and no central tyre pressure regulation system. Also known as Model A.

BTR-152V1

This has an open top, front-mounted winch and a tyre pressure regulation system with external air lines. Also known as the Model B.

BTR-152V2

This is a BTR-152 modified to have internal air lines but no winch.

BTR-152V3

This has an open top, front-mounted winch, internal air lines and infra-red driving lights. Also known as Model C.

BTR-152K

This is the same as the BTR-152V3 but in addition has overhead armour protection for the troop compartment. The roof has two hatches which hinge on the right side. The front hatch is provided with one firing port and the rear hatch with two firing ports. This is also known as the Model D or Model 1961.

BTR-152U

This is a command vehicle and normally uses a BTR-152V1 or BTR-152V3 chassis. The BTR-152U is easily recognisable as it has a much higher roof and normally has additional equipment on the roof. It often tows a trailer with further equipment, i.e. a generator.

BTR-152A Anti-Aircraft Vehicle

This is basically a BTR-152V chassis fitted with a turret mounting twin KPV heavy machine-guns. An identical turret is fitted to the BTR-40A anti-aircraft vehicle. The turret has manual elevation and traverse. The guns have a maximum elevation of +80° and a depression of −5°, total traverse being 360°. The KPV machine-gun has a cyclic rate of fire of 600 rounds per minute, per barrel, and a practical rate of fire of 150 rounds per minute per barrel. Maximum effective range in the ground role is 2,000m and in the anti-aircraft role 1,400m. The API (Armour Piercing Incendiary) round has an m/v of 1,000m/s and its projectile, which weighs 64.4 grams, will penetrate 32mm of armour at 500m. There are also towed models of the KPV machine-gun – the ZPU-1, ZPU-2 and ZPU-4.

BTR-152 with Quad 12.7mm MG M53s

The Egyptians have reported to have fitted a number of their BTR-152s with the Czechoslovakian Quad 12.7mm machine-gun M53. This is basically four Soviet DShK machine-guns on a Czechoslovakian designed mount (normally towed on a two-wheeled trailer). Each barrel has a cyclic rate of fire of 550/600 rounds per minute but practical rate of fire is 80 rounds per minute. Each barrel has one drum of 50 rounds, and maximum effective range is 1,000m. Its API projectile, which weighs 49.5 grams, will penetrate 20mm of armour at 500m.

BTR-152 with ATGWs

It has been reported that the Soviets have fitted a number of their BTR-152s with ATGWs. No further information is available at this time, although the Sagger is the most likely missile.

Right The basic BTR-152 Armoured Personnel Carrier.
Above The BTR-152A Anti-Aircraft Vehicle with twin 14.5 machine-guns.

The BTR-152U Command Post which has a higher roof.

SOVIET UNION

BTR-40 SERIES – ARMOURED PERSONNEL CARRIER
MANUFACTURER – Soviet State Arsenals
CURRENT STATUS – In service with Afghanistan, Albania, Algeria, Bulgaria, China (built in China as the type 55 Armoured Personnel Carrier), Cuba, Czechoslovakia, East Germany, Egypt, Guinea, Hungary, Indonesia, Iran, Laos, Libya, Mali, North Korea, Vietnam, North Yemen, Poland, Somalia, Soviet Union, Sudan, Syria, Tanzania, Uganda, Yemen, Yugoslavia and a number of 'Liberation' forces. Production of the BTR-40 is complete.

BASIC DATA

CREW:	2 + 8	VERTICAL OBSTACLE:	.47m
WEIGHT:	5,300kg	TILT:	20-25°
LENGTH:	5m	TRENCH:	.7m (with channels)
WIDTH:	1.9m	ENGINE:	GAZ-40 6-cylinder in-line water-cooled petrol engine developing 80HP at 3,400rpm
HEIGHT:	1.75m (without armament)		
GROUND CLEARANCE:	.275m		
TRACK:	1.588m (front)	ARMAMENT:	1×7.62mm SGMB MG with an elevation of $+23\frac{1}{2}°$, depression of $-6°$ and a total traverse of 90°.
	1.6m (rear)		
WHEELBASE:	2.7m		
TYRES:	9.75×18		
MAXIMUM SPEED:	80km/hr		
RANGE:	285km	ARMOUR:	8mm (maximum)
FUEL CAPACITY:	120 litres		
FUEL CONSUMPTION:	42 litres per 100km		
FORDING:	.9m		
GRADIENT:	30°		

DEVELOPMENT

The BTR-40 (4 × 4) APC was the second Soviet APC to enter service, the first being the BTR-152. The BTR-40 entered production in 1951 and is based on the GAZ-63 (4 × 4) truck, though the BTR-40 has a shorter wheelbase than the GAZ-63 (3.3m).

DESCRIPTION

The hull is of all-welded construction with the engine at the front of the vehicle and the personnel compartment at the rear. The commander and driver are in the centre of the vehicle and are each provided with a windscreen. When in action this is covered by a steel hatch with an integral viewing block. They also each have a side door, the top of which can be folded down if required, and there is a vision slit over each door. Normal means of entry for the infantry is via the twin doors at the rear of the hull. There is no bulkhead between the driver's compartment and the crew compartment. Most later production vehicles have three firing ports in each side of the hull and two firing ports in the rear of the hull.

The BTR-40 is not amphibious, has no infra-red driving or fighting equipment, has no NBC system and does not have the central tyre pressure regulation system. It is, however, fitted with a winch at the front of the vehicle.

Although called an armoured personnel carrier it was used more as a command and reconnaissance vehicle, and has been replaced in front line Soviet units by more recent vehicles such as the BRDM-1 and BDRM-2 vehicles.

VARIANTS

BTR-40A Anti-Aircraft Vehicle

This is a basic BTR-40 fitted with the same turret as that mounted on the BTR-152A Anti-Aircraft Vehicle. This turret mounts twin 14.5mm KPV heavy machine-guns and has manual elevation and traverse. Maximum elevation is + 80° and depression is − 5°, total traverse being 360°. The KPV machine-gun has a cyclic rate of fire of 600 rounds per minute per barrel, but its practical rate of fire is 150 rounds per minute per barrel. Maximum effective range in the ground role is 2,000m and in the anti-aircraft role 1,400m. The API (Armour Piercing Incendiary) round has an m/v of 1,000m/s and its projectile, which weighs 64.4 grams, will penetrate 32mm of armour at 500m. There are also towed models of the KPV machine-gun – the ZPU-1, ZPU-2 and ZPU4. Basic data of the anti-aircraft model are similar to those of the standard BTR-40 except that it is slightly heavier and has an overall height of 2.5m.

BTR-40K (or BTR-40B)

This is simply a basic BTR-40 with the addition of four armoured roof hatches, each of which is provided with a single firing port.

BTR-40kh

This is a chemical decontamination reconnaissance vehicle and has special equipment at the rear which enables it to dispense marking-flags into the ground.

Above The basic BTR-40 Armoured Personnel Carrier.
Left The BTR-40A with twin 14.5mm machine-guns for use in the anti-aircraft role.

SOVIET UNION

AT-P – ARMOURED TRACKED ARTILLERY TRACTOR
MANUFACTURER – Soviet State Arsenals
STATUS – In service only with the Russian Army. Production complete.

BASIC DATA

CREW:	3 + 6	FORDING:	.7m
WEIGHT LOADED:	6,300kg	GRADIENT:	60%
LENGTH:	4.45m	VERTICAL OBSTACLE:	.7m
WIDTH:	2.5m	TRENCH:	1.22m
HEIGHT:	1.83m	ENGINE:	ZIL-123F, 6-cylinder
GROUND CLEARANCE:	.33m		water-cooled petrol
TRACK:	2m		developing 110HP at
TRACK WIDTH:	300mm		2,900rpm
LENGTH OF TRACK		ARMAMENT:	1 × 7.62mm Goryunov
ON GROUND:	3m		SGMT bow-mounted
GROUND PRESSURE:	.4kg/cm^2 (unloaded)		MG
MAXIMUM ROAD SPEED:	50km/hr	ARMOUR:	12mm (maximum)
RANGE:	500km		

DEVELOPMENT/DESCRIPTION

The AT-P is a light, full-tracked tractor that has been designed to tow artillery as well as carrying the crew for the gun and a supply of ammunition. The vehicle was first seen in the late 1950s. Some reports have indicated that the vehicle uses some components of the ASU-57 Assault Gun which appeared at about the same time.

The driver is seated at the front of the vehicle on the left and to his right is a ball-mounted machine-gun operated by a gunner who also acts as the radio operator. Some models have had the ball mounting replaced by a machine-gun in a fully rotating turret. The driver's hatch opens to the left and the gunner's hatch opens to the rear. Both are provided with vision blocks. The commander is seated behind the driver and is provided with a square hatch cover that opens to the rear, with a periscope mounted in it. The engine is to the right of the commander and the exhaust pipe leads out to the right side of the hull.

The AT-P has five road wheels with the driving sprocket at the front. There are two track return rollers and the suspension is of the torsion-bar type.

The troop compartment at the rear of the hull has vertical sides and an open roof and the six men are seated across the vehicle. If required, the troop compartment can be covered by a tarpaulin cover. Ammunition is normally carried externally in ready-use boxes.

As far as it is known the AT-P has no amphibious capabilities and is not fitted with an NBC system. Some models have a single infra-red driving light. Its total cargo capacity is 1,200kg. Various types of artillery and mortars can be towed by the AT-P, including the 85mm D-44 ATG, 100mm M1955 or T-12 ATG, 122mm Howitzer M1938 (M-30) or the 122mm Howitzer D-30.

VARIANTS

AT-P (Command)
This has overhead armour for the troop compartment and the twin doors at the rear are each provided with a vision/firing port. There are external stowage boxes and the commander is provided with a fully rotating cupola. The exhaust pipe has been removed from the side of the hull and is now in the roof.

AT-P (Fire Control)
This is similar to the above and in addition has a full width rear compartment.

AT-P Armoured Tracked Artillery Tractor.

SPAIN

PEGASO 6 × 6 ARMOURED PERSONNEL CARRIER
MANUFACTURER – Pegaso S.A., Madrid
STATUS – Trials.

GENERAL

For some time there have been reports that Pegaso has developed, under contract to the Spanish Army, a 6 × 6 armoured personnel carrier. It is believed that it has a body of welded aluminium construction which has been supplied by Britain. Suspension is of the hydro-pneumatic type and an NBC system is provided. Firing ports are provided in the hull sides and rear. No further information is available at this time.

SWEDEN

PANSARBANDVAGN 302 – ARMOURED PERSONNEL CARRIER
MANUFACTURER – AB Hägglunds and Soner, Örnsköldsvik
STATUS – In service with the Swedish Army. Production complete.

BASIC DATA

CREW:	2 + 10 (driver, gunner and 10 men)	RANGE:	300km at 45km/hr
		FUEL:	285 litres
WEIGHT LOADED:	13,500kg	FORDING:	Amphibious
LENGTH:	5.35m	GRADIENT:	60%
WIDTH:	2.86m	VERTICAL OBSTACLE:	.61m
HEIGHT:	2.5m (including turret)	TRENCH:	1.8m
	2.06m (without turret)	ENGINE:	Volvo-Penta Model
GROUND CLEARANCE:	.4m		THD 100B horizontal,
TRACK:	2.42m		4-stroke turbo-charged
TRACK WIDTH:	380mm		6-cylinder, in-line,
LENGTH OF TRACK ON GROUND:	2.98m		diesel developing 280HP
GROUND PRESSURE:	.6kg/cm^2		at 2.200rpm. 9.6 litres
POWER-TO-WEIGHT RATIO:	20BHP/ton	ARMAMENT:	1 × 20mm cannon
MAXIMUM ROAD SPEED:	66km/hr		2 × 5 smoke dischargers
MAXIMUM WATER SPEED:	8km/hr		

DEVELOPMENT

Hägglund first became involved in armoured fighting vehicles in 1958 when they built a prototype of the Pbv 301 armoured personnel carrier. This was basically the old Strv.m/41 light tank with a new hull. From 1962 to 1963 they converted many Strv.m/41s to the APC role. The Pbv.301 has now been replaced by the Pbv.302.

Early in 1961 the Swedish Army drew up requirements for a new tracked armoured personnel carrier and late in 1961 Hägglunds were awarded a contract to develop this new vehicle. The first of two prototypes was completed in December 1962, and in October 1963 Hägglunds were awarded a production contract for an initial batch of 700 vehicles. The first production vehicles were completed in February 1966 with final vehicles being completed in December 1971. Since then Hägglunds have developed from the Pbv.302 the Bgbv 82 ARV, Brobv 941 Bridgelayer and the Ikv 91 Tank Destroyer.

DESCRIPTION

The hull of the Pansarbandvagn 302 or (Pbv 302 for short) is of all-welded rolled steel construction. The sides of the hull are of double skinned construction which provides increased buoyancy as well as additional protection against attack from anti-tank projectiles. Some items of equipment such as the batteries are mounted between the hull sides.

The gunner is seated at the front of the vehicle on the left. The driver is seated in the centre of the hull at the front and is provided with a single-piece hatch cover that opens to the rear and three periscopes for driving whilst closed down. The commander is seated at the front on the right side. He has a single-piece hatch cover and a total of five periscopes for observation purposes. The engine is mounted in the forward part of the vehicle and the complete engine, clutch and gearbox are built as one unit.

The nine infantry are seated at the rear of the vehicle, the tenth being the commander who is seated at the front. In the roof of the troop compartment are hinged hydraulically-operated hatches (one each side), enabling the crew to use their small arms from within the vehicle.

The hatches are controlled by the vehicle commander and if required they can be opened half way to give maximum protection to the infantry. Along the edge of each hatch is a sensitive pressure bar which prevents a man having a hand or weapon trapped when the hatch is closed. Normal means of entry and exit is via the two doors in the rear of the hull which can be locked in the open position if required.

The suspension consists of five road wheels supported by trailing arms and individually syspended by traversal torsion bars. Shock absorbers are provided for the first and fifth road wheel stations. The drive sprocket is at the front and the idler at the rear. The first vehicles had the American T130 track but more recently Hägglunds have developed the new M70 track. During trials it was found that these gave up to 20% increased traction on soft soil as well as an increase in water speed. They have a life in excess of 10,000km. The tops of the tracks are covered by a shroud to improve water flow.

The gearbox is a manual Volvo-Penta T60 with 8F and 2R gears. A clutch-and-brake steering system is provided. The steering clutch is of the double dry-plate type and the steering brakes at each end of the drive shafts are servo-assisted high-power disc brakes. There are two access panels in the glacis plate. The complete engine/transmission layout is as follows: engine, clutch, gearbox, curved tooth coupling, steering brake, final drive, bevel gear, steering clutch and then via drive shafts to the drive sprocket. The turret is armed with a Hispano Suiza 20mm type 804 cannon. This has a cyclic rate of fire of 500 rounds per minute. Two types of ammunition are carried: armour piercing with an m/v of 800m/s and high explosive. Three belts each of 135 rounds of HE are carried and ten magazines of AP, each magazine holding ten rounds. Total ammunition capacity is 505 rounds.

The gun has an elevation of $+50°$ and a depression of $-10°$, traverse being a full 360°. Traverse and elevation are achieved by hand cranking, and in traverse the gunner can select from 4° to 12° per handle revolution. The gunner is provided with a $\times 8$ monocular sight for use against ground targets and there are three periscopes in the forward part of the turret for general observation, plus one in the turret rear. For use against aircraft the gunner opens a hatch in the turret roof and uses the open sights mounted on the gun cradle. When the 20mm gun is being fired torque is automatically compensated by a mechanical turn-compensator. The turret is provided with a roof hatch for the gunner. Smoke dischargers are mounted on the roof of the vehicle towards the rear.

The basic vehicle can be quickly adopted for the following roles:

Ambulance

The standard APC can carry four stretchers in its basic form and can be modified to carry six-eight stretchers.

Recovery Vehicle

A hydraulic winch can be mounted in the rear troop compartment and spades fitted to the rear of the hull.

Load carrier

The basic vehicle can carry 2,000kg of cargo.

The Pbv 302 is fully amphibious being propelled in the water by its tracks. Before entering the water a trim vane is erected at the front of the hull and the two electric bilge pumps are switched on. Infra-red driving lights are provided but there is no NBC system. The latter could be fitted if required.

VARIANTS

Stripbv 3021 Armoured Command Vehicle

This has a crew of three plus four command staff and is provided with radios and tables. Externally it is recognisable by its additional radio antennae, the basic vehicle having two antennae.

Epbv 3022 Armoured Observation Post Vehicle

Ten of these are issued to each armoured Brigade. The driver and gunner are in the normal position. A cupola has been fitted over the normal commander's station which is where the Fire-Control Officer is seated. The cupola has a combined binocular and optical rangefinder and the commander can change between the $\times 4$ binocular and the $\times 10$ coincidence rangefinder using the same eyepieces. The rangefinder has an 800mm base. An azimuth sensor driven by the turret ring gives accurate azimuth to the target. The cupola is hand-cranked in traverse and the line of sight is manually elevated. In the rear are three radios and two wire links, and the fire-control system includes a navigation system. The direction of travel is fed from a gyro and displayed to one of the operators.

Bplpbv 3023 Armoured Fire Direction Post Vehicle
This has four radios and a fire direction computer mounted in the rear troop compartment. The crew consists of gunner, driver, battery commander and a ranging section of seven men.

Product Improved Pbv 302
Hägglunds have suggested that the Pbv 302 could be modified to fulfil a full MICV role with the following modifications which could be carried out to existing vehicles or incorporated in new production vehicles:
1. A reduced complement of infantry with their backs to each other facing outwards. The top part of the sides of the troop compartment would be sloped, each side having three vision ports and three spherical firing ports.
2. It would be powered by the later Volvo THD 100C diesel engine which develops 310HP.
3. An automatic Allison HT 740 gearbox would be installed in place of the manual gearbox.
4. A Hägglunds hydrostatic steering system as used in the latter Hägglunds vehicles would be fitted and trials have already been carried out with this.
5. The 20mm cannon would be replaced by the Oerlikon 25mm KBA cannon. If required the armament would be stabilised with power traverse and elevation.

Above left The Pbv.302 Armoured Personnel Carrier.
Above right One of the early Pbv.302 APCs showing its amphibious capabilities.
Below left The Epbv.3022 Armoured Observation Post Vehicle.
Below right The Bplpbv.3023 Armoured Fire Direction Post Vehicle.

SWITZERLAND

MOWAG PIRANHA – ARMOURED PERSONNEL CARRIER
MANUFACTURER – Mowag Motorwagenfabrik AG, Kreuzlingen.
STATUS – Trials completed. Available for production.

BASIC DATA	4 × 4	6 × 6	8 × 8
CREW:	9	12	14
WEIGHT LOADED:	7,000kg	9,600kg	12,500kg
WEIGHT EMPTY:	5,830kg	7,100kg	8,500kg
LENGTH:	5.26m	5.84m	6.235m
WIDTH:	2.5m	2.5m	2.5m
HEIGHT (w/o armament):	1.85m	1.85m	1.85m
GROUND CLEARANCE			
hull:	.5m	.5m	.5m
differential:	.39m	.39m	.39m
TRACK:	2.18m	2.18m	2.18m
WHEELBASE:	2.5m	2.04m + 1.04m	1.1m + 1.335m + 1.04m
TYRES:	11.00 × 16	11.00 × 16	11.00 × 16
TURNING RADIUS:	5.6m	5.65m	6.2m
MAXIMUM ROAD SPEED:	100km/hr	100km/hr	100km/hr
MAXIMUM WATER SPEED:	9.5km/hr	10km/hr	10km/hr
RANGE ROAD:	750km	1000km	800km
FUEL CAPACITY:	275 litres	300 litres	300 litres
FORDING:	Amphibious	Amphibious	Amphibious
GRADIENT:	70%	70%	70%
ANGLE OF APPROACH:	45°	45°	45°
ANGLE OF DEPARTURE:	45°	45°	45°
ENGINE TYPE:	Petrol	Diesel	Diesel
HP/RPM:	190/4,000	300/2,800	325/2,800

Note: For armament details, refer to text. Weight of vehicle and height depend on armament installation.

DEVELOPMENT/DESCRIPTION

The Piranha series is the most recent range of vehicles from Mowag. The range consists of 4 × 4, 6 × 6 and 8 × 8 models, which have a large number of interchangeable components including wheels, suspension, steering, propellers, hull front and rear, hatches, doors and so on. Mowag suggest that the series is suitable for a wide variety of roles including use as an armoured personnel carrier, command and radio vehicle, mortar carrier, anti-aircraft or anti-tank vehicle, fire support vehicle, load carrier, ambulance and internal security vehicle.

DESCRIPTION

The hull of the Piranha is of all-welded construction and this provides the crew with protection from small arms fire. The driver is seated at the front of the hull on the left side and is provided with a single-piece hatch cover and a total of three periscopes for driving whilst closed down. The engine is to the right of the driver. The weapon installation is in the forward part of the vehicle behind the driver, with the personnel compartment at the rear.

There are two Mowag type ball mounts in each side of the hull , with a vision block over the top of each mount, enabling the crew to fire their weapons in safety from within the hull. There are two hatch covers over the top of the personnel compartment and normal means of entry and exit is via twin doors in the rear of the hull. Each of these doors is provided with a Mowag type ball mount.

The suspension consists of independent torsion bars with coil springs, maximum vertical travel being 320/340mm. Each wheel also has a hydraulic shock absorber. Automatic locking differentials are mounted inside the hull. Run-flat tyres are fitted.

The Piranha is fully amphibious being propelled in the water by two propellers, one each side at the rear of the hull. Before entering the water a trim vane is erected at the front of the hull. Electrical system is 24V and an NBC system is provided.

VARIANTS
4 × 4
This is powered by a 190HP petrol engine coupled to a Chrysler manual five-speed gearbox. A variety of 12.7mm and 20mm armament installations are available.

6 × 6

This is powered by a 300HP turbo-charged diesel coupled to an automatic Allison five-speed gearbox. Acceleration is from 0 to 44km/hr in ten seconds. A wide range of armament installations are available including 12.7mm machine-guns, 20mm, 25mm and 30mm turret-mounted cannon, 90mm anti-tank guns and an 81mm or 120mm mortar. An extra 75 litre fuel tank can be fitted which increases the vehicles' operating range of 1,200km.

8 × 8

This is powered by a 350HP turbo-charged diesel coupled to an automatic Allison five-speed gearbox. A wide range of armament installations is available, including 20mm and 30mm cannon, twin 30mm anti-aircraft guns, 81mm or 120mm mortars, twin 80mm rocket launchers, and in addition a remote-controlled 7.62mm machine-gun is mounted at the rear on the troop compartment in the roof. Other armament installations are possible for all these vehicles.

Above The Mowag Piranha 4×4 vehicle with remote-controlled 7.62mm machine-gun.
Below The Mowag Piranha 8×8 vehicle with turret-mounted 30mm cannon and a remote-controlled 7.62mm machine-gun at the rear.

SWITZERLAND

MOWAG TORNADO – MECHANIZED INFANTRY COMBAT VEHICLE
MANUFACTURER – Mowag Motorwagenfabrik AG, Kreuzlingen
STATUS – Trials. Not yet in production.

BASIC DATA

CREW:	10 (commander, driver, gunner and 7 infantrymen)	FUEL CAPACITY: FORDING:	550 litres 1.3m (without preparation) 1.8m (with preparation)
WEIGHT LOADED:	20,500kg		
WEIGHT EMPTY:	17,200kg	GRADIENT:	60%
LENGTH:	6.05m	SIDE SLOPE:	40%
WIDTH:	3.15m	VERTICAL OBSTACLE:	.85m
HEIGHT:	2.94m (top of turret) 1.9m (top of hull)	TRENCH: ENGINE:	2.2m Mowag M 8DV-TLK,
GROUND CLEARANCE:	.45m		8-cylinder multi-fuel
TRACK WIDTH:	450mm		engine developing 430HP
LENGTH OF TRACK			at 2,100rpm
ON GROUND:	3.7m	ARMAMENT:	1 × 25mm Oerlikon B 20
GROUND PRESSURE:	.6kg/cm^2		cannon turret-mounted.
POWER-TO-WEIGHT			2 × 7.62mm MGs in
RATIO:	20.97HP/ton		individual turrets on
MAXIMUM ROAD SPEED:	70km/hr		rear of hull top
RANGE:	600km (road)		

DEVELOPMENT

Mowag have been designing and developing tracked armoured personnel carriers for some 20 years. The Tornado 2 is a logical development of the Mowag Pirate APC which was developed in the 1950s. The Pirate did not enter production and is not therefore described here. Mowag were involved in designing and building some of the prototypes of the German Marder MICV and have built a number of components for the Marder, which is in production in Germany.

There have in fact been at least two models of the Tornado. The first model (the data above relate to the latest model) was a little smaller than the current model, had narrow tracks and was fitted with the Mowag M 150-6S transmission. It was armed with a turret-mounted 20mm cannon, remote-controlled machineguns at the rear, a single ball mount in each side of the fighting compartment, and two ball mounts in the twin doors at the rear of the vehicle. In addition a launching ramp was provided for the Swedish Bantam Anti-Tank Guided Weapon.

At the time of writing no production order for the Tornado had been announced although the vehicle has been tested by the Swiss Army who are believed to have a requirement for an MICV type of vehicle. The Swiss Army currently use the American M-113A1 APC. A further development of the Tornado is the Taifun, which is slightly larger and is powered by a 540HP engine (see entry under 'Italy').

DESCRIPTION

The hull of the Tornado is of all-welded steel armour. The glacis plate provides complete protection from 20mm projectiles whilst the hull side armour is proof against 12.7mm projectiles. Two escape hatches are provided in the floor of the vehicle.

The driver is seated at the front of the vehicle on the left side of the hull, with the engine to his right. The driver is provided with three periscopes to his front and one to his left, and in addition there is a single periscope in his hatch cover. One of his periscopes can be fitted with an infra-red viewer for driving at night. The driver's seat is adjustable so that he can drive in the head-out position. The commander is seated behind the driver and is provided with a one-piece hatch cover and a cupola that can be rotated through 360°. This is provided with a periscope which has an elevation of +.60° and a depression of − 15°.

The gunner is seated in the turret which is in the centre of the vehicle, and there are a total of six vision blocks arranged around the turret. In addition the gunner has a Z 11 optical sight for aiming the main armament, which has a ×2 to ×6 magnification.

The seven infantrymen are seated in the rear of the vehicle. One to the rear and left of the main turret, the other six, three either side, back to back at the rear of the hull. The infantry enter and leave the vehicle via a large power-operated ramp at the rear of the hull.

There are two firing ports in the rear fighting compartment which allow the infantry to fire sub-machine guns from within the vehicle. Over each of the firing ports is a vision block. There are also two hatches in the roof of the vehicle and two remote-control machine-gun mounts.

The engine, transmission and cooling system are mounted as a complete unit at the front of the vehicle and can be quickly removed for replacement. The hydro-mechanical six-speed transmission is provided with a torque converter with an automatic lock-up clutch. The Tornado can travel the same speed backwards as it can forwards. It is slightly faster than the Marder and can accelerate from 0 to 70km/hr in 45 seconds.

The suspension system is of the torsion-bar type and consists of six dual road wheels with the idler at the rear and the drive sprocket at the front, and there are three track return rollers. The two front and rear wheels are provided with hydraulic shock absorbers. The steel tracks are fitted with rubber blocks which can be quickly removed, and special rubber blocks with ice spikes are also available.

For normal purposes the Tornado's fording capability of 1.3m is sufficient, but with preparation it can ford to a depth of 1.8m. Electric bilge pumps are provided.

The Tornado is fitted with a ventilation and NBC protection system. This includes a primary and a fine filter. The ventilation system has two modes of operation – normal ventilation with an air flow rate of 4m³ per minute, and protection ventilation with an air flow of 3m³ per minute. The filter cartridges can be quickly changed when required. In addition, the interior of the hull is provided with a lining of plastic material for protection against radiation.

Various types of radio installation are available according to the requirements of the user. The vehicle has a 24V electrical system which consists of four batteries of 200Amp/hr and a 9kw generator to supply power to the various systems on the vehicle. The engine is provided with an automatic fire-extinguisher system. Various night driving and night fighting aids are available.

The 25mm Oerlikon cannon is mounted in a turret with a traverse of 360°, the gun having an elevation of + 60° and a depression of − 12°. The turret is power-operated and can be used against both ground and air targets and can fire a variety of ammunition including HE and armour piercing rounds. If required the turret could be fitted with an stabilization system which allows the turret to be laid and fired whilst the vehicle is moving, or manual controls could replace the powered controls. Another optional fit is to replace the turret with the same turret as fitted to the Marder MICV. Finally the existing turret could be fitted with a 20mm cannon and a 7.62mm machine-gun mounted co-axially.

The two Mowag-developed remote-controlled machine-gun turrets are identical to those used on the German Marder and each of these has a traverse of 230°, the 7.62mm machine-guns having an elevation of + 60° and a depression of − 15°. These turrets are controlled from within the vehicle and each is provided with two vision blocks and a PERI Z 12 sighting telescope.

The firing ports have also been developed by Mowag, and are identical to those of the German Marder, as they are of Mowag design and construction. This allows a sub-machine gun, ie the Uzi, to be fired from within the vehicle. The SMG can be used from + 18° to − 18° and 42° in azimuth, and when closed they are water-tight. The following quantities of ammunition are carried for the weapons installed in the vehicle—800 rounds of 25mm and 5,000 rounds of 7.62mm machine-gun ammunition. In addition the crew have their own weapons which would include automatic rifles, SMGs and anti-tank weapons.

The Mowag Tornado MICV.

VARIANTS

Mowag have drawn up proposals for a number of variants of the Tornado vehicle. These include a recovery vehicle complete with dozer blade and crane, ambulance, command vehicle, anti-tank vehicle fitted with anti-tank guided weapons, 120mm self-propelled mortar and an ammunition or load carrier. Mowag have also developed to prototype stage a 90mm self-propelled anti-tank gun which they call the Gepard. This is similar to the German Jagdpanzer Kanone (JPZ 4-5). Mowag did in fact build some of the prototypes of the German tank destroyer.

The Mowag 90mm Self-Propelled Anti-Tank Gun, the Gepard.

SWITZERLAND

MOWAG GRENADIER – ARMOURED CAR/ARMOURED PERSONNEL CARRIER
MANUFACTURER – Mowag Motorwagenfabrik AG, Kreuzlingen
STATUS – Ready for production.

BASIC DATA

CREW:	1 + 8 (driver and up to 8 men)	MAXIMUM ROAD SPEED:	100km/hr
		MAXIMUM WATER	
WEIGHT LOADED:	6,100kg	SPEED:	9km/hr
WEIGHT EMPTY:	4,400kg	RANGE:	550km
LENGTH:	4.84m	FUEL:	180 litres
HEIGHT:	2.12m (turret top)	FORDING:	Amphibious
	1.7m (hull top)	GRADIENT:	60%
GROUND CLEARANCE:	.25m (axles	ANGLE OF APPROACH:	41°
	.4m (hull)	ANGLE OF DEPARTURE:	36°
TRACK:	1.99m (front)	ENGINE:	8-cylinder, 4-stroke,
	2m (rear)		water-cooled petrol
WHEELBASE:	2.5m		developing 202HP at
TURNING RADIUS:	6.45m		3,900rpm

DEVELOPMENT

The Mowag Grenadier is yet another Mowag product designed for the export market. It is not known if the vehicle has been produced in any quantity.

DESCRIPTION

The hull of the Grenadier is of all-welded construction which gives the crew complete protection from attack from small arms fire. The driver is seated at the front of the hull on the left with the engine to his

A Mowag Grenadier showing its amphibious capabilities. This vehicle is armed with 8cm multiple rocket launchers.

right. The driver is provided with a single-piece hatch cover and a total of three periscopes for observation purposes. The armament is installed in the centre of the roof and there is also a smaller circular hatch in the rear of the hull, one of these doors being provided with a vision block. Mowag type firing ports and vision blocks can be mounted in the hull sides and rear if required.

The NP 435 gearbox has 4F and 1R gears. Differentials are fitted in the front and rear axles with a self-locking device. The steering is power-assisted. Rigid axles are fitted and the suspension consists of springs and hydraulic shock absorbers.

The Grenadier is fully amphibious being propelled in the water by a three-bladed propeller at the rear. Before entering the water a trim vane is erected at the front of the hull. The propeller is engaged when moving into second gear, and the two parallel rudders are connected with the steering wheel. An electric bilge pump is fitted.

The electrical system consists of 2 × 12V batteries with a capacity of 100A6hr, and a 450Watt alternator is also fitted.

Optional equipment includes an air-conditioning system, infra-red driving lights, electric ventilator and bullet-proof tyres.

VARIANTS
The Grenadier can be fitted with a variety of armament installations, including the following:
Turret-mounted 20mm cannon
8cm Multiple Rocket-Launcher
Anti-Tank weapons
Remote-controlled 7.62mm machine-gun with a × 4 sight.

SWITZERLAND

MOWAG ROLAND – ARMOURED PERSONNEL CARRIER/INTERNAL SECURITY VEHICLE
MANUFACTURER – Mowag Motorwagenfabrik, Kreuzlingen, Switzerland
STATUS – In service with a number of countries, including Greece and Peru and especially South America. Manufactured as and when orders are received. It has been reported that this vehicle is also being built in Argentina.

BASIC DATA

CREW:	3 + 3/4 (commander, driver, gunner and 3/4 men)	ANGLE OF DEPARTURE:	36°
		MAXIMUM ROAD SPEED:	110km/hr
			80km/hr (with bullet-proof tyres)
WEIGHT LOADED:	4,700kg		
WEIGHT EMPTY:	3,900kg	RANGE:	550km
LENGTH:	4.44m	FUEL CONSUMPTION:	28 litres per 100km
WIDTH:	2.01m	FORDING:	1m
HEIGHT:	2.03m (top of turret)	GRADIENT:	60%
	1.62m (top of hull)	VERTICAL OBSTACLE:	.4m
GROUND CLEARANCE:	.4m	ENGINE:	Chrysler 8-cylinder, water-cooled petrol engine developing 202BHP at 3,900rpm
TRACK:	1.71m (front)		
	1.655m (rear)		
WHEELBASE:	2.5m		
TYRES:	9.00 × 16	ARMAMENT:	Various armament can be installed including turret-mounted 7.62mm MGs
TURNING RADIUS:	6.45m		
ANGLE OF APPROACH:	40°		

The Mowag Roland fitted with obstacle-clearing blade.

The Mowag Roland with doors and turret open.

DEVELOPMENT/DESCRIPTION

The Roland has been designed by Mowag for a variety of roles including use as an armoured personnel carrier and as an internal security vehicle. The other roles suggested by Mowag include use as a command and radio vehicle, ambulance, supply carrier, and as an armed reconnaissance vehicle.

The hull of the Roland is of all-welded steel armour plate of approx. 110kg/cm² strength.

The driver is seated at the front of the vehicle and is provided with a one-piece hatch cover that opens to the right, and three periscopes for use when driving closed down. A special windscreen complete with a wiper has been developed so that the driver can drive head-out in wet weather. In the centre is the turret which can be adopted to mount a variety of armament installations. The basic turret is provided with a single vision block and a firing port which will accept various machine-guns. The turret is not provided with a basket, but the gunner has an adjustable seat. There is also a single hatch in the roof of the vehicle, behind and to the right of the turret.

Entry doors are provided in both sides of the hull and each of these is provided with a firing port and above this a vision block. There is a further door at the rear of the vehicle on the right side and this is also provided with a vision block and a firing port. In addition, there is a vision block in each side of the hull between the driver's position and the side doors. Normally one passenger sits near each of the side doors and the other two men sit to the right of the engine compartment.

The engine is at the rear of the hull on the left side. The gearbox has 4F and 1R gears and a two-speed transfer case. The suspension consists of semi-elliptical leaf-type springs with hydraulic shock-absorbers on all four wheels. Non-spin differentials are fitted in both front and rear axles. The vehicle's brakes are hydraulic with vacuum boosters, and the hand brake is mechanical and operates on all the rear wheels. The electrical system is 12V and a 12V battery (125Amp/hr) is provided. The alternator is 12V, 30Amp. A heater is installed as standard equipment.

VARIANTS

A wide range of optional equipment is available, including a front-mounted obstacle-clearing blade, blue flashing lights, wire mesh protection for headlamps, various radio installations, remote-control unit for a 7.62mm machine-gun, special gun ports for sub-machine-guns, bullet-proof tyres, infra-red night driving equipment, searchlights and a complete air-conditioning system.

SWITZERLAND

MOWAG MR 8-01 SERIES – ARMOURED PERSONNEL CARRIER
MANUFACTURERS – Mowag of Kreuzlingen and Büssing and Henschel in Germany
STATUS – In service with German Border Police and German Police. Production complete.

BASIC DATA

CREW:	3-5	ANGLE OF APPROACH:	45°
WEIGHT:	8,200kg	ANGLE OF DEPARTURE:	44°
LENGTH:	5.31m	MAXIMUM ROAD SPEED:	80km/hr
WIDTH:	2.2m	GRADIENT	60%
HEIGHT:	2.2m (including turret)	ENGINE:	Chrysler Type R361
	1.88m (top of hull)		6-cylinder petrol engine
GROUND CLEARANCE:	.5m (hull)		developing 161HP
	.3m (axles)	ARMAMENT:	1 × 20mm cannon
TRACK:	1.95m		2 × 4 smoke
WHEELBASE:	2.6m		dischargers
TYRES:	10.00 × 20		

DEVELOPMENTS

In the 1950s Mowag built a number of prototypes of the MR 8-01 series of 4 × 4 armoured personnel carriers. A small number of these were sold to Germany and a large number (reported to be 300/400) were subsequently built in Germany. As far as is known no other country uses this vehicle.

DESCRIPTION

The hull of the MR 8-01 is of all-welded steel construction with the driver at the front of the vehicle on the left side. The turret (when fitted) is in the centre and the engine at the rear on the left side. The vehicle is not amphibious, does not have an NBC system and has no infra-red equipment installed for night operations.

VARIANTS

The Federal German Border Police (Bundesgrenzschutz or BGS) have two models of this vehicle, these being known as the SW1 and SW2:
SW1 is the Geschützter Sonderwagen 1 (Kfz 91) and has no armament as it is used as an APC and carries seven men.
SW2 is the Geschützter Sonderwagen 11 (Kfz 91) and is armed with a turret-mounted 20mm cannon, with four smoke dischargers either side of the turret. This has a crew of four.
The German Police have used some of the SW1 with an obstacle-clearing blade mounted at the front of the hull.
Other Mowag variants included the following, most of which were built as prototypes:
MR 8-09 with 20mm cannon, MR 8-23 with turret-mounted 90mm Mecar gun, MR 8-30 with twin 8cm multiple rocket-launchers, MR 9-32 with a 120mm mortar.

Left SW1 of the Federal German Border Police.
Above SW11 of the Federal German Border Police, armed with 20mm cannon.

UNITED STATES

XM723 – MECHANIZED INFANTRY COMBAT VEHICLE
MANUFACTURER – FMC Corporation, San Jose, California
STATUS – Trials. Should enter production in 1978/79.

BASIC DATA

CREW:	11-12 (commander, gunner, driver and 9 infantry)	MAXIMUM WATER SPEED:	6/9km/hr
		RANGE:	483km
WEIGHT LOADED:	19,505kg	FUEL:	746 litres
WEIGHT EMPTY:	17,690kg	FORDING:	Amphibious
WEIGHT AIR-PORTABLE:	15,876kg	GRADIENT:	60%
LENGTH:	6.35m	SIDE SLOPE:	40%
WIDTH:	3.2m (o/a) 2.971m (over tracks)	VERTICAL OBSTACLE:	.914m
		TRENCH:	2.54m
HEIGHT:	2.768m (o/a) 2.616m (turret roof) 1.981m (hull top)	ENGINE:	Cummins VTA-903 water-cooled, turbo-charged, 4-cycle diesel engine developing 450HP at 2,600rpm
GROUND CLEARANCE:	.482m		
TRACK WIDTH:	533mm		
LENGTH OF TRACK ON GROUND:	3.81m	ARMAMENT:	1 × 25mm cannon (prototypes have 20mm cannon)
GROUND PRESSURE:	.49kg/cm^2		1 × 7.62mm MG co-axial with above
POWER-TO-WEIGHT RATIO:	24.8HP/ton		
MAXIMUM ROAD SPEED:	72.4km/hr		

Note: The above data relate to prototype vehicles; production models may well differ.

DEVELOPMENT

In the early 1960s the Pacific Car and Foundry Company of Renton, Washington, built five prototypes of a vehicle called the XM701 Mechanized Infantry Combat Vehicle, based on the M107/M110 self-propelled gun chassis. It was found however that this vehicle was too large. FMC then built two prototypes of an MICV called the XM765. This was not adopted by the United States Army but was developed by the FMC Corporation into the Product Improved M113A1 and later still the Armoured Infantry Fighting Vehicle which is now in production for the Royal Netherlands Army. There is a separate entry for this vehicle.

The United States Army then issued a requirement for another Mechanized Infantry Combat Vehicle and three companies were shortlisted: Chrysler, FMC and Pacific Car and Foundry.

In November 1972 the FMC Corporation was awarded a $29.3 million contract to run for four years to build 17 prototypes for testing. At the present time these are undergoing extensive trials and some problems have been encountered with the suspension, as is normal during the early development cycle of any armoured vehicle. Recently it has been stated that the XM723 should enter production in 1978 at a unit cost of about $233,000. The XM723 will not replace all current M113A1s, but simply on a selective basis.

DESCRIPTION

The hull of the XM723 is of all-welded aluminium construction, the front, vertical hull sides and hull rear having a sheet of steel armour placed a short distance from the aluminium armour. This provides added protection against anti-tank weapons of the HEAT type. The vehicle has been designed to carry an infantry squad and its equipment, the latter including four LAWs and 3 Dragon ATGWs.

The driver is seated at the front of the vehicle on the left side and is provided with a single-piece hatch cover that opens to the left and a total of four periscopes. The commander is seated behind the driver and has a single-piece hatch cover and a total of six periscopes. The gun turret is in the centre of the hull, slightly offset to the right. The eight or nine infantrymen are seated at the rear of the vehicle, the number carried depending on the seating arrangement. Two men are seated to the left of the turret, one behind the other facing forwards, and the other six in the rear. In each side of the hull are two vision ports and two firing ports, and there are also two firing and two vision ports in the hull rear. Normal means of entry and exit for the infantry is via a hydraulically-operated ramp at the rear of the hull, and this is also provided with a single door in case the ramp should jam shut. There is a single-piece hatch cover over the rear troop compartment and this opens to the rear to enable the crew to use their anti-tank weapons.

The suspension of the XM723 is of the torsion-bar-in-tube type with a total vertical road wheel travel of 355mm. The suspension consists of six road wheels with the drive sprocket at the front and the idler at the rear and track return rollers are also provided. Three shock absorbers are provided for each track. The steel track is of the single-pin type and is provided with detachable rubber pads.

The engine and transmission are mounted to the right of the driver. The transmission is a General Electric HMPT-500 automatic hydro-mechanical model. The hydrostatic transmission is mounted at the front of the hull.

The electrical system is 24V and a 220Amp generator is provided, plus four 6TN batteries with a capacity of 100Amp/hr each.

The turret is provided with a single-piece hatch cover that opens to the rear, six periscopes and an M36E2 day/night sight. The turret has full powered traverse through 360°, elevation being +60° and depression −9°. An electro-hydraulic stabilization system developed by the national Water Lift Corporation enables the gunner to lay and fire his weapons whilst the vehicle is on the move.

Prototypes are armed with a 20mm M129 cannon and a 7.62mm mounted co-axially to the left of the 20mm cannon. Production vehicles will, it is anticipated, be armed with the 25mm Bushmaster cannon now being developed for a variety of roles by the Aeronutronic Ford Company, and a co-axial M60E2 7.62mm machine-gun. The gunner can select which type of ammunition he wants to use with the 20/25mm cannon and the empty cartridge cases are automatically ejected outside the vehicle. Total ammunition capacity is 600 rounds of 25mm and 3,400 rounds of 7.62mm ammunition.

The firing ports in the hull sides and rear have been designed for use with the old .45 M3A1 sub-machine-gun; six of these and 4,000 rounds of ammunition are carried. A new weapon for these firing ports may well be developed.

The XM723 is fully amphibious being propelled in the water by its tracks, and a propeller kit is believed to be under development. Fixed fire-extinguishing systems are provided in both the crew and engine compartments. Night driving equipment is provided.

VARIANTS
The only two possible variants announced so far are:
  1. Anti-Tank Vehicle with TOW missile system under armour.
  2. Anti-Aircraft Vehicle with the Roland SAM system installed.

The XM723 MICV at speed during trials.

Above XM723 MICV from the rear. The side armour is clearly shown in this photograph.
Below The General Electric HMPT-500 Hydro-mechanical Transmission as fitted to the XM723 MICV.

UNITED STATES

ARMOURED INFANTRY FIGHTING VEHICLE – MECHANIZED INFANTRY COMBAT VEHICLE
MANUFACTURER – FMC Corporation, San Jose, California
STATUS – In production. 850 AIFVs have been ordered by the Netherlands Army for delivery in 1977/78.

BASIC DATA

CREW:	10 (commander, driver, gunner and 7 infantry)	ACCELERATION:	0-32km/hr in 10 seconds 0-48km/hr in 23.1 seconds
WEIGHT LOADED:	13,470kg		
WEIGHT EMPTY:	11,292kg	RANGE (road):	490km
LENGTH:	5.258m	FUEL:	416 litres
WIDTH:	2.819m	FORDING:	Amphibious
	2.54m (over tracks)	GRADIENT:	60%
HEIGHT:	2.784m (including periscope)	SIDE SLOPE:	40%
		VERTICAL OBSTACLE:	.635m
	2.619m (top of turret)	TRENCH:	1.676m
	2.007m (top of hull)	ENGINE:	Detroit Diesel Model 6V53T, V-6, 2-cycle, turbo-charged, liquid-cooled diesel developing 264BHP at 2,800rpm
GROUND CLEARANCE:	.432m		
TRACK:	2.159m		
TRACK WIDTH:	381mm		
LENGTH OF TRACK			
ON GROUND:	2.7m	ARMAMENT:	1 × 25mm cannon 1 × 7.62mm MG co-axial with above
GROUND PRESSURE:	.66kg/cm²		
MAXIMUM ROAD SPEED:	61.2 km/hr		
MAXIMUM WATER SPEED:	6.3km/hr		

DEVELOPMENT

About ten years ago the United States Army placed an order with FMC for a modified M113A1 fitted with a turret-mounted gun and firing ports. This was called the XM765. Two were built for the Army and were tested in both the United States and Korea. FMC went on to develop this vehicle further and the end result was the Armoured Infantry Fighting Vehicle, the first prototype of which was completed in 1970. The United States Army then placed a development contract with FMC for a new MICV which became the XM723, for which there is a separate entry. The AIFV was demonstrated in Europe in 1973/74 and the first production order was placed by the Netherlands Army early in 1975.

The AIFV is much cheaper than the XM723 and uses many components of the M113A1 series of armoured personnel carriers, which should make it an attractive proposition for many countries.

DESCRIPTION

The hull of the AIFV is of all-welded aluminium construction. The vertical sides are of spaced laminate armour; ie a layer of steel has been bolted on to the aluminium and the space between has been filled with foam. This gives added protection against HEAT rounds as well as increasing the buoyancy of the vehicle. If required an appliqué steel armour kit can be bolted to the floor to give added protection against mines.

The driver is seated at the front of the hull on the left side and is provided with a single-piece hatch cover and a total of four M27 periscopes for observation purposes. A UA9630 passive periscope can replace one of the M27 for use at night.

The commander is seated behind the driver and also has a single-piece hatch cover. The commander is provided with four M27 and one M20A1 periscopes, the latter having a magnification of ×6. A passive night periscope can replace one of the day periscopes if required. The turret is in the centre of the hull, slightly offset to the right.

A total of seven infantrymen are carried. One man is seated between the commander and the turret and the other six men are in the hull rear, three each side back to back. There is a single-piece hatch cover over the hull rear which opens to the rear. The infantry enter and leave the vehicle via a hydraulically-operated ramp in the rear of the hull. There are a total of five firing ports and five periscopes arranged round the rear troop compartment. There are two firing ports each side and one in the rear ramp and the side firing ports are each provided with an M17 periscope whilst the rear firing port has an M27 periscope.

The suspension of the AIFV is of the torsion-bar-in-tube type. There are a total of five road wheels with the drive sprocket at the front and the idler at the rear, and no track return rollers. Dual action hydraulic shock absorbers are provided for the first and fifth wheel stations. Track tension is provided by a simple grease-gun actuation of the rear idler wheel. The track fitted is the T130E1 single-pin, steel-block, rubber-bushed pin with a removable rubber pad.

The engine is mounted to the right of the driver and is similar to that mounted in the M113A1 except that it has a turbo-charger. A larger capacity radiator, modified transmission with heavy duty components, heavy duty universal joint and final drives as fitted to the M548 tracked cargo carrier. Air for the engine enters a grill centred in the engine compartment cover and exhausts through grilles to the right. The engine can be removed as a complete unit through a hinged hatch in the front and top of the hull. The transmission is an Allison TX100-1A automatic with 3F and 1R gears and a torque converter and lock-up clutch. The steering is an FMC DS200 mechanical controlled and pivot steer.

Normal steering and braking is accomplished by oil-cooled band-type brakes located in the controlled differential. A set of air-cooled disc brakes are located on the differential output shafts for pivot steering in the water. The fuel is carried in two armoured cells in the rear of the hull, and an armour plate separates the cells from the troop compartment.

The AIFVs being delivered to the Netherlands are armed with an Oerlikon 25mm KBA cannon and a co-axial Belgian 7.62mm MAG machine-gun. The Netherlands are also arming their C and R vehicles with the KBA cannon. Ready-use ammunition consists of 165 rounds of 25mm and 230 rounds of 7.62mm. Stowed ammunition consists of 150 rounds of 25mm and 1,610 rounds of 7.62mm. The turret has an electro-hydraulic traverse mechanism with manual controls for use in an emergency. Turret can be traversed through 360° at a speed of 45°/sec. Elevation is from $-10°$ to $+55°$ at 60°/sec. The gunner is provided with four M27 periscopes for observation purposes as well as a Philips ×2 (day) and ×6 (night) sight. He also has an open anti-aircraft emergency gun sight and a 150watt infra-red/white searchlight is synchronized with the main armament.

It is possible to fit an add-on electro-hydraulic stabilization system as well as launchers for chaffe or smoke grenades. It would be possible to fit other 20/25mm weapons, for example the German Rh.202 20mm cannon.

The electrical system is 24V and two 6TN batteries with a capacity of 100Amp/hr are provided.

The AIFV is fully amphibious being propelled in the water by its tracks. Before entering the water a trim vane is erected at the front of the hull, and electrical bilge pumps are provided.

The vehicle is not provided with an NBC system although a ventilator is installed in the roof. Heaters can be provided for the engine coolant, battery and crew compartments.

VARIANTS

AIFV with Low Profile Weapon Installation
This can be armed with a variety of weapons including 20mm M139, 25mm Oerlikon KBA or the Rheinmetall 20mm gun. The turret has a traverse of 45° a second and an elevation of 60° a second. Elevation is from +60° to −15°. It is provided with an M34 day sight and can also be fitted with an M36 night sight. In addition it has four M27 periscopes.

AIFV with Low Profile .50 MG Installation
This is armed with a .50 (12.7mm) machine-gun which is aimed and fired from within the vehicle. The gun is linked to an M28C sight and four M27 periscopes are also provided.

Additional roles possible with kits
Kits are available to enable the AIFV to be used in the following roles:
Command Post–with tables, radios and, if required, radar.
TOW–This is still under development and will consist of twin launchers in a one-man turret. In addition ten missiles will be carried inside the hull.
Mortar–This will carry 51 rounds of 120mm mortar bombs and tow a 120mm mortar. Total crew will be seven men.
Ambulance–No armament. This will carry four stretchers, three sitting wounded plus crew.
Cargo carrier–Crew of two and armed with a pintle-mounted .50 (12.7mm) machine-gun.
Recovery–Fitted with winch, heavy duty crane and pintle-mounted .50 (12.7mm) machine-gun.

Left Armoured Infantry Fighting Vehicle with turret mounted 25mm cannon and co-axial 7.62mm machine-gun.
Above Armoured Infantry Fighting Vehicle with low profile 12.7mm machine-gun mounting.
Below Armoured Infantry Fighting Vehicle with different roof arrangement and 20mm low profile cannon.

UNITED STATES

COMMANDO SERIES–MULTI-MISSION VEHICLE
MANUFACTURER–Cadillac Gage Company, Warren, Michigan
STATUS–In service with Bolivia, Ethiopia, Laos, Lebanon, Malaysia, Muscat and Oman, Peru, Portugal, Saudi Arabia, Singapore, Somalia, Sudan, Turkey, United States and Vietnam. In production.

BASIC DATA	V-100	V-150	V-200
CREW:	12	12	12
WEIGHT LOADED:	7,370kg	9,550kg	12,730kg
WEIGHT EMPTY:	5,910kg	6,820kg	9,298kg
LENGTH:	5.689m	5.689m	6.121m
WIDTH:	2.26m	2.26m	2.438m
HEIGHT			
without armament:	1.93m	1.955m	1.981m
turret top:	2.438m	2.54m	2.489m
GROUND CLEARANCE (axles):	.406m	.381m	.431m
TRACK:	1.866m	1.942m	2.038m(f) 2.076m(r)
WHEELBASE:	2.667m	2.667m	3.263m
TYRES:	14.00 × 20	14.00 × 20	16.00 × 20
GROUND PRESSURE:	1.476kg/cm²	1.5kg/cm²	1.265kg/cm²
TURNING RADIUS:	8.534m	8.382m	9.753m
MAXIMUM ROAD SPEED:	100km/hr	88km/hr	96km/hr
WATER SPEED:	4.8km/hr	4.8km/hr	4.8km/hr
RANGE			
road:	500-965km	500-965km	600km
cross-country:	400-680km	400-680km	300-400km
FUEL:	303 litres	303 litres	379 litres
FORDING:	Amphibious	Amphibious	Amphibious
GRADIENT:	50%	60%	60%
SIDE SLOPE:	30%	30%	30%
VERTICAL OBSTACLE:	.609m	.609m	.609m
ANGLE OF APPROACH:	55°	55°	50°
ANGLE OF DEPARTURE:	53°	53°	50°
ENGINE:	Chrysler 361 V-8 petrol, 200HP	Chrysler 361 V-8 petrol or Cummins V-6 diesel developing 155HP	Chrysler 440 CID, 275HP
WINCH CAPACITY:	4,536kg	4,536kg	6,804kg

DEVELOPMENT

Design work on the Commando armoured vehicle started in 1962/63 with the first prototype being completed in March 1963 and production vehicles following early in 1964.

The Commando saw extensive service in Vietnam with the United States Army, United States Air Force, ARVN and Thai forces. It was mostly used in the convoy escort role.

The V-100 was followed by the larger V-200 which in turn has been followed by the V-150. Both the V-200 and V-150 are currently available. By 1975 over 2,000 Commando armoured vehicles had been delivered. According to Cadillac Gage, the United States has not supplied any Commandos to Portugal; however, Commando type vehicles have been seen in large numbers in Portugal and it is reliably reported that the Commando is now being built in Portugal under the name of Bravia Cgaimite.

DESCRIPTION

The description below relates to the V-150 Commando–the V-100 and V-200 are very similar.

The hull of the Commando is of all-welded construction and provides the crew with protection from small arms fire up to and including .30 ball. The driver is seated at the front of the hull with a further seat to his right. A total of five vision blocks are arranged around the front and sides of his compartment and twin hatches that open left and right are provided in the roof of the driver's compartment. The turret is mounted in the centre of the hull and turrets with a 20mm or 90mm gun have two hatch covers that open to the rear whilst turrets with twin 7.62mm or one 7.62mm and one 12.7mm machine-gun have a single-piece hatch cover that opens to the rear. There is a hatch in each side of the hull, the top opening sideways whilst the bottom half folds downwards to form a step. There is a further hatch in the hull rear on the right and the top half of this hinges upwards whilst the bottom half hinges downwards. All three hatches have a vision block and a firing port.

There are a further six firing ports and vision blocks arranged around the sides of the hull. In addition there is a roof hatch to the right of the engine compartment.

The engine and transmission are at the rear of the hull on the left side, and this is provided with access hatches in the roof and the sides of the hull. A fire-bomb shroud is mounted over the engine which prevents flaming liquids from entering the engine compartment.

The Commando has 4 × 4 drive and a gearbox with 5F and 1R gears. A fully automatic gearbox with 3F and 1R gear is also being offered.

The axles are modified five-ton truck axles and have locking differentials. The suspension consists of leaf springs and hydraulic shock absorbers. Tyres are of the run-flat type and steering is power assisted. The electrical system is 24V and is radio suppressed. The Commando is fully amphibious, being propelled in the water by its wheels, and two electric bilge pumps are fitted. All models have a winch mounted in the front of the hull. The Commando does not have an NBC system. Infra-red driving lights are not normally fitted although provision has been made for these.

VARIANTS
V-100
1. Fitted with turret-mounted twin 7.62mm or .30 machine-guns, elevation +59°, depression −14°, traverse 360°. Ammunition supply consists of 1,000 rounds for ready-use and 9,000 rounds in reserve. Six smoke dischargers can be mounted either side of turret if required.
2. Similar turret to above but armed with one .30 (7.62mm) and one .50 machine-guns.
3. Fitted with a pod for use in the command role, communications role or as armoured personnel carrier.
4. Open-top model which can be fitted with a variety of systems, ie various turrets, pod or machine-guns.
5. Mortar carrier with 81mm mortar.
6. Riot-Control, Police or fire-fighting vehicle.
7. Anti-Tank vehicle with TOW or Dragon missiles.
8. Turret-mounted General Electric 7.62mm six-barrelled minigun.
9. Recovery vehicle.
There have also been other projects including a Commando with a multiple rocket system.

Commando V-100 in Vietnam armed with one single .50 (12.7mm) and twin .30 (7.62mm) machine-guns.

V-150

This was introduced in 1971 and has the following improvements over the earlier V-100:

Increased payload (up from 1,360kg to 2,268kg). Increased cross-country mobility. Increased armour protection. Improvements in human engineering.

The following variants are available:

1. Armoured Personnel Carrier carrying twelve. Armed with similar turret to No. 1 above.
2. Mortar carrier with a crew of five men. Armed with an 81mm mortar and a total of 60-80 mortar bombs. Up to three 7.62mm machine-guns and 2,000 rounds of ammunition can be carried. Smoke dischargers can also be fitted.
3. Fitted with a larger turret armed with a 20mm Oerlikon cannon and a co-axial 7.62mm machine-gun, a further 7.62mm machine-gun is mounted on top of the turret for use in the anti-aircraft role. The 20mm cannon has an elevation of +60° and a depression of −8°. A Cadillac Gage electro-hydraulic elevation/traverse mechanism is provided. Total ammunition capacity is 400 rounds of 20mm and 3,000 rounds of 7.62mm ammunition, and smoke dischargers can be mounted on the turret rear if required. This model has a crew of eight.
4. Fitted with the same turret as the above but with a 90mm Mecar gun, co-axial 7.62mm machine-gun and a 7.62mm anti-aircraft machine-gun. Total ammunition capacity is 40 rounds of 90mm and 3,000 rounds of 7.62mm. Crew consists of four men.
5. Recovery vehicle with 'A' frame.
6. Anti-Tank vehicle with TOW or Dragon ATGW.
7. Riot-Control vehicle.
8. Command/Radio vehicle.

V-200

This was developed in 1969 and is essentially a larger V-100 with bigger tyres, larger fuel tanks and a more powerful engine. The following models have been offered:

1. Armoured Personnel Carrier with seats for twelve men, armed with 7.62mm machine-guns, total ammunition supply 5,000 rounds. Gross vehicle weight is 12,730kg; empty weight 9,298kg.
2. Armed with turret-mounted 90mm gun, co-axial 7.62mm machine-gun, 7.62mm anti-aircraft gun and smoke dischargers. Empty weight is 11,248kg.
3. Armed with turret-mounted 20mm cannon, 7.62mm co-axial machine-gun, 7.62mm anti-aircraft machine-gun and twelve smoke dischargers. Total ammunition capacity is 525 rounds of 20mm and 5,000 rounds of 7.62mm. Crew of eleven. Empty weight 11,112kg.
4. Mortar carrier with 81mm mortar and a 7.62mm machine-gun. Total ammunition supply is 96 81mm mortar bombs and 2,500 rounds of 7.62mm machine-gun ammunition. Crew of five. Curb weight is 10,433kg.
5. 120mm mortar carrier. Total ammunition supply is 75 mortar bombs and 2,500 rounds of 7.62mm machine-gun ammunition. Crew of seven. Curb weight is 10,976kg.
6. Recovery vehicle with tools and an 'A' frame mounted on the front of the hull. Maximum crew is eight. Armed with a 7.62mm machine-gun.
7. Command vehicle with a crew of seven and a curb weight of 10,250kg.

The Commando can be fitted with various other armament installations as required by the user.

Left Commando V-150 with turret-mounted Oerlikon 20mm cannon.
Above Commando V-150 armed with a Mecar 90mm gun, and 7.62mm co-axial and 7.62mm anti-aircraft machine-guns.

V-150 Commando with pod and a single 7.62mm machine-gun.

Above V-150 with 81mm mortar installed.

V-200 with turret-mounted 20mm cannon. Note the larger wheel arches on the V-200 when compared with the V-100 and V-150.

UNITED STATES

M113 SERIES–ARMOURED PERSONNEL CARRIER AND VARIANTS
MANUFACTURERS–FMC Corporation, San Jose, California and Oto Melara, La Spezia, Italy
STATUS–In service with Argentina, Australia, Bolivia, Brazil, Cambodia, Canada, Chile, Denmark, Ecuador, Ethiopia, Germany, Guatamala, Greece, Haiti, Iran, Israel, Italy, Laos, Lebanon, Libya, Netherlands, New Zealand, Norway, Pakistan, Peru, Philippines, Somalia, South Korea, Spain, Switzerland, Taiwan, Thailand, Turkey, United States, Uruguay, Vietnam. In production.

BASIC DATA	M106A1	M113A1	M125A1	M548A1	M577A1	XM806E1
CREW:	6	13	6	4	5	4
WEIGHT						
loaded:	11,996kg	11,156kg	11,261kg	12,880kg	11,513kg	11,567kg
empty:	11,274kg	9,702kg	10,539kg	7,435kg	10,865kg	10,355kg
LENGTH:.	4.926m	4.863m	4.863m	5.892m	4.863m	5.339m
WIDTH:	2.863m	2.686m	2.686m	2.686m	2.686m	2.686m
reduced:	2.54m	2.54m	2.54m	2.54m	2.54m	2.54m
HEIGHT						
overall:	2.5m	2.5m	2.5m	2.68m	2.68m	2.5m
hull top:	1.828	1.828m	1.828m	1.93m	2.469m	1.828m
GROUND CLEARANCE:	.406m	.406m	.406m	.406m	.406m	.406m
TRACK:	2.159m	2.159m	2.159m	2.159m	2.159m	2.159m
TRACK WIDTH:	381mm	381mm	381mm	381mm	381mm	381mm
LENGTH OF TRACK ON GROUND:	2.667m	2.667m	2.667m	2.819m	2.667m	2.667m
POWER-TO-WEIGHT RATIO:	17.92	19.27	19.09	16.9	18.67	18.59
(HP/TON):						
GROUND PRESSURE:	.59kg/cm^2	.55kg/cm^2	.55kg/cm^2	.6kg/cm^2	.57kg/cm^2	.57kg/cm^2
MAXIMUM ROAD SPEED:	67.59km/hr	67.59km/hr	67.59km/hr	62.2km/hr	67.59km/hr	67.59km/hr
MAXIMUM WATER SPEED:	5.8km/hr	5.8km/hr	5.8km/hr	5.6km/hr	5.8km/hr	5.3km/hr
ACCELERATION 0-48km/hr:	29sec	25.4sec	28.5sec	34.5sec	26.7sec	26.9sec
RANGE:	483km	483km	483km	483km	595km	483km
FUEL, LITRES:	360	360	360	397	454	360
FORDING:	Amp	Amp	Amp	Amp	Amp	Amp
GRADIENT:	60%	60%	60%	60%	60%	60%
SIDE SLOPE:	30%	30%	30%	30%	30%	30%
VERTICAL OBSTACLE:	.61m	.61m	.61m	.61m	.61m	.61m
TRENCH:	1.68m	1.68m	1.68m	1.68m	1.68m	1.68m
ENGINE:	GMC Diesel Model 6V53, 6-cylinder water-cooled developing 215BHP at 2,800rpm					
ARMOUR:	12-38mm	12-38mm	12-38mm	12-38mm	12-38mm	12-38mm

Note: Above data are from FMC. US Army data differs slightly. M113 was powered by a Chrysler Model 75M, V-8 water-cooled petrol engine which developed 209BHP at 4,000rpm.

DEVELOPMENT
In 1954 characteristics were laid down for a new tracked air transportable family of armoured personnel carriers. These were to replace the current M59 and M75 tracked APCs. Prototypes were built in 1958 and were known as the T113E1 and T113E2. Four of each type were built. The T113s were of all-aluminium construction whilst the similar T117 was of all-steel construction. In June 1959 a production order was awarded to FMC for the construction of an initial batch of 900 M113s, the first of which was completed in 1960. In June 1959 FMC were awarded a further contract to study the feasibility of fitting a diesel engine in place of the petrol engine. This was known as the M113E2 and was standardised as the M113A1 in May 1963, with the first production vehicle following in 1964. Since then all production has been concentrated on the M113A1 with the diesel engine. By 1975 well over 60,000 M113s and its many variants had been built by FMC, and Oto Melara of Italy had built about 4,000 vehicles for delivery to Italy, Libya and Greece.

DESCRIPTION (M113A1)
The hull of the M113A1 is of all-welded aluminium construction. The driver is seated at the front of the hull on the left side and is provided with a single-piece hatch cover that opens to the rear. His vision equipment consists of four M17 periscopes and a single M19 periscope in the hatch roof, which can be replaced by an infra-red periscope. The engine is mounted to the right of the driver with the air inlet and air outlet louvres in the roof of the hull. The Allison TX-100 transmission consists of a three-speed gearbox and a two-stage torque converter, giving a total of 6F and 2R gears. There is an access plate in the front of the hull.

The commander is in the centre of the hull and has a cupola with a single-piece hatch cover. The cupola has a total of five M17 periscopes and can be traversed through 360° by hand. A single Browning .50 (12.7mm) M2 machine-gun is mounted on the commander's cupola. This has an elevation of +53° and a depression of −21°. 2,000 rounds of ammunition are carried for this. Five infantry sit along each side of the hull facing each other and there is a single seat to the rear of the commander's station. A hatch is provided over the rear troop compartment. The normal means of entry and exit is via a large hydraulically-operated ramp in the hull rear, which is provided with an integral door in the left side should the ramp fail to open.

The suspension is of torsion-bar type and consists of five road wheels with the drive sprocket at the front and the idler at the rear. There are no track support rollers. The top half of the track is covered by a rubber skirt. The first and last road wheel stations are provided with hydraulic shock absorbers. The electrical system is 24V and consists of two 12V batteries. Charging is carried out by an engine-mounted generator. Two electric bilge pumps are provided.

The M113A1 is fully amphibious being propelled in the water by its tracks. Before entering the water the trim vane is erected at the front of the hull.

Infra-red driving lights are provided. The M113A1 does not have an NBC system as a normal part of its equipment. The engine compartment is provided with a fire-warning and fire-extinguishing system.

The following individual kits are available:

Heater kit for personnel compartment −Heater kit for engine coolant and battery−Windshield kit−Non-skid ramp plate kit−Anti-mine armour kit−Buoyant side pods−Various gun shield kits−Capstan drums attached to drive sprockets for use as self-recovery winches−Anchor kit for use with above−Litter kit enabling the vehicle to be used as an ambulance−NBC detector and automatic alarm kit-NBC kit for up to four men including commander and driver−Closure kit.

VARIANTS
Below are some of the many variants of the M113 series:

Australian models
Light Reconnaissance vehicle
This has the commander's cupola replaced by a T50 turret mounting a .30 (7.62mm) and a .50 (12.7mm) machine-gun. Total ammunition supply consists of 2,500 rounds of .30 and 3,000 rounds of .50 ammunition. This vehicle has a crew of three men–commander, gunner and driver.

Fire Support Vehicle
The Australian Army has 18 of these in service. They consist of an M113A1 chassis with the complete turret of the British Saladin armoured car (the Saladin is no longer in service with the Australian Army). Loaded weight is 11,930kg and empty weight 11,113kg. It has a crew of three. Total ammunition capacity is 55 rounds of 76mm and 5,500 rounds of .30.

Armoured Personnel Carrier
Most of these have a T50 turret mounting twin .30 machine-guns, and 5,000 rounds of ammunition. The Lebanon uses a number of these vehicles.

New Fire Support Vehicle
The Australian Army has a requirement for 45 additional Fire Support Vehicles. In 1975 three M113A1s were fitted with a modified British Scorpion turret . These were tested between May and October 1975. As the turret has increased the weight of the vehicle foam-filled aluminium pods have been fitted to the front and sides of the hull. A .30 machine-gun has been fitted to the turret for use against low flying aircraft. Basic data are: crew three, length 4.864m, width 2.69m and height 2.73m.

Bulldozer Kit
The dozer blade consists of an aluminium structure filled with closed-cell polyurethane foam to create buoyancy. When afloat the blade is raised and acts as a trim vane, the standard M113 type trim vane having been removed. The blade has a replaceable steel blade and can be angled at 30° to the right for use as a snow plough. The dozer blade is operated by the driver.

M113 Bridgelayer
This was developed by the United States Army Mobility Equipment R & D Centre for use in Vietnam and was preceded by an 'expedient' bridgelayer which could take an M41 light tank. A total of 29 M113 Bridgelayers were ordered early in 1969. These have a bridge which weighs 1,225kg and can span a gap 10m in width.

Modified M113A1 for Infantry

In 1975 an M113A1 had racks welded to the outside of its hull for the storage of equipment and supplies. This resulted in increased stowage capacity inside the vehicle. This model weighs 12,121kg and carries the following quantities of ammunition:
.50 ammunition capacity increased from 1,995 to 3,570 rounds – 7.62mm ammunition increased from 1,320 to 8,400 rounds – 7.62mm rifle ammunition increased from 3,100 to 5,050 rounds – 40mm grenades increased from 60 to 144 – four Claymore mines – 5.4kg of TNT – 10 M21 anti-tank mines – 3 Dragon missiles – 6 LAWs

M113 with Radar

The M113 has been adopted by a number of Armies to carry various types of tactical and mortar-locating radar systems. For example, the Dutch and Germans have M113s with the British Green Archer radar. Other radar installations include the AN/TPS-25, AN/TPS-33 and AN/PPS-4 and 5.

M113 with TOW

Many M113s are fitted with the Hughes TOW anti-tank missile system.

M113 with HOT

Euromissile have designed a twin HOT installation and fitted it on to an M113 for trials. It has yet to enter service.

M113 with Rheinmetall Turret

Rheinmetall are offering a Rh.10 turret with the Rh.202 20mm cannon. This has not yet been adopted.

M113 with Hägglunds Turret

The Swiss Army has a number of vehicles fitted with the same turret as that fitted to the Pbv.302 APC of the Swedish Army. This is armed with a 20mm cannon. The Swiss designation is Spz.63/73.

M113 Fire-Control Vehicles

Many countries use the M113 for fire artillery fire-control duties. The Swiss call theirs the Feuerleitpanzer 63.

M113 with Fox Turret

The British MoD are offering the Fox turret for export. This can be fitted to the M113.

M113 with Rarden Turret

The Peak Engineering Company have designed a turret with a 30mm gun which can be fitted to an M113 vehicle.

M113 with Oerlikon Weapons

Oerlikon offer a wide range of armament installations for the M113. These include the new 25mm GBD weapon as fitted to Dutch Lynx vehicles.

M113 with Oto Melara Weapons

Oto Melara of Italy offer a number of armament installations including a 20mm cupola-mounted cannon.

M113 ACAV

This was developed for use in Vietnam and has a single .50 machine–gun and two 7.62mm M60 machine-guns, all of which are provided with shields.

M113 with SS-11

A number of countries have fitted the SS-11 ATGW to the M113.

M113 with Gas Turbine

This was a trials model.

M113 Command and Reconnaissance Vehicle

There is a separate entry for this.

Armoured Infantry Fighting Vehicle

There is a separate entry for this.

Mauler Anti-Aircraft Vehicle XM546/XM546E1

This was cancelled some years ago.

M113 Cargo

The M113's seats fold flat against the sides of the hull enabling it to be used in the cargo role.

M113 with Grenade Launchers

The M113 can be fitted with a 40mm grenade launcher.

XM734 MICV
This was for trials only, no production.

XM765 MICV
This was for trials only, no production. FMC further developed this into the AIFV (previously known as the M113A1 PI).

M113 with 'A' Frame
This was a field modification in Vietnam.

Fitter's Vehicle
This is sometimes referred to as the M579. It is a basic M113A1 which has been modified by the installation of a large hatch which opens to the right. This has an integral commander's hatch and a cargo hatch. An HIAB crane is mounted on the left side of the roof and this can be slewed through 190°. The crane's tip cargo-handling hook is attached to the winch cable, and an intermediate hook is attached directly to the crane. Cargo handled at the tip hook can be raised or lowered either by the hydraulic lifting cylinder or independently by the winch. The Gearmatic model 6E winch has a total of 15.2m of rope and has a capacity of 1,360kg on a full drum or 1,770kg on a bare drum.

Recovery Vehicle
This is a basic M113A1 APC that has been modified by the installation of a hydraulically driven winch and fairlead assembly for retrieving disabled vehicles. Two spades are fitted at the rear of the hull and an auxiliary spade unit can be used between the two outer spades for soft soil conditions. The winch is a Model P30 hydraulic and is provided with 91.4m of .06m diameter cable. This has a capacity on a full drum of 5,103kg, or 9,070kg on a bare drum. A Blackhawk MC 3,000 hydraulic crane is mounted on the left side of the hull roof, and this has a capacity of 1,361kg at 1.52m reach. This vehicle is armed with a .50 machine-gun and 2,000 rounds of ammunition. The designation is M806A1.

M113 with Mortar (Germany)
Rheinstahl have converted over 500 M113s for the German Army. A new two-piece hatch cover that opens to the left and right is provided over the rear troop compartment. A 120mm Tampella mortar is mounted in the rear, which fires to the rear of the vehicle and has a traverse of $18\frac{1}{2}°$ left and 25° right, elevation limits being +45° to +80°. A total of 63 rounds of 120mm mortar ammunition are carried, or 23 when afloat. A 7.62mm machine-gun is mounted on the commander's cupola and eight smoke dischargers are fitted at the front of the hull. Loaded weight is 11,300kg. Soltam of Israel are offering a similar M113 kit.

M106A1 Mortar Carrier
The first model was the M106 which had a petrol engine. The current model is the M106A1 which has a diesel engine. This carries a 107mm (4.2inch) mortar in the rear and a total of 88 mortar bombs. A .50 M2 machine-gun is fitted to the commander's cupola and 2,000 rounds of ammunition are carried for this.

M125A1 Mortar Carrier
The first models came off the production line in 1966, these being the M125 with petrol engine. Current models have a diesel engine. An 81mm mortar is mounted in the rear of the hull and this is on a turntable which has a traverse of 360°, elevation limits being from $+41\frac{1}{2}°$ to +63°. A total of 120 mortar bombs are carried. A .50 (12.7mm) machine-gun is mounted on the commander's cupola and 2,000 rounds of ammunition are carried for this.

M132A1 Flamethrower
This is an M113A1 with the commander's cupola replaced by an M10-8 flame gun. This has a traverse of 360°, elevation limits being from −8° to +55°. A 7.62mm M73 machine-gun is mounted with the flame gun. The flame can be projected to a maximum range of 150m and this can last up to 32 seconds. Loaded weight is 10,838kg. The system was developed by Aircraft Armaments Incorporated of Cockeysville, Maryland, the first prototype being completed in 1962. It first saw service in Vietnam from 1963. In 1965 the Consolidated Diesel Electric Corporation of Schenectady, New York, were awarded a contract to convert 201 M113A1s to M132A1 standard.

The M132A1 is supported in action by the M45 vehicle. This is based on the M548 carrier, and is armoured and carries additional fuel for the flame gun.

M577A1 Command Post
This has a higher roof than the basic APC and is used as a command, communications or fire-control vehicle. The first four prototypes were completed in 1962 and the vehicle was placed in production in December 1962. The first order was for 250 vehicles and the second for 674 vehicles. A tent can be erected at the rear of the vehicle if required.

M163 Vulcan Air Defence System

This consists of a modified M113A1 chassis, the chassis being designated M741. A turret mounting a six-barrelled 20mm M61 cannon is mounted on the roof of the vehicle. This was developed by the General Electric Company and is also used in a towed system designated the M167. The turret has powered traverse and elevation, traverse is a full 360°, elevation being from −5° to +80°. Turret slewing rate in azimuth is 60°/second and in elevation 45°/second. A range only radar is mounted on the right side of the turret. The 20mm gun has two rates of fire – 1,000 or 3,000 rounds per minute. A total of 1,110 rounds of ready-use ammunition is carried and a further 800 rounds in reserve. A recent trials version has been designated Autotrack Vulcan ADS. The Vulcan system is also used by the Israeli Army.

The M163's suspension can be locked during firing to give a more stable firing platform.

M548 Tracked Cargo Carrier

This uses many components of the M113A1 but has some different components such as modified torsion bars. The prototype was powered by a petrol engine and was designated XM548, the diesel model being the XM548E1. It has a payload of 5,443kg and a towed load of 6,350kg. A winch with a capacity of 9,072kg is provided. A 7.62mm (with 660 rounds) or a .50 (with 300 rounds) machine-gun can be mounted over the four-seat cab at the front of the hull. There have been a number of trials versions including one with twin 20mm cannon, another with twin 40mm cannon and the XM696 recovery vehicle. It is also being used as a trials vehicle for a number of radar systems.

M548 with Rapier SAM

This is under development by the British Aircraft Corporation for the Iranian Army. The prototype had a launcher for four Rapier missiles but production models will have eight missiles in the ready-to-launch position. If required another M113 or M548 will carry the Blindfire all-weather radar system.

M548 with SAM-D

The SAM-D missile system was to have been mounted on the M548 but will now be installed on trailers.

M548 with Skyguard

The Swiss Company of Contraves have fitted an M548 with the Skyguard radar for trials purposes.

M548 with Indigo SAM System

The Italians are developing a self-propelled model of the Indigo SAM system. One M548 will carry four missiles and another the fire control centre.

M548 for Lance System

The M548 chassis is also used for the Lance surface-to-surface missile system. The M688 vehicle being the loader transporter and the M752 being the launch vehicle. The basic chassis is designated the M667. The suspension can be locked whilst the missile is being launched.

M727 HAWK Missile Carrier

This carries three HAWK missiles on a launcher at the hull rear and was first shown in 1966. The vehicle has a loaded weight of 12,925kg. Two other units are required with the system: (1) the continuous wave acquisition radar for target acquisition and (2) high-powered illuminator radar for acquiring, tracking and illuminating the target. The suspension on the M727 can be locked.

M730 Chaparral Carrier

This has a total of four Chaparral short-range SAMs mounted on a launcher at the rear of the hull, a further eight missiles being carried in reserve. Total weight of this model is 12,600kg. The Chaparral vehicle is used also by Israel.

Pershing Missile System

When first introduced this was mounted on the XM474 chassis series. These have now been withdrawn from service and the Pershing is now on 8 × 8 trucks.

Top The M113E1 showing its amphibious capabilities.
Centre The M113A1 Armoured Personnel Carrier.
Right M113 of the Swiss Army, their designation being Spz.63.
Far right M113 APC with TOW Anti-Tank Missile System fitted.

1

2

3▼

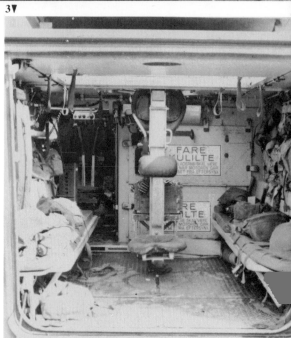

▼4

1 M113 of the Swiss Army fitted with a
hydraulically-operated bulldozer blade.
2 Italian Oto Melara Infantry Armoured Fighting
Vehicle.
3 Interior view of an M113 APC from the rear.
4 The M125A1 with 81mm mortar.
5 The M106A1 with 107mm (4.2 inch) mortar.
6 Swiss Mv.Pz.64 which has a Swiss 120mm mortar.
7 German M113 with 120mm mortar. Conversion work
carried out by Rheinstahl.
8 M113 Light Reconnaissance Vehicle of the
Australian Army.
9 M113A1 Fire Support Vehicle of the Australian
Army.

5

6

7▲

▼8

▼9

Top M113A1 Fire Support Vehicle of the Australian
Army. This is a trials vehicle with a British Scorpion
turret with some modifications.
Above M132A1 Flamethrower in action.
Right The new Autotrack Vulcan Air Defense System.

Top The M577A1 Command Vehicle.
Above XM806E1 Recovery Vehicle from the rear.
Left Fitters' Vehicle complete with jib folded.

1

2

3   ▼4

1 The M752 vehicle complete with Lance
surface-to-surface missile.
2 The M548 Load Carrier.
3 Modified M548 with Rapier SAM being launched.
4 M548 with Chaparral surface-to-air missiles.
5 Model of final version of M548 with a total of eight
Rapier SAMs.
6 M727 carrier with three Hawk surface-to-air
missiles.
7 Series of photographs showing an M113 Launched
Light Assault Bridge.

5

6

▼7

UNITED STATES

M59 – ARMOURED PERSONNEL CARRIER
MANUFACTURER – FMC Corporation, San Jose, California
STATUS – In service with Brazil, Ethiopia, Greece, Lebanon, Turkey, Vietnam. Production now complete.

BASIC DATA

CREW:	2 + 10 (commander, driver and 10 infantry)	FUEL:	518 litres
		FORDING:	Amphibious
WEIGHT LOADED:	19,323kg	GRADIENT:	60%
WEIGHT EMPTY:	17,916kg	VERTICAL OBSTACLE:	.46m
LENGTH:	5.163m	TRENCH:	1.676m
WIDTH:	3.263m	ENGINE:	2 × General Motors
	3.149m (reduced)		Corporation Model 302,
HEIGHT:	2.387m (cupola)		6-cylinder, water-cooled,
	2.235m (top of hull)		in-line petrol engines
GROUND CLEARANCE:	.457m		developing 127HP at
TRACK:	2.616m		3,350rpm, *each*
TRACK WIDTH:	533mm	ARMOUR (estimates):	
LENGTH OF TRACK		hull front:	16mm
ON GROUND:	3.079m	hull sides and rear:	12.7mm
GROUND PRESSURE:	.51kg/cm²	roof:	10mm
MAXIMUM ROAD SPEED:	51.5km/hr	ARMAMENT:	1 × calibre .50 (12.7mm)
MAXIMUM WATER			Browning M2 HMG
SPEED:	6.9km/hr		with 2,000 rounds of
RANGE:	164km		ammunition (see text)

DEVELOPMENT

The M59 (full designation being Carrier, Personnel, Full Tracked: Armoured, M59) was designed and built by the FMC Corporation as a replacement for the earlier M75 APC. The M59 was itself replaced in United States Army service by the M113 APC, also designed and built by the FMC Corporation. The development designation was T59 and the T59 was powered by Two Cadillac engines whilst the T59E1 was powered by two General Motors M302 liquid-cooled engines as used in the M135 6 × 6 truck of that period. The T59E1 was standardized as the M59 in December 1953 and was in production from February 1954 to March 1959. Without doubt the M59 was a considerable improvement over the earlier M75 and was much cheaper to build. It was, however, underpowered and somewhat difficult to maintain.

DESCRIPTION

The hull of the M59 is of all-welded steel construction with the driver seated at the left front and the commander to his right. The driver is provided with three periscopes for observation when closed down with a further periscope in the hatch cover. The circular hatch opens to the rear. The commander also operates the .50 machine-gun and the following armament installations were fitted to production vehicles: vehicles numbers 7 to 1312 had a circular rotating cupola with six vision blocks and an externally operated machine-gun; vehicles numbers 1313 to 2941 had a cupola with four periscopes, and vehicles 2942 onwards had the M13 cupola which had a traverse of 360° and the machine-gun could be elevated from −11° to +57°. M59s fitted with this were known as the M59A1, and the M13 cupola was also fitted to the M84 Mortar Carrier as standard.

There are two hatches over the personnel compartment, the troops normally entering and leaving the vehicles via the hydraulically-operated ramp at the rear of the vehicle. A door is provided in the centre of this ramp in case the ramp should jam. There is a bench seat down each side of the troop compartment and this can be folded up when cargo is being carried.

The suspension is of the torsion-bar type and five road wheels are provided with the drive sprocket at the front and the idler at the rear. There are three track return rollers. The first and fifth road wheel stations are provided with hydraulic shock absorbers.

The engines are mounted one in each side of the hull, next to the personnel compartment and the air inlet/outlet louvres are in the roof of the vehicle. Two General Motors Corporation Model 300 MG or 301 MG hydramatic transmission with two ranges are provided.

The M59 is fully amphibious being propelled in the water by its tracks. Before entering the water a trim board is erected at the front of the hull and a bilge pump mounted in the hull. Infra-red headlamps are fitted and one of the driver's periscopes can be replaced by an infra-red periscope.

VARIANTS

The basic vehicle could also be used as an ambulance, load carrier, command vehicle and weapons carrier. The only other variant to enter service was the M84 Mortar Carrier. Development designation was T84 and it was standardized in November 1955 as the M84, entering production in January 1957.

The physical characteristics of the M84 are almost identical to the M59 except that it had a loaded weight of 21,364kg, and a crew of six. The 4.2″ (107mm) mortar could also be fired away from the vehicle and a baseplate was carried on the rear of the hull for this purpose. A total of 88 mortar bombs were carried and it was fitted with the M13 cupola as fitted to late production M59s. The mortar fires through the roof of the vehicle. As the M84 was slightly heavier than the standard M59 a total of four collapsible rectangular boxes were provided for fitting around the four air inlet/outlets (ie two each side). The ramp on the M84 differed from that of the M59 in that the escape door was on the right side rather than in the centre.

There were also many experimental models of the M59 including a flamethrower version. This was, however, late in development and the system was fitted to the M113, becoming the M132/M132A1. A whole series of amphibians were developed including howitzer and anti-aircraft vehicles, the end result being the LVTP-6 which was not adopted by the United States Marine Corps. Various other armament installations were tried on standard M59s, including remote-controlled machine-guns and a 106mm M40 Recoilless Rifle.

Above M59 Armoured Personnel Carrier.

UNITED STATES

M75 – ARMOURED PERSONNEL CARRIER
MANUFACTURERS – International Harvester Company and FMC Corporation
STATUS – In service with Belgian Army. Production of the M75 is complete.

BASIC DATA

CREW:	2 + 10 (commander, driver and 10 infantry)	VERTICAL OBSTACLE:	.457m
		TRENCH CROSSING:	1.676m
WEIGHT LADEN:	18,828kg	ENGINE:	Continental Model
WEIGHT EMPTY:	16,632kg		AO-895-4, 6-cylinder,
LENGTH:	5.193m		air-cooled, petrol engine
WIDTH:	2.844m		developing 295BHP
HEIGHT:	3.041m (top of MG)		at 2,660rpm
	2.755m (top of cupola)	ARMAMENT:	1 × calibre .50 (12.7mm)
GROUND CLEARANCE:	.457m		M2 MG with 1,800
TRACK:	2.209m		rounds of ammunition
TRACK WIDTH:	533mm	ARMOUR	
LENGTH OF TRACK		front hull upper:	12.7mm at 73°
ON GROUND:	3.048m	front hull lower:	15.9mm at 32°
GROUND PRESSURE:	.57kg/cm²	hull sides:	15.9mm
MAXIMUM ROAD SPEED:	71km/hr	hull rear:	15.9mm
RANGE:	185km	hull top (vehicle numbers	
FUEL:	568 litres	7-376 and 1007-1326):	9.5mm
FORDING:	1.219m	hull top (vehicle numbers	
	2.032m (with kit)	377-1006 and 1327-1736):	12.7mm
GRADIENT:	60%	hull floor:	25.4mm

Below M75 of the Belgian Army. This photograph was taken in 1973.
Right M75 of the United States Army with engine and transmission being taken out.

DEVELOPMENT

In September 1945 a requirement was drawn up for a full-tracked armoured personnel carrier using components of the T43 Cargo Tractor, which later became the T43E1. In September 1946 the development of the T18 (Vehicle, Utility, Armoured) was approved, later prototypes being the T18E1 and the T18E2. Various armament installations were tried on the prototypes including remote-controlled 12.7mm machine-guns, pintle-mounted machine-guns and a cupola-mounted twin 12.7mm machine-gun.

In December 1952 the T18E1 was standardized as the M75 and replaced the older M44 Utility Vehicle. The first production model was completed in March 1952 and the last vehicle in February 1954. Both International Harvester and FMC built the vehicle. Total production amounted to 1,729 vehicles.

The full designation of the M75 is Vehicle, Armored Infantry, Full Track, M75. Many components such as engine, transmission and track of the M75 are also used on the M41 Light Tank.

DESCRIPTION

The hull of the M75 is of welded armour plate and steel. The driver is seated at the left front with the commander to his rear and in the centre. The driver has a one-piece hatch cover and a total of three periscopes. The commander is provided with a cupola which can be traversed through 360°. There are six vision blocks around the cupola. The commander has to expose his body to fire the machine-gun which has an elevation of +45° and a depression of −25°. There are two hatches over the roof of the personnel compartment and the crew enter and leave the vehicle via the two doors in the rear of the hull.

The engine and transmission are mounted in the front of the vehicle as one unit to assist in easy removal from the vehicle. There is also a maintenance door in the right side of the hull. The transmission is a General Motors Corporation Allison Division Model CD-500-4 cross drive with three ranges – low, high and reverse.

The suspension is of the torsion-bar type and there are a total of five road wheels with the drive sprocket at the front and the idler at the rear. Vehicles numbers 7-376 and 1007-1326 had four shock absorbers – on the first, second and fifth stations, whilst vehicles numbers 377-1006 and 1327-1376 had shock absorbers on the first and fifth wheels stations only. All vehicles have three track return rollers.

The M75 is not amphibious and has no NBC system. Infra-red driving lights are provided and an infra-red periscope can be fitted if required. Maximum towed load of the M75 is 6,350kg.

It is recognizable by its large size, lack of trim vane on the front of the hull, exhaust pipe across the front of the hull and the two doors in the rear of the hull.

VARIANTS

There are no variants in service although a mortar carrier designated T64 (4.2″) was developed as was the T73 Infantry Vehicle.

UNITED STATES

HALF-TRACK VEHICLES – ARMOURED PERSONNEL CARRIERS
MANUFACTURERS – Autocar Company, White Motor Company, Diamond T Motor Company and
International Harvester Company
STATUS – In service with Argentina, Belgium, Brazil, Colombia, Cuba, Dominican Republic, Greece,
Israel, Guatemala, Italy, Japan, Mexico, Morocco, Portugal Philippines, Spain, Taiwan, Thailand,
Turkey, Uruguay, Venezuela, Yugoslavia. Production complete.

BASIC DATA	M2A1 HALF-TRACK CAR	M16 A/A VEHICLE		M2A1 HALF-TRACK CAR	M16 A/A VEHICLE
CREW:	10	5	FUEL:	227 litres	227 litres
WEIGHT LOADED:	8,890kg	9,810kg	FORDING:	.812m	.812m
WEIGHT EMPTY:	6,940kg	8,450kg	GRADIENT:	60%	60%
LENGTH:	6.137m	6.501m	VERTICAL OBSTACLE:	.304m	.304m
WIDTH:	2.221m	2.159m	ENGINE:	White 160 AX 6-cylinder	
HEIGHT:	2.692m	2.616m		petrol developing 128HP	
GROUND CLEARANCE:	.223m	.284m		at 2,800rpm	
TRACK:	1.637m (front)	1.637m (front)	ARMAMENT:	1 × .50	4 × .50
	1.722m (rear)	1.722m (rear)		(12.7mm) MG	(12.7mm) MGs
TRACK WIDTH:	305mm	305mm		1 × .30	—
LENGTH OF TRACK				(7.62mm) MG	—
ON GROUND:	1.187m	1.187m	AMMUNITION .50:	700	700
TYRES:	8.25 × 20	8.25 × 20	.30:	7,750	—
MAXIMUM ROAD SPEED:	64km/hr	64km/hr	ARMOUR	7-13mm	7-13mm
RANGE:	280km	250km			

DEVELOPMENT

Development of Half-Track vehicles in the United States Army can be traced back to 1925, when the
Ordnance Department purchased a Citroen Half-Track from France for trials. Further developments took
place in the 1930s and in September 1940 the first production orders were issued to Autocar (for the M2
and M3), White Motor Company (M2) and Diamond T Motor Company (M3), first production vehicles
being completed in May 1941. Late in the war International Harvester built Half-Tracks.

DESCRIPTION

The hull is of armoured plate with the engine at the front of the vehicle. The transmission has 4F and 1R
gears. Half-Tracks will be found in service with either a winch mounted on the front, a roller, which
helped it cross ditches and other obstacles, or without either of these. The driver is seated on the left and
there are a further two seats to this right. There are doors in each side of the driving compartment and the
tops, which are provided with a vision port, can be folded down if required. The driver's windscreen is
covered by an armoured visor which can be raised horizontally if required, and this also has vision ports.
The troop compartment is at the rear of the hull and a single door is provided in the hull rear. Machine-
guns are normally mounted around the top of the hull on pedestals, or a single 12.7mm machine-gun is
mounted to the right of the driver.

VARIANTS

There are the following models of the Half-Track: Half-Track Carrier M2 and M2A1, Half-Track
Personnel Carrier M3, M3A1 and M3A2, Half-Track Car M9A1, Half-Track Personnel Carrier M5 and
M5A1, Half-Track Carrier M5A2, Half-Track Car M2, Half-Track Personnel Carrier M3, Half-Track Car
M2A1, Half-Track Personnel Carrier M3A1, Half-Track Car M3A2. They were all generally similar with
minor differences such as different wings, different hull tops, different engines and so on. The 81mm
Mortar Carriers were designated M4, M4A1, and M21, and carried a total of 97 rounds of 81mm mortar
bombs.

   The following Multiple Gun Motor Carriages were also built: M16, M14 and M27, each with four .50
(12.7mm) Browning machine-guns in a turret and a total of 5,000 rounds of ammunition, and the M13
which has twin .50 anti-aircraft machine-guns in a turret. The M15 and M15A1 anti-aircraft vehicles were
armed with a 37mm gun and twin .50 (12.7mm) machine-guns on a single mount. The guns had an elevation
of +85° and a depression of −5°, traverse was a full 360°, and total ammunition capacity was 200 rounds of
37mm and 1,200 rounds of .50 (12.7mm). As far as is known, Yugoslavia is the only country that still uses
the M15A1.

   In addition there were many experimental models and other production models but only those known to
be in service are included above.

Right A Half-Track of the Israeli Army.
Below A Half-Track of the Israeli Army armed with twin 20mm cannon.

Israeli Half-Tracks

Israel is perhaps the largest user of Half-Tracks in the world and has adapted these vehicles for a wide variety of roles including the following:

Basic Vehicles– these are normally armed with up to four 7.62mm or 12.7mm machine-guns mounted around the top of the hull, and in addition most vehicles have a .30 (7.62mm) machine-gun in a ball mount to the right of the driver.

Anti-Aircraft Vehicle– this is armed with a powered turret with twin 20mm cannon, designed and built by Ramta Structures and Systems. It is also available in the towed role.

Mortar Carrier– the Israeli Army has many Half-Tracks fitted with a 120mm Soltam mortar in the hull rear. This has a range of 400-6,500m and over 30 mortar bombs are carried. A base plate is carried on the rear of the vehicle so that the mortar can be dismounted and fired away from the carrier if required.

Anti-Tank Missile– Israel did have a number of Half-Tracks with four French SS-11 ATGWs mounted over the top of the troop compartment in the ready-to-launch position. It is doubtful if any of these remain in service today.

Anti-Tank Gun– a number of Half-Tracks were fitted with a 106mm M40 recoilless rifle in the rear troop compartment. These were built in Israel by Israel Military Industries. They also have some vehicles armed with a 90mm Mecar gun on a modified British 6-pounder carriage. These are either carried in the troop compartment or towed behind the truck.

In addition they have command vehicles with a raised roof, ambulances, load and ammunition carriers.

UNITED STATES

LANDING VEHICLE ASSAULT
MANUFACTURER – Bell Aerospace, New York
STATUS – Development.

GENERAL
In 1975 Bell Aerospace was awarded a twelve month $278,000 contract to carry out initial development of
a new Landing Vehicle Assault. This programme is under the direction of the United States Naval Sea
Systems Command and is directed towards finding a replacement for the current LVTP-7 vehicle in the
1980-1985 time frame.

It is expected that the LVA will operate in the water at speeds of between 56 and 112km/hr and on land
at between 64 and 88km/hr. The initial concept is believed to include fitting an LVTP-7 type hull with an air
cushion system and a hydro-pneumatic track suspension system.

Other companies involved in this project are known to include:

Allison Division of General Motors Corporation (transmission)
National Water Lift Company (land running gear and primary weapon system)
Carborundum Corporation (parasitic armour)
Alcoa (aluminium armour)
Rosenblatt and Son of New York (hydrodynamic consultants).
Apart from Bell Aerospace, two other American companies have been awarded similar contracts.

Below Artist's concept of the Bell Aerospace Landing Vehicle Assault in action.

UNITED STATES

LVTP-7 – AMPHIBIOUS ASSAULT VEHICLE
MANUFACTURER – FMC Corporation, San Jose, California
STATUS – In service with Argentina, Italy, Spain, Thailand and United States Marine Corps. Production complete.

BASIC DATA

CREW:	3 + 25 (commander, gunner, driver and 25 Marines)	FORDING:	Amphibious
		GRADIENT:	70%
		SIDE SLOPE:	60%
WEIGHT LOADED:	23,655kg	VERTICAL OBSTACLE:	.914m
WEIGHT EMPTY:	18,257kg	TRENCH:	2.438m
LENGTH:	7.943m	ENGINE:	Detroit Diesel Model
WIDTH:	3.27m		8V53T, 8-cylinder,
HEIGHT:	3.263m (o/a)		water-cooled, turbo-
	3.12m (top of turret)		charged diesel
GROUND CLEARANCE:	.406m		developing 400HP
TRACK:	2.609m		at 2,800rpm
TRACK WIDTH:	533mm	ARMAMENT:	1 × M85 .50 (12.7mm)
LENGTH OF TRACK ON			MG
GROUND:	3.94m	ARMOUR:	
GROUND PRESSURE:	.57kg/cm²	ramp outer:	12.7mm
MAXIMUM ROAD SPEED:	63.37km/hr	ramp inner:	6.72mm
MAXIMUM WATER SPEED:	13.5km/hr	hull sides;	31mm—45mm
RANGE:	482km at 40km/hr (land)	hull floor and roof:	30mm
	7 hours at 2,600rpm (water)	hull rear:	35mm
FUEL CAPACITY:	681 litres		

DEVELOPMENT

In March 1964 the United States Marine Corps issued a requirement for a new tracked amphibian to replace the then current LVTP-5 series of amphibians which had been in service for over ten years. The contract was awarded to the FMC Corporation and engineering development started in February 1966. The overall programme was under the direction of the Naval Ships Systems Command. A total of 17 prototypes were built, the first one being completed in September 1967 and handed over to the United States Marine Corps on 19th October 1967. The prototypes were designated LVTPX-12 and the 17 included 14 LVTPX-12s, one LVTCX-2 (command) and two LVTRX-2 (repair) vehicles. Trials were undertaken from late 1967 to early September 1969. In June 1970 FMC were awarded a contract to build a total of 942 vehicles at a total cost of $78.5 million. The vehicles cost $129,000 each, some of the components being supplied as GFE (Government Furnished Equipment). The production models were designated LVTP-7 (Landing Vehicle Tracked Personnel Model 7) and the first production model was handed over on 26th August 1971, the first unit being equipped by 31st March 1972. The last LVTP-7 was handed over to the Marine Corps in September 1974 and the vehicle has now completely replaced the earlier LVTP-5 series of amphibians which have been withdrawn from service.

DESCRIPTION

The hull of the LVTP-7 is of all-welded aluminium construction. The driver is seated at the front of the vehicle on the left side and is provided with a one-piece hatch cover that opens to the rear and a total of seven vision blocks. An M24 infra-red periscope is also available. The commander is seated behind the driver and also has a single-piece hatch cover and a total of seven vision blocks. In addition he has an M17C periscope. The gunner's turret is on the right side of the hull and the gunner is provided with vision blocks and a ×1 and ×6 sight. The turret has full powered traverse through 360° at a speed of 60° per second. The .50 (12.7mm) M85 machine-gun has an elevation of +60° and a depression of −15°. A total of 1,000 rounds of ammunition are carried, of which 400 are for ready-use.

The engine and transmission are at the front of the hull and the engine can be removed as a complete unit in about 30 minutes. It can also be run outside the vehicle for test purposes.

The HS-400-1 transmission utilizes a torque converter with lock-up, electro-hydraulically controlled clutches, a hydrostatic steering system and internal, multiple disc brakes. A power take-off mounted on the converter housing supplies power to the water jets and the cooling fan through electro-hydraulically controlled clutches. Power is taken from the transmission to the drive sprockets through hull-mounted final drives.

The troop compartment is at the rear of the hull and the 25 Marines sit on benches parallel to the sides of the hull. These can be quickly stowed to load cargo and supplies. There are a total of three roof hatches, normally used for loading supplies alongside a ship. Normal means of entry and exit for the Marines is via the hydraulically-operated ramp in the rear of the hull, which has an integral door should the ramp jam.

The suspension is of the torsion-bar and tube type and consists of six road wheels with the drive sprocket at the front and the last road wheel acting as the idler. The first and sixth road wheel stations are provided with hydraulic shock absorbers.

The tracks are steel with replaceable rubber pads. The LVTP-7 is fully amphibious being propelled in the water by two water jets, one each side of the hull. The water jets are driven through right-angled gearboxes located on top of the sponsons. Deflectors are used for steering and reverse. The vehicle can also be propelled in the water by its tracks and the tracks are also used when approaching land.

The electrical system is 24V and the generator has a capacity of 180Amps. Four type 6TN 12V batteries are carried.

The LVTP-7 is not provided with an NBC system, but infra-red driving lights are provided. The following kits are available for the LVTP-7: litter kit for the ambulance role, winterization kit, visor kit and navigation light kit. When being used in the cargo role the LVTP-7 can carry 4,536kg of cargo.

VARIANTS
LVTR-7 (Landing Vehicle, Tracked, Recovery, Model 7)
The first prototype was built in 1968 and was designated the LVTRX-2. The hull is similar to that of the basic LVTP-7 but it does not have a machine-gun turret and instead is armed with a 7.62mm M60 machine-gun, pintle-mounted. The LVTR-7 is provided with a full range of repair equipment including an air compressor, battery charger, generator, portable pump, a welding kit and a full range of tools. A hydraulic crane is mounted on the roof, and this can be elevated from 0° to +65°. It is also provided with an extending boom which can lift 4,309kg at 4.114m, or a load of 2,722kg at 6.552m. The vehicle is also provided with a two-speed (high and low) winch. This can pull a maximum of 14,151kg on a bare drum at low speed, down to 1,978kg on a full drum at high speed. If required a tent can be erected at the rear of the hull. The LVTR-7 has a crew of five and a loaded weight of 24,398kg.

LVTC-7 (Landing Vehicle, Tracked, Command, Model 7)
The eighth prototype LVTPX-12 was rebuilt to the LVTCX-2. Externally the vehicle is almost identical to the standard LVTP-7 apart from its additional radio aerials. A tent can be erected at the rear of the hull to give the personnel additional working area. The LVTC-7 has a total crew of 13 men, comprising the commander, driver, gunner, five command staff and five radio operators. The additional radios require additional power and a generator powered by a four-cylinder engine has been provided. This model also has an air filtration system. Total loaded weight is 21,754kg.

Above LVTP-7 Amphibious Assault Vehicle of the USMC.

LVTE-7 (Landing Vehicle, Tracked, Engineer, Model 7)

The prototype of this was completed in 1970 and designated the LVTEX-3. To date it has not been placed in production. The hull is similar to the standard LVTP-7 but a dozer blade has been provided at the front of the hull. The main role of this vehicle is to clear a patch through minefields. To do this it is provided with a rocket propelled line charge. This is fired over the minefield and then detonated; a total of three line charges are carried in the rear compartment. It has a total crew of six – commander, gunner, driver and three men to operate and load the line charge. Total loaded weight is 24,321kg.

LVTH-7

There was to have been a model armed with a 105mm howitzer to replace the LVTH-6 vehicle but this was not built and the LVTH-6 has been withdrawn from service and not replaced.

Mobile Test Unit

This was first announced late in 1974. It is being used by the United States Army at Redstone Arsenal under the High Energy Laser Research Programme. The troop compartment is now filled with equipment and on the roof is a laser and a target tracking system. It is believed that this is being used in the anti-aircraft role rather than the ground role. Companies concerned with the project include Avco-Everett, (laser), Perkin-Elmer, (SCI systems), and the Northrop Corporation (automatic viewing system for night operations).

Below Prototype LVTRX-2 Recovery Vehicle which has entered service as the LVTR-7.
Right Rear view of the LVTC-7 (Landing Vehicle, Tracked, Command) showing seats, tables and radio installations.

UNITED STATES

LVT-4 – AMPHIBIOUS ASSAULT VEHICLE

MANUFACTURER – FMC (3 plants), Graham-Paige Motor Company of Detroit and St Louis Car Company of St Louis

STATUS – In service with Taiwan and Thailand. Production complete. (Thailand is now receiving the LVTP-7 so their LVT-4 will soon be phased out.)

BASIC DATA

CREW:	2-7	RANGE WATER:	160km
WEIGHT LOADED:	16,510kg	FUEL:	617 litres
WEIGHT EMPTY:	12,428kg	FORDING:	Amphibious
LENGTH:	7.974m	GRADIENT:	60%
WIDTH:	3.251m	VERTICAL OBSTACLE:	.914m
HEIGHT:	3.073m (without armament)	TRENCH:	1.524m
GROUND CLEARANCE:	.457m (hard ground) .387m (soft ground)	ENGINE:	Continental W670-9A, 4-cycle, 7-cylinder radial developing 250BHP at 2,400rpm
TRACK:	2.895m		
TRACK WIDTH:	355mm	ARMAMENT:	2 × .50 (12.7mm) Browning HB M2 MGs
LENGTH OF TRACK ON GROUND:	3.962m		2 × .30 (7.62mm) M1919A4 MGs
GROUND PRESSURE:	.59kg/cm² (hard ground)		1 × .30 (7.62mm) M1919A4 in ball mount
MAXIMUM ROAD SPEED:	24km/hr		
MAXIMUM WATER SPEED:	11km/hr		
RANGE LAND:	240km		

DEVELOPMENT

In the 1930s Donald Roebling, who lived in Florida, developed a tracked vehicle for use in the Florida Everglades. This vehicle was known as the Alligator. The Marine Corps became interested in this vehicle for ship-to-ship transport and ordered three prototypes. These were followed by a production order for 200 vehicles, these being known as the LVT-1 (Landing Vehicle Tracked). The first vehicles were unarmoured although they were used in combat. The next model was the LVT-2 which came in 1943. The LVT(A)1 had the turret of the Stuart Light Tank and the LVT(A)2 was armoured. The LVT-3 and LVT-4 had a redesigned hull with a ramp at the hull rear. The LVT(A)4 had the same turret as that fitted to the M8 75mm SPH, and the LVT(A)-5 was similar but also had a stabilization system for the turret. Post-war many LVTs were brought up to LVT-3C standard with overhead armour.

Total production of LVT (all types) amounted to some 18,620 vehicles, with the following companies building them: Donald Roebling of Florida, FMC with plants at Lakeland (California), Riverside (California) and San Jose (California), Graham-Paige Motor Company of Detroit, Michigan, Ingersoll Steel and Disc Division of Borg-Warner Corporation at Kalamazoo, Michigan, and the St Louis Car Company of St Louis, Missouri.

In addition there were many trials versions both during and after World War II. After the war the LVTs continued in service until they were replaced in the mid-1950s by the LVTP-5 and LVTH-6. After the war they saw service in Korea with the United States Marine Corps, in Vietnam with French Forces and at Suez with the British Army. They have only recently gone out of service with Italy and Spain who replaced them with the new LVTP-7.

DESCRIPTION

The hull of the LVT-4 is of all-welded construction and first models were unarmoured but later production models had armoured crew compartments, although additional bolt-on armour kits were used on most models. The three crew members sat at the front of the vehicle, driver in the centre, commander to the left and bow machine-gunner to the right. On the LVT-4 the engine and transmission (a Spicer with 5F and 1R gears) were in the forward part of the vehicle (on earlier models it was at the rear) and this allowed a ramp to be fitted at the rear of the hull. The LVT-4 could carry a total of 30 troops or a Jeep or an anti-tank gun. Total ammunition capacity was 5,000 rounds of .50 and 4,000 rounds of .30. The French Army have recently used an LVT-4 fitted with equipment for their projected Entrac amphibious engineer vehicle.

VARIANTS

See above.

LVT-4 Amphibious Assault Vehicle.

YUGOSLAVIA

M60–ARMOURED PERSONNEL CARRIER
MANUFACTURER–Yugoslav State Arsenals
CURRENT STATUS–In service with Cyprus and Yugoslavia. Production complete.

BASIC DATA

CREW:	3 + 10 (commander, gunner, driver and 10 infantry)	GRADIENT:	60%
		VERTICAL OBSTACLE:	.6m
		TILT:	26°
WEIGHT LOADED:	9,500kg	TRENCH:	2m
LENGTH OVERALL:	5.05m	GROUND PRESSURE:	.6kg/cm²
WIDTH:	2.75m	ENGINE:	FAMOS 6-cylinder in-line, water-cooled diesel developing 140HP
HEIGHT:	1.8m (without 12.7mm MG)		
GROUND CLEARANCE:	.35m		
TRACK:	2.37m	ARMAMENT:	1 × 12.7mm M2 HB MG on roof 1 × 7.9mm M53 MG in bow
LENGTH OF TRACK ON GROUND:	3m		
TRACK WIDTH:	300mm		
MAXIMUM ROAD SPEED:	45km/hr	ARMOUR:	25mm (maximum–glacis plate) 10mm (sides and rear)
WATER SPEED:	6km/hr		
RANGE:	400km (cruising)		
FUEL CAPACITY:	130 litres		
FUEL CONSUMPTION:	38 litres per 100 km		

DEVELOPMENT

The M60 Armoured Personnel Carrier was first seen during a parade held in Yugoslavia on May 1st 1965, and for some time was known simply as the M-1965 APC. It has also been called the M-590. The M60 has not been manufactured in large numbers.

The Yugoslav M60 Armoured Personnel Carrier, armed with a 12.7mm machine-gun.

DESCRIPTION

The M60 is of Yugoslav design and construction, although a number of features of earlier foreign designed APCs have been incorporated into the vehicle. The hull is of all-welded construction and as far as it is known no NBC system is fitted. The suspension and track are based on that of the Soviet SU-76 SPG which Yugoslavia acquired in some numbers after the Second World War. The drive sprocket is at the front and the idler is at the rear. There are five road wheels and three return rollers. The suspension and track are well outside the hull and sand/dirt guards are provided.

The M60 is fully amphibious, being propelled in the water by its tracks, and before entering the water a trim vane is erected at the front of the vehicle. The FAMOS engine is an Austrian Saurer diesel built under licence in Yugoslavia, and it also powers a number of Yugoslav trucks and the Hungarian K800 Tracked Artillery Tractor.

The infantry dismount from the vehicle via the twin doors in the rear of the hull and each of these doors is provided with a single firing port. There are also three firing ports in each side of the hull.

The driver is seated at the front on the left side of the vehicle and is provided with a single-piece hatch cover that opens upwards and to the rear. It is provided with a periscope and there is a similar hatch to the right of the driver. The commander's position is behind the driver and has a single-piece hatch cover that opens to the rear. The gunner's position is to the right of the commander, and a two-piece hatch is provided for the gunner. The M2 HB (Heavy Barrel) machine-gun is of American design and construction and can be used against both ground and air targets. Ammunition types include ball and AP rounds. The 7.9mm M53 machine-gun mounted in the glacis plate is operated by the gunner or another member of the crew. The M53 is a Yugoslav copy of the German Second World War MG42 machine-gun.

VARIANTS

There are no known variants of the M60 although it is quite probable that radio, command, ambulance and cargo models exist.

TANK DESTROYERS

There are two types of tank destroyer: tank destroyer gun and tank destroyer missile. A tank destroyer relies on its speed and firepower and in all cases has the minimum of armour. The Soviets call their ASU-57 and ASU-85 Assault Guns but they are used in the tank destroyer role. Listed below are the current tank destroyer gun/missile vehicles together with a listing of other tank destroyers, details of which will be found in their respective entries. It should be remembered that most APCs can be fitted with an ATGW system or a Recoilless Rifle which gives them A/T capability.

Tank Destroyers

Country	Designation	Type
Austria	Panzerjäger K	Gun
Germany	Jagdpanzer Kanone	Gun
	Jagdpanzer Rakete	Missile
Great Britain	Charioteer	Gun
Japan	Type 60 SPRR	Recoilless Rifle
Soviet Union	ASU-85	Gun
	ASU-57	Gun
United States	M56	Gun
	M18	Gun
	M10 and M36	Gun

Other tank destroyers, details of which will be found in their respective entries:

Country	Refer to entry	A/T Designation (if any)
Czechoslovakia	OT-64	OT-64 with Sagger ATGW
	OT-810	OT-810 with Recoilless Rifle
France	AML	AML with NA2 ATGW turret
	M3	M3 with HOT
	AMX10P	AMX10P with HOT
	AMX VCI	AMX VCI with ENTAC or TOW
Germany	Marder	Marder with Milan
	Spz.12-3	Jpz.3-3
Great Britain	Scorpion	Striker ATGW Vehicle
	Ferret	Mk.2/6 and Mk.5 ATGW
	FV432	FV432 with Wombat
	FV432	FV438 ATGW Vehicle
Soviet Union	BRDM-2	BRDM-2 with Sagger
	BRDM-1	BRDM-1 with Snapper, Swatter or Sagger ATGW
Sweden	Ikv-91	Light Tank/Tank Destroyer
Switzerland	Mowag Tornado	Gepard Tank Destroyer
United States	M113	M113 with HOT or TOW
	Half-Track	Half-Track with R/R or ATGW

AUSTRIA

PANZERJÄGER K, 4KH6FA, FL-120S – TANK DESTROYER
MANUFACTURER – Steyr-Daimler-Puch AG, Vienna
STATUS – In service only with the Austrian Army. Production complete.

BASIC DATA

CREW:	3 (commander, gunner, driver)	SIDE SLOPE:	40%
		VERTICAL OBSTACLE:	.8m
WEIGHT LOADED:	17,500kg	TRENCH:	2.4m
LENGTH:	7.778m (gun forward) 5.582m (hull)	ENGINE:	Steyr Model 6FA, 6-cylinder diesel,
WIDTH:	2.5m		9.981 litres,
HEIGHT:	2.355m (base of commander's cupola)		developing 300HP at 2,300rpm
	1.945m (axis of bore)	ARMAMENT:	1 × 105mm gun
	1.408m (top of hull)		1 × 7.62mm MG 42
GROUND CLEARANCE:	.38m		co-axial MG
TRACK:	2.12m		2 × 3 smoke dischargers
TRACK WIDTH:	380mm	ARMOUR	
LENGTH OF TRACK ON		glacis:	20mm
GROUND:	3.04m	nose:	20mm
GROUND PRESSURE:	.68 kg/cm²	hull side:	14mm
POWER TO WEIGHT		hull rear:	12mm
RATIO:	17.8HP/ton	hull roof:	8mm
RANGE:	530km	turret front:	40mm
FUEL CAPACITY:	400 litres	turret sides:	20mm
FORDING:	1m	turret roof:	10mm
GRADIENT:	70%		

DEVELOPMENT

The Panzerjäger K (which is nicknamed the Cuirassier) is a development of the Saurer armoured personnel carrier. Development was started in 1965 by Saurer-Werke, who were taken over in 1970 by the Steyr-Daimler-Puch Company. The first prototype was completed in 1967 with the second prototype following in 1969. Five pre-production vehicles were built in 1971 and since then about 120 production vehicles have been built for the Austrian Army.

DESCRIPTION

The hull of the vehicle is of all-welded construction and is a complete re-design of the Saurer APC hull. The driver is seated at the front of the hull on the left side and is provided with a total of three periscopes for observation when driving closed down, and a single-piece hatch cover. When driving in wet weather a small windscreen complete with a wiper can be erected. The turret is in the centre of the hull and is a French FL-12 built in France by Fives-Lille-Cail with final assembly in Austria. The turret is of the oscillating type as fitted to the AMX-13 light tank. According to some reports the turret as fitted to this vehicle has more room than the standard French turrets. The turret is traversed hydraulically with one complete rotation taking 12-13 seconds. The commander is seated on the left of the turret and the gunner to the right. The commander is provided with a cupola with a total of eight vision blocks and a one-piece hatch cover. The gunner also has a one-piece hatch cover which is of the lift and swivel type. He also has an observation periscope, a ×8 (8.5° field of view) sight and a periscopic sight with a double sight—ie ×1.6 and 28° field of view and a ×7.5 with a 9° field of view.

The turret has an elevation of +13° and a depression of −6°, elevation, like the traverse, being hydraulic. The gun is aimed by the gunner with the commander having override capability. Hand controls are provided for use in an emergency. The 105mm gun is provided with a muzzle brake and fires a hollow-charge stabilized projectile with an m/v of 800m/s and a maximum effective range of 2,700m. In addition High Explosive and Smoke rounds are available, with an m/v of 700m/s.

The gun is fed from two revolver-like magazines each of which holds six rounds of ammunition, enabling the gun to fire one round every five seconds. The empty cartridge cases are ejected through a small hatch in the turret rear. A co-axial 7.62mm machine-gun is mounted to the right of the main armament and there are three smoke dischargers either side of the turret. Total ammunition capacity is 43 rounds of 105mm and 2,000 rounds of 7.62mm. Trials have been carried out with a laser rangefinder mounted on the roof of the turret towards the rear.

The Saurer diesel is mounted at the rear of the hull and is provided with a turbo-compressor worked by the exhaust gases. The Fitchel and Sachs gearbox has 6F (2nd to 6th being synchronized) and 1R gears.

The engine permanently drives an oil pump with a variable output, and this is linked to a hydraulic engine acting on the differential which controls the tracks. By acting on the steering gear and speed of the hydraulic engine, the driver can continuously modify the speed ratio of both tracks. All-turning radii can thus be obtained until pivoting 'on the spot' takes place (both tracks turning in an opposite direction at the same speed). Since such a system needs no action from the brakes, the whole power produced by the engine is constantly available on the tracks. The main brakes are hydraulically applied with the foot, and once stopped the hand brake is applied.

The suspension is of the torsion-bar type and consists of five road wheels, drive sprocket at the rear, idler at the front and three track support rollers. The first and fifth road wheels are provided with a telescopic dampener and an additional spring.

There are a total of 78 shoes per track and each of these is provided with a rubber block. Steel spikes can be fitted for operating in ice and snow. The vehicle is provided with an oil heater and there is a fan fixed on the turret roof which draws out fumes when the gun is fired. Other equipment includes a 28V/4.5kw generator, two batteries of 12V 180Amp and a full set of tools.

The vehicle has no amphibious capability and no NBC equipment. Infra-red driving lights have not yet been provided although both an infra-red searchlight and an infra-red sight ($\times$ 6 magnification and 7° field of view) are provided.

VARIANTS

The only known variant is the armoured recovery vehicle 4KH6FA-B which uses a similar chassis to the 4KH6FA. The prototype was completed in 1974 and is known as the Bergepanzer K. The vehicle is provided with a hydraulically operated folding crane and two winches.

Basic data of the ARV, which is also known as the Greif, are as follows:

CREW: 4 WEIGHT: 20,500kg LENGTH: 6.27m WIDTH: 2.5m HEIGHT: 2.38m MAXIMUM ROAD SPEED: 63km/hr RANGE: 450km GROUND PRESSURE: .66kg/cm² GRADIENT: 70% ENGINE: As for Panzerjäger, 300HP diesel ARMAMENT: 1 × 7.62mm MG

It has been reported that an armoured load carrier based on the ARV is being developed.

Left and previous page The Panzerjäger K, 4KH6FA with 105mm gun.
Below Front photograph of the Armoured Recovery Vehicle 4KH6FA-B with dozer blade in travelling position.
Bottom Side photograph of the Armoured Recovery Vehicle 4KH6FA-B.

GERMANY (FEDERAL GERMAN REPUBLIC)

JAGDPANZER KANONE (JPZ 4-5)—SELF-PROPELLED ANTI-TANK GUN
MANUFACTURER—Rheinstahl Sonderfertigung, Kassel (See text)
STATUS—In service with Belgium and Germany. Production complete.

BASIC DATA

CREW:	4 (commander, gunner, loader, driver)	FORDING:	1.4m (w/o kit) 2.1m (with kit)
WEIGHT LOADED:	27,500kg	GRADIENT:	60%
LENGTH:	8.75mm (including gun) 6.238m (hull)	SIDE SLOPE:	30%
		VERTICAL OBSTACLE:	.75m
WIDTH:	2.98m	TRENCH:	.2m
HEIGHT:	2.085m (w/o A/A MG)	ENGINE:	Daimler-Benz Model
GROUND CLEARANCE:	.45m (front) .44m (rear)		MB 837 Aa 8-cylinder water-cooled
TRACK WIDTH:	450mm		diesel developing
LENGTH OF TRACK ON			500HP at 2,200rpm
GROUND:	3.8m	ARMAMENT:	1 × 90mm gun
GROUND PRESSURE:	.75kg/cm²		1 × 7.62mm MG co-
POWER-TO-WEIGHT			axial with main
RATIO:	19.5HP/ton		armament
MAXIMUM ROAD SPEED:	70km/hr (forwards and reverse)		1 × 7.62mm A/A MG 8 smoke dischargers
RANGE:	400km	ARMOUR:	12mm–50mm
FUEL:	470 litres		

DEVELOPMENT

The German Army made large-scale use of tank destroyers during the Second World War and continued development of these after the war. They first tried mounting a 90mm gun on the HS-30 armoured personnel carrier which was then entering service with the German Army but this was not a success and development was stopped. It was then decided to use the same basic chassis for a self-propelled anti-tank gun and anti-tank missile system, a light reconnaissance tank and a new armoured personnel carrier. As there was not an urgent requirement for the latter, work was initially concentrated on the anti-tank vehicles. The APC eventually became the Marder whilst the reconnaissance tank was developed to prototype stage only. There is a separate entry for the Jagdpanzer Rakete although this has an identical hull to the Jagdpanzer Kanone. The first series of five prototypes were built in 1960/62 and consisted of:
Hanomag built two vehicles known as the 1 RU 3/1 and 1 RU 3/2
Henschel built two vehicles known as the 1 HK 3/1 and 1 HK 3/2
Mowag (of Switzerland) built one prototype known as the HM 3, and recently as a private venture Mowag have built a similar vehicle on the Tornado MICV chassis called the Gepard.
    These were followed by a second series of six prototypes in 1963/64:
Hanomag built three vehicles called the 2 RU 3/1,2 RU 3/2 and 2 RU 3/3
Henschel built three vehicles called the 2 HK 3/1,2 HK 3/2 and 2 HK 3/3.
    Finally came the third series of six prototypes:
Hanomag built the RU 331, RU 332 and RU 333
Henschel built the RU 334, RU 335, RU 336.
    These prototypes were followed by a total of 750 production vehicles which were built between 1965 and 1967, ie 375 by Henschel and 375 by Hanomag—both companies are now Rheinstahl.
    The JPZ 4-5 are used by the German Panzerjäger Companies, each of which has two JPZ 4-5s at HQ, two sections each of 5 JPZ 4-5s and one section of Jagdpanzer Rakete.
    In December 1972 the Belgian Army ordered 80 vehicles (at first they ordered 84) and these were assembled at Anvers in Belgium, the first one being completed in 1975. They use many automative components of the Marder MICV including the transmission, improved sights, a new fire-control system which includes a SABCA laser rangefinder, Lyran mortar for illuminating targets at night, passive night viewing equipment and FN MAG 7.62mm machine-guns in place of the German MG 3 machine-guns. The total order was worth some 1,100 million Belgian Francs. Eight Belgian infantry battalions have each got two platoons each of four Jagdpanzer Kanones with the remainder being held in reserve.

DESCRIPTION

The hull of the JPZ 4-5 is of all-welded construction. The driver is seated at the front of the hull on the left side and steers the vehicle with a steering wheel. He is provided with a one-piece hatch that opens to the right and three periscopes for driving whilst closed down. The 90mm gun is in the glacis plate, slightly offset to the right of the centre line. The gunner is to the right of the gun and is provided with a sight with a magnification of × 8.

The loader's hatch is behind the driver's hatch and is of the lift and swing type. It is provided with periscopes and in addition there is a swivelling periscope in front of the loader's hatch.

The commander's hatch is in the roof at the rear of the fighting compartment on the right side. His hatch is also of the lift and swing type and is provided with periscopes around the hatch. In addition there is a swivelling periscope with a magnification of × 6 to × 20 in front of his hatch. The engine and transmission are at the rear of the hull and an automatic fire extinguishing system is mounted in the engine compartment.

The suspension consists of torsion bars, bumper springs and hydraulic shock absorbers. The transmission is a Renk HSWL 123 3 and the hydrostatic steering gear is combined with a differential gear.

An NBC system is provided, as are infra-red driving lights. Most JPZ 4-5s have an infra-red searchlight mounted over the 90mm gun and when not required this is stowed in a box on the rear of the hull.

The 90mm gun has an elevation of +15° and a depression of −8° and traverse is 15° left and 15° right. Both elevation and traverse are manual. A 7.62mm MG 3 machine-gun is mounted to the right of the main armament and an additional 7.62mm machine-gun is mounted on the commander's hatch. It can also be mounted on the loader's hatch if required. The eight smoke dischargers are mounted on the rear decking.

The 90mm (40.4 calibre) gun was made by Rheinmetall and fires the same HEAT-T and HEP-T rounds as the M48 tank still used by the German Army. This has a maximum effective range of 2,000m. An electro-mechanical firing mechanism is provided and maximum stated rate of fire is twelve rounds per minute. The barrel is provided with a double-baffle muzzle brake and a fume extractor.

VARIANTS
There are no variants in service although during the development of the JPZ 4-5 many variants were projected (refer to the Marder entry for these vehicles). More recently Rheinstahl have suggested that the JPZ 4-5 could be fitted with the 105mm L7A3 gun, but at the present time this is a proposal only.

Above Jagdpanzer Kanone (Jpz.4-5) with infra-red searchlight over main armament.
Below Jagdpanzer Kanone (Jpz.4-5) from the rear.

GERMANY (FEDERAL GERMAN REPUBLIC)

JAGDPANZER RAKETE (RJPZ-2)
MANUFACTURER – Rheinstahl Sonderfertigung, Kassel (see text)
STATUS – In service only with the German Army.

BASIC DATA

CREW:	4 (commander, missile controller, missile loader and driver)	FORDING:	1.4m 2.1m (with kit)
		GRADIENT:	60%
WEIGHT LOADED:	23,000kg	SIDE SLOPE:	30%
LENGTH:	6.43m	VERTICAL OBSTACLE:	.75m
WIDTH:	2.98m	TRENCH:	2m
HEIGHT:	2.6m (with missiles) 1.98m (hull top)	ENGINE:	Daimler-Benz Model MB 837 Aa, 8-cylinder, water-cooled diesel developing 500HP at 200rpm
GROUND CLEARANCE:	.45m (front) .44m (rear)		
TRACK WIDTH:	450mm		
LENGTH OF TRACK ON GROUND:	3.8m	ARMAMENT:	2 launchers for SS 11 ATGW
GROUND PRESSURE:	.63kg/cm²		1×7.62mm MG in bow
POWER TO WEIGHT RATIO:	21.7HP/ton		1×7.62mm A/A MG
MAXIMUM ROAD SPEED:	70km/hr (forward and reverse)		8 smoke dischargers
RANGE:	400km		
FUEL:	470 litres		

Jadgpanzer Rakete (RJPZ-2) from the front, showing both SS 11 launchers and missiles deployed.

DEVELOPMENT

The Jagdpanzer Rakete (RJPZ-2) has an almost identical hull to the Jagdpanzer Kanone (JPZ 4-5) for which there is a separate entry. The first prototype was built by Hanomag and was known as the RU 234. This was followed in 1963 by a further three prototypes by Hanomag known as the RU 341, RU 342 and RU 343, as well as three prototypes by Henschel known as the RU 344, RU 345 and RU 346. Each company then built 185 production vehicles, the first being completed in 1967 and the last in 1968.

DESCRIPTION

The hull is of all-welded construction. The driver is seated at the front of the hull on the left side and steers the vehicle with a steering wheel. He is provided with a one-piece hatch cover that opens to the left and has a total of three periscopes for driving whilst closed down. The bow machine-gunner is seated on the right side of the hull and also has a single-piece hatch cover opening to the right, and three periscopes.

The engine and transmission are at the rear of the hull and an automatic fire extinguishing system is mounted in the engine compartment. The transmission is a Renk HSWL 123 3 and the hydrostatic steering gear is combined with a differential gear.

The suspension consists of torsion bars, bumper springs and hydraulic shock absorbers. There are five road wheels with the drive sprocket at the rear and the idler at the front and there are three track return rollers.

The Jagdpanzer Rakete is provided with an NBC system and infra-red driving lights.

There are two launchers for the SS 11 ATGW. The left launcher can be traversed from 270° to 360° whilst the right launcher can be traversed from 0° to 90°, covering an arc of 180°. The launchers can be elevated from 0° to +20°. The SS 11 missile was developed and built by Nord-Aviation (now Aérospatiale) of France. It is 1.2m in length and has a minimum range of 500m and a maximum range of 3,000m. Its maximum speed is 580km/hr. A total of 14 missiles are carried inside the hull. Whilst a missile is being guided to the target the other launcher is being reloaded. The missile controller keeps track of the missile via a periscope mounted in the roof of the hull. A 7.62mm MG3 machine-gun is mounted in the bow of the vehicle on the right side, and this has a traverse of 15° left and 15° right, elevation limits are −8° to +15°. A further 7.62mm MG3 machine-gun is mounted over the driver's hatch. Eight smoke dischargers are mounted on the rear hull decking. A total of 3,200 rounds of 7.62mm machine-gun ammunition are carried.

VARIANTS

Jagdpanzer Rakete with TOW installation

This was suggested as an alternative to the HOT installation. This model would have had two launchers for the American Hughes TOW missile and would have carried a total of 20 missiles.

Jagdpanzer Rakete with HOT K3S installation

This has a single launcher for the French/German HOT missile and a total of 19 missiles are carried inside the hull. The HOT missile is 1.275m in length and its warhead has a diameter of 136mm. It has a minimum range of 75m and a maximum range of 4,000m. Speed is 260m/s. The missile is launched from a tube which is 1.3m in length and 175mm in diameter, and weighs 27kg. The missile aimer is provided with a day sight with two magnification settings of ×4 and ×12, and there is also a night sight of the image-intensification type which has a magnification of ×6. The missile aimer has simply to keep his sight on the target until the missile hits the target. It was announced late in 1975 that the German Army would be refitting all these vehicles with the HOT installation over the next five years.

Above Jagdpanzer Rakete (RJPZ-2) from the rear, showing smoke dischargers on rear hull decking.
Left HOT missile being launched from a Jagdpanzer Rakete (RJPZ-2) during trials.

GREAT BRITAIN

CHARIOTEER – TANK DESTROYER
MANUFACTURER – Conversions were carried out by Royal Ordnance Factories.
STATUS – In service with Finland, Lebanon. Conversion complete.

BASIC DATA

CREW	4 (commander, gunner, loader and driver)	ENGINE:	Rolls-Royce Meteor Mk.1, 2 or 3, 12-cylinder petrol engine developing 600HP at 2,550rpm
WEIGHT LOADED:	28,958kg		
LENGTH:	8.839m (gun forward) 6.425m (hull)		
WIDTH:	3.067m	ARMAMENT:	1 × 20-pounder (83.4mm) gun with an elevation of +10° and a depression of −5°
HEIGHT:	2.59m		
GROUND CLEARANCE:	.406m		
TRACK WIDTH:	394mm		1 × .30 Browning (7.62mm) MG co-axial with main armament
GROUND PRESSURE:	.98kg/cm²		
POWER TO WEIGHT RATIO:	21HP/ton		2 × 6 smoke dischargers 25 rounds of 83.4mm ammunition and 3,375 rounds of .30 ammunition
MAXIMUM ROAD SPEED:	51.5km/hr		
RANGE:	240km		
FUEL CAPACITY:	526 litres		
FORDING:	1.041m		
GRADIENT:	50%	ARMOUR:	
VERTICAL OBSTACLE:	.914m	hull front:	64mm
TRENCH:	2.362m	glacis plate:	25mm
		turret front:	30mm
		floor:	14mm (early models had a 6.35mm floor at the rear)

DEVELOPMENT/DESCRIPTION/VARIANTS

The Charioteer (FV 4101) was developed to fulfil a requirement for a tank destroyer for the Royal Armoured Corps. Essentially it consists of a Cromwell hull fitted with a new turret mounting the 20-pounder gun of the Centurion tank of that period. The hull machine-gun of the Cromwell was deleted and the position plated over. Development started in 1950 and conversions started in 1952. The Charioteer was phased out of service with the Royal Armoured Corps in 1956. The new turret was provided with twin hatches for both the commander and loader. Turret rotation was at a maximum speed of 18° a second, this being powered with manual controls for use in an emergency.

The suspension was of the Christie-type and consisted of five road wheels with the drive sprocket at the rear and the idler at the front. There were no track support rollers. Hydraulic shock absorbers were fitted to the first, second, fourth and fifth road wheels. The gearbox was the Merrit-Brown Type Z 5 with 5F and 1R gears. The Charioteer is not amphibious although a deep-fording kit was developed. No night-fighting or NBC system is provided.

Below Charioteer tank of the Finnish Army.

JAPAN

TYPE 60 – SELF-PROPELLED RECOILLESS RIFLE
MANUFACTURER – Komatsu Manufacturing Company
STATUS – In service only with the Japanese Self-Defence Force. Production complete.

BASIC DATA

CREW:	3 (commander, loader and driver)	GRADIENT:	67%
		VERTICAL OBSTACLE:	.53m
WEIGHT:	8,020kg (loaded)	TRENCH:	1.78m
	7,600kg (empty)	ENGINE:	Komatsu T120 6-cylinder
LENGTH:	4.3m		air-cooled diesel engine
WIDTH:	2.23m		developing 120HP at
HEIGHT:	1.38m		2,400rpm
GROUND CLEARANCE:	.35m	ARMAMENT:	2 × 106mm recoilless
TRACK WIDTH:	260mm		rifles
GROUND PRESSURE:	.63kg/cm²		2 × 12.7mm ranging
MAXIMUM ROAD SPEED:	48km/hr		MGs
RANGE:	130km (road)	ARMOUR	
FUEL:	77 litres	hull front:	30mm
FORDING:	.8m	hull sides and rear:	10–15mm

DEVELOPMENT

Design of the Type 60 Self-Propelled Recoilless Rifle (SPRR) commenced in 1954, with the programme being managed by the Technical Research and Development Headquarters of the Japanese Self-Defence Force.

Prototypes were built by two Japanese companies, Komatsu (SS1) and Mitsubishi (SS2). The first prototypes were completed late in 1955. The SS1 had its engine at the front of the hull, drive sprocket at the rear, torsion-bar suspension with rubber cushioning, and was armed with twin 105mm recoilless rifles. The SS2 had its engine at the rear, drive sprocket at the front, torsion-bar suspension with hydraulic shock absorbers, and was armed with twin 106mm recoilless rifles. The SS2 was found to be slightly better than the SS1.

Komatsu then built the SS3 which had a number of improvements including a more powerful engine. It was completed in 1956. Next came the SS4 in 1959. This featured improved cooling for the modified engine and the steering system was changed from a clutch and brake system to a controlled differential type.

The SS4 was standardized as the Type 60 Self-Propelled Recoilless Rifle in 1960. Sub-contractors to the Komatsu Company included the Japan Steel Works which built the Recoilless Rifles and the Howa Machinery Company. At the time of writing no replacement for the Type 60 had been announced although it is logical that a replacement, probably armed with ATGWs, is under development.

Above Type 60 Self-Propelled Recoilless Rifle from the front, with mount and weapons in the raised position.
Left Close up of the rear of the twin recoilless rifles on the Type 60 Self-Propelled Recoilless Rifle.

DESCRIPTION

The hull of the Type 60 is of all-welded rolled plate construction. The driver is seated on the left side of the hull and is provided with three periscopes and a single-piece hatch cover that opens to the rear.

The commander/gunner sits to the left of the twin recoilless rifles and is provided with a single-piece hatch cover that opens to the rear and a total of four vision blocks. There is a single vision block in the rear of the commander's position. The loader's station is to the left of the commander's position when travelling. The twin 106mm recoilless rifles are mounted parallel to each other on the right side of the hull. Elevation and traverse are accomplished by a combined hydraulic/electric system. When lowered the rifles have an elevation of +10° and a depression of −5°, traverse being 10° left and right. However, when the mount, complete with the commander's position is raised, the rifles have an elevation of 15° and a depression of −20°, traverse being 30° left and 30° right. The fire control system comprises a rangefinder, optical sight and a .50 (12.7mm) ranging rifle/machine-gun over each recoilless rifle. The 106mm recoilless rifle fires an HE or HESH round, effective range being 1,100m and maximum range 7,700m. Rate of fire is six rounds per minute and a total of ten rounds are carried. The rifles are loaded from the rear by the loader. The recoilless rifles weigh 114kg each and have an overall length of 3.408m, length of barrel being 3.332m.

The engine and transmission are at the rear of the hull. The suspension is of the torsion-bar type and consists of five road wheels with the drive sprocket at the front and the idler at the rear and there are three track support rollers. The first, second and fifth road wheel stations are provided with hydraulic shock absorbers. The prototypes could be fitted with much wider tracks for operations in the snow. The Type 60 has no infra-red night fighting or driving equipment and does not have an NBC system. It is not amphibious.

VARIANTS

There are no variants of the Type 60 SPRR.

SOVIET UNION

ASU-85 – AIR-PORTABLE SELF-PROPELLED ANTI-TANK GUN
MANUFACTURER – Soviet State Arsenals
STATUS – In service with East Germany, Poland and the Soviet Union. Production of the ASU-85 is now complete.

BASIC DATA

CREW:	4 (commander, gunner, loader & driver)	GRADIENT:	70%
		VERTICAL OBSTACLE:	1.1m
WEIGHT LOADED:	14,000kg	TRENCH:	2.8m
LENGTH:	8.49m (including armament) 6m (hull only)	ENGINE:	Model V-6, 6-cylinder in-line water-cooled diesel developing 240HP at 1,800rpm
WIDTH:	2.8m		
HEIGHT:	2.1m	ARMAMENT:	1 × 85mm gun with
GROUND CLEARANCE:	.4m		an elevation of +15° and
TRACK:	2.66m		a depression of −4°, total
TRACK WIDTH:	360mm		traverse 12°, axis of
LENGTH OF TRACK ON GROUND:	4.195m		bore 1.57m 1 × 7.62mm PKT MG
GROUND PRESSURE:	.44kg/cm²		co-axial with main
POWER TO WEIGHT RATIO:	17.1HP/ton		armament A total of 40 rounds
MAXIMUM ROAD SPEED:	44km/hr		of 85mm ammunition
RANGE:	260km	ARMOUR	
FUEL CAPACITY:	250 litres	glacis:	40mm at 60°
FUEL CONSUMPTION:	96 litres per 100km	upper hull side:	15mm at 30°
FORDING:	1.1m	mantlet:	40mm at 60°

DEVELOPMENT
The ASU-85 was first seen in public during the annual May Day Parade held in Moscow in 1962. As far as it is known the ASU-85 is only employed with the Airborne Divisions, each of which has a battalion with a total of 18 ASU-85s. The ASU-85 is air-portable in such aircraft as the AN-12 and can also be air-dropped.

DESCRIPTION
The ASU-85 is based on PT-76 Light Tank components. The hull of the vehicle is of all-welded construction with a sloping glacis plate and sloping sides to the superstructure. The driver is seated at the very front of the vehicle on the right and is provided with two viewing devices to his front and a further viewing block to his right in the side of the hull. The commander's hatch is in the forward part of the roof and opens to the front and there is a further hatch to the left of the commander's hatch which opens to the left. There are a further two square type hatches behind the first two and these open to the front. There is a further viewing block on the left of the hull and another at the very rear of the fighting compartment on the right side.

The engine and transmission are at the rear of the hull and both are as fitted to the PT-76, the gearbox having 4F and 1R gears. The suspension is of the torsion-bar type and consists of six road wheels, driving sprocket at the rear and idler at the front.

Two additional drum-type fuel tanks are often fitted on the rear of the hull and there is a large stowage box between these drums.

The 85mm gun is mounted slightly to the left of the centreline and has hand traverse and elevation. This is provided with a double baffle muzzle brake and a bore evacuator is fitted two thirds of the way up the barrel. The 85mm gun is a development of the M-1943 weapon and fires fixed rounds. Maximum rate of fire (aimed) is stated to be four rounds per minute. The following types of ammunition are available:
HE projectile weighing 9.5kg with an m/v of 792m/s.
APHE projectile weighing 9.3kg with an m/v of 792m/s, which will penetrate 102mm of armour at 1,000m.
HVAP projectile weighing 5kg with an m/v of 1,030m/s, which will penetrate 130mm of armour at 1,000m.
A full range of night fighting and driving aids is fitted. These include infra-red driving lights and an infra-red searchlight fitted over the main armament. The commander is also provided with an infra-red searchlight in front of his hatch. It is not known if the ASU-85 is fitted with NBC equipment. It is not amphibious but a splash plate is fitted to the glacis plate so that when the vehicle is fording the water does not rush up the glacis plate.

VARIANTS
There are no known variants of the ASU-85.

Above ASU-85s on exercise in the snow.
Left ASU-85 Airportable Self-Propelled Anti-Tank Gun.

SOVIET UNION

ASU-57 – AIR-PORTABLE SELF-PROPELLED ANTI-TANK GUN
MANUFACTURER – Soviet State Arsenals
STATUS – In service with Egypt, East Germany, Poland, Soviet Union and Yugoslavia. Production complete.

BASIC DATA

CREW:	3 (commander, driver, loader)	FORDING:	.7m
		GRADIENT:	60%
WEIGHT LOADED:	3,350kg	VERTICAL OBSTACLE:	.5m
LENGTH:	4.995m (including gun)	TRENCH:	1.4m
	3.48m (hull only)	ENGINE:	M-20E, 4-cylinder, in-line,
WIDTH:	2.086m		water-cooled petrol
HEIGHT:	1.18m		engine developing 55HP
GROUND CLEARANCE:	.204m	ARMAMENT:	1 × 57mm gun with an
TRACK:	1.87m		elevation of +12° and
TRACK WIDTH:	300mm		a depression of −5°,
LENGTH OF TRACK ON			total traverse 22°. A
GROUND:	2.375m		total of 30 rounds of
GROUND PRESSURE:	.35kg/cm²		57mm ammunition
MAXIMUM ROAD SPEED:	45km/hr	ARMOUR	
RANGE:	250km	glacis plate:	6mm at 60°
FUEL CAPACITY:	140 litres	upper hull sides:	6mm at 90°
FUEL CONSUMPTION:	56km per 100 litres	mantlet:	6mm at 39°

DEVELOPMENT

The ASU-57 (ASU=Russian designation for airborne assault gun and 57 for the calibre of the gun) was first seen during the May Day Parade held in Moscow in 1957. Until the introduction of the larger ASU-85 in 1962, the ASU-57 was the only Soviet self-propelled air-portable anti-tank gun.

The first models built were of conventional steel armour and these were powered by a six-cylinder in-line ZIL-123 petrol engine that developed 110HP. Total combat weight was 5,400kg and other basic data were as follows: length of hull 3.44m, width 2.2m, height 1.4m, maximum road speed 64km/hr, range 320km and a maximum armour thickness of 13mm.

These steel models were followed by a slightly smaller model constructed largely of aluminium. This is the current model and the data above relate to this vehicle.

DESCRIPTION

First production models had the Ch-51 gun with a total of 34 slots in its muzzle brake. Later production models had the Ch-51M gun which has a double baffle muzzle brake. The gun has no bore evacuator and is offset slightly to the left of the centre line. It has an axis of bore of .975m and a travelling lock is provided.

The 57mm gun was developed from the Second World War M-1943 (ZIS-2) anti-tank gun and fires the same ammunition. It has a semi-automatic vertical sliding breech-block and a hydro-spring recoil system. Maximum rate of fire is ten rounds per minute.

The following types of ammunition are available:
HE projectile weight 2.8kg, m/v 695m/s.
APHE projectile weight 3.1kg, m/v 980m/s, will penetrate 85mm of armour at 1,200m.
HVAP projectile weight 1.8kg, m/v 1,255m/s, will penetrate 100mm of armour at 1,000m.
Maximum range of the gun is 6,100m at maximum elevation.

The hull is of welded construction with the engine (mounted transversely) and transmission at the front of the hull. There are a total of four road wheels and two track return rollers each side, and the drive sprocket is at the front. The commander, who also acts as the gun layer (he is provided with a PO2-50 sight), is seated on the left side of the gun with the driver on the right. The third member of the crew acts as the loader. In addition the vehicle can carry three infantrymen. A machine-gun is often carried for use in the ground role. There is a vision block each side of the gun for the use of the commander and driver, and an additional single vision port each side.

The ASU-57 has no NBC system as its fighting compartment has an open top. It has no amphibious capability. Some models have infra-red driving lights, although no infra-red fighting equipment is fitted.

The ASU-57 is deployed at Regimental level, ie each Soviet Parachute Regiment has a battery consisting of nine ASU-57s and three are detached to individual Parachute battalions as required. The ASU-57 is normally air-dropped. The An-12 (CUB) carries two pallets each with an ASU-57.

VARIANTS

There are no known variants in service.

Above ASU-57 Model B moving across country.
Left ASU-57 Model A moving into action after being air-dropped.
Right The M56 90mm Self-Propelled Anti-Tank Gun. The rubber tyred road wheels are clearly shown in this photograph.

UNITED STATES

M56–SELF-PROPELLED ANTI-TANK GUN
MANUFACTURER–Cadillac Motor Car Division of General Motors Corporation
STATUS–In service with Morocco and Spanish Marines. Production complete.

BASIC DATA

CREW:	4	FUEL:	208 litres
WEIGHT LOADED:	7,030kg	FORDING:	1.066m
WEIGHT EMPTY:	5,783kg		1.524m with special kit
LENGTH OVERALL:	5.841m	GRADIENT:	60%
LENGTH HULL:	4.555m	VERTICAL OBSTACLE:	.762m
WIDTH:	2.577m	TRENCH CROSSING:	1.524m
HEIGHT:	2.057m	ENGINE:	Continental A01-403-5,
	1.676m (axis of bore)		6-cylinder air-cooled
GROUND CLEARANCE:	.38m		opposed fuel-injection
TRACK:	1.981m		petrol engine developing
TRACK WIDTH:	508mm		200BHP at 3,000rpm
GROUND PRESSURE:	.316kg/cm^2	ARMOUR:	Nil (See text)
MAX. ROAD SPEED:	45km/hr	ARMAMENT:	1 × 90mm gun
RANGE:	225km		

DEVELOPMENT

In 1948 a requirement was established for an air-portable self-propelled anti-tank gun. The end result was the M56 which is often known as the Scorpion, its full American Army designation being Gun, Anti-Tank, Self-Propelled: 90mm, M56. The prototypes were known as the T101/T101E1 and three prototypes were built by the Cadillac Motor Car Division of General Motors, who also undertook production. The M56 was in production from 1953 to 1959 and was used by the 82nd and 101st Airborne Divisions. It has been replaced in the United States Army by the M-551 Sheridan tank. The M56 was similar in chassis concept to the M76 Otter amphibious load carrier of that period.

The M56 90mm Self-Propelled Anti-Tank Gun from above.

DESCRIPTION

The hull of the M56 is of welded and riveted aluminium construction with the engine and transmission at the front of the vehicle, the gun in the centre and the loading area at the rear. The transmission used is the General Motors Allison Division Model CD-150-4 cross drive with torque converter, and this has two forward and one reverse ranges. The suspension is of the torsion-bar type with hydraulic shock absorbers. There are four road wheels which have conventional rubber tyres, the drive sprocket is at the front and the idler at the rear and there are no track return rollers. The track is an endless rubber band with reinforced steel cables.

The 90mm gun M54 (T125) in mount M88 (T170E1). It has a traverse of 30° left and 30° right, elevation is +15° and depression −10°, elevation and traverse being manual. The driver is seated on the left of the gun with the gunner to the right of the gun.

The gun can be fired electrically or mechanically and has a vertical sliding breech-block. Life of the gun barrel itself is about 700 rounds. A hydro-spring recoil mechanism is provided, maximum recoil being 1.1m. The breech is opened manually for loading the first round and remains open after the first round has been fired. Total ammunition supply is 29 rounds and this is stowed horizontally under the breech of the gun. Ammunition is of the fixed type and is similar to that used for the M48 tank but with a reduced charge. The following types of ammunition are available:

Type	Muzzle velocity	Range at elevation
APC-T	853m/s	4,572m at 2° 30 min
HEAT	853m/s	4,572m at 4° 5 min
AP-T	914m/s	4,572m at 2° 16 min
TP-T	914m/s	4,572m at 2° 16 min
HE	823m/s	4,572m at 2° 41 min
WP	823m/s	4,572m at 2° 41 min
HEAT-T	1,219m/s	4,572m at 6° 14 min

Also, HE-T, WP-T, HVAP-T and HVTP-T rounds are available.

When the gun was fired the vehicle would tend to jump towards the rear as the chassis was so light. Often, one of the crew would stand away from the vehicle to observe the fall of shot and give corrections, especially in dusty weather. The only part of the vehicle that was armoured was the small shield, and the crew were very vulnerable to small arms fire and shell bursts. No NBC system was provided and it was not amphibious though a deep fording kit was available. Infra-red driving lights were provided.

VARIANTS

There are no variants in service although many different models were developed to prototype stage including an amphibious armoured personnel carrier, anti-aircraft vehicle with four 12.7mm machine-guns, recoilless rifle vehicle, mortar carriers (81mm and 107mm), missile launching vehicle, and one was also fitted with a gas turbine engine for trials.

UNITED STATES

M18 – SELF-PROPELLED ANTI-TANK GUN
MANUFACTURER – Buick Motor Division of General Motors Corporation
STATUS – In service with Nationalist China, South Korea, Venezuela and Yugoslavia. No longer in production.

BASIC DATA

CREW:	5 (commander, gunner, loader, driver and co-driver)	ENGINE:	Continental Model R-975-C1 developing 350HP at 2,400 rpm, or Model R-975-C4 developing 400HP at 2,400 rpm. Both are 9-cylinder, air-cooled petrol engines. Model R-975-C1 was fitted to vehicles from 1 to 1350, and the R-975-C4 from vehicles 1351 onwards.
WEIGHT LOADED:	17,650 – 18,144kg		
WEIGHT EMPTY:	16,120kg		
LENGTH:	6.654m (gun forward) 5.282m (chassis)		
WIDTH:	2.87m (with T69 tracks)		
HEIGHT:	2.565m (with A/A MG) 2.368m (w/o A/A MG)		
GROUND CLEARANCE:	.355m		
TRACK:	2.413m		
TRACK WIDTH:	365mm (T69 track) 533mm (T85E1 track)	ARMAMENT:	1 × 76mm gun M1A1 or M1A2, elevation +19½° depression −10° 1 × .50 (12.7mm) M2 heavy barrel MG for A/A use on ring mount
LENGTH OF TRACK ON GROUND:	2.946m		
GROUND PRESSURE:	.83 – .85kg/cm²		
MAXIMUM ROAD SPEED:	88.5km/hr		
RANGE:	240km (cruising)	ARMOUR	
FUEL CAPACITY:	625 litres	hull front:	12.7mm
FORDING:	1.22m	hull sides:	12.7mm
GRADIENT:	60%	hull rear:	12.7mm
VERTICAL OBSTACLE:	.914m	hull top:	7.9mm
TRENCH:	1.879m	hull floor:	6.35mm
		turret front:	19.05mm – 25.4mm
		turret sides and rear:	12.7mm

Note. The weight, width and ground pressure depends on the type of track fitted.

This photograph was taken in 1964 and shows M18s of the Chinese Nationalist Army on the firing range at the Armour School at Taichung. These vehicles have a .30 machine-gun mounted on the turret top in addition to the standard .50 machine-gun.

DEVELOPMENT

The M18 Self-Propelled Anti-Tank Gun (its official designation was M18 Gun Motor Carriage) was the final result of three years of development which started with the 37mm Gun Motor Carriage T22 and T23. These were followed by the 57mm Gun Motor Carriage T49, the 75mm Gun Motor Carriage T67 and finally the 75mm Gun Motor Carriage T70 which was standardized as the M18. Six pilot models of the T70 were built and an immediate production order for 1,000 vehicles was placed before the pilots were completed. Production of the T70 commenced in mid-1943 and a total of 2,507 were built when production was completed in October 1944. The T70 was actually standardized as the M18 in February 1944.

The M18 was used by the Tank Destroyer battalions in Europe from 1944 and it continued in service with the United States Army after World War II. The M18 was nicknamed the Hellcat as it relied on its speed to get itself out of trouble. Its armour was very thin and only protected the crew from shell splinters and small arms fire.

DESCRIPTION

The hull of the M18 is of all-welded construction. The driver and co-driver are seated at the front of the hull, with the driver on the left and the co-driver on the right. Each man is provided with a two-piece hatch cover, the forward part, which contains the viewing periscope, opening forwards, and the rear half opening to the left or right (ie the driver's to the left and the co-driver's to the right). An escape hatch is provided in the floor. The turret is in the centre of the hull and the engine at the rear. The transmission is at the front of the hull between the driver and co-driver and is of the torqmatic type with 3F and 1R gears. The suspension is of the torsion-bar type and consists of five road wheels, each of which is provided with a shock absorber, drive sprocket at the front, idler at the rear and four track return rollers.

The turret has an open roof and powered traverse through 360°. The ring mount for the anti-aircraft machine-gun is at the rear of the turret on the left side.

The 76mm gun is the same as that fitted to late Sherman tanks. A muzzle brake was fitted when required to the M1A2 gun. Elevation was manual. A total of 45 rounds of 76mm ammunition could be carried and 800 rounds of .50 machine-gun ammunition.

The following types of 76mm ammunition were available: Armour Piercing Capped M62 which could penetrate 102mm of armour at a range of 914m, m/v was 792m/s, Armour Piercing M79, High Explosive M42A1, Smoke M88 and Illuminating. The M18 has no amphibious capability (although many experimental models were tested), no infra-red equipment and no NBC equipment.

VARIANTS

There were many variants of the M18 including the M39 and M44 Armoured Utility Vehicles which were based on M18 components. None of these remain in service.

UNITED STATES

M10/M10A1 and M36/M36B1/M36B2 – SELF-PROPELLED ANTI-TANK GUNS
MANUFACTURERS – M10 – Grand Blanc Tank Arsenal. M10A1 – Grand Blanc Tank Arsenal, Ford Motor Company. M36 – Grand Blanc Tank Arsenal, American Locomotive Company, Massey Harris Company, Montreal Locomotive Works. M36B1 – Grand Blanc Tank Arsenal. M36B2 – American Locomotive Works.
STATUS – M10 – Denmark (Achilles) and South Korea
M36 – Pakistan (including M36B2), South Korea, Turkey and Yugoslavia (including M36B2). Production of these has now been completed.

BASIC DATA	M10	M10A1	M36	M36B1	M36B2
CREW:	5	5	5	5	5
WEIGHT LOADED:	29,940kg	29,030kg	27,670kg	30,840kg	29,940kg
LENGTH W/O ARMAMENT:	5.975m	5.975m	5.975m	6.27m	5.975m
WIDTH:	3.048m	3.048m	3.048m	2.55m	3.048m
HEIGHT:	2.47m	2.47m	3.19m	2.66m	3.15m
GROUND CLEARANCE:	.43m	.43m	.44m	.43m	.46m
TRACK:	2.108m	2.108m	2.108m	2.108m	2.108m
TRACK WIDTH:	419mm	419mm	419mm	419mm	419mm

LENGTH OF TRACK ON GROUND:	3.733m	3.733m	3.733m	3.733m	3.733m
GROUND PRESSURE:	.86kg/cm²	.86kg/cm²	.95kg/cm²	.96kg/cm²	.86kg/cm²
MAXIMUM ROAD SPEED:	48km/hr	48km/hr	42km/hr	42km/hr	40km/hr
RANGE:	320km	260km	180km	160km	180km
FUEL CAPACITY:	621 litres	727 litres	727 litres	636 litres	625 litres
FORDING:	.914m	.914m	.914m	.914m	1.07m
GRADIENT:	60%	60%	60%	60%	60%
VERTICAL OBSTACLE:	.609m	.609m	.46m	.609m	.48m
TRENCH:	2.286m	2.286m	2.286m	2.286m	2.286m
ENGINE TYPE:	GMC × 2	Ford GAA	Ford GAA	Ford GAA	GMC × 2
ENGINE HP/RPM:	375/2,100	450/2,600	450/2,600	450/2,600	375/2,100
ARMAMENT:					
main:	76.2mm	76.2mm	90mm	90mm	90mm
bow:	—	—	—	.30 (7.62mm)	—
A/A MG:	.50 (12.7mm)	.50 (12.7mm)	.50 (12.7mm)	.50 (12.7mm)	.50 (12.7mm)
AMMUNITION					
main:	54	54	47	47	47
bow MG:	—	—	—	450	—
A/A MG:	300	300	1,000	1,000	1,000
ARMOUR					
hull front:	12.7mm/50.8mm		38.1/50.8mm		50.8mm
hull sides:	19/25.4mm		19/38mm		38/50mm
hull rear:	25.4mm/38mm		19/38mm		38mm
hull roof:	9.52/19.05mm		9.52/19mm		25.4mm
hull floor:	6.35mm		12.7mm		12.7mm/25.4mm
turret front:	63.5mm		76.2mm		76.2mm
turret sides:	12.7mm		31.75mm		31.75mm
turret top:	19.05mm		28.57mm		28.57mm

Note on Armour: Some vehicles were re-worked and armour thickness may vary.

Above The M10 with the British 17-pounder gun was known as the Achilles.

GENERAL

The driver and co-driver are seated at the front of the vehicle and each is provided with a single-piece hatch cover with an integral periscope. The other three crew members are seated in the turret, the top of which is open. The engine is at the rear and the transmission at the front of the hull. The suspension consists of three bogies, each of which has two road wheels and a return roller at the top. The drive sprocket is at the front and the idler at the rear.

DEVELOPMENT/VARIANTS M10 and M10A1

In April 1942 design work on a three-inch (76.2mm) Gun Motor Carriage called the T35 commenced. This consisted of a M4A2 tank chassis and a T1 tank turret. An improved model was known as the T35E1 and this was standardized in June 1942 as the M10 Gun Motor Carriage. The M10 is essentially an M4A2 chassis with a new hull top and a new turret. The M10A1 was almost identical but used the M4A3 chassis. Most of these were retained in the USA and some had their turrets removed and were used as prime movers under the designation M35.

The three-inch (76.2mm) gun M7 is in mount M5, elevation is +19° and depression −10°, turret has full traverse through 360°. It fires the HE M42A1 round or the M62 APC round. This has an m/v of 792.5m/s and would penetrate 102mm of armour at 914m. The British fitted many M10s with their 17-pounder anti-tank gun and called them the Achilles IC, or Achilles IIC in the case of the M10A1. They remained in service for many years after the Second World War. A .50 (12.7mm) Browning M2 machine-gun is mounted on the turret for anti-aircraft use.

DEVELOPMENT/VARIANTS M36, M36B1 and M36B2

In October 1942 it was decided to mount a 90mm gun on a Gun Motor Carriage. This idea was first tried on an M10 but the turret was found to be unsatisfactory. Design work on the T71 Gun Motor Carriage started in March 1943 and this was basically an M10A1 chassis with a new turret mounting a 90mm gun. In November 1943 it was decided to place the vehicle in production and it was standardized as the M36 Gun Motor Carriage in June 1944. The M36B1 was simply an M4A3 chassis and hull with the new turret and only 187 of these were built. The M36B2 used the M10 hull, although many M10s were brought up to M36 standard, and was provided with a new turret and gun.

The vehicle is armed with a 90mm gun M3 in mount M4, elevation is +20° and depression −10°. It fires the M71 HE round and the M82 APC round. The latter has an m/v of 814m/s and would penetrate 76mm of armour at a range of 4,300m. A .50 (12.7mm) Browning M2 machine-gun was mounted on the turret for anti-aircraft defence.

M36 Self-Propelled Anti-Tank Gun.

SELF-PROPELLED GUNS

This covers self-propelled guns and howitzers. Tank destroyers and mobile anti-aircraft systems each have their own sections.

The majority of self-propelled guns in service are based on an MBT or light tank chassis, although the United States developed a series of light-weight chassis specifically for self-propelled guns: eg the M108/M109 and M107/M110.

Most self-propelled guns (except the heavier weapons such as the 203mm weapons) normally carry a small number of anti-tank rounds in case they find themselves without armour or infantry cover. Apart from the older weapons and some of the heavier weapons the armament is normally mounted in a turret which can be traversed through 360°, which enables it to lay on different targets without moving its position.

Artillery has now become more effective with the introduction of advanced fire-control equipment, computers (including laser rangefinders), rocket-assisted projectiles, and the accurate Cannon Launched Guided Projectiles to come into service in the not too distant future. Automatic loading systems are being developed (eg the French GCT) which enable high rates of fire to be achieved. With the introduction of accurate artillery and mortar locating equipment, artillery must now fire as many rounds as accurately as possible in the shortest time, and then redeploy to a new fire position.

The following SPGs are covered in this section:

Canada	Sexton	88mm
France	AMX 155mm GCT	155mm
	155mm SPH Mk.F3	155mm
	105mm SPH	105mm
Great Britain	Abbot	105mm
Israel	L-33	155mm
Soviet Union	122mm M1974	122mm
	152mm M1973	152mm
	ISU-122/152	122mm/152mm
	SU-100	100mm
	SU-76	76mm
Sweden	155mm Bandkanon 1A	155mm
United States	M110	203mm
	M55	203mm
	M107	175mm
	M109	155mm
	M44	155mm
	M108	105mm
	M52	105mm
	M7	105mm

Other SPGs will be found in the following sections:

COUNTRY	REFER TO ENTRY	SPG DESIGNATION
Germany	Leopard MBT	155mm GCT
Japan	Type 74 MBT	155mm SPG
Soviet Union	IS-3	155mm M1957
	IS-3	420mm M1960
	T34/85	122mm SPG
Switzerland	Pz.68	Panzer Kanone 68
United States	M3/M5 Light Tank	M8 75mm SPH
	Sherman	155mm SPG

CANADA

SEXTON – SELF-PROPELLED GUN
MANUFACTURER – Montreal Locomotive Works, Montreal
STATUS – In service with India, Italy, Portugal and South Africa. Production of the Sexton was completed in 1945.

BASIC DATA

CREW:	6 (commander, driver, gunner, gun-layer, loader and wireless operator)	FORDING:	.914m
		GRADIENT:	60%
		VERTICAL OBSTACLE:	.609m
		TRENCH:	1.879m
WEIGHT LOADED:	25,855kg	ENGINE:	Continental R975-C1, 9-cylinder air-cooled petrol engine developing 400HP at 2,400rpm. Later Sextons were powered by a Continental R975-C4 engine developing 475HP at 2,400rpm
LENGTH:	6.121m		
WIDTH:	2.717m		
HEIGHT:	2.438m (top of superstructure) 2.87m (with canvas cover erected)		
GROUND CLEARANCE:	.431 (with 3-piece transmission) .466m (with 1-piece transmission)	ARMAMENT:	1 × 25-pounder (88mm) Mk. 2 gun on mount Mk. 1 2 × .303 (Bren) LMG
TRACK:	419mm (early models) 394mm (late models with CDP tracks)		
		AMMUNITION:	112 cartridges 87 HE or Smoke projectiles 18 Anti-Tank projectiles 1,500 rounds of .303 ammunition: ie 50 × 30 round magazines
LENGTH OF TRACK ON GROUND:	3.733m		
GROUND PRESSURE:	.81kg/cm² (with 419mm tracks) .85g/cm² (with 394 tracks)		
POWER TO WEIGHT RATIO:	15.47HP/ton (R975-C1 engine) 18.37HP/ton (R975-C4 engine)	ARMOUR superstructure: front:	19mm
		superstructure sides:	12.7mm
		hull sides:	12.7mm – 25.4mm
MAXIMUM ROAD SPEED:	40.23km/hr	hull floor front:	25.4mm
RANGE:	290km (roads)	hull floor rear:	12.7mm
FUEL CAPACITY:	682 litres		

Above Side photograph of a Sexton Self-Propelled Gun.
Right A Sexton of the South African Army with non-standard type tracks.

DEVELOPMENT

The Sexton was designed and developed in Canada during the Second World War to a British General Staff Requirement. The first pilot model was completed late in 1942 with production commencing early in 1943. Production continued until late 1945 by which time 2,150 had been built. The Sexton continued in service with the British Army until the 1950s.

DESCRIPTION

The full designation of the Sexton was 25-pounder Self-Propelled Tracked Sexton. It was basically the lower half of a Grizzly 1 tank chassis (which was similar to the American M-4A1 chassis) on which was welded a new superstructure mounting the famous British 25-pounder Field Gun.

The engine is at the rear of the hull and the transmission at the front, the latter with 5F and 1R gears and the final drive of the controlled differential type. The suspension each side consists of three two-wheeled bogie assemblies, with the drive sprocket at the front and the idler at the rear, and there are three track support rollers, ie one on the top of each bogie assembly. Early Sextons had a $16\frac{1}{2}''$ (419mm) track but these were replaced by the $15\frac{1}{2}''$ (394mm) CDP (Canadian Dry Pin) tracks. Late production Sextons had a one-piece transmission rather than the three-piece transmission of the early models. In addition late production vehicles were fitted with the more powerful and more reliable Continental R975-C4 engine.

The 25-pounder gun was mounted in the front of the superstructure and had a traverse of 25° left and 15° right, elevation being +40° and depression −9°. The recoil was limited from the 1.016m of the standard field gun to .508m on the Sexton. Standard 25-pounder sights were provided for both direct and indirect fire. Various types of separate loading HE, smoke and anti-tank rounds were carried, these being stored under the floor and in the fighting compartment itself. In bad weather a canvas cover could be erected over the fighting compartment.

VARIANTS

Gun Position Officer Vehicle

The Gun Position Officer (GPO) vehicle was produced in limited numbers and was basically a Sexton with no armament and the gun position plated over. Internally tables and chairs were provided and additional radios and communications equipment were installed.

FRANCE

AMX 155mm GCT–SELF-PROPELLED GUN
MANUFACTURER–ATS Roanne (see text)
STATUS–Trials with the French Army. Will enter production and service in 1977.

BASIC DATA

CREW:	4 (commander, 2 gunners, driver)	MAXIMUM ROAD SPEED:	60km/hr
		RANGE:	450km
WEIGHT LOADED:	41,000kg	FUEL CAPACITY:	970 litres
WEIGHT EMPTY:	37,000kg	FORDING:	2.2m
LENGTH:	10.4m (gun forward)	GRADIENT:	60%
	9.5m (gun rear)	VERTICAL OBSTACLE:	.93m
	6.485m (chassis)	TRENCH:	2.9m
WIDTH:	3.15m (over turret)	ENGINE:	Hispano-Suiza
	3.115m (over chassis)		HS-110, 12-cylinder,
HEIGHT:	3.3m (including MG)		multi-fuel, water-
	2.995m (turret roof)		cooled engine
	2.16m (axis of bore)		developing
GROUND CLEARANCE:	.42m		700HP at 2,400rpm
TRACK WIDTH:	570mm	ARMAMENT:	1 × 155mm gun
LENGTH OF TRACK ON GROUND:	4.12m		1 × 7.62mm A/A MG
			2 × 2 smoke
GROUND PRESSURE:	.9kg/cm²		dischargers

DEVELOPMENT

Development of the GCT (Grande Cadence de Tir) started in 1969/70 with the first two prototypes being completed in 1972/73. It was shown for the first time in public at the 1973 Satory Exhibition near Paris. In addition a GCT turret has been mounted for trials purposes on a Leopard 1 MBT tank chassis and the French have suggested that a number of current MBT chassis could be easily adapted to take the turret. The prototypes were followed by ten pre-production vehicles in 1974. It is expected that it will enter production in 1976/77 and enter French Army service in 1977/78. It will replace the 105mm and 155mm self-propelled weapons at present used by the French Army. Each GCT battalion will have three batteries each of six guns, all of which will be controlled by the new Atila Artillery Automation System under development by Compagnie Internationale pour l'Information.

DESCRIPTION

The hull of the GCT is similar to that of the AMX-30 MBT apart from the following: ammunition racks in the hull have been removed, a 5kVA 28V generator has been installed and a ventilation system has been fitted to supply the turret with cold air. The result is that the chassis itself is about 2,000kg lighter than the basic AMX-30 chassis. The engine, transmission, suspension and so on are identical to the standard MBT so are not repeated here.

The turret is of all-welded steel construction and is mounted in the centre of the hull. The commander's cupola is on the right and the loader's hatch on the left. The latter is provided with a 7.62mm machine-gun with a traverse of 360°, elevation limits being −20° to +50°. A total of 2,000 rounds of 7.62mm ammunition are carried for the machine-gun. There is an access door in each side of the turret. The turret has full power traverse through 360° at a speed of 10°/second with manual controls for use in an emergency. The gun can be elevated from −5° to +66° and, like traverse, this is powered (hydraulic), elevation speed being 5°/second. The turret can be locked with the gun to the front or rear. Average rate of fire with automatic loading is eight rounds per minute, ie four rounds in the first 25 seconds and six rounds in 40/45 seconds. With manual loading two/three rounds per minute can be fired.

The fire control systems provided on the standard GCT are:
1. Gimbal suspension providing for the attachment of the goniometer in the turret and permitting it to move freely by 12° relative to the axis in all directions.
2. One hermetically sealed conventional optical goniometer. Traverse angles are read on standard engraved drums and elevation angles appear on an elevation scale.
3. One azimuth plate that can be manually adjusted, provided with a spirit level to set the goniometer vertically.
4. Direct sight for anti-tank use.

The following can be provided if required:

1. Replacing the manually adjusted traverse plate of the firing control by an automatically adjusted traverse plate.
2. Replacing the conventional optical goniometer by an electronic goniometer with a digital display.
3. Remote control display of the firing data.
4. Manually adjusted traversing plate of the firing control replaced by a contra-rotating device to maintain vertical position of the goniometer.

Ammunition is stowed in racks at the rear of the turret and loaded hydraulically, total ammunition capacity being: 42 projectiles and 42 slow bags arranged in seven racks of six identical shells and seven racks of six bags. In addition there are 40 quick charges in a fixed container in the turret basket. The turret is resupplied via the twin doors at the rear of the turret. Four men take 20 minutes or three men take 30 minutes to reload the turret with fresh ammunition and the turret can also be resupplied whilst the gun is firing.

The 155mm/40 calibre weapon has a vertical sliding wedge breech-block hermetically sealed by a metal obturator. Breech is opened and closed hydraulically and recoil system is of the constant type. The barrel is provided with a double baffle muzzle brake.

Ammunition. The charge range, organized around the 155mm hollow-base shell, is a six charge range, +1 charge for the 155 Model 56 shell, though the latter cannot be fired at such a high pressure as the 155mm hollow-base shell (m/v 300/810m/s).

Charge 1   Quick charge composed of an empty powder bag and a small quantity of black powder.
Charge 2   Quick charge composed of two bags of type 1.
Charges 3, 4, 5, 7   Slow charges.
Charge 6   Used for firing 155mm Model 56 shell.

This range of charges permits an overlap higher than 20% in plunging fire (elevation lower than 45°) for all charges and an overlap from 5% to 7% for all charges in vertical fire (elevation +45° to +66°).

The 155mm Ct TA 68 hollow-base shell weighs 43.2kg of which 8.355kg is RDX-Tolite explosive, m/v is 810m/s and maximum range is 23,500m. The weapon also fires smoke and illuminating projectiles, the American M107 (HE, Illuminating, Smoke) projectiles and the French type 155 Model 56/59 (HE and Smoke), and under development are Rocket Assisted Projectiles with a range of 30,000m. The French also state that ammunition for the British/German/Italian FH70/SP70 programme will be able to be used in the GCT. The GCT can be fitted with an NBC system and infra-red or image-intensification night driving equipment.

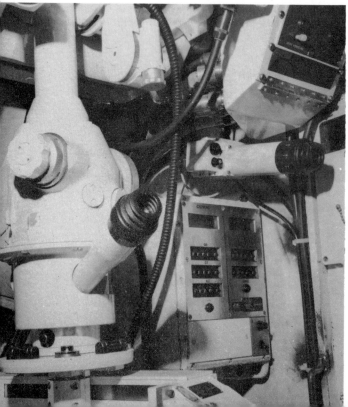

Top and previous page AMX 155mm GCT
Self-Propelled Gun.
Above AMX 155mm GCT Self-Propelled Gun from
the rear with reloading doors open.
Left The Sopelem M 363 Fire-Control Unit fitted in a
AMX 155mm CGT Self-Propelled Gun.

FRANCE

155mm SELF-PROPELLED HOWITZER Mk. F3
MANUFACTURER – Creusot-Loire, Chalon-sur-Saone
STATUS – In service with Abu Dhabi, Argentina (they may have been assembled in Argentina), Chile, Ecuador, France, Kuwait, Venezuela. In production.

BASIC DATA

CREW:	1 + 1 (commander and driver). The other 8 crew members are in AMX-VCA which also carries ammunition	RANGE:	300km
		FUEL CAPACITY:	450 litres
		FORDING:	.65m
		GRADIENT:	50%
		VERTICAL OBSTACLE:	.6m (forwards) .4m (reverse)
WEIGHT LOADED:	17,400kg	TRENCH:	1.5m
LENGTH:	6.22m (travelling) 4.88m (front of drive sprocket to rear of fifth road wheel)	ENGINE:	SOFAM Model 8 GXb, 8-cylinder, water-cooled petrol engine developing 250HP at 3,200rpm, 8.25 litres
WIDTH:	2.72m		
HEIGHT:	2.1m (travelling)		
GROUND CLEARANCE:	.47m	ARMAMENT:	1 × 155mm howitzer, 33-calibre barrel
TRACK:	2.159m		
TRACK WIDTH:	350mm	ARMOUR	
LENGTH OF TRACK ON GROUND:	2.997m	glacis:	15mm at 55°
		hull sides:	20mm
GROUND PRESSURE:	.8kg/cm²	hull floor front:	20mm
MAXIMUM ROAD SPEED:	65km/hr	hull floor rear:	10mm

DEVELOPMENT

The 155mm Self-Propelled Howitzer Mk. F3 (Obusier de 155mm sur Affût Automoteur) was developed in the early 1960s. It consists of a modified AMX-13 chassis with a 155mm howitzer mounted on the rear. The howitzer was designed and built by ATS (Atelier de Construction de Tarbes), whilst the chassis was designed and built by ARE (Atelier de Construction de Roanne). The mounting and trials were carried out by the EFAB (Établissements d'Études et de Fabrication d'Armament de Bourges). By the middle 1960s the Roanne tank plant was very much involved in the AMX-30 programme so the vehicle is now built and marketed by Creusot-Loire. The weapon will be replaced from the late 1970s by the 155mm SPG GCT which is based on the AMX-30 chassis.

DESCRIPTION

The hull is of all-welded construction with the driver seated at the front of the chassis on the left side. He is provided with three periscopes for observation when closed down and a single-piece hatch cover. The commander is seated behind the driver and has a cupola with split hatch covers.

The suspension is of the torsion-bar type and consists of five road wheels with the last road wheel acting as the idler, the drive sprocket is at the front and there are three track return rollers. Shock absorbers are provided on the first and fifth road wheels. There are two spades at the rear of the hull, one on each side, and these are released manually and the vehicle reversed so that they are pushed into the ground. The gearbox has 5F and 1R gears with steering through a Cleveland type differential. Infra-red driving lights are provided.

When in the travelling position the gun barrel is locked 8° to the right of the vehicle's centre line. It is elevated and traversed manually. Elevation limits are 0° to +67°, traverse being 20° left and 30° right (elevation 0° to +50°) and 16° left and 30° right (elevation +50° to +67°).

The weapon can fire the following types of ammunition:
155mm High Explosive Projectile Mk. 56 with a range of 18,000m, projectile weight 43.75kg.
155mm High Explosive Projectile M107 (USA) with a range of 18,000m.
French 155mm TA 64 Hollow-Base projectile with a range of 21,500m.
American T-387 projectile with a range of 18,000m. These include smoke and illuminating.

Average rate of fire is one round per minute, or three rounds per minute for a short period. For details of the tracked support vehicle refer to the entry on the AMX-VCI.

VARIANTS

There are no variants in service.

Left The 155mm Self-Propelled Howitzer Mk.F3 with weapon at high elevation.
Below The 155 Self-Propelled Howitzer Mk.F3 travelling across country.
Bottom The 155mm Self-Propelled Howitzer Mk.F3 in the firing position. Note that the spades have been positioned.

FRANCE

105mm SELF-PROPELLED HOWITZER
MANUFACTURER – French State Arsenals
STATUS – In service with France, Israel, Morocco and the Netherlands. Israel has very probably phased out this weapon as she has introduced large numbers of 155mm Self-Propelled Howitzers (M-109, M-109A1 and L-33s). The Netherlands uses the model with the 30 calibre barrel, the other countries use the 23 calibre barrel. The only model to enter production is the Model A which has no turret. Production has now been completed. If a foreign country did wish to purchase this weapon then Creusot-Loire would build the vehicle.

BASIC DATA	Fixed Model A	Turret Model B		Fixed Model A	Turret Model B
CREW:	5	5	VERTICAL OBSTACLE:	.65m (forwards)	.65m (forwards)
	(commander, driver, gun			.45m (reverse)	.45m (reverse)
	layer and two loaders)		TRENCH:	1.9m	1.9m
WEIGHT LOADED:	16,500kg	17,000kg	ENGINE:	SOFAM 8 GXb, 8-cylinder,	
LENGTH:	6.4m	5.9m		water-cooled petrol engine	
WIDTH:	2.65m	2.5m		developing 250HP at 3,200rpm.	
HEIGHT:	2.7m (with	2.7m (with		Engine is now built by	
	cupola)	cupola)		Saviem	
	—	2.3m (without	ARMAMENT:	1 × 105mm	1 × 105mm
		cupola)		howitzer	howitzer
GROUND CLEARANCE:	.32m (front)	.45m (front)		1 or 2 × 7.5mm or	1 or 2 × 7.5mm or
	.275m (rear)	.34m (rear)		7.62mm MGs	7.62mm MGs
TRACK WIDTH:	350mm	350mm	AMMUNITION:	56 rounds of	80 rounds of
GROUND PRESSURE:	.8kg/cm²	.82kg/cm²		105mm	105mm
POWER-TO-WEIGHT			ARMOUR		
RATIO:	15.15HP/ton	14.7HP/ton	glacis plate:	15mm at 55°	15mm at 55°
MAXIMUM ROAD SPEED:	60km/hr	60km/hr	hull sides:	20mm	20mm
RANGE:	350km	300km	hull floor front:	20mm	20mm
FUEL CAPACITY:	415 litres	450 litres	hull floor rear:	10mm	10mm
FUEL CONSUMPTION:	130 litres per	150 litres per	superstructure front and		
	100km (road)	100km (road)	sides:	20mm	20mm
FORDING:	.8m	.6m	superstructure rear:	15mm	15mm
GRADIENT:	60%	60%	turret sides and rear:	12mm	12mm

DEVELOPMENT/DESCRIPTION

Both of these vehicles basically consist of a modified AMX-13 Light Tank chassis with a 105mm howitzer mounted at the rear of the hull. The driver is seated at the left front of the vehicle with the transmission to his front and the engine to his right. The driver is provided with three periscopes and a single-piece hatch cover that swings to the left. The transmission has 5F and 1R gears and its steering gear is of the Cleveland differential type. The suspension is of the torsion-bar type and consists of five road wheels, drive sprocket at the front, idler at the rear and three track support rollers. The first and fifth road wheels are provided with hydraulic shock absorbers.

Model A (Fixed)

This is known either as the Self-Propelled Howitzer Mk.61 or, to give it its full title, Obusier de 105 Model 1950 sur Affût Automoteur. The first prototype was built in 1950 with production vehicles being delivered to the French Army in 1952. It is armed with the 105mm M1950 howitzer which was also developed as a towed weapon. The howitzer has an elevation of +70° and a depression of −4° 30′, total traverse is 20° left and 20° right, elevation and traverse is by hand. The gun has a maximum range of 15km, m/v being from 220/670m/s. There are two types of barrel, one of 23 and the other of 30 calibre, and the barrel is provided with a double baffle muzzle brake. Of the 56 rounds of ammunition carried, six are for anti-tank use. A telescope with a magnification of ×6 is provided for anti-tank use with a ×4 sight for normal artillery work. A 7.5mm AA 52 or 7.62mm AA 52 machine-gun is carried inside the vehicle and a similar machine-gun is mounted on the commander's hatch which is on the right side of the fighting compartment at the front. The fighting compartment has hatches in the roof and doors in the rear.

This weapon will be replaced by the new 155mm GCT SPG which is based on the AMX-30 MBT chassis.

Model B (Turret)

This has not entered service. The Swiss Army purchased four for trials purposes but as they have also developed a 155mm SPG called the Panzer-Kanone 68, it is very unlikely that they will order the French 105mm SPG.

The turret can be traversed through 360° and the howitzer can be elevated from −7° to +70°. A total of 80 rounds of ammunition are carried, of which six are for anti-tank use. An anti-tank sight with a magnification of ×8 is provided whilst the standard artillery sight has a magnification of ×4.

It will fire an HE projectile weighing 16kg to a maximum range of 15,000m, m/v being 220/670m/s.

The commander's cupola is on the right side of the roof and can be fitted with a 7.5mm AA 54 or 7.62mm AA 52 machine-gun, and an additional machine-gun can be carried inside. There is another hatch on the left side of the turret that opens to the rear. There are twin doors in the rear of the turret. The commander's cupola could be replaced by the same cupola as that fitted to the AMX VCI armoured personnel carrier, giving the commander full protection when using the machine-gun.

Above and previous page The AMX 105mm Self-Propelled Howitzer Mk.61 with the fixed type turret.
Left AMX 105mm Self-Propelled Gun Model B with turret. This particular vehicle belongs to the Swiss Army which purchased a few for trials purposes.

GERMANY/GREAT BRITAIN/ITALY

SP-70 – 155mm SELF-PROPELLED HOWITZER
STATUS – Development

GENERAL

In August 1968 Germany and Britain agreed to develop a new 155mm towed howitzer and later a self-propelled weapon, these being known as the FH-70 and SP-70. In 1970 the Italians joined the programme. By 1975 the final series of prototypes of the FH-70 were undergoing trials and it is expected that it will enter service in 1978/80.

The SP-70 will use the same engine, transmission, suspension and tracks as the Kampfpanzer 3/FMBT-80 which is still being developed, but with a hull of aluminium construction.

The German side of the programme is being handled by Rheinmetall with MaK (Kiel) as a main sub-contractor for the chassis. In 1975 it was reported that MaK had started to build five prototypes of the SP-70. In Great Britain the project is being handled by Vickers (Elswick) and a number of Royal Ordnance Factories. In Italy the project is being handled by Oto-Melara, who have already built a mock-up of SP-70 as well as adopting an M109 to fire FH-70 ammunition. The FH-70/SP-70 will fire the following types of separate loading ammunition: HE, Illuminating, Smoke, Direct Anti-Tank, Indirect Anti-Tank (ie dropping stick mines) and an Extended Range HE round. The standard HE round will have a range of 24,000m whilst the extended range round will have a range of 30,000 plus.

The mock-up of the SP-70 which was shown several years ago had the turret towards the front and the engine and transmission at the rear. The suspension consisted of seven road wheels with the drive sprocket at the rear and the idler at the front, and three track return rollers were provided. The 155mm gun was provided with a double baffle muzzle brake and a fume extractor. The turret had a traverse of 360°, elevation limits are not known but the towed FH-70 has an elevation of +70° and a depression of −5½°. Four smoke dischargers are mounted on each side of the turret.

GREAT BRITAIN

ABBOT – 105mm SELF-PROPELLED GUN
FALCON – SELF-PROPELLED ANTI-AIRCRAFT GUN SYSTEM
MANUFACTURER – Vickers Limited, Elswick, Newcastle-upon-Tyne
STATUS – Abbot is in service with the British Army. Value Engineered Abbot is in service with the British Army (4) and the Indian Army. Production of the Abbot has been completed but can be placed back in production if required.
The Falcon has completed its trials and is available for production.

BASIC DATA	ABBOT	V/E ABBOT	FALCON
CREW:	4	4	3
WEIGHT LOADED:	16,556kg	15,090kg	15,850kg
WEIGHT EMPTY:	14,878kg	14,200kg	14,300kg
LENGTH o/a:	5.84m	5.714m	5.333m
LENGTH HULL:	5.709m	5.333m	5.333m
WIDTH:	2.641m	2.641m	2.641m
HEIGHT (w/o A/A MG):	2.489m	2.489m	2.514m
GROUND CLEARANCE:	.406m	.406m	.406m
TRACK:	2.184m	2.184m	2.184m
TRACK WIDTH:	343mm	343mm	343mm
LENGTH OF TRACK ON GROUND:	2.844m	2.844m	2.844m
GROUND PRESSURE:	.89kg/cm²	.81kg/cm²	.81kg/cm²
MAXIMUM ROAD SPEED:	48km/hr	48km/hr	48km/hr
MAXIMUM WATER SPEED:	5km/hr	—	—
RANGE:	390km	390km	390km
FUEL CAPACITY:	386 litres	386 litres	386 litres
FORDING:	1.219m	1.117m	1.117m

GRADIENT:	60%	60%	60%
VERTICAL OBSTACLE:	.609m	.609m	.609m
TRENCH:	2.057m	2.057m	2.057m
ENGINE:	See text	See text	See text
ARMAMENT:	1 × 105mm 1 × 7.62mm A/A MG 2 × 3 smoke dischargers	1 × 105mm	2 × 30mm
ARMOUR			
hull sides and nose:	12mm	12mm	12mm
hull top and rear:	10mm	10mm	10mm
hull floor:	6mm	6mm	6mm
turret front, sides and rear:	10mm	10mm	10mm
turret top:	12mm	12mm	12mm

DEVELOPMENT/DESCRIPTION/VARIANTS
ABBOT SELF-PROPELLED GUN
The Abbot (105mm Artillery Self-Propelled) uses many components of the FV432 series of armoured personnel carriers. The first of twelve prototypes was completed in 1961. Six of these were powered by a Rolls-Royce B.81 petrol engine and six by the Rolls-Royce K.60 multi-fuel engine. The Abbot was in production from 1964 to 1967. It is deployed by the Royal Artillery in both the United Kingdom and Germany, each Abbot regiment consisting of three batteries, each with six Abbots. The Abbot is used in conjunction with the Field Artillery Computer Equipment (FACE) and is supported in action by the Alvis Stalwart load carrier which carries additional ammunition.

The hull of the Abbot is of all-welded construction. The differential is at the very front of the hull and the driver is seated towards the front on the right side. He is provided with a single wide-angle periscope and twin hatch covers that open left and right.

The Rolls-Royce K.60 Mk. 4G in-line, 6-cylinder, vertically-opposed, multi-fuel engine develops 240BPH at 2,750rpm and is mounted together with the gearbox as a complete unit and can be removed from the hull as such.

The turret is at the rear of the hull with the commander and gunner on the right and the loader on the left. The commander has a single-piece hatch cover and a total of three periscopes. The loader has a single-piece hatch cover that opens to the rear. There is a small door in the turret rear and a larger door in the rear of the hull for ammunition resupply. The suspension consists of five road wheels with the drive sprocket at the front and the idler at the rear, two track support rollers, and shock absorbers on the first and fifth road wheels stations. The tracks are of manganese steel with rubber pads. Drive from the engine is taken to a Rolls-Royce transfer box to an Allison (GMC) TX.200 6-speed (6F and 1R) automatic gear box, built in England under licence by Rolls-Royce.

The electrical system is 24V with one set of batteries with a capacity of 100Amp/hr in the hull for vehicle requirements and a similar set in the turret for the radio. Charging is carried out by means of two air-cooled alternators driven by the engine.

The turret has powered traverse through a full 360° and elevation is manual from −5° to +70°. The gun, which is made by the Royal Ordnance Factory at Nottingham, is provided with a double baffle muzzle brake, a fume extractor and a semi-automatic vertical sliding breech. The weapon is mounted in a ring type cradle with twin hydraulic buffers and a single hydro-pneumatic recuperator. An electrically power-operated rammer is provided and this is operated by the loader.

The gun is laid for azimuth using a periscope dial sight which protrudes through the turret roof and this is protected by a rotating cupola. A sight is also provided for direct fire, ie against tanks.

Ammunition is of the separate loading type and the following types are available:
High Explosive (projectile weight 15.1kg)
Smoke-Base Ejection (projectile weight 15.98kg)
Target Indicating
Illuminating
High Explosive Squash Head (projectile weight 10.49kg)
Squash Head Practice

There are eight charges in the cartridge system. These are fired from two separate cartridges: Supercharge cartridge containing supercharge only; normal cartridge containing charges 1-5. In addition to supercharge and charge 1-5, two sub-zone charges (A and B) are provided. These are fired from a normal cartridge case, emptied of its original charge bags.

The 105mm gun has a maximum range of 17,000m and a maximum rate of fire of twelve rounds per minute. A total of 40 rounds of ammunition are carried, of which six are HESH.

A 7.62mm Bren Light Machine-gun is mounted on the commander's cupola and a total of 1,200 rounds of ammunition are carried for this. A three-barrelled smoke discharger is mounted each side of the turret.

The Abbot is provided with a flotation screen which can be erected by the crew in about 15 minutes. It is then propelled in the water by its tracks. An NBC pack is provided and infra-red driving lights are fitted as standard. A fire-warning system is installed.

Vickers are also offering Abbot fitted with the General Motors diesel developing 216HP at 3,750rpm coupled to a semi-automatic gearbox.

VALUE-ENGINEERED ABBOT

The first prototype Value Engineered Abbot was completed in 1967 and a number of these were subsequently purchased by the Indian Army. The British Army has four of these in use in the Suffield Training Area in Canada. The Value Engineered Abbot differs from the standard Abbot in the following:

A flotation screen is not provided.

The Rolls-Royce K.60 Mk. 60G/1 runs on diesel fuel only and develops 213BHP at 3,750rpm.

The manganese steel tracks are not fitted with rubber pads.

Only one set of batteries with a capacity of 100Amp/hr is provided.

Charging is carried out by means of an air-cooled alternator driven from the engine.

Turret is traversed by a two-speed hand wheel.

Fire-warning equipment is not provided.

The British dial sight has been replaced by a German sight in an unarmoured hood.

Commander's cupola has a single periscope, twin hatch covers, and does not rotate.

The loader hatch has split hatch covers.

No light machine-gun or smoke dischargers are provided.

Infra-red driving lights are not provided.

NBC system is not installed.

Any of these could be fitted during or after production if required.

FALCON

The Falcon is a joint development between Vickers Limited and the British Manufacture and Research Company of Grantham. The first prototype was completed in 1970 and this has been subjected to extensive trials. It basically consists of a Value Engineered Abbot chassis with a new turret mounting twin Hispano-Suiza (now Oerlikon) HSS 831L 30mm guns. It is powered by a Rolls-Royce K.60 Mk. 60G/2 engine which develops 213BHP at 3,750rpm.

The turret is of all-welded construction and the commander and gunner are seated side by side in the turret rear, each having a single-piece hatch cover that opens to the rear. The crew compartment is sealed from the guns and ammunition.

The turret has power elevation and traverse and can be traversed through a full 360°, elevation is from −10° to +85°. Elevation tracking velocity is 40°/second maximum, traverse velocity (slew) is 80°/second, traverse velocity (tracking) is 45°/second.

The gunner has a periscope gunsight with a ×1 magnification and automatic lead angle display for anti-aircraft and ×6 magnification for ground targets. The commander has a similar sight but without the anti-aircraft display. He also has two periscopes for observation purposes.

The gunner tracks the target by operating a two-motion joystick which is energised when a foot pedal is depressed.

The guns are cocked and fired electrically and single shot and automatic fire from both or either gun can be selected. The weapons have an effective anti-aircraft range of 3,000m and a combined cyclic rate of fire of 1,300 rounds a minute. A total of 620 rounds of ammunition are carried and empty cases and belt links are ejected sideways through the elevation trunnion bearings. The weapons are stabilized which enables the weapons to be fired whilst the Falcon is moving.

The following types of ammunition are available:

High Explosive Incendiary (HEI)

High Explosive Incendiary-Tracer (HEI-T)

Armour Piercing Incendiary with hard metal core and tracer (APIC-T)

Armour Piercing Incendiary with self-destruct base fuse (APHEI)

Plus two practice rounds – HE-P and HET-P.

Two alternators provide all power requirements. Optional equipment includes flotation screen, infra-red driving lights, NBC pack, smoke-dischargers, multi-fuel engine and so on.

A laser rangefinder is being incorporated to feed continuously updated range information to the computer. At the present this has to be put in manually by the commander. It is anticipated that this will be tested in 1976.

Top Abbot 105mm Self-Propelled Gun with flotation screen erected.
Centre The Falcon anti-aircraft system with twin 30mm cannon.
Above and left Abbot 105mm Self-Propelled Gun with 105mm gun elevated.

ISRAEL

L-33 – SELF-PROPELLED GUN/HOWITZER
MANUFACTURER – Chassis from United States. Conversion carried out by Soltam Company of Israel
STATUS – In service only with the Israeli Army.

BASIC DATA

CREW:	8	GROUND PRESSURE:	.83kg/cm² (estimate)
WEIGHT LOADED:	41,500kg	MAXIMUM ROAD SPEED:	36.8km/hr
LENGTH:	8.55m (including	RANGE:	260km
	armament)	FUEL:	636 litres (estimate)
	6.4m (hull only,	FORDING:	.914m (estimate)
	estimate)	GRADIENT:	60%
WIDTH:	3.33m	VERTICAL OBSTACLE:	.6m
HEIGHT:	2.46m	TRENCH:	2.3m
GROUND CLEARANCE:	.43m (estimate)	ENGINE:	Cummins Diesel
TRACK:	2.108m	ARMAMENT:	1 × 155mm gun/howitzer
TRACK WIDTH:	584m		1 × 7.62mm MG
LENGTH OF TRACK		ARMOUR:	12mm-64mm (hull)
ON GROUND:	3.74m		

Note: The above estimated data have been taken from the basic M4A3E8 Tank. In some cases, eg the fuel capacity, the figure may be higher, since if the Israelis have installed a new engine it is more probable that they have also installed larger fuel tanks for extended desert operations.

Below The Israeli L-33 155mm Self-Propelled Gun/Howitzer.

DEVELOPMENT/DESCRIPTION/VARIANTS

The existence of the L-33 became known early in 1973 and the weapon was used in some numbers during the 1973 Middle East Campaign. It is essentially a Sherman M4A3E8 Tank chassis (with horizontal volute suspension), which has been fitted with a new all-welded hull and a new engine.

The driver is seated at the front of the vehicle on the left and has a bullet-proof window to his side and front, and also a single-piece hatch cover that opens to the rear. The commander's position is to the rear and above the driver's position. He also has a bullet-proof window to his front and side, as well as a single-piece hatch cover.

The machine-gun which can be used in both the ground and anti-aircraft roles, is mounted on the right of the vehicle at the front and access to this is via a twin hatch cover. There is also an observation window in the right side of the superstructure near this position. The crew enter and leave the L-33 by a single door in each side of the hull.

The crew are provided with a complete communications system as well as individual seat belts.

The 155mm (33 calibre) gun/howitzer is identical to that used in the towed M68 weapon, which is also made in Israel by Soltam. The weapon has an elevation of $+52°$ and a depression of $-3°$, traverse is 30° left and 30° right. It can fire a variety of ammunition including HE which has an m/v of 725m/s and weighs 43.7kg, maximum range being 21,500m. According to most reports the L-33 is provided with a pneumatic lifting/loading mechanism which allows it to achieve a high rate of fire. The gun has a semi-automatic breech-block, a muzzle brake, fume extractor and a travelling lock. Ammunition stowage has not been revealed but at least 30 rounds of separate loading ammunition are carried. Soltam have also built a 160mm self-propelled mortar and details of this will be found in the entry for the Sherman tank.

The Israeli L-33 155mm Self-Propelled Gun/Howitzer with some of its crew and ammunition displayed.

SOVIET UNION

M-1974 122mm SELF-PROPELLED HOWITZER (also known as the SP74)
M-1973 152mm SELF-PROPELLED HOWITZER (also known as the SP73)
MANUFACTURER – Soviet State Arsenals
STATUS – In service with the Soviet Army, the M-1974 is also in service with the Polish Army. In production.

GENERAL

Development of a new series of self-propelled guns commenced in the 1960s. The M-1974 was first seen in public during a parade held in Poland in 1974. In appearance the M-1974 is very similar to the M109 155mm SPH of the United States Army.

The driver is seated at the front of the hull on the left side with the engine to his right. The turret is at the rear of the hull and is provided with two hatches. The suspension consists of seven road wheels with the drive sprockets at the front and the idler at the rear, and the road wheels are similar to those of the PT-76 Amphibious Light Tank family. The 122mm howitzer is believed to be a modified version of the towed 122mm M-1955 (D-74), but with a fume extractor on the barrel, though it retains the double baffle muzzle brake. This fires an HE projectile weighing 25.5kg (m/v 900m/s) to a maximum range of 21,900m. An APHE round is also available: the projectile weighs 25kg and has an effective range of 1,200m. Maximum rate of fire is given as six/seven rounds per minute.

The M-1973 152mm Self-Propelled Howitzer is said to be based on the SA-4 Ganef surface-to-air missile system. This is believed to be armed with a modified version of the towed 155mm M-1955 (D-20) field howitzer. This fires an HE projectile weighing 43.6kg to a maximum range of 17,300m. An APHE projectile weighing 48.8kg is also available. Some reports have indicated that a Rocket Assisted Projectile has been developed for both the M-1974 and M-1975.

The new M-1974 122mm Self-Propelled Howitzer, which was first seen in Poland in 1974.

SOVIET UNION

ISU-122 and ISU-152 – SELF-PROPELLED ASSAULT GUNS
MANUFACTURER – Soviet State Arsenals
STATUS – ISU-122 is in service with Algeria, Bulgaria, China, Czechoslovakia, Vietnam, Poland, Romania
ISU-152 is in service with Algeria, China, Czechoslovakia, Egypt, Iraq, Poland and Syria.
Most Warsaw Pact countries have these vehicles in reserve, as does the Soviet Union.

BASIC DATA	ISU-122A	ISU-152		ISU-122A	ISU-152
CREW:	5	5	FUEL CAPACITY:	520 litres	520 litres
WEIGHT LOADED:	46,500kg	46,500kg	FUEL CONSUMPTION:	350 litres per	350 litres per
LENGTH:	10.06m (gun	9.05m (gun		100km	100km
	forward)	forward)	FORDING:	1.3m	1.3m
	6.77m (hull)	6.77m (hull)	GRADIENT:	60%	60%
WIDTH:	3.07m	3.07m	VERTICAL OBSTACLE:	1m	1m
HEIGHT:	2.47m (w/o	2.47m (w/o	TRENCH:	2.5m	2.5m
	A/A MG)	A/A MG)	ENGINE:	Both are powered by a Model	
GROUND CLEARANCE:	.46m	.46m		V-2, IS, V-12, water-cooled	
TRACK:	2.41m	2.41m		diesel developing 520HP at	
TRACK WIDTH:	650mm	650mm		2,100rpm	
LENGTH OF TRACK			ARMAMENT:	1 × 122mm	1 × 152mm
ON GROUND:	4.265m	4.265m		1 × 12.7mm	1 × 12.7mm
GROUND PRESSURE:	.84kg/cm²	.84kg/cm²		A/A MG	A/A MG
POWER-TO-WEIGHT			ARMOUR		
RATIO:	11.18HP/ton	11.18HP/ton	glacis:	110mm at 70°	110mm at 70°
MAXIMUM ROAD SPEED:	37km/hr	37km/hr	upper hull side:	90mm at 0°	90mm at 0°
RANGE:	150km	150km	mantlet:	90mm	90mm

Note: Additional fuel tanks can be fitted on both models and these increase its range to approx. 520km.

ISU-122

This entered production towards the end of 1943 and used components of the IS heavy tank. The gun is the M-1931/44 (A-19S), wartime designation being the M-1944, and was a development of the 122mm M-1931/37 (A-19) towed weapon. This model is recognizable as the barrel has no muzzle brake or bore evacuator. The breech was of the screw-type and hand-operated. The ST-18 direct sight was fitted. The gun has an elevation of +16° and a depression of −3°, total traverse was 14° and axis of bore was 1.8m. Elevation and traverse were manual. A 12.7mm DShK anti-aircraft machine-gun was fitted on the roof of the vehicle. A total of 30 rounds of separate loading 122mm ammunition were carried as well as 250 rounds of 12.7mm machine-gun ammunition. Average rate of fire was three rounds per minute. The following types of ammunition were available:
HE with the projectile weighing 25.5kg with an m/v of 781m/s.
APHE with the projectile weighing 25kg with an m/v of 781m/s. This would penetrate 160mm of armour at 900m. Maximum range of the gun was 13,400m at maximum elevation.

ISU-122A

This entered service in 1944. The ISU-122A is armed with the Model 1944 gun D-25S (wartime designation being M-1943), this being a modification of the 122mm tank gun M-1943 (D-25). This weapon has a similar elevation and traverse to the basic ISU-122, and fires the same ammunition as well as carrying the same quantities of ammunition. For anti-aircraft defence a 12.7mm DShK machine-gun was mounted on the roof. The YSh-17 sight is fitted for direct laying.

The gun has a semi-automatic vertical sliding wedge breech-block and this gives it a higher rate of fire than the earlier model.

The ISU-122A can be distinguished from the early ISU-122 as the ISU-122A has a barrel which is not only thinner but also has a double baffle muzzle brake and a different mantlet.

ISU-152

This is armed with the 152mm (actual calibre is 152.4m) M-1937/43 (ML-20S) (wartime designation being M-1944), which was developed from the 152mm gun/howitzer M-1937 (ML-20) and was also used in the earlier SU-152. This has manual elevation and traverse; elevation of +20° and a depression of −3°, total traverse is 10° and axis of bore is 1.85m. It has a short barrel with a multi-baffle muzzle brake and no bore evacuator. Recoil system is the same as that fitted to the ISU-122 (A-19S). It fires 152mm rounds of the separate loading type, rate of fire being two-three rounds per minute. The following types of ammunition are available:

HE with the projectile weighing 43.6kg, m/v being 655m/s.

APHE with the projectile weight 48.8kg, m/v being 600m/s, and this will penetrate 124mm of armour at 800m. An ST-10 direct sight is provided and the weapon has a maximum range of 9,000m. A 12.7mm DShK machine-gun is mounted on the roof. Total ammunition capacity is 20 rounds of 152mm and 250 rounds of 12.7mm.

ISU Armoured Recovery Vehicles

There are five different models of the ISU used in the recovery role, these being designated ISU-T Models A, B, C, D and E:

ISU-T Model A

This was the first model to enter service and is simply an ISU with armament removed and a winch installed. It is therefore limited to towing operations and recovering light vehicles.

ISU-T Model B

This is similar to the Model A but in addition has a jib crane and a stowage platform fitted over the hull rear enabling it to carry spare parts.

ISU-T Model C

This is similar to the above and also has a winch and a large spade mounted at the rear of the hull which enables it to recover heavier vehicles.

ISU-T Model D

This is similar to the Model C but in addition has two push bars on the front of the hull. It does not have a spade, but can be fitted with a schnorkel. Basic data on this model are:

Crew: 4 Weight: 45,500kg Length: 8.325m Width: 3.07m Height: 3.5m Ground clearance: .46m Range: 150km Fording: 1.3m Other data are similar to ISU.

ISU-T Model E

This is provided with an 'A' frame which is swung to the rear when not in use as it is pivoted at the front. This has a capacity of 5,700kg. It is provided with a spade at the rear but does not have a schnorkel.

Above right ISU Model E Armoured Recovery Vehicle.
Above left ISU-122 with D-25S 122mm gun.
Left ISU-152 Self-Propelled Assault Gun.

SOVIET UNION

SU-100–SELF-PROPELLED ASSAULT GUN
MANUFACTURER–Czechoslovakian and Soviet State Arsenals
STATUS–In service with Albania, Algeria, Bulgaria, Communist China, Cuba, Czechoslovakia, East Germany, Egypt, Iraq, Mongolia, Morocco, North Korea, North Yemen, Romania, Soviet Union, Syria, Yugoslavia. Production of the SU-100 is now complete.

BASIC DATA

CREW:	4 (commander, gunner, loader and driver)	TRENCH:	2.5m
WEIGHT LOADED:	31,600kg	ENGINE:	Early models are powered by a V-2-34M, V-12, water--cooled diesel developing 500HP at 1,800rpm. Later models are powered by a V-2-34II which develops 530HP at 2,100rpm
LENGTH:	9.45m (including main armament) 6.19m (hull only)		
WIDTH:	3.05m		
HEIGHT:	2.245m		
GROUND CLEARANCE:	.4m		
TRACK:	2.45m	ARMAMENT:	1 × 100mm gun D-10S M-1944, elevation +17°, depression −2°, total traverse 16°, axis of bore 1.63m. Some models (late production) have an elevation of +20° and a depression of −3°. 34 rounds of 100mm ammunition are carried
TRACK WIDTH:	500mm		
LENGTH OF TRACK ON GROUND:	3.85m		
GROUND PRESSURE:	.83kg/cm²		
POWER-TO-WEIGHT RATIO:	15.8HP/ton		
MAXIMUM ROAD SPEED:	55km/hr		
RANGE:	300km		
FUEL CAPACITY:	560 litres (internal tanks only. A further four tanks can be fitted to the rear of the vehicle, two each side of the engine compartment)	ARMOUR	
		glacis plate:	45mm at 50°
		nose:	45mm at 60°
		side hull:	45mm at 0°
FUEL CONSUMPTION:	190 litres per 100km	side of superstructure:	45mm at 20°
FORDING:	1.3m	belly:	20mm
GRADIENT:	60%	mantlet:	75mm
VERTICAL OBSTACLE:	.73m		

DEVELOPMENT

The earlier SU-85 was developed in 1943 and entered production towards the end of the same year. The chassis was that of the T-34 tank and the 85mm gun was an adaptation of the M-1939 85mm anti-aircraft gun. As far as it is known there are now no SU-85s in service at all. The SU-122 also used the T-34 chassis, and this is no longer in service.

The SU-100 was a logical development of the earlier SU-85 and entered production in 1944. Production of the vehicle continued after the Second World War both in the Soviet Union and also in Czechoslovakia, where a production line was established after the war. The SU-100 was used both in the fire support role and in the anti-tank role.

DESCRIPTION

The hull of the SU-100 is of all-welded construction with the armament and fighting compartment at the front and the engine and transmission at the rear. The gearbox has 4F and 1R gears. The suspension is of the Christie type with five road wheels each side, the idler at the front and the drive sprocket at the rear.

The driver is seated to the left of the main armament and is provided with a large hatch cover that opens upwards (externally). The commander is provided with a cupola on the right side of the superstructure and projecting outside the superstructure. He has a one-piece hatch cover that opens forward. Around the roof of his cupola are direct viewing blocks and there is a periscope with a traverse of 360° in the forward part of the cupola roof.

In the roof of the fighting compartment there are also twin hatch covers to the rear and left of the main armament and a further hatch cover at the very rear of the fighting compartment. This also continued for a short distance below to the rear of the superstructure. Most post-war SU-100s have an additional stowage box on the right side of the superstructure, forward of the commander's cupola.

The 100mm gun D-10S is similar to that used on the early models of the T-54 MBT and is a development of a naval weapon; it is mounted to the right of the centreline. The recoil mechanism consists of a hydraulic buffer and a hydro-pneumatic recuperator. Its breech-block is of the semi-automatic sliding wedge type. The long barrel has no muzzle brake and no bore evacuator. The gun is hand traversed and elevated and its very low depression was often a severe handicap. It fires 100mm fixed rounds, maximum rate of fire being seven/eight rounds per minute. A TSh-19 or TSh-20 direct sight is fitted. The following types of ammunition are available, all being of the fixed type, ie complete rounds, ready to fire:

HE projectile weighs 15.7kg and has an m/v of 900m/s.

APHE projectile weighs 15.9kg and has an m/v of 1,000m/s. This will penetrate 185mm of armour at 1,000m.

HEAT projectile has an m/v of 900m/s and will penetrate 380mm of armour. The maximum range of the 100mm gun is 15,400m, the limitation being the amount of elevation that can be obtained.

The SU-100 has no NBC system and no infra-red driving or fighting equipment. In fact most models have only one headlamp for driving at night. It has no deep fording or amphibious capabilities.

VARIANTS
SU-85 and SU-100 Armoured Recovery Vehicles
These are designated SU-85-T and SU-100-T respectively. Both are simply SU-85s and SU-100s with their main armament removed and some also have winches fitted. Both of these are now rarely seen as they are rather limited in their capabilities. Some SU-100s were known to have been fitted with dozer blades on the front and their armament removed – this was a post-war modification.

SU-100 Command Vehicles
This is seldom seen now and is an SU-100 with armament removed and plated over. Internally radios and map tables were fitted. Additional aerials enable this model to be distinguished from the SU-85-T and SU-100-T ARVs.

Above SU-100 Self-Propelled Assault Gun.
Below SU-85-T Armoured Recovery Vehicle.

SOVIET UNION

SU-76–SELF-PROPELLED GUN
MANUFACTURER–Soviet State Arsenals at Uralmashzavod
STATUS–In service with Albania, Communist China, East Germany, North Korea, Vietnam, Yugoslavia. Production of the SU-76 was completed in 1945.

BASIC DATA

CREW:	4 (commander, gunner, loader, driver)		GAZ-203 engine which develops 80HP at
WEIGHT LOADED:	11,200kg		3,400rpm, giving the
LENGTH:	5m		vehicle a slightly
WIDTH:	2.74m		higher speed but a
HEIGHT:	2.1m		reduced range. This
GROUND CLEARANCE:	.3m		model is designated
TRACK:	2.4m		SU-76M
TRACK WIDTH:	300mm	ARMAMENT:	1 × 76.2mm gun
LENGTH OF TRACK			M1942/43 with an
ON GROUND:	3.11m		elevation of +25°
GROUND PRESSURE	.57kg/cm²		and a depression
POWER-TO-WEIGHT			of −5°, traverse is
RATIO:	12.5HP/ton		20° left and 12° right,
MAXIMUM ROAD SPEED:	45km/hr		axis of bore is 1.72m.
RANGE:	360km		1 × 7.62mm Degtyarev
FUEL CAPACITY:	400 litres		MG for A/A use.
FUEL CONSUMPTION:	110 litres per 100km		60 rounds of 76mm
FORDING:	.9m		ammunition are carried.
GRADIENT:	47%	ARMOUR	
VERTICAL OBSTACLE:	.65m	glacis plate:	25mm at 30°
TRENCH:	2m	nose:	35mm at 60°
ENGINES:	2 × GAZ-202, 6-cylinder	front superstructure:	25mm at 27°
	in-line water-cooled	lower hull sides:	16mm at 0°
	petrol engines	superstructure sides:	12mm at 17°
	developing 70HP	superstructure rear:	15mm at 0°
	each at 3,600rpm.	floor:	10mm
	Late SU-76 have the	mantlet:	14mm

DEVELOPMENT

The SU-76 (Samokhodnaya Ustanovka) entered production late in 1942 and is based on the T-70 Light Tank chassis of the period. It has been fitted with a modified version of the standard towed 76mm divisional gun M-1942 (ZIS-3). It was first employed as a tank destroyer but was soon relegated to the infantry support role as it had insufficient armour and its gun lacked the penetration against the newer German tanks that were entering service in 1943/44. Today it is only found in second-line units and workers' militias.

DESCRIPTION

The SU-76 has a hull of all-welded construction which is both wider and longer than that of the T-70, and also has an additional road wheel each side. The differential, gearbox (4F and 1R gears), engines (mounted in tandem) and radiators are all mounted on the right side of the hull. On the left side of the hull are the batteries, fuel and ammunition. The driver is seated in the centre of the glacis plate and is provided with a single-piece hatch cover and a periscope. Components taken from the T-70 include the engines, transmission, suspension, track, road wheels and a number of other hull fittings.

The suspension is of the torsion-bar type and consists of six road wheels, drive sprocket at the front and idler at the rear, and a total of three track support rollers.

The fighting compartment is at the rear of the vehicle and has no overhead protection. Entry is via a door in the rear of the hull. The rear of the fighting compartment is only armoured for half its height. A tubular framework is provided over the fighting compartment so that a tarpaulin can be fitted in bad weather, and in addition the frame is used to mount a 7.62mm anti-aircraft machine-gun when required.

The 76mm gun has a double baffle muzzle brake and is mounted to the left of the centreline. Elevation and traverse is by hand. The recoil system consists of a hydraulic buffer and a hydro-pneumatic recuperator, and the breech-block is of the semi-automatic vertical sliding type. The gun fires the following types of fixed ammunition, as also used in the PT-76 Light Amphibious Tank:

HE projectile weighing 6.2kg with an m/v of 680m/s.
APHE projectile weighing 6.5kg with an m/v of 655m/s which will penetrate 61mm of armour at 1,000m.
HVAP projectile weighing 3.1kg with an m/v of 965m/s, which will penetrate 58mm of armour at 1,000m.
HEAT projectile weighing 4kg with an m/v of 325m/s, which will penetrate 120mm of armour at 1,000m.

Maximum range of the 76mm gun is 11,200m, this being achieved with maximum elevation. The gunner is to the left of the gun, the loader behind and the vehicle commander to the right.

Late production SU-76s had the side armour on the superstructure without the cut-off corners and also their rear hull armour was extended to the roof. There were at least two other models of the SU-76, one of which had the gun mounted on the vehicle centre line and also had a full armoured rear hull with a three-part door. The other also had the gun mounted on the vehicle centre line but also had overhead armour and a cupola on the left of the turret roof. The latter vehicle is thought to have existed as a prototype only. The SU-76 has no infra-red equipment, no NBC system and no amphibious capability.

VARIANTS

SU-37 Self-Propelled Anti-Aircraft Vehicle
This had a similar hull to the SU-76 and there were two models: the SU-37/1 had a single 37mm anti-aircraft gun and the SU-37/2 had twin 37mm anti-aircraft guns. Neither of these are in service having been phased out in 1946.

PSAF 76/137A
This is a modified SU-76 used for gunnery training by the East Germans.

SU-76 Armoured Workshop Vehicle
This is basically an SU-76 with the armament removed. The armour has been extended to the front of the vehicle just behind the driver's position, and overhead armour is provided. Inside the vehicle the ammunition racks have been removed and the following fitted: lathe, small forge, drill press, bench, welding kit, vice and a generator to power the equipment. Additional stowage boxes are provided on the outside of the vehicle. The vehicle is powered by a German EM 6, 6-cylinder in-line diesel developing 120HP. This gives it a top road speed of 45km per hour and a range of 360km. Loaded weight is 11,000kg.

Below SU-76 Self-Propelled Gun from the rear. This particular vehicle is on display with a cover over the fighting compartment.

Above SU-76 Self-Propelled Gun.

SWEDEN

155mm BANDKANON 1A – SELF-PROPELLED GUN
MANUFACTURER – AB Bofors, Bofors
STATUS – In service with the Swedish Army. Production complete.

BASIC DATA

CREW:	6 (commander, layer, radio operator, loader, A/A gunner and driver)	FUEL:	1,445 litres
		FORDING:	1m
		GRADIENT:	60%
WEIGHT LOADED:	53,000kg	VERTICAL OBSTACLE:	.95m
LENGTH:	11m (including armament)	TRENCH:	2m
		ENGINES:	Rolls-Royce K60 diesel
	6.55m (hull only)		developing 240HP at
WIDTH:	3.37m		3,750rpm and a Boeing
HEIGHT:	3.85m (with A/A MG)		Model 502/10MA gas
	3.35m (w/o A/A MG)		turbine developing
GROUND CLEARANCE:	.42m (centre of hull)		300SHP at 38,000rpm
TRACK:	2.59m	ARMAMENT:	1 × 155mm gun
TRACK WIDTH:	670mm		1 × 7.62mm A/A MG
LENGTH OF TRACK		ARMOUR	
ON GROUND:	4.57m	hull:	15mm
GROUND PRESSURE:	.85kg/cm²	turret:	20mm
MAXIMUM ROAD SPEED:	28km/hr	magazine:	15mm
RANGE:	230km		

DEVELOPMENT

The 155mm Bandkanon 1A (or VK-155) was designed and developed by Bofors in the 1950s. The first prototype was completed in 1960. This differed from production vehicles in that its suspension consisted of six road wheels, idler at the rear, drive sprocket at the front and three track return rollers. It also had a different shaped hull. This was followed by six pre-production vehicles.

In 1965 a production order worth 60 million kroner was awarded to Bofors for production models and the VK-155 was in production from 1966 to 1968. Volvo and Landsverk were also involved in the production of the vehicle.

The VK-155 uses many components of the S-tank which was also built by Bofors, including the same engines, transmission and suspension. The vehicle has a very high rate of fire but is also very heavy, has a rather low speed and was expensive to build.

DESCRIPTION

The hull is of all-welded construction with the engine and transmission at the front of the hull and the turret at the rear. The driver is seated in the hull just in front of the turret, slightly to the left. His compartment can be reached from the turret.

The turret is in two halves, left and right. The commander, layer and radio operator are in the left part whilst the loader and machine-gunner are in the right half which also houses the auxiliary engine. There is an access door in the front of each side of the turret and each side is also provided with a single-piece hatch cover in the roof.

The hydro-pneumatic suspension can be locked in position when the gun is fired. There are six road wheels with the last road wheel acting as the idler, the drive sprocket is at the front.

The two engines and transmission are mounted as a single unit and can be removed as a complete unit.

The 155mm L/50 gun has powered elevation for $+2°$ to $+38°$ and manual elevation for $-3°$ to $+40°$ at a speed of 5° a second. Traverse is 15° left and 15° right apart from when the gun is below 0° when the traverse is 15° left and 4° right. When in the travelling position the gun barrel is held in position by a lock.

The rifled gun is provided with a muzzle brake with very small holes in it. The semi-automatic, wedge-shaped breech-block opens downwards. The gun is fed from a fourteen round magazine which has two layers each of seven rounds. The first round is hand loaded and thereafter it is fully automatic. A full magazine can be fired in less than 60 seconds. A selector allows either single shots or full automatic.

When a new magazine is required the gun is elevated and the two covers on top of the magazine are opened vertically. The hoist on the vehicle slides along to the end of the slide bar where it picks up a new clip from a truck. It then places the clip of 14 rounds into the magazine and the doors are closed. It takes two minutes to load a fresh magazine.

There are two spring-operated ammunition feeds which operate alternately to take the complete rounds to the central feed platform under the magazine. They are then fed to the breech by a rammer.

The VK-155 fires an HE round to a maximum range of 25,600m. It has been recently reported that a rocket-assisted round is being developed for this weapon. The complete round weighs 85kg and there are three propelling charges. No. 1 has an m/v of 600m/s and No. 3 an m/v of 865m/s.

Infra-red driving lights are provided but it has no amphibious capability.

VARIANTS

There are no variants of this vehicle.

Above Prototype of the 155mm Bandkanon 1A.
Left Production model of the 155mm Bandkanon 1A.

UNITED STATES

M109 – SELF-PROPELLED HOWITZER
MANUFACTURER – Allison Division of General Motors Corporation at Cleveland Tank-Automotive Plant
STATUS – In service with Austria, Belgium, Canada, Denmark, Germany, Great Britain (early in 1975 two M109A1s were being tested), Iran, Israel (including M109A1s), Italy (armament built in Italy by Oto Melara), Libya (from Italy), Netherlands, Norway, Spain (and M109A1s), Switzerland, United States (Army and Marine Corps). Still in production.

BASIC DATA

CREW:	6 (commander, gunner, 3 ammunition men, driver)	MAXIMUM WATER SPEED:	6.43km/hr
		RANGE:	360/390km
WEIGHT LOADED:	23,786 kg	FUEL CAPACITY:	511 litres
WEIGHT EMPTY:	19,730kg	FORDING:	1.828m
LENGTH:	6.612m (including gun)		Amphibious with kit
	6.256mm (w/o armament)	GRADIENT:	60%
WIDTH:	3.295m	VERTICAL OBSTACLE:	.533m
	3.149m (with fenders removed)	TRENCH:	1.828m
HEIGHT:	3.289m (with A/A MG)	ENGINE:	Model 8V71T Detroit Diesel (General Motors Corporation), turbo-charged, 2-stroke, liquid-cooled, 8-cylinder developing 405BHP at 2,300rpm
	3.06m (w/o A/A MG)		
GROUND CLEARANCE:	.467m		
TRACK:	2.768m		
TRACK WIDTH:	381mm		
LENGTH OF TRACK ON GROUND:	3.962m	ARMAMENT:	1 × 155mm M126 Howitzer in Mount M127
GROUND PRESSURE:	.766kg/cm^2		
MAXIMUM ROAD SPEED:	56km/hr		1 × .50 (12.7mm) M2 HB A/A MG

DEVELOPMENT

In 1952 the development of a new 156mm Howitzer (SP) designated T196 started. This was to have the same chassis as the 110mm T195 (SP) Howitzer and the latter ended up as the 105mm M108. In 1956 it was decided to mount a 155mm weapon in place of the 156mm weapon. The first prototype T196 was completed in March 1959 and this was powered by a petrol engine. Further work resulted in the T196E1 which was completed in mid-1960 with a diesel engine. The T196E1 was cleared for limited production in 1961 and the first production contract was awarded to the Cadillac Motor Car Division of General Motors Corporation in October 1961, production being undertaken at the Cleveland Tank Automotive Plant. The first production M109 was completed in November 1962 and it was not until July 1963 that the T196E1 was made 'Standard A' when it became the M109. The second year's production was also awarded to General Motors Corporation whilst the third year's production went to Chrysler at Detroit. Production is now at General Motors Corporation again at Cleveland Tank Automotive Plant and total production has now reached over 2,500 vehicles.

The M109 replaced the 155mm M44 SPH. The full designation of the M109 is Howitzer Medium Self-Propelled M109. It is deployed in the United States Army in batteries of six, each battalion having three batteries. Each armoured and mechanized division has three battalions of M109s.

DESCRIPTION

The hull, turret, suspension and mechanical components of the M109 are identical to those of the M108 (105mm) SPH.

The hull and turret of the M109 are of all-welded aluminium construction. The driver is seated at the front of the vehicle on the left side and is provided with a one-piece hatch cover that is pivoted on the left, and a total of three M45 periscopes for use when driving closed down. The periscopes can be covered by small metal flaps to prevent damage.

The XTG-411-2A transmission is at the front of the hull. The engine and radiators are to the right of the driver and together can be removed as one complete unit. The commander's cupola is on the right side of the turret and can be traversed through 360°. He is provided with a single M27 periscope and a one-piece hatch cover that opens to the rear. There is also a rectangular hatch cover to the left of the commander's cupola which opens to the right.

In each side of the turret is a hatch and there are twin doors in the turret rear. There is a single hatch in the rear of the hull which opens to the right and is used to resupply the vehicle with ammunition. There is a spade each side of the rear of the hull though these are not always used. When required they are dropped manually and the vehicle is reversed on to them.

The turret has full traverse through 360°. The 155mm howitzer has an elevation of + 75° and a depression of − 3°. The breech-block is of the semi-automatic screw type and a hydro-pneumatic recoil system is provided. The barrel is provided with a large muzzle brake. Ammunition is of the separate loading type and average rate of fire is three rounds per minute. The following types of ammunition are available for the M109:

Type	Muzzle Velocity	Maximum Range	Weight
M107 HE	561m/s	14,700m	43.88kg
M116 Smoke BE	561m/s	14,700m	39.2kg
M118 Illuminating	536m/s	11,595m	46.74kg

Other rounds include dummy, tactical nuclear, canister, gas and various types of smoke.

A .50 (12.7mm) machine-gun is mounted in front of the commander's cupola for anti-aircraft use. A total of 28 rounds of 155mm and 500 rounds of .50 ammunition are carried.

The suspension is of the torsion-bar type and consists of seven road wheels with the drive sprocket at the front and the idler at the rear. There are no track support rollers. The top half of the tracks are covered by a rubber skirt which can be removed if required. Electrical system is 24V and 4 × 12V batteries are carried.

Infra-red driving lights can be provided as can an NBC pack. The amphibious kit consists of nine air bags attached to the front of the hull (1) and each side of the hull (4 + 4) and inflated from the vehicle. When in the water the vehicle is propelled by its tracks. These flotation bags are not carried as a part of normal equipment.

Above M109 of 176 Abu Klea Medium Battery, Royal Artillery (39 Medium Regiment) of the British Army.

VARIANTS
M109A1
Development of the M109A1 (M109E1) started in 1967. It is basically an M109 with a new cannon designated M185. This has a total length of 6.045m and fires a round with a bigger charge. The barrel is provided with a fume extractor. It has a maximum range of 18,000m against 14,700m of the standard M109. In 1972 the United States Army started to bring M109s up to M109A1 standard, this being carried out at base workshop level with the aid of kits. The M109A1 weighs 24,070kg and is 9.042m long. Other data and performance are similar to the basic M109. The M109 was to have been replaced by the XM179 155mm SPH but development of this has been cancelled.

Driver Training M109
The Netherlands Army has a number of M109s with their turrets removed and replaced by a large greenhouse-type cabin. These are used for driver training.

XM138
This was a project only and was an M109 chassis with a 155mm weapon in an unarmoured turret.

M109A1 with CLGPs
The M109A1 is being tested with the new Cannon Launched Guided Projectiles at present being developed by Texas Instruments and Martin Marietta Aerospace. The latter company's CLGPs have been the most successful and have hit targets at 4km, 8km and 12km. The first round being developed is the XM712 anti-tank round. The basic idea is that a laser beam is directed at the target by a director mounted on the ground or in a helicopter and the CLGP homes on to the target.

German M109s
The German Army has a total of 587 weapons designated M109G. These have a German Rheinmetall horizontal sliding breech-block rather than the screw type fitted to the American weapons and German sights are fitted. It has been stated that these models have a range of 18,500m and it is assumed that the Germans have improved ammunition. German M109Gs are fitted with four smoke dischargers on each side of the turret front.

Italian M109s
Italy purchased a number of M109s from the United States minus their armament, which has been built in Italy by Oto Melara. It is assumed that the armament is identical to the American models. Oto Melara have fitted an M109 with a much longer barrel with a fume extractor, designed to fire the ammunition that has been developed for the FH-70. Using standard 155mm ammunition this has a range of 22,000m or 24,000m with FH-70 standard ammunition. An extended range projectile with a range of 30,000m is under development.

Swiss M109s
The M109s used by Switzerland are designated M109U. The Swiss Army call them the Panzerhaubitze 66 or Pz.Hb.66 for short. They have a semi-automatic loader of Swiss design and can fire six rounds a minute.

Left Rear view of an M109 with spades in travelling position.
Below M109A1 with spades lowered and gun elevated.
Bottom right M109 with turret removed and used as a driver training vehicle by the Royal Netherlands Army.
Bottom left M109G of the German Army. Note the German smoke dischargers on the side of the turret.

UNITED STATES

M108 – SELF-PROPELLED HOWITZER
MANUFACTURER – General Motors Corporation
STATUS – In service with Belgium, Brazil, Spain and United States. Production of the M108 has been completed.

BASIC DATA

CREW:	5 (commander, gunner, two ammunition members and driver). When used in static role another two ammunition members are used	GROUND:	3.962m
		GROUND PRESSURE:	.71kg/cm²
		MAXIMUM ROAD SPEED:	56km/hr
		MAXIMUM WATER SPEED:	6.43km/hr
		RANGE:	360/390km
		FUEL CAPACITY:	511 litres
WEIGHT LOADED:	22,452kg	FORDING:	1.828m
WEIGHT EMPTY:	18,436kg		Amphibious with kit
LENGTH:	6.114m (there is no gun overhang on the M108 when the gun in traversed forwards)	GRADIENT:	60%
		VERTICAL OBSTACLE:	.533m
		TRENCH:	1.828m
		ENGINE:	Model 8V71T Detroit Diesel (General Motors Corporation), turbo-charged, 2-stroke, liquid-cooled, 8-cylinder, developing 405 BHP at 2,300 rpm
WIDTH:	3.295m / 3.149m (with fenders removed)		
HEIGHT:	3.155m (including A/A MG) / 2.794m (reduced)		
GROUND CLEARANCE:	.451m	ARMAMENT:	1 × 105mm Howitzer M103 in Mount M139 / 1 × .50 (12.7mm) M2 HB A/A MG
TRACK:	2.768m		
TRACK WIDTH:	381mm		
LENGTH OF TRACK ON			

DEVELOPMENT

In April 1953 development of a 110mm self-propelled howitzer designated the T195 commenced. Later it was decided that the T195 would have a 105mm rather than a 110mm howitzer. The first mock-up was completed in March 1954. The prototypes of the T195 were powered by a Continental petrol engine and the suspension used components of the T113 armoured personnel carrier. Next came the T195E1, which had a diesel engine rather than a petrol engine. The T195/T195E1 differed in a number of points from production vehicles: different shaped turret, different glacis and hull front, twin doors in the rear of the fighting compartment, a muzzle brake on the 105mm howitzer and no idler. The seventh road wheel acted as the idler on the T195 but the T195E1 had the idler. In December 1961 the T195E1 was cleared for limited production and designated the M108, or to give the vehicle its full designation: Howitzer, Light, Self-Propelled, 105mm, M108.

Production commenced in October 1962 and was completed in September 1963. Prime contractors were the Cadillac Motor Car Division of the General Motors Corporation. Final assembly was carried out at the Cleveland Tank Plant. The M108 was the replacement for the M52. The M108 was built in small numbers as the United States Army decided that the M109 with a 155mm howitzer was a better weapon and the latter remains in production today. The M108 and M109 are identical apart from armament, fire-control equipment and shell racks.

DESCRIPTION

The hull and turret of the M108 is of all-welded aluminium construction. The driver is seated at the front of the vehicle on the left side and is provided with a one-piece hatch cover that is pivoted on the left and a total of three periscopes for use when driving closed down. These periscopes can be covered with small metal flaps to prevent damage.

The transmission is at the front of the hull and the engine is to the right of the driver. The turret is at the rear of the chassis. The commander's cupola is on the right side of the turret and can be traversed through 360°. He is provided with a one-piece hatch cover that opens to the rear and a single periscope. There is also a rectangular hatch cover to the left of the commander's cupola and this opens to the right.

There is a hatch in each side of the turret and twin doors in the rear of the turret. There is also a large single hatch at the rear of the hull which opens to the right and is used to resupply ammunition to the gun. The M108 has no spades at the rear.

The turret has a traverse of 360°. Elevation and traverse is manual. Elevation of the 105mm howitzer is +74° and depression −4°. The breech-block is of the vertical sliding wedge type. The firing mechanism consists of a concentric hydrospring. The maximum range of the 105mm howitzer is 12,000m and a wide range of HE (m/v 472m/s), chemical, smoke ammunition can be fired. Sustained rate of fire is three rounds per minute. A .50 anti-aircraft machine-gun is mounted in front of the commander's cupola. A total of 87 rounds of 105mm and 500 rounds of .50 (12.7mm) ammunition are carried.

The suspension is of the torsion-bar type and consists of seven road wheels with the drive sprocket at the front and the idler at the rear. There are no track support rollers. The top half of the tracks are covered by a rubber skirt which can be removed if required. In fact most vehicles in service have their skirts removed.

Power is transmitted by the engine to a General Motors Corporation, Allison Division, cross-drive transmission with 4F and 2R ranges. Infra-red driving lights can be fitted as can an NBC pack. The amphibious kit consists of a total of nine air bags which are attached to the front of the hull (1) and each side of the hull (4 + 4), and are inflated from the vehicle. When in the water it is propelled by its tracks. These flotation bags are not carried on the vehicle as a part of normal equipment.

VARIANTS
There are no variants of the M108 in service.

Above The T195 which was the forerunner of the T195E1 which became the M108.
Left M108 of the Belgian Army.

UNITED STATES

M110–SELF-PROPELLED HOWITZER

MANUFACTURERS–FMC Corporation (San Jose, California), Pacific Car and Foundry Company (Renton, Washington), Bowen-McLaughlin-York (York, Pennsylvania)

STATUS–In service with Belgium, Germany, Great Britain, Greece, Iran, Israel, Netherlands, South Korea, United States (Army and Marines). Production complete, although facilities are available for additional production if required.

BASIC DATA

CREW:	5 on gun (commander, driver and 3 gun crew). Other 8 men in M548 carrying ammunition	GROUND PRESSURE:	.76kg/cm^2
		MAXIMUM ROAD SPEED:	56km/hr
		RANGE:	725km
		FUEL CAPACITY;	1,137 litres
WEIGHT LOADED:	26,534kg	FORDING:	1.066m
WEIGHT EMPTY:	24,312kg	GRADIENT:	60%
LENGTH:	7.467m (gun forward, spade up)	VERTICAL OBSTACLE:	1.016m
		TRENCH:	2.362m
	5.72m (w/o gun or spade)	ENGINE:	Model 8V71T Detroit Diesel (General Motors Corporation), turbo-charged, 2-stroke, liquid-cooled, 8-cylinder developing 405HP at 2,300rpm
WIDTH:	3.149m		
HEIGHT:	2.93m (to top of barrel, travelling)		
	2.809m (top of mount)		
	1.475m (top of hull)		
GROUND CLEARANCE:	.44m	ARMAMENT:	× 8″ (203mm) M2A1E1 Howitzer in Mount M158
TRACK:	2.692m		
TRACK WIDTH:	457mm		
LENGTH OF TRACK ON GROUND:	3.936m		

DEVELOPMENT

In 1956 requirements were drawn up for a new family of airportable self-propelled artillery weapons. In September 1956 the Pacific Car and Foundry Company was awarded a contract to build three 8″ (203mm) self-propelled howitzers designated T236, two 175mm self-propelled guns designated T235 (these became the current M107) and one 155mm self-propelled gun designated T245 (this only reached the prototype stage). The basic idea was to have the same chassis and gun mount and fit different barrels. In 1957 it was decided to build ARVs on the chassis and these were the T119, T120 (this became the current M578) and the T121. The first prototype T236 was completed in early 1958 and was powered by a petrol engine. In 1959, however, it was decided that future vehicles would have a diesel engine and the T236 when fitted with a diesel became the T236E1. After trials the T236E1 was adopted as the M110 in March 1961. The first production contract was awarded to Pacific Car and Foundry in June 1961 and the first production vehicles were completed in August 1962 with the first battalion being formed at Fort Sill early in 1963. Since then the M110 has been built by both FMC and Bowen-McLaughlin-York. The M108 (105mm) and M109 (155mm) SPHs have the same engine and transmission as the M110.

DESCRIPTION

The hull is of all-welded construction with the driver seated at the front of the vehicle on the left. He is provided with a single-piece hatch cover and a total of three M17 periscopes for driving whilst closed down. The Allison (General Motors Division) cross-drive transmission is mounted at the front of the hull. It is a Model XTG-411-2A and has 4F and 2R gears. The engine is mounted to the right of the driver.

The suspension is of the torsion-bar type and consists of five road wheels with the drive sprocket at the front. A hydraulic cylinder is attached to each road wheel arm which serves as a shock absorber, hydraulic bump-stop and suspension lockout when the gun is being fired. The electrical system is 24V and a generator with a capacity of 300 Amps is provided. There are a total of four type 6TN 100 Amp batteries.

The other four crew members are seated two each side of the gun. The M110 is supported in action by an FMC M548 tracked vehicle carrying the rest of the gun crew and ammunition. Some armies used 6 × 6 trucks for the supporting role whilst the British Army use the Alvis Stalwart.

The 8″ (203 mm) Howitzer has a traverse of 30° left and 30° right, elevation being +65° and depression −2°. Elevation and traverse are power assisted with manual control if required. The barrel has a hydro-pneumatic recoil system; minimum recoil is .635m and maximum recoil is 1.778m. The breech-block is of the interrupted screw, stepped-thread type. A hydraulically operated spade is provided at the rear of the hull and there is also a hydraulic device on the left of the gun for loading projectiles. Ammunition is of the separate loading type and two rounds are carried on the gun. Average rate of fire is one round per minute. The following types of ammunition are available: tactical nuclear, M106 High Explosive (this has an m/v of 594m/s and a maximum range of 16,800m, the projectile itself weighing 90.72 kg), and the M426 gas projectile (which has similar range but weighs 90.27kg). The M110 is provided with infra-red driving lights but has not been provided with an NBC system. It is not amphibious.

VARIANTS

M110E1

After the M110 had been in service for a few years a number of weaknesses showed up and new production vehicles had these corrected. The new vehicles were known as M110 (Mod), development designation being M110E1. The main improvements concerned the engine cooling, hydraulic system, electrical system, hydraulic spade and the loader/rammer.

M110E2

Development of the M110E2 commenced in December 1969 under the direction of Weapons Command at Rock Island, Illinois. The M110E2 will replace both the current M110 and the M107 (175mm) SP weapons. The M110E2 has a much longer barrel (2.438m longer than the standard barrel) and the complete vehicle weighs 28,168kg and has an overall length of 10.261m. Minimum recoil is .771m and maximum recoil is 1.828m. The weapon uses the same mount but the equilibrators have a 260psi (18.28kg/cm²) increase in pressure. The M110E2 will fire the following types of ammunition: High Explosive, Incendiary, Tactical Nuclear, Dual Purpose and Improved Conventional Munitions. No range has been released but it is known that it will have a greater range than the existing M110 but less than that of the current M107 whose range is 32,600m.

According to a recent American Government report, replacement of M110 and M107 barrels with the new barrel will start in FY 1976 and a total of 28 million dollars was requested for this, 26 million for the Army and 2 million for the Marine Corps. A further 12 million dollars will be required to complete the programme in FY 1977. It is known that a Rocket Assisted Projectile is being developed for the M110E2.

Above The M110 8" (203mm) Self-Propelled Howitzer.

Above The M110E2 8″ (203mm) Self-Propelled Howitzer which is scheduled to replace both the M107 (175mm) and M110 (203mm) weapons in the near future.
Below The M110 8″ (203mm) Self-Propelled Howitzer with spade down.

UNITED STATES

M107–SELF-PROPELLED GUN

MANUFACTURERS–FMC Corporation (San Jose, California), Pacific Car and Foundry Company (Renton, Washington), Bowen-McLaughlin-York (York, Pennsylvania)

STATUS–In service with Germany, Great Britain, Greece, Iran, Israel, Italy, Netherlands, Spain, United States (Army and Marines), Vietnam. No longer in production.

BASIC DATA

CREW:	5 on gun (commander, driver and 3 gun crew). Other 8 men are in M548 carrying ammunition	LENGTH OF TRACK ON GROUND:	3.936m
		GROUND PRESSURE:	.81kg/cm²
		MAXIMUM ROAD SPEED:	56km/hr
		RANGE:	725km
WEIGHT LOADED:	28,168kg	FUEL:	1,137 litres
WEIGHT EMPTY:	25,915kg	FORDING:	1.066m
LENGTH:	11.256m (gun forward, spade up) 5.72m (w/o gun or spade)	GRADIENT:	60%
		VERTICAL OBSTACLE:	1.016m
		TRENCH:	2.362m
		ENGINE:	Model 8V71T Detroit Diesel (General Motors Corporation), turbo-charged, 2-stroke, liquid-cooled, 8-cylinder, developing 405HP at 2,300rpm
WIDTH:	3.149m		
HEIGHT:	3.679m (to top of barrel, travelling) 2.809m (top of mount) 1.475m (top of hull)		
GROUND CLEARANCE:	.466m	ARMAMENT:	1 × 175mm gun M113 in Mount M158
TRACK:	2.692m		
TRACK WIDTH:	457mm		

DEVELOPMENT

The development of the M107 is identical to that of the M110 and the reader is referred to this entry. The only point is that the development designation of the M107 was T235 and later the T235E1.

Above M107 of the Royal Artillery Wing, Royal Armoured Corps Centre, travelling across rough country.

DESCRIPTION

The chassis of the M107 is identical to that of the M110 and the reader is referred to this entry for full details.

The M107 is armed with a 175mm gun M113 (T256E3) in Mount M158. This has an elevation of +65° and a depression of −2°, traverse is 30° left and 30° right. The weapon has a hydro-pneumatic recoil mechanism, minimum recoil being .711m and maximum recoil being 1.778m. The breech-block is of the welin-slip thread type. The rammer and loader assembly lift the projectile from the ground, and position it for ramming, and then ram it into the barrel. Maximum rate of fire is two rounds per minute. The M107 fires an HE round to a maximum range of 32,800 metres with an m/v of 914.4m/s. The M437A1 projectile has 13.608kg of TNT whilst the M437A2 HE projectile has a weight of 66.81kg and has a filling of 14.061kg of Comp. B. The ammunition is of the separate loading type.

VARIANTS

M107E1

After the M107 had been in service for several years a number of faults became apparent. These were corrected in later production vehicles which were known as M107 (Mod), although in service use they are still simply called M107s. The main improvements were the engine cooling, hydraulic system, electrical system, hydraulic spade and the loader/rammer. The M107/M110 chassis was also used as the basis for the now defunct MICV-70 project. Both the United States and British Armies have fitted the gun mount and crew area with nylon or canvas covers to provide the crew with protection from bad weather or NBC.

In the United States Army the M107 is to be replaced in the near future by the M110E2 8″ (203mm) Howitzer.

Above M107 of the 42nd Regiment, Royal Artillery, firing on the ranges near Fallingbostel, Germany.
Left M107 of the German Army.
Right M55 8″ Self-Propelled Howitzer travelling across country.

UNITED STATES

M55 – SELF-PROPELLED HOWITZER
MANUFACTURER – Pacific Car and Foundry Company, Renton, Washington
STATUS – In service with Belgium and Italy. Production complete.

BASIC DATA

CREW:	6	RANGE:	257km
WEIGHT LOADED:	44,452kg	FUEL:	1,438 litres
WEIGHT EMPTY:	40,823kg	FORDING:	1.219m
LENGTH:	7.908m (o/a with spade up)	GRADIENT:	60%
	7.14m (w/o spade)	VERTICAL OBSTACLE:	1.016m
WIDTH:	3.58m	TRENCH:	2.26m
HEIGHT:	3.469m (top of cupola)	ENGINE:	Continental Model AV-1790-5B, 5C or 5D, V-12 air-cooled petrol engine developing 704BHP at 2,800 rpm
	3.124m (top of turret)		
GROUND CLEARANCE:	.469m		
TRACK:	2.794m		
TRACK WIDTH:	584mm		
LENGTH OF TRACK ON GROUND:	4.673m	ARMAMENT:	1 × 8″ (203mm) Howitzer 1 × .50 (12.7mm) Browning M2 MG
GROUND PRESSURE:	.78kg/cm²		
MAXIMUM ROAD SPEED:	48km/hr		

DEVELOPMENT

The requirement for a 155mm Gun Motor Carriage was established in 1946. In April 1948 a contract was awarded to the Pacific Car and Foundry Company of Renton, Washington, to design a vehicle that would accept a 155mm gun or an 8″ howitzer. In April 1950 a contract for one prototype of a 155mm self-propelled gun designated T97 was awarded to the Pacific Car and Foundry. This was followed in April 1951 by a further contract for a prototype of an 8″ self-propelled gun designated the T108. The prototype T97 was handed over in April 1952 and the prototype of the T108 in July 1952.

Both weapons were placed in immediate production and production continued until April 1955. The current designation of the weapons are:

Gun Field Artillery Self-Propelled: 155mm, M53
Howitzer Heavy Self-Propelled: Full Tracked, 8″, M55

After a very short period numerous faults developed in the vehicles and a full modification programme was started at Pacific Car and Foundry in July 1955 and was completed in November 1956. At that time it was decided that all United States Army M53s (155mm) would be converted to M55 (8″) standard, though the Marine Corps held on to their M53s for a number of years. As far as it is known there are now no M53s in service anywhere at all. Both vehicles are identical apart from their main armament, and their ammunition racks were interchangeable. Many components of the M55 are used in the first M48 tanks, for example the engine, transmission and the A41-1 auxiliary engine.

DESCRIPTION

The hull of the M55 is of all-welded construction with the engine and transmission at the front of the vehicle and the turret at the rear. All the crew are in the turret, including the driver. The driver is seated on the left side of the turret and is provided with a door in the side of the turret. There is also a door on the right side of the turret. The commander's cupola is on the right side of the turret. The rear of the turret is provided with two large hatches, one opening upwards whilst the other folds down to provide a working platform for the gun crew.

The suspension is of the torsion-bar type and consists of seven road wheels, the drive-sprocket is at the front and there are three track return rollers. The last road wheels are mounted on eccentric shafts and maintain constant tension on the tracks when the vehicle is moving. Power is transmitted from the engine to a General Motors Corporation (Allison Division) Model CD-850-4, 4A or 4B cross-drive transmission with 2F and 1R ranges. When in action the spade is hydraulically lowered into position. Infra-red driving lights are provided.

The M55 is armed with an 8″ howitzer M47 (T89) in Mount M86 (T58) – the same mount was also used for the 155mm gun in the M53. The howitzer has an elevation of +65° and a depression of −5°, the turret has a traverse of 30° left and 30° right. Traverse and elevation are powered and there are two speeds:

Traverse 1–5 ratio 10° per second
          1–1 ratio 3° per second
Elevation 1–5 ratio 7.5° per second
          1–1 ratio 1.5° per second

The howitzer has a stepped thread, interrupted-screw, horizontal swing, breech-block and percussion inertia firing mechanism. Recoil system is of the hydrospring type. Ammunition is of the separate loading type and power ramming is provided. It can fire a High Explosive shell with a muzzle velocity of 594m/s to a maximum range of 16,916m. When in the travel position the barrel is held in place by a lock. A total of ten rounds of 8″ ammunition are carried. A .50 (12.7mm) machine-gun is mounted in front of the commander's cupola for anti-aircraft use. This has a traverse of 360° and a maximum elevation of +60°. A total of 900 rounds of .50 machine-gun ammunition are carried. The M55 does not have an NBC system and has no deep fording capabilities.

VARIANTS

There are no variants of the M55 in service although the M55E1 was developed to prototype stage.

Left M55 8″ Self-Propelled Howitzer in firing position.

UNITED STATES

M52 and M52A1 – SELF PROPELLED HOWITZER

STATUS – In service with Belgium (reserve), Greece, Japan, Jordan, United States (reserve). They are no longer in service with the German Army. Production of the M52 has now been completed.

BASIC DATA

CREW:	5	ENGINE:	The M52 is powered by
WEIGHT LOADED:	24,040kg		a Continental AOS-895-3,
WEIGHT EMPTY:	22,588kg		6-cylinder, air-cooled,
LENGTH:	5.8m		supercharged petrol
WIDTH:	3.149m		engine developing
HEIGHT WITH A/A MG:	3.316m		500BHP at 2,800rpm.
HEIGHT WITHOUT A/A MG:	3.056m		The M52A1 has a
GROUND CLEARANCE:	.491m		Continental AOSI-895-5
TRACK:	2.602m		engine but with fuel
TRACK WIDTH:	533mm		injection. A GMC
LENGTH OF TRACK ON	3.793m		Model A41-1 auxiliary
GROUND:			engine is also fitted.
GROUND PRESSURE:	.6kg/cm²	ARMOUR	
MAXIMUM ROAD SPEED:	56.3km/hr (M52)	hull front:	12.7mm
	67.59km/hr (M52A1)	hull top:	12.7mm
RANGE:	160km	hull floor:	12.7mm
FUEL CAPACITY:	678 litres	turret front:	12.7mm
FORDING:	1.219m	turret sides:	12.7mm
GRADIENT:	60%	turret rear:	12.7mm
VERTICAL OBSTACLE:	.914m	turret roof:	12.7mm
TRENCH:	1.828m	ARMAMENT:	1 × M49 105mm Howitzer
			1 × calibre .50 (12.7mm) M2 Browning A/A MG

DEVELOPMENT

In February 1948 development started of a 105mm Howitzer Motor Carriage called the T98. Two prototypes were built at Detroit Tank Arsenal and these used many components of the T37 and T41 (later known as the M41) light tanks at that time under development. The first pilot model was completed in 1950. The T41 became the T41E1 and as the T98 was to have the maximum number of interchangeable components, ie engine, transmission, tracks and suspension, the T98 became the T98E1.

The T98E1 was standardized as the M52 Howitzer Self-Propelled Full Tracked 105mm and a total of 684 M52s were built. The M52A1 is essentially an M52 with a fuel injection system fitted which gave the vehicle a higher road speed. The M52A1 was standardized in August 1956. The M52 has an almost identical chassis to that of the M44 and M44A1 155mm self-propelled howitzer. The M44 does however have wider tracks.

DESCRIPTION

The hull of the M52 is of all-welded construction with the engine and transmission at the front of the vehicle and the turret at the rear. The M52 is fitted with a General Motors Corporation (Allison Division) Model CD-500-3 cross-drive transmission which has high, low and reverse ranges.

The suspension is of the torsion-bar type and consists of six road wheels with the drive sprocket at the front, the sixth road wheel acting as the idler, and with a total of four track support rollers. Hydraulic shock absorbers are fitted on the first, second, fourth and fifth road wheel stations.

All the crew are seated in the turret at the rear of the vehicle. The driver is on the left side and is provided with a cupola and a door in the left side of the turret. The layer is on the right side of the weapon and has a small hatch in the right side of the turret. The commander's cupola is at the rear of the turret on the right side. The calibre .50 machine-gun is mounted in front of the commander's cupola and this has an elevation of +85° and a depression of −15°, total traverse being 360°. There are doors and hatches in the rear of the turret. No spade is fitted as this is not required on a weapon of this type.

The turret has a traverse of 60° left and right of the centreline. The 105mm M49(T96E1) howitzer is in mount M85(T67E1) and has an elevation of +65° and a depression of −10°. Elevation and traverse are manual.

The breech-block is of the vertical sliding type and it has a spring actuated, inertia percussion firing mechanism. The recoil mechanism is of the concentric hydrospring type.

A total of 102–105 rounds of 105mm ammunition are carried as well as 900 rounds of .50 machine-gun ammunition.

The following types of semi-fixed ammunition are carried: HE Type M1 (complete round weighs 19.05kg, m/v 472m/s and maximum range 11,270m), HEP and HEP-T Type M327, HEAT and HEAT-T Type M67 (complete round weighs 16.78kg and has an m/v of 381m/s, maximum range being 7,854m). In addition it can fire chemical, smoke and illuminating rounds. The HEP and HEAT rounds are of the fixed type. In the semi-fixed round the cartridge case is a loose fit over the projectile, enabling access to the propellent for adjustment.

The ammunition is stowed both in the turret and underneath the turret. In the turret is a revolver type drum on the left side which holds a total of 21 rounds of ready-use ammunition. The vehicle is not fitted with an NBC system although a large ventilating blower is mounted in the roof of the turret, and hot air-heaters are also provided. Infra-red driving lights are provided as are bilge pumps. A fixed fire extinguisher system is provided which can be operated internally or externally.

VARIANTS
There are no variants in service.

Above M52 105mm self-propelled howitzer.
Left Rear view of the turret with the doors open showing the revolver type drum on the left which held ready-use ammunition.

UNITED STATES

M44 – SELF-PROPELLED HOWITZER
MANUFACTURER – Massey Harris
STATUS – In service with Greece, Italy, Japan, Jordan, Spain, Turkey and the United States (Reserve). Production of the M44 has been completed.

BASIC DATA

CREW:	5	TRENCH:	1.828m
WEIGHT LOADED:	28,350kg (M44)	ENGINE:	M44 is powered by a
	29,030kg (M44A1)		Continental AOS-895-3,
WEIGHT EMPTY:	26,308kg (M44)		6-cylinder air-cooled
	26,980kg (M44A1)		petrol engine developing
LENGTH:	6.159m (spade up)		500HP at 2,800rpm. The
WIDTH:	3.238m		M44A1 has a
HEIGHT:	3.111m (tarpaulin in		Continental AOSI-895-5
	position)		fuel-injection engine. A
GROUND CLEARANCE:	.48m		Model 4-41-2 GMC
TRACK:	2.602m		Auxiliary engine
TRACK WIDTH:	635mm		is provided
LENGTH OF TRACK ON GROUND:	3.793m	ARMOUR:	
		hull front:	12.7mm
GROUND PRESSURE:	.66kg/cm^2 (M44)	hull top:	12.7mm
	.67kg/cm^2 (M44A1)	hull floor:	12.7mm
MAXIMUM ROAD SPEED:	56.3km/hr	compartment front:	12.7mm
RANGE:	122km (M44)	compartment sides:	12.7mm
	132km (M44A1)	compartment rear:	12.7mm
FUEL CAPACITY:	568 litres	ARMAMENT:	1 × 155mm Howitzer M45
FORDING:	1.066m		1 × Calibre .50 (12.7mm)
GRADIENT:	60%		Browning MG A/A
VERTICAL OBSTACLE:	.762m		MG

M44 with howitzer at high elevation and spades in travelling position.

DEVELOPMENT

Development started in 1947 as the T99 and two pilot models were built. As the vehicle was to have as many components as possible of the T41E1 light tank, the T99 became the T99E1. A production order for a total of 608 T99E1s was given, but in October 1952 changes were made to the vehicle and it was given the new designation of T194. By that time 250 T99E1s had already been built and these were subsequently brought up to T194/M44 standards. In November 1953 the T194 was standardised as the Howitzer 155mm Self-Propelled M44 and was to replace the older M41 155mm Self-Propelled Howitzer. The M44A1 was standardised in August 1956 with a fuel injection engine.

DESCRIPTION

The hull of the M44 is of all-welded construction. The engine and transmission are at the front of the vehicle and the gun and crew compartment at the rear. The vehicle is fitted with a General Motors Corporation (Allison Division) Model CD-500-3 cross-drive transmission with 2F and 1R ranges. The suspension is of the torsion-bar type and consists of six road wheels with the drive sprocket at the front, the sixth road wheel acting as the idler, and a total of four track support rollers. Hydraulic shock absorbers are fitted to the first, second and fourth wheel stations.

All the crew are in the fighting compartment at the rear of the hull. This has an open roof. A model with overhead armour was built but was not adopted for service. If required, bows and a tarpaulin cover can be fitted over the fighting compartment of the vehicle.

When in action a spade is lowered at the rear of the hull and the rear doors are swung out as these contain ammunition. The driver is seated on the left side of the compartment and behind him is the ring mount for the anti-aircraft machine-gun. The machine-gun can be traversed through 360°, elevation limits being +52° and depression −21°.

The 155mm Howitzer M45 (T186E1) is mounted in Mount M80 (T167), traverse is 30° left and 30° right at a speed of 10° per second. Elevation is +65° and depression is −5°, at a speed of 20° per second. Elevation and depression are hydraulic with manual controls for use in an emergency.

The breech-block is of the interrupted stepped thread type with a hydrospring recoil mechanism. Ammunition is of the separate loading type and the following types are available: HE M107 (projectile weight 43,885kg), maximum range with M3 charge being 9700m, (372m/s) or with a M4A1 charge 14,600m (564m/s), Chemical, Nuclear, Illuminating M118 Series (projectile weight 46.72kg), Smoke M110 Series, and BE Smoke M116 Series (projectile weight 38.3kg). Average rate of fire is about one round per minute.

The M44 is not provided with an NBC system and does not normally have infra-red driving lights.

VARIANTS

There are no variants of the M44 or M44A1 in service.

M44 in firing position with spades down and rear doors open.

UNITED STATES

M7 – SELF-PROPELLED HOWITZER
MANUFACTURER – M7 American Locomotive Company. M7/M7B1 Pressed Steel Company. M7B2
Federal Machine and Welder Company
STATUS – In service with Belgium, Brazil, Israel, Italy, Jordan, Pakistan, Portugal, South Africa, Turkey
and Yugoslavia. No longer in production.

BASIC DATA

CREW:	7 (commander, gunner, 4 ammunition handlers, driver)	TRENCH:	2.286m
		ENGINE:	M7 is powered by a Continental R-975-C1,
WEIGHT LOADED:	22,970kg (M7), 22,680kg (M7B1)		9-cylinder radial petrol engine developing 350HP
LENGTH:	6.019m (M7), 6.184m (M7B1) (there is no gun overhang on this vehicle)		at 2,400rpm. M7B1 is powered by a Ford GAA, V-8 petrol engine developing 450HP
WIDTH:	2.878m (M7), 2.933m (M7B2 with sand shields)		at 2,600rpm
		ARMAMENT:	1 × 105mm Howitzer M2A1 with an elevation
HEIGHT:	2.946m (including A/A MG) 2.54m (excluding A/A MG)		of +35° and a depression of −5°, traverse 30° left and 15° right 1 × .50 (12.7mm) M2
GROUND CLEARANCE:	.43m (M7), .44m (M7B1)		Heavy Barrel MG for
TRACK:	2.108m		A/A use on a ring
LENGTH OF TRACK ON GROUND:	3.733m		mount
GROUND PRESSURE:	.73kg/cm^2	ARMOUR:	
MAXIMUM ROAD SPEED:	40km/hr (approx)	hull front upper:	12.7mm
RANGE:	137-201km	hull front lower:	50.8-114.3mm
FUEL CAPACITY:	677 litres (M7), 636 litres (M7B1)	hull sides upper:	12.7mm
		hull sides lower:	38mm
FORDING:	1.219m (M7), .914m (M7B1)	hull rear upper:	12.7mm
		hull rear lower:	38mm
GRADIENT:	60%	hull bottom front:	25.4mm
VERTICAL OBSTACLE:	.609m	hull bottom rear:	12.7mm

DEVELOPMENT

Development of the 105mm Howitzer Motor Carriage T32 started in June 1941. It is essentially an M3 tank chassis with a new superstructure mounting a standard 105mm howitzer offset to the right with limited traverse. Two pilot models were built by the Baldwin Locomotive Company and the vehicle was standardised as the M7 in February 1942. A total of 4,267 M7s were built between 1942 and 1945 by three different manufacturers and at different times.

It was first used in action by the British 8th Army in North Africa and the British continued to use the M7 until they replaced it by the Sexton. The M7 was called the Priest by the British Army as its 12.7mm anti-aircraft machine-gun was mounted in a pulpit-type tower on the right side of the front superstructure. Later production models were known as the M7B1 which was standardized in September 1943. This could be fitted for deep-wading operations. The final production models were the M7B2, only 127 of which were built. They had a slightly different pulpit and detailed alterations to the right of the 105mm howitzer. M7s had a three-piece bolted nose whilst most M7B1s and all M7B2s had a cast one-piece nose.

DESCRIPTION

The hull of the vehicle was of all-welded construction apart from the nose. The driver is seated to the left of the 105mm howitzer and is provided with a one-piece observation hatch which hinges upwards, and a vision block is provided in the hatch. All crew members are seated in the fighting compartment which has an open roof. If required, a canopy could be erected over the fighting compartment, and tubular stays for this purpose were carried on the sides of the hull.

The transmission is at the front of the vehicle and the engine at the rear. The gearbox has 5F and 1R gears. The suspension is of the vertical volute type and consists of three bogies, each of which has two small road wheels and a return roller. The drive sprocket is at the front and the idler at the rear.

The 105mm howitzer had manual traverse and elevation and fired the same ammunition as the standard 105mm towed howitzer. Maximum range is 11,160m. A total of 69 rounds of 105mm and 300 rounds of 12.7mm machine-gun ammunition are carried.

The M7 has no NBC system, no infra-red equipment and no amphibious capability.

VARIANTS
Many trials variants were built during World War II. There are no variants in service today.

M7 Priest on display at Aberdeen Testing Ground in Maryland.

MOBILE ANTI-AIRCRAFT SYSTEMS

There are two basic types of mobile anti-aircraft systems: gun and missile. Either of these types can be an all-weather system (eg the German Gepard) or a daylight/clear-weather system (eg the American M42), though most of the missiles are all-weather systems, with the exception of the Roland 1, SAM-9 and Chaparral. The Rapier in its basic form is a clear-weather system but when coupled to the Blindfire radar system it becomes an all-weather system.

COUNTRY	SYSTEM	TYPE
Czechoslovakia	M53/59	Gun
France	AMX-13 DCA	Gun
	Crotale	Missile
Germany	Gepard	Gun
Soviet Union	ZSU-23-4	Gun
	ZSU-57-2	Gun
	SA-8	Missile
	SA-6	Missile
	SA-4	Missile
United States	ARGADS/GLADS	Gun
	M42	Gun

Below is a listing of other vehicles fitted with anti-aircraft armament. Details of these will be found under their respective entries.

COUNTRY	SYSTEM	REFER TO ENTRY ON
France	Javelot	AMX-30
	DCA	AMX-30
	Shahine	AMX-30
	Roland	AMX-30 and Marder
	VDA	Panhard M3
	S 530	Panhard AML
Germany	—	Leopard 2
	Roland	Marder
Great Britain	Falcon	Abbot
	FV432 A/A	FV432
Soviet Union	BTR-152 A/A	BTR-152
	BTR-40 A/A	BTR-40
	T-34/85 A/A	T-34/85
	SA-9	BRDM-2
United States	M163 VADS	M113
	SAM-D	M113
	HAWK	M113
	Chaparral	M113
United States/GB	Rapier	M113
United States/Italy	Indigo	M113
United States/Switzerland	Skyguard	M113
United States	Half-Track A/A	Half-Track

Right The M53/59 self-propelled anti-aircraft system with turret traversed to the rear. The vertical magazines can be clearly seen.

CZECHOSLOVAKIA

M53/59 – SELF-PROPELLED ANTI-AIRCRAFT GUN SYSTEM
MANUFACTURER – Avia Zavody NP (chassis) and Czechoslovakian State Arsenals (body and guns)
CURRENT STATUS – In service with Czechoslovakia and Yugoslavia. Production complete.

BASIC DATA

CREW:	1 + 2	FUEL CONSUMPTION:	27 litres per 100km
WEIGHT LOADED:	9,500kg	FORDING:	.8m
LENGTH:	6.984m	GRADIENT:	31°
WIDTH:	2.41m	VERTICAL OBSTACLE:	.46m
HEIGHT:	3.06m	TRENCH:	.69m
GROUND CLEARANCE:	.4m	ENGINE:	Tatra T 912-2,
TRACK:	1.87m (front)		6-cylinder, in-line,
	1.755m (rear)		air-cooled diesel
WHEELBASE:	3.58m + 1.12m		developing 110HP
TYRES:	8.25m × 20		at 2,000rpm
MAXIMUM ROAD SPEED:	60km/hr	ARMAMENT:	2 × 30mm M53
RANGE:	500km		cannon
FUEL CAPACITY:	120 litres	ARMOUR:	10mm

DEVELOPMENT/DESCRIPTION

The M53/59 entered service in 1959 and is basically a modified Praga V3S (6 × 6) truck chassis that has been fitted with an armoured body with twin 30mm cannon at the rear.

The engine is at the front of the vehicle and its gearbox has 4F and 1R gears and a two-speed transfer case. The cab has seats for the driver on the left and the commander on the right. The commander is provided with a transparent observation dome in the roof of the cab. Both the commander and driver are provided with a side door, the top of which can be folded down, and in addition there is an observation slit above this door. They are also each provided with a windscreen for normal vision, which can be covered by steel hatches if required. The cab extends some way back and this has sufficient space for additional ammunition and supplies and an additional vision slit is provided in each side towards the rear. At the rear of the cab are two hatches which give direct access to the rear deck.

Above The M53/59 self-propelled anti-aircraft gun travelling.

The twin 30mm guns have hydraulic traverse and elevation. Maximum elevation is + 90° and maximum depression is − 10°, total traverse is 360° and axis of bore is 2.41m. The guns can be removed from the vehicle and fired from the ground if required. These guns have also been built in a towed version mounted on a four-wheeled carriage, these being known simply as the M53. The major difference between the towed and self-propelled model is that the latter is fed by 50-round vertical magazines whilst the towed model is fed by 10-round clips that are fed horizontally.

The 30mm cannon are gas operated and fully automatic, and have a cyclic rate of fire of 450/500 rounds per minute per barrel, but the practical rate of fire is 100/150 rounds per minute per barrel. Both HE and API rounds can be used. These both have an m/v of 1,000m/s and the complete round weighs .9kg with the projectile itself weighing .45kg. The API round will penetrate 60mm of armour at 500m. Maximum horizontal range is 10,000m and maximum vertical range is 7,000m, though effective range is 2,000m. The barrels can be quickly changed and additional magazines are carried on the rear decking. It is a clear-weather anti-aircraft system and is only provided with optical sights. Early models had multi-baffle muzzle brakes, but more recently these have been replaced on many vehicles by conical type flash eliminators.

The gunner sits on the left side of the turret at the rear and this position is armoured. The driver and commander would normally remain under cover in the cab but one of the crew would have to leave the cab in order to change the magazines.

The M53/59 has no infra-red driving equipment, no NBC system, no radar fire control system and no provision for deep wading. It can easily be recognized not only by the unusual layout of the vehicle but also by its dual rear tyres and the lack of any sort of tyre pressure regulation system.

VARIANTS
There are no known variants of the M53/59 in service.

FRANCE

AMX-13 DCA – SELF-PROPELLED ANTI-AIRCRAFT GUN SYSTEM
MANUFACTURER – Creusot-Loire
STATUS – In service with the French Army. Production has now been completed.

BASIC DATA

CREW:	3 (commander, gunner and driver)	TRENCH:	1.9m
		ENGINE:	SOFAM 8 GXb,
WEIGHT LOADED:	17,200kg		8-cylinder, water-cooled
LENGTH:	5.373m		petrol engine developing
WIDTH:	2.5m		250HP at 3,200rpm
HEIGHT:	3.794m (radar operational)	ARMAMENT:	2 × 30mm HSS 831A cannon
	2.716m (radar retracted)		2 × 2 smoke dischargers
GROUND CLEARANCE:	.37m		600 rounds of 30mm
TRACK WIDTH:	350mm		anmmunition and 12
GROUND PRESSURE:	.84kg/cm^2		smoke bombs are
POWER TO WEIGHT			carried
RATIO:	14.53HP/ton	ARMOUR	
MAXIMUM ROAD SPEED:	60km/hr	glacis plate:	15mm at 55°
RANGE:	300km (road)	hull side:	20mm
FUEL CAPACITY:	450 litres	hull floor front:	20mm
FORDING:	.6m	hull floor rear:	10mm
GRADIENT:	50%	turret:	20mm
VERTICAL OBSTACLE:	.65m (forwards) .45m (reverse)		

DEVELOPMENT

The AMX-13 DCA, the latter standing for Défence Contre Avions, was developed by a number of French and Swiss Companies to meet a requirement for a mobile self-propelled anti-aircraft system. The overall system was constructed by the Direction des Études et Fabrications d'Armement with the assistance of the following Companies: Société d'Applications des Machines Motrices (France) who designed the turret, Compagnie Générale de Télégraphie sans Fil (France—now part of the Thomson-CSF Organisation) who designed the radar system and Hispano-Suiza (Switzerland) who built the guns (Hispano-Suiza are now part of the Oerlikon-Bührle Group).

Development started in 1960 with the first prototypes being completed in 1962. The very first prototypes were not fitted with the radar system. After trials the system entered production in 1964 with first deliveries to the French Army starting the following year. According to most reports a total of 60 systems were built for the French Army and these currently equip two anti-aircraft battalions. More recently the complete turret of the AMX-13 DCA has been fitted on to the AMX-30 MBT chassis which is being offered for export by the GIAT although the French may well decide to place an order for the vehicle. The main advantages of the AMX-30 DCA are that the chassis is larger and the vehicle's main engine can be used to provide power for the system.

In the 1950s a number of anti-aircraft vehicles were developed using the AMX-13 chassis. These included one model with a single Bofors 40mm gun with standard optical sights whilst Oerlikon fitted a similar chassis with four 20mm cannon and a radar ranging system. None of these entered service however.

DESCRIPTION

The AMX-13 DCA is essentially an AMX-13 Self-Propelled Gun chassis with a new turret (Model S 401A) complete with a radar system. The hull is of all-welded construction with the engine, transmission and driver at the front of the vehicle and the turret at the rear. The transmission has 5F and 1R gears and a Cleveland type differential is fitted.

The suspension is of the torsion-bar type and consists of five road wheels, drive sprocket at the front, idler at the rear and three track support rollers. The first and fifth wheel stations are provided with hydraulic shock absorbers. The turret has complete traverse through 360°, elevation being +85° and depression −8°. Both elevation and traverse are electro/hydraulic. Maximum traverse speed is 80° per second with acceleration starting at 120° a second, maximum elevation speed is 45° a second. Minimum traverse and elevation speed is a 2 mils a second.

The twin Hispano-Suiza HSS 831A guns have a maximum rate of fire of 650 rounds per minute per gun. 300 rounds of belted ammunition are provided for each gun. The gun itself is gas operated and weighs 156.5kg complete with belt feed mechanism. The empty cartridge cases are automatically ejected outside the turret and the rate of fire can be pre-set by a burst limiter, ie 1, 5, 15 rounds or a continuous burst. The maximum range of the guns is 10,200m and their effective range is 3000m.

The following types of fixed rounds are available: Practice, High Explosive and Armour Piercing.

Practice
Type EP which is an inert practice shell without tracer, and type ET which is an inert practice shell with tracer.

High Explosive
UIA which is an HE incendiary round with a high blast effect, shell weighs 360 grammes and the cartridge 870 grammes.
UIAT which is similar to the above but also has a tracer, shell weighs 360 grammes with the cartridge weighing 870 grammes.

Armour Piercing
RT which is an armour-piercing round with tracer, shell weighs 390 grammes and the cartridge weighs 900 grammes. This will penetrate 45mm of armour.
RI which is an armour-piercing incendiary shell without tracer, weighs the same as the RT round and will penetrate 45mm of armour.
RIA which is an armour-piercing incendiary shell, self-destruct, will penetrate 40mm of armour. The shell weighs 360 grammes and the cartridge weighs 870 grammes.
RINT which is an armour-piercing incendiary shell with hard core and tracer. The shell weighs 360 grammes and the cartridge weighs 870 grammes and this will penetrate 60mm of armour. Optical sights are provided for use against both ground and aerial targets, the commander's sight being a × 1 whilst the gunner's are × 4. The commander is seated on the left of the turret and the gunner on the right, both being provided with a single-piece hatch cover.
The RD 515 (Oeil Noir 1 Black Eye) radar is mounted at the rear of the turret and has a maximum range of 15km. It is of the pulse doppler type and can be hydraulically folded down behind the turret when not required.

Basically the system operates in the five following stages:

Omnidirectional Watch
In this the radar scanner rotates at 60rpm and the targets appear on the commander's PPI (plan position indicator) tube in a number of range selection gates.

Bearing Acquisition
When a target is considered a threat by the commander he rotates the turret in the direction of the target. The radar than makes a sector scan about this position over an angle of 30°, the commander gradually correcting the direction of the turret to hold its axis in line with the direction of the target.

Elevation Optical Acquisition
The gun layer then takes over control of the turret and scans in elevation so acquiring the target.

Range Finding
At the end of the three previous phases, target designation (bearing and elevation speed) is secured. The target distance is measured by operating the radar in the range-finding mode. In this mode a range-finding gate locks on to the target echo. The target distance is transmitted continuously to the corrector and at the same time it is displayed on the sight of the commander.

Firing
During this phase the corrector is supplied with the bearing, elevation speed and target distance. The layer introduces the correction in the sight and remote control chains. Firing takes place as soon as the target enters the weapon optimum zone of efficiency. The burst of the 30mm cannon are automatically adjusted to a number of salvos preselected by limiters.

The gun turret is air-conditioned, this being provided by two air-blowers mounted behind the crew.

Above AMX-13 DCA in action with radar scanner erected.
Below AMX-13 DCA with radar scanner retracted.

FRANCE

CROTALE – ANTI-AIRCRAFT MISSILE SYSTEM
MANUFACTURER – Thomson-CSF (Electronics Systems Division), Bagneux. See text.
STATUS – In service with French Air Force, Libya, Pakistan, Spain (reported), and South Africa. In production.

BASIC DATA	ACQUISITION VEHICLE	LAUNCH VEHICLE			
CREW:	3	3	MAXIMUM ROAD SPEED:	70km/hr	70km/hr
WEIGHT LOADED:	12,500kg	14,800kg	RANGE:	500km	500km
LENGTH:	6.22m	6.22m	FORDING:	.68m	.68m
WIDTH:	2.65m	2.65m	GRADIENT:	40% at 2km/hr	40% at 2km/hr
HEIGHT:	2.04m (air transport)	2.04m (air transport)		10% at 15km/hr	10% at 15km/hr
GROUND CLEARANCE:	.45m (travelling)	.45m (travelling)	VERTICAL OBSTACLE:	.3m	.3m
			ENGINE:	See text	See text
WHEELBASE:	3.6m	3.6m	ARMOUR:	3mm-5mm	3mm-5mm

DEVELOPMENT

Development of the Crotale surface-to-air missile system commenced in 1964, the two prime contractors being Thomson-CSF (for the radar and electronics) and Engines Matra (for the missile). It has been reported that South Africa paid for 85% of the initial development costs of the Crotale with France contributing the remaining 15%. The first of three batteries were delivered to South Africa in 1971, although later contracts may well have raised this figure. The South Africans call the system Cactus. In 1971 the French Air Force placed an order for 1 acquisition and 2 firing units, this being followed by a production order. The French Air Force use the system to protect their strategic nuclear air fields. Lebanon did place an order for Crotale but this was subsequently cancelled. Crotale was entered for the American SHORADS competition but this was won early in 1975 by the German/French Roland 2 missile system. A naval version of the Crotale has been developed. A further development of the Crotale called the Shahine is being developed for Saudi-Arabia. This will be mounted on an AMX-30 tank chassis but will not enter service until 1980.

Below The Crotale firing unit from the rear with a total of four missiles in their launcher cells.
Right The Crotale acquisition vehicle with its surveillance radar.

DESCRIPTION

First the vehicles themselves. The first vehicles were built by Hotchkiss-Brandt but several years ago they stopped all production of armoured and wheeled vehicles and then Creusot-Loire built the hulls. The hull is of all-welded construction. The driver is at the front of the vehicle with the power pack at the rear.

The vehicle is unique in that it is powered by a thermal motor and has an electric transmission. The electric transmission was developed by the Belgian company of Ateliers de Constructions Électriques de Charleroi (ACEC). It consists of an alternator the output of which is rectified and then fed to a series of wound dc motors which in turn drive the wheels by means of built-in epicyclic reduction gears. The motor also provides power for the electrical system and the air-conditioning system.

The hydraulic system works the jacks (three jacks are lowered when the vehicle is in the firing or action position), steering, suspension and brakes. The front brakes are hydraulic whilst the rear are hydraulic and mechanical. The four hydraulic and pneumatic suspension units act as pneumatic springs, suspension springs and pneumatic suspension jacks. The driver can adjust the jacks to suit the operational requirement. The suspension jacks, like the brakes, are made by Messier Auto Industrie.

There are two vehicles in the Crotale system: the acquisition unit and the launch unit. Data are transmitted from one vehicle to the other by means of a data link (up to 500m) or a radio link (up to 5,000m).

First the acquisition unit. This carries out target surveillance, identification and designation. It is provided with a Doppler pulse search and surveillance radar which rotates at 60rpm and has a detection range of at least 18km. Its transmitter frequency is in the S band, an IFF system is provided.

Second is the firing unit. This tracks the target, launches a missile and guides it to its target. Its radar transmits in the Ku band, and can guide two missiles simultaneously. The launch radar takes over the missile in flight by a signal from a responder mounted in the missile and guides it by a command system. The missile is aimed during the first phase of flight by means of an infra-red receiver sensitive to the wave length emitted by the propellent flame.

A total of four missiles in their launcher cells are carried on the launch unit, and it takes about two minutes to load four new missiles with the aid of a crane.

The missile itself weighs about 85kg and is 2.89m in length. One missile in its container weighs about 100kg. The missile has an HE fragmentation warhead in the centre of the missile with an infra-red proximity fuze and the warhead weighs 15kg. The missile has a solid propellent motor and it reaches a top speed of Mach 2.3 in 2.3 seconds. The system has an effective range of between 500m (minimum) and 8,500m (maximum) in range and maximum altitude of approx 3,000m. According to the manufacturers it takes six seconds from when the target is detected until the missile is launched. It is an all-weather system.

A typical battery would consist of an acquisition unit and three firing units. It takes five minutes to bring the system into action as it cannot be fired on the move.

GERMAN (FEDERAL GERMAN REPUBLIC)

FLAKPANZER 1 GEPARD – SELF-PROPELLED ANTI-AIRCRAFT GUN SYSTEM
MANUFACTURER – Krauss-Maffei AG, Munich
STATUS – In production. On order for Belgium, Germany and the Netherlands.

BASIC DATA

CREW:	3 (commander, gunner and driver)	POWER-TO-WEIGHT RATIO:	18.2HP/ton
WEIGHT LOADED:	45,100kg	MAXIMUM ROAD SPEED:	65km/hr
WEIGHT EMPTY:	43,500kg	MAXIMUM ROAD RANGE:	600km
LENGTH:	7.7m (guns forward)	MAXIMUM CROSS	
	7.27m (hull)	COUNTRY RANGE:	450km
WIDTH:	3.25m	FUEL CAPACITY:	985 litres
HEIGHT:	3m (with radar down)	FORDING:	2.25m
	4.03m (with radar operating)	GRADIENT:	60%
		VERTICAL OBSTACLE:	1.15m
GROUND CLEARANCE:	.44m	TRENCH:	3m
TRACK:	2.74m	ENGINE:	MTU MB 838 Ca.500
TRACK WIDTH:	550mm		10-cylinder multi-fuel
LENGTH OF TRACK ON			engine developing
GROUND:	4.23m		830HP at 2,200rpm
GROUND PRESSURE:	.97kg/cm^2	ARMAMENT:	2 × 35mm cannon
			2 × 4 smoke dischargers

DEVELOPMENT

In the 1960s the German Army issued a requirement for a new self-propelled all-weather anti-aircraft gun system to replace the M42 system used by the German Army. Two companies built prototype vehicles. The German company of Rheinmetall built two prototypes of the Matador ZLA. This was armed with twin 30mm cannon and had a Siemens surveillance radar and a fire-control radar and computer built by AEG-Telefunken.

Below and right The Flakpanzer 1 Gepard type 5PZF-B which is now in production for the German Army.

Contraves AG of Zurich Switzerland built three prototypes of a vehicle known as the 5PZF-A, armed with twin 35mm cannon. Other companies associated with this model were Oerlikon-Bührle of Zurich (guns and ammunition), Siemens AG of Munich (search radar and IFF) and Siemens-Albis AG of Zurich (tracking radar). These prototypes were subjected to extensive trials and the 5PZF-A was found to be the superior system. The German Army then placed orders for six modified models called the 5PZF-B and a total of twelve pre-production models. The German Army has a requirement for a total of 420 of these, production has now commenced and the Gepard should enter service in 1977/78. The Belgian Army has ordered 55 Gepards.

The Netherlands decided to have their own model and this is called the 5PZF-C. It has the same armament as the German model but has a Dutch Hollandse Signaalapparaten integrated search and tracking radar. One prototype of this was built, followed by five pre-production vehicles. The Netherlands have placed a first order for 60 vehicles which may be followed by a further order for 35.

DESCRIPTION

The hull of the Gepard is almost identical to that of the Leopard 1 MBT and the reader is referred to this entry for full details of this. The only major modification to the chassis has been the installation of a 95HP auxiliary diesel engine in the forward part of the hull.

The driver is seated in the front of the hull with the other two crew members in the turret towards the front. The turret has a large one-piece hatch. Both crew members are provided with a fully stabilized panoramic telescope which can be used for target acquisition, observation purposes and for laying the guns on to ground targets.

The two 35mm Oerlikon cannons are belt-fed and the empty cartridge cases are automatically ejected outside the turret. The guns have a cyclic rate of fire of 550 rounds per barrel per minute. The gunner can select single shots, bursts or continuous fire. Total ammunition supply is 660 rounds of anti-aircraft ammunition and 40 anti-tank rounds, the latter carried externally in an armoured magazine. The gunner can quickly select either A/A or A/T ammunition. Once the magazines have been used it takes between 20 and 30 minutes to reload them.

The following types of ammunition have been developed for the Gepard:

Ammunition type	Wt of complete round	Fuze wt.	Projectile wt.	M/V
APHE	1,562gr	47gr	550gr	1,175m/s
HEAT	1,562gr	31gr	550gr	1,175m/s
AP-T	1,562gr	—	550gr	1,200m/s

The guns have an effective operational range of 4,000m and a projectile takes 6.05 seconds to reach this range. According to Oerlikon Bührle there is 75% chance that the target will be hit.

The turret has full powered traverse through 360°, elevation being +85° and depression −5°. Azimuth acquisition speed is 90°/second, azimuth tracking speed being 56°/second. Elevation acquisition speed is 42°/second and elevation tracking speed is also 42°/second.

The main differences between the models are:

	5PZF-B	5PZF-C
SEARCH RADAR FREQUENCY	S-Band	X-Band
MAXIMUM RANGE OF ABOVE	15km	15km
EVALUATION TECHNIQUE	Pulse Doppler fully coherent	Digital MTI
IFF	Integrated in Search Radar	Integrated in Search Radar
TRACKING RADAR FREQUENCY	Ku-Band	X-Band
MAXIMUM RANGE OF ABOVE	15km	15km
EVALUATING TECHNIQUE	Pulse Doppler, coherent reception/peak	Pulse Doppler, coherent reception

The system operates as follows. The search radar is mounted on the turret rear (when travelling this can, if required, be folded down to reduce the overall height of the vehicle). The radar can be used when the vehicle is travelling. The search radar sweeps through a full 360° and carries out continuous surveillance. When aircraft are approaching they show up on the screen and an audible alarm also sounds. A marker is positioned on the target which is on the PPI scope. If there are a number of targets, then the one which poses the greatest threat is marked. The target is displayed in terms of azimuth angle and range. If required this information from the scope can be transmitted to the air defence HQ so they also have a picture of the overall scene.

If the target does not respond to the IFF system the pulse-doppler tracking radar acquires and tracks the target in terms of azimuth and elevation angles. The search radar operates continuously. The tracking radar sweeps through approx. 200° and can be traversed through 180° so that the front faces the front of the turret.

The analogue main computer calculates the lead angles taking into account the weather conditions, muzzle velocity of ammunition, cant angles and so on. A stand-by computer is provided in case the main computer fails. The rate of fire is programmed as a function of range.

The Gepard is provided with an NBC system. It also has a navigational system both for cross-country navigation and to ensure that the screens are oriented to the north. Four smoke dischargers are mounted either side of the turret. The Dutch Army have named their model the Cheetah and this will have six smoke dischargers mounted either side of the turret.

The type 5PZF-C which has a Dutch Signaalapparaten integrated search and tracking radar. This model has been adopted by the Dutch Army.

SOVIET UNION

ZSU-23-4 – SELF-PROPELLED ANTI-AIRCRAFT GUN SYSTEM
MANUFACTURER – Soviet State Arsenals
CURRENT STATUS – In service with Bulgaria, Czechoslovakia, East Germany, Egypt, Finland, Hungary, India, Iraq, Iran, Poland, Soviet Union, Syria, S. Yemen. Still in production.

BASIC DATA

CREW:	4	FUEL CONSUMPTION:	96 litres per 100km
WEIGHT LOADED:	14,000kg	FORDING:	1.07m
LENGTH:	6.3m	GRADIENT:	30°
WIDTH:	2.95m	VERTICAL OBSTACLE:	1.1m
HEIGHT:	2.25m (radar in retracted position)	TRENCH:	2.8m
		ENGINE:	Model V-6, 6-cylinder, in-line water-cooled diesel developing 240HP at 1,800rpm
GROUND CLEARANCE:	.4m		
TRACK:	2.67m		
TRACK WIDTH:	360mm		
LENGTH OF TRACK ON		ARMAMENT:	4 × 23mm Zu 23 cannon
GROUND:	3.8m		
GROUND PRESSURE:	.479kg/cm^2	ARMOUR	
MAXIMUM ROAD SPEED:	44km/hr	glacis plate:	15mm at 55°
RANGE:	260km	upper hull sides:	15mm at 0°
FUEL CAPACITY:	250 litres	mantlet:	10mm at 15°

DEVELOPMENT/DESCRIPTION

The ZSU-23-4 was first seen during the parade held in Moscow on the 7th of November 1965. Since then it has been manufactured in very large numbers, not only for members of the Warsaw Pact but also for a number of countries in the Middle East. Each Soviet Motor Rifle Regiment has an anti-aircraft battery of four ZSU-23-4s whilst each Soviet Tank Regiment has one anti-aircraft battery of eight ZSU-23-4s.

The chassis of the ZSU-23-4 is based on that of the PT-76 Light Tank and has six road wheels with the drive sprocket at the rear and the idler at the front. It has the same type of track as the PT-76 and also has torsion-bar suspension.

The hull of the ZSU-23-4 is of all-welded construction with the driver at the front, turret in the centre and engine and transmission at the rear. At present there are no firm details of the transmission, but as it has the same engine and similar chassis to that of the PT-76 it most probably has the same gear box which has 5F and 1R gears.

The driver is seated on the left and is provided with a windscreen, which is covered by a steel hatch cover when in action. This is provided with an integral viewing block. The turret is square in shape and is provided with two roof hatches, a circular one for the commander on the left and a much larger one to the right of this. Infra-red driving lights are provided and it is assumed that the vehicle has an NBC system fitted. It has however no amphibious or deep wading capability.

ZSU-23-4s of the Soviet Army on parade in Moscow.

The turret has power traverse and elevation, maximum elevation is + 80° and depression is − 7°, total traverse is 360° and axis of the lower guns is 1.83m.

The 23mm cannon are gas operated and have vertically moving breech-block locking systems which drop to unlock. These guns are also in service on a twin mobile mounting known as the ZU-23. The four 23mm cannon of the ZSU-23-4 are water-cooled and have a cyclic rate of fire of 800/1,000 rounds per gun per minute. They have, in fact, the highest cyclic rate of fire of any anti-aircraft gun in service at the present time. Even the American Vulcan system only fires at a maximum of 3,000 rounds per minute.

The ZSU-23-4 normally fires in bursts of 50 rounds per barrel. Its practical rate of fire is 200 rounds per barrel per minute. The weapon can fire both HEI and API rounds. The HEI projectile weighs .19kg and the API projectile weighs .189kg, both have an m/v of 970m/s and the API projectile will penetrate 25mm of armour at 500m. The maximum horizontal range is 7,000m and their maximum vertical range is 5,100m. Effective anti-aircraft range however is between 2,000m and 2,500m, whilst effective range in the ground role is 2,000m. The guns can be trained and fired whilst the vehicle is on the move. A total of 2,000 rounds of ammunition are carried, ie 500 rounds per gun.

The B-76 radar is mounted at the rear of the turret and has both target acquisition and fire-control capabilities. The radar has been given the code name of 'Gun Dish' and operates in the Ku band and can pick up aircraft up to 20km away. An MTI (Moving Target Indicator) is provided as is an analogue computer. Optical sights are provided and there is an auxiliary gas turbine which supplies the power to the radar.

If required the radar scanner can be rotated to the rear and folded down behind the turret.

The ZSU-23-4 was extensively used in the Middle East campaign of October 1973, and is accredited with shooting down a large percentage of the 110 or so Israeli aircraft lost during the campaign. Although the ZSU-23-4 has now been in service for some ten years, it is still one of the most advanced mobile anti-aircraft guns in service at the present time.

VARIANTS
There are no known variants in service. Recently some ZSU-23-4s have been seen with a slightly modified turret but the exact nature of the internal modifications, if any, is not known at the present time.

Close-up of the four 23mm water-cooled cannon on an Egyptian ZSU-23-4.

SOVIET UNION

ZSU-57-2 – SELF-PROPELLED ANTI-AIRCRAFT GUN SYSTEM
MANUFACTURER – Soviet State Arsenals
STATUS – In service with Bulgaria, Czechoslovakia, East Germany, Egypt, Finland, Hungary, Iran, Iraq, North Korea, Poland, Romania, Soviet Union, Syria, Vietnam, Yugoslavia. Production complete.

BASIC DATA

CREW:	6	FUEL CAPACITY:	812 litres
WEIGHT:	28,100kg	FUEL CONSUMPTION:	190 litres per 100km
LENGTH:	8.48m (guns forward)	FORDING:	1.4m
	7.43m (guns rear)	GRADIENT:	30°
	6.22m (hull only)	VERTICAL OBSTACLE:	.8m
WIDTH:	3.27m	TRENCH:	2.7m
HEIGHT:	2.75m	ENGINE:	Model V-54, V-12,
GROUND CLEARANCE:	.425m		water-cooled diesel
TRACK:	2.64m		developing 520HP at
TRACK WIDTH:	580mm		2,000rpm
LENGTH OF TRACK ON		ARMAMENT:	2 × S-68 57mm guns
GROUND:	3.84m	ARMOUR	
GROUND PRESSURE:	.63kg/cm^2	glacis plate:	15mm at 60°
MAXIMUM ROAD SPEED:	48km/hr	upper hull side:	15mm at 0°
RANGE:	400km	mantlet:	15mm

DEVELOPMENT/DESCRIPTION

The ZSU-57-2 was first seen in public on 7th November 1957. It basically consists of a modified T-54 tank chassis with a new turret mounting twin 57mm guns. The ZSU-57-2 has been replaced in many front line units by the more recent ZSU-23-4. Each Soviet Tank Regiment had a battery of eight ZSU-57-2s.

The modifications to the chassis have been extensive and include much thinner armour, especially at the front, and the elimination of one road wheel on each side, the ZSU-57-2 having only four road wheels each side with quite large spaces between them, the idler at the front and the drive sprocket at the rear. Due to its lighter turret and thinner armour the ZSU-57-2 weighs only just over 28 tons compared with the 36 tons of the T-54. This gives the ZSU-57-2 slightly superior cross-country performance.

The driver is at the front of the hull on the left and is provided with a windscreen which can be covered by a steel hatch when in action. He is also provided with a hatch cover and periscopes. The other five crew members are seated in the turret, the loader, gunner and fuze setter on the left and the other loader and the vehicle commander on the right.

ZSU-57-2s on parade viewed from the rear.

Above ZSU-57-2 with turret traversed to the left.

The twin S-68 fully automatic 57mm guns are mounted in a large open-topped turret with a total traverse of 360°. The guns have a maximum elevation of +85° and a maximum depression of −5°, axis of bore being 2.05m. The turret is power-operated with manual controls for use in an emergency.

The guns have a cyclic rate of fire of 105/120 rounds per minute per barrel, though practical rate of fire is 70 rounds per minute per barrel. The ammunition is in clips of four rounds and is fed into two magazines, one for each gun. The empty cartridge cases and clips are dropped on to a conveyor belt which takes them to the rear of the turret where they fall into the large external wire basket on the rear of the turret.

The S-68 gun is a twin model of the single 57mm S-60 anti-aircraft gun which is mounted on a four-wheeled carriage. They both fire the same ammunition, and this ammunition cannot be used with the 57mm anti-tank or assault guns (ASU-57).

The weapons fire both HE/HEI and AP/API rounds with a proximity fuze, and both have an m/v of 1000m/s. The HE round used is the model UOR-281 Frag-T round, and although designed for use against aircraft it can also be used against ground targets, the complete round consisting of a point detonating, self-destruction fuze, high-explosive filled steel projectile, tracer assembly, brass cartridge case, propellant and a percussion primer. The complete round weighs 6.48kg. projectile weight being 2.85kg, total length 536mm. The concise data on the HE round do however conflict with other information which states that all rounds have a proximity fuze. The AP/API projectile weighs 3.1kg and will penetrate 106mm of armour at 500m. The ZSU-57-2 carries a total of 316 rounds of 57mm ammunition in clips of four. Of these 264 are ready for immediate use, the remainder being stowed below the turret. The maximum range of the 57mm guns is given as 12,000m in the ground role and 8,800m in the anti-aircraft role, but practical range in the anti-aircraft role is 4,000m and in the ground role less than 4,000m.

The ZSU-57-2 has only optical sights and is therefore limited to clear-weather operations. When in action one of the crew has been seen standing on the rear deck holding an optical heightfinder. The ZSU-57-2 is also most useful in the anti-tank and anti-APC roles.

No NBC system is fitted and it has no amphibious or deep wading capabilities. Infra-red driving lights are provided.

VARIANTS
There are no known variants in service although there have been some reports of ZSU-57-2s being fitted with a radar system.

SOVIET UNION

SA-8 – SELF-PROPELLED ANTI-AIRCRAFT MISSILE SYSTEM
MANUFACTURER – Soviet State Arsenals
STATUS – In service with the Soviet Army.

GENERAL
This new surface-to-air missile system was first shown in public during a parade held in Moscow in November 1975.

The four missiles, two each side, are mounted on a turret with a traverse of 360°. A surveillance radar scanner is mounted on top of the turret and this can be folded down behind the turret when travelling. A dish-shaped radar is mounted on the front of the turret and is used for target tracking. There is also a dish-shaped object each side of the tracking radar. The exact role of these is uncertain. According to some reports they could be target illuminators, or for transmitting instructions to the missiles. A TV camera is mounted on top of the radar assembly for optical tracking.

The 6 × 6 chassis has not been seen before and the tyres appear to be provided with a central tyre pressure regulation system. The vehicle is most probably amphibious. The crew are seated at the front of the hull and the windscreen can be covered by a visor when the missiles are being launched.

The missile itself has a proximity fuze and is about 3.1m in length. According to some reports it may well be that the Naval missile designated the SA-N-4 is also the SAM-8. It is estimated that the missile has a range of between 10 and 12km.

SOVIET UNION

SA-6 GAINFUL – SELF-PROPELLED ANTI-AIRCRAFT MISSILE SYSTEM
MANUFACTURER – Soviet State Arsenals
STATUS – In service with Warsaw Pact Forces, Egypt, India, Iraq, Libya, Syria and Vietnam.

BASIC DATA

CREW:	3
WEIGHT LOADED:	14,000kg
LENGTH:	6.8m
WIDTH:	3.18m
HEIGHT:	3.45m
GROUND CLEARANCE:	.4m
TRACK:	2.67m
TRACK WIDTH:	360mm
LENGTH OF TRACK ON GROUND:	3.8m
GROUND PRESSURE:	.48g/cm^2

MAXIMUM ROAD SPEED:	44km/hr
RANGE:	260km
FUEL CAPACITY:	250 litres
FORDING:	1m
GRADIENT:	60%
VERTICAL OBSTACLE:	1.1m
TRENCH:	2.8m
ENGINE:	Model V-6, 6-cylinder, in-line, water-cooled diesel developing 240HP at 1,800rpm

DEVELOPMENT/DESCRIPTION

The SA-6 (or SAM-6) was first seen during a parade held in Moscow in 1967. Its first operational use, however, was by Egyptian and Syrian forces in the October 1973 Middle East campaign. In this, the SA-6 is accredited with shooting down about 35% of the 110 Israeli aircraft lost.

A typical SA-6 battery consists of the following vehicles:

1. Flat Face long-range radar mounted on a standard 6×6 ZIL-157 chassis. This radar is also used with the SA-3 (GOA) and provides long-range target detection.

2. Straight Flush fire-control vehicle which has a similar chassis to the missile carrier. It has two radars—target tracking and illuminating radar on top and the acquisition radar underneath.

3. Three tracked launcher vehicles each with three missiles. The launcher can be traversed through 360° and elevation to +85°.

4. Missile resupply vehicles, three per battery.

Each Soviet Army Group in Europe has five batteries of SA-6 missiles. The missile itself is 6.2m in length and its body has a diameter of 355mm. It weighs approx 550kg, of which 80kg is the warhead. The warhead has 40kg of HE and a proximity fuze. The missile has a minimum range (horizontal) of 4km. Maximum range in the low role is said to be 30/35km and in the high role 50/60km. Its operational altitude ranges from 100m to 18,000m.

System of operation. The Flat Face radar (maximum range 250km) detects the enemy aircraft and passes information to the Straight Flush acquisition radar which locates the target and confirms that it is an enemy aircraft (ie IFF). The tracking and target illuminating radar then takes over, locks on to the target, and a missile is launched. An optical mode is also provided.

The chassis is believed to be based on the ZSU-23-4 chassis, which is in turn based on the PT-76 Amphibious Light Tank chassis. The crew compartment is at the front, launcher in the centre and engine and transmission at the rear. The suspension consists of six road wheels with the drive sprocket at the rear and the idler at the front.

The vehicle is not amphibious and is believed to be fitted with an NBC system. Infra-red driving lights are provided. The United States has acquired a complete SA-6 battery and this has been tested in the United States.

Left SA-6 launcher being prepared for action.
Below Rear view of an SA-6 Launcher of the Egyptian Army.

SOVIET UNION

SA-4 GANEF – SELF-PROPELLED ANTI-AIRCRAFT MISSILE SYSTEM
MANUFACTURER – Soviet State Arsenals
STATUS – In service with Soviet Forces. Systems supplied to Egypt have been replaced by SA-6.

DESCRIPTION

The SA-4 (or SAM-4) Ganef was first seen in public during a parade held in Moscow in 1964. It consists of a tracked chassis with a launcher with two missiles. The chassis is not based on any existing vehicle and its suspension consists of seven road wheels with the drive sprocket at the front and the idler at the rear and four track return rollers. It is believed that this chassis is identical to that used on the tracked minelaying vehicle. The engine is in the forward part of the hull thus leaving the rear clear for equipment.

The Ganef missile itself is about 9m in length and has a diameter of 80cm. Its weight at launch is believed to be 1,000kg. Four solid propellent boosters are arranged around the missile and a ramjet is mounted in the missile itself. Its maximum horizontal range in the anti-aircraft role is about 70km and some sources have stated that it has some ground-to-ground capability. Its warhead is HE.

A Ganef battery in a Soviet Army Group consists of a Pat Hand Radar, three launchers and three missile resupply vehicles. It is air-portable in the An-22 transport aircraft.

The system is used in conjunction with the Long Track long-range surveillance radar and the Pat Hand radar at battery level for target acquisition and fire control.

Above and left The Soviet Ganef mobile anti-aircraft missile system.

UNITED STATES

ADVANCED RADAR-DIRECTED GUN AIR DEFENCE SYSTEM (ARGADS)
GUN LOW ALTITUDE AIR-DEFENCE SYSTEM (GLADS)
STATUS – Development

GENERAL

The United States Army has a requirement for a system to replace the current Vulcan 20mm air-defence system which is in service in two models, the M 163 (on M113A1 chassis) and the towed M 167. Initially this replacement was known as the GLADS but more recently the designation ARGADS has been mentioned. The United States Army has a requirement for between 600 and 1,000 of these and the system would probably be mounted on an M60 MBT chassis, an M 109 chassis or the new MICV chassis. The following is a list of the known contenders for the ARGADS/GLADS requirement:

Javelot anti-aircraft system (refer to entry for AMX-30 MBT).

The German Gepard, one of which has been tested in the United States. If this was adopted the Raytheon Company would be the prime contractor.

A modified version of the existing 20mm Vulcan gun system.

The General Electric GAU-8 30mm cannon as fitted to the A-10 attack aircraft but installed on a tracked chassis with radar fire-control system.

The Hughes chain gun being developed for the new Hughes attack helicopter.

Twin 40mm Bofors guns, being developed by Aeronutronic Ford.

UNITED STATES

M-42 – SELF-PROPELLED ANTI-AIRCRAFT GUN SYSTEM
MANUFACTURER – Most M-42s were built by the Cadillac Motor Car Division of General Motors Corporation
STATUS – In service with Austria, Germany (FGR), Japan, Jordan, Lebanon, Vietnam and the United States (Reserve). Production of the M-42 is complete.

BASIC DATA

CREW:	6	ENGINE:	Continental or Lycoming
WEIGHT LOADED:	22,452kg		6-cylinder, horizontally
WEIGHT EMPTY:	20,094kg		opposed, air-cooled super-
LENGTH o/a:	6.356m (guns forward)		charged petrol engine
LENGTH HULL:	5.819m		developing 500BHP
WIDTH:	3.225m		at 2,800rpm
HEIGHT:	2.847m		M-42 has AOS-895-3
GROUND CLEARANCE:	.438m		and the M-42A1 has
TRACK:	2.603m		AOSI-895-5
TRACK WIDTH:	533mm	ARMAMENT:	Twin 40mm cannon in
GROUND PRESSURE (LOADED):	.65kg/cm²		turret with traverse of 360°.
MAXIMUM ROAD SPEED:	72.4km/hr		One cal. .30 MG is
RANGE:	161km		mounted on turret for
FUEL CAPACITY:	530 litres		local defence
FORDING:	1.016m	ARMOUR:	
GRADIENT:	60%	front plate lower:	25.4mm at 45°
VERTICAL OBSTACLE:	.711m	front plate upper:	12.7mm at 33°
TRENCH:	1.828m	floor:	9.5mm-31mm
		sides:	12.7mm hull
		gun shield:	9.52mm-15.87mm

DEVELOPMENT

In August 1951 the United States Army authorized the design and development of a self-propelled anti-aircraft gun T-141 (interim vehicle) and the T-141E1 (ultimate vehicle), as well as the development of a fire-control vehicle called the T-53. In May 1952, however, the T-141E1 was cancelled as was the T-53. Design and production of the T-141 was undertaken by the Cadillac Motor Car Division of the General Motors Corporation at the Cleveland Tank Plant.

The first prototype was built in 1951 and handed over to the Army in August 1951. After trials the T-141 was standardized as the M-42 in October 1953. The full designation of the M-42 is Gun Anti-Aircraft Artillery Self-Propelled: Twin 40mm, M-42, it has often been called 'The Duster'. In addition to Cadillac some vehicles were built by ACF Industries Incorporated of Berwick, Pa, whose first vehicle was completed in April 1952 and last vehicle in December 1953. Production of the M-42 was finally completed by Cadillac in July 1957 after 3,700 had been built.

Many components of the M-42 are also used in the M-41 Light Tank and the M-44 (155mm) and M-52 (105mm) self-propelled guns.

DESCRIPTION

The driver and radio operator are in the front of the hull and each of these are provided with a single-piece hatch cover. The other four crew members are in the turret in the centre of the vehicle.

The engine and transmission are at the rear of the hull. Transmission is a GMC (Allison Division) Model CD 500-3 and has 2F and 1R ranges. The suspension is of the torsion-bar type. There are five road wheels with the drive sprocket at the rear and the idler at the front, and three track return rollers. The first, second and fifth road wheel stations have hydraulic shock absorbers.

The M-42 is not fitted with an NBC system and it has no provision for deep fording. Infra-red driving lights are often fitted.

The M-42A1 was standardized in February 1956. This has the AOSI-895-3B engine fitted with a fuel injection system, the engine thus designated AOSI-895-5 and giving the M-42A1 a 20% increase in range over the earlier M-42.

The turret has full power traverse through 360°, traverse speed being 40° a second. The guns have an elevation from −3° to +85° when powered and from −5° to +85° when manually operated. Powered elevation speed is 25° per second.

The twin 40mm M2A1 cannon are fitted in Mount M2A1. The M2A1 cannon is recoil-operated and has a vertical sliding breech-block. It can fire single rounds or fully automatic and its maximum rate of fire is 120 rounds per minute, per barrel. The following types of ammunition are available: AP-T with a muzzle velocity of 874m/s, which has a maximum range in the horizontal role of 8,663m, though its effective range is 2,000/3,000m when being used in the ground role; HE-T with a muzzle velocity of 874m/s, which has an effective range in the anti-aircraft role of 4,663m or 4,754m in the ground role. All ammunition is in clips and is of the fixed type. A total of 480 rounds of ammunition are carried, this being stowed in the turret and in lockers along either side of the hull. In addition there is a calibre .30 (7.62mm) M-1919A4 machine-gun on the right side of the turret, and 1,750 rounds of ammunition are carried for this weapon. Some vehicles have had this old machine-gun replaced by the more recent M-60 7.62mm machine-gun. The computing sight M38 is designed to provide an effective means of controlling fire of the guns against both ground and aerial targets. The M24C sight is designed to superimpose a reticle pattern in the gunner's line of sight and is used in conjunction with the computing sight M38 during power operation. The Speed Ring Sight is used during manual operations if a power failure occurs.

The M-42 is a clear-weather anti-aircraft system and has no provision for operating at night

VARIANTS
There are no variants in service although trials were carried out with an M-42 with a range only radar scanner mounted on the right side of the turret. Some vehicles were fitted with wire-mesh screens over the rear part of the turret to give some protection against hand grenades.

Above and previous page The M42 twin 40mm self-propelled anti-aircraft gun system.

OTHER ARMOURED VEHICLES

Included in this section are combat engineer vehicles, armoured minelayers, armoured recovery vehicles, bridgelayers and armoured cargo carriers. A full listing of this section is given below together with a list of armoured recovery vehicles and bridgelayers found under other entries. Most armoured personnel carriers can be used for the cargo role but the French VAB wheeled vehicle has been designed for both the APC and cargo-carrying roles and details of this are in the entry for the VAB in APC section. The M548 tracked cargo carrier is based on M113 components and details of this will be found in the M113 entry.

Vehicles covered in this section:

Great Britain	FV180 Combat Engineer Tractor
United States	Universal Engineer Tractor
Soviet Union	Full-Tracked Armoured Minelayer
Sweden	Brobandvagn 941 Bridgelayer
	Bärgningsbandvagn 82 Armoured Recovery Vehicle
United States	M578 Armoured Recovery Vehicle
	M88 Armoured Recovery Vehicle
Germany (FGR)	Transportpanzer 1 and 2 (Load Carriers)

Other Vehicles:
Bridgelayers

Country	Entry
France	AMX-30
	AMX-13
Germany	Leopard 1
Great Britain	Vickers MBT
	Chieftain
	Centurion
Japan	Type 61
Soviet Union	T-54/T-55
	T-34/85
Switzerland	Pz.68
United States	M551
	M60
	M48
	M47
	Sherman
	M113

Armoured Recovery Vehicles and Engineer Vehicles

Austria	Pänzerjager K	ARV
Czechoslovakia	OT-62	ARV
France	AMX-30	ARV
	AMX-13	ARV, AEV
	AMX VCI	AEV
Germany	Leopard	ARV, AEV
Great Britain	Vickers MBT	ARV
	Chieftain	ARV, AEV
	Centurion	ARV, AEV, BARV
	Scorpion	ARV
	FV432	ARV
Japan	Type 61	ARV, AEV
Soviet Union	T-54/T-55	ARV
	IS-3	ARV
	T-34/85	ARV
	SU-100/SU-85	ARV
	ISU-122/152	ARV

Switzerland	Pz.61 and Pz.68	ARV
United States	M60	AEV
	M47	ARV, AEV
	Sherman	ARV
	M113	ARV
	LVTP-7	ARV

GREAT BRITAIN

FV180 COMBAT ENGINEER TRACTOR
MANUFACTURER – Royal Ordnance Factory, Leeds
STATUS – Undergoing trials, should enter production 1976/77.

BASIC DATA

CREW:	2 (driver and operator)	GROUND PRESSURE:	.435kg/cm²
WEIGHT:	17,100kg	MAXIMUM ROAD SPEED:	56km/hr
LENGTH:	7.544m (o/a)	MAXIMUM WATER	
	5.334m (hull)	SPEED:	8/9 km/hr
WIDTH:	2.896m (including	FUEL:	430 litres
	bucket)	FORDING:	1.829m
	2.793m (hull)	GRADIENT:	60%
	2.769m (tracks)	VERTICAL OBSTACLE:	.61m
HEIGHT:	2.667m (o/a)	TRENCH:	2.06m
	2.286m (top of hull)	ENGINE:	Rolls-Royce C6TFR,
GROUND CLEARANCE:	.457m		6-cylinder, in-line
TRACK WIDTH:	508mm		diesel developing 320HP
LENGTH OF TRACK ON			at 2,100rpm
GROUND:	3.758m		

DEVELOPMENT

In the 1960s the Military Engineering Experimental Establishment at Christchurch (which is now part of the Military Vehicles and Engineering Establishment) commenced design work on a new vehicle called the Combat Engineer Tractor. Initially both France and Germany were involved but France dropped out in 1967 and Germany dropped out several years later.

The first of two running test rigs was completed in January 1968 with the second rig being completed in April 1968. These proved the basic idea and in 1970 it was decided to build a total of seven prototypes. The first of these was completed in February 1973 and the last in January 1974 and they were built at the Royal Ordnance Factory at Leeds. These prototypes are now undergoing extensive trials as well as a sales tour and it is expected that production will start in 1976/77.

The CET will be used to support front line units and for a wide range of roles including dozing, tracklaying, preparing crossings, towing trailers as well as assisting vehicles across water obstacles. It is expected that this will replace the Centurion AVRE in the dozer role.

DESCRIPTION

The hull of the FV 180 Combat Engineer Tractor is of all-welded aluminium armour construction. The vehicle is normally driven with the bucket to the rear. The layout of the CET from the front is as follows:
The final drives are at the front of the hull with the driver and operator on the left. Each man is provided with a single hatch cover that opens to the rear and there are a total of ten vision blocks for observation purposes. Both crew members can reverse their seats and essential controls are duplicated so that either man can operate the vehicle. The engine and transmission are to the right of the crew compartment.

The suspension is of the torsion-bar type and consists of five road wheels with the drive sprocket at the front and the rear wheel acting as the idler. Hydraulic double acting ram type dampers are fitted on the first and last wheel stations. To provide a firm platform when operating, the front and rear wheel stations can be locked from the crew compartment. The tracks are cast steel link of the single horn type with rubber bushes and rubber pads for operating on roads.

Power is transmitted from the turbo-charged engine through two gearboxes to a Rolls-Royce CGS 312 steering unit and then to the final drives. The first gearbox, the transfer box, provides PTOs for the water jets and hydraulic pumps. The main TN 26 gearbox has four gears in both directions. For normal road and cross country travel controlled differential steering is used. A clutch and brake steering system is provided for dozing operations.

The FV180 is powered in the water by two Dowty water jets mounted one each side of the rear, and steering is achieved by deflecting the thrust from the unit on the inside of the turn; deflecting both units gives reverse. For amphibious operations the trim board is erected at the front of the hull and a rubberized fabric buoyancy unit is erected at the front of the hull. The rear unit is a plastic cased polyurethane foam block fitted to the bucket.

The bucket is of light alloy construction with steel cutting edges and tynes, it holds 1.72m³ of earth. It is hydraulically operated and can be used for digging—for example to prepare gun positions, bulldozing or as an earth anchor. It can remove 300m³ per hour over a 100m hauling distance. The hydraulically operated capstan winch is provided with 107m of 16mm rope and can be led to the front or rear by direction changing blocks. Maximum winching speed is 113m/minute.

The self emplacing earth anchor is mounted on the top of the hull and can be rocket propelled over the front of the vehicle to a distance of 91.4m. A rope is attached to this anchor which in turn is attached to the winch. This is used to assist the CET in leaving rivers and other obstacles.

Passive night viewing equipment can be provided. An NBC system is fitted and smoke dischargers are mounted on the front of the hull. The electrical system is 24V and an AC140 generator with an output of 140Amps at 28V is mounted. There are four UK6TN batteries rated at 100Amps.

A crane can be quickly erected in the bucket and this is used to handle stores and supplies. A pusher bar can be provided for launching bridging pontoons. The CET can also tow a four-wheeled trailer fitted with the Giant Viper Mine Clearing System. This basically fires a rocket-propelled explosive line across the minefield, which then falls on the minefield and is exploded, hopefully clearing the emplaced mines.

VARIANTS
There are no variants of the CET at the present time.

Above A Combat Engineer Tractor undergoing trials.
Below A Combat Engineer Tractor showing its amphibious capabilities. The buoyancy bag on the front of the hull was designed and built by FPT Limited of Portsmouth.

UNITED STATES

UNIVERSAL ENGINEER TRACTOR
MANUFACTURER – Caterpillar Tractor Company, Peoria, Illinois
STATUS – Trials.

BASIC DATA

CREW:	1	TRACK:	2.235m
WEIGHT:	24,494kg (fully loaded)	TRACK WIDTH:	457mm
	14,515kg (empty)	GROUND PRESSURE:	.58kg/cm^2
LENGTH:	6.48m	MAXIMUM ROAD SPEED:	48.28km/hr
WIDTH:	2.794m (w/o dozer wings)	MAXIMUM WATER SPEED:	4.82km/hr
	2.946m (with dozer wings)	RANGE:	322km
		GRADIENT:	60%
HEIGHT:	2.387m (reduced)	SIDE SLOPE:	35%
GROUND CLEARANCE:	.457m	ENGINE:	Diesel 285HP

DEVELOPMENT

The Universal Engineer Tractor (UET) has been under development for the Corps of Engineers for ten years. A further four pre-production units were delivered for trials purposes in 1975. The UET has been developed by the Caterpillar Tractor Company and the United States Army Mobility Research and Development Centre at Fort Belvoir, Virginia.

DESCRIPTION

The UET has been designed to carry out a wide variety of roles in the battlefield area, including dozing, scraping, rough grading, excavating and hauling operations. In addition it can be used to transport troops and equipment. Its hull is of all-welded aluminium construction and it is air-transportable. The UET is fully amphibious being propelled in the water by its tracks.

The scraper bowl is at the front of the vehicle with the driver at the rear on the left and the engine to his right. The operator has full armour protection whilst the personnel when carried in the scraper bowl only have front and side armour protection.

The dozer blade is mounted on the apron and dozing and scraping is accomplished by raising and lowering the front of the vehicle by means of the hydro-pneumatic suspension. A positive load factor elector is provided for the scraper bowl. If required the scraper bowl can be filled with ballast.

Its hydro-pneumatic suspension system has four aluminium road wheels and a drive sprocket at the rear. The Powershift Planetary transmission has 6F and 2R gears.

The UET has a maximum drawbar pull of 21,319kg. A winch with a capacity of 11,340kg is provided, as is a bilge pump.

Above and previous page A Universal Engineer Tractor (UET) undergoing trials.

SOVIET UNION

FULL TRACKED ARMOURED MINELAYER
MANUFACTURER – Soviet State Arsenals
STATUS – In service with the Soviet Army.

GENERAL

Although this has been in existence for over five years, few details have become available so far. It has the same chassis as the SA-4 Ganef surface-to-air missile system.

Its suspension consists of seven road wheels with the drive sprocket at the front and the idler at the rear, and a total of four track return rollers. The engine and transmission are at the front of the hull which leaves the rear of the hull clear for the plough type minelaying system and for the storage of mines.

SWEDEN

BROBANDVAGN 941 – ARMOURED BRIDGELAYER
MANUFACTURER – AB Hägglund and Soner, Örnsköldsvik
STATUS – In service with the Swedish Army. Production complete.

BASIC DATA

CREW:	4 (commander, driver, gunner and bridge operator)	POWER-TO-WEIGHT RATIO:	11BHP/ton
WEIGHT:	29,400kg (with bridge)	MAXIMUM ROAD SPEED:	56km/hr
	22,400kg (w/o bridge)	MAXIMUM WATER SPEED:	8km/hr
	7000kg (bridge)	RANGE:	400km
LENGTH:	17m (with bridge)	FUEL CAPACITY:	550 litres
	6.71m (hull only)	FORDING:	Amphibious
WIDTH:	4m (with bridge)	GRADIENT:	60%
	3.23m (hull)	VERTICAL OBSTACLE:	.6m
HEIGHT:	3.5m (with bridge)	TRENCH:	2.5m
	1.75m (w/o bridge)	ENGINE:	Volvo-Penta Model THD
GROUND CLEARANCE:	.4m (centre of hull)		100C, 6-cylinder in-line
TRACK WIDTH:	450mm		turbo-charged diesel
LENGTH OF TRACK ON GROUND:	3.6m		developing 310BHP at 2,200rpm. 9.6 litres
GROUND PRESSURE:	.91kg/cm²	ARMAMENT:	1 × 7.62mm MG
			2 × 6 smoke dischargers

DEVELOPMENT
The Brobandvagn 941 (or Brobv 941 for short) has an almost identical hull to that of the Bgbv 82 ARV. The first prototype of the Brobv 941 was completed in December 1968 with production being undertaken in 1972/73.

DESCRIPTION
The hull of the Brobv 941 is of all-welded steel construction with the crew compartment at the front and the bridge and laying equipment at the rear. The front plate gives the crew full protection against attack from projectiles up to and including 20mm calibre. The sides of the hull are of double skinned construction.

There are a total of four hatches or cupolas in the roof of the crew compartment. The driver is seated at the front in the centre and is provided with a one-piece hatch cover that opens to the rear and a total of three periscopes. The commander is to the right of the driver and also has a single-piece hatch cover that opens to the rear as well as a total of five periscopes. There are two further hatches in the rear of the crew compartment, one on the left (the gunner's) and one on the right. Each of these positions has two periscopes.

The engine, torque converter, clutch, gearbox and steering gear (including bevel gear) are built in one complete unit. The variable hydraulic pump of the hydrostatic steering system is mounted in front of the engine and the hydraulic motor is mounted on the steering gearbox. The servo-assisted disc brakes and the final drives connect the power plant to the drive sprockets. The transmission, clutch and gearbox are all built by Volvo-Penta. The gearbox is a Model R61 and has 8F and 2R gears. The steering gear is Hägglunds and the hydrostatic transmission is a Lucas Model PM 300. The fuel tank is at the rear of the hull under the engine.

The suspension is of the torsion-bar type and consists of six road wheels with the idler at the front and the drive sprocket at the rear. The first and sixth road wheel stations are provided with hydraulic shock absorbers. Track tension is automatically adjusted by a hydraulic system.

The bridge is 15m in length (an 11m bridge is also available) and will take a maximum load of 50 tons. It is laid in position hydraulically and it takes three to five minutes to place or retract the bridge, this being carried out from within the crew compartment. The bridgelaying mechanism is journalled in the chassis with two supporting legs and two hydraulic cylinders.

A hydraulically-operated dozer blade is mounted at the front of the vehicle, and is used to level the ground if required and also to stabilize the vehicle when the bridge is being laid.

On arriving at the stream or ditch, the telescopic beam under the bridge is slid across until it reaches firm ground on the other side. The light alloy bridge is then slid across on this beam and the beam is withdrawn as the bridge is laid in the correct position. The Brobv can then cross and pick up the bridge from the far

1. If needed the nearest bridge abutment can be levelled with the bulldozer blade. Then the bulldozer blade is depressed to stabilize the vehicle.

Launching sequence for the Brobandvagn 941 Bridgelayer.

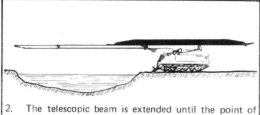

2. The telescopic beam is extended until the point of the beam reaches the other bridge abutment.

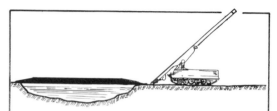

4. By tilting the whole bridgelaying mechanism the bridge is laid down in the right position.

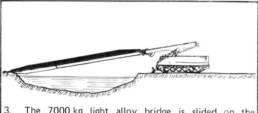

3. The 7000 kg light alloy bridge is slided on the telescopic beam.

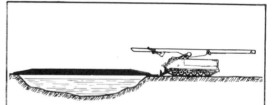

5. The bridgelaying mechanism is operated back to transport position and the first vehicle can pass the bridge.

The Brobandvagn 941 Bridgelayer complete with bridge.

side. When laying the bridge in very rough terrain one of the crew members can be outside the vehicle and give instructions to the crew inside via a wire link.

The gunner can fire his machine-gun from his open hatch cover or from an alternative position on top of the bridgelaying mechanism. It can also be mounted near the commander's hatch or in the rear platform area. The Brobv 941 is fully amphibious being propelled in the water by its tracks. Before entering the water a trim vane is erected at the front of the hull and the bilge pumps are switched on. The bridge, which floats, is towed behind the vehicle in the water.

Infra-red driving lights are provided. Provision was made in the design of the vehicle for the installation of an NBC pack but this has not been fitted so far.

SWEDEN

BÄRGNINGSBANDVAGN 82 – ARMOURED RECOVERY VEHICLE
MANUFACTURER – AB Hägglund and Soner, Örnsköldsvik
STATUS – In service with the Swedish Army. Production complete.

BASIC DATA

CREW:	4 (driver, gunner, commander and fitter)	MAXIMUM ROAD SPEED:	56km/hr
WEIGHT LOADED:	26,300kg (with S Tank powerpack)	MAXIMUM WATER SPEED:	8km/hr
WEIGHT EMPTY:	23,300kg	RANGE:	400km
LENGTH:	7.23m	FUEL CAPACITY:	550 litres
WIDTH:	3.25m	FORDING:	Amphibious
HEIGHT:	2.63m (spades up) 2.45m (top of turret)	GRADIENT:	60%
		VERTICAL OBSTACLE:	.6m
GROUND CLEARANCE:	.45m (centre of hull)	TRENCH:	2.5m
TRACK WIDTH:	450mm	ENGINE:	Volvo-Penta Model THD 100C, 6-cylinder, in-line turbo-charged diesel developing 310BHP at 2,200rpm, 9.6 litres
LENGTH OF TRACK ON GROUND:	3.6m		
GROUND PRESSURE:	.82kg/cm^2		
POWER-TO-WEIGHT RATIO:	12BHP/ton	ARMAMENT:	1 × 20mm cannon 16 smoke dischargers

DEVELOPMENT

Hägglunds started design work on the Bärgningsbandvagn 82 (or Bgbv 82 for short) in June 1966. The first prototype was completed in July 1968 and this was followed by a total of 24 production vehicles which were built between April and December 1973. The vehicle has been designed to recover other members of the Hägglunds family as well as carrying out repair work on larger armoured vehicles, for example changing the engine on the S Tank. A complete S Tank power pack can be carried in the rear of the Bgbv 82. The vehicle uses many components that are common to the Brobv 941 Bridgelayer and the Ikv 91 Tank Destroyer.

DESCRIPTION

The hull is of all-welded rolled steel construction with the crew compartment at the front and the recovery/load compartment at the rear. The front plate gives the crew full protection against attack from projectiles up to and including 20mm calibre. The sides of the hull are, like the Pbv.302, of double skinned construction. Prototypes had a total of three cupolas/turrets but production vehicles have four. The turret is at the front of the left side with the driver's position in the centre. The driver is provided with a one-piece hatch cover that opens to the rear and a total of three periscopes for driving whilst closed down. The commander is to the right of the driver and has a single-piece hatch cover and a total of five periscopes. Behind the commander's cupola is a further cupola for the fitter.

The engine, torque converter, clutch, gearbox and steering gear (including bevel gear) are built in one complete unit. The variable hydraulic pump of the hydrostatic steering system is mounted in front of the engine and the hydraulic motor is mounted on the steering gearbox. The servo-assisted disc brakes and the final drives connect the power plant to the drive sprockets. The transmission, clutch and gearbox are all built by Volvo-Penta. The gearbox is the Model R61 and has 8F and 2R gears. The steering gear is Hägglunds and the hydrostatic transmission is a Lucas Model PM 300. The fuel tank is at the rear of the hull under the engine.

The suspension is of the torsion-bar type and consists of six road wheels with the idler at the front and the drive sprocket at the rear. The first and sixth road wheel stations are provided with hydraulic shock absorbers. Track tension is automatically adjusted by a hydraulic system.

A hydraulically-operated bulldozer blade is mounted at the front of the hull, this can be used for both dozing purposes and for stabilizing the vehicle when the crane or winch are being used.

The HM 20 winch is mounted just behind the crew compartment and is driven by a Hägglunds high torque hydraulic motor giving 20 tons pulling force on the 145m of wire rope. It has two ranges, and speed varies from 0 to .6 metres per second. The two hydraulically operated anchor spades are carried on the vertical position and when in position together absorb a force of 60 tons which is the maximum for a three-part pull. The wire rope runs out through a guide hole in the rear of the hull.

The Hiab-Foco 9000 lifting crane is mounted in the rear of the vehicle on the right side and is provided with a special hydraulic valve which limits the lifting torque and locks the crane when moving the load. This crane can lift 5,500kg with 1.5m jib, 3,500kg with 2.5m jib and 1,500kg with 5.5m jib. When lifting heavy loads the spades are positioned. All recovery equipment is hydraulically controlled from within the crew compartment. The Bgbv 82 carries a full range of tools and welding equipment.

The turret is identical to that fitted to the Pbv 302 APC and is armed with a 20mm cannon with an elevation of $+50°$ and a depression of $-10°$. It can be used against both ground and aerial targets. Total ammunition capacity is 505 rounds. In addition there are eight smoke dischargers mounted either side of the turret. The Bgbv 82 is fully amphibious being propelled in the water by its tracks. Before entering the water the trim vane is erected at the front of the hull and the bilge pumps are switched on. If the vehicle is carrying a load then a flotation screen must be erected around the rear cargo area. Infra-red driving lights are provided and provision has been made for fitting an NBC system though this has not so far been fitted.

VARIANTS
There are no variants of the Bgbv 82.

Above The Bärgningsbandvagn 82 ARV from the front.
Left The Bärgningsbandvagn 82 ARV recovering a disabled vehicle.

UNITED STATES

M578-LIGHT ARMOURED RECOVERY VEHICLE
MANUFACTURER – Bowen-McLaughlin-York Incorporated of York, Pennsylvania
STATUS – In service with Brazil, Canada, Denmark, Great Britain, the Netherlands, Norway, Spain and the United States. In production.

BASIC DATA

CREW:	3	FUEL CAPACITY:	1,137 litres
WEIGHT LOADED:	24,470kg	FORDING:	1.066m
WEIGHT REDUCED:	21,319kg (for air transportation)	GRADIENT:	60%
		VERTICAL OBSTACLE:	1.016m
LENGTH o/a:	6.42m or 6.356m (early models)	TRENCH:	2.362m
		ENGINE:	General Motors Model
LENGTH HULL:	5.937m or 5.562m (early models)		8V71T, 8-cylinder,
WIDTH:	3.149m		liquid-cooled, turbo-
HEIGHT:	3.314m (with MG)		charged, two-cycle
	2.921m (top of cupola)		diesel developing
GROUND CLEARANCE:	.47m		425BHP at 1,700rpm
TRACK:	2.692m	ARMAMENT:	1 × calibre .50 (12.7mm)
TRACK WIDTH:	457mm		Browning MG with 500
LENGTH OF TRACK ON			rounds of ammunition.
GROUND:	3.764m		Some NATO countries
GROUND PRESSURE:	.71kg/cm²		(eg The Netherlands)
MAXIMUM ROAD SPEED:	59.5km/hr		have fitted their vehicles
RANGE:	725km		with smoke dischargers.

DEVELOPMENT

In 1956 the Pacific Car and Foundry Company of Renton, Washington, was awarded a contract to build prototypes of a new range of self-propelled guns all using the same basic chassis. These were the T236 (later the M110), T235 (later the M107) and the T245. In 1957 the programme was expanded to include a series of light armoured recovery vehicles. These were designated T119, T120 and T121. The T119 and T121 had a crane with a traverse of 360° and was not armoured, but did not develop beyond the prototype stage. The T120 was initially powered by a petrol engine which was later replaced by a diesel engine and became the T120E1. The T120E1 was standardized as the M578 and the first production vehicle was completed by the FMC Corporation in October 1962. Since then the Pacific Car and Foundry Company and Bowen-McLaughlin-York Incorporated have built the vehicle. The current manufacturer is Bowen-McLaughlin-York and, according to the Pentagon, the United States Army will receive 178 vehicles at a total cost of 27.6 million dollars in FY 1975 and 210 vehicles at a total cost of 38.9 million dollars in FY 1976. The M578 is used by all arms including self-propelled artillery battalions, mechanized infantry battalions and armoured cavalry squadrons.

The full designation of the vehicle is: Recovery Vehicle Full-Tracked: Light Armoured M578.

DESCRIPTION

As has been previously stated, the chassis of the M578 is identical to that of the M107 and M110 self-propelled guns. The driver is seated towards the front of the vehicle on the left side. He is provided with a one-piece hatch cover and a total of three periscopes for driving when closed down. The XTG-411-2A transmission (automatic) has four forward and two reverse ranges and is mounted at the front of the vehicle. This is made by the Allison Division of GMC. The engine is to the right of the driver.

The suspension consists of five road wheels with the drive sprocket at the front of the vehicle. The suspension is of the torsion-bar type and a hydraulic cylinder is attached to each road arm, serving as a shock absorber, hydraulic bump-stop and suspension lockout. A spade is mounted at the rear of the hull.

The other two crew members are seated in the large turret at the rear of the vehicle. Both are provided with a single-piece hatch cover, and a total of six periscopes each. The machine-gun is mounted on a pintle in the front of the left hatch cover. Normal means of entry and exit for the turret crew is via a door in each side of the turret. There are also double doors in the rear of the turret. The M578 does not have an NBC system and is normally provided with infra-red driving lights.

The M578 has been designed to recover vehicles weighing up to approx. 30,000kg. It has a tow-winch capacity of 27,216kg (bare drum) and a hoisting capacity of 6,804kg. The turret can be traversed through 360°.

Boom and Winch Data:
    The tow/winch cable has 70.10m of 25.4mm diameter cable, and has the following capacity: Bare drum 27,240kg at 6.10m/min, low gear; bare drum 6,724kg at 24.38m/min, high gear; full drum 17,343kg at 14.33m/min, low gear; full drum 4,290kg at 58.52m/min, high gear.
    The hoist/winch cable has 76.2m of 15.87mm diameter cable, and has the following capacities: Bare drum 6,810kg at 9.14m/min, low gear; bare drum 1,553kg at 40.23m/min, high gear; full drum 4,159kg at 14.94m/min, low gear; full drum 944kg at 65.84m/min, high gear.
Hoisting Capacity:
    13,620kg at 3.58m distance from the rear of the vehicle, with spade emplaced.
    13,620kg at 1.72m distance from the rear of the vehicle with spade retracted.
    Maximum distance from ground to hook with boom at minimum reach is 5.51m.
    Maximum distance from ground to hook with boom at maximum reach is 1.9m.

VARIANTS
There are no variants of the M578 in service.

Above M578 Armoured Recovery Vehicle of the Canadian Armed Forces.
Left M578 Armoured Recovery Vehicle of the United States Army.

UNITED STATES

M88 – ARMOURED RECOVERY VEHICLE
MANUFACTURER – Bowen-McLaughlin-York, York, Pennsylvania
STATUS – In service with Austria, Germany (FGR), Israel, Norway and the United States (Army and Marines). Production of the M88 has now been completed. See also text.

BASIC DATA

CREW:	4 (commander, driver, co-driver and mechanic)	RANGE:	360km
		FUEL CAPACITY:	1,685 litres
WEIGHT:	50,800kg	FORDING:	1.625m
LENGTH:	8.254m (w/o dozer blade)	GRADIENT:	60%
WIDTH:	3.428m	VERTICAL OBSTACLE:	1.066m
HEIGHT:	3.225m (with MG)	TRENCH:	2.616m
	2.921m (top of machine-gunner's hatch)	ENGINE:	Continental AVSI-1790-6A, 12-cylinder, air-cooled, super-charged, fuel-injection petrol engine developing 980BHP at 2,800rpm
GROUND CLEARANCE:	.457m		
TRACK:	2.717m		
TRACK WIDTH:	711mm		
LENGTH OF TRACK ON GROUND:	4.572m	ARMAMENT:	1 × .50 (12.7mm) M2 Browning MG with a total of 1,500 rounds of ammunition
GROUND PRESSURE:	.74kg/cm^2		
MAXIMUM ROAD SPEED:	48km/hr		

DEVELOPMENT

The project to develop a new medium armoured recovery vehicle to replace the then current M74, was started in 1954. Three prototypes, designated T88, were built by Bowen-McLaughlin-York Incorporated of York, Pennsylvania. Ten companies were approached to build the production vehicles, and the contract was finally awarded to Bowen-McLaughlin-York. The first pre-production vehicles were completed early in 1960. The M88, or to give the vehicle its full designation – Recovery Vehicle Full-Tracked: Medium M88 – was in production from February 1961 to February 1964, and approx. 1,000 vehicles were built. All these were built at Bowen-McLaughlin-York's Bair facility which is about 15km from York. The basic hull was provided from another company and BMY assembled the vehicle, making two complete vehicles each working day. According to BMY, there were some 385 sub-contractors to the company.

The M88 can recover damaged and disabled vehicles up to and including the M60 and XM1 series tanks. The M88 cost approx. 150,000 dollars each to build and they use many components of the M48 Medium Tank. The M51 Heavy Armoured Recovery Vehicle has now been withdrawn from service, the last users being the United States Marine Corps.

DESCRIPTION

The upper hull of the M88 is cast in one piece and provides the crew with full protection from small arms fire, mortar fire and land mines. The crew compartment is at the front of the vehicle with the engine and transmission at the rear. The crew can enter the vehicle through any of the following hatches: there is a single hatch in each side of the hull, both the driver and co-driver at the very front of the hull are each provided with a hatch cover and the machine-gunner has a hatch in the centre of the hull. The transmission is the XT 1410-2 cross-drive. The suspension is of the torsion-bar type. There are a total of six road wheels with the idler at the front and the drive sprocket at the rear. There are three track return rollers.

Early models were fitted with a cupola-mounted .50 machine-gun but all vehicles now have the machine-gun pintle-mounted.

A full range of recovery equipment is provided. This includes a hydraulically operated blade at the front of the hull, normally used to stabilize the vehicle when the boom is being used, but in addition to clear away obstacles. The boom is mounted at the front of the vehicle and when not required it rests on top of the hull towards the rear. The boom has a capacity of six tons with the spade up and 25 tons with the spade in position. Maximum boom lift weight to 2.438m is 5.79t and at 1.219m is 7.62t.

The two winches are in the lower part of the hull, under the crew compartment.

The main winch has 60.96m of 31.75mm cable, line pull and speed being: bare drum 40,823kg at 8.229m/min, low speed, 32.91m/min, high speed; full drum 23,314kg at 12.801m/min, low speed, 51.82m/min, high speed.

The hoist winch is provided with 121.9m of 15.87mm cable. Line pull and lifting speed: bare drum – 4 part line: 22,680kg at 2.59m/min, low speed, 10.668m/min, high speed; full drum – 4 part line: 13,608kg at 4.876m/min, low speed; 19.812m/min, high speed.

The M88 can also tow a vehicle up to 36,740kg in weight.

The vehicle is fitted with an auxiliary fuel pump which allows it to transfer fuel to other vehicles. Infra-red driving lights are provided and infra-red binoculars are provided for the commander. No NBC system is provided. Trials were carried out with a schnorkel fitted to the top of the hull to increase the fording capabilities of the vehicle, but this was not adopted. A total of eight fixed-fire extinguishers are fitted inside the hull.

M88A1

Several years ago the United States Army fitted a basic M88 with the same engine as that fitted to the M60 MBT. This was given the designation M88E1. In the FY 1976 United States Department of Defence Report the following was stated: '110 million dollars is requested for the M88A1 programme, consisting of 82 million dollars for 159 vehicles (144 for the Army and 15 for the Marine Corps) and a further 29 million dollars for the conversion of 189 existing M88 vehicles to M88A1 standard. And for FY 1977 the following is requested. 89 million dollars for 168 M88A1s for the Army and a further 27 million dollars for the conversion of 240 M88s to M88A1 standard. Conversion of the final increment of M88s to M88A1 standard is planned for FY 1978.' The complete modification of the M88 to M88A1 standard covers many areas including the fitting of the AVDS-1790-2A diesel engine in place of the earlier petrol engine, a diesel auxiliary power unit installed and a personnel heater installed.

It would therefore appear that the M88 will be put back into production after 12 years, in addition to the modification programme.

Right M88 Armoured Recovery Vehicle with 'A' frame in position and blade in position for lifting operations.
Below M88 of the Austrian Army lifting a Saurer Armoured Personnel Carrier.

GERMANY (FEDERAL GERMAN REPUBLIC)

TRANSPORTPANZER 1 (6 × 6) and 2 (4 × 4) — ARMOURED CARGO VEHICLES
MANUFACTURER – Not yet announced
STATUS – Trials completed, ready for production (6 × 6).

BASIC DATA	4 × 4	6 × 6			
CREW:	2 + 10	2 + 12	RANGE:	800km	800km
WEIGHT LOADED:	12,000kg	16,400kg	FORDING:	Amphibious	Amphibious
WEIGHT EMPTY:	10,000kg	13,400kg	ANGLE OF APPROACH:	45°	45°
LENGTH:	5.89m	6.74m	ANGLE OF DEPARTURE:	45°	45°
WIDTH:	2.917m	2.94m	ENGINE:	Mercedes-Benz	Mercedes-Benz
HEIGHT:	2.15m	2.3m		Model OM 402 VA	Model OM 403 VA
GROUND CLEARANCE:	.405m (axles)	.405m (axles)		8-cylinder	10-cylinder
	.5m (hull)	.5m (hull)		multi-fuel	multi-fuel
TRACK:	2.5m	2.5m		water-cooled	water-cooled
WHEELBASE:	3.35m	1.4m + 2.7m		diesel develop-	diesel develop-
TYRES:	14.00 × 20	14.00 × 20		ing 310HP at	ing 390HP at
TURNING RADIUS:	7.65m	5.8m (using all		1,800rpm	1,800rpm
		3 axles)			
MAXIMUM ROAD SPEED:	90km/hr	90km/hr			
MAXIMUM WATER SPEED:	9km/hr	10km/hr			

Note: The above data relate to prototype vehicles and production models may well differ.

DEVELOPMENT

Development of these vehicles was carried out by Büssing, Daimler Benz, Klöckner-Humboldt-Deutz, Krupp, MAN and Rheinstahl. Wherever possible standard commercial components have been used in these vehicles and many of these will be interchangeable with those of the new German range of tactical trucks. The 4 × 4 Model has been shelved but is included to give an overall picture of the programme. The German Army has an initial requirement for 1,000 Transportpanzer 1s and these will be used to carry troops and supplies in the battlefield area. They will also be used for command, radio and ambulance roles. Studies are being carried out to fit various types of armament installations.

VARIANTS

Transportpanzer 2 (4 × 4) LG 496

This has a hull of all-welded steel construction. The driver and commander are seated at the front of the hull with the engine behind them, the load compartment being at the rear of the hull.

Both the driver and commander are provided with a side door which has an integral observation hatch. Over their compartment are two circular hatches. The windscreen can be covered by an armoured cover if required. The engine, cooling system and air cleaner can be removed for repair or replacement as a complete unit. The transmission is a ZF four-speed fully automatic. The suspension consists of rigid axles with control rods in conjunction with coil springs and hydraulic shock absorbers and differential locks. The brakes are hydraulic and power-assisted steering is standard.

The Transportpanzer 2 is fitted with an NBC system and is fully amphibious, being propelled in the water by two propellers at the rear, one each side. Before entering the water a trim vane is erected at the front of the hull.

Armament consists of a 7.62mm MG 3 machine-gun and smoke dischargers. The cargo compartment is 3m long, 1.45m wide and 1.26m high. Hatches are provided over the cargo compartment and there is an observation flap in each side of the compartment.

Transportpanzer 1 (6 × 6) LG 493

This is similar to the above but can carry 3,000kg of cargo. All three axles can be steered on this model. The cargo compartment is 3.79m long, 1.45m wide and 1.26m high.

Transportpanzer 3 (8 × 8) LG 495

This 8 × 8 armoured load carrier was a project only and was not built. It was to have used the Spähpanzer 2 (8 × 8) reconnaissance vehicle chassis suitably modified.

One of the prototypes of the Transportpanzer 1 (6×6) vehicles undergoing trials.

The Transportpanzer 2 (4×4) vehicle.

OTHER ARMOURED VEHICLES

Listed below are those armoured vehicles which have now been withdrawn from service, or their development stopped, or they are in service in very small numbers.

Armoured Vehicle Name	Country	Type	Status
CATI	Belgium	Tank Destroyer	No longer in service
Churchill	Great Britain	Tank	Some used by Eire
Conqueror	Great Britain	Tank	No longer in service
Daimler Dingo	Great Britain	Scout Car	Some used by Angola, Cyprus and Portugal
G-13	Czechoslovakia/ Germany	Tank Destroyer	No longer in service
Hornet/Malkara	Great Britain	Tank Destroyer	No longer in service
Hotchkiss LFU	France	Light AFV	Development cancelled
Hotchkiss TT A 12	France	APC	Development cancelled
Ikv-102 and Ikv-103	Sweden	SPG	No longer in service
Landsverk 180	Sweden	Armoured Car	Some used by Eire
LVTP-5	United States	APC (Amphibious)	No longer in service
MAC-1	United States	Armoured Car	Some used by Mexico
Marmon-Herrington Mk. 1V/F	South Africa	Armoured Car	Some used by Cyprus
MOWAG Pirate	Switzerland	APC	Development cancelled
MOWAG Puma	Switzerland	APC	Development cancelled
MBT-70	USA/Germany	MBT	Development cancelled
m/43	Sweden	SPG	No longer in service
M39	United States	APC/Recce	No longer in service
M40	United States	SPG	No longer in service
M41	United States	SPG	No longer in service
M50	United States	Tank Destroyer	No longer in service
M51	United States	ARV	No longer in service
M53	United States	SPG	No longer in service
M103	United States	Tank	No longer in service
Pbv.301	Sweden	APC	No longer in service
RAMS	United States	APC/Assault	Development cancelled
Strv.40	Sweden	Tank	Some used in Dominica
Strv.74	Sweden	Tank	Being replaced by Ikv-91
SKP and VKP m/42	Sweden	APC	Some in UN service
SWAT	United States	APC/IS	Development cancelled
Truck, Armoured	Canada	APC	No longer in service
Twister	United States	8 × 8 Recce	Development cancelled
Unimog	Germany/Sweden	APC	Some used in Eire
Valentine	Great Britain	Tank	Some reported in Sudan
VBB	Brazil	APC	Prototypes only
VEAK 40	Sweden	AA System	Development cancelled
Vixen	Great Britain	Scout Car	Development cancelled
XM179	United States	SPG	Development cancelled
XM701	United States	MICV	Development cancelled
XM803	United States	MBT	Development cancelled
YP104	Netherlands	Scout Car	Development cancelled

ADDENDA

AMX-30 Main Battle Tank—The French Army will have a total of 5 regiments with the Pluton tactical nuclear missile system on the AMX-30 and not six regiments as previously announced. Four of these regiments have been formed so far (3rd, 25th, 60th and 74th) with the final regiment, the 32nd, becoming operational in 1977.

Leopard 2(AV) Main Battle Tank—The Leopard 2 (Austere Version) was completed early in 1976 and should start its trials in the United States in September 1976. These trials are scheduled to run through to February 1977. It is then expected that there will be a further trial with the Leopard 2(AV) and the best of the XM1 tanks, i.e. the Chrysler or the General Motors version. The Leopard 2(AV) is armed with a standard NATO 105mm rifled tank gun, a co-axial 7.62mm machine gun, there is also a 7.62mm machine gun on both the commander's and gunner's cupolas. Four smoke dischargers are mounted either side of the turret.

Basic data of the Leopard 1 (AV) is as follows: Crew 4. Length gun forward 9.641m, length of hull 7.403m. Width 3.54m. Width without skirts 3.42m. Height turret top 2.454m, height with machine gun 2.884m. Ground clearance front .55m and rear .505m. Weight loaded 54,000kg. Ground pressure .91kg/cm^2. Power to weight ratio 27.5 HP/T. Maximum road speed 68 km/hr. Gradient 60%. Side slope 30%. Vertical obstacle 1.15m. Trench crossing 3m. Fording without preparation 1.2m, with preparation 2.35m.

German 105mm and 120mm Smoothbore Guns—The German Rheinmetall Company, who has developed the 105mm and 120mm smoothbore tank guns for the Leopard 2 MBT, are now offering these weapons as a refit programme for such tanks as the Leopard 1, M47, M48 and the M60.

Leopard 1 MBT—The first Australian Leopard 1 MBT was handed over in June 1976. The Canadian Army has placed an order for up to 120 Leopard 1 MBTs as a replacement for the Centurion tanks currently deployed in Canada and Europe.

Chobham Armour—In June 1975 the British Ministry of Defence announced that the MVEE had developed a new type of armour called "Chobham Armour." This will not however be fitted to the British Army Chieftains. Its first application will be on the second production batch of Chieftains for Iran, these will be known as the Shir Iran (Lion of Persia). From the limited amount of information available it would appear that this armour is of a laminate rather than the spaced armour type which has been adopted for the American XM1 and the German Leopard 2. The Shir Iran will be powered by a new Rolls-Royce CV12TCA twelve cylinder diesel which develops 1200 BHP at 2300 rpm, this has a dry weight of 2041kg. This engine will be coupled to a new David Brown TN 37 transmission with four forward and three reverse gears. The Improved Fire Control System includes a new commander's cupola designated the No. 21, this has been developed by MEL. It includes a light intensifier night sight, a thermal head and non-reflecting periscopes. A variety of sensors are provided including traverse displacement, elevation displacement, trunnion tilt, angle of sight, crosswind, air density, headwind and barrel wear. It was also announced in early 1976 that Kuwait had in fact ordered a total of 165 Chieftain tanks.

British 105mm and 120mm tank guns—It was announced in 1976 that the Royal Armament Research and Development Establishment was developing new 105mm and 120mm tank ammunition. The new 120mm rounds will have an effective range of well over 2000m with increased armour penetration, new core materials and a new high energy propellant are being used. The following 120mm rounds are under development: Fin Stabilized Armour Piercing Discarding Sabot, Product Improved APDS, HEAT, Product Improved HESH, Illuminating, Canister, Product Improved Smoke. It was also stated that a new 105mm round was under development, presumably this is a Fin Stabilized APDS round.

Chieftain Replacement—It is known that a number of British companies are working on components for the replacement for the Chieftain. This will probably use the new Rolls-Royce diesel, the TN 37 transmission and a new suspension of the hydro-pneumatic type. Airscrew Howden Limited are believed to be working on the engine cooling side. The FCS will incorporate a laser rangefinder.

Soviet T-64 MBT—It has been reported that the T-64 is armed with a 125mm rather than a 122mm gun and that this is fed from an automatic loader which holds 28 rounds.

New Swedish MBT—The Swedish Army has a requirement for a new MBT to replace its S Tanks and Centurion tanks in the 1980s. In the short term the Centurion tank will probably be updated with a new engine and a new FCS.

Swiss Pz.68AA2 MBT—It has been announced that the Swiss Army has placed an order for 110 PZ.68 AA2 MBTs, these will be built at the Federal Engineering Works at Thun. This tank has the following improvements over the earlier models: thermal sleeve on main armament, improved fire control system and stabilization system, new oil cooling system, modified gun control equipment, improved crew heaters, new dry air filter in place of the previous oil filter, increased number of ready rounds and an improved NBC system.

XM1 MBT—Prototypes were handed over to the Army in February, 1976. At this time the following information was released:

	Chrysler	General Motors
CREW:	4	4
COMBAT WEIGHT:	52,616kg	52,616kg
LENGTH CHASSIS:	7.797m	7.62m
WIDTH:	3.555m	3.657m
HEIGHT TO ROOF:	2.348m	2.413m
ROAD SPEED:	72.4km/hr	77.24km/hr
SPEED CROSS COUNTRY:	56km/hr	56km/hr
RANGE:	480km	480km
VERTICAL OBSTACLE:	1.066m	.914m
GRADIENT:	60%	60%
GROUND PRESSURE:	.84kg/cm^2	.84kg/cm^2
MAIN ARMAMENT:	105mm	105mm
CO-AXIAL ARMAMENT:	7.62mm	7.62mm
LOADER'S ARMAMENT:	7.62mm	7.62mm
COMMANDER'S ARMAMENT:	12.7mm	12.7mm

It is anticipated that production tanks will have a 40mm grenade launcher in place of the loader's 7.62mm machine gun.

M60 Series MBT—Further improvements in the M60 series may include: improved crew heaters, more reliable air cleaner blower motors, individual round ready rack handles, improved driver's escape hatch, low profile commander's cupola and a smoke generating system. As of early 1976, the laser rangefinder and solid state computer had not been placed in production for the M60 series.

M48 Series MBT—The Jordanian Army has started a refit programme on its M48 tanks, this is believed to include a 105mm gun and a new engine. The first M48A5 tanks were delivered in December 1975, the first unit to receive them being the South Carolina National Guard (2nd Battalion 263rd Armour and Troop E, 19th Armoured Cavalry). Total number of 105mm rounds carried is 43.

Above: The Leopard 2 (AV) with 105mm rifled tank gun.

The experimental vehicle with the new British "Chobham Armour."

Shillelagh Missile System—In mid-1976 trials were under way with a Shillelagh missile (as used with the M60A2 and M551 Sheridan) modified for laser beam-riding guidance.

CVR(W)Fox—Fox vehicles delivered to the British Army will not have the flotation screen fitted, this will be available as an optional extra for export. The Peak Engineering Company are offering a 7.62mm machine gun turret for installation on a Fox vehicle and this was shown at the BAEE in June 1976.

Shorland Armoured Patrol Vehicle—A Shorland modified to mount a sniper's rifle has been ordered by the Dutch Police, this will be used at airports. The RUC have placed an order for the Short SB.301 APC; a total of 8 countries have now ordered the SB.301.

American ARSV—The M114 C & R vehicle was to have been replaced by the ARSV, prototypes of which have been built by Lockheed (6×6) and FMC (tracked). These have now been cancelled and in the short term the ARSV requirement will be filled by a modified M113A1 APC and in the long term by a modified version of the XM723 MICV.

MOWAG Taifun MICV—This has been demonstrated in Saudi Arabia and a number of other countries.

M113 APC—The United States Army has a requirement for a TOW equipped M113A1, two types are being studied. One will have the missile in an elevated pod with the other being a cupola-type installation.

M-980 Yugoslav APC—The new Yugoslav MICV is now known as the M-980. It has a crew of three (commander, gunner and driver) and can carry 6 to 8 fully equipped infantry. It is powered by a HS 115-2 eight cylinder water-cooled diesel which developes 280 HP at 3000 rpm, this is the same as that fitted to the French AMX-10P MICV. The engine is coupled to a hydraulic torque converter and a preselective gearbox with 4F and 1R gears. It is armed with a 20mm cannon and a co-axial 7.92mm machine gun and there are two launchers for the Sagger ATGW to the turret rear. The vehicle is fully amphibious and is provided with a NBC system and a full range of night vision equipment. Basic data is as follows: Weight loaded 12,000kg. Weight empty 11,000kg. Length 6.25m. Width 2.85m. Height without turret 2.16m. Height with turret 2.5m. Track 2.47m. Track width 300mm. Maximum road speed 70km/hr. Maximum water speed 8km/hr. Range 500km. Gradient 60%. Side slope 30°.

Soviet 122mm M1974 SPG—Basic data is: Crew 4. Weight 30,000kg. Length 7.3m. Width 3m. Height overall 2.42m. Track width 380mm. Length of track on ground 4.4m.

M109 SPG—The British Army will convert its M109s to M109A1 standard. The Martin CLGP has now been selected for further development and the company have given it the name of Copperhead.

SAM-8 Missile System—This now has the NATO code name of GECKO.

Roland SAM—The American Army was to have mounted the Roland SAM on the GOER (4×4) chassis or a XM723 MICV chassis. It is now looking at the possibility of mounting the system on the M109 SPG chassis.

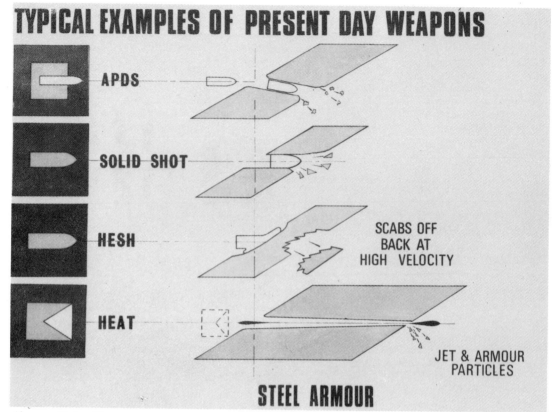

Above and below: The current armour and the new Chobham armour showing the effect of attack from various types of ammunition.

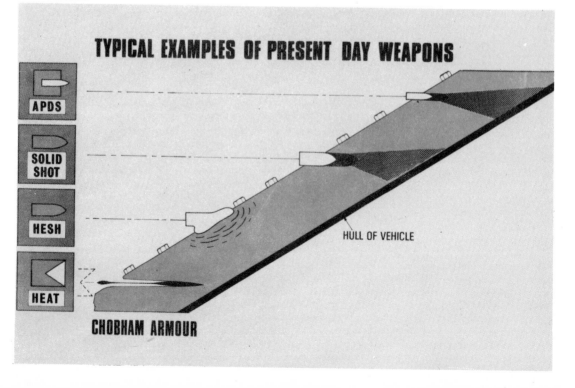

Above: The Chrysler XM1 Main Battle Tank.
Below: The General Motors XM1 Main Battle Tank.

GLAADS USA—Early in 1976 trials started with a GLAADS at Fort Bliss, Texas. This consists of a XM701 MICV chassis with a new turret armed with twin 25mm guns. The system was developed under the direction of the United States Army Armament Command and the Rodman Laboratory at Rock Island, and Frankford Arsenal. Design work was carried out by Aeronutronic-Ford Corporation at Newport Beach. The twin 25mm guns are fed from two feed chutes (i.e. two per gun). The advanced fire control system includes a fully integrated and stabilized optical, infrared and laser sensors. The sensors feed data to a computer developed by Rockwell (Autonetiçs), and this computers the necessary lead and elevation angles.

Norwegian SSM System—The Norwegian Company of A/S Kongsberg Vaapenfabrikk are developing a tracked version of their Penguin SSM System. This is for coastal defence and will be mounted on a Hägglunds (Swedish) tracked chassis.

Turkey has stated that it hopes to set up both tank and APC production lines. It is thought that the Leopard tank and the M113A1 or Marder vehicles will be built.

Russian Tracked Minelayer GMZ—The new Russian minelayer is now known to be called the GMZ and is based on the Ganef chassis. The engine is at the front and mines and mine plough mechanism is at the rear. It is armed with a 14.5mm machine gun and night vision equipment is provided. Basic data is: Length 7.5m (or 10.3m with plough travelling). Width 3.2m. Height 2.5m or 2.7m with searchlight. Track width 540mm. Length of track on ground 5m. It has a crew of four and is powered by a water-cooled diesel engine.

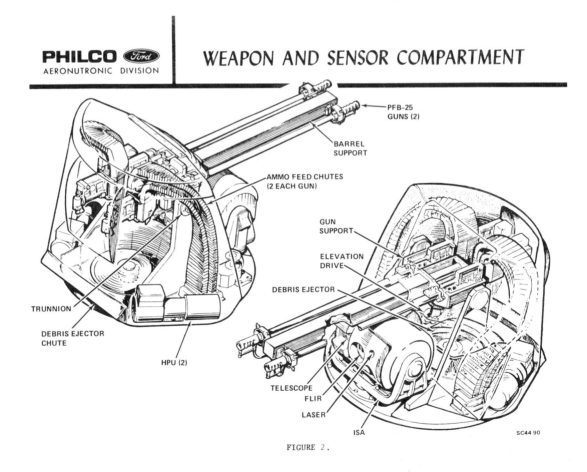

FIGURE 2.

The turret of the GLAADS (Gun Low Altitude Air Defense System)

PHOTO CREDITS

The author would like to thank the many Governments, Units, Companies and Individuals who have supplied photographs for this publication. These sources are given below:

Alvis Limited (Great Britain)
Associated Press (Great Britain)
Astra SpA (Italy)
Australian Army
Austrian Army
Barr and Stroud Limited (Great Britain)
Bell Aerospace (United States)
Bell, T.
Berliet Company (France)
Bofors AB (Sweden)
British Aircraft Corporation (Guided Weapons Division)
British Ministry of Defence Army (CCR)
Bundesgrenzshutz (German Border Police)
Cadillac Gage Company (United States)
Canadian Armed Forces
Central Office of Information (Great Britain)
CILAS Company (France)
Cohen, Irvine
DAF (Holland)
ECP Armées (France)
Egyptian Army
Engesa SA (Brazil)
Euromissile
Fiat Company (Italy)
Finnish Army
FMC Corporation (United States)
FN Herstal (Belgium)
FPT Industries Limited (Great Britain)
Foss, Christopher F.
General Electric Company (United States)
German Army
GIAT (France)
GKN Sankey Limited (Great Britain)
Hägglund and Soner (Sweden)
Hughes Aerospace (United States)
Icks, R. J.
Indian Army
Irish Army

Israel Aircraft Industries
Israeli Army
Jungner Instruments AB (Sweden)
Krauss-Maffei AG (Germany)
Lockheed Missiles and Space Company (United States)
MEL Equipment Company (Great Britain)
Mercedes-Benz Company (Germany)
Messerschmitt-Bölkow-Blohm (Germany)
Mitsubishi Heavy Industries (Japan)
Mowag Company (Switzerland)
Oerlikon-Bührle Limited (Switzerland)
Oto Melara SpA (Italy)
Panhard and Levassor (France)
Philco Ford Corporation (United States)
Rank Precision Industries Limited (Great Britain)
Rheinstahl AG (Germany)
Royal Armoured Corps Tank Museum
Royal Netherlands Army
SAMM Company (France)
Saurer Werke (Austria)
Saviem (France)
Short Brothers and Harland Limited (Great Britain)
Solartron Electronic Group (Great Britain)
Soltam Company (Israel)
Sopelem (France)
Steyr Company (Austria)
Swedish Army
Swiss Army
TASS
Technology Investments Limited (Eire)
Thomson-Brandt (France)
Thomson (CSF)
Tunbridge, S.
United Scientific Group Limited (Great Britain)
United States Army
United States Marine Corps
Vickers Limited (Great Britain)
Yamada, S.

INDEX